D0209090

THE SHORTER
CAMBRIDGE MEDIEVAL HISTORY

THE SHORTER CAMBRIDGE
MEDIEVAL HISTORY

BY THE LATE
C. W. PREVITÉ-ORTON

IN TWO VOLUMES

VOLUME I
THE LATER ROMAN EMPIRE TO
THE TWELFTH CENTURY

WITHDRAWN

ST. FRANCIS SEMINARY
SALZMANN
LIBRARY
Milwaukee, Wis. 53207

CAMBRIDGE UNIVERSITY PRESS
CAMBRIDGE
LONDON · NEW YORK · MELBOURNE

PUBLISHED BY
THE SYNDICS OF THE CAMBRIDGE UNIVERSITY PRESS

The Pitt Building, Trumpington Street, Cambridge CB2 1RP
Bentley House, 200 Euston Road, London NW1 2DB
32 East 57th Street, New York, NY 10022, USA
296 Beaconsfield Parade, Middle Park, Melbourne 3206, Australia

Library of Congress catalogue card number: 75-31398

ISBN 0 521 20963 3 hard covers
ISBN 0 521 09977 3 paperbacks
ISBN 0 521 05993 3 set of two volumes (hard covers)

First Edition 1952
Reprinted with corrections 1953 1960 1962
Reprinted 1966 1971
First paperback edition 1975
Reprinted 1977

First printed in Great Britain at the University Printing House, Cambridge
Reprinted at the Alden Press, Oxford

EDITORIAL NOTE

The late Professor C. W. Previté-Orton was invited by the Syndics of the Press in 1939 to write his own, concise version of the *Cambridge Medieval History*, of which he had been one of the editors. The *History* is essentially a work of reference, so vast that no student seeking a general view of the development of medieval Europe is ever likely to contemplate reading the whole of it. The new book which the Syndics had in mind was one of such dimensions as would make it possible for the student to regard it as a continuous history, intended to be read as such. At the same time, it was to be planned on a scale large enough for it to retain the essential value of the major *History* as a work of reference. The writer was to have complete discretion in the use he chose to make of the words and phrases of the original authors. He could incorporate them as they stood, or he could ignore them, as seemed to him best in each individual case.

The manuscript was left complete at Professor Previté-Orton's death, and at the request of the Syndics I have revised it for the printer. The text itself required little attention. Professor Previté-Orton had endeavoured to take account of advances in knowledge since the earlier volumes of the *Cambridge Medieval History* were published, and had in many cases modified and corrected the statements of his authors. I have followed the same policy, as I know he would have wished me to do, and have not hesitated to amend his text in places where more recent research seemed to me to require it. Professor Previté-Orton's knowledge was so extensive, and his judgment so sure, that such changes have been few in number. But the field of medieval studies is wide, and if the changes made by either of us have been insufficient, I can only plead, as with little reason he once did, *indocta ignorantia*.

The one major alteration which has been made in the text is in the matter of arrangement. It was apparent from his manuscript that Professor Previté-Orton, when half-way through his task, had altered his original plan, and a series of relatively short chapters was followed by a number of very long ones. I have broken these into chapters of more moderate size, and to some extent have had to change the order of the sections in the process. For any faults in the arrangement of the chapters, and for any inappositeness in the titles of chapters and sections, I am therefore solely responsible.

It was at first proposed to publish this *Shorter Medieval History* without maps and, like the *Cambridge Medieval History* itself, without either genealogical tables or illustrations. The character of the work, which was intended to appeal to the general reader, who was not likely to have the necessary reference books at his elbow, seemed to make their insertion desirable. A selection of genealogical tables, some lists of rulers, and a number of maps have therefore been included. None of these has claim to independent value; they are intended to do no more than assist the reader in the understanding of the text. A higher function and a greater importance can be assigned to the illustrations, since, like the text of the *History* itself, they illuminate not only the highway but many of the smaller side-tracks of medieval history. In choosing them, the Syndics were fortunate enough to enlist the help of Dr S. H. Steinberg, who has had considerable experience in this field. It is probable that even professed medievalists will discover among them many things that are unfamiliar and of exceptional interest.

PHILIP GRIERSON

Gonville and Caius College
14 February 1952

CONTENTS

BOOK I

THE LATER ROMAN EMPIRE

BOOK II

THE BREAK-UP OF THE EMPIRE

BOOK III

BYZANTIUM AND ISLAM

BOOK IV

THE DARK AGES IN THE WEST

CONTENTS

BOOK V

THE FOUNDATION OF WESTERN EUROPE

BOOK VI

THE TWELFTH CENTURY

LIST OF ILLUSTRATIONS

Most of the illustrations have been greatly reduced

xi

xix

LIST OF MAPS

LIST OF GENEALOGICAL TABLES

BOOK I
THE LATER ROMAN EMPIRE

CHAPTER 1

THE ROMAN EMPIRE UNDER CONSTANTINE THE GREAT

This history of the Middle Ages begins with the double revolution worked by the Emperor Constantine the Great within the ancient and decaying Roman Empire and the declining civilization of Antiquity which the Empire embodied. The first of these revolutions was the transfer of the imperial capital to Byzantium on the Bosphorus, an act which sealed the transference, long in preparation, of the centre of gravity of the Empire to its less anaemic Eastern half. The second was the adoption of Christianity as the dominant religion of the Empire. It is not that these epoch-making events created or began the Middle Ages, for medieval times were still some two centuries in the future and, when they came, there were other elements which had no less effect on their origin and development. But these two decisions of one man did lay down conditions without which medieval and modern Europe could hardly have been shaped and grown.

To himself, we may guess, Constantine seemed no innovator, but the divinely led preserver of a civilization hardly won and now in pressing danger, the successor of the long line of autocrats who safeguarded the peace and the existence of the Roman Empire, the only state where human life was truly civilized. To appreciate his task and the evolution he could not foresee we must first reconstruct the Empire of his day, its geography, populations, structure, and economics, its mentality and its armaments, its strength, its internal weaknesses and its external foes.

(I) THE GEOGRAPHY OF THE EMPIRE

The Roman Empire under Constantine formed a natural unity cleft into two no less natural halves. Its unity was due to the fact that it essentially consisted of the lands and peoples clustered round the Mediterranean Sea. There its civilization had grown. There its dominion had spread. The way of life of its peoples was formed by Mediterranean climate and conditions. Under the long Roman peace the inland sea had been the easiest and widest

1

route of its commerce, supplemented by the rivers of Italy, Spain, and Gaul. The long Roman roads which spanned the Empire were military and governmental links in the first place, and only secondarily commercial arteries: industrial and commercial cities were predominantly on or near

Fig. 1. Rome and Constantinople. Ivory diptych

the Mediterranean coasts. The expansion of the Empire was limited in part by climatic conditions. If we follow on the map the isothermal lines of midwinter we find that the average temperature of its European provinces does not fall below freezing-point: beyond that line are obvious military frontiers on or beyond the Danube. If we take the midsummer, the average temperature on the frontier in Asia and Africa stands at near 86° Fahrenheit. The frozen north and the torrid south were equally outside of and alien to the Empire, and the city-life of the Mediterranean was with difficulty adapted even to the edge of its native zone. Further afield, as in Britain, the Romano-British country house, the villa, had to be modified to suit its non-Mediterranean surroundings.

If only by reason of its vast extent, with the manifold variations of soil, configuration, racial composition, and in a subordinate degree of climate which it implied, the Empire had from the first fallen into natural divisions which impaired its overruling and largely political unity. As the central power grew weaker in the political convulsions and disasters of the third century A.D., as the subject populations were taken up into Roman citizenship and furnished the army and the official classes, as the memory of crushing conquest by the Empire evaporated, it was no wonder that the underlying provincial characteristics should pierce through and modify the common culture imposed upon them. Chief of all these divisions, however, were those of East and West, which were due to the dual character of that common civilization itself. The East was the Greek or Hellenized, the West the Latin or Romanized half of the Empire. Though Rome had borrowed its culture from Greece, it did so with a difference, and in turn imbued the West, which had been barbaric, with its own version of civilization, with its unsubtle but dynamic cult of law and authority and with its native Latin tongue, the fit vehicle of both and of its plain, matter-of-fact, if rhetorical, thought. The West was the Latin part of the Empire, however vulgarized and slipshod its common speech might be. Against the West stood the East, home of ancient civilizations which had received directly the vivifying, transforming imprint of Greece before the Roman conquest. Here the language and literature of civilization were Greek. Much of the Greek spirit had been infused into alien peoples, inquisitive, speculative, turning the material world which the Roman took for granted into themes for creative thought. This Greek world was a borrower, too; from Rome it took law and state organization; from the East, as we shall see, it took religious conceptions and mysticism which it in turn passed on to the West. But although they had so much in common, the two halves were separate in language and ethos, and if they had drawn closer to one another in the cosmopolitan first two centuries of our era, they were steadily falling apart in the third. The cultivated class was ceasing to be bilingual.

Both East and West enjoyed but an imperfect inner unity resting on the educated, official classes, for the lower men's positions were in the social scale, the more they were divided by provincial, local conditions and the less they shared in the common culture of the Empire. Peasant and craftsman might have little Roman about them save their reverence—it was hardly modern patriotism—for the majestic Empire which ruled and

Map 1

4

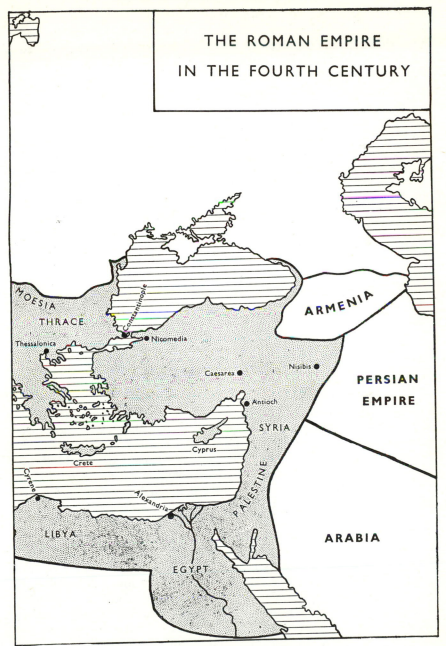

THE ROMAN EMPIRE
IN THE FOURTH CENTURY

MOESIA

THRACE

Thessalonica

Constantinople

Nicomedia

Caesarea

ARMENIA

Nisibis

PERSIAN

EMPIRE

Antioch

SYRIA

Cyprus

Crete

PALESTINE

Cyrene

Alexandria

LIBYA

ARABIA

EGYPT

Map 1

protected them, and their uncouth varieties of vulgar Latin or unpolished Greek. There were great territorial aggregates within the Empire, marked out by natural frontiers and conditions as well as by history, which possessed a certain self-consciousness of their separate being. We cannot call it a national or tribal sentiment; it was rather an ever stronger provincialism, which could and did become more disruptive to the Empire than unifying to the territory itself.

To take the West first. There was the imperial, or ex-imperial, land of Italy, now stretching over all the peninsula south of the Alps, impoverished, depopulated, and dethroned, but still encircled by a halo of past greatness, and possessing the eternal city of Rome itself, the maker of the Empire. Save in a scanty resident aristocracy, dignified and idle, the Romans of 300, the offspring of countless immigrants, might have little in common with the Romans of old, but the material city they dwelt in retained all its prestige. It was still in imagination the mistress of the world, a marble monument compact of temples, palaces and triumphal buildings, enshrining the imperishable glories of the past, and seeming throughout the Empire she had made to be a pledge for perpetuity. Yet Italy, with her annex Rhaetia, seems to have the least identity of all the lands of the Empire. We can speak of Gauls and Spaniards, but hardly of Italians, when this history begins.

To the east of the Adriatic lay the mountainous lands of the north-western Balkan peninsula, which may be somewhat loosely termed Illyricum. Latin as the spoken language reached here as far as Naïssus and Scupi (the modern Nish and Skoplje), though the ultimate political frontier, largely for geographical reasons, left both these places in the eastern half of the Empire. These lands, with their extension, partly mountainous (Noricum) and partly plain (Pannonia), to the Danube, inhabited by a rude and hardy peasantry, had in the years 250–300 furnished the best of the Roman troops, the generals, and the Emperors. They had in fact borne the weight of the Empire's defence against its external foes and by consequence had ruled it. But they had spent themselves in the task, and their depopulation owing to this and to barbarian inroads was by 300 annulling their preponderance and levelling them with other exhausted provinces.

To the north-west of Italy came the provinces of Gaul, defined by its natural boundaries of the Alps, the Pyrenees, the sea, and the river Rhine. This most Romanized country mainly consisted of two fertile plains, the greater in the north and west stretching from the lower Rhine to the Pyrenees, the lesser in the south on the Mediterranean Sea. Between them rose the mountain range of the Cevennes. The land was linked by ample water-systems, the Rhone in the south-east, the Garonne and the Loire in the west and centre, the Seine in the north, and the Rhine on the north-eastern German frontier. No territory was more fitted to be a bulwark of the Empire and a reservoir of men, but its blood had been drained in the effort, and its eastern districts, half-Germanic at its conquest, were becoming further Germanized by the settlements of the German soldiery.

Across the Channel lay the somewhat detached territory of Roman Britain, with whose physical characters the reader may be assumed to be familiar. But it is to be remembered that much, especially the Midlands, lay under woodland, and that marshy riverine districts tended to be thinly populated. Only the south-east, bounded roughly by a line from the Wash to the Bristol Channel, was thoroughly Romanized, and even there the towns and country houses, the villas, were surrounded by barbaric peasants. In the north-west, save for a few towns like Chester and Viriconium, there were military settlements and camps, such as those along the Roman Wall or at York, but little Romanization of the scanty British population. Britain was a bastion worth having, but its part in imperial politics was occasional and secondary—the very recruits it provided served mostly on more critical frontiers. Its own frontier, however, had some amplitude. By land the free barbarians of the north reached up to the Wall of Hadrian; across the western sea lay Ireland, a less and less peaceful barbaric neighbour; to the east, as we shall see, the Germans were becoming nearer enemies.

In contrast to Gaul and Britain, and even to Italy if we reckon with Italy her alpine Rhaetian appendage, the territory of Spain in 300 had no external frontiers. The Pyrenees, with their few and lofty passes, separated it from Gaul, the Mediterranean from the inner provinces and from Africa, the Atlantic as yet from the outer world. Spain internally was divided by its mountain ridges into several sections of plateau or fertile plain. The most northerly of these latter, the Cantabrian range, continued the Pyrenees westward to the Atlantic. South of it lay the barren mountain plateau divided by the Guadarrama range and watered by the upper Douro and the upper Tagus rivers. But Lusitania, the lower plains of these two rivers on the Atlantic, was rainy and fertile. South of the Pyrenees came the rich Mediterranean watershed of the river Ebro and its kindred eastern coast, Tarraconensis. Most southerly of all, divided from the central plateau by the Sierra Morena, extended the fertile, sub-tropic land of Baetica, fringed near its seaboard by the Sierra Nevada. All these provinces had given men and natural wealth to the Empire.

Across the Straits of Gibraltar lay the African territories. From the Atlantic to the Gulf of Gabes (the Syrtes) they were dominated by the branches of the Atlas range, on the slopes of which or between which lay fertile Roman provinces, the Mauretanias to the west, Numidia (the most Roman) in the centre, and Africa, roughly corresponding to modern Tunis, to the east. Here there were bred the formidable light horse who fought

7

Fig. 2. Road map of Gaul

on other frontiers. Their own limit, at the edge of the desert of Sahara, was held against their barbaric kinsmen, the free Moors, by troops from Syria.

As we have seen, Latin and Greek met in the Balkan peninsula that stretched south from the river Danube to the Mediterranean, varying from a continental to a Mediterranean climate. Its dominating feature was the great mass of mountains covering the centre, with its eastern offshoots of Haemus and Rhodope. Around them and parted by them lay wide plains: Moesia, which was the southern watershed of the Danube, Thrace between

8

Fig. 2. Road map of Gaul

Haemus, Rhodope and the Propontis, Macedonia round the city of Thessalonica, Thessaly south of Mount Olympus, and the lesser hollows farther south still in Boeotia, Attica, and the Peloponnese. The whole was a land naturally variegated and divided, which had been brought to a unity by Roman rule. True Greece to the south enjoyed still the prestige of its history and its civilization—it was a centre of culture—but it had always been infertile as a whole, and had long been terribly depopulated. Macedonia and Thrace were still populous and wealthy, but Moesia, like Illyricum, had lost the best of its peasantry in the wars and for the legions.

3   9

It was now a home for Dacians withdrawn south of the Danube when their native province was abandoned to the barbarians.

On the eastern edge of Thrace, between the Black Sea and the Aegean, flowed the all-but inland waters which divided Europe and Asia, the two Straits of the Bosphorus and the Hellespont or Dardanelles and the land-locked Propontis or Sea of Marmora. These coasts were the key-point of both sea and land-routes between east and west and north and south, and it is, perhaps, a testimony to the strength of the Empire which could beat back its separate foes on its many frontiers that it was only towards 300 that an Emperor in search of a strategic centre from which to defend the East fixed his residence on the Propontis at Nicomedia.

Nicomedia was on the Asiatic coast in the peninsular territory now called Asia Minor, which already in prosperity and population was in a way to become the kernel of the eastern Empire. On its wide and productive tableland, girt with a rim of mountain ranges, and in its river-valleys on the west and outer edge of fertile coastland, there dwelt a numerous and hardy people of peasant tillers and herdsmen, with fishermen and traders in the port towns. It could rank as an extension of Hellas, if alloyed. The mountain ranges of the eastern border as far as the upper Euphrates were higher with few passes, so that with their warlike highlanders they formed in Armenia Minor a natural defensible frontier; and the same rarity of practicable passes in the southern range of the Taurus mountains cut off the Cilician coast more from Asia Minor than from Syria.

Much of the Syrian territory, the watersheds of the Orontes and the middle Euphrates, was among the most prosperous of the Empire, and the barren Phoenician coastland flourished on trade and navigation. The large towns were thoroughly Hellenized. Even the frontier land of Mesopotamia could be populous while the Persians were kept at bay beyond Nisibis. Palestine on the south was at any rate a route of transit trade.

Lastly came the river land of Egypt, still, though over-exploited, a chief granary of the Empire. Here lay a great centre of Hellenism at Alexandria, one of the wealthiest of ports, and the Greek element was strong in the Delta and beyond, as it was in Cyrenaica, which was really an appendage to Egypt between the desert and the sea.

(2) THE FOUNDING OF CONSTANTINOPLE AND THE ADOPTION OF CHRISTIANITY

It can easily be seen how difficult it was to find a suitable administrative centre, a real capital, for this vast Empire and its divergent provinces, when once the pressure of outer foes had become persistent and severe and the cohesion of its parts was diminished. The wonderful system of strategic roads might lessen physical obstacles to the movement of troops and speed up the receipt of intelligence, but it could not obviate the necessity of the Emperor being within convenient reach of his frontier armies, and able with as little loss of time as might be to hurry to important provinces to quell internal revolt. The problem of a centre of the whole Empire was in fact insoluble. It had already led to the desertion of Rome by the Emperors and their residence in more conveniently placed cities like Milan. Together with the ever tighter centralization needed to hold the Empire together and galvanize the flagging energies of its populations, and with the enormous increase of business at headquarters which accompanied this, it had in- spired a short-lived scheme of Diocletian for the division of the Roman world among four co-regent rulers, the two Augusti and their satellite Caesars, each taking charge of a section of the provinces and frontiers. The arrangement had foreshadowed the division between East and West.

But while no single centre fit to control the whole West could be found, the genius of Diocletian perceived that the region of the Propontis was the natural centre of the East. Thence in the heart of the Empire watch could be kept on the frontier of the lower Danube and the still more endangered frontier of Persia. There was the crossing of the routes of trade and armies, east to west and north to south. Even isolated Egypt was barely less accessible by sea from Asia Minor than by land across the desert from Antioch. Diocletian had chosen Nicomedia on the Asiatic shore, with its more sheltered climate, for his residence; the still more gifted Constantine, taught by the experience of his war with his rival Licinius and perhaps by its three years' siege 130 years earlier by the troops of the Emperor Severus, had the imaginative insight to choose Byzantium for his new eastern capi- tal. There is no need to credit him with an impossible prescience of later history. What he could see was that Byzantium added to the advantages of the Propontine general situation those of an all-but impregnable port, citadel, and arsenal. With the new extent he gave it on its promontory on the inner mouth of the Bosphorus, with its unequalled harbour of the Golden Horn, it commanded the transit between Europe and Asia, between the Black Sea and the inner Mediterranean. It could be the bulwark of either continent if invasion swept one or the other. It could reach out to either for administration and conquest. It was a natural emporium. Once made, the choice seems so inevitable that the blindness of earlier rulers for a capital they did not, in their circumstances, require, can be unfairly blamed. It took fifty years for Constantine's New Rome, which he founded in 330 and which was known as his city—Constantinople—to become the habitual residence and capital of the peripatetic Emperors, but that evolution Constantine foresaw and planned. He gave it its Senate, which his son made the equal of Old Rome's, its Forum, its statues, the spoils of Greece, and its games; he gave it, too, its corn-supply from Egypt, like that of Old Rome from Africa, extending an abuse to create a capital. He made it also pre-eminently a Christian city. Its heathen temples were ghosts left by Byzantium; all that was new, living, and Constantinian was Christian, like his basilica, whose foundations can still be seen beside St Sophia.

We may glance at the future unknown to Constantine. The new creation intensified the division between East and West, for Constantinople gave cohesion to the East and was bound to be a chief, as it was the most secure, seat of Empire. Yet an Emperor there was too far off to control and defend the West; he must have a Western colleague, and his own interests, indeed

Fig. 3. Constantine and Justinian

his mere successes, were to divert the barbarian pressure from the Lower Danube to the Rhine. Thus Constantinople's prosperity and safety meant a fatal weakening of the more straggling, more exhausted West. It also entailed the survival of the Eastern Empire for 1100 years. With that strong heart and behind that bulwark, the East could repel the attacks of enemies divided by the Propontis and the Straits; it had time for many centuries to reform itself, not once only, and to survive. Not till the recruiting grounds of Asia Minor were largely lost in the eleventh century was its strength fatally impaired; not till its sea-power was lost in the twelfth century did Constantinople cease to be impregnable and fall a victim to the Latins. Even then, when the Greeks recovered it, it could still hold out 200 more years as a frontier fortress of Europe and as the remaining citadel of the ancient world and of Greek thought and literature, which were to be an inspiring guide and teacher to the modern evolution of Europe.

This was possible because Constantinople was a profoundly Greek city and the heir of ancient Hellas. But its Hellenic character was one of the factors which co-operated to cut short the dominions of the Eastern Emperors. It was not only the exhaustion of the Persian wars and the irresistible eruption of the Moslem Arabs which shore off Syria and Egypt from the Empire; it was also the mental incompatibility of the main populations of those Asiatic provinces with the Greek core of Asia Minor and the Balkans. Lack of spiritual sympathy alienated Syrians and Egyptians from their old masters, while an inner resemblance reconciled them to their new ones. This was the political significance of the contest between orthodoxy and Monophysitism in religion, then the one free sphere of the mind in which all, however illiterate, could take a side.

It was in September 323 that Constantine had vanquished his remaining rival Licinius in the battle of Chrysopolis (Skutari). In the November following he traced the line of the walls of New Rome on the opposite shore of the Bosphorus. He had conquered as a Christian Emperor, and it was as such and in charge of the Christian Church that he summoned the First Œcumenical Council to meet at Nicaea in Bithynia in the summer of 325. The Council was to complete the work of the Emperor, who had already reconciled the Christians to the Roman State, by reconciling the Christians among themselves.

It is hard to say exactly at what moment Constantine had definitely adopted his new faith. The exigencies of a ruler, whose subjects were mainly pagan, the ebb and flow of a convert's opinions 'this way and that dividing the swift mind', would make his steps ambiguous. But at any rate, after the victory of the Milvian Bridge over the heathen Maxentius in 312 *instinctu divinitatis*, 'by divine prompting,' it would be incredulous to deny that Constantine had exchanged the semi-monotheistic worship of Sol Invictus, 'the unconquered Sun', for the God of the Christians. But this was as yet the religion of Flavius Constantinus, not of the Emperor. The agreed policy of toleration, put into effect next year, when he met his colleague and then ally, Licinius, which is known as the 'Edict' of Milan, shows how far his favour to the Christians might safely go with the approval of pagan opinion. Not only was freedom of worship permitted to all, but the churches and property confiscated from Christian communities in the persecution of Diocletian were restored to them, and private pagan claims were bought out from imperial funds. Heathen deities, even 'Sol Invictus', soon disappeared from his coinage. The clergy of the Catholic Church received in 313 the exemption from public burdens which certain

13

pagan priesthoods enjoyed; manumissions of slaves in churches were to be valid as they were in certain temples. It was a 'most favoured religion' privilege applied to Christianity. More marked was his personal intervention in the Donatist schism. He laid the Donatists' appeal before the bishops in synod at Rome and Arles in 313–14 and upheld their decision. He issued on provocation a decree of persecution against these dissident and disobedient Christians in 316, a measure which he revoked on its failure in 321. In 317 his guards were bearing the monogram ☧, 'Christos', on their shields, as all his troops had done by his order at the Milvian Bridge. Its meaning must by then have been unmistakable, and it was the Christian Emperor who defeated the heathen Licinius, now again a persecutor, at Chrysopolis. The conversion which had begun, perhaps, as an opinion, had ended in the mystical, inspiring belief that he was the chosen instrument of the One True God and Saviour, the Giver of Victory.

That conviction, not unalloyed with superstition, was powerfully backed by the policy which it sanctioned. Constantine, himself inclined to and then convinced of the new religion with the multiplying proofs of his success, had the native insight to perceive the strength and cohesion of the Christians. They had a universal creed, contrasting with the wavering speculations of the pagans, their local, competing deities, their inconsistent traditions, their mixture of discordant philosophies and ethics combined with popular superstitions and dubious practices. They, he may have felt—for he was not unlettered—were still writing a literature which showed life and contemporary inspiration apart from the endless imitation of masterpieces far in the past. The universal church, with its appeal to every class and province, seemed designed to be the support and the solidifying force of the universal empire. It had been a cardinal error of his predecessors not to recognize the value of this unifying, vivifying force. They had declared war against a mighty potential ally in the name of outworn beliefs which were yearly losing their appeal. The deified Emperor had for forty years already sunk to be the favourite of the god of one or other cult. It was better to be the hallowed vicegerent of the one almighty *Summus Deus*. Christianity could be a new and living form of patriotism and loyalty, imposing obedience and inspiring veneration. Nor were the immediate gains to be despised. By favouring and then professing Christianity Constantine acquired the support of an active and stubborn minority throughout the Empire: his rivals had only the tepid adherence of interested supporters and habitual, disorganized pagans. And Constantine would know well that imperial favour would be rapidly increasing that minority by the facile conversion of all who wished to rise in this present world. These were powerful political motives to second that confidence in himself and his divine mission which his experience inspired.

As with the foundation of Constantinople, we may look forward to the future then unknown. The revolution worked by Constantine was irrevocable. The abounding life of Christianity could not fail to triumph over the anaemic gods of paganism, and the nostalgic longing for the past was unable to provide more than evanescent attempts at reaction. Only the crasser superstitions of the populace, the underworld of pagan beliefs, had vitality to survive either furtively in an acknowledged magic and spirit-worship or disguised and reputable in a Christian transmutation. The Roman Empire and ancient civilization became bound up with Christianity, from which they received new life, new power to survive, new ability to be imparted to the oncoming barbarians. Medieval Europe was to evolve and become civilized, to improve in ethical ideals, motives, and behaviour under the guidance of Christianity, through which it also received the remnants of the heritage of the ancient world. In spite of immense inner diversities, Europe was to develop its common distinctive character from its Christian mould.

(3) THE GOVERNMENT OF THE EMPIRE

The government of the Roman Empire, in which Constantine the Great carried through his religious revolution, was an autocracy based on the support of the armies, but also conforming to the rule of law inherited from the days when Rome was a free republic and still permeating thought and life. This reign of law was the hall-mark of the Empire, which it never lost and which it bequeathed to Europe. The monarch could make and alter the law at pleasure, but arbitrary, capricious infringement of it was against the spirit of his office and the Roman State. By constitutional theory all the powers of the Roman people had been transferred irrevocably to the elect of the Senate and armies. Now the Senate was not even a sleeping partner, and the choice or the assent of the armies made the despot. The whole of government, including the association of a colleague or successor, was in his hands, yet not even that could create a right of hereditary succession. The nature of his office derived from its founder, the Emperor Augustus whose name was still his title, and indeed the ever-recurring crises of the Empire forbade the expedient of hereditary rule, however much loyalty and habit might tend to maintain a dynasty which had once attained the throne. The consequent uncertainty was a weakness in that it encouraged revolt and civil war, but a strength in that it helped to ensure the capacity of the Emperors, for the ablest ruler could fight his way to a legitimate crown. The Empire suffered its worst misfortunes when loyalty to incompetent heirs was strongest. It was partly to diminish the danger of military revolts that Diocletian had adopted for the Emperors the oriental pomp and aloofness of the Persian kings. They wore the diadem with the purple[1] robe and shoes; their life became a ceremonial,

[1] I.e. the colour now called cardinal red.

15

surrounded by eunuchs and guards; their subjects admitted to audience fell prone in adoration to kiss the hem of their robe. If with the Christian dispensation they ceased to be divine, their persons, acts and possessions were 'sacred'. An aureole of majesty was made to seclude them from common humanity. But if there was shrewd policy in the system, there was also weakness: the Emperor might not know the Empire and the peoples he ruled. An active life in the world before his accession might compensate for his seclusion after it, but it was hard for him to penetrate the veil of his household and ministers, and if he succeeded to the throne in boyhood, he might become their puppet.

Centralization and despotism required the services of an immense, hierarchic bureaucracy to administer the Empire, and since the days of Diocletian, as a precaution against revolt, the civil administration had been rigidly separated from the military commands. At the head of it stood the Sacred Consistory, the Privy Council of high functionaries which advised the Emperor. Certain chiefs of departments invariably became members. Of these the chief eunuch, the Praepositus Sacri Cubiculi, became one of the most influential, and often the most hated and corrupt. He was in charge of the palace. The Count of the Sacred Largesses was the Treasurer, while the Count of the Res Privatae managed the immense imperial estates. The Quaestor of the Sacred Palace was the chief legal officer: he drafted laws and interpreted them, and advised the answers to petitions. The Master of the Offices was head of the secretariat with its manifold duties. Under him were the central *scrinia* headed by their *magistri*, which dealt with all documents, but he also commanded the imperial guards and controlled the arsenals. Perhaps his most formidable charge was that of the *agentes in rebus*, the imperial secret service. These multitudinous and ubiquitous official spies superintended the imperial postal service, conveyed official commands, and reported real or imaginary delinquencies of all and sundry. They were worse than the abuses they were supposed to prevent; their corruption was notorious, and they added to the ills and oppression of the Empire. Unlike the Master of the Offices, the Pretorian Prefects were an old institution, but although they were officials of the central administration, they were not so closely connected by necessity with the person of the Emperor. There were never less than three, and sometimes there were four among whom the Empire was divided, and unless there were two or more Augusti, only one was in immediate touch with his monarch. The East, Italy, and Gaul were the three certain centres of the prefects' spheres: when there was a fourth, he was entrusted with Illyricum, i.e. the Balkans. The duties of all may be described as those of minister of the interior and chief justice of appeal. It was a post, like that of the Quaestor, particularly fitted for an eminent lawyer, yet for a trained administrator as well. The pretorian prefect received appeals from the governors in his sphere, but he also superintended the levy of taxes, the furnishing of supplies to the army, and the conduct of the provincial executive officials. The discretion allowed to him was great; he judged without appeal; yet he appears as more important for routine efficiency than for policy.

For the purposes of civil government the Empire was divided into some 120 provinces which were grouped in twelve dioceses. In the West lay the dioceses of Britain, Gaul, Spain, Africa, and Illyricum; in the East Dacia, Macedonia, Thrace, Asia, Pontus, the East (Syria), and Egypt. The vicar of each diocese assisted the pretorian prefect to supervise the provincial governors, and was an alternative judge of appeal from them, appeals from the vicar not going to the prefect but to the Emperor. The provincial governors themselves, most of whom bore the title of President (*Praeses*), also united executive and judicial authority. Below them were the oligarchies of Curiales, who ruled the cities through their chiefs, the local Senates, the members of which were styled Decurions. An exceptional government was enjoyed by Rome itself. The Prefect of the City, whose office went back to the reign of Augustus, and who alone among officials still wore the ancient Roman toga, ruled the capital and presided in the Senate, while his appellate jurisdiction extended over a circuit of 100 miles. But although the cities with their dependent countryside were the typical units which made up the province, they did not cover all its expanse. The domains (*saltus*) of the Emperor and the great landowners, mostly senators, were largely exempt from them and the governors and controlled by imperial procurators or private stewards. It was an anticipation of medieval feudalism.

In itself this elaborate hierarchy was cumbrous, but corruption and suspicion made it burdensome to the last degree. Every official was watched and duplicated by the *agentes in rebus*, whose sins in corruption and extortion were worse than his own. *Defensores* from among the wealthy were appointed to supervise the cities and aid the oppressed, but the most efficient check was provided by the Christian bishop whose voluntary arbitration was authorized and encouraged by the Emperors: he was the most equitable judge obtainable, and as a refuge to the oppressed deservedly gained much of the influence which he expended in the doctrinal disputes of the age. Here again the coming Middle Age cast its shadow before.

Except in certain frontier districts, where the *dux* or general of the troops exercised the civil government also, military command was completely separated from civilian rule. The highest office was that of Master of the Soldiers (*magister militum*), either of the horse (*m. equitum*) or of the foot (*m. peditum*), or of both (*m. utriusque militiae*). In the latter days of Constantine there were four Magistri; eventually there were eight. Two of them accompanied the Emperor, but the function of all was much the same: to

17

command an army and conduct a war. Beneath them the forces on the frontier were commanded by some thirty-five dukes (*duces*), of whom ten were known by the higher title of counts (*comites*), i.e. 'companions' of the Emperor. Besides these there were the two Counts of the Domestics, the guards of the Emperor, composed at first of *Protectores*, who were selected veterans, and of Domestics proper, who were well-born officers in training. The rest of the army fell into three main classes, the *limitanei*, the *comitatenses*, and the *palatini*. The *limitanei* were almost a garrison militia stationed on the fortified frontiers where they had their hereditary farms in return for military service: they were largely of barbarian extraction, the descendants of the captives of old wars or the residuum of old migrations. The *comitatenses*, on the other hand, together with the *pseudo-comitatenses* which Constantine had drawn from the *limitanei* to reinforce them, were mobile troops, who could take the field anywhere. The *palatini* formed a similar field-army but were cantoned in the provinces near the Emperor's residence. The strength of the legions, who were the heavy infantry, was now about 1000 men, for even the older legions, who still numbered 6000 men, were divided in practice into similar regiments. They were levied by a mixture of heredity, conscription, and voluntary enlistment. The *auxilia*, in contrast, who were cavalry and light infantry, were mainly barbarian mercenaries from outside the Empire, and were of higher repute for their fighting qualities. Among them the heavy cavalry, cataphracts trained in the Persian method, were growing in importance. They wore scale armour, and carried long spears as well as bows. Their charge and volleys were becoming a decisive element in victory even in the non-Persian wars.

The army as a whole was a disciplined and formidable array, but the proportion of barbarians and semi-barbarians within it was a grave danger not because of disloyalty, but because it proved the increasingly unwarlike character of the civilized population of the Empire. The long-continued cult of callous ferocity and sadistic sensationalism in the gladiatorial shows of the amphitheatre had debased the people without preserving their virility. The appetite for this supremely selfish, insane pleasure was fostered by the popularity-hunting government to the destruction of public spirit. In Italy and Egypt self-mutilation, by amputating the thumb, was practised to escape conscription. Yet war was nearer to men than ever before in imperial times. The disastrous civil contests of the third century had been accompanied and followed by barbarian invasions which pierced far beyond the fortified frontier zones and all but wrecked the Empire. It was a sad sequel to the erstwhile Roman peace when the Emperor Aurelian (270–5) undertook the fortification of the cities and even of Rome itself, and the small circumference of the walls of the provincial towns is a striking witness to the decrease in the numbers of a population which had never attained the density of modern Europe. The plague under Marcus Aurelius (165–6), succeeded by a century of war and devastation, had reduced the human assets of the state beyond danger point.

Since the edict of the Emperor Caracalla in 212 every citizen of a city in the Empire was also a Roman citizen and subject to the Roman Law. But that was far from implying the equality or homogeneity of the citizen body. Rather it was becoming ever more split up into classes and occupations which were in process of being hereditary castes. The first cleft was that between the *honestiores* (honourable) and the *humiliores* (lower). The *honestiores* included the senatorial order, the equestrian order (both transformed inheritances from the Republic), the soldiers, and the decurions: their punishments for crime were lighter, and they could only be tortured on special counts. The *humiliores* were the rest of the population. Among the *honestiores* the highest in rank were another survival, the two ordinary consuls who gave their name to the year. Surrounded with extraordinary pomp and burdened with expense which only great wealth could bear, the consulship was an empty honour conferred on high birth or eminent services: the Emperors themselves took the office at least once in their reign. Below the consuls came the patricians, since Constantine a personal dignity, unconnected save in name with the hereditary patricians of earlier times. The next rank was that of high officials, like the pretorian prefect, who were styled *viri illustres*, the next that of officials who were entitled *spectabiles*, below them again came the *clarissimi*, who all belonged to the senatorial order, which was much wider than the actual members of the two Senates of Rome and Constantinople. The *clarissimi* were in the main the descendants of imperial soldiers, officials, and contractors who had made fortunes. But few could trace their male lineage to the nobles of the Republic. Below them came other titles, *eminentissimus*, *perfectissimus* and the like, which denoted the precedence an office held in the official hierarchy. The fulsomeness of these titles, disguised by habit, was an expression, as they were invented, of a courtly, servile age and its pompous, privileged bureaucracy.

The class of *curiales*, or town-dwelling landowners of middle fortune, governed the cities as a hereditary duty. But craftsmen and traders, too, bakers, shipmen and the like, were turned into hereditary corporations from which there was no escape. Even the class of paupers (*proletarii*) who received the public dole of food at Rome seems itself to have been hereditary. The peasant class of *coloni* in like manner were tied to their paternal holdings (*adscripticii glebae*) which they cultivated as a state duty. Freedom of life and occupation had in short largely vanished from the Roman Empire. Men existed to pay their dues to the State and to keep the anaemic fabric of society in working order. The dreadful, callous practice of legal infanticide by the exposure of new-born children, whether unwanted girls or weakly boys, which was endemic in parts at least, and those the most

19

civilized, of the Empire, is perhaps evidence of the small hope men placed in the future, just as the fierce degrading shows of captives forced to fight and criminals exposed to wild beasts in the amphitheatres suggest the jaded boredom of the present to the town dwellers. Both practices were frowned upon by the Christian Church and Constantine.

The causes of this rigid, government-driven system lay partly in the drab and aimless life of men outside the imperial bureaucracy, partly in the economic decline of the overtasked Empire, both perhaps to be summarized as the senility of a civilization and its inducements to action. That civilization had been formed and had made its advance in the free city-states, in an atmosphere of city pride, of patriotic competition, and of dazzling opportunity. City politics were world politics: each citizen could take his part in the common effort and could hope for his share in gain and fame. When monarchy came with Alexander the Great, there was still a civilization to spread and an empire to exploit. The Roman conquest reduced political activity to local affairs, but there was still the Graeco-Roman civilization to impart to pupil races, still the native city to be adorned and to excel its neighbours in an age of peace, still the sense of expanding energy and increasing activity. This was the age of private munificence and municipal extravagance, encouraged by the government. Temples, baths, basilicas for public business, theatres, amphitheatres, spectacles were lavished on the townsmen by their wealthier fellows and their magistrates. But it was largely unproductive expenditure which slowly drained the wealth of each locality without facilitating its renewal. Over parts of the Empire, such as Britain, the city was an artificial institution set up by the government, a luxury only maintainable in times of prosperity. The imperial government was provoked to supervise municipal administration more and more, and to place the towns in leading-strings. Town notables, as town autonomy vanished, found they had become subordinate implements of the imperial bureaucracy, and the life went out of their public functions, which grew every decade more disagreeable, more profitless and more oppressive. They had to be driven to their unwelcome tasks and burdens, which brought no real honour and gratified no ambition. Like beasts at the water-wheel, they plodded a dreary round to haul up the taxes needed by their rulers. Provincial sentiment, although it played a part in the army revolts which had rent the Empire in the third century, did not as yet provide more than a disintegrating force in civil life. It made men sluggish in imperial concerns, rather than energetic in their own. In short, Roman patriotism, though not Roman pride, was in a way the business of the army and the bureaucracy.

(4) ECONOMIC LIFE

The economic decline of the Empire was a still more potent factor in this moral paralysis of its citizens. A long story must here be cut short. The peace of the early Empire and its victories had produced a vigorous inter-provincial trade seconded by the labour of a multitude of cheap slaves, won in the wars, and employed on great estates or in workshops. But with the spread of civilization, especially westward, and with the equality of universal citizenship, the provinces provided more and more for their own ordinary wants; inter-provincial trade became far more restricted to the luxuries or quasi-luxuries which had always formed its staple. Indeed, the civil wars of the third century and the dislocation of the Empire must have put an end to most of it, and a full recovery from those disasters never happened. Then, too, with the end of expansion and conquest and with the adoption of the policy of settling barbarian captives as military peasants on the depleted frontiers, the supply of cheap slaves gave out: slaves became a costly luxury. Thus the means of production on a large scale for distribution at a distance were severely limited.

One of the worst evils of the third century had been the debasement of the coinage, when the Emperors were attempting to provide for increasing military and civil expenditure from the taxes of a population reduced in numbers and prosperity by plague and war. The debasement, besides diminishing in the end the value of the revenue, was pernicious to trade near and far and bore its full share in the economic decline of the Empire. So debased and disorganized was the coin that the sacks (*folles*) of what was really base metal, issued by the mints, were passed from hand to hand unopened, the clumsiest, bulkiest form of a circulating medium. Still more significant was the custom that taxes and salaries, even the soldiers' pay, were rendered more and more in kind. This avoided the uncertainties of depreciated money, but the ease which it might thereby give the taxpayer was more than counter-balanced by the burden of transport which it imposed upon him and by the waste and expense of storage and deterioration when the crops were on the way to and when they reached the government magazines. Diocletian and Constantine between them did indeed restore the coinage. The new gold *solidus* retained its fineness for centuries. The new silver coins were genuine silver. But both gold and silver were only legal tender when weighed. Clipping and abrasion no doubt produced a diffidence which the government felt as much as any one. Only the tiny *follis* (now meaning the separate coin) was merely counted. The gold and silver coins, too, were less plentiful for currency, it seems. The mines in the Empire were less productive. A considerable quantity of the precious metals had leaked to the East in the purchase of luxuries, there being little counter-exports to exchange for jewels, silks, and spices from India and

China. Still more perhaps was hoarded in various ways, as a treasury reserve, as the household equipment of the court and the wealthy, as the ornament of temples and then of churches. It did not assist in the revivification of moribund commerce, which might in fact seem to be a risky and needless investment. Nor did it supersede the custom of taxes and payments in kind, which remained to clog and burden the administration and economic life of the Empire.

The luxury trade manufacture within the Empire had its strongest home in the East. Syria produced its dyed webs. There were celebrated wines there, in Asia Minor, and in Italy. Trade in necessaries was scantier, but oil with which food was cooked was sent from the olive-bearing zone elsewhere, and the corn-tribute from Egypt for Constantinople and from Africa for Rome had to be handled under government control. Again, iron and the metals and pottery had their producing centres, whence they journeyed to government arsenals, to the mints, or to shops and private buyers. The profits of this and of local trade cannot, however, have been alluring, for the Emperors made the membership of the trading corporations hereditary and compulsory. It was a crime to fly from an occupation and even in some cases to marry outside its circle. The desire to escape from the burdens of life in the decadent and overtaxed towns was obvious as the fourth century grew old.

Yet there was wealth in the Empire, though vegetative and not producing greater wealth. Strewn over the provinces lay the estates, the *latifundia*, of the senatorial order, yielding an ample revenue and supplying all save luxury needs to their proprietors. Some of these estates and incomes reached fabulous proportions, and as residence in the capital was no longer required, the *clarissimi* were becoming in large part a provincial, rural nobility. Given to country sports and imitative, lifeless culture, they lived in their spacious villas or country houses amid their dependants. The domestic manufactures of the estate were almost departments of a self-sufficing area under the control of its lord. A certain portion of the cultivated land was reserved as a home-farm; the rest was divided into small holdings, which supported the *coloni* and their families, who gave as rent a share of the crops, and supplemented it by prescribed work on the home-farm. The system all tended to a self-sufficing, stagnant economy.

The class of *coloni* was formed from very different elements. There were the descendants of pre-Roman serfs, whose condition had changed but little; there were those of barbarian captives settled on the land; there were slaves planted out in tenements; there were former free peasants who found life easier and safer by becoming the tenants or protégés of the great landowner; there were absconding *curiales* and others from the towns fleeing the taxes. But the general picture is fairly uniform. The peasant was bound to his hereditary plot to which he had an hereditary right. He suffered from the oppressions of his landlord and the government, but each afforded some protection from the other, the landlord the most. Apart from barbarian invasions, such as those which desolated Illyricum, he enjoyed a measure of stability and security. In the course of the fourth century, he was made to pay his taxes through his landlord, which was possibly a benefit, and was deprived of the power to bring a civil action against his landlord, an almost certain grievance. The landlord was his magistrate, and might illegally keep his private prison and his private armed troop. It was a life far on the way to medieval feudalism. The peasant's best protection lay not in the law, but in the private, obvious interest of the lord, which led him to keep his estate populated and prosperous. Better terms were obtainable by the varieties of tenure under *emphyteusis*. This was the lease of land with a light rent to redeem it from uncultivation or to turn it into olive-grove or vineyard. The land would be forfeited if the conditions were broken, but otherwise the tenure was in practice perpetual. A valuable tenant was not to be lost. In fact the fear of land going out of cultivation was a constant preoccupation of government and landlord. Derelict land had by law to be taken over by the neighbours; land could not be sold without its *coloni*. Yet in the fertile lands of Campania, Ionia and Egypt there is evidence of derelict arable, and this was not due to barbarian devastation. The fleeing peasant might take to begging or brigandage or, if he were a devout Christian, to monasticism.

A chief cause of the economic distress, visible in town and country in spite of transient improvement, was the severe pressure of the wasteful taxation needed to keep the revived Empire solvent. It would probably have been bearable if it had not been for the extortions and corruption of the officials and the oppression of the powerful, and these vices no laws, no remedies, no machinery (such as the *agentes in rebus*) devised by the Emperors were able to prevent: indeed, they were possibly more rampant on the vast imperial estates than on those of the great landowners. The system of taxation had been reformed by Diocletian; it was equitable in intention, and perhaps in practice had it been honestly administered, but at its best it was cumbrous and obscure, even to officials, at least with regard to its chief component, the land-tax or *annona*. The land of each city and great domain was surveyed and roughly classed in separate units (*iuga*) according to its extent, its produce, its working resources and fertility. By the combination of these factors, it was liable to a proportion of the *annona* on the territory to which it belonged, the amount of which was fixed by imperial edict (*indictio*) for each year. It was supplemented by a poll-tax on the inhabitants. In the towns the tradesmen (*collegiati*) paid an oppressive tax, the *chrysargyrion*, and the *curiales* the five-yearly *aurum coronarium*, while the *clarissimi* were subject to the heavy *aurum oblaticium*. To these

23

taxes we must add that on sales and the various *angariae*, such as the imperial post, which scarred the districts along the roads.

The worst lot in the system of taxation fell to the *curiales*. It was their duty to supplement the insufficient income of their town out of their own property in order to cover its expenses. But more onerous still was their function of collecting the imperial taxes which were assessed to their city and its dependent territory. In any case this was a difficult and odious task—in 383 the domains of the *clarissimi* were removed from their area, which must have been a measure of relief—but the fact that they were obliged to make up any deficiency in the receipts made it intolerable. Flight was forbidden under heavy penalties; they were legally tethered to their city and caste; the land of an absconding *curialis* or of an extinct family had to be taken over by their fellows. Late in the fourth century inscription as a member of the *curia* was used as a punishment for certain offences. To live concealed as a *colonus* on a great estate seemed to many a preferable life if it could be achieved. In self-defence they were extortionate and corrupt when they had the power to be so. In fact, although the East as a whole was better off than the West, the city organization of the Empire was breaking down under its burdens. The lesser landowner, the trader, the peasant-freeholder, and the *colonus* all had to be chained to their hereditary tasks so as to support the overladen State and provide it with funds and food to carry on. The benefits of civilized life and the pleasure in its activities seemed to be outweighed by its miseries.

(5) CULTURE

It is to be remembered that an appreciable proportion of the Empire's inhabitants had no share in either its Greek or its Latin civilization. In Britain the majority of the country folk still spoke their native Celtic language, the ancestor of Welsh, Cornish and Breton. Round Trier and elsewhere in Gaul allied tongues were living; St Irenaeus (*ob.* 202) had preached in Gaulish as well as in Greek and Latin. On each side of the Pyrenees, Basque, which survives to-day, maintained itself. Germanic was spoken in considerable areas west of the Rhine. In Africa the Moors kept up their still living Berber dialects, and the settled upper class retained the Semitic Punic, introduced by the Carthaginians, and still possibly alive in Malta. In Illyricum, in spite of widespread Latin, the native idiom held its own and has produced modern Albanian. When we look at the East, the pre-Greek languages assume national proportions and possess national literatures which repel Greek with but subordinate infiltration of Hellenism. Copts in Egypt, Aramaeans in Syria, Armenians in the northern mountains, not to mention the Asiatic tribesmen of the Taurus and the Celtic Galatians, who were illiterate, clung firmly to their ancient languages, which embodied their distinctive habits of thought and steadily sapped their co-hesion with the Empire.

The Greek and Latin speakers, however, were largely illiterate peasants and artisans, whose varying patois by no means allowed them to appreciate the conservative literary tongue. That was a privilege of the educated classes, and they were perhaps more alive to the externals than to the inner spirit of the heritage that they revered. The investigating curiosity of the Greeks had not survived the Roman conquest; knowledge of natural science had ceased to grow. The system of education in rhetoric, although implying much more than oratory, had concentrated men's attention on declamatory, exaggerated phrases, on the art of spinning sentences to a patient audience, on the resources of a pleader with a view to his career. Where there were points of law to be discussed, principles of law to be applied, and plain facts to reason on, this society could be highly ration-alistic; but in general the rationalism of an earlier generation had dis-appeared. It was an age of signs and wonders, of emotional credulity and vulgar magic. Partly this may have been due to the mere predominance of the average citizen whether hellenized or romanized, now that, so to say, society had been denuded of those thin intellectual strata which had produced Western civilization. The more primitive rocks now made the landscape. Partly it was the effect of the steady penetration of oriental influences, which had life and originality now denied to the West, and pre-ferred the marvellous and esoteric to the matter-of-fact, which sought for mystical illumination rather than for explanation. The continued disasters of the times, the long absence of the political liberty in which ancient habits of thought had been formed, the loss of even personal freedom in the regimented state organized by Diocletian, the very dead-weight of insuper-able, unattainable models in literature, thought, and art, all combined to drive both eastern and western men into themselves, to spin a visionary universe from the unreachable ego. The worship of the stately, idealized Olympian gods had palled and become an ancient custom, that of sheer human power in the deified Emperors seemed less natural as unity dis-appeared and fleeting rulers were slain or carried captive in civil and foreign wars; the little or local deities who gave fertility, the real, heartfelt religion of average folk, were always perhaps more like familiar spirits than gods, and were less attractive amid derelict fields and scanty offspring. The eastern cult of Mithras seems to have been a soldier's creed which supplied a divine personal protector by a magical ceremony, which appealed more to credulity than to evidence. Other similar cults like that of Isis differed less in method and aim than in the public they addressed. The official cult of Sol Invictus, the unconquered sun, looks like an attempt to acclimatize a speculative monotheism with 'a local habitation and a name'. Save in Syria, whence it spread, it was a governmental creed.

The most philosophic form of pagan illuminism appeared in the Neo-Platonism founded by the Egyptian Plotinus (*ob.* 269) and propagated by the Phoenician Porphyry (*ob.* 304). An exalted pantheistic monotheism was grafted by Plotinus with subtlety and fervour on Platonic thought. The material world was an emanation from the indescribable spiritual unity and yet a glorious hindrance to the reunion of the soul with its unalloyed original. Oriental asceticism and ecstatic vision were natural concomitants of the system, and the pagan gods were without difficulty accepted, nay cherished, as embodiments, aspects, and glimpses of the One. With the Aramaean Iamblichus (*ob.* 330) the degenerate, fanatic side of this philosophy took the lead. Magic and miracles, the boosting of any and every superstition so long as it was not Christian, testified to the desperate efforts of educated pagans to retain belief in their multitudinous deities. Unable to be sceptics, averse from a revolutionary monotheism, they slid down from Platonic heights, grasping at any tuft of grass or withered thorn. There must have been a competition, however unacknowledged, for the suffrage of the primitive masses of the population, a suffrage easiest to be gained by an appeal to their ingrained belief in spells and charms and the mystery of petty ritual. But that it should be congenial to the Neo-Platonists reveals the mentality of their credulous age.

The law was a favourite study of the upper-class Roman citizen, whether in the civil service or out of it. But it is noticeable that, although schools of law flourished, the series of the creative commentators, those great jurisconsults who had done so much to develop it, had ended in the middle of the third century. The age of Constantine saw codifiers and collectors. None the less legal studies retained their influence. The education of the schools of rhetoric was largely directed to produce good pleading in the courts. A successful pleader might rise in the imperial service and become a governor or a minister. Lawyers still shared with soldiers the government of the Roman world.

The cultured men of the day, when they were not engrossed in law, philosophy, or Christian theology, tended to an anecdotic antiquarianism which required more learning than intellect. One of the best of these students was the friend of Constantine, the ultra-learned Christian Eusebius, bishop of Caesarea in Palestine. Bred, one may say, in the ample library left by Origen in Caesarea, Eusebius had a critical sense of documentary evidence and a large conception of universal history. His *Chronography* was to be the basis of general historical knowledge for centuries; his *Ecclesiastical History* preserved and arranged a mass of carefully compiled information. It is true that precision of statement yields to overcharged general rhetoric. An objective treatment of facts was beyond the reach and the desires of an age devoted to flattery, controversy, and propaganda, but Eusebius is an instance of the intellectual superiority of the

Christian writers over their pagan contemporaries. They had a consistent scheme of knowledge, a concrete object of research; they had something to say and still had liberty to say it.

The art of the age is in its turn self-revealing. We find an imitative largeness of conception natural to an ecumenic empire, and the skilful engineering of long experience in practical building—the arch, the apse, and the cupola were great stand-bys for the architect. Withal there spread from the East, from Egypt and Syria, an originality and emotionalism and a sense of colour and gorgeousness which make the hues of their predecessors seem elementary. Of craftsmanship in glass, ivory, metal and stone there was plenty, mostly oriental in origin. But in the West especially, there was in building the curse of official bigness and pomposity. The intellectual grasp of reality, the rationalism of Greek art, the delicate, unrelaxing vigilance, the apt simplicity of earlier times were gone. They were not of facile manufacture nor did they produce quick effects; and mere imitation of past masterpieces had little inspiration and ceased to be desired. They were replaced in smaller objects by rich decoration of varied device, often the most effective when least Hellenic in tradition: the barbaric art of the steppes was invading the Empire. And though the same shop might produce for pagan and Christian, the Christian themes, however much they reproduced older emblems and scenes, had a new interpretation, a new conviction of appeal, which made them more living—in short, better art. Ancient statuary and the zeal to represent the human and animal forms with the exquisiteness of nature seem to have died; lumpish, inexact energy in the limbs, a stolid glare in the coarse faces, a tailor-like truth in the dress were the effects aimed at and achieved, unless sculptures were plundered from old monuments to deck the new. But there was both emotion, splendour, and beauty in the schemes of coloured marbles which encrusted the inner walls, and in the variegated glass mosaics which adorned the curved ceilings. Here again Christian beliefs gave the best and novel themes, just as the Christian churches could give meaning and use to the creative invention of the architect. The favourite form among several was the basilica, the rectangular hall ending in an apse, in front of which stood the altar and around which were the seats of the clergy. It was a design which had served for halls of justice and audience, and in the first century appears in a subterranean temple at Rome. But besides its own variants, such as three to five aisles, subsidiary apses, transepts which suggested the cross, and an entrance hall, there were rivals such as the round church, suitable for a baptistery, all of them with appropriateness for Christian ritual and freely designed from the accumulated traditions which no longer oppressed the builder.

The Christian art, like the Christian literature of the age, was in fact a part of the general culture of the Empire, giving greater scope to its

Fig. 4. Constantine's Arch, Rome

practitioners by reason of its new purposes, its new heartfelt subject-matter, and perhaps still more by its new freedom when all else was bound down in thought and action, in caste and livelihood under a bureaucratic, suspicious despotism. The Christians were only a minority in most parts, a half in some eastern provinces, a tenth or merely a twentieth in others and the west, when the Empire in the person of Constantine made its peace with them. But, whether left alone as mostly happened or fiercely assailed in the persecutions, they were an independent community in their religion, with their own way of life, their own theology and inner controversies, and their own officials and institutions. They formed an adult world-wide organization, not derived from the Empire but allied with it, almost a state within the state, accustomed to self-management, where every member counted for something and could take sides in what concerned his church and its beliefs. The Emperor, now a Christian, could share in the Church's life and influence it, but he could not dominate what the Empire had not created. He was inevitably immensely powerful in the Church, but he interfered chiefly in dangerous crises of disputes affecting the unity of the whole body. In the normal life of the Church, it was self-governing. This external fact agreed with a fundamental tenet of Christianity itself. Pagan religion had been a civic or family function for earthly welfare. The Christian faith was the way for the individual believer of any rank or race to attain eternal salvation. It was not a part of civil life, but beside it and in essence superior to it. The problem of Church and State begins for Europe with Constantine.

(6) THE ORGANIZATION OF THE CHURCH

The Christian organization may be described as a loose confederation of autonomous communities, held together by the conviction of unity and fraternity in a common faith, fortified in practice by continuous mutual intercourse. Since Christianity had grown up amid the city-state organization of the Empire, its autonomous communities, its 'churches',[1] were mostly city-communities, although rural communities, where cities were sparse and great estates, imperial or other, wide, did make their appearance. Of each church the ruler, focus and embodiment of its tradition, was its bishop, elected by the community and considered to be the successor of the Apostles even when the church was not of immediate apostolic foundation. He was assisted in his pastoral office by the presbyters, who in many dioceses, to use a later term, were also taking charge of the districts and their several churches into which the ever-increasing Christian population was divided. Like the bishops, but with a more unanimous assent, they were now considered as a separate order in the Church, possessed by the laying on of hands of the power to consecrate the bread and wine in the Eucharist, the central act of Christian worship. The presbyter was a *sacerdos*, ἱερεύς, a priest like those of the Jews; the bishop was a *summus sacerdos*. In the bishop's administrative duties, he was assisted by the order of deacons. Below these again came the sub-deacons, the exorcists, acolytes, and readers (lectors), and the deaconesses, the minor orders of a later time. A growing custom approved the slow promotion in ordination from the lesser dignity to the higher, but in actual importance the deacons who had charge of church property often outweighed the more sacred presbyters. Here two facts of high significance stand out. Christianity gave to women a position as personalities, not merely as mothers, which paganism had denied them. The old fertility cults had ceased to appeal to the educated class. Women as well as men were martyrs and confessors. Chastity, virginity and the gentler virtues were held in the highest honour; indeed the severity of oriental asceticism

---

[1] It will be convenient to recall the variant meanings of 'Church', (1) the whole Christian body or a dissident body of Christians, (2) the local community under its bishop, (3) the building for Christian worship. Later in the Middle Ages there emerges (4) the Christian organization within a large territory, e.g. the Gallican or the German Church.

had made its way into Egyptian and Syrian Christianity and was rapidly spreading. Constantine's social legislation, which punished, sometimes with desperate cruelty, offences against morals, is evidence of his conversion to Christianity as well as of his diagnosis of social evils. He discountenanced the callous exposure of unwanted infants and the savage gladiatorial shows. Women were the most zealous of converts and the most effectual of domestic missionaries, for they were in charge in the impressionable years of life. To them was likewise largely due the second fact. In 321 Constantine decreed that the Christian churches could receive by gift or legacy anything from anybody, an unexampled privilege which no pagan temple had ever enjoyed. The result was that wealth flowed into them with rapid profusion, much of it derived from the piety of devout ladies. By a phenomenon which has recurred in other times, the extinction of the male line and the accumulation of wealth by heiresses were not uncommon among the wealthy and well-to-do, and their benefactions, seconded by imperial and other liberality, rendered in a century the Bishop of Rome, for instance, among the greatest of the landed proprietors of the Empire. If some of these riches provided a too alluring bait to the ambitious and worldly and were spent in sumptuous luxury, they also provided means which were zealously used to relieve the poor and distressed, to finance orphanages and hospitals, to build and adorn churches. The spate of conversions to Christianity which set in when the Emperor was a Christian was not exclusively owing to self-interested ambition or fashion any more than to the moral and intellectual appeal of the faith; there was always the active benevolence of the churches to attract the poor and oppressed. The bishop was an intercessor for the unfortunate, his church an asylum for the harshly or unjustly condemned; his arbitration was fairer and less costly than the tribunal's judgement; Constantine seems to have encouraged his judicial powers. And he was the choice of the people. He could freely persuade them from the pulpit. Can we wonder at the unbridled fervour with which they flung themselves into the doctrinal disputes which affected the whole being and teaching of their community, and which they were free to debate in contrast to the chained submission of the rest of their lives?

While in each city its church under its bishop was effectively organized, it was not the same with the whole body of Christians. Yet the local churches had always been in close touch with one another by personal intercourse and by letters. The bishops of a province and even of a civil diocese were accustomed to act together. Councils of bishops to settle disputed points were growing in frequency: in 314, under Constantine's patronage, a council of Western bishops met at Arles to adjudicate on the Donatist schism in Africa, and Constantine for some years endeavoured to enforce their decision by persecuting the recalcitrant Donatists. But the most effectual bond of unity lay in the influence of the great sees. The bishop of a provincial capital in the East was the metropolitan of the lesser cities of its province: this was modelled on secular divisions, and the custom became universal in the century after Constantine. More important were the churches of the super-eminent cities. Here, as was natural, the believers were most numerous, the city's secular rank most impressive, the line of bishops and martyrs most illustrious, the tradition of the past best attested and most ancient, and lastly the prestige of apostolic foundation best remembered and accepted. Rome, Alexandria and Antioch stood out among competitors. Rome, with all the glamour of the Eternal City, declared its bishop the successor of St Peter, the prince of the Apostles, and of St Paul, over whose relics Constantine had built two famous basilicas. Its church claimed that its pure tradition was never sullied with heretical opinions. Antioch, the capital of the East, where the name of Christian was first given, also claimed St Peter as its first bishop. The learned church of Alexandria, the capital of Egypt, was said to have been founded by the evangelist St Mark, the disciple of St Peter, and in secular matters the corn-supply and the artistic productions which went to Rome had long bound it closely to the centre of the Empire. While the influence of other sees depended more on the personality of a particular bishop during his life, Rome, Antioch, and Alexandria gave pre-eminence to each temporary occupant, and how much they owed to their secular standing was shown by the swift rise of the New Rome, Constantinople, to an equal rank.

(7) STRENGTH AND WEAKNESSES OF THE EMPIRE

In traversing the catalogue of the characteristics and the weaknesses of the 'late classical' Roman Empire, it is a hard task to give a harmonious picture in which the lights and shades should fall in a just proportion, and in their variety and detail should form a whole and provide some reasonable estimate of the reasons why the Eastern half of the Empire survived for long centuries and the Western half broke up under barbarian conquerors and descended to a lower stage of civilization. Stress may be rightly laid on the share of 'contingency', the chance of certain events which drew a long train of consequences after them. The Empire, terribly exhausted by plague and civil war in the third century after Christ, was exposed to the violent pressure of barbaric invasions, which in their turn were due to external developments partly caused by events in the distant East and wholly, wherever they happened, outside Roman control. The Empire was temporarily saved by a succession of most able rulers, but the very means, the rigid centralized organization which they found necessary for survival, were themselves an evil, and time was never given in the West, though it was in the East, for their full effect and at least partial transmutation for the better. But while 'contingencies' may give us the deciding immediate

31

impulses to what actually happened, they cannot tell us what would have occurred without them, nor can they throw light on the fundamental state of things which made them so effectual. It may be suggested that the Roman Empire and 'Ancient' classical civilization was suffering from senescence and spiritual exhaustion in its polity, in its ideas and culture, in the lack of depth in its contact with the masses of the population, into which it was ceasing to infiltrate, in the stagnant economic system which decayed in material wealth when increasing wealth was urgently needed. Able men in practical affairs abounded, but the rationalism of ancient thought was absent in literature and art, perhaps, too, one may say, in politics; how much the life of ancient, imaginative polytheism had vanished is obvious from the apathy whith which the pagan majority accepted a malevolent toleration and then suppression from the Christian Emperors. Tolerated paganism, losing adherents day by day, was the religion of cultured *honestiores* for old times' sake with Neo-Platonism as its intellectual backing, and of rude peasants still in awe of the gods of tilth and woodland. The self-administering city was largely an artificial structure west of the Alps, and where it was indigenous had lost its half-free character and therewith its vitality. Under the crushing burden of taxation and with the retrogression of trade, men had to be chained and forced to their occupations as a duty to the State. Universal compulsion succeeded and completed the demise of zeal. The swarming bureaucracy employed to keep the flagging Empire in action was oppressive, corrupt, wasteful, and unmanageable. The very strength of provincial, separatist feeling was a danger to the unity of the ecumenic Empire and therefore to be checked and feared. The most warlike provinces, such as Illyricum, had been depopulated; others, such as Italy, had been drained of their adventurous elements; and the result was that the army was largely made up of barbarian mercenaries or of half-barbarians settled as military tenants on the frontiers. The dangers of the system were immense, for the armies were the source of power, and it would not be long before barbarian generals, uneducated or half-educated, though surprisingly loyal, disposed of the Empire. It is true that this army was cheaper to maintain than the native volunteer, but its discipline and efficiency decayed with its barbarization, and its numbers, perhaps some 300,000 or 400,000 men in all, were in any case too few to protect the interminable frontier and hold back more powerful and more desperate foes.

If this were all, the Empire might have been expected to crumble any moment instead of experiencing a genuine revival under Constantine. But there were better symptoms too. There was still a great reservoir of human capacity in the Empire, men who could plan, act, and govern; there was still a population of hardy peasants and industrious townsmen. In the East there were wealthy, trading towns which had not lost their resilience under their burdens; the Asiatic provinces had suffered less than most others. There were well-chosen defensible frontiers with an elaborate system of fortification scientifically guarded. The Empire indeed, even in its evils, was a triumph of organization worthy of the civilized, ancient world. The Roman law, confusing as might be its sources and its local variants, was a common possession of the citizens, binding the Empire together by its civilized excellence. And the sense of unity and pride in being Roman, a member of the one truly civilized society with its overwhelming prestige, was strong still, if passively obedient. Given time to recuperate, given a faith to revivify men's trust in themselves and devotion to a cause, given, too, a contraction of the frontiers able to convert provincial preferences into an imperial patriotism which should be identical with a fervently held imperial religion, given in fact what happened in the East and was cut short prematurely in the West, the Empire and its civilization could be preserved and renovated, but not, as its history showed, be rejuvenated. The weight of the past was too oppressive for more than a stabilized vitality.

CHAPTER 2

THE NEIGHBOURS OF THE EMPIRE

The map of the Roman Empire reveals one of its major misfortunes, that save on a part of the Atlantic seaboard it was encircled by a ring of actual or potential foes. In Africa the plundering Moorish tribes of the Sahara demanded a frontier garrison at the least; if that was depleted, their inroads meant loss of territory, for they would be joined by provincial Moors, little more civilized than themselves. The Nubians of Ethiopia were indeed inoffensive, and the disunited Arabs across the Red Sea were as yet no danger, while their northern tribes along the Syrian frontier were useful, if predatory, allies. But the great oriental monarchy of Persia or Iran under the Sassanian dynasty was a rival empire and a most formidable enemy.

(1) THE PERSIAN EMPIRE

Sassanian Persia claimed to be, and indeed was, the heir of the Persian Empire of Cyrus and Darius, which had ruled Nearer Asia from the Aegean to the Indus centuries earlier. That eclectic empire had collected, added to, and continued the earlier civilizations, such as the Babylonian, within its area. But the Greek conquest by Alexander had intervened and spread over it a Hellenistic layer, percolating into the native population, deeply in Asia Minor and Syria, more superficially farther east. Then had begun a resurgence of the older culture, a reaction of orientalism, led at first by the Parthian dynasty of the Arsacids, which reconstituted the Iranian empire east of Mesopotamia. In 227 the Arsacids were overthrown and replaced by the vassal King of Persis (Persia proper), the Sassanian Ardashir (Artaxerxes) I. Thus the true Persians of the south recovered the leadership of Iran. But the change of dynasty did not merely mean a change in the particular province which held the hegemony in Iran. It meant a stronger central control: vassal kingships no longer turned the monarchy into a kind of federation. It meant a vividly conscious nationalism: far more than the Arsacids did the Sassanians feel themselves the heirs of Cyrus and the champions of Iran against the European power of Rome in a kind of competition for world dominion. Lastly, as was to happen to the Byzantine Empire, that nationalism was inspired and fortified by a national religion, Zoroastrianism. Though the Arsacids had been Zoroastrians, their zeal was pale beside that of the Sassanians who had begun as priests of the fire-temple of Istakhr. With the accession of Ardashir I a new energy was let loose. Fortunately for Rome, Sassanian Persia had ambitious and

34

deadly foes in Central Asia, on the Oxus and towards the Indus, as well as in the West.

The religion of Zoroaster, or Mazdaism, as it was expounded in Sassanian times, was based on the strife of Ormazd, the good god who was to triumph, and Ahriman, the evil creator whose power and followers were to be resisted by the devout Zoroastrian until their eventual defeat. Only Ormazd and his subordinate deities were to be worshipped. Thus, in its dualism, the religion was essentially a monotheism with a lofty and intolerant doctrine of life and morals. But it was a religion both sacerdotal and ritualistic to a high degree. The priests or Magi were a power in the State. The worship of the sacred fires, the observance of ceremonial purity, the chanting by the Magi of the spell-like hymns of their later sacred books, the

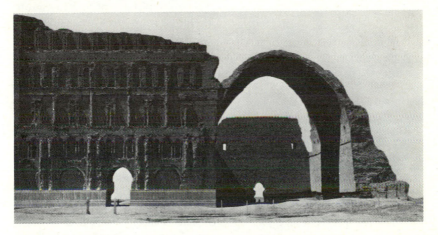

Fig. 5. Ctesiphon palace

dread of polluting the holy elements of fire, earth, and water which led to the exposure of the dead to be eaten by birds of prey, all tended to prevent the expansion of Zoroastrianism outside its native Iran, and to make it a burden even there, although its dualistic cosmogony, borrowed by the eclectic theories of Mani (*ob.* 273) in his new religion of Manichaeism, found an easy way into both Europe and Asia in spite of persecution on all sides.

Sub-kings, when they existed, were merely highly titled governors; yet great noble families, with wide domains, were a power in Iran. The backbone of the army consisted of the numerous lesser nobles, who in return for their fiefs formed the heavy mailed cavalry. They were splendid lancers and archers, and such deadly adversaries to the Roman legions that they were imitated in the regiments of cataphracts.

While the Sassanians drew their strength from Iran, the centre of administration and commerce lay for geographical reasons outside Iran in

Mesopotamia, on the Tigris in the city of Ctesiphon. There the trade-caravans from India, Central Asia, and the Mediterranean met and exchanged their wares. Babylonia was still and was long to be a fertile, wealthy land, only to be ruined by the ruin of its canals. But with the capital so far to the west, it is no wonder that the Sassanians, besides the rage for conquest, found the Roman frontier dangerously near. The first series of Persian wars had closed with the peace of the Caesar Galerius and King Narses in 296. It was a triumph for Rome. Not only was northern Mesopotamia from Nisibis westward kept by the Empire, but the five provinces east of the Tigris and south of Lake Van were ceded by Narses, and the kingdom of Armenia north of them was admitted to be a Roman vassal. For defence and offence the Empire was content, but no able King of Persia could be expected to endure the situation, and a warrior-king was now adult, Shapur (Sapor) II (309–80).

Fig. 6. A Sassanian king hunting lions

The five ceded provinces, roughly modern Kurdistan, were important both as mountain ramparts and gateways, but the mountain kingdom of Armenia was an invaluable bastion of the Empire. Stretching between the rivers Araxes and Kur and including the upper waters of the Euphrates, its warlike nobility under a branch of the Arsacids obstinately resisted Sassanian conquest with the aid of the little Caucasian kingdoms of Iberia (Georgia) and Albania. It was inspired by a strong national consciousness, which was invigorated by its special Indo-European language and at this very time by its whole-hearted conversion to Christianity under King Tiridates III (288–314). Henceforth the fire-worshipping Persian conqueror was the religious as well as national enemy of Armenia, while the less dangerous Roman was its often ineffectual ally. But as Armenia could not maintain itself alone, it added to the strain on Roman frontier defence.

(2) THE GERMANIC PEOPLES

There is a fundamental contrast between the foes of the Empire north and south of the Caucasus range. Southwards there were cultured stable monarchies, however fierce their ambitions or unfixed their frontiers: even in North Africa the barbaric Moors were the ancient dwellers in the land and tenacious of it. But northwards it is a world in flux, peoples and tribes in continuous migration, attempted when not achieved. Not only will a tribe pass from end to end of Europe, but large fragments of it will appear in opposite quarters at the same time, and tribes and fragments will form new units under new names. Here the position of the various peoples will be cursorily indicated as they were placed at the close of the reign of Constantine.

On the greater part of its European frontier, beyond the rivers Rhine and Danube which marked it, the Roman Empire was faced by Germanic tribes, speakers of one of the chief branches of the Indo-European group, a branch which was already dividing into separate languages. They were a stalwart, blond, fighting race, both prolific and adventurous. So much of their territories was still covered by primeval forest and their passion for war was so strong that for centuries they had been expanding from their original lands on the coasts of the North Sea and the Baltic, and the larger number of them had acquired a thoroughly migratory character in the search of wider, more fertile homes and of plunder on the way. Their numbers have been exaggerated, but were formidably large. Losses in war, though there were cases of extermination, were easily made up by their fecundity: every tribesman was a warrior. Often enough the Roman Empire had thrust them back, only to find the pressure resumed with greater numbers. These plundering, restless tribesmen, though always ready to migrate, were by no means mere herdsmen: they ploughed their cornfields with a heavy wheeled plough in characteristically long strips which did not require frequent turning of the plough nor so much fencing against the cattle. But they preferred to add to their lands by conquest rather than by clearing the sacred primeval forest. Better land, ready cultivated, could be won by the sword, to which their fighting spirit and all their ideas of honourable activity inclined them: the conquered had the choice of remaining as half-freemen (*liti, laten* in the West) or slaves, or of migrating, too, *en masse*. Thus the victories of one tribe set other tribes in motion, and the numbers of the victors were swelled by conquered dependants. While there was a democratic tendency in the institutions of most tribes, in which important decisions were taken in the assembly of the freemen, the *thing*, and in ordinary life the group of kinsmen was important for law and mutual responsibility, a leading feature of Germanic society was the chieftain with his band of voluntary warrior companions whom he maintained in peace and who followed him to war. The chiefs or nobles had wider lands than the plain freeman, tilled with the help of serfs and slaves, and used their wealth to maintain their followers (*comitatus*), who naturally thronged to take service with a warlike and adventurous lord. Their fidelity was inviolable—it superseded the bond of kindred; they died round a fallen chief rather than escape or surrender. Nothing

could have more fostered a restless, warlike spirit among chiefs and followers. They produced the dynamic force which thrust the tribes on raids
and wanderings. A successful warrior might become a chief; a chief was
eager to increase his following and power by increasing his wealth and fame.
The institution implied nearly continuous war, and war fostered the power,
when it did not cause the appearance, of a central institution, the kingship
of a whole tribe or sub-tribe. The majority of the chieftains of a tribe came
of families already recognized as noble, but among them there was usually
a pre-eminently noble family, which claimed descent from the gods, and
from whose members alone the tribal king, if he was desired, could rightly
be elected. The oldest of these kingships possibly originated from priesthoods of ancient fertility cults, but the effective cause of the election of
a king among the migrating tribes was the need of unity of command in
war. Most of the tribes adopted permanent kingship sooner or later, and
the strong feeling that only the race of divine descent could rightfully occupy
the throne had, even among Christians, important political consequences.
If the privileged family became extinct, tribal cohesion was seriously
damaged: any great noble felt he had an equal right to reign with the
successful competitor. Loyalty and common action gave way to rebellion and
treason. On the other hand, the continued existence of the acknowledged
royal house, even in decadence and civil strife, gave a concrete embodiment
of tribal unity and common tradition which appealed to a barbaric age.

The god from whom the royal families usually traced their descent was
Woden (Odin), the war-god and wily magician, whose character expressed
the qualities of the war-chief united to the priest of a magic ritual. It
would appear that the nobles and their followers were specially devoted to
his worship. Among them, later at any rate in Scandinavia, he was exalted
as the Allfather, whose mantle was the starry sky, and who had learnt the
secrets of the Fates. He was the death-dealing god who slew his own
favourites, the god of the fighting hero in battle and feasting in hall, the
god of spells and the lays in which the warriors' deeds were celebrated.
Beside him was the plain war-god Tiu (Tyr), somewhat, it seems, outshone
by his cunning compeer. Of wider attributes, though warlike also, was
Thunor (Thor), the thunder-god of farmers and of lawful possession.
Dimmer gods and goddesses of primeval fertility existed besides these
three, though lessened in honour, not to mention the minor spirits of soil
and water, spring and woodland. The impression is given of a natural
polytheism changing under the influence of the warlike migrations and ill
fitted to resist a consistent, stable religion presented with all the glamour of
higher civilization. But the ethos which it produced survived it.

The Germanic tribes in the fourth century fell into three main divisions;
the Scandinavians, whose activities were barely observable in the background, the West Germans, and the East Germans. The two latter were

roughly divided by the river Elbe, and although possessing much in common, were markedly distinct in their tribal habits and destiny. The West Germans between the Rhine and Elbe were, so to say, taking root by now in their territories; they were expansionist rather than migratory; only on the coast did their colonists migrating across the sea slowly lose touch with their former homes. The East Germans, between the Elbe, the Baltic, the Vistula and the Black Sea, were completely migratory, ready to change their habitations entirely in search of richer lands; it was they who really broke down the fabric of the Western Empire in their wanderings and by the foundation of their transitory states.

The most numerous of the East Germanic peoples was that of the Goths, who had crossed, like most of their fellows, from Scandinavia to the opposite coast of the Baltic some centuries before. Thence, soon after 200 they had moved south-east to the steppeland north of the Black Sea, where they had adopted the nomadic life of the region and soon became the most pressing danger of the Empire. Under their king, Kniwa, they had ravaged the Balkans and destroyed (251) the Emperor Decius and his army. Eighteen years later they received a crushing defeat from the Emperor Claudius Gothicus near Naissus (Nish), which kept them from more than passing raids for several generations, but Illyricum was fatally exhausted by their ravages. Constantine himself had to intervene in 331–2 to repel a Gothic invasion of Moesia. Mcantime they engaged in inter-tribal wars which accentuated their divisions. About 300 their eastern tribe, the Greutungi or Ostrogoths, under a king, held the steppes between the rivers Dniester and Don with a wide supremacy over their neighbours. The Tervingi or Visigoths[1] occupied the steppe and forest between the Dniester and the Danube; they seem to have lacked a king. In modern Transylvania were settled the allied, less active, tribe of the Gepids, while on the Sea of Azov was a fraction of the much scattered tribe of the Heruli, by all accounts the most savage of these Teutonic stocks. Between the Gepids and the Danube, there appeared in Constantine's last years a part of another East Germanic tribe, the Asding Vandals, who drove out the older inhabitants; the other principal Vandal tribe, the Silings, were settled in modern Silesia, which retains their name.

It is easier to say where the lesser East Germanic tribes had been than where their main branches were in the time of Constantine. The Rugians had been on the Baltic and have left their name in the island of Rügen; they were now, perhaps, north of the Carpathians with the Sciri and part of the Heruli. The Langobards had been on the lower Elbe, where the Bardengau long preserved their memory; now they, too, were somewhere north of the Erzgebirge. The Burgundians, some of whom had appeared on the

---

[1] Ostrogoths and Visigoths may mean East and West Goths respectively. It may be doubted whether Greutungi and Tervingi were completely coincident with them.

Don, have left traces of themselves in the island of Bornholm (Burgundar-holm) in the Baltic; they had been between the rivers Oder and Vistula; lately they had forced their way westward and were now settled on the river Main and the adjacent Rhineland, pressing earlier invaders farther south.

A more permanent, though not motionless, picture is presented by the West Germans. The Marcomanni and the Quadi, both of the group of tribes known as Suevi, kept their seats in modern Bohemia and Moravia respectively, whence they raided the Empire across the Danube. North-west of them the Thuringians, the ancient Hermunduri, possessed the present Thuringia with wider extension to south and north. Far more enterprising was the recent confederacy of the Alemanni, a mixture, as their name implies, of several clans, among whom the latest come were the Suevic Semnones from beyond the Elbe, who eventually provided an alternative name, Swabia, to Alemannia. The confederacy was in bitter enmity with Rome. The Alemanni were old raiders of Gaul. Driven from the Main by the Burgundians, they had occupied the once Roman territory of the Agri Decumates (in modern Baden and Württemberg) and were now pressing furiously on the Roman frontiers of the upper Rhine and upper Danube. North of them along the east bank of the Rhine had arisen another loose confederacy also with a new name, the Franks, composed of tribes long settled there, such as the Sugambri, Chamavi, Chatti, Chattoarii, with perhaps some reinforcement from defeated tribes, like the Chauci, moving west. Both Franks and Alemanni were ruled by kinglets (*gau-kings*) who were not mere chieftains. Further north again, in the coastal marshlands of modern Holland and Hanover, dwelt the Frisians on their *terpen* or artificial hillocks, where they had been for centuries. Although they had slowly spread over a greater area, the Frisians made no collective conquests; but some are found taking a part in the raids of other tribes. East of the Frisians and Franks were the fierce group of Saxons, the men of the cutlass, a lax confederation whose leading people, the Saxons proper, had spread from Holstein beyond the Elbe, which they still retained; the class of half-free *laten*, like the *liti* of the Franks and Frisians, presumably was made up of the remnants of conquered tribes, such as the Chauci. Whether marshmen on the coast or heath-dwellers inland, the Saxons took readily to the sea and were formidable pirates who plundered the coasts of Britain and Gaul. They were much resembled in dialect and habits by the kindred tribe of Angles, who inhabited the peninsular modern Slesvig to the north, but the Angles, unlike the Saxons, seem to have possessed a kingship. North again, the peninsula of Jutland was or had been held in part probably by the Jutes, while the adjacent islands were already occupied by the Danes from Scandinavia. All these coastland tribes were increasing in numbers; they jostled, pressed upon, and allied with one another, broke up and united; all were seafarers, and their migratory

Fig. 7. The Broch of Mousa, Shetlands

instinct led them over seas familiar to them by trade and piracy. Though not impervious to Roman and oriental influences, their barbaric culture was in essentials homegrown. Their religion and their lays and legends expressed the turmoil, the exploits and hardy cunning of their lives, their 'Heroic Age'.

(3) CELTS AND SLAVS

Equally hostile to the Empire, but less dangerous because of their narrower and isolated zone of attack, were the Picts and Scots of the British Isles. Both invaders had escaped the Roman conquest and retained their barbaric tribalism and culture; they too, were in their 'Heroic Age'. The Picts or 'painted (tattooed) people' were the tribes to the north of the Forth who had never been annexed to the Empire. Possibly they were already coalescing into the loose tribal kingdom of Alban. Their southerly division certainly spoke a Celtic Brythonic dialect akin to ancient Welsh; their northerly members round the Moray Firth, although eminent specialists claim them as Brythonic, are of more dubious origin, and some of their royal names and the 'Pictish succession' of their kings, which was not patriarchal but descended through females, suggest that they were, partially, of non-Celtic speech and customs. In any case both divisions assailed their more civilized British neighbours by land and sea. The Scots, although like other peoples of mingled race, were more homogeneous in speech and institutions. They were the Celtic tribes of Ireland, speaking the Goidelic branch of the Celtic languages, the ancestor of modern Gaelic, and organized in clans of kindreds under the rule of patriarchal chiefs. Their civilization much resembled that of the Britons four centuries earlier. Their paganism exhibited a rich mythology, and they were accumulating a store of mythic and historic tales, the substance of which is partly preserved in later lays. They too were tending to coalesce in loosely federate kingdoms and to employ their surplus energies in sea-raids on Roman Britain.

From the present we turn to the future enemies of the Empire. Only a cursory mention need as yet be made of the Slavs, known to their German neighbours as Wends. These prolific tribes, speaking a conservative branch of the Indo-European group of languages, were steadily spreading from their centre of dispersion, the modern Polesia, in and around the Pripet marshes; westward they had reached the Vistula and perhaps the Oder and its mouth on the Baltic, as these lands were evacuated by the East Germans. Northward they were extending towards Novgorod, but were held back by the still more conservative Indo-European Balts in the forests and marshes of Lithuania and Prussia proper. Southward they were roughly bounded by the grass steppes of the modern Ukraine. Deficient in organization and living in their villages under a simple patriarchal system, they were a ready prey to aggressive neighbours such as the Ostrogoths, and their vegetarian diet has been attributed to the impossibility of retaining herds amid their plundering enemies. They were barely known to the Romans.

(4) THE NOMADS OF THE STEPPES

Far more potentially dangerous and destructive near and far were the nomad horsemen of the vast steppes of Central Asia and south-east Europe, ranging from the mouth of the Danube to the Pacific Ocean, and to some extent divided by the mountain mass north of the Pamirs. They were by no means all of the same race or group of languages, for much of their life and customs was imposed by their habitat, and intermixture of blood by conquest or alliance was common. The Goths during their residence in the Ukraine took up in some measure nomad ways; the blond Alans between the Don, the Volga, and Mount Caucasus were Iranian in speech and partly in blood, and remnants of other Iranian nomads, not to mention descendants of captive women and slaves, were no doubt absorbed into newcoming tribes from the East. But the main and typical mass of the nomads east of the Volga belonged to the yellow Ural-Altaian race which had peopled the eastern steppes from time immemorial. Their languages, in spite of their variety, were of the same group, and their physique and character were all but identical. The Ural-Altaian, or Mongolian as he is often called, was thick set and wiry, but soon corpulent, and bandy legged; his hair was straight and black, and the beard was scanty; his cheek-bones were high and his eyes slanted upward and outward, the lids showing the 'Mongolian fold'. To other peoples he seemed excessively ugly, and his ferocity deepened the shades. Fearless, enduring, and cruel, he appeared everywhere as a ruthless destroyer, a heartless and incessant plunderer and slave-taker, and, until long intermixture had changed his racial characteristics, incapable of a higher civilization than the simple habits prescribed by the steppes.

Those habits were due to the necessities of a horseman, hunter, and sheepmaster, who changed his camping ground yearly from the winter-pastures of the south or sheltered valleys, burnt up in the hot weather, to the summer-pastures of the north or the uplands, frozen when the cold set in. The distance covered between them might be anything up to 1000 miles, and over this the nomads rode on their horses, their best wealth, famous for their endurance and speed. The horse conditioned their whole existence. Their favourite food was *kumiz*, fermented mare's milk. The hours they did not pass in their felt tents were spent on horseback. Their riding and archery were superb, and their ubiquity and elusiveness in war exaggerated their numbers and wore down resistance in a slower foe. It was hard to bring them to close quarters in battle, until they saw their opponents exhausted: their feigned flights proved the most effective tactics; they were never more dangerous than when they tempted pursuit.

Their invasions were partly the result of an overflowing population, and they were allured by the wealth of settled, agricultural races around them; but still more important were migrations due to wars among themselves. One collection of tribes would drive out another from the best pastures. Those of the conquered who did not submit to the victors migrated to treat more distant tribes in the same way. The process ended in an attack on the settled, civilized peoples beyond the steppes. The accumulation of large hordes of invaders was made easier by the elementary organization of the Ural-Altaians. A few families under a patriarchal rule formed a camp, a few camps a clan, a few clans a tribe, all very loosely held together. It would happen that under an able leader tribes would gather in a horde, clans of different tribes would form new combinations and a new but temporary people would arise and conquer. There is a probability that some of the tribes on the frontier of China, whose name the Chinese transcribed as Hiung-nu, retreated westward and passed, doubtless with fresh recruits and with losses on the route, to the steppes east of the Caspian

Sea, where they appeared as the Huns. In any case they were a horde hitherto unknown to westerners and set in motion by events farther east. Distant, incalculable upheavals had prepared a revolution in Europe.

The paganism of the nomads had but little advanced beyond a belief in the numberless spirits, good and ill, of earth, water, and air, who could be propitiated and controlled by offerings and magical ritual. Among them the spirits of the dead held a prominent place in the religion of their living kinsmen, and ancestor-worship might be described as their chief cult. But superior creative spirits also appeared in their cosmogony, even perhaps an originating god of heaven. The ancient sword, however, which their king Attila worshipped, was rather the habitation or symbol of his tutelary spirit of war.

Although so barbaric, the Ural-Altaians were not without an art and culture which they shared with and partly borrowed from the old nomad Iranian art of the western steppes. This art, preponderantly the work of the smith, had received potent influences from the Greeks, the Persians, and the Chinese, but it had absorbed and transformed them according to its own aesthetic tendencies. Vigorous, fierce, but stylized animal forms, blended into spirals and volutes for decoration, inlaid enamels of bright colours, these ornamented their weapons, clothing, armour, and utensils. The style was barbaric but impressive; it spread not only with the nomads but to other receptive peoples. Its influence can be traced among the most westerly Germanic and Celtic tribes.

It is very evident that neither Moor nor Persian, neither German nor Celt required external pressure to induce them to invade the Roman Empire. They saw there wealth, fertility, and civilization which were irresistibly attractive. Persia was an expanding monarchy. German and Celt were prolific barbarians little inclined to find room by forest clearance or more laborious agriculture. Their institutions, such as the chief with his sworn followers, and their whole ethos with its glorification of warlike adventure, impelled them to gain fame, land, and wealth by the sword. The Empire had held them back by main force for centuries. Now the Empire was weakened in cohesion, population and morale; it was depending more and more on hired levies from the barbarians themselves. Resistance grew more and more exhausting and difficult, and then, as we shall see, the barbarians were in their turn thrust forward by the hordes from Asia. It is little wonder that the frontiers were permanently broken, and that the overtasked, more straggling western half of the Empire was submerged, while the eastern half with its fortunate capital survived. The sea, which divided the Balkans from Asia Minor made it less vulnerable from the north, and the Persians had their own eastern frontier to protect against the nomads. They, too, were obliged to fight on two fronts.

CHAPTER 3

THE SUCCESSORS OF CONSTANTINE, 337–395

(I) THE FLAVIAN DYNASTY AND THE PERSIAN WAR

The chief external dangers to the Roman Empire lay on three frontiers, those of Persia, the Danube and the Rhine, and the course of the struggle on each frontier is clearest when told consecutively. But the three theatres interacted on one another; a defeat on the Rhine might divert or withhold sorely needed troops from the Persian war: the Roman armies and revenues were not sufficient for all the calls upon them. Dynastic questions, too, and rivalries for the throne affected the Empire's government and defence beyond any group of provinces. There was a contest between the hereditary, dynastic principle, which appealed to men longing for peace and order, and the elective principle inherent in the constitution, which allured the mutinous soldiers of localized armies and the private ambitions of their discontented, distrusted generals. The effects of rebellion could not be localized in fact, although the narrative may have to separate civil wars according to their geographical scene. None the less, as the weightiest and most critical events in each period fall in the range of a particular frontier, some continuity may be observed. The first in order of time may be described in connexion with the Persian war.

While the genius of Constantine, his capacity as a general and ruler, his insight into the world before him, the amazing, sustained audacity of his decisions, stand out consistently, his character exhibits conflicting traits, which have led to very diverse interpretations. Contemporary dishonest panegyric and ill-informed malicious detraction obscure his portrait. The practical shrewd veteran, chaste and humane, degenerated into an elderly fop, devoted to the new politic pomp of the throne, and led by his venal and corrupt entourage of eunuchs and sycophants who fleeced his subjects. It was partly the penalty of an Asiatic secluded despotism, but perhaps the wear and tear of a hectic career had left scars on the mind. He was capable of a mystic enthusiasm which sustained his self-confidence, but made him more liable to bursts of imperious anger; moreover a rational explanation of irrational acts is not to be expected when the acts themselves are scantly known. There was in him as in so many of his successors a strain of savagery. After all they were half-civilized, and the degrading amphitheatre had long been brutalizing the Roman world.

It seems that Constantine was strongly attached to the dynastic principle. The Empire was too vast and centralized to be governed for long by a single man. The system of imperial partners, hastily allied by political

45

Fig. 8. Constantine, the Empress Fausta and their three sons

marriages, had proved a complete failure; close blood-relationship within the Flavian house offered a better chance of harmony. Yet in 326 Constantine put to death his eldest and promising son Crispus and his wife the Empress Fausta. There may have been mere family discord, for Fausta is accused of contriving the death of her stepson Crispus, or perhaps there was a real plot, or the Emperor may have been egged on to a fever of suspicion and jealousy. His subsequent arrangements show that he hoped for concord and collaboration within the imperial house. His three sons by Fausta were carefully bred to rule, and were given shares of the Empire as Caesars. Constantine II, the eldest, was put in charge of the West beyond the Alps; Constans, the youngest, of the centre with Italy and Illyricum; Constantius II of the East; while two nephews, Delmatius and Hanniballianus, were to rule the lower Danube frontier and north-east Asia Minor respectively, the latter with the oriental title of King of Kings, which suggests a hoped-for expansion eastwards. But scarcely had Constantine breathed his last at Nicomedia in 337, after a baptism more than usually delayed, when the scheme broke down. The soldiers of the army of the East massacred the nephews, brothers, and the hated chief minister of

Constantine, only leaving alive two children, Gallus and Julian: none but the sons of the Emperor should rule.

The Persian war had begun. Shapur II had already driven out the Armenian King Arsaces and had vainly besieged the frontier town of Nisibis. Constantius II restored Arsaces, but adopted for years a defensive policy, punctuated by a victory near Singara. His main work was to reform the Eastern army. Henceforward the cataphracts, the heavy mailed cavalry on the Persian model, were the chief arm of the East Roman forces. Not till 359 did Shapur win a dear success by the capture of the key town of Amida (Diarbakr) on the Tigris, and Constantius prepare for more decisive action in the desultory war.

1. The House of Constantine

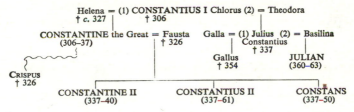

Events within the Empire had held his hands so long. In 340 Constantine II, the senior Augustus, attempted to dispossess the young Constans, but perished in an ambuscade near Aquileia. The valiant Constans took over his brother's lands without resistance, and proved himself an untiring defender of his frontiers until his vices and misgovernment led to a revolt of the Gallic troops and his murder (350). The old days seemed coming back, for the usurper accepted by the troops was a soldier, Magnentius, of German extraction. Italy and Africa submitted to him, and the army of Illyricum was only kept from full revolt by the elevation to the Empire of its commander, Vetranio, in collusion with Constantius. Fortunately the Persians once again failed to take Nisibis, so that Constantius could move westwards. In a dramatic scene before the armies Vetranio abdicated, and Constantius could advance to inflict a crushing defeat (351) on Magnentius at Mursa (Esseg or Osijek) on the Drave. The cataphracts decisively proved their superiority as a fighting arm over the Gallic legions, but the loss of some 54,000 men in this internecine struggle weakened the Empire's defensive forces for years. The usurper was not driven to suicide in Gaul till 353.

His brother's murder, the usurpation by a half-barbarian soldier, and his own childlessness forced on Constantius the problem of the succession and the harmony of the Empire. In 351 he called his elder cousin Gallus from seclusion and made him Caesar with Antioch for his residence and the East for his sphere of government. The choice was unfortunate: the bloodthirsty Caesar exercised a reign of terror without compensating ability, and his wife Constantina, the Emperor's sister, made his tyranny worse. He became a danger to the Empire. Constantius' remedy was to invite him to his presence in Italy, where he was tried and beheaded (354). There was now only one Flavian left, Julian, the half-brother of Gallus, and to him the Emperor turned after long years of suspicion and neglect. Both were natural. Julian's father had been murdered in the massacre of 337 with Constantius' assent; his half-brother had just been executed; and Julian's tastes and occupations were studious and literary. His sympathy for paganism was as yet unknown. While he had inherited the energy of the Flavians, his upright, kindly temper stood in contrast to the fierce passions of his cousins and may have been derived from his mother's family, the Anicians, the most illustrious of the older senatorial houses. Constantius, however, in spite of the dissuasions of his eunuch favourites, appointed his cousin Caesar, gave him a sister to wife, and sent him to Gaul. Julian's success in administration and war surpassed the Emperor's hopes, and aroused the suspicions which he was always prone to adopt and which were fanned by jealous or corrupt officials and courtiers. He was already estranged when the revival of the Persian war and the loss of Amida gave him the opportunity to weaken his too popular Caesar.

More troops were urgently needed in the East for a major campaign, and Constantius sent the fatal order—not to Julian but to subordinates—that the pick of the Gallic army should march to Asia. Julian prepared to obey, but the order was hated by the soldiers and they almost forced him to accept the style of Augustus at Paris (360). This was rebellion, which Julian attempted to cover by asking for recognition from the senior Augustus. Constantius, whose sense of duty detained him and his army in the East on the frontier, replied by demanding abdication and submission. A compromise became impossible, and Julian took the plunge into civil war before the Eastern army could advance against him. By rapid and risky converging movements through Rhaetia and North Italy, he first seized the key-city of Sirmium (Mitrovitsa) among the marshes on the Save and then the pass of Succi (Trajan's Gate, Troyanova Vrata), which commanded the ascent from the Thracian plain to the Haemus range. The threat could not be neglected, and Constantius started from Syria to oppose it. On the way he died in Cilicia in November 361. The Empire fell unresisting to his cousin. A grim, Dantesque face looks from the statue of Constantius II. If not a great or attractive ruler, he was no weakling; he possessed the tireless energy of his house; he knew how to exact obedience from the tried ministers and generals he promoted; and he felt deeply his responsibility for the safety of the Empire. Himself no brilliant general, he improved the efficiency of the army by his changes. But his merits were vitiated by his intolerance of opposition and his fear of treason, which led him to indiscriminate, cruel injustice and made him a persecuting theologian. He distrusted eminent ability, and listened easily to sycophants who used his favour for extortion and oppression. 'He had much influence', it was said, 'with Eusebius', the eunuch who was his chief chamberlain. This was the resource of a second-rate prince to whom the possession of high talents meant a potential rebel, and the ineligibility of a eunuch was a recommendation. The strict separation of military and civil commands was a safeguard, but even so the untrustworthiness of Roman-born generals was a permanent disease of the Empire.

The pagan reaction of Julian, like the Christian proselytizing zeal of his predecessor, must be left to the appropriate chapter. In external affairs, during a temporary lull in the West, Julian was free to devote himself to the Persian war in the vain hope of giving a lasting check to Persian aggression. In 363 he assembled his mobile army, 65,000 men—a revealing figure—including the Gallic legions, in Syria, sent a division due east to hold Mesopotamia, and himself struck deep southwards along the Euphrates to capture the capital, Ctesiphon, and paralyse the enemy. In spite of the flooding of central Iraq by the Persians, who cut the canals, Julian reached and crossed the Tigris, but he was in no condition to assault the city: retreat up the eastern bank of the Tigris was the only resource. The northwards march in the heat of summer, through country wasted by Shapur's order, harassed by the swarms of the Persian heavy and light cavalry, was arduous. Julian's plans had miscarried. Shapur was a different foe from the haphazard German chiefs he knew and he was forced to fight at a disadvantage. It may be that he had hoped for a diversion from Arsaces of Armenia, who remained prudently neutral; and the Mesopotamian division probably hardly knew their Emperor's whereabouts. The final blow was a mortal wound to Julian himself on 26 June 363, which deprived his men of a resolute and inspiring leader. The new Emperor, elected by them almost by chance on the extinction of the Flavian house, was the captain of the guard, the Christian Jovian, whose delays rendered an escape that was difficult impossible. At Dura he accepted the 'shameful peace' offered by the Persians as the price of a safe retreat. Shapur's terms were obviously devised to secure a defensible strategic frontier. Singara and Nisibis, the two strong, loyal frontier towns, and the Kurdish provinces east of the Tigris which had been won by Galerius, were ceded to him; Armenia was to be left in the Persian sphere.

This was a peace which the Empire might and did accept as tolerable for the actual frontier, but Armenia as a Persian vassal opened a gate into Asia Minor and the Black Sea. Shapur's endeavours to annex Armenia—he captured the temporizing Arsaces—and Caucasian Iberia and to convert them both to Mazdaism provoked Valens, Jovian's successor in the East, to counter-measures; he was successful in Iberia and supported the Christian Armenians who won some victories, but he was called off to the Gothic war, and the death of the great Shapur (380) only partially softened the conflict. With his hands full in Europe, Theodosius the Great, Valens' successor, was willing to agree to a compromise (387) with the then King of Persia, Shapur III. Four-fifths of Armenia became a vassal state of Persia under a Christian king; the remainder was left to the Empire, first as a vassal kingdom and finally as a province defended by the new city of Theodosiopolis. The Empire had at least barred the gate into Asia Minor, and in spite of subsequent rivalries which ended in Persarmenia being reduced to a Persian province, the frontier assumed a character of bickering permanence. Besides their gains under the compromise, the defence of their own eastern frontier no doubt made the kings of Persia more pacific towards the Empire.

(2) THE DEFENCE OF THE RHINE AND UPPER DANUBE

While the defence of the Rhine frontier lacked the grandiose appearance of a conflict of great powers which characterized the Persian war, it was in essentials far more critical, nay disastrous, for the Empire, for it devastated the stronghold of the West; the loss of Gallic man-power, not to mention wealth, was not to be remedied. The evil had begun in the bad days before Diocletian, and Constantine the Great had won his early laurels through his crushing victories over Franks and Alemanni, so crushing and so bloody in reprisals that there was comparative peace on the Rhine till his death. He exposed two Frankish kinglets and a host of their followers to the wild beasts in the amphitheatre at Trier, for he was then still a pagan. But the depopulation of eastern Gaul was shown by the fact that his father Constantius I Chlorus had settled thousands of Franks and Alemanni as *laeti*, bound to military service, west of the Rhine, which meant steady Germanization and barbarization, while free Franks and Alemanni from beyond the Rhine flocked in as recruits for the field-army. The usurper Magnentius was a Frank by blood. These more peaceful years restored the Germans' numbers, and Constans was obliged to repress the Franks in 341–2, but the disastrous civil war between Constantius II and the rebel Magnentius brought the usual consequences. The frontier garrisons were depleted, the field-army was moved away and decimated at Mursia, and Franks and Alemanni ranged plundering and slaying over Gaul. Though Constantius attacked the Alemanni, they remained in possession of Alsace, and the Salian Franks, a newly mentioned, perhaps newly formed, sub-tribe, crossed the lower Rhine and occupied Toxandria, which is now Brabant. Cologne fell to the Ripuarian Franks, a similar conglomeration on the middle Rhine. The Germanization of these regions became all but complete.

Fig. 9. The Emperor raised on a shield

It was the Caesar Julian who with inadequate forces and disloyal colleagues had to meet this inundation. In brilliant campaigns (356–8) he cleared Gaul of the Alemanni, winning one decisive victory at Strasbourg, and quelled them in their homes beyond the Rhine. He recaptured Cologne from the Ripuarians, and expelled the Chamavi to their old home

51

on the Yssel; but he was obliged to leave the Salians as *foederati* (vassal allies owing contingents of troops) in Toxandria. The Empire's armour had here been pierced. A mild and just administration and the repression of extortion did something to heal the wounds of Gaul; so did the repatriation of 20,000 captives carried off by the Alemanni; the frontier defences were restored along the Rhine. But the province needed years of peace, which it did not get, and abundant armies, which were drawn off to the East. When Valentinian succeeded Jovian (364), he saw that a single ruler of the Empire was quite impossible. He left his brother Valens as Emperor in the securer East, and himself undertook the crucial task of defending the imperilled West.

The reign of Jovian had been as brief as it was inglorious. He died suddenly in Asia Minor in February 364. The careful choice that was made of his successor by the council at Nicaea shows that the needs of the Empire were well understood by them. They elected a Christian and a distinguished

2. The House of Valentinian

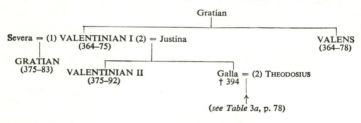

(see Table 3a, p. 78)

soldier. Valentinian I was the son of a Pannonian peasant, Gratian, who had entered the army and risen to high rank and wealth. His son had served in Gaul and was an officer in the imperial guards. His energy and soldierly qualities were conspicuous even among these Emperors from Illyricum, and his reign was occupied in the defence of the frontiers. But as a civil ruler he was less efficient. That the Emperor disliked men of birth and breeding and knew no Greek did little harm in the Latin West he ruled, yet it shows his lack of education in all but war. He tightened the regime of castes and the harsh centralization of the Empire in his endeavours to combat the evils of the time. But he could be hoodwinked by his corrupt entourage, and his wayward outbursts of despotic passion and cruelty were harmful to justice and good government. The wicked tyranny of Count Romanus in Africa escaped punishment and was redoubled in spite of complaints and commissions of inquiry, for he had friends at court; it was the honest accusers who were put to death.

Valentinian's main preoccupations were with the defence of Gaul and Britain. In Gaul the Alemanni were the worst danger. They crossed the frozen Rhine at midwinter, defeated Roman generals, and spread desolation.

At last in three victories Jovinus, master of the cavalry, drove them back. Valentinian was able to retaliate by wasting Alemannia, never so effectual a process, as the Germans could flee to the forests. None the less by 375 the Alemanni had been taught a lesson, and peace was arranged with their king Macrianus. The brigandage of uprooted peasants, which followed the raids and was the curse of Gaul, was sternly and ferociously repressed for a season. Meanwhile the Emperor refortified the Rhine frontier and overawed the Franks, whose recruits formed a valuable part of his army. When he was dead and news came of the war of Valens with the Goths, an invasion by the Alemannian tribe of the Lentienses reached no farther than Alsace, and was decisively routed by the Emperor Gratian at Argentaria, near Colmar (378).

It was in Valentinian's reign that Britain suffered irremediable disaster. Events there and in Gaul reacted on one another. The rumour of invasions spread; the Romans were hard put to it to defend themselves on all sides, and it is the strongest testimony to Valentinian that he quenched for a time the wildfire of ubiquitous ravage. At the very opening of the century Constantius Chlorus had been obliged to undertake a major campaign against Picts, Scots, and Saxons and reorganize the defences of Britain, where he died (306). Besides restoring the Wall of Hadrian in the north against the Picts, he instituted fortifications on the coast against the Saxons under an officer styled significantly the Count of the Saxon Shore. Coast castles, serving as bases for the old-established and enlarged fleet, were built from the Wash to the Isle of Wight. Other harbour forts were built on the Irish Sea. The command of the bulk of the garrison belonged to the Duke of the Britains stationed at York. Britain in fact was now all frontier. But the new system worked, and, although Constans in 342 had to intervene in person, the raids were kept within bounds. But from Julian's death, or even earlier, they assumed dangerous proportions. Picts, Scots, Saxons, and, it is curious to note, Franks descended on the country from all sides. The villas of the landed proprietors began to be deserted as devastation went farther. The Franks must have been Salians in part, although at this time the Salians were mainly loyal *foederati*; but it is a legitimate conjecture that they were largely Jutes, whose traditions bring them from Jutland, yet whose culture and customs at a later date show a close connexion with Frisia and the Rhine. They may well have formed part of the Frankish conglomerate. In any case the situation of Britain was desperate: the Wall was lost, overrun by Scots from the west and Germans from the east, and the count and the duke were both slain in their defeat. In 368 Valentinian sent over his best general, Count Theodosius, to Britain, with picked troops as reinforcements. The tables were turned, the marauding bands intercepted, rounded up, and driven out; a mutiny was repressed, the Wall restored, and punitive raids carried out. The Saxon Shore was furnished with signal towers in Yorkshire, and a new province, Valentia, was created, perhaps in Wales, to keep settled invaders down. Yet the respite was transitory owing to the internal revolutions of the West.

The Roman provinces of Rhaetia, Noricum, and Pannonia under the Flavian dynasty enjoyed comparative peace from the barbarians across the upper Danube. Rhaetia served more as a Roman base against than as a victim of the Alemanni. Constantine the Great dealt so effectually with the Sarmatians, a Dacian tribe between the Danube and the Theiss, carrying off the majority of them to be peasant-soldiers in Pannonia, that the remnant were quiet neighbours at the close of his reign. The next generation, however, renewed the assault, and in 357-9 Constantius II crushed the Sarmatians and curbed the Suevic Quadi of modern Moravia. Valentinian's fortifications, which he extended beyond the Danube in disregard of the treaty, provoked both Quadi and Sarmatians to fresh devastations. The Emperor's reprisals were decisive, and the cowed barbarians came to beg for mercy at Brigetio not far from the southward bend of the Danube. At their appearance Valentinian in a transport of rage was struck by apoplexy (February 375). His death was a disaster for the Empire. It would have had worse immediate consequences had it not been for the amiable character of his son Gratian, whom he had associated (367) with him as Emperor of the West. The Illyrian army proclaimed Gratian's step-brother Valentinian II, a child of six, their Emperor, and Gratian accepted his colleague in the spirit of an affectionate guardian. But in spite of soldierly qualities and success against marauding Franks and Vandals, who now were raiding across the Rhine, Gratian lost his hold on the armies. He neglected administration for sport, and his open preference for Alan mercenaries, if justified by their fighting qualities, lost him the devotion of the Gallic troops. This was to give an opening for the ruinous disease of mutiny and private ambition which afflicted the Empire. On the defeat and death of his uncle Valens by the Goths (378), Gratian made the admirable choice of a colleague to save the East in Theodosius the Great, but thereby the rivalry and hopes of another distinguished general, not of the imperial family, were aroused.

The Spaniard Maximus commanded in Britain, where the attacks of Picts and Scots were being renewed. He accepted his army's proclamation of him as Augustus and sailed with it to Gaul in complete disregard of the island's interests. The Gallic troops went over to him; the deserted Gratian was treacherously murdered at Lyons (August 383); and the usurper was acknowledged in Spain and Africa. Theodosius saved the Italian diocese for the young Valentinian II at the cost of recognizing Maximus. It was a hollow peace. Maximus tried in vain to trap the Italian Augustus into a meeting; Bauto the Frank held the Alpine passes against an attempt at invasion, while Theodosius prepared for war. Levies of men, principally barbarians, and extortion of money to pay them went on through both halves of the Empire. In 387 Maximus moved, and easily drove the feeble Valentinian II from Italy to Theodosius. The Eastern Emperor advanced through Illyricum. Three hard-fought battles, the last at Aquileia, achieved the overthrow of Maximus; he was captured and put to death (July 388), and his son Victor shared his fate in Gaul. There had been a manly energy in the rule of Maximus, who discarded the employment of eunuchs, which was lacking in the young Valentinian, now made sole Emperor of the West by the conqueror. He was an amiable second Gratian without experience or power, which was in the hands of a general, the Frankish Count Arbogast. In May 392 he was strangled in the night. Arbogast was ambitious, but he was a barbarian and dared not usurp the Empire. Instead he was king-maker of an imperial puppet, Eugenius, who had been his secretary, and who was in touch with the votaries of moribund paganism. In the war that followed Theodosius depended more on Gothic, Arbogast more on Frankish auxiliaries. The issue was decided in the battle of the river Frigidus (Vipao, Wippach) at the head of the Adriatic. Eugenius was executed; Arbogast committed suicide; and the victorious Theodosius united East and West for the last time till his death in 395.

The civil wars from the revolt of Maximus had dealt incurable and unnecessary wounds on the Western Empire. At their close it is evident that the mobile army was composed not only of barbarian levies but of barbarian tribal allies, *foederati*, fighting in their own fashion and under their own kinglets and chiefs. Not only that, but the highest commands in the army were held by barbarian generals, Bauto, Arbogast, Stilicho, who thus disposed of the fate of the Empire. Meanwhile, barbarian raiders, in the absence of the field-armies, were piercing the frontiers and laying waste the exhausted, dispeopled provinces. When Maximus left Britain the raids there redoubled. The Wall of Hadrian was finally deserted. The landowners fled from their villas even in the south. The diocese was sinking back into barbarism under assaults from all sides. This was the time when Niall of the Nine Hostages, High-king of Ireland (389–405), was the scourge of Britain and even of the Gallic coast. His power is obvious from his suzerainty of his own country. It was in these raids that the British boy, St Patrick, son of a decurion, was captured (389) in his father's little villa and taken to slavery in north Ireland, whither he was to return years after as a missionary. At the same time Ripuarian Franks and Alemanni were crossing the Rhine into Gaul. Count Arbogast repelled them and retaliated and then levied them for the army which he was to lead against Theodosius. The danger on the frontier was undiminished when the Emperor died (395).

(3) THE GOTHS AND THE CROSSING OF THE DANUBE

For many years the Flavian dynasty succeeded in maintaining a stable situation on the lower Danube. Constantine the Great was aided in the Black Sea against Ostrogoth aggression by the alliance of the Greek republic of Cherson in the Crimea. His eldest son and namesake inflicted a severe defeat on the Visigoths (332) when they invaded Moesia. The river fortifications were strengthened and a wall built across the Dobrudzha to the Black Sea, where the delta of the Danube did not provide a defensible line. But in the main peace prevailed. Ermanaric, the king of the Ostrogoths, famed in legend as Hermanrich, extended his suzerainty northwards, perhaps to the Baltic, and thus turned away from the Empire. The Visigoths seemed to be settling down under several chieftains. They were *foederati* of the Empire, and supplied troops under their own leaders at call in return for annual subsidies. Whether from their proximity to the Empire or the number of their Christian captives and serfs or from the decadence of their paganism in their wanderings, a momentous change was penetrating them, the adoption of Arian Christianity. But whatever sporadic Christians there may have been among the Goths, the apostle of the nation and through them of all the East German tribes was Wulfila (Ulfilas) (310–81). He belonged to a Cappadocian family which had been carried away captive in a Gothic raid, and it is significant that he was a Goth by language and 'nationality'. As a boy he was a hostage in Constantinople, where *c.* 341 he was ordained bishop for the Goths by the Arian bishop Eusebius. For seven years he preached and organized Christianity among the Visigoths, gaining over large numbers to the Faith. But there was still a powerful heathen party led by one of the greatest chiefs, Athanaric, who conducted a fierce persecution in which those who would not worship the old gods were burnt alive. Wulfila himself with a considerable band took refuge in the Empire, where they were given by Constantius land in Moesia and were known as the Lesser Goths. But many Christians remained, and by degrees the whole tribe was converted. Nameless missionaries carried Christianity to the other East Germans, Ostrogoths, Gepids, Vandals, Heruli, and Burgundians, even to the West German Longobards; by 400 all had embraced the Arian faith. Part of this rapid conversion, which left the more settled West Germans as a whole untouched, was due to the genius of Wulfila, who provided his countrymen with a Christian written literature. He replaced their native script, the runes, which were only fitted for the briefest incised sentences, by a modification of the Greek alphabet with supplementary letters to express the sounds of the Gothic language, and he translated the Scriptures into Gothic. A manuscript of his New Testament, dating from the fifth or sixth century, still survives. In this way the elements of Christianity and Graeco-Roman civilization were acquired by the East Germans who ruined the Western Empire. The benefits of their conversion were real, if slow, but unhappily they were ardent Arians. Their heresy deepened the offence of their barbarism to their Catholic subjects, and made the gulf between the two peoples unbridgeable. Good relations between conquerors and conquered would have been difficult to create in any case; the hostility in religion made them impossible. But it was better than if the East Germans had remained incorrigible, unteachable heathens.

Meanwhile the Visigoths had been tempted by its civil wars to attack the Empire. In 365 Procopius, a cousin of Julian, persecuted by Valens and a fugitive because of his kinship to the apostate, raised a revolt in Constantinople and gained the Balkans. He was only overthrown by the arrival of the eastern army from Syria (366). But he had called in Gothic aid, and Valens decided on a punitive war (367–9) across the Danube. He drove Athanaric into the Transylvanian mountains and enforced a peace. The first effect was civil war among the Visigoths, and fierce persecution of

Fig. 10. Luke v, 5–10. Bishop Wulfila's Gothic translation

the Christians by Athanaric. But he lost ground, and Fritigern, who adopted Christianity, took the lead among the chiefs. Then came a cataclysm. The Huns started to move from the east of the Caspian Sea. In 372 they overthrew the Alans, most of whose remnants[1] came fleeing west. Next came the turn of the Ostrogoths. They were broken by the Hunnic onslaught after a desperate resistance and subjected; the aged Ermanaric killed himself, and his son King Withimir was slain in battle. The Visigoths, too, were unable to resist. They were defeated under Athanaric in 375 on the bank of the Dniester. Athanaric withdrew to Transylvania shorn of most of his power; years after he took refuge in Constantinople and died there. But the greater part of the tribe fled under Fritigern and other chiefs to the Danube and clamoured for admission into the Empire. Valens decided to grant their petition on terms. It was a momentous decision to allow so numerous a people to pass the defences *en masse*. But there were wide vacant lands in Moesia, the Visigoths would provide admirable recruits for the army, and on a smaller scale the same policy had been

[1] A fragment of the Alans remains in the Caucasus as the Ossetes.

followed without ill result. The Visigoths, too, were largely Christians, and were required to give up their arms. Once they were ferried tumultuously across the Danube, however, the arrangements broke down. The shameless extortion and corruption of the imperial officials, who kept them in semi-starvation yet left them their arms in return for bribes, drove the barbarians to desperation. Brawls were inevitable. One occurred while Fritigern was entertained by Count Lupicinus at a feast in Marcianopolis, and the count ordered the massacre of such of the chief's *comitatus* as were in the city. Fritigern escaped by a ruse, and the war began. The other Gothic chieftains joined him with their clans, as well as a part of the Ostrogoths with their boy-king Witheric. Not only Moesia, but the untouched province of Thrace south of the Haemus range was desolated and the inhabitants carried away captive. Yet the cities held out securely, and in open fighting the Roman troops at least held their own. The enemy, however, was too strong to be overcome by the forces at hand. Valens brought up the army from the eastern frontier, while his nephew Gratian sent detachments in aid and followed with his army from the West. By ill advice Valens, who had reached Adrianople, refused to wait for his nephew and offered battle on 9 August 378. He was completely outmanoeuvred by Fritigern. His cavalry were too weak against the Ostrogothic horsemen, his infantry were mishandled, and he himself fell with two-thirds of the Roman army. They had fought as well as ever, but incompetent leadership and the disadvantage of too weak a force of cavalry produced a major disaster. The Goths were now inside the frontier, the Balkans were still more dispeopled, and the regular army fatally depleted. The defeat of Adrianople is a landmark in the decline of the Roman Empire.

The Emperor Gratian did the best in his power to remedy the catastrophe. He summoned from retirement in Spain the most able general of the Empire, Theodosius, put him in command, and soon created him Emperor of the East. In view of the disloyalty of Roman generals this was a risky measure, and Theodosius had wrongs which he might have avenged. His father, Count Theodosius, after his success in Britain had subdued a serious Moorish revolt, but he had also revealed the crimes of Count Romanus and the miscarriage of justice that followed. This made him powerful enemies, who obtained his execution on the death of his master Valentinian (376). His son, already distinguished, had been disgraced at the same time. Now the son, Theodosius the Great, was called on to save the Empire. He did so as much by diplomacy as by arms and at great cost. He reformed the army, repelled the Goths from the siege of Thessalonica, his headquarters, drove back a fresh invasion of Ostrogoths at the Danube delta, and hemmed in the Visigoths in Moesia. But in the war they had devastated Macedonia and Thessaly, while the Ostrogoths and Alans invaded Pannonia. At last, with Fritigern dead, a treaty was made in 382. The Visigoths were settled as *foederati* in Moesia, and besides their obligations as self-governing vassals they supplied plentiful recruits to the Eastern army. A little earlier Gratian had adopted the same course with the Ostrogoths, who were given Pannonia. It was an unsatisfactory peace. The Danube had ceased to be a frontier; barbarian states were inside the Empire, providing much of its armed force,

Fig. 11. Theodosius I with Valentinian II and Arcadius

and many of the Goths were in favour of renewing the war and continuing their conquests. It was, in fact, only a respite. In 390, with the aid of Huns from beyond the Danube, Alaric led a part of the Visigoths to devastate Thrace and was not rounded up till 392. It is significant that the victorious general was Stilicho, a Vandal bred in the Roman service. By the end of Theodosius' reign (395) the Roman generals were mostly barbarian mercenaries and the Roman armies largely composed of barbarian *foederati*.

CHAPTER 4

THE TRIUMPH AND DIVISIONS OF
CHRISTIANITY

(I) THE ARIAN CONTROVERSY

When Constantine the Great took over the Eastern provinces of the Empire from the fallen Licinius, he was met by a controversy which threatened to cleave the unity of the Christian Church. It concerned the most fundamental of Christian beliefs, the divinity of Christ, and both as a convert and as a statesman the Emperor had every reason to desire that his instructors should agree on the basis of his new faith, and that the Church as a whole should continue to be a solid support for the throne and a cement for the Empire. Thus nothing could be more natural than that he should use all his influence to end the Arian schism.

The controversy arose from the difficulty of combining the divinity of Christ, the incarnate Logos, with the unity of God. Already in the third century Sabellius had stressed monotheism to the extent of declaring that the Logos was a function of God the Father rather than a separate Person, but his view had comparatively few adherents. The majority of Eastern Christians held firmly to the separate Person of the Redeemer without defining too plainly the sense in which the Father and the Son were the One God. The doctrine of Arius, in which he had precursors, was that there was an eternity when the Son was not, that he had been begotten by a once lonely Creator, and that the Incarnation was the dwelling of the Logos in the human body of Christ. In his endeavour to be monotheistic, Arius taught the existence of a secondary, inferior God, whose humanity was merely physical. He was a respected presbyter of Alexandria, and his bishop Alexander vigorously opposed his theology. Arius was driven to Palestine, but though he was condemned by a small Council of bishops at Antioch (324), his partisans were numerous; he had crystallized a type of Christian thought by what seemed a simple explanation, if its ease was superficial, and although it made the worship of Christ as God almost contradictory to its monotheism. It might, too, be more congenial and seem more natural to recent converts from paganism, accustomed to a gradation of deities in existence, rank, and power. It certainly attracted the East Germans, as we have seen, when they were converted. But the opposition to it in the Graeco-Roman world was intense, and produced a more definite form of the counter-doctrine, which should not be either Sabellian or polytheistic. This asserted in terms that the Son was the co-eternal Logos of the Father and had taken on Himself human nature at the Incarnation.

60

It was now that Constantine intervened. He first vainly urged reconciliation on a basis of live and let live with an irreducible minimum in the divinity of the Redeemer, a policy to which he steadfastly adhered. Then he took control of the situation by summoning the proposed synod at Ancyra in Cappadocia to sit in his presence at Nicaea in Bithynia as an Ecumenical Council of the Christian Church. Some 300 bishops came at his call in 325. They were almost all Easterners, though deputies represented the Bishop of Rome, and a most important member was Bishop Hosius of Cordova, much in the Emperor's confidence. Other leading figures were Arius himself, Bishop Marcellus of Ancyra, the Sabellian, Alexander of Alexandria and his deacon Athanasius, and the two Eusebiuses, the Bishop of Nicomedia and the learned Bishop of Caesarea, who belonged to the conservative, inclusive majority of the East. It was easy to agree in condemning the extreme opinions of Arianism and Sabellianism, but a common formula to unite the other parties was hard to reach. At last, under the Emperor's influence, the Council devised and accepted with only two dissentients the original Nicene Creed.[1] The Only-begotten Son, the Lord Jesus Christ, was declared to be of the same substance, ὁμοούσιος, with the Father. The Council dissolved, leaving an indelible mark on Christian doctrine and government as well, for it had legislated in canons binding on the whole Church, besides formulating articles of faith in the creed which were to prove permanent. Constantine hoped that on its broad basis reunion and reconciliation of the disputants might take place.

He was prepared to enforce subscription to the new creed by banishing the recalcitrants, and even Arius subscribed at last. But the obstacles were greater than the practical Emperor thought. On the one hand, the definitely Nicene party, headed by Athanasius, now Bishop or Patriarch of Alexandria, insisted that the creed, with ὁμοούσιος, should be understood in their strict sense, and that Arius should not be forgiven without express acceptance of his adversaries' meaning. On the other, the conservatives of various shades, headed by Eusebius of Nicomedia, who feared Sabellianism most of all, distrusted the word ὁμοούσιος, and looked on Arius as a pardonable, too-precise extremist. They formed the wide, amorphous party of semi-Arians, whose difficulty was to find a common formula save by the addition of fresh anathemas on the solutions proposed. They began, however, by attacking the chief members of the Nicene party, and in 335 a Council at Tyre deposed Athanasius on trumped-up charges. The Patriarch appealed in person to Constantine, at first with success, but soon he was banished to Gaul, though no fresh Patriarch filled his see. At Tyre Arius had been readmitted to communion, just as the Emperor wished: his enemies rejoiced that he died suddenly the day before the formal ceremony.

[1] The Nicene Creed of the liturgy was probably produced in the General Council of Constantinople of 381, but was only adopted in 451.

St Athanasius is the hero of the Arian controversy. A subtle Greek metaphysician and theologian, bred to the law, he was too ingenious a case-maker, but his grasp of principles and what they implied was profound, his courage and firmness were unshakable, his insight into men and affairs was piercing. His generosity of temper and his leadership gained him the devotion of the Egyptians and the respect of the outside world. With magnificent persistence he maintained and propagated the Nicene doctrine of the Incarnation against skilful opponents who had the Emperors on their side.

On the death of Constantine (337) Athanasius returned to his see. The new Eastern Emperor Constantius II was personally opposed to him; he had theological tastes and was easily influenced by court Arianizers. In 341 he expelled Athanasius and other bishops by force, and one new version of the creed after another was devised by Eastern synods. But now the West was being roused to the theological problem. Less metaphysical and less given to subtle distinctions than the East, the West venerated the Council of Nicaea and was content with its creed. Julius, the Bishop of Rome, gave the vast authority of his church to the support of Athanasius. The Emperor Constans, a sordid champion, demanded a new General Council. It met (343) in two discordant halves, the Westerns at Sardica (the modern Sofia) and the Easterns at Philippopolis. The Westerns under Hosius restored Athanasius, the Easterns under Stephen, Patriarch of Antioch, condemned him. But the victory was won for Sardica later, when Stephen was detected in an infamous plot to discredit the Western Bishop of Cologne on a mission to Antioch. In 346 Constantius was obliged to consent to the restoration of Athanasius.

The lull in the controversy, however, only lasted until Constantius became master of the West by the overthrow of Magnentius. From 353 he renewed the attack on Athanasius and the Nicene leaders by councils which acted under pressure. Hosius of Cordova was imprisoned; Liberius of Rome and Hilary of Poitiers were exiled, the one the head of the greatest of the churches, the other the best Western theologian. A surprise attack (356) was made by the soldiery on Athanasius, who barely escaped to a secret life as a fugitive for six years among the desert monks and the devout of Egypt. His rival Patriarch, George of Cappadocia, a dubious character, who had been a pork-contractor, was obliged to flee from the mob in a year or two.

Meantime changes were taking place in the anti-Nicene ranks. The moderates preferred the word ὁμοιούσιος, 'of like substance', to ὁμοούσιος, 'of the same substance', but held to the eternity of the Logos who became incarnate. The real extremists were the utter Arians, Anomoeans, who denied even the likeness, and between these grew up a temporizing party, the Homoeans, who omitted the substance while asserting the likeness. It was the latter who enjoyed the vacillating support of Constantius. After

Fig. 12. (a) Orthodox priests exposed at sea.
(b) Arians burn an Orthodox church

a mêlée of councils, which provoked the pagan jibe that the imperial post-horse service was crippled by bishops rushing to and fro to attend them, the Homoeans won. At Constantinople in 360 a colourless Homoean creed (the fourth of Sirmium[1]) was adopted under imperial pressure, and the moderate semi-Arian chiefs were sent into exile. But this decision had no effect in the West, where Arians and semi-Arians were few. In the East the sympathies of the moderate semi-Arians were becoming more Nicene and they were listening to friendly overtures from Athanasius. By contrast the Homoeans were definitely Arian in doctrine. When the Patriarch of Antioch, Meletius, preached a Nicene sermon, he was exiled and an Arian set in his stead.

[1] Also called 'the Dated Creed', for it was dated by the consuls of the year.

(2) JULIAN AND THE PAGAN REACTION

The imperial support, not only of the Homoeans but of Christianity, was lost by the accession of the pagan Julian and by his attempt to put new life into the worship of the old gods. Julian had been brought up, mainly in seclusion, as a Christian and as an enthusiast for the literature of ancient Hellas. The Arianism in which he was bred had scant attractions for him; paganism to him was Hellenism, and at Nicomedia he willingly fell under the influence of a cultured pagan circle which gathered round the great rhetorician and teacher Libanius. In a credulous age Julian was outstripped by none in credulity. The Neo-Platonism of the time was thick with prodigies and marvellous séances, which found him an eager believer. He formed an admiring friendship with the impressive philosophic charlatan, Maximus. He himself was guided by divine voices. Iamblichus seemed to him to have written the final truths of religion. His new pagan education was completed in the schools of Athens, which were the stronghold of the ancient gods. There he became an initiate of the Eleusinian mysteries. Doubtless the secrecy of his conversion and the hypocrisy which as an outward Christian he was bound to practise account in part for the neurotic and highly strung character of Julian. It is to his credit that he showed a humanity, uprightness and chastity rare in the declining Empire. If he was vain and pedantic, he was neither treacherous nor cruel in his pagan fanaticism. He did not have time to develop the ruthless spleen of despotism.

It was not till Julian rebelled against Constantius that he could reveal his true religion as a proselytizing pagan determined to revivify the worship of the gods. His Gallic troops were largely heathen, and from the moment when he reached Sirmium in 361 he spared no pains to increase their fervour and gain over apostates like himself, if less sincere, in the army, court, and administration. No great success attended his efforts at conversion, but the purging of the corrupt civil service and the dispersal of the swarm of court menials and officials which the cult of oriental despotism had fostered gave opportunities for the promotion of pagans, who were numerous in the educated classes. Julian, whose incessant activity and literary tastes allowed him to be a voluminous author, endeavoured to reanimate the pagans and confound the Christians by his polemic writings. They had a vivacious, witty brilliance. As we might expect from the spirit of the age, they are better in criticism and learning than in constructive or penetrating thought. Intended to convince, their appeal was to the Neo-Platonic enthusiast, not to his opponents.

Julian trusted most of all to the exercise of his authority as Pontifex Maximus, high priest of the ancient religion, backed by his absolute power as Emperor. This office had been from the time of Augustus one of the constituent elements of the imperial regime, and had continued to be held by Constantine and his sons, who had employed deputies for its religious functions. Their attitude to paganism had been one of unfriendly toleration. The best statues of the gods were taken to adorn Christian Constantinople. Temples had been despoiled of their lands and revenues for the benefit of court favourites or of Christian churches. The lapse of temple services and sacrifices, as pagan devotion decayed, was encouraged. The temples themselves, in some parts, were allowed to be destroyed or converted to other uses. Constantius II had even removed the altar of Victory from the Senate-house when he visited Rome, in spite of the pagan majority in the Senate (357). But in general the maintenance of the pagan cults had been left to depend on the varying zeal of local magistrates and the proportion of pagans in the population. Julian now set out to use his powers to restore everywhere the rites and endowments of the temples, to rekindle devotion to them, and to reorganize the disconnected cults of the whole amorphous assemblage of gods, Greek, Roman, barbaric, and oriental, as a state church of paganism. He saw the strength that Christianity possessed in its unity and organization, and imitated them in his new creation. But the philosophic, doctrinal basis of his pagan church was to be Neo-Platonic monotheism with its emanations, expressed in the devout worship of the multitudinous departmental gods of tradition. All the temples were to be reopened and all cults zealously performed, however forgotten. The Empire smoked with sacrifices and hecatombs. Julian himself was tireless in his participation in public worship. The priests were to be virtuous and professional; they were even to preach. The provinces were to have their metropolitans, the cities their high priests in an orderly hierarchy. They should organize charitable relief for the religious poor. It is evident how the Emperor took his lesson from the Christianity he hated and hoped to outvie.

But the appeal showed no signs of success. It not only failed with the Christians, who might, as in Cappadocia, embrace the whole population, but it did not inspire the pagans beyond a small circle of Neo-Platonists. The cultured conservatives had no wish to see their ancestral usages brigaded into a religion of enthusiasm. If they wished for religious consolation and visionary ecstasy, they sought them as initiates in the secret rites of the mystery religions of Mithras or Isis or the like, in which Julian himself was an adept. These were experiences for the individual or a select group, not for public worship of state or city-gods. The pagan populace preferred to his austere puritan revival the cruel or sensational games of the amphitheatre and circus, to which Julian gave the minimum of his countenance, and the magical invocation of the rustic gods. Indeed the Emperor was at one with the majority of his subjects only in his credulity, which gave them an unquestioning faith in omens, oracles, spells and magicians. It was the underworld of paganism which had the most tenacious

Fig. 13. Roman horsemen with dragon standard

life. Even the Christian Emperors, who punished the practice of magic as a heinous crime, believed in its efficacy.

Julian, when he re-established paganism as the imperial religion, proclaimed universal toleration. But the effects of his abolition of Christian privileges were harsh enough. State subventions were to cease; so were the exemptions granted to the clergy and the right to receive bequests to the churches. Temple lands and sites were to be restored to their former use, and if the temples had been destroyed, they were to be rebuilt by the destroyers. He hoped much from Christian divisions, the clash of Arian and Catholic. Even his justice was quibbling in his desire to foment them. He revoked the sentences of exile and confiscation which Constantius had decreed against the Catholic bishops, but when Athanasius re-entered on the see of Alexandria, which was vacant by the murder of the Arian George of Cappadocia in a riot provoked by his greed and tyranny, Julian drove him once more into exile as an unauthorized intruder; it is true that he might well fear the influence of the Patriarch. Towards the close of his reign he entered on a path which led to persecution. He forbade Christians to teach in the schools of rhetoric on the masterpieces of ancient literature even to their co-religionists. How should Christians expound the heathen works which they denounced, and which were almost the scriptures of paganism? Tolerant pagans, as well as Christians, condemned the edict, for the culture and education of the day depended on these works; it was an attempt to deprive the Christians of a common cultural inheritance, to make them intellectual plebeians. Julian wished to handicap his antagonists. The vanity of his hopes was shown at his death, when his own army elected the Christian Jovian as his successor.

(3) THE ESTABLISHMENT OF CATHOLICISM

The change of ruler marked the end of the pagan reaction. Whether from weakness or good sense the new Emperor had just time before his sudden death in 364 to proclaim universal toleration and to recognize Athanasius as Patriarch of Alexandria. Valentinian followed in his footsteps in the West. He adhered to the Nicene party, which steadily grew, but let the Arians and pagans be. Valens, however, who in other matters was loyally subservient to the brother to whom he owed his throne, in religion was a convinced and even persecuting Arian. His personal adherence helped to sustain opinions that were losing ground, for Valens, when his cruelty was not roused by fear, was a good administrator. He reduced the taxes, fortified the frontier, and built splendidly. Until the Gothic migration confronted him with a crisis, his indecision and delays did little harm in secular affairs, while he was fixed in his religious policy by the influence of the Homoean bishops left by Constantius, and especially by Eudoxius, the Patriarch of Constantinople.

During his brief return to his see under Julian, Athanasius had reinvigorated the Nicene party in the East, but he had also alarmed the conservatives by the express acknowledgement of the Holy Spirit as the Third co-equal Person in the Trinity. Valens, who expelled the returning Nicene bishops, failed to depose Athanasius permanently, nor was he able to quell the opposition to Arianism. When he fell at Adrianople, Athanasius was already dead (373); his place as leader of the Eastern Nicenes was taken by the ascetic St Basil, Bishop of Cappadocian Caesarea, whom Valens had not dared to depose. Although the Arians were strong in some districts, such as Constantinople, the tendency of conservatives and semi-Arians was to accept the Nicene Creed and the full doctrine of the Trinity expounded by Athanasius. It was only the support of Valens which maintained the Arians in power. His death left the Nicene Emperor Gratian in control, and in January 379 Gratian appointed the Spaniard Theodosius, a rigid Nicene, to be his colleague in the East. In 380 Theodosius commanded all his Christian subjects to follow the Nicene doctrine professed by the churches of Rome and Alexandria; next year he ordered the churches of the East to be given over to the Nicenes. An Eastern Council, later recognized as ecumenical, was held at Constantinople in May 381 and reaffirmed the Nicene Creed. It was followed up by new persecuting edicts of the Emperor, which went far beyond the partisanship of Valens: the Arians were forbidden to build themselves new churches even outside the walls of cities; their ordinations were proscribed; they were subjected to civil disabilities. Constantinople, which was their stronghold, if somewhat influenced by the missionary efforts of the preacher, St Gregory Nazianzen of Cappadocia, was in fact forcibly converted by Theodosius. From this time the Arians were a persecuted and dwindling minority in the East as well as in the West. When the young Western Emperor Valentinian II, under the influence of his Arian mother, the Empress Justina, ordered two churches in Milan to be given to the Arians, he was baffled by the indignant protests of the archbishop, St Ambrose, one of the pillars of his throne. Even this passing favour was ended by the conversion of Valentinian to orthodoxy under the influence of his protector, Theodosius. But if Arian Romans became few, the East German tribes who invaded the Empire remained steadfast to the Arian doctrine. Arianism became the badge of barbarian Christianity, and the religious dissidence deepened and widened the cleft between them and their subjects, who clung passionately to their orthodox faith.

The Council of Constantinople took a further step in the development of church organization. It gave to the Bishop of Constantinople the second place in the ecclesiastical hierarchy immediately after the Bishop of Rome, and before those of Antioch and Alexandria. The title of Patriarch came into use for the bishops of these super-eminent sees, to whom was added in the fifth century the Bishop of the holy city of Jerusalem. The Roman world during this period fell under the authority of these patriarchates. Other cities, like Carthage, Milan, or Ephesus, however high in rank or illustrated by famous bishops, took a secondary place. Constantinople achieved its position as the New Rome, the capital of the Eastern Empire, but its secular claims were resented and denied by the ancient capital of Rome, which asserted a universal authority based on its Petrine foundation. The Western Council of Sardica (343) had given the right of an appeal to Rome to a bishop deposed by a local synod. It was under the statesmanlike if worldly minded Damasus (366–84), who obtained his bishopric after fierce faction fights, that the see of Rome put forth its first official definition of its primacy over all other churches, as their type and model and supervisor. While the claim was admitted in the sense of an honoured pre-eminence in the East, it was confirmed as an appellate jurisdiction in the West by an edict of the Emperor Valentinian III.

The establishment of Christianity as the religion of the State undoubtedly brought evil effects in its train to the religion of the Gospel. For one thing, with the power of the Empire at its back, the spirit of persecution, bred among passionately held convictions on the true faith and made familiar by the anti-Christian persecutions of the pagan Emperors, had become endemic in the Church. Not only were Jews, Manichees and pagans penalized, but heretics, i.e. Christians of scantly held or defeated opinions, were subjected to harsh persecution. The despotism of the Empire entered the Church in the endeavour to control men's thoughts as well as their actions. The toleration of Arian worship appeared a scandalous sin to the eyes of the saintly Ambrose, which may have led him even to countenance pious fraud in the opportune discovery of the bodies of the unknown martyrs, St Gervasius and St Protasius, during his conflict with Justina. On another count, the character of the bishops deteriorated under the influence of court favour and wealthy sees. While many maintained a standard which won the respect of unbelievers, too many were sycophants and careerists, whose lives did little credit to the Church. Again, when the profession of Christianity became profitable and fashionable, swarms of converts entered the Christian community, bringing with them a general decline in Christian morals and behaviour. When all the Roman world had become Christian, it seemed much the same world as it had been before conversion.

Yet there are signs of the beneficial, renovating action of Christianity on that fatigued civilization and its ingrained defects. Men found they had a sacred cause, beyond self-preservation, to plan and strive for. A fresh and vivid interest in things of the mind, which involved the eternal destiny of each and all, sprang up instead of the passive acquiescence in government orders and the little-heeded speculations of cliques of philosophers. It was the doctrine of redemption by the Incarnate Saviour which awoke men from their apathy and servitude. It gave energy and freedom to the disputes on the creed, a nobility to life in spite of mob violence and persecution, and it won the victory for the Nicenes, its most efficient champions.

The beneficial effect of the Church's authority and its spirit of independence amid the servility and spasmodic ferocity of a decadent age were evident in the reign of Theodosius the Great. Devout and benevolent as the Emperor was in the main, he was liable to fits of passionate wrath which knew no bounds of mercy or equity. When a disloyal riot broke out (383) in the excitable city of Antioch on the occasion of new and grinding taxation, it was the intercession of the Bishop Flavian with Theodosius which put a stop to the executions and obtained the revocation of his edict degrading the offending capital from its rank and privileges. Still more cruel was the Emperor's action towards Thessalonica, after Constantinople the most important city of the Balkans. In 390 the mob, long irritated by the billeting of barbarian troops on them, savagely murdered Botheric, who commanded the garrison. By the Emperor's order, given from Milan, in spite of the pleas of St Ambrose, the soldiers treacherously massacred some 7000 citizens gathered in the circus. St Ambrose at once refused the communion until penance was done by the culprit, and the Roman world was amazed to see the Emperor without his purple standing as a penitent in the cathedral of Milan. Perhaps only St Ambrose with his courage and fame could have won such a victory, but he won it by the power of a Christian bishop, who could overawe the temporal autocrat of the State. The dead weight of military despotism and the callous brutality fostered by the amphitheatre found at last an opponent they could not subdue.

The influence of Christian ethics may be traced in the humanitarian legislation, however ineffective and marred by desperately ferocious penalties, of the Christian Emperors. Constantine abolished the cruel punishment of crucifixion, although burning at the stake became customary, and quite vainly denounced the inhuman sports of the amphitheatre. Valentinian had more success in forbidding the condemnation of Christian criminals at least to the arena. It was Valentinian, too, who punished the callous practice of exposing unwanted infants as murder. Constantine had done something to protect the slave from ill usage: to kill him was to be punished like the murder of a freeman. It was forbidden to break up the families of slaves or *coloni* by sales. Sexual crimes, like rape, were threatened with punishments of such fierceness as to suggest that their prevalence had far passed the danger-point. Parental tyranny was limited; and by a law of Theodosius the conviction of the father was not to involve the complete ruin of his dependants. When the courts were arbitrary and corrupt and spies and informers were a public evil, the right of asylum given to the churches was a protection to the oppressed in spite of its abuse. But more important was the free access given to the bishops' courts on civil suits and the binding force of their decisions: it showed their fairness and the evil reputation of the civil tribunals. The great St Ambrose, who had been a lawyer and a governor before his election to Milan, was overwhelmed by his judicial duties as archbishop. That the clergy were freed from curial responsibilities and trade-taxes was justified by the abundant charities and humane activity of the Church, but it led to a rush of the unfit for ordination, and Constantine already in 320 forbade a *curialis* to take orders. The reform cannot have conduced to the recruiting of an educated priesthood, nor did it keep out the careerist: Valentinian found it necessary to cancel the free reception of legacies by clerics who courted the favour of wealthy ladies.

The Church, however, did not only influence the imperial laws and their administration; it had become a new source of law, the scope of which was widened as the number of Christians increased. The Councils which were held legislated on Christian institutions and conduct as well as on the creed. Only certain canons, or church laws, had as yet an ecumenic vogue. The difference between East and West was shown in their laws. In the East bishops only were bound to celibacy, while in the West priests and deacons also were forbidden to marry by the canons. The East accepted the canons of Eastern Councils only; in the West, besides the canons of Nicaea and some other Greek Councils, those of Sardica and of a number of provincial Councils were in force, although the last applied to restricted areas. In the West, too, a new source of Canon Law was appearing in the decretals, or authoritative letters, of the Bishops of Rome. Current usage was applying to the primate of the West the title of Pope (Papa), which effectually distinguished him from his fellow-bishops, and his pronouncements had a corresponding weight.

The veneration of saints and martyrs and a belief in their authority and intercession had long been a characteristic of Christianity. Their relics were treasured; miracles wrought by them in life or after death were readily believed; churches were dedicated to them; the days of their death were held in special honour; the importance of sees depended in part on their apostolic foundation or the Saints who had occupied them. But the hasty conversion of the majority of heathens in the fourth century added enormously to this veneration and credulity. The new converts were accustomed to numerous, varied and local objects of worship and prayer, and they turned willingly from their old gods to the saints and holy relics.

Fig. 14. Baptism of Christ

Nothing was more in accord with their prepossessions than the array of saints which was almost a new pantheon. Such an event as St Ambrose's discovery of St Gervasius and St Protasius aroused a storm of enthusiasm. Indeed, apocryphal saints were invented by the wish to convert and to believe. At times and in certain places the old divinity in a Christian disguise retained his ancient worship. Some of the pagan festivals, which occurred at fit seasons of the year for prayer or rejoicing, were adapted to the Christian calendar.

(4) EARLY MONASTICISM

Along with these developments resulting from the rapid extension of Christianity, there were others due to the depth of the religious convictions of the age, the growth of asceticism and monasticism. Ascetic tendencies were of old date and authorized by Scripture. The insistence on celibacy for the higher clergy shows their influence. Celibacy was upheld as one of the highest virtues. So an ascetic life appeared among the devout laity, especially among women: widows and virgins devoted themselves to a religious life and good works. Two factors played a great part in transforming these ascetic tendencies into the monastic movement which so powerfully affected the life and ideas of Europe during the Middle Ages. One, the more external, was the evils of the times. It was in the close of the third century that the great impulse to monasticism began, the flight from the evil world, sinful, disordered, unjust, oppressed, extortionately taxed, where a more ordinary life of Christian austerity and renunciation seemed barely practicable. Men fled from the natural ties and duties of life in search of liberty to pray and contemplate. The other factor was the strong influence of oriental ideas on the Empire. The solitary ascetic who undertook a life of religious exercises and self-mortification was an Eastern growth, which naturally appealed to the Eastern provinces and spread from them with Christian theology to the West. There was a general conviction that the ascetic life was the only fully Christian life, the ideal and surest way to salvation. It is significant of the creative power which returned to the Roman world with Christianity that these ascetic impulses formed new and lasting institutions outside the rigid framework of secular society.

The fathers of monasticism were two Egyptians, St Anthony and St Pachomius. St Anthony (c. 250–356) was an Egyptian peasant, who, after an ascetic novitiate of fifteen years, secluded himself in a deserted fort for twenty years of solitary devotion. His renown brought a colony of ascetics round him, and at their petition he organized (c. 305) a form of co-operative hermit-life. It allowed a wide variety in the degree of seclusion. North of Lycopolis (Asyut) the desert fringe of Lower Egypt was populated by Antonian hermits, either singly or in small or large groups. At Nitria (Wady Natrun) in the Libyan Desert, the largest settlement, there were communal bakeries, the monks could live either alone or several together, there was a common discipline by the scourge for faults, they all wove linen for their clothes, but they only gathered for common worship on Saturday and Sunday. At Cellia, a few miles off, however, the hermits lived in complete solitude save for the Saturday and Sunday services. The individual hermit, in short, arranging his life as he wished, was the Antonian ideal. St Pachomius (c. 290–345), on the other hand, was the founder of cenobitic or community monasticism. He began life as a pagan recluse of the god Serapis in the Thebaid, and became a Christian hermit at the age of twenty. Love of the brethren led him to establish (c. 315–20) his first monastery at Tabennisi near Tentyra (Denderah) on the Nile; other foundations followed over Upper Egypt. He established real communities under a Rule. The monks had a common kitchen and eating-room, which they served in turn, and a great variety of work made them a self-sufficing colony. Their day was divided by a fixed routine of church services, Bible reading, and the exercise of the occupations for which they were qualified. They were marked more by their tonsure than their garb. It was a rule which appealed to women as well as men, and there were Pachomian nunneries besides Antonian anchoresses. Taken together, the two saints had given a new expression to the Christian ideal.

The movement spread rapidly outside Egypt. In Palestine, where Hilarion introduced Antonian hermit-life, and in Syria, where it met Asiatic ascetic influences, it remained predominantly eremitical. The cenobia were looked on as training grounds for hermits. In the fifth century, besides the cenobia which followed St Basil's Rule, there were the *lauras*, to which St Sabas gave a semi-eremitical constitution. But the Syrian monks and hermits differed from the Egyptians by adopting artificial methods of mortifying the body by self-torture. Such were the pillar-saints, like St Simeon Stylites (395–461), and the hermits who afflicted themselves with chains and weights or those who grazed like cattle. In Asia Minor an advance in cenobitic monasticism was made by St Basil (329–79), Archbishop of Caesarea. He was the father of Greek and Slav monasticism, of which his two Rules set the type. About 360 he retired to a spot near Neocaesarea in Pontus and thence legislated for his new monastery and the others which sprang up in imitation. The Basilian monastery was thoroughly cenobitical. The monks lived under the same roof, ate together, and assembled six times a day in the church. Work, largely agricultural, rather than ascetic practices was insisted upon. The education of boys and the care of orphanages were among their virtues. Not the least important duty of their profession was strict obedience to abbot and superiors, now made an essential, like chastity and poverty, of the monastic life. For St Basil the hermit was not even theoretically more holy than the cenobitic monk.

It was from Egypt that St Athanasius (339) introduced both hermits and cenobites to Rome and Italy. Their increase was speedy. Eusebius, Bishop of Vercelli (*ob.* 371), made the innovation of placing the clerics of his cathedral under a cenobitic rule, and in this he was imitated by St Augustine in Africa. St Martin, Bishop of Tours, was the founder of monastic life in

Gaul (*c*. 363). He appears to have kept close to the Pachomian model. In one way or another the ascetics spread over the West. Whether men fled most from the burdens or from the sins of society, it was a sign of the whole-hearted and ever wider acceptance of Christian belief.

The numbers of the monks, especially in Egypt and the East, presented a problem to the government. In 390 there were 5000 Antonian hermits in Nitria alone; the Pachomian monks of Egypt numbered some 7000 in all. It was among these indomitable ascetics that St Athanasius possessed a secure refuge from the government. The Arian Valens endeavoured in vain to bend them to his creed by conscripting the young and able bodied at Nitria for the army. Among the crowd of hermits or individualistic monks there existed, indeed, a growing number of impostors who feigned or made capital out of their austerities, an evil which led to canons prescribing episcopal supervision. A profound and not entirely desirable influence on the life of the Empire was exercised by the veneration which the ascetics, and especially the more spectacular among them, like the pillar saints, enjoyed among all classes. It produced a hectic mob emotion which distorted the religion of the time. The monks, drawn from the peasantry and indiscriminately recruited, invaded theological and even political controversy with a wild fanaticism with which they infected the populace.

(5) THE END OF PAGANISM

The triumph of Christianity implied its concomitant, the decay of paganism. Julian's reign had merely suspended the progress of desertion. The rule of Valens in the East was marked by the ruin of numerous temples, if only for lack of repair: their revenues were diverted to public or private use, and where the maintenance of their worship depended on the local magistrates those overtaxed notables, though pagan, cannot have been eager to provide for their upkeep. It was in the great cities and by the support of wealthy senatorial families that the worship of the Olympian deities could be carried on. In Rome the resident senators still maintained paganism as the established religion; the altar of Victory had been restored by Julian; the ancient ceremonies were performed at the government's expense. In Athens the schools of philosophers were heathen. The Eleusinian mysteries, the Olympic games continued. It was the Emperor Gratian who began to employ more effectual measures against this kind of toleration. He refused to take the title of Pontifex Maximus, confiscated the revenues of the Roman priesthoods, and removed once more the altar of Victory from the senate-house in spite of the forlorn appeals of the pagan senators (382). His action was upheld by Valentinian II, who listened to St Ambrose against the pagan spokesman Symmachus. The conservatives' hopes were revived when Arbogast placed on the throne Eugenius, who, though a

Christian, restored the altar and made an exuberant pagan, Flavian, praetorian prefect. But this wishful thinking was dispelled by the battle of the Frigidus and the supremacy of Theodosius the Great.

The altar of Victory now disappeared for good and all. Theodosius closed the temples, of which many were destroyed by ardent bishops, like that of Serapis at Alexandria (391) by the Patriarch Theophilus. The temple properties were confiscated in East and West. The Olympic games ceased (394). Sacrifices to the heathen gods in any form were prohibited as treasonable. Yet paganism survived as a private, almost quietistic, belief for over a century. Imperial officials could be employed and promoted in spite of their adherence to it. The Eleusinian mysteries only came to an end in 396 (?), when Alaric destroyed the temple of Demeter. Till the reign of Justinian the teachers of Athens were pagans and Neo-Platonists. In literary circles, steeped in the ancient poets, paganism died hard. Indeed the great Christian writers, like St Jerome and St Augustine, were remorseful for the hold that heathen literature kept upon themselves. Pagan philosophy still coloured the intimate thoughts of Boethius, a Christian and a theologian, in the sixth century, when as a creed it had vanished. The old faith lived longest in the more primitive strata of the population, not as a religion but as a magical practice to conciliate or compel familiar spirits or demons who had once been Olympian or petty local deities. But even among these feeble folk the Christian saints were triumphantly superior. The Roman world had accepted Christianity.

BOOK II

THE BREAK-UP OF THE EMPIRE

※※※

CHAPTER 5

THE CRUMBLING OF THE EMPIRE
IN THE WEST, 395–476

(I) STILICHO AND ALARIC, 395–410

Until the death of Theodosius the Great at Milan on 17 January 395 the
Roman Empire had weathered the barbarian storm in spite of disasters
and the civil wars. Yet its situation had changed definitely for the worse.
Not to mention the economic distress caused by over-taxation and barbarian ravages, there was the loss of territory and valuable recruiting
grounds within the old fortified frontier. Salian Franks had settled in
north-east Gaul, Ostrogoths in Pannonia, Visigoths in Moesia, all under
their native princes. Most serious of all evils was the depletion of the
field-armies and garrisons, and the fact that these consisted of barbarian
mercenaries. The depletion compelled the use of the federate Goths at the
Frigidus and raised the ambition of their chiefs. That the regular armies
were composed of barbarian mercenaries meant that their officers and
generals were barbarians too, only half-Romanized, and these held the
destinies of the Empire in their hands. When the generals were Romans,
they had usually, if eminent, aspired to become Emperors, a main cause of
the Empire's weakness. Now that they were Germans, ineligible men in
their own eyes for the crown, they aspired to be Emperor-makers and to
rule in the name of an Emperor-puppet. This had been the aim of Arbogast
the Frank when he murdered Valentinian II and installed the powerless
Eugenius. He had the advantage that the Western frontiers required a
single commander-in-chief: the enemies on the Rhine and upper Danube
were too closely connected. Nor could Theodosius alter the geographical
necessity. The East with its separate frontiers and foes must divide the
supreme command.

It was, perhaps, fortunate at first for the Empire that the two sons of
Theodosius were nullities whom no barbarian general would wish to
dethrone. Arcadius, who took the East with half Illyricum, was only
seventeen at his accession, and remained sluggish and malleable all his life.

3. The Emperors of the Fifth and Sixth Centuries

(a) The House of Theodosius

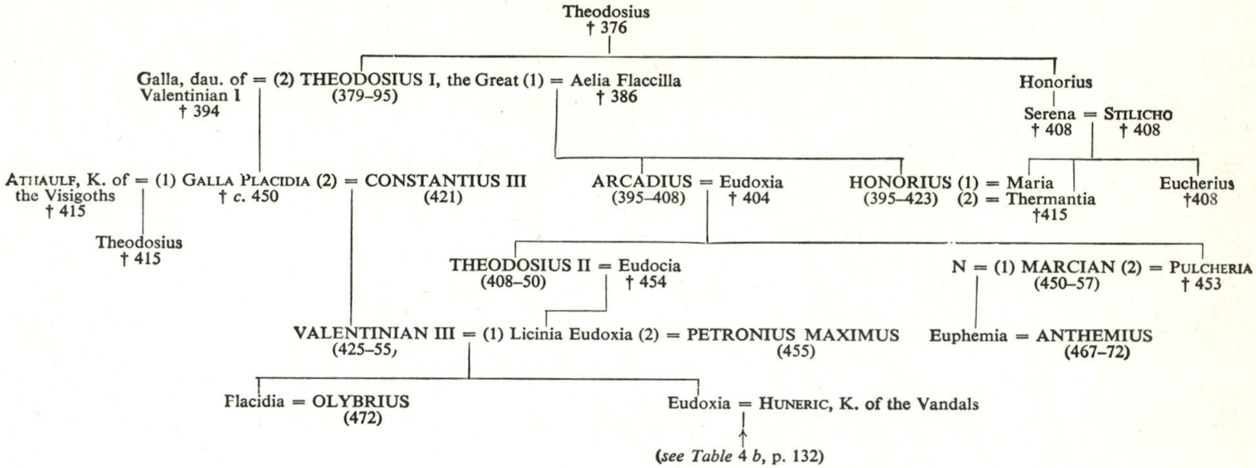

Theodosius † 376

THEODOSIUS I, the Great (1) = Aelia Flacilla † 386
Galla, dau. of Valentinian I † 394 = (2) THEODOSIUS I

Honorius

Serena = STILICHO † 408

Eucherius † 408

ARCADIUS (395–408) = Eudoxia † 404

HONORIUS (1) = Maria (2) = Thermantia † 415
(395–423)

N = (1) MARCIAN (2) = PULCHERIA † 453
(450–57)

Euphemia = ANTHEMIUS (467–72)

ATHAULF, K. of the Visigoths † 415 = (1) GALLA PLACIDIA (2) = CONSTANTIUS III (421)
† c. 450

Theodosius † 415

THEODOSIUS II (408–50) = Eudocia † 454

VALENTINIAN III (425–55) = (1) Licinia Eudoxia (2) = PETRONIUS MAXIMUS (455)

Flacidia = OLYBRIUS (472)

Eudoxia = HUNERIC, K. of the Vandals

(see Table 4 b, p. 132)

(b) The Family of Leo I

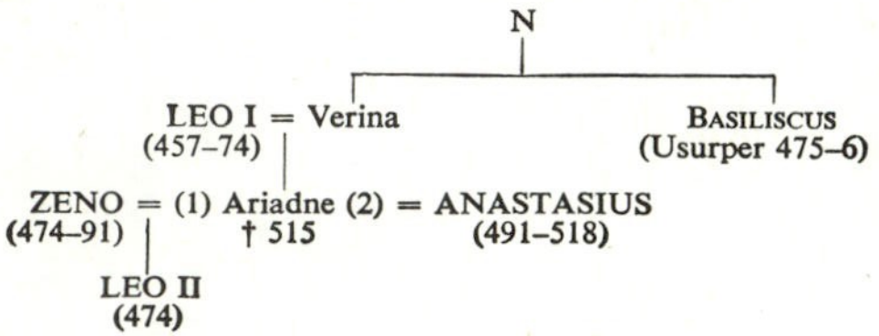

N

BASILISCUS (Usurper 475–6)

LEO I (457–74) = Verina

ZENO (474–91) = (1) Ariadne (2) = ANASTASIUS (491–518)
† 515

LEO II (474)

(c) The House of Justin

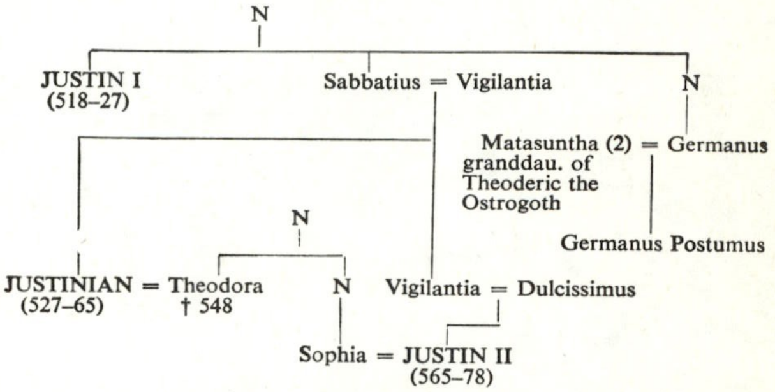

N

Matasuntha (2) = Germanus granddau. of Theoderic the Ostrogoth

Germanus Postumus

JUSTIN I (518–27)

Sabbatius = Vigilantia

Vigilantia = Dulcissimus

JUSTINIAN (527–65) = Theodora † 548

N

Sophia = JUSTIN II (565–78)

Fig. 15. Stilicho, Serena and their son Eucherius. Ivory diptych

Honorius, who received the West at the age of eleven, was little better than a child who never grew up. His dying father had placed in command of the West his best general, Stilicho, a Vandal long in the Roman service, to whom he had married his niece Serena, while in the East the praetorian prefect Rufinus of Aquitaine had the charge of Arcadius. Both were able men, but Stilicho had the disadvantage of his barbarian extraction and Rufinus that of being a civilian unconnected with the imperial house. Stilicho aimed perhaps at the regency of the whole Empire and at least at the reannexation of eastern Illyricum to the West. The two governments thus became unfriendly to each other while he lived. But there arose a third candidate for power who utilized their dissensions. While Goths, both Arians and heathens, swarmed in the army, the larger part of the Visigoths were federates settled in Moesia. On the death of Theodosius these elected a king, Alaric, and he, disappointed in his hopes of military command, revolted and with his tribe ravaged the Balkans. The best

Eastern troops were still in Italy, a band of Huns had crossed the Caucasus and reached Syria, and when Stilicho came nominally to the rescue to Thessaly his conduct was so dubious that he received peremptory orders to evacuate Illyricum and send back the Eastern troops to Constantinople. He was unable to refuse obedience, but those troops under their leader, the Goth Gainas, promptly massacred Rufinus. Power fell into the hands of the chief eunuch Eutropius, who had already found a wife for Arcadius in a Frankish lady Eudoxia, daughter of Bauto, a mercenary general like Arbogast. Alaric was left to ravage Greece and play off the two courts against one another. Only Thebes was strong enough to hold out against him.

Stilicho's obedience was probably influenced by the revolt of the Moors. Prince Gildo, brother of the earlier rebel Firmus, who had been conquered by Count Theodosius, and himself once prefect of Mauretania and master of the horse and foot in the army, had rebelled in 394; he ruled the interior, but not the fortified cities, which he attacked with the aim of founding a Moorish kingdom of North Africa. None the less Stilicho led his army once more to Greece in 397, and blockaded Alaric in Elis. Yet no victory was attempted. The counter-move of Eutropius, who evidently looked on Stilicho as the worse enemy, was to receive favourably an offer of the rebel Gildo to hold North Africa as a vassal of the Eastern Empire. This led to the rapid return of Stilicho to Italy to meet the danger. He had come to some agreement with Alaric, whom he left to be a terror to the East. A terrible devastation of Epirus by the Visigoths was the first result; the next was an adroit *volte face* of Eutropius. Alaric, who may like his predecessors have found the fortifications of the Eastern cities too strong for him, was placated by bribes and the title of *magister militum* of Illyricum with the possession of Epirus, a poorer land than Moesia. He was now to be a thorn in the side of the Western Empire. Stilicho was declared a public enemy by Arcadius, to which an inadequate reply was the refusal of the West to recognize Eutropius as a consul for 399. The two halves of the Empire had become open foes to their common detriment.

The revolt of Gildo was the more dangerous because he was able to cut off the African corn-supply which was sent to Rome, but Stilicho was equal to the emergency. He brought the corn and also troops from Gaul, thereby weakening the Gallic defences, and he sent his army to Africa under Gildo's brother and bitter enemy Mascezel, whose children had been murdered by the rebel. Gildo's forces dissolved before his opponent (398). He met his death as a hunted fugitive. The victor died by a suspicious accident in Stilicho's entourage. In the same year Stilicho riveted his hold on the Emperor by marrying him to his daughter Maria.

Meantime revolutions succeeded one another in the East, all connected with what may be called its domestic Gothic question. Gainas was now a *magister militum*, and supported by the Gothic mercenaries was aiming to be another Stilicho. The revolt of Goths settled in Asia Minor under Tribigild and the failure to subdue them (399), while a band of Huns ravaged Thrace, gave him his opportunity. The Empress Eudoxia had turned against Eutropius, who was dismissed and executed. Gainas, at the head of the troops and in alliance with Tribigild, was for a time supreme, but the Goths were hated and disunited as well. When Gainas demanded a church in Constantinople for his Arian countryman, he roused even the lethargic Arcadius. He felt uneasy in the city and withdrew to the suburbs with most of his troops (400). The remainder were massacred, while the loyal forces were put under the command of the heathen veteran Fravitta, a Goth of the ancient school. The old Gothic inability to take fortified towns, the command of the Straits by the East Roman fleet which marooned the rebels in devastated Thrace, and the generalship of Fravitta ended the campaign in the Romans' favour. Many Goths were drowned in trying to cross to Asia Minor, Tribigild was killed, and Gainas himself died in a battle with Uldin the Hun beyond the Danube, which he had passed with the remnant of his men. Both Alaric and Stilicho had remained quiet the while. The one could not wish for a rival Gothic chief, the other for an imitation of himself in the East.

It was now the turn of the West to feel the renewed ferment of the frontier tribes. The Visigoths had given the example, and the Huns were pressing upon them. On the middle Danube a confederacy was forming under the leadership of a Goth, Radagaisus, which included Goths, Asding Vandals, and Alans. It would seem that Radagaisus and Alaric concerted invasions of Italy. Stilicho gathered and increased his forces: Uldin the Hun and Alans appeared in his army. In 401 a campaign near the Danube ended in victory and compromise. Godegisel, King of the Vandals, and his tribe were allowed to take Noricum and Vindelicia. Thus the upper Danube frontier was submerged. Then in November Alaric entered Italy and besieged Honorius in Milan. But Stilicho hurried south, driving the Visigoths westward. A bloody battle was fought at Pollentia (Pollenzo) on 6 April 402, and Alaric's wife and children were taken prisoner. He found Stilicho ready for another compromise. Alaric withdrew to Illyricum and was given the Western rank of *magister militum*; he was to co-operate in the annexation of East Illyricum to the West. He broke the treaty almost at once, for in 403 he advanced to besiege Verona. Once more Stilicho defeated and could have crushed him, but preferred a treaty. A joint invasion of the East was arranged. Here again Stilicho's plans were upset by Radagaisus, who in 405 entered Italy with a horde of Ostrogoths, Vandals, Alans and Quadian Suevi. Stilicho was equal to the emergency. He now had a body of Visigothic deserters, under a chief, Sarus, in his army. With his usual skill he trapped Radagaisus at Faesulae (Fiesole) in

Tuscany. The invading host suffered heavy loss in its attempt to break through, and Radagaisus was taken and killed: the survivors were allowed to journey back to Noricum. Italy was saved once more, and so was the Eastern Empire.

Stilicho's half-hearted use of his successes may have been partly due to his shortage of troops and his desire to retain the barbarian tribes as recruiting grounds. The divisions, which are obvious among the Visigoths, may have made him look upon Alaric as a passing danger only. At any rate during these wars the defence of the Rhine had to be left to the Frankish federates. The fact tempted the coalition formed by the dead Radagaisus. The Vandals, Alans and Suevi moved west instead of south. On the river Main they joined the Siling Vandals and then defeated the federate Franks, although King Godegisel fell in battle. On the night of 31 December 406 they crossed the frozen Rhine at Mainz, which they destroyed, and harried defenceless Gaul to the Pyrenees, where they were stopped by the fortified passes. They showed a power to take walled cities unusual in these hordes. Trier, Arras, Amiens, Paris, Orleans and Tours fell victims to their predatory march over the plainland of Gaul. The sufferings of the Gauls were intense and without precedent for centuries. But the worst was that the Rhine frontier had been broken and was never to be restored. The fall of the Western Empire had begun.

While the Vandals and their allies halted in Narbonensis, other tribes followed in their wake. The Alemanni resumed their invasions, and took possession of Alsace. The Burgundians, pressing down the Main, also crossed into Gaul round Worms. But Stilicho did not take his eyes off the East. The invasion and the lack of defence made the garrisons restive. In Britain the troops set up a common soldier, Constantine, as Emperor. He crossed over to Gaul with them (407), and they never came back. The provincials were left to their own devices to repel the raiders from overseas. Constantine was accepted by such troops as were left in Gaul. Sarus the Goth, sent against him by Stilicho, had to buy a passage back to Italy by bribing the brigand peasants called Bagaudae, who infested the country and held the passes of the Alps. The Pyrenees were forced and Spain fell to the usurper. He did not, however, possess all Gaul, for the Armoricans of the north-west revolted against the officials and maintained some kind of independence; in Britain, too, there was a similar rebellion among the Celtic countrymen, and perhaps it was at this time that Cunedda led a part of the Votadini from the north-east to the west, where, driving out the Irish tribesmen settled there, he founded the little kingdom of Venedotia (Gwynedd) or North Wales.

None of these disasters deflected the main policy of Stilicho: he was still bent on aggression towards the East, to which he had closed the Italian ports, and on friendship with the federate Germanic tribes. On the death of his daughter the Empress Maria he married Honorius to her sister Thermantia so as to maintain his control. But Alaric, who had been kept waiting for the Eastern campaign, saw his opportunity for fresh blackmail. He marched from Epirus to Noricum, now vacated by the Vandals, and demanded an enormous payment (8000 pounds of gold) for his services. Even the Roman Senate, accustomed to servility, only consented to the payment with fiery protests. Then came the news that Arcadius had died (1 May 408), leaving a child of seven, Theodosius II, as his heir. Stilicho at once showed his hand: he would proceed to Constantinople to secure the regency for Honorius, i.e. for himself, while Alaric and his Visigoths should trek to Gaul and put down the rebel Constantine. But he had not reckoned on the disaffection of the regular legions and the Roman population. Stilicho seemed to be always favouring the 'federate' tribes and almost looking for lands to give them in the Empire. Even though they were mainly barbarian mercenaries, the legionaries felt a professional indignation, and there were still Roman officers and men among them. After all, Constantine, who was to be ruined by Alaric, had been elevated by the army. Although Stilicho had been invariably successful, he had not prevented the devastation of Illyricum, North Italy and Gaul. In fact his treaties had allowed its recurrence. Roman hatred rose high in the civilian population and in the Romanized army against the half-barbarian who appeared to be sacrificing the Empire to his ambitions. It is noticeable that among the military malcontents was Sarus the Visigoth mercenary, who had his own ambitions. A first mutiny was fomented by him at Ravenna on the Adriatic coast. This city, since the battle of Pollentia, had acquired a new importance as the chief imperial residence in the West. Like the later Venice it was almost impregnable among the marshes and lagoons,[1] one of which provided it with an admirable harbour. Stilicho quieted this outbreak, but the greater part of the troops were at Pavia, whither Honorius proceeded. There both Emperor and troops were worked on by a palace official, Olympius, a Greek by birth, who reported that Stilicho intended to murder the child Theodosius II and place his own son Eucherius on the throne. By visiting sick soldiers in a pretence of Christian charity Olympius spread his tale. The troops burst into mutiny against the government, massacring their generals and the high officials, including the pretorian prefects of Italy and Gaul, all of them nominees of Stilicho. The news reached Stilicho at Bologna, where his Germanic generals, with Sarus among them, urged immediate civil war. When Stilicho refused, Sarus led a massacre of his bodyguard of Huns. Stilicho escaped to Ravenna, where an order for his arrest followed him from Honorius, now as obedient to Olympius as he had been to the Master of Both Services. Stilicho was lured from sanctuary, and a second imperial letter ordered his execution (23 August 408). He

[1] The coast has now receded five miles, and both lagoon and marsh are drained.

might, perhaps, have saved himself had he appealed to the Germanic soldiery, but he was put to death. Thermantia was divorced, Eucherius was soon murdered, Stilicho's friends were tortured in the hope of proving a plot, and by an insane policy the Roman soldiers were allowed to slaughter the families of their Germanic comrades. Most of these deserted in a body to Alaric in Noricum.

Although Stilicho's policy may have been wrong-headed and warped by his ambitions, he was the best general of the day and a born ruler. The only advantage gained by his death was the reconciliation of East and West. The worst of the many disadvantages was the regency of Olympius, the Master of the Offices, for Honorius remained a cipher. Olympius had only cunning and no statesmanship. With the army half destroyed and out of hand, he refused Alaric's demand for more money and a settlement in Pannonia; he dared not make the able, treacherous Sarus commander of the troops. This was to invite the deluge. Alaric with his main army entered Italy and marched without resistance straight on Rome itself. Honorius lurked safe in Ravenna with the government. Since his accession the Senate had played a real part in public affairs, for ministers like Stilicho sought naturally to gain over the great landowning class, whose richest members lived in ostentatious, futile luxury in Rome amid their thousands of slaves. It now had to deal with Alaric as a government. When the Gothic blockade of the city began, its first measure was to execute Stilicho's widow Serena, suspected of an understanding with Alaric. Then when famine appeared it asked for terms. They were exorbitant—all valuables and all Germanic slaves—but were lowered to an enormous ransom and the Senate's influence with Honorius for peace. Although there was a large pagan group of senators, it is significant that the temple treasures were taken to spare their private fortunes. Alaric withdrew to Tuscany (December 408), where he was joined by swarms of fugitive slaves from Rome, and negotiated with the Emperor. Olympius now hoped for help from the usurper Constantine, whom he recognized as co-Emperor, and from reinforcements from Dalmatia. The last came, but were cut to pieces by Alaric. Meanwhile Alaric's brother-in-law Athaulf came from Pannonia with a force of Goths and Huns. On this, Olympius fell from power (he was later scourged to death), and Jovius the praetorian prefect became chief minister. But the court of Ravenna remained uncomplying even to reduced demands of Alaric, sponsored by Pope Innocent I, which asked for Noricum and the office of *magister militum*. The arrival of 10,000 newly levied Huns and the Goths' shortage of provisions may account for this obduracy.

Alaric's counter-move was reminiscent of Arbogast. He seized the Roman corn-magazines at Portus by Ostia and compelled the Senate to elect the prefect of the city, Attalus, as Emperor (end of 409). Attalus was a pagan, but he was duly baptized by an Arian bishop of the Goths. He made Alaric his commander-in-chief and then presumed to contradict him. The corn-supply was derived from Africa, where Count Heraclian, the slayer of Stilicho, held sway for Honorius and would not send it to rebel Rome. Alaric wished to dispatch a Gothic force over sea, but Attalus insisted on Roman levies, who failed utterly. Meantime Alaric was besieging Ravenna, which was saved by the long-expected help from the East, 4000 efficient soldiers. It became clear that Attalus, the self-willed puppet, was of no use to the Goths, and Alaric deposed him (May 410) as a preliminary to fresh parleys with Honorius during a truce. This was broken by Sarus, hitherto standing aloof, in a treacherous attack on the Gothic camp in the name of Honorius. The result was to fix Alaric's resolution to loot all he could from Rome and transport his army to Africa, the land of plenty, for settlement.

In August 410 he invested Rome once more. Starvation quickly followed, and in the night of 23 August the Salarian gate was opened by treachery. For three days Goths and slaves ranged through the Eternal City. There was much destruction, considerable slaughter and outrage, and immense plunder, although the churches seem to have been spared. The stored plate, jewels, and silks of the senators were at last dissipated; captives were held to ransom or slavery; fugitives found their way to Africa or Palestine with the tale that Rome, the eternal mistress of the world, had fallen before the barbarians. 'The human race is included in the ruins', wrote St Jerome in his cell at Bethlehem, and St Augustine amid his sneers at the helpless gods of the past admitted that the whole world groaned at the fall of Rome. To the pagan remnant, living on ancient glories, it must have seemed that the genius they idolized had fled the violated sanctuary. Even the quick recovery could not restore its lost glamour: the new prestige of Rome was to be Christian and papal.

Alaric had no mind to remain in Italy. On 27 August he marched south to Reggio, which he burnt and where he collected the ships for the conquest of Africa. But the seas round Sicily were dangerous even to sailors, and his ships were scattered and wrecked in a sudden storm. Alaric and his Goths were landsmen and flinched. Scarcely had he turned back before he died at Cosenza (410), and was buried in the bed of the river Busento, the place being concealed by the massacre of the slaves, who first diverted and then restored the stream. He had been a great destroyer.

(2) THE SHRINKAGE OF THE EMPIRE:
CONSTANTIUS III AND AËTIUS

The Visigoths at once elected the dead king's brother-in-law Athaulf as his successor. For a year or two he remained in Italy living on the country, but the dream of a Gothic empire, which he had cherished, faded as he realized the barbarism of his tribe and the civilization that lay prostrate. Since the siege of Rome the Goths had held as a hostage Placidia, the sister of Honorius. Athaulf married her, and chose, he said, 'the glory of seeking to restore and to increase by Gothic strength the name of Rome'. His aims were perhaps not unlike the views of Stilicho, as they appeared to a would-be federate. But for their accomplishment peace and alliance with the childless Honorius were necessary. As it happened, events beyond the Alps prepared the way.

The usurper Constantine had taken possession of Spain by an expedition of his son Constans, whom he made his colleague, and the latter had left the Briton Gerontius in charge. Gerontius proved a traitor in every way: he proclaimed an insignificant follower, Maximus, Emperor, and opened the Pyrenean passes to the united Vandals, Alans and Suevi, who were still looting southern Gaul. They entered Spain (409) and spread over the land. Meantime Gerontius attacked Gaul, killed Constans, and besieged Constantine in Arles (411). But Honorius now had an army again, and a general, the Roman Constantius, master of the soldiers. He was a striking personality from Illyricum like the Flavian Emperors, for he was born at Naïssus (Nish). Men felt he was worthy of the purple as he rode bending over his horse's mane and glancing with flashing eyes to right and left. He inspired instant loyalty from the troops. Gerontius was deserted by his own men; the Franks who came to help Constantine were defeated; and the usurper surrendered, soon to be executed by Honorius.

This success did not mean the pacification of either Gaul or Spain. The Franks, Burgundians and Alemanni, who held the north-east, set up a new usurper, the Gaul Jovinus, to legalize their conquests. Constantius was obliged to quiet Spain by a pact (411) with the invaders, who were recognized as *foederati*: the Asdings and Suevi took the north-west, the Silings the south, while the more numerous Alans took the land between. Constantius may have been called back to Italy by the movements of Athaulf. At any rate in 412 the Visigoth left Italy for southern Gaul. He at first treated with Jovinus, but they soon fell out—the slaughter of Sarus, his ancient enemy, who had joined Jovinus, was one cause—and Athaulf, in a momentary alliance with Honorius, sent the head of the usurper to Ravenna (413). In return he should have been supplied with corn by the Emperor, for southern Gaul was wasted, but a fresh revolt prevented this. Count Heraclian of Africa, like other Roman generals, made a bid for the

Empire. He stopped the corn-ships once more, and himself sailed with a fleet to Italy. His defeat, flight and execution followed in quick succession. The effect of his rebellion was to renew the war between the Visigoths and the Empire.

There was, however, another question in dispute, the possession of Placidia, sister and heiress of Honorius. Through all these anarchic years one chief cause of the paralysis of the Romans had been the problem of replacing or succeeding the simpleton Honorius. Stilicho, perhaps, was content to rule in his name. Constantine, Heraclian and others tried rebellion. Constantius hoped to gain the crown by marrying Placidia. Here Athaulf was the obstacle, for, although himself a barbarian, a son of his by his captive might reign in the future. In January 414 he celebrated his marriage at Narbonne with full Roman rites. This was to challenge Constantius, who advanced into Gaul. Although Athaulf vainly wooed the Gallo-Romans by re-creating Attalus, who had followed the Gothic camp, his puppet-Emperor, he was outgeneralled and forced into Spain with his starving Goths. At Barcelona he was murdered in his stables (415) by a servant of the dead Sarus, whose brother Sigeric was killed in his turn after a reign of seven days, during which he had wreaked his blood-feud and treated Placidia with ignominy. Athaulf's reign had been an ambitious failure.

King Wallia, who was now elected, returned to the search for land as a so-called *foederatus* with practical success. His first plan was to invade Africa like Alaric, but a storm, which wrecked the van of his fleet near Gibraltar (416) had the same effect on him as on his predecessor. He found Constantius ready for a deal. In fact Constantius had made up his mind to accept the settlement of the barbarians on the fringes of Gaul: it was the policy of Stilicho. He had already agreed to the settlement of the Burgundians round Worms. By the treaty the Visigoths were to be at last supplied with corn; in return they restored Placidia and agreed to attack the Vandals and Alans in Spain. Wallia performed his contract. The Silings were exterminated and the remnant of the Alans were driven into Galicia, where they were absorbed by the Asdings, cooped up with the Suevi in that province. Then (418) the Visigoths received their reward in Gaul, where they settled as federates in Aquitania Secunda from the Loire to Bordeaux with the addition of Toulouse.

Some kind of peace was now restored in the West, though with the loss of territory, by Constantius. For some time the imperial government had been trying to heal some of the wounds inflicted by misgovernment and war. In 408 the bishops were given civil jurisdiction in their dioceses, which alleviated the corrupt justice of the secular courts. Remission of taxation, which could hardly have been levied in any case, was granted to Italy. Population was only too successfully attracted back to Rome. In southern Gaul Constantius set up an annual assembly at Arles (418), which was to ventilate grievances and link the subjects to the bureaucracy. These remedial measures came too late to achieve much, and the prime evils—invading barbarians, grasping officials, selfish great landowners, and disloyal generals—remained. For the time Constantius was supreme. He was given the rank of *patricius*, which placed him next to the consuls; in 417 he was married to the unwilling Placidia; and in 421 was at last declared Augustus and co-Emperor. The appointment might have led to war with the East, where the dread of a new and capable dynasty made Theodosian descent a condition of the crown and a court principle, but the conflict was averted and the continued misfortunes of the West ensured by the death of Constantius III within the year of his accession.

The death of Constantius was followed by another period of turmoil and disasters, while rivals struggled for the control of the Roman government and barbarian kings used the opportunity to tear fresh provinces from the Empire of the West. The losses suffered were not to be retrieved, and a long step was taken to the Empire's dissolution. The first to grasp power at Ravenna was Castinus, whose rule was a series of calamities. A rival, Count Boniface, fled to Africa, where he set up a half-independent authority. Placidia had lost control of the exuberant fraternal affection of Honorius, and was banished (423) with her children, Valentinian and Honoria, to Constantinople, whither Boniface sent her a maintenance. Meanwhile peace had vanished from Spain. Gunderic, King of the Vandals and the Alans, after a vain attempt to enlarge his cramped borders by attacking the Suevi, broke loose into southern Spain. Castinus marched against him with the assistance of a Visigothic corps, sent by the federate Theodoric I, a grandson of Alaric, who had succeeded Wallia in 419. When it came to fighting, the Visigoths basely assaulted their Roman comrades in the rear, giving to Gunderic a crushing victory (422). The Vandals were now unchecked in Spain, captured the ports, and, alone of these invaders, took to the sea as pirates. Theodoric in Gaul threw off the mask, and proceeded to conquer Narbonensis as far as the Rhone.

In this confusion the problem of the succession engrossed the Roman generals; one cannot call them statesmen. In 423 Honorius faded out of the life in which he had trifled so long. Even in the clumsy portraiture of his own time he shows a lack-lustre, flabby face which tells its own tale. There were two main alternatives in the choice of his successor. One was to recognize the hereditary claim of the Theodosian house. In that case the crown would come to Valentinian, the son of Placidia and Constantius III, living in exile at Constantinople. This would give the friendship of the East, a valuable asset. But Valentinian was a child of four, which meant that real control would be a question of armed competition. The other alternative was to elect a Western Emperor. This was adopted by Castinus in the elevation of John, an experienced bureaucrat. The action was possible because the Western Empire possessed a new recruiting ground in the confederacy of Hunnish tribes, which made up in some degree for the failing supply of the old source of mercenaries owing to the hostility and migrations of the Germans. As it happened, there was an eminent officer in the Western service who had a great personal influence with the Huns. This was Aëtius, 'the last of the Romans', born at Silistria on the lower Danube, the son of a cavalry general and his Italian wife. He had been a hostage among the Huns, and he was now dispatched to levy a fresh Hunnish army to support the usurping John. There was also Count Boniface to reckon with in Africa, against whom a force was sent. The Eastern government, however, acted with promptitude. Theodosius II had for a moment thought of reuniting the Empire under himself: the obvious independence of the West led him to send Valentinian with an army under his best generals (425). John was quickly overthrown and executed. When Aëtius arrived, three days too late, he was pacified by the command in Gaul as count, and his large Hunnish army was dismissed with pay. Valentinian III became Emperor under the regency of his mother, who resumed the title of Augusta, with Felix as commander-in-chief.

Gaul indeed required immediate action, for Theodoric the Visigoth was besieging Arles. Franks and Burgundians were stirring. Britons were emigrating from their harried land to Armorica, where they settled in independence, bringing in, it may be noticed, their native language, not Latin, and giving the land the name of Brittany. Aëtius took the situation in hand; he repulsed Theodoric and recovered Narbonensis at the price of acknowledging the independence of the Visigoths. Roman rule was restored in south and central Gaul. About 431 he threw back King Clodio of the Salian Franks from Arras and the river Somme. He had already checked the Ripuarians. He even campaigned on the upper Danube. The preservation of Roman Gaul was one key-note of his policy; his personal understanding with the Huns, from whom his armies were recruited, was the other.

The defence of Gaul was not the only preoccupation of Aëtius. He took a steadily more ambitious part in the struggle for power at Ravenna round the changeful Placidia. The conduct of Count Boniface in Africa was giving anxiety to the Patrician Felix. In any case the position in Africa was serious. The Moors had forced back the frontier and raided the fertile provinces in the coastal region. Even there rebellion was always simmering among the numerous Donatists, who hated the persecuting orthodoxy of Ravenna. Count Boniface, hitherto a loyal partisan of Placidia and a devout friend of the great St Augustine, Bishop of Hippo, was disappointed in his hopes of succeeding Castinus. His second wife was an Arian, and he may have begun to toy with the ambition of becoming ruler of an African dominion with the support of the disaffected heretics. In 427 Felix recalled him, and he rebelled. After defeating a first army, he was hard pressed by a second, mostly composed of Visigothic mercenaries under Sigisvult. But now a third competitor for Africa appeared.

The Vandal King Gunderic was succeeded in 428 by his brother, the famous Gaiseric, by far the ablest general and statesman of his day. Lame and taciturn, he could both lead his tribe to victory and weave political combinations over half Europe. For the rest he was a cruel, grasping barbarian, on whom the only effect of his Arian Christianity was to make him a persecutor. It was said that Boniface invited him to his aid and perhaps Sigisvult did the same, but Gaiseric needed no invitation. Unplundered Africa, whence the corn which supplied the exhausted Western provinces was shipped to Rome, had already been the goal of the Visigoths, and the Vandals had taken to the sea in Spain. In Spain he had rivals in the Suevi, on whom he inflicted a parting defeat. In May 429 he crossed the Straits from Tarifa to Mauretania with his whole people. It throws light on the size of these East German tribes who overran the Empire that the Vandals numbered 80,000 souls, i.e. about 15,000 fighting men. Gaiseric's rapid and formidable advance through Numidia quickly reconciled the Roman generals, but Boniface was defeated by him and besieged (430) in the coast town of Hippo, where St Augustine was the soul of the defence till his death (28 August 430). Only a few fortified cities, Carthage, Cirta and Hippo were able to hold out behind their walls, which were not to be stormed by the barbarians. The Vandal conquest was now threatening the whole Empire, for not only was Africa the granary of the West but its ports in Vandal hands would imperil the Roman command of the Mediterranean and deprive the provinces of their best barrier and defence. So the East, too, sent an army under Aspar the Alan, who had vanquished the usurper John. This army in its turn was defeated by Gaiseric (431), when the policy of Placidia took another turn.

Felix had been murdered at Ravenna in 430 by the soldiers at the instigation of Aëtius, who took his place as commander-in-chief and resumed his campaigns on the Rhine and the Danube. Placidia, however, chafed at his tutelage: she may, too, with Italy as her first thought, have laid more stress on the defence of Africa than on that of Gaul. She summoned Count Boniface to Ravenna and made him Master of the Soldiers in place of Aëtius. The rivals fought it out near Rimini. Aëtius was defeated and fled to the Huns, but Boniface died shortly after. His successor Sebastian was soon ousted by Aëtius and his Hunnish army (433), and Aëtius as patrician became unchallenged ruler of the West. Once more rival ambitions and policies had been put to the arbitrament of civil war. These struggles showed how the Western Empire was disintegrating into a collection of provinces and armies when unity and loyal cohesion were its first need. No Roman general would postpone his ambitions to co-operation.

If the chief of the state was to be selected by civil war, it must be owned that the victory of Aëtius was the survival of the fittest. He displayed military and diplomatic talent of the first order, and his three consulships, an unparalleled record for a subject under the Empire, were well earned. Nevertheless the odds against him were now too great: the Western Empire shrank still further in his days. The first loss, due in part to Aëtius' underestimate both of Africa and Gaiseric, was that of Africa to the Vandals. A compromise treaty of 435 ceded the central part, Numidia, to Gaiseric as a federate. The faithless Vandal used his settlement to equip a piratical fleet, and then on 19 October 439 he suddenly entered Carthage without fighting. The capture gave him the best harbour in the western Mediterranean and the long-desired cornfields. When his fleet ravaged the two other corn-lands of Italy, Sicily and Sardinia, East and West combined to avert the danger. But their naval expedition was blundered, and in 442 Aëtius acknowledged the independence of the Vandals and their possession of modern Tunisia and Morocco. The less valuable central and eastern coastlands, the modern Algeria and Tripolitana, were reserved as detached provinces of Rome. Further Vandal attacks were only averted by the ingenious diplomacy of Aëtius, who played on the greedy ambition of Gaiseric by offering Valentinian's child-daughter as a bride for Gaiseric's son Huneric. The bait induced Gaiseric to send (445) the Visigothic wife his son had married back to her father Theodoric I on a false accusation of treason, for which he cut off her nose and ears. This outrage broke up an old alliance and produced a fragile peace. But the fatal wound to the western half of the Empire remained bleeding, for it was threatened by sea as well as land.

Spain, too, was half lost to another barbarian foe of no unconquerable strength. The often defeated Suevi, cantoned in the north-west, conquered all but the north-east under their King Rechiar between 438 and 448. The conquest was made easier by peasant revolts against the great landowners, which had become endemic in Spain as well as in Gaul. The Empire was crumbling under its own social stress as much as under the blows of the barbarians.

Britain was already lost, although a simulacrum of Roman rule may possibly have been kept up for a while by the conferment of official titles on its native leaders. In 429 St Germanus, Bishop of Auxerre, on a visit to Verulamium (St Albans) to combat the sparse followers of the heretic Pelagius, could apply the military knowledge of his secular youth to lead the Britons to victory against an army of Saxons and Picts. But the Romanized towns were being deserted, and such government as could be exercised was in the hands of tribal kings. The last effort of the Roman party may be seen in the 'Groans of the Britons', a vain appeal for help to Aëtius in 446. Yet in 442 a Gallic chronicler could say, although inaccurately, that Britain had become subject to the Saxons, and tradition placed the alliance of Vortigern, a British king, with a long-famous raiding chief, Hengest the Jute, and the permanent settlement of the Jutes in Kent at about the same date.

In Gaul, however, Aëtius was bent on preserving the imperial rule. It is true that the Bretons were taking over western Armorica, and the Saxons, besides their raids, were making small settlements on the north coast near Boulogne and Bayeux. But he defeated the Burgundians (435), and next year their king Gundahar and much of his tribe were cut to pieces by Aëtius' friends, the Huns—a defeat which gave birth to famous German legends. In 443 Aëtius established the principal remnant as *foederati* in Savoy, where they recuperated. Meantime the patrician was subduing the brigand peasant Bagaudae (437) and combating the Visigoths. Narbonne, which they were besieging, was relieved (437); one battle went in favour of Aëtius; in another at Toulouse his pagan lieutenant, Litorius, lost the day (439). Mutual exhaustion produced a peace restoring the *status quo ante*, while Aëtius blocked the main crossing of the Loire by a federate colony of Alan troops at Orleans. Thus in spite of losses Roman Gaul was given some kind of peace for a few years.

(3) THE EMPIRE AND THE HUNS

While the main direction of the State was in the hands of the patrician Aëtius, the control of the palace at Ravenna and the education of Valentinian III seem to have been left to the Empress Galla Placidia. Under her tuition the Emperor grew up indolent and dissolute: the energy of his father had evaporated. Yet the court was a useful instrument in keeping up the good understanding with Constantinople which was desirable for the tottering West. In 437 Valentinian visited the eastern capital to marry his cousin Eudoxia, the daughter of Theodosius II, and in return for Eastern help against the Vandals ceded that part of Illyricum which had been allotted to the West on the death of Theodosius the Great. The transfer was a concession to natural geographical grouping, for the Balkans were thus united, and it relieved the West of a stretch of the frontier. Next year the constitutional unity of the whole Empire was affirmed by the solemn reception by the Roman Senate of the Theodosian Code, the collection just promulgated in the East of the imperial edicts from Constantine the Great downwards. Yet the real separation of the Greek and Latin halves was shown at the same time by the declaration that future edicts should only be valid in the dominions of the Emperor who decreed them. When Valentinian in 445 confirmed and extended the appellate jurisdiction of the Pope over all bishops, his edict affected the West alone, although the Emperors acted in concert over the General Council of Chalcedon.

The separate existence and policy of the two Empires were shown clearly in their relations with their northern neighbours, the Huns. These tribes, after their overthrow of the Ostrogoths (375) and the flight of the Visigoths, had spread westward in a loose confederacy from the Caucasus to the bend of the Danube near the modern Budapest. They retained their nomadic, pastoral way of life and themselves only inhabited the steppelands which favoured it, but they raided and subjected the peoples of the hills, woodlands, and marshlands around and between the steppes. The Gothic remnant in the Crimea, the Gepids in Transylvania, the Ostrogoths in Pannonia were their vassals or allies, while a Slav population was extending north and even south of the Carpathians as their subjects. Owing perhaps to their tribal divisions as well as to the natural obstacles of the Danube frontier, the Huns for many years inflicted little molestation on the Empire, but in the early fifth century they were given greater unity by the rise of a King, Rua or Rugila, whose own horde was cantoned in the steppes along the river Theiss in modern Hungary, and they at once became formidable. It was Rua who had been the friend and ally of Aëtius and provided him with mercenaries and auxiliaries. When he died (c. 433), he was succeeded by his two nephews, Bleda and Attila. Their rule continued jointly, with Bleda much in the background, until 445 when Attila murdered his brother and reigned alone. 'The Scourge of God', as Attila was deservedly called, was a thorough Altaian in physique and character, a ruthless, destroying conqueror, a genius of rapine and war. His portrait in the description of the historian Priscus, who saw him in his permanent wooden encampment in Hungary, might stand as the type of his people— short, broad-shouldered, flat-nosed, with fierce, sunken eyes and impassive mouth in an almost beardless face, dealing out rough justice to his subjects amid a medley of tongues, Hunnic, Gothic, and Latin, and temperate amid the boisterous feasting of his vassal kings and chiefs. Yet this absolute ruler had little idea of government beyond conquest, slave-hunting, and looting, and it was perhaps the fact that his Empire had reached the Rhine, the Baltic, and the Caspian, rather than the incitements of the Vandal Gaiseric, who certainly needed an ally, that made him in 441 turn to the spoliation of the still wealthy Roman Empire.

It was the richer eastern half that Attila first victimized. By a treaty concluded in 434 the East agreed to an annual blackmail of 700 pounds of gold, and promised to deliver up such fugitives as escaped from Attila's wrath. Arrears of the blackmail and incomplete surrender of the refugees were Attila's excuse for war when the Eastern armies were busy elsewhere. Two terrible invasions (441–2 and 447) devastated the Balkans as far as Constantinople and Thermopylae. Each was followed by a humiliating peace with enormous payments impossible to discharge. In desperation the eunuch Chrysaphius, who directed affairs, endeavoured to suborn one of Attila's envoys, the Scirian chief Edeco, to murder him. Edeco revealed the plot to his master, but it is curious that Attila contented himself with publicly flouting the contemptible Theodosius II, and even relaxed his demand that the land between the Danube and Naïssus (Nish) should be left waste. He must have felt that there was little more to be got by a fresh attack on the East. Constantinople and the Straits had once more proved the bulwark of the Empire.

The West was an easier if less profitable prey, and against the West Attila, breaking off his old friendship with Aëtius, declared war. There were several pretexts. The Franks were fighting among themselves: one prince appealed to Attila, the other with success to Aëtius. Gaiseric urged the Huns on against the Visigoths. The Emperor Marcian, who (450) brought back good government and strength to the East, refused the blackmail. But another *casus belli* is so strange that it has been disbelieved. Honoria, Valentinian's sister, had an intrigue with the chamberlain Eugenius. Her lover was executed, and she was in disgrace (449). Her revenge was to appeal to Attila, sending him her ring in authentication. The Hun, rightly or wrongly, took the ring as an emblem of betrothal, and claimed that his additional bride should be delivered to him with part of the West as her dower. The flimsiness of the pretext was shown by Attila's choice of Gaul as the most eligible land to invade, not Italy where court and princess were to be found.

Attila collected all his powers for the attack on Gaul, although the numbers given for his host are absurd. With the Huns marched their Germanic vassals, Gepids under Ardaric, Ostrogoths from Pannonia, Thuringians, Rugians, Sciri, Heruli, Burgundians of the Main, and Ripuarian Franks. Aëtius must have foreseen his danger in the gathering of so great a muster, but he lacked troops, for hitherto he had depended on Hunnish mercenaries. Attila had pretended to him he was merely attacking the Visigoths, for which Roman Gaul offered the only route; to Theodoric the Visigoth he explained he was only invading Roman territory. But the common danger was obvious, and with some difficulty Aëtius gained the Visigoths' alliance. The Salian Franks, too, under the legendary Merovech, the Armoricans, and the Burgundians of Savoy, joined him. Early in 451 Attila sacked Metz and moved towards Orleans, where he found the Romans and Visigoths awaiting him. Their position was too strong, and the Alans settled there, whom he had hoped would desert to him, chose, though with suspicious fidelity, not to break with Aëtius. Then the Hun swerved back towards Troyes, where the Catalaunian plains of Champagne gave his horsemen scope. Near Mauriacus the armies met. Aëtius showed his generalship by seizing a height which was the key of the field. Holding it and on his right were the Visigoths; in the centre were the untrustworthy Alans; on his left he led his own troops and his other auxiliaries. The Huns round Attila broke the Alans and turned on the Visigoths, already hotly engaged, but here they attacked in vain. The battle raged all day with enormous carnage till the Huns were driven back to their laager. Aëtius refused to attempt to storm it next day, which has caused the battle to be represented as drawn, but Attila was in no case to renew it. He withdrew across the Rhine, while Aëtius persuaded the new Visigothic King, Thorismud, whose father Theodoric had fallen in the fight, that he must return to Toulouse to secure his succession. It may be conjectured that Aëtius would not again risk his army, weakened as it was by the slaughter—he had won the campaign—but much ink has been spent in divining his motives for an action in which presumably generalship, not much cultivated by his barbarian allies, had the chief share.

Was the battle of Mauriacus a decisive battle of the world? Attila certainly remained as rapacious and aggressive as ever—it was the condition of his empire—but he never again offered a pitched battle. What might have happened if he had won is naturally impossible to say. He was a mere ravager, but much could have been destroyed which, in fact, survived. As it was, no fresh invaders entered Gaul; the tribes already lodged there were left to fight for extension and supremacy and to unite as well as they could with the Gallo-Romans. In Gaul the era of the migrations was drawing to its close. The far result was the blended beginnings of a new medieval civilization.

Attila, however, for whom fresh raids were imperative, turned on an easier prey. In 452 he led a host to Italy. The great city of Aquileia was so sacked that it never recovered; Milan and Pavia suffered a less wrecking plunder. It seemed as if nothing could save Rome, for Aëtius now had no allied armies as in Gaul. None the less Attila might well hesitate. North Italy had been stricken by famine in 450, and the pestilence which followed infected his northern tribesmen as the summer came on: hunger and plague were deadly enemies. Reinforcements were reaching impregnable Ravenna from the Eastern Empire. At the critical moment a Roman embassy appeared, led by Pope Leo the Great, whose personality might well overawe the superstitious Hun and his Arian Germans. The arguments they used and the promises they made are not recorded, but Attila turned back with his spoils to Hungary. One result of his raid and the destruction of Aquileia had been an influx of refugees into the fishing townlets among the marshes, which gave rise to the later legend that the city of Venice owed its origin to this invasion.

Attila, however, defeated in Gaul by arms and in Italy by the climate, lived by and for his plundering wars, and he was preparing another invasion of the Balkans when (453) he broke a blood-vessel in the night he took a new wife, the German Ildico who became in legend the Kriemhild of the *Nibelungenlied*. The very partial success of his last wars and the division of his Huns among three of his sons were together tempting provocation to the subject East Germanic tribes, who, encouraged perhaps by the Emperor Marcian, rose in revolt. They were led by Ardaric the Gepid and inflicted (454) a crushing defeat on the Huns at Nedao in Hungary. Most of the vanquished nomads rejoined their kindred tribes on the steppes north of the Black Sea, whence they continued to supply mercenaries, this time to East Rome. The best part of the Hungarian steppe was taken by the Gepids, while the Rugians held the north bank of the Danube opposite Vienna and the Sciri and Heruli occupied northern Hungary. Thence they sent recruits to the West Roman army, which from being mainly Hunnish became in a few years mainly Germanic. It was a fresh danger to the Empire, for they were more ambitious of lands and commands than Aëtius' Huns had been. As for the Ostrogoths, they lived south of the Danube in Pannonia under three royal brothers of the Amal house as federates of the Eastern Empire.

(4) THE END OF THE EMPIRE IN THE WEST

The removal of immediate danger and the loss of his Hunnish troops were fatal to Aëtius. In 450 the Empress Placidia was entombed at Ravenna in her mausoleum, whose severe beauty shows that the arts at least were not dead in Italy. Her influence over the worthless Valentinian fell not to Aëtius but to the eunuch Heraclius, who egged him on to revolt against the all-powerful patrician. There was a grudge among the senators against the general who had not defended Italy with a non-existent army and had left the repulse of Attila, as was thought, to the awe-inspiring intervention of the Pope; and this grudge was linked to his own ambition by the richest senator, Maximus, head of the great Anician house. Valentinian was screwed up to action when he had to betroth one of his daughters to Aëtius' son Gaudentius, which created a claim to the succession, since the Emperor had no son. So he suddenly picked a quarrel during an interview and stabbed the patrician with his own hand. The murder was completed by Heraclius, and in this way, as a court wit said, Valentinian 'used his left hand to cut off his right' (September 454). He had also prepared his own death. Maximus was disappointed because he had not succeeded to the position of Aëtius, and in March 455 induced two followers of the murdered patrician to kill both Valentinian and Heraclius in a review of the troops at Rome. The assassination, which was unpunished, closed the line of quasi-hereditary Emperors in the West, and to that extent it was a misfortune. The throne now was open once more to any competitor, whether forceful or a puppet. For the rest the few public acts of Valentinian, like those of Honorius, had been disastrous to the Western Empire.

Maximus was soon awakened from his ambitious delusions. The Senate elected him Emperor; he forced Valentinian's widow, Eudoxia, to marry him so as to acquire an hereditary claim; but more he could not achieve without troops and the skill to use them. The opportunity had been given to the deadliest foe of the Empire. Gaiseric had his fleet in readiness—it was some months since Aëtius was dead—and the wealth of Rome, spared by Alaric or accumulated since, was to be had for the taking. The Vandals landed at Porto unopposed and marched up the Tiber on the city. Maximus was killed in his flight (31 May), and on 2 June Gaiseric entered Rome, received by Pope Leo who induced him to refrain from fire and slaughter. For a fortnight the Vandals plundered at their leisure all that was portable in palaces and temples. The spoils of the Temple of Jerusalem, brought by Titus at its sack, and even half the gilded roof of the temple of Jupiter on the Capitol, were carried away. Christian churches as a rule were spared and unremunerative destruction of buildings or works of art was not committed. But Gaiseric took away numerous prisoners, a source of ransoms, including the Empress Eudoxia and her daughters, Eudoxia and Placidia. The Vandal fleet mastered the western Mediterranean and plundered its shores, while the Roman remnants of Africa from Tripolis westward submitted to the king.

The dissolving Empire now received an Emperor from Gaul. Thorismud the Visigoth had subdued the Alans of Orleans and attacked the Empire before he was murdered and succeeded by his brother Theodoric II (453), who covered his aggressions with a philo-Roman varnish. He intervened in Spain to check the recrudescent Bagaudian revolt. Then on the death of Maximus he sent a force to Italy to establish his old friend, the Gallo-Roman noble Avitus, as Emperor, and himself marched to Spain (456), defeating the Suevi and taking part of the land for himself in the Emperor's name. Avitus was no trifler, but his sole personal following was in central Gaul, and in Italy both successes and failures were harmful to him. Gaiseric attacked by sea, and starved Rome by withholding the corn-supply. Ricimer, the Suevic mercenary general, justified Avitus' choice of him by a land victory over the Vandals at Agrigento in Sicily and a sea victory off Corsica, which gave him the real allegiance of the Germanic troops, but to pay off his departing Visigothic allies the Emperor was forced to strip the bronze roofs of the public buildings of Rome. It was thus easy for Ricimer to join with the unreasoning Senate in deposing Avitus in 456 and to take control. Avitus gallantly brought some Gallic troops to be defeated at Piacenza, was consecrated a bishop to disqualify him for the throne, and died within the year.

The control of Italy now passed finally to the Germanic mercenaries quartered in the country. Ricimer, who led them, appeared in the role of a somewhat embarrassed Emperor-maker. Being a barbarian, he could not seize the crown himself; that would make the entire civilian population his enemies and incur the hostility of the Eastern Empire, his necessary ally against Vandal and Visigoth. If he chose an able, warlike Emperor, he lessened his own power; if he took a nominee from the East, he could only count on half his submission; if he appointed an Italian puppet, his government lost credit in Italy and the support of the East. Trial was made of all these expedients. After a brief period in which there was no separate Emperor of the West, Ricimer obtained his own appointment as patrician from the Eastern Emperor Leo I and the sanction of the choice by Senate and army of his ablest Roman subordinate, Majorian, as Emperor (457–61).

If energy, talent and good intentions without the loyalty of the indispensable Germanic mercenaries could have restored the Western Empire, Majorian would have been the restorer. His decrees endeavoured to reform the corrupt administration by alleviating the taxes and the abuses of collection, especially the liability of the *curiales* for the city quotas. He tried to revivify the institution of *defensor civitatis* as a protection against officials. He forbade the destruction of ancient monuments for the sake of their materials, which had become a habit in the impoverished state, and to which the Vandals have undeservedly given their name. More urgent was the recovery of the provinces and the defeat of Gaiseric. In 458 Majorian gathered an army, marched to Gaul, repressed the Burgundians, drove the openly hostile Visigoths from the siege of Arles, and compelled Theodoric II to accept again the position of a *foederatus*. He then proceeded to Spain, where he collected a fleet at Alicante for the invasion of Africa. It shows the real weakness of the Vandals when faced by a competent foe that Gaiseric sued vainly for peace. But Gaiseric's genius did not desert him. Aided by treason, he pounced on the unready Roman fleet and, what with fire and capture, made it useless (461). Majorian could only make a peace recognizing his conquests. It was fatal to the Emperor. Ricimer was jealous of his ability, the bureaucrats hated his reforms, and the barbarian soldiers without victory turned from him. On his re-entry into Italy he was deposed and murdered at Tortona.

Ricimer now tried a puppet, Severus (461–5), but the western half of the Empire was sadly shorn. Two of Majorian's lieutenants, Marcellinus in Dalmatia and Aegidius in northern Gaul, refused to take orders from Ravenna. The Alps, too, had slipped from Roman control. After the death of Aëtius the Alemanni crossed the uppermost Rhine and settled in what is now German Switzerland. The Rugians raided Noricum, where Severinus the saintly abbot did his best to protect and guide his flock. In Gaul Theodoric II attempted to overthrow Aegidius, but his army was defeated (463) near Orleans with the aid of Childeric of the Salian Franks. Aegidius turned to Gaiseric for an ally, but died in 464, leaving his 'kingdom of Soissons' to his son Syagrius. It was Childeric who, as a loyal federate, saved Angers from the attack of a Saxon chief, Odovacar. Thus only a truncated Gaul, threatened by Visigoths and Burgundians, remained to the Empire.

The most dangerous foe was the crafty Gaiseric with his sea-power. He married the captive princess Eudoxia to his son Huneric, and sent her sister Placidia to Constantinople, where she was married to the senator Olybrius. Gaiseric not only obtained a dowry with Eudoxia but demanded the Western throne for Olybrius. Meantime his corsair fleets yearly ravaged the Italian coast. At last Ricimer and the Senate agreed to ask for an Emperor from the East, and received by the Emperor Leo's nomination an eminent official Anthemius (467–72), the son-in-law of the late Emperor Marcian. This meant that the Roman world was allied together against Gaiseric. Count Marcellinus of Dalmatia led a fleet and army to Italy with the new Emperor, who wedded his daughter to Ricimer, and the full forces of the allies were deployed against the Vandals under Marcellinus' command. Heraclius marched from Egypt and recaptured Tripoli, Marcellinus reconquered Sardinia and part of Sicily, Basiliscus with the main Byzantine fleet sailed to Africa. Gaiseric seemed doomed, but, besides his central position, he possessed the secret friendship of Aspar, the powerful general at Constantinople, and perhaps of Ricimer: they neither of them wished to see the barbarians utterly overcome and themselves outshone. Helped once more by treason, Gaiseric employed fire-ships to burn half the armada of the incompetent Basiliscus; and the able Marcellinus was assassinated in Sicily (468). Meanwhile Vandal corsairs plundered the coasts of Illyricum and Greece. The Empire was exhausted and Leo made a peace. It only lasted a few years, for on Leo's death (474) Gaiseric resumed his piratical attacks, and forced the new Eastern Emperor to conclude a new treaty (476), by which the Vandal dominion in Africa, Sicily, Sardinia, Corsica and the Balearic Isles was recognized. In return Gaiseric gave up his own Roman prisoners and slaves, and allowed those of other Vandals to be ransomed. The aged Vandal king's moderation may be accounted for by his approaching death and his knowledge of the weakness of his kingdom. The Vandals had always been few and hated by their subjects; they were now degenerate in African luxury, and their pirate fleet was largely manned by Moors and outlaws. It was the cruel genius of Gaiseric which upheld his power, and with his death in 477 the Vandal danger was at an end.

The Emperor Anthemius was not only unfortunate in the course of the Vandalic war. He found another persistent and victorious enemy in Gaul. This was Euric, who gained the kingship of the Visigoths in 466 by murdering his brother Theodoric II, also a fratricide. Euric was much the ablest of the Visigothic princes and he was a man of large ambitions—the conquest of the derelict Roman provinces in Gaul and Spain—in which he was mainly successful. Theodoric II had already acquired Narbonne and a strip of the Mediterranean coast. In 470 Euric reached the Rhone by the capture of Arles and the middle Loire by that of Bourges: only Clermont in Auvergne held out, led by the heroic son of Avitus, the patrician Ecdicius. At the same time the Visigoths, no longer under the mask of federates, were invading Spain. These reverses gave a chance to Ricimer, already jealous of a too independent Emperor and an ally of his own nephew, the federate Burgundian Gundobad, who took over the coastland of Provence. The *magister militum* revolted, defeated and slew Anthemius, and set up Olybrius, the son-in-law of Valentinian, who had come to Italy on a mysterious mission. In his few months' reign (472) Olybrius passed from one master to another, for Ricimer died, leaving Gundobad in control. It may be said of Ricimer that he never forgot that he was a Roman *magister militum* and that he kept some understanding with the East. Indeed it was his only possible way of playing for his own hand in Italy, for his troops were mostly not of his own tribe and were disunited.

King Gundobad's interest lay in Gaul, in the extension of the lands of his not too numerous tribe. Before he left Italy he set up as Emperor (March 473) a certain Glycerius, whose reign was marked by the passage of a section of the Ostrogoths under Widimir to join Euric in Gaul. The proximity to the East still protected Italy, but not Glycerius. The Emperor Leo could at last intervene, and early in 474 sent Marcellinus' nephew and successor in Dalmatia, Julius Nepos, to Rome with an army to be his colleague in the West. Glycerius was rendered innocuous by being consecrated bishop of Salona in Dalmatia.

Nepos might have retained power in Italy had not civil war broken out in the East and deprived him of support. In 475, through the mediation of Bishop Epiphanius of Pavia, he concluded a peace of surrender with the Visigoths. Clermont was ceded against its will, and Euric was acknowledged to be sovereign ruler west of the Rhone. Gaul in fact was lost to the Empire, for Syagrius of Soissons and the Bretons were independent. But the mercenaries in Italy were restive with hopes when they saw their civilian ruler weak, and they found a leader in a barbarized Roman. Orestes was a Pannonian who had been a secretary of Attila; he had after 454 entered the Roman service and married the daughter of a Count Romulus. Such a man was a natural choice for Nepos to make for *magister militum*, but Orestes wished to be another Ricimer. He easily drove Nepos back to Dalmatia, where he reigned till his murder in 480, and the Senate in October 475 elected Orestes' young son Romulus Augustulus to be Emperor under his father's regency.

The discontent of the Germanic mercenaries was not to be appeased by the promotion of their Roman commander. These Heruli, Sciri and Rugii desired to be put on the same footing as the German *foederati* and conquerors they saw around them. As soldiers they themselves were quartered in billets and barracks in certain towns. They saw Visigoths and the like become landowners great and small by the system known as *hospitalitas*. The individual tribesmen received a share (one- or two-thirds) of the land and stock of the Roman proprietors; in return they served in the tribal host when it was called out for war. This system the mercenaries now demanded: each Roman proprietor should surrender one-third of his property to a military *hospes*. On Orestes' refusal they elected a Scirian, Odovacar, their king, and slaughtered Orestes. His son, the boy Romulus Augustulus, was captured in Ravenna (September 476) and relegated to a Campanian villa on a pension.

King Odovacar was thus master of Italy at the head of the mercenary tribesmen, and his first business was to defend his frontiers against barbarian competitors. From the dying Gaiseric he obtained the cession of Sicily, all but the western port of Lilybaeum (Marsala), in return for a tribute. Euric, again on the warpath, was more formidable. He crossed the Rhone and defeated the Burgundian Gundobad; peace was only granted on the cession of the coastland of Provence as far as the Alps (481). As the Burgundians occupied Lyons, Autun and Langres, nothing was left to the Empire in Gaul, except the 'kingdom' of Syagrius. In Spain the Visigothic bands conquered the whole country save the north-west and some Roman enclaves: by 478, from his capital of Toulouse, Euric ruled from the Loire to the Pillars of Hercules.

The elevation of Odovacar and the deposition of the boy who by a curious irony of history bore the names of the founder of Rome and the founder of Empire mark the end of the Roman Empire of the West. It was now partitioned among the barbarians. But Odovacar's position was peculiar: he was king, not of a tribe, but of an assortment of mercenaries; and, weakened by the fact, he was too near the East to disregard the wishes of his Roman subjects or the claims of the Eastern Emperor, who in their eyes and his own was, with Nepos, the legitimate ruler and source of authority in the Roman world, especially since in 476 the Emperor Zeno had triumphed in the civil war. Odovacar therefore assumed the attitude of a magnified Ricimer. By his orders the Roman Senate sent a solemn embassy with the imperial insignia to Constantinople, declaring they did not need a separate Emperor and begging Zeno to grant to Odovacar as his lieutenant in Italy the title of patrician. Zeno replied with much diplomatic adroitness. He praised the pro-Roman sentiments of Odovacar and conferred on him the title of patrician, if Nepos had not already done so. This reserved acquiescence was enough for Odovacar, though not satisfying. When Nepos was murdered (480), he annexed Dalmatia and punished the assassins as if he had been his rival's deputy. The façade of imperial rule was thus maintained.

101

This unity and continuance of the Empire, however, was not all a fiction. The Roman Senate, i.e. Odovacar, still nominated one of the consuls for the year. The Roman civil administration survived intact under a pretorian prefect, who was Odovacar's minister. In obeying the Germanic king-patrician, whose Arianism they loathed, the Romans felt that they were loyal to their distant Emperor. What was even more important, Roman civilization, in spite of loss and deterioration, was still living in Italy and dominated by Catholic Christianity. The Arian Germanic patrician and tribesmen were still only an all-powerful garrison. The Senate, and far more the Pope and the Italian bishops, retained the moral guidance of the population and of its civil government. So though the Emperors had been replaced by barbaric Germanic kings in the West, the echo of the Empire's fall was deadened and its consequences mitigated and delayed by this persistent make-believe. None the less the truth could not but slip out. 'The Western Roman Empire perished with this Augustulus', wrote Count Marcellinus in the next generation.

CHAPTER 6

THE SURVIVAL OF THE EMPIRE IN THE EAST

(1) THE RESISTANCE AND REFORM OF THE EASTERN EMPIRE

When Alaric with the main body of the Visigoths was turning his eyes westward from his lodgement in Illyricum, the prospects of the Eastern Empire seemed almost as dark as those of the West. The Emperor Arcadius was a nullity, the Frankish Empress Eudoxia was engrossed by her personal likings and resentments. The Empire, although preserved from the remaining Goths in its service by the destruction of them and their leaders, was thereby left nearly without an army. Stilicho in the West was an enemy, the Balkans were exhausted by their long harrying, in Asia Minor the brigand-like hillsmen of Isauria were plundering their peaceful neighbours from their stronghold in the Taurus Mountains, and Constantinople was distracted by a feud between Eudoxia and the eloquent and censorious Patriarch, St John Chrysostom. When the Empress obtained his deposition in 404, his riotous partisans set the first St Sophia and the Senate House aflame, thereby destroying some of the masterpieces of ancient Greek art.

The East, however, was not lacking in men of uprightness and capacity if they could be put in power. When Eudoxia died of a miscarriage on 6 October 404, some happy influence secured the appointment of Anthemius as pretorian prefect. His administration, which lasted till 414, was most fortunate for the Empire, and it is to be noted that his chief adviser is said to have been Troilus, a sophist or professional teacher, who had not been a bureaucrat. The execution of Stilicho (408) was a piece of good fortune for the East, since it removed a persistent enemy. The death of Arcadius was probably also beneficial, for it secured the power of the prefect, who acted as regent for his son, the child Theodosius II. In these years of good government the Empire was strengthened within and without. On the eastern frontier, cordial relations, fortified by a commercial treaty, were maintained with the Persian king, Yezdegerd I. In Asia Minor the brigandage of the Isaurians was somehow checked. In the Balkans the raiding Huns were driven back, while their clients, the Germanic Sciri, were rounded up and settled as serf-cultivators in Asia Minor. The fleet on the Danube was made adequate to prevent incursions from the north, and the Illyrian cities were refortified. As important was the building (413) of the famous Theodosian Wall of Constantinople, which still exists. It stretched, like the old wall, from the Golden Horn to the Propontis, and included the new suburbs of the growing capital. It was not to be breached

103

Fig. 16. The Theodosian Wall, Istanbul

until the final fall of the Empire. The reorganization of the essential corn-supplies from Egypt secured peace and prosperity to New Rome, while the cancelling of enormous arrears of taxation relieved the hard-hit provinces. Only a solvent government could have done this.

Anthemius found a capable successor in the first woman to rule the Empire, the Augusta Pulcheria, elder sister of the Emperor. Theodosius II, who was only two years her junior,[1] was a weakling, though not such a dullard as his father. He was of an amiable disposition, and was carefully educated by his sister in the fashion of the day. He was given to pious observances, was a calligrapher, a fair scholar, a hunter and horseman, exemplary in morals. But this sheltered court-life left him a puppet of his sister, his wife, and his eunuchs in turn. Pulcheria, on the other hand, to whom it was her native element, showed from the first, at the age of 15, both character and intellect and a resolve to rule. For the sake rather of politics than religion, she took a vow of virginity, and her sisters followed suit. Spinning and devotion filled the time she spared from government, and the Empire gained by the general wisdom of her rule, although the sale of offices again became notorious and fiscal oppression revived. That authority was somewhat shaken incited transient disorders, of which the most notable were the riots of Alexandria and the barbarous murder of

---

[1] See Genealogical Table 3 above, p. 78.

Hypatia. In that turbulent city the population was divided among Christians, Jews and pagans. The Patriarch Cyril was the focus of trouble in his unscrupulous grasp at power. After prolonged rioting between Christians and Jews, he instigated his followers to expel the Jews from the city, and this fresh outrage provoked the prefect of Egypt, Orestes, to complain to the Emperor. He was attacked with stones by some fanatical monks, the chief of whom he put to death by torture, providing Cyril with a martyr. It was said that Orestes was under the influence of the pagan teacher and philosopher Hypatia, celebrated for her beauty, ability and charm of character. This was enough to rouse the *parabolani* (sick-attendants) to drag her from her chariot to a church and there horribly kill her with tiles. Even the government took action at the atrocity. The *parabolani* were limited to the number of 500, selected by the prefect, and forbidden to appear in assemblies and spectacles. Yet within two years Cyril reobtained their selection and an increase in their personnel.

The marriage of Theodosius was a necessity of State, and Pulcheria schemed to promote a docile Empress. The pagan Athenais, the daughter of an Athenian sophist, had come to the capital as a petitioner against her brothers, who had usurped her share of her father's property. Pulcheria introduced her to the Emperor, who was duly attracted and made her his wife (421). She was baptized under the name of Eudocia. Her literary tastes and ability, besides her beauty, made her a suitable consort to Theodosius, and, in addition to theological poems, she composed an epic on one eastern war. A lasting harmony between her and her sister-in-law was hardly to be expected. Eudocia began to show opinions of her own in theology and appointments. Eventually after an open quarrel Pulcheria retired from court. But Eudocia made a long pilgrimage to Jerusalem (437–9), which must have loosened her control over her ever-guided husband. In 441 her personal friend, the eminent and popular pretorian prefect Cyrus, was dismissed from office, and the eunuch Chrysaphius, who had fomented the disagreements between her and Pulcheria, obtained the chief influence. Eudocia found herself accused of adultery with Paulinus, the master of the offices, who was executed. She asked permission in 443 to retire to Jerusalem, where she lived for years in pious occupations, soon deprived of imperial honours but left with an ample income. Chrysaphius could now misgovern the Empire till his master's death through a hunting accident (28 July 450).

In spite of over-taxation and the troubles due to the barbarians of Europe, the internal government of the Eastern Empire continued in some degree the beneficial work of Anthemius until the eunuch Chrysaphius obtained control. Frequent remissions of taxation, if they showed the extent of impoverishment, showed also the effort to relieve it. More permanent was the positive attempt to clarify the law, and thereby to improve its administration, which Theodosius II was induced to authorize. In concert with his Western colleague, the child Valentinian III, he issued in 426 a decree prescribing the method in which the works of the authoritative jurists of the past were to be used by judges, thus bringing some sort of certainty and order among their often conflicting decisions. In 438 he issued with Valentinian's assent the Theodosian Code, a classified collection of the edicts of the Christian Emperors. The most important statutes for ordinary life were thus made clearer and more accessible to judges and suitors. The new Code achieved a speedy success and in Italy remained the basis of traditional Roman Law. It will be referred to in a subsequent chapter, but here it may again be said that it marks the end of the unity of the law of East and West. It applied to both, but the edicts of later date were declared by it to be valid only for the dominions of the Emperor who decreed them. The separation was emphasized when the prefect Cyrus published for the first time decrees in Greek. Another reform, which suggests the influence of the highly educated Eudocia, was the foundation of the university of Constantinople. A staff of twenty-eight teachers was endowed to lecture in Greek and Latin learning (27 February 425) in the capital; it was a Christian counterpoise to the still pagan schools of Athens.

In foreign affairs the great success of the reign was the relief obtained from the dangerous pressure on the eastern frontier. So far as the Roman government was concerned, it was due to the conciliatory defensive policy adopted by Theodosius the Great, and perhaps by the much blamed Jovian. When Yezdegerd I of Persia placed a son of his own on the Persarmenian throne, Roman Armenia was converted into a mere province (415–6), and Persarmenia soon underwent the same fate from Persia (428). Persian persecution of the Christians led to a brief war (421–2), in which the Alan general Ardaburius defeated the armies of the Great King. As a result Bahram V relinquished hostilities, and in 422 the Hundred Years' Peace between the Empire and Persia was concluded. The persecution was to cease, and neither party was to abet the restless, plundering Arab vassal tribes of the other's borderland between Mesopotamia and Syria. Doubtless this peace, which was lasting in spite of interruptions, was due largely to the increasing weakness of the Sassanids before their priests and great nobles and to the constant peril of the Persian eastern frontier from the nomads beyond the Caspian Sea, but something is due to the wisdom of the East Roman government, which was content with a reasonable, stable division of interests. It was a great achievement which freed the Romans' hands for defence in the West for many years. Even when Yezdegerd II took advantage of the Vandal war to make an attack, he quickly renewed the peace in order to defend himself (441) from the Ephthalite Huns, a more aggressive foe than the Kushans, whom they replaced (c. 425) on the Oxus.

On the western border, in spite of some successes, the experiences of the reign were less happy. The aggressive, expanding barbarians, led by able chieftains, were not to be checked like Persia by dangers in the rear, and the Western Empire, although it acted as a buffer, was more a liability than an asset. Yet the elevation of Valentinian III to the Western throne by armed intervention was a notable triumph, and the acquisition (438) of Dalmatia and west Illyricum as the price of his marriage to Theodosius' daughter Eudoxia was a substantial gain which strengthened the frontier of the Balkans. The two divisions of the Empire were also drawn together by their common danger from the sea, the menace of the Vandal Gaiseric in Africa and the Mediterranean. In 431 the Eastern *Magister militum* Aspar was sent with fleet and army to aid in the defence of Africa. After three years he had only saved Carthage, and after the treaty of 435 he seems to have become a secret ally of Gaiseric. The fact was that Aspar was an Alan, whose fellow tribesmen formed part of Gaiseric's following, and the best of his own troops were Germanic mercenaries. All alike were Arians and a danger to the Empire which they served. The loss of Carthage (439) caused another Eastern fleet to be sent to Sicily, but it did nothing useful, and the Persian War and the Hun invasion caused its recall. The western Huns under Attila had become a worse danger. In 434, after a Hunnish raid, a humiliating treaty was made with Attila: the East Roman tribute or rather blackmail was doubled, and the Empire was not to receive deserters, i.e. probable recruits, from Attila. At Gaiseric's instigation, a terrible Hun invasion (441) devastated the Balkans as far as the Aegean: the tribute was trebled and a lump sum paid as well (443). It was almost impossible to discharge the blackmail, and in 447 a still more destructive raid reached Thermopylae. While submitting to Attila's terms, the eunuch Chrysaphius laid a plot to murder him. This miserable scheme was unveiled, but fortunately Attila was turning westward for a less exhausted prey. In the meantime a virile Emperor ascended the Eastern throne.

As Theodosius II lay dying without a son, the problem of the succession was ingeniously solved. Valentinian III was impossible. Aspar, who commanded the forces and would have wished for the throne, was an Alan and an Arian. But his chief of staff, Marcian, was a Roman veteran from Thrace, and fitter to rule than Aspar perhaps foresaw. This soldier was associated as Emperor by the Augusta Pulcheria, and to him, a widower, she was nominally married. This gave him the legitimacy of the Theodosian house (450–7), while his connexion with Aspar and the army ensured him their support. The break with past misrule was at once marked by the deserved execution of Chrysaphius. A restraint was placed on the sale of offices, the remission of arrears eased the burdens on the taxpayer, and senators and reformers were equally pleased when the compulsory and senseless outlay by the consuls of the year on public games was corrected into a contribution to the upkeep of the aqueducts. Internal disorder due to the Isaurians, who had been raiding again since 441, was lessened by the lucky death of their leader Zeno, while Arab and Nubian incursions on

Syria and Egypt were checked. Forty years later a new Emperor could be greeted with shouts of 'Reign like Marcian'.

Meantime Marcian, who wisely kept peace with Persia and the Vandals, was free to defy the Huns and refuse the ruinous blackmail. The dubious result of this spirited policy was determined by Attila's sudden death and the break-up of his empire. Marcian used it to protect the Danube frontier by taking the curiously lethargic Gepids into alliance as *foederati* and by settling the Ostrogoths in eastern Pannonia on the same terms— a more risky experiment of which he did not live to see the sequel. He died in 457 without nominating a successor. Pulcheria had died four years earlier, and the choice of an Emperor was at Aspar's mercy. His Arianism and race excluded himself, and he selected another subordinate, his steward, the Roman Leo I. But he did not thereby secure a grateful puppet, for Leo was a man of ability and resource. He eluded Aspar's advice and raised up a rival to him.

With external foes Leo's reign was marked by indecisive friction and one great disaster. He was a rival of Piroz, the king of Persia, for the suzerainty of the little Christian kingdom of Lazica, the ancient Colchis, on the

Fig. 17. The Emperor Marcian

Black Sea coast between the Empire and the Caucasus, but while Lazica suffered from both powers, they did not fight one another. More serious were the troubles with the Ostrogoths in Pannonia. They raided Illyricum and took Dyrrachium (Durazzo), since their subsidy was withheld. This was granted anew, but Theodemir, one of the three Amal brothers who ruled

108

them, had to give his son Theodoric, afterwards famous, to be brought up in Constantinople as a hostage (459). The restless tribe soon fell out with their neighbours the Sciri, from whom they met defeat with the death of Walamir, one of the brother kings. A later raid of Huns and Goths ended in their quarrel and mutual extermination (467). But Leo's most serious effort against the barbarians was his formidable expedition sent to aid his Western protégé, the Emperor Anthemius, Marcian's son-in-law, against Gaiseric (468). This came utterly to grief owing to the incompetence of its commander, Basiliscus, the brother of Leo's wife, Verina. The effect of the disaster was to imperil the Empire's solvency, and to reduce its power of self-defence.

Meantime the covert struggle with Aspar was maturing. While mercenary Goths and other Germans formed the best of the army, there was a pressing danger that Aspar would seize complete control. To avert it Leo turned to the Isaurian mountaineers who had so long vexed Asia Minor. He levied a new bodyguard, the excubitors, from among them, and brought their most noted chieftain, Tarasicodissa, to Constantinople, where he took the name of Zeno and was married to the Emperor's daughter Ariadne (467?).[1] This meant the revival of a native Roman soldiery. The weakness of the arrangement lay in the hatred felt in the capital for the Isaurian brigands. Leo found himself obliged to dispatch his son-in-law to Cilicia as *magister militum* of the East. Without his support he was obliged to marry his second daughter to Aspar's younger son, Patricius, and confer on him, although an Arian, the rank of Caesar or heir-presumptive (470). This unpopular act perhaps really strengthened the Emperor's hands. Zeno could return, Aspar and his eldest son were murdered in the palace, and an attack by Aspar's Gothic guards was warded off by the excubitors (471).

Thus the Emperor-maker was removed from the scene and with him the imminent danger of barbarian rule of the Empire. But the Gothic mercenaries, on whom he had rested his power, remained in arms in Thrace under another Theodoric, 'the squinter', son of Triarius, who aspired both to take Aspar's place and to be king of all the Ostrogoths. The latter ambition, however, opened a rift between him and the kingly house of the Amals which was never likely to be really closed, and Leo with premature cunning hastened to restore the hostage Theodoric to his father. The immediate effect of the action was fraught with harm to the Empire, for Leo had no hold now on the Ostrogoths. King Widimir, the third Amal brother, promptly invaded Italy, and then passed on to join the Visigoths in Gaul. Theodemir and his son, after capturing Singidunum (Belgrade) from the Sarmatians, seized on Naïssus. Leo was forced to allot them lands in Moesia, where Theodoric soon (471) succeeded his father. There was still the problem of Theodoric the Squinter, who pursued leisurely hostilities

[1] See Genealogical Table 3 above, p. 78.

in Thrace. It was only lack of food and his inability to take more than one city which induced him to accept the Emperor's ample concessions—the position of *magister militum*, the chieftainship of his Goths in Thrace, and a heavy annual subsidy, in return for services which were not to be used against the Vandals (473). The net result was that the federate Goths of both Theodorics were cantoned in the best Balkan lands. The marvel was that in spite of all Leo left the treasury full. If there was oppression, there must also have been prosperity in the Asiatic provinces.

Leo's health, however, was failing, and a successor had to be found. His son-in-law Zeno was his obvious choice, but he and his Isaurians were hated in the capital. A curious subterfuge was thought necessary. Leo created his grandson and namesake, Zeno's son, Emperor (November 473), and on his death (February 474) the child Leo II in his turn associated Zeno, whom he left sole Emperor by his own death a few months later. But the shifty, shrewd Isaurian had gained a most unstable throne. The Arabs were raiding Syria, the western Hunnish clans of the Ukraine steppe, now known as Bulgarians, made incursions south of the Danube, Theodoric the Squinter was again in revolt in Thrace, and the Vandals sacked Nicopolis, the memorial of the battle of Actium, in Epirus. Over this last misfortune Zeno won a great diplomatic triumph. His envoy, Severus, persuaded Gaiseric (474) to release his own and allow the ransom of his nobles' Roman captives in a permanent peace. The age of the Vandal king and his foresight of his people's decline may have been the main cause of the treaty, but for whatever reason the Vandal danger, which had been so formidable, was over.

Worse than all these foes were the Roman malcontents. Intrigue, rivalry, ambition, and treason seethed among the principal personages of the court and army, including the Isaurians themselves, while the theological disputes of the day, which will be described later, rent the Church and the populace. It was Zeno's greatest merit that, indifferent character as he might be, he weathered these storms, and conjured at the last after a multitude of shifts the Ostrogothic peril. Even a simplified sketch of the political and military tangle of events must separate the domestic and Gothic series which were in fact closely allied.

The evil genius of the court was Leo I's widow, the Empress Verina, who hungered to recover power. She wove a plot with her brother Basiliscus and the able Isaurian chieftain Illus, hitherto Zeno's ally. Theodoric the Squinter favoured it. In January 475 she frightened Zeno into fleeing to Isauria, only to find herself cheated by Basiliscus, who became Emperor. Basiliscus soon showed all his old incompetence. He declared for Monophysite opinions and degraded the bishop of Constantinople from his patriarchal rank. He appointed Armatus, his nephew and his wife's paramour, a mere dandy, to be *magister militum* in place of

Theodoric the Squinter. Illus was sent to subdue Zeno, but changed sides, while Armatus, sent to conquer them, was bribed to do the same by the promise of a life-tenure of his command and the rank of Caesar for his son. Zeno returned to his throne (August 476), saw that Basiliscus was executed and Armatus murdered, and courted Theodoric the Amal, whom he adopted in Germanic fashion as his son-in-arms. The sordid contest for power was quickly renewed. Verina's attempts to assassinate her faithless ally, Illus, led to his withdrawal to Isauria, and his return to save the capital from the Goths was only purchased by her surrender to him as his prisoner. The Empress Ariadne continued her mother's feud. Although Illus subdued a city revolt to place Marcian, son of the Western Emperor Anthemius and son-in-law of Leo I, on the throne, he withdrew again, this time to Antioch, as *magister militum* of the eastern frontier. There he revolted in alliance with his captive Verina, with a puppet Leontius as nominal Emperor. But he had little support outside Isauria, and his ally, King Piroz of Persia, was killed in a disastrous defeat by the Ephthalite Huns of the Oxus. Four years of petty warfare ended in his capture by betrayal in the Isaurian fortress of Cherris, when he and his puppet were put to death (488).

During all these years Zeno had been playing fast and loose with the Ostrogothic chiefs, equally hostile to him and one another. He was saved by their mutual enmity and the fighting qualities of the Isaurians, but the Balkan population was depleted by their ravages. First Zeno held by Theodoric the Amal, but so feebly supported him that both Theodorics united against him. Then he bought over Theodoric the Squinter (478). The Amal was driven from Thrace, ravaged Macedonia, and then made Dyrrachium in Epirus his headquarters. There he was held in check by an able general Sabinianus, while the Squinter endeavoured to surprise Constantinople after the Theodosian Wall had been breached by an earthquake. The Isaurians twice prevented his assault (479, 481), and he was defeated at sea in an attempt to cross to Bithynia. Thrace was plundered by him and, when he died by an accident, more brutally by his son Recitach (481). Meantime Sabinianus was murdered by the ungrateful Zeno, and Theodoric the Amal was able to ravage Macedonia and Thessaly. He was temporarily pacified by the rank of patrician and the consulship of the year, and still more by the permission to assassinate Recitach—a substantial bribe, for he thus became sole king of the Ostrogoths, who were settled now in Moesia. Fresh hostilities produced at last a satisfactory treaty (487): Theodoric was to invade Italy. It is to be remembered that from the abdication of Romulus Augustulus, or at least from the death of Julius Nepos (480), Zeno had been the legal, though nominal, ruler of Italy as the sole Emperor of the Roman state. He had, in legal form, allowed the Patrician Odovacar to be his vicegerent; now he authorized the Patrician Theodoric to drive out Odovacar and take his place. The benefit to the East was immense. In 488 the plundering Ostrogoths and their formidable ruler were removed from the Balkans. Constantinople ceased to be threatened. A more trustworthy native soldiery could defend the Empire without the perpetual embarrassment of active or potential foes by their side.

In spite of his discreditable methods Zeno's reign had been of marked service in the preservation of the Empire. Germanic predominance in the army had ceased; the Vandal peril and the Ostrogothic peril were ended. If new foes, the Bulgarians and Slavs, raided across the Danube, they were not yet more than troublesome. In internal affairs he was less successful. The *Henoticon*, by which he hoped to heal the doctrinal breach between the orthodox and the Monophysites, did little more than call a truce. The ecclesiastical conflict was mainly, though not wholly, a sign of the growth of particularism within the Empire, the estrangement of Syrians and Egyptians from the Hellenized Balkans and Asia Minor. Disastrous as the cleavage was, it went too deep for closing.

Zeno died in April 491. With his usual clannishness he had timorously worked for the succession of his disreputable brother Longinus, but his widow, the Augusta Ariadne, had the wisdom to choose the Epirote Anastasius (491–518) as Emperor and consort. He was a silentiary, i.e. a member of the personal bodyguard of the late ruler, an elderly pious man of 61, whose reputation was so good that he had been considered for the patriarchate of Antioch. His defect in the eyes of the orthodox was his Monophysite opinions. None the less he was greeted with the cry of 'Reign like Marcian! Reign as you have lived!' There was no Emperor to crown him, and according to the custom which had grown up in the last forty years for Emperors elected during a vacancy of the throne, he was crowned by the Patriarch of Constantinople.

The talents of the mild Anastasius were for administration and finance. His ill fate and his religious opinions compelled him to meet insurrections and foreign wars, but it is noticeable that in these uncongenial tasks he chose able men to command. His first troubles were with the Isaurians, whom he removed from Constantinople, where they were hated. Longinus was got rid of by compulsory ordination and banishment, but the revolt of Isauria lasted seven years till 498, when large numbers of the rebels were transported to the empty lands of Thrace. They still furnished useful recruits for the army, for the lessons of the preceding century were not forgotten, and barbarian auxiliaries henceforth supplemented but did not replace the native troops of the Empire.

The miseries of the Balkans, however, were not over. They were now subject to the raids of the savage Bulgarians, who roamed between the Dniester and the Danube, as well as of the Slavs who came in their wake.

112

The situation was complicated by the fact that numbers of Bulgarians were in the Empire's service as *foederati*. From time to time the nomads defeated the imperial forces: the Slavs in 517 reached Thessaly. To secure the capital and its food supply still further the Emperor built the new Long Wall, roughly on the modern lines of Chatalja, from the Black Sea to the Propontis. One attempt to aid repopulation was the settlement of a remnant of the Heruli fleeing from the Lombards. With Theodoric the Ostrogoth the relations of the Epirote Anastasius were seldom cordial. Not till 497 did he give formal recognition of the Gothic king's rule in Italy, when he oddly also returned the imperial insignia sent to Zeno by Odovacar. Was it a hint that he would accept an imperial colleague in the West? But in 505 the two powers fell out, when the Goths had defeated the Gepids and intervened south of the Danube in favour of the barbarian brigand Mundo, gaining him a victory. Anastasius in 508 retaliated by sending a fleet to ravage the Italian coast and granting the Frank Clovis the consular insignia at a time when Theodoric wished to check the Frankish advance. The reconciliation with the Empire which followed was but grudging.

These were not the only frontier raids the Empire had to parry. In Africa, the Berbers of the desert attacked Cyrenaica and Upper Egypt. In Asia, the Arabs, whether Roman or Persian vassals or independent, increased their plundering incursions on Syria. Although they were driven back, and aimed only at plunder, their frequent attacks were the shadows of coming events, the first mutterings of the storm that long afterwards was to sweep over Nearer Asia and Africa. The immediate danger to the Empire came from Sassanid Persia. An able and aggressive king, Kavad, having been deposed, was restored to the throne by the Ephthalite Huns, to whom he had promised an ample payment (499). He applied to the thrifty Anastasius for help in discharging his debt, and when he received only the offer of a loan to be repaid, he took his revenge in war. He brought Ephthalites and Arabs into the field as well as Persians. The treason of Constantine, count of Roman Armenia, gave him the frontier town of Theodosiopolis (502), and he then besieged the more important Amida (Diarbakr), which was gallantly defended by its citizens until a night attack of the Persians carried a part of the wall which was guarded by some monks who were in a drunken sleep (11 January 503). The Amidans were massacred and their city was garrisoned by Kavad, but although he won a victory over the discordant Roman generals, he could take no other fortified town in Roman Mesopotamia. His attention was soon distracted by an invasion of the Huns from beyond the Caucasus, while Celer, the master of the offices, was placed by Anastasius in supreme command. The Romans took the offensive, crossing the Persian border. An Arab and an Armenian chief changed sides (504), and Kavad, at war with his neighbours and engaged in internal reforms which reinvigorated his monarchical power, proposed a peace. Celer paid a sum of money for the surrender of Amida, both sides restrained their Arab raiders, and Anastasius took the opportunity to build an immensely strong fortress at Dara as a curb to the similar city of Nisibis, not far away, which had been lost to Persia by Jovian. This was a breach of the treaty of 442, and was atoned for in the definite peace (November 506) by a further payment to the Persian king. The net result of the war was that Anastasius, in spite of the damage done to the wasted lands, had maintained and strengthened the Roman frontier.

The mildness and good administration of Anastasius were almost universally praised. Like other good Emperors he discouraged informers and is said to have abolished the sale of offices. Remittances of taxation to hard-pressed or ravaged provinces were common form, but, advised by the able and greedy Syrian Marinus, he endeavoured at the same time to relieve the taxpayers, especially the townsmen, and to increase the receipts of the government. His most celebrated measure was the abolition of the *chrysargyron*, the oppressive tax on the stock and plant of tradesmen (498), and of the right of requisition for the troops. This caused general rejoicings. He reformed the currency (498) by replacing the small copper coins of miserable fabric, which from the beginning of the century had had to satisfy the public demand for small change, by four denominations of substantial size which were easy to handle and which played a conspicuous part in the economic revival of the Empire. A new land-tax, the *chrysoteleia*, was applied to the pay and upkeep of the soldiers, to whom he endeavoured to secure their full due. Another beneficial reform was the abolition of the collective responsibility of the *curiales* for the tax-quota of their cities, and the institution of tax-collectors called *vindices*. The *curiales*, however, were still involved in their unwelcome task after his reign, and complaints of heavy extortion remained rife. But he left the treasury full and Marinus rich. Considering the devastation of the Balkans and Mesopotamia, this suggests that, in spite of wars and taxes, trade was reviving under his economic rule.

It was on the insoluble religious question that Anastasius lost his hold on his capital and the Hellenized part of his subjects. His Monophysite opinions, which became more pronounced as he grew older, were distasteful to them, and the peace of Constantinople was constantly disturbed by serious riots, which were frequent also in Alexandria and Antioch. In 512 Marinus induced him to insert the Monophysite addition to the *Tersanctus* in the liturgy and almost caused a revolution in Constantinople, which was only prevented by Anastasius showing himself in the Circus without his crown and promising concessions. All the same, something like a persecution of the orthodox continued, and led to an armed revolt.

Vitalian, the commander of the Bulgarian *foederati* in Thrace, provoked by the expulsion of his close friend Flavian, the Patriarch of Antioch, seized on Odessus (Varna) on the Moesian coast. Thence, gathering other insurgents, he marched on Constantinople with the cry of justice for the banished patriarchs and the removal of the Monophysite insertion in the *Tersanctus.* The promise that grievances should be remedied and the religious differences settled in concert with the Pope led his officers, who clearly did not wish the overthrow of Anastasius, to insist on his retreat. But the promise was not kept, and Vitalian again revolted. He was kept at bay by troops, promises, and bribes, yet he held the field. In 515 he made another attack, his third, on Constantinople, encamping to the north of the Golden Horn in the later Galata while his fleet lay in the Bosphorus. This time he was defeated by land and sea. He retired with his Bulgarians to Anchialus (Burghas), where he stayed until the sudden death of the octogenarian Emperor on 9 July 518. This closed a period in the history of the Eastern Empire, the period of recuperation, in which Anastasius had played a most efficient part.

Drab, confused, tedious, and often sordid as is the story of the defence and recuperation, with its revolts, its court intrigues, its mercenary armies, its self-seeking generals, its corrupt ministers, its faithless cunning and its treasons, yet the Empire's survival shows the strength of its sounder elements. There was high ability and solid organization in the bureaucracy, industry and wealth in the townsmen, hardiness in the peasantry, military skill in the generals, and a fighting, patriotic spirit in the population which needed only to be utilized and disciplined. And there were eminent men—Anthemius, Cyrus, Marcian, Anastasius—whose patient statesmanship slowly guided the Empire from desperation to security. They possessed in Constantinople and its Straits an invaluable citadel; they could and did divert the Goths to the unhappy West. But they could not heal the religious divergencies which cleft the East, for they were both the expression and the exacerbation of growing particularism as the Romano-Hellenic unity dissolved.

(2) THE CHURCH AND DOCTRINAL ISSUES IN THE FIFTH CENTURY

While the Empire and perhaps the Church gained certain advantages by their close alliance from the days of Constantine, both also suffered severe losses from their association. The Empire was involved in the bitter disputes over the development of doctrine, almost inevitable in the intellectual activity which the acceptance of Christianity brought about, and in the rivalry of the great sees for leadership. These quarrels and controversies all tended to disruption, for the patriarchates were in their nature territorial, and

115

the opinions they championed became mainly territorial too: in the lands beyond the Taurus they became non-Greek as against the Hellenic core of the Empire and eventually as against the Roman West as well. The Church, and especially its hierarchy, suffered above all in morale. The bishoprics were too valuable a prize for ambition to ignore, and more and more turbulent, intriguing careerists, often able theologians, filled them. Bitterness and fanaticism had been present in the Church before Constantine's conversion; they now had freer scope and were increased by the distorted zeal of so many monks. Finally, the mob, becoming Christian, did not cease to be a mob, riotous and superstitious, and its susceptibility to eloquence and catchwords gave it a lively interest in doctrinal questions and an excuse for its own impulses.

It was not the older Arian controversy which now divided the Roman world. Arianism divided Roman from Germanic barbarian, but its supporters among the Romans were a dwindling remnant. The great sees now found matter of dispute and rivalry within the Trinitarian creed of Nicaea. Alexandria was arrayed against Antioch and against the new-made claims of Constantinople, which rested on its secular rank as capital, although it discovered that it too possessed an apostolic founder in St Andrew. Rome, with its assumption of a universal pre-eminence as the see of St Peter, never acknowledged the canon of 381 which gave New Rome the second place as the new capital. To bid for the support of the Pope who led all the West was an obvious tactic of the contending sees, yet they would not admit papal prerogative in the papal sense. To bid for the support of the Emperor was another obvious tactic in a state church which led towards Caesaropapism.

There were four major ecclesiastical conflicts arising in the East in the fifth century: (1) that concerning St John Chrysostom (Alexandria against Constantinople); (2) the Nestorian controversy (Alexandria, aided by Rome, against Constantinople and Antioch); (3) the Eutychian or Monophysite controversy (Alexandria against Constantinople, in which after a preliminary defeat Rome succeeded in giving the victory to Constantinople); (4) the *Henoticon* controversy, in which the Emperors, in pursuit of the Empire's unity, endeavoured to impose a half-way truce, which had but poor success in the East, and alienated the West almost to the point of schism.

In the first conflict only a modicum of doctrinal enmity was mingled with personal rivalry and ambition. Its originator was Theophilus, Patriarch of Alexandria (385–412), a cultivated personage who bears a bad name for violence and duplicity. The prestige of his see, the riotousness of his divided city, and the swarms of fanatical monks in the neighbouring desert gave every opportunity to an unscrupulous man of his temper to encroach on the secular authority of the imperial prefect. His mathematical learning enabled him to compose a table of the difficult Easter Cycle which bulked large in the formal piety of the age. He was literary enough to enjoy works he publicly anathematized, diplomat enough to adjust the quarrels of his neighbours when he had a mind. Domineering ambition seems to have been his leading motive. He endeavoured to gain more control over the desert monks by imposing by violent means, episcopal consecration on some leading ascetics. He set himself up also as the ally of the grossest and most ignorant theology of the day because it was popular among them. This was 'Anthropomorphism', the creed of the unhappy monk who wept that 'they had taken away his God' when the doctrine of Origen that God is invisible, incorporeal and incomprehensible was maintained. It was against the philosophic doctrines of Origen and against what may be called his philosophic speculations that Theophilus first proceeded in a synod. Then he attacked by armed force a settlement of monks who held Origenistic opinions. Their leaders, the four 'Tall Brethren', fled to Constantinople, where they appealed to the Patriarch, St John Chrysostom, for protection.

John, whose eloquence won him the lasting surname of 'the golden mouth', deserved a worthier and less cunning foe than Theophilus. He had won fame as a monk and preacher at Antioch, which was enough to make him suspect at Alexandria, for besides mere rivalry the two patriarchates were the centres of opposing schools of thought. The Antiochenes were literal and, one might say, matter-of-fact, the Alexandrines from Origen onwards allegorical and speculative in the interpretation of Scripture, though oddly enough, so far as his action was not due to personal motives, Theophilus was now calling a halt to the pregnant suggestions of Origen which might conceivably lead far away from current Christianity. Chrysostom was no persecutor in doctrine, but, ascetic himself, he was a harsh reformer in discipline and morals and intemperate in his 'golden' eloquence. The ways of court and clergy provided him with much to denounce and chastise. While he gained warm adherents and popularity, he naturally made bitter enemies. In 401 he conducted a visitation of the Churches of Ephesus and western Asia Minor, which greatly needed reform, and thus raised the question of his patriarchal rights over them. On his return, although he had been appointed by the court, he lost the favour of the Empress Eudoxia, who preferred the more soothing sermons of his *locum tenens* and was indignant with Chrysostom for adjudging him to have been in the wrong in an ecclesiastical quarrel. In this atmosphere the four Tall Brethren appeared. They were received with cautious kindness by Chrysostom, but from the Empress, to whom they appealed, they obtained the citation of Theophilus to Constantinople to answer for his persecution. This was to allow an arch-tactician to deploy his forces. Theophilus first prepared the ground by sending an aged episcopal partisan to denounce Origenism and flout Chrysostom in his own see. Then he came himself with a train of bishops, made an alliance with the Empress, and in 404 held a packed synod at Chalcedon. Chrysostom, who held a synod of his own adherents, refused to attend his enemies', and was promptly deposed by them. When the angry mob of Constantinople broke out in wrath, he withdrew, but returned to his see, unfortunately for himself, three days later, when an earthquake and the people's ferment alarmed Arcadius into recalling him.

His next misfortune was due to his own hasty temper and unchecked tongue. The noisy revellings which accompanied the erection of a statue of the Empress disturbed the divine service in the church near by where he was officiating. He not only protested, but preached in unmeasured terms against the offenders, with allusions to Herodias and Jezebel which glanced at Eudoxia. Another packed synod was convoked to depose him, this time for returning at the Emperor's request after deposition without a synodical restoration. The canon infringed had been passed by an Arian Council in 341, but that was disregarded. Arcadius reluctantly removed him to exile (20 June 404), in which he died in 407. But he retained the affection of the Byzantines, and public opinion was for him. Pope Innocent I and Honorius demanded a Council in vain, while in Constantinople there broke out the riot disastrous to ancient art. The breach between parties was not healed till his name was restored to the list recited from the diptychs in the Eucharist. His vicissitudes showed clearly the degeneration of the official Church, its divisions, and its subordination in the East to the Emperor's will, even the will of Arcadius.

If theology played a small part in the persecution of Chrysostom, it dominated in its most subtle and venturous form the Nestorian controversy, although here too the rivalry of Alexandria with Antioch and Constantinople embittered the contention. Nestorius the Isaurian, educated at Antioch and a follower of the learned Antiochene scholar, Theodore of Mopsuestia, became Patriarch of Constantinople in 428. His views have been exaggerated and misrepresented for centuries, but from his own rediscovered writings it appears that he differed from the finally authorized doctrine more in the subtle choice of terms to express the mystery of the Incarnation than in their essential meaning. He insisted on the distinction of the two natures, the Divine and the human, indissolubly conjoined in Christ, and objected to the growing use of the epithet Θεοτόκος—Mother of God—for the Virgin Mary, which was especially favoured in Alexandria. This was to rouse the Alexandrian Patriarch Cyril (412–44), more ambitious and astute than Nestorius, and as penetrating a theologian as he. Cyril declared for the indissoluble *union* of the two natures in the single Person and for the title Theotokos. His view was, perhaps, a more fitting expression for the doctrine of the Incarnation; the title Mother of God, too, appealed to a generation which was devoted to the efficacy of the intercession of the Saints. But Cyril relied on court intrigues and bribes as well as arguments, and he gained the valuable support of the Pope, Celestine I, in denouncing Nestorius as a heretic. The Emperor Theodosius endeavoured to lull the storm by a General Council at Ephesus in 431, but the expedient had the opposite effect. The bishops divided rapidly into two rival Councils. The majority, largely Egyptian, under Cyril, backed by the papal delegates, deposed Nestorius and John the Patriarch of Antioch and condemned their terminology as heretical; the minority, under John, in their turn deposed Cyril and the Bishop of Ephesus. The Emperor at first recognized both decisions; indeed Nestorius was willing to retire to a monastery. He had made himself personally disliked by his harsh ways, especially at court where Pulcheria was his enemy; he was also out of favour at Rome, where he was regarded as leaning towards Pelagianism in opposition to the absolute predestination of St Augustine. So Cyril was soon restored, and under pressure a formula which the Antiochenes could accept was adopted by the bishops. Cyril was triumphant except that he could not secure the condemnation of the teaching of Theodore of Mopsuestia, the learned and cautious originator of what Nestorius had maintained. The unfortunate Nestorius, the victim of patriarchal rivalries, personal dislikes, and a too adroit antagonist, was later sent in persecuted banishment to Egypt. There he lived to approve the Council of Chalcedon, in spite of its condemnation of himself, and was murdered late in 451 by the fanatical monk, Senuti. His opinions retained a number of adherents in North Syria, where under persecution they developed into the full-blown Nestorianism of the two Natures, which he never professed.

In the wake of the Nestorian controversy came the Monophysite. The subtle compromise of the General Council of Ephesus appealed to neither extreme party, and when Cyril was succeeded in 444 by the equally ambitious but violent and immoral Dioscorus, the tempest broke forth again with redoubled fury. It was the extreme doctrine of the single Divine Nature of the Incarnate Christ which was held by the turbulent, fanatical Egyptian and Syrian monks as well as by a considerable portion of monks elsewhere; it was also favoured by numbers of the lay population, most markedly in the non-Greek areas of the Empire. The strife became overt when the aged Eutyches, an abbot at Constantinople, was prosecuted for heresy by his Patriarch Flavian in the local synod. He maintained that the human nature assumed by God the Son was absorbed into the divine nature—i.e. Monophysitism—and was condemned. He appealed to the Emperor and the Pope. Theodosius II was at heart a Monophysite, and summoned a Council to meet at Ephesus on 1 August 449, with Dioscorus as president. This was to abet Alexandrian ambitions and to give their chance to the Monophysites. Pope Leo the Great took the side of Flavian, and it may be said, of the conservatives. With far more decorum, for he had the instincts of a statesman, he denied the need of a Council, urged that, if held, it should be in the West, and claimed that he as successor to St Peter should lay down the orthodox faith by his statement, the famous *Tome*. But Dioscorus, strong in imperial support and the riotous bands of monks who thronged in his company, pursued his aims with a violence which earned the assembly the name of the 'Robber Council'. Monophysite or intimidated bishops refused to permit the Tome to be read, deposed Flavian and his adherents, and declared Eutyches orthodox; Flavian soon died of the physical maltreatment to which he had been subjected. Monophysitism seemed to have won the day, while Leo protested in the distance. Then the death of Theodosius in 450 changed the scene. The new rulers Marcian and Pulcheria leaned to the other side. They had a difficult game to play. A new Council must be held in the East in imperial leading strings; the proceedings of the Robber Council must be annulled; the overweening dictation of Alexandria must be rebutted; the Pope's Tome must be accepted as correct in doctrine, but not as decisive of it, as Leo demanded; and the much humiliated see of Constantinople must be established in a pre-eminence second only to Old Rome in rank rather than in powers. In 451 the General Council of over 600 bishops met by the Emperor's summons at Chalcedon with the Pope's legates acting as ecclesiastical presidents. Violent party feeling was shown from the outset; yet it was clear that the Emperor's will would prevail. Intimidated or insincere bishops rapidly changed sides, while Anatolius, who had succeeded Flavian at Constantinople as a Monophysite, had already left his old party. Dioscorus was now condemned in his turn. The creeds of Nicaea and of Constantinople (381) were confirmed—the latter indeed came to replace the Nicene in the liturgy. More important was the approval after discussion of Leo's Tome, but it was not made the formal definition of doctrine, although that definition was based on it. Last of all, in Canon XXVIII, the precedence of the see of Constantinople as New Rome immediately after Old Rome was decreed in spite of the protests of the papal legates and of Leo when he heard of it. The sting lay, not in the power and dignity adjudged to Constantinople, but in the reasons given, that each Rome possessed its rank because it was a capital of the Empire, whereas the Pope claimed to be head of the Church as successor to St Peter.

The definitions of Chalcedon may be praised for establishing an accepted Christology for European Christendom and for giving a common faith to Greek as well as Roman patriotism. But even Greek unanimity took long to obtain, while the non-Hellenic provincials were firm in their Monophysitism. The Copts of Egypt, the Aramaic-speaking Syrians, and the Armenians were more and more estranged from the official Church, while oddly enough the Dyophysitism of the pronounced Nestorians also survived and spread beyond the Euphrates under the leadership of Ibas, Bishop of Edessa.

The death of Marcian in 457 loosened the hold of the government on these movements. A certain Timothy, nicknamed 'the Cat', was riotously elected Patriarch of Alexandria on the murder of his orthodox predecessor Proterius, and though he was driven out, he still headed the Monophysite Copts in the background. In Antioch, a violent Monophysite, Peter the Fuller, intruded himself, and added to the discord by an innovation in the ritual: he inserted in the Tersanctus the words 'Who was crucified for us'. These troubles came to a head when Basiliscus usurped the Empire in 475. The rebel Emperor was a Monophysite. He restored Timothy the Cat and Peter the Fuller to their sees, and in a circular letter (the *Encyclical*) anathematized the Council of Chalcedon. But if he pleased the Egyptians and Syrians, he enraged most of the Greeks. He was forced to recall the Encyclical. When Zeno recovered the throne (476), the ferment was still heaving. The Emperor's policy seems to have been intended to be neutral with an obvious leaning to the Monophysites. With the aid of the supple Acacius of Constantinople and of Peter the Stammerer, whom he recognized as Timothy the Cat's successor in Alexandria, he issued the *Henoticon* (482). In it he anathematized Nestorius and Eutyches, declared the sufficiency of the creeds of Nicaea and Constantinople, and denounced any contrary doctrine 'whether taught at Chalcedon or elsewhere'. This manifesto was enough for most Monophysites, who felt released from the definitions of Chalcedon, while it allowed a certain loophole and satisfaction to the orthodox, who saw Eutyches condemned and the definitions not overtly denied. A deceptive peace was to reign in the Empire by lulling the controversy to sleep. But if this was for a time the case in the Eastern Empire, there was no such submission in the West or by the Papacy, which was so nearly concerned with the Tome of Leo and the decisions at Chalcedon. After an angry controversy Pope Simplicius solemnly excommunicated Acacius, Peter, and Zeno himself, and the first ecclesiastical schism between East and West began. It lasted for years, in spite of attempts to heal it. The Emperor Anastasius made matters worse by markedly leaning towards the Monophysite doctrine. He fell out with two successive Patriarchs for being too yielding in the recurrent negotiations with the Papacy. His own unpopularity was thereby augmented, for Monophysitism was weak west of the Taurus Mountains just as it was strong in Syria and Egypt. On his death it was easy for the Illyrian Emperor Justin to abolish the Henoticon and restore orthodoxy as the one permitted belief, while Rome was satisfied by the removal of Acacius's name from the diptychs. It was, however, one thing to decree this and another to subdue the resistance of Syrians, Copts and Armenians. The deposed Patriarch of Antioch, Severus the Pisidian, continued to organize the

Monophysite communities in spite of persecution. Thus, although the influence of the Empire increased in the West, an ever deepening wedge was driven into the rift within the Empire, that between the Hellenized and the mainly non-Hellenic provinces.

Meanwhile, the brief period during which the Monophysites had held the upper hand had furthered the spread of Nestorianism in the distant East. The theological school which Ibas had maintained at Edessa was closed by Zeno in 489; many of its scholars migrated to Nisibis in Persian territory, where Barsumas, a zealous Antiochene and Nestorian, was bishop. In the result, the Christians in Persia, perforce hostile to the Monophysite and orthodox Empire which persecuted them, grew and flourished under their Catholicos, the Bishop of Ctesiphon. The Nestorians formed for centuries the Christian Church of Asia from Nisibis to India, and they even established a mission at Si-ngan-fu in Northern China.

The subtle Christological disputes which engrossed and were for long to engross the metaphysical East roused far less passion in the Latin West. Even the Tome of Leo was due perhaps rather to the determination of the Pope to assert a decisive voice in an endless controversy than to a wish to revise the creed. The Arian debate, dying in the East, was indeed still alive in the West, for the Germanic tribesmen, whose faith was Arianism, were rulers there, to be conquered by words if not by arms. That Greek speculation should make so little impression on the Latins was doubtless partly due to their more practical temperament. It was also due to cultural estrangement, the cessation of the knowledge of Greek. The bilingual man of letters was becoming rare. It is significant that the greatest Latin doctor of the Church, who shaped the theology and political ideas of Western Europe for many centuries, St Augustine of Hippo, refused to learn Greek. Yet he was bred a rhetorician, learned in all other knowledge of the schools. He was an African, born at Thagasta in 354, son of a pagan father and a Christian mother, St Monica. It was in 373 that the reading of Cicero's now lost *Hortensius* called him from dissipation to the pursuit of wisdom, and for years he was attracted by the dualism of the Manichees. Then he fell under the influence of Neo-Platonism, which had a lasting effect on his theology. The philosophic idealism that colours his utterance and forms the real basis of his thought is Platonic in its origins. As a professional rhetorician he came from Carthage to Rome and thence to Milan, where the great St Ambrose held the see. When his mistress, by whom he had a much-loved son, Adeodatus, took a vow of chastity, he gave her a successor, for philosophy had not conquered his passions, and he acquiesced in schemes of a marriage. But his mother and other influences were drawing him to Christianity. It was in 386 that he overheard the child's voice saying 'Tolle, lege', 'Take and read', and opened the New Testament at the passage of St Paul which clinched his resolution. In 387 he was baptized. In 396, after years of teaching, writing, and study in an ascetic life, he became bishop of the coast town of Hippo in his native Africa, where he remained till his death during the Vandal siege in 430. He became the indefatigable champion, the instructor, and the philosopher of Western Christendom. His genius was so rich in ideas that he affected every subsequent thinker; like sparks from a furnace they kindled fires in the most divergent intellects and inspired the most opposed reasonings. His very Latinity, which varied with its theme, was next to the Vulgate of St Jerome the most potent influence on medieval writers. The legacy which the Middle Ages derived from Antiquity is typified by him, and in the realm of thought largely consists of his works.

Two among the controversies in which St Augustine engaged require special mention for their far-reaching effects on later times. One (411–18) was with the British monk Pelagius and concerned the doctrines of Original Sin, Divine Grace, and Predestination. Pelagius, the quiet monk, denied the inheritance of original sin, maintained that divine grace was an aid to, not the only source of, human righteousness, and denied that God had predestined men to hell or heaven. St Augustine, the reformed rake, held that man's will was evil through original sin derived from Adam, that Grace to a man was necessary before an approach to righteousness was possible, and that the recipients of Grace were elected by God from all eternity; others were doomed to hell in like manner. It was the grim doctrine of St Augustine which won the suffrage of the Western Church with its submission to absolute power and its open-eyed knowledge of human infirmity. The doctrine formed a powerful incentive to obedience to the Church and its dictates and towards the ascetic monastic life and its flight from the world. But by its terrors it helped the development of assuaging doctrines, which offered the intercession of the saints and the rites of religion as means to diffuse Grace more widely than a strict account might suggest.

The second controversy was provoked by the disasters of the times, and in especial by the sack of Rome herself, the Eternal City, by Alaric. The pagans declared it the punishment for the desertion of the gods who had made Rome great. Christianity was to blame. St Augustine answered the charge in *De Civitate Dei*, written from 413 to 426. The protection of the heathen gods was a delusion; the history of heathen Rome was dark with calamity. His Spanish pupil Orosius attempted in his *Historia* to prove that the Empire, now Christian, was really more prosperous than of old. This was a victory of the spirit over the sense, of blind conviction over patent facts. But St Augustine followed it up by a Christian philosophy of history, far more profound and cogent. It was based on the true purpose of human life and society, which could only find felicity in eternal salvation.

To St Augustine the meaning of human history was not primarily the organization of human society into states and the achievements of those states, it was the vicissitudes of the conflict between Good and Evil, the City of God and the Earthly City, which for mankind began with the Fall. The City of God in the full sense is composed of those in Heaven and Earth whose ruling motive is the love of God and the righteousness He enjoins; the *Civitas Terrena* of those on Earth who are led by the love of self, however ennobled by the loftiness of their chosen gratifications or the beneficence of their actions. No heathen can have the love of God or render Him His due, the all-important due; that is to say, the heathen is fundamentally unjust and unrighteous. The heathen republics, kingdoms, and empires therefore embody the evil spirit of the Earthly City; their very wars and conquests show it. Human society indeed is designed by God, but the Fall has distorted and degraded it to this sinful form. The good objects for which it was ordained, though still partly present, are enfeebled and adulterated. But the City of God has also its embodied history, however stained and alloyed, for in it the love of God and the true Faith persisted. It was to be found in the Patriarchs, the Jewish monarchy, and the Christian Church. This did not mean that Church and State were eternal opposites. St Augustine, far from being a Church politician, thought of men as individuals, candidates for salvation. If members of the Christian Church were orthodox and righteous, they were members of the City of God in this life. When the Empire became Christian, its rulers and citizens were on the same conditions acceptable; their institutions were acquiring a sanctity. Neither the Christian Empire nor the Church coincided exactly with the City of God on earth. But they professed the primary conditions of a just society. Within their limits were numbered the living inhabitants of the City of God. Yet St Augustine's conception of history saw his hostile cities embodied in actually organized states and institutions. He made it difficult for his followers to fuse the Church with the converted Christian Empire. And, theory apart, there was the practical problem, which he did not solve, of the mutual relations of the existing fully organized ecclesiastical and secular hierarchies, both Christian, the problem of Church and State. Answers to that problem were produced by his interpreters and dominated medieval political theory. They were not his answers, but they took rise from his history of his mystical cities, which he traced in a succession of temporal, embodied states.

In the Eastern Empire the relation of Church and State was more and more settling down, as we have seen, to a common, if sometimes mutinous, dependence on the Emperor. In the dissolving Empire of the West the weakening Emperors were glad to fortify unity by encouraging the growing prerogatives of the Pope of Rome. Pope Innocent I (401–17) continued the tradition of Damasus, and asserted both that he ought to give judgement on appeals from bishops, and that the Roman Church was the founder

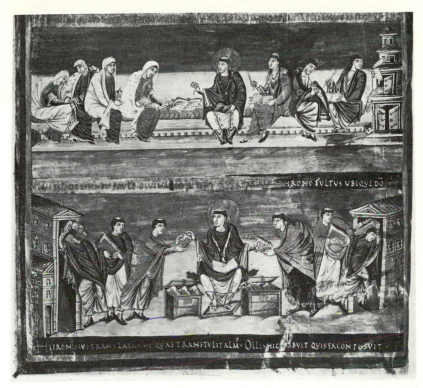

Fig. 18. (*a*) *St Jerome dictating his translation of the Bible;*
(*b*) *distribution of the first copies of the Vulgate in Rome*

and therefore the model of all the churches of the West. Pope Zosimus
(417–18) established a papal vicariate in Gaul. But it was Leo the Great
(440–61) who more definitely formulated papal claims, and not only at
Chalcedon with his Tome. In the see of St Peter, he said, 'there lives on his
power and the excellence of his authority'. In Gaul, he annulled the decree
of a synod and deposed, though ineffectually, St Hilary of Arles. He also
obtained what authority the Emperor could give him, when Valentinian III
(445) issued more precisely the edict giving the Pope appellate jurisdiction
over bishops and metropolitans, and ordering the civil governors to enforce
obedience. To Pope Gelasius I (492–6), when the Western Empire was no
more, belongs the celebrated and long-lasting definition of the spheres and
rank of the rulers of Church and State. In a letter to the Emperor Anastasius he declared that there were two powers which ruled this world, 'the
sacred authority of pontiffs and the royal power', and that of the priests
was the weightier because they had to render account to God even for

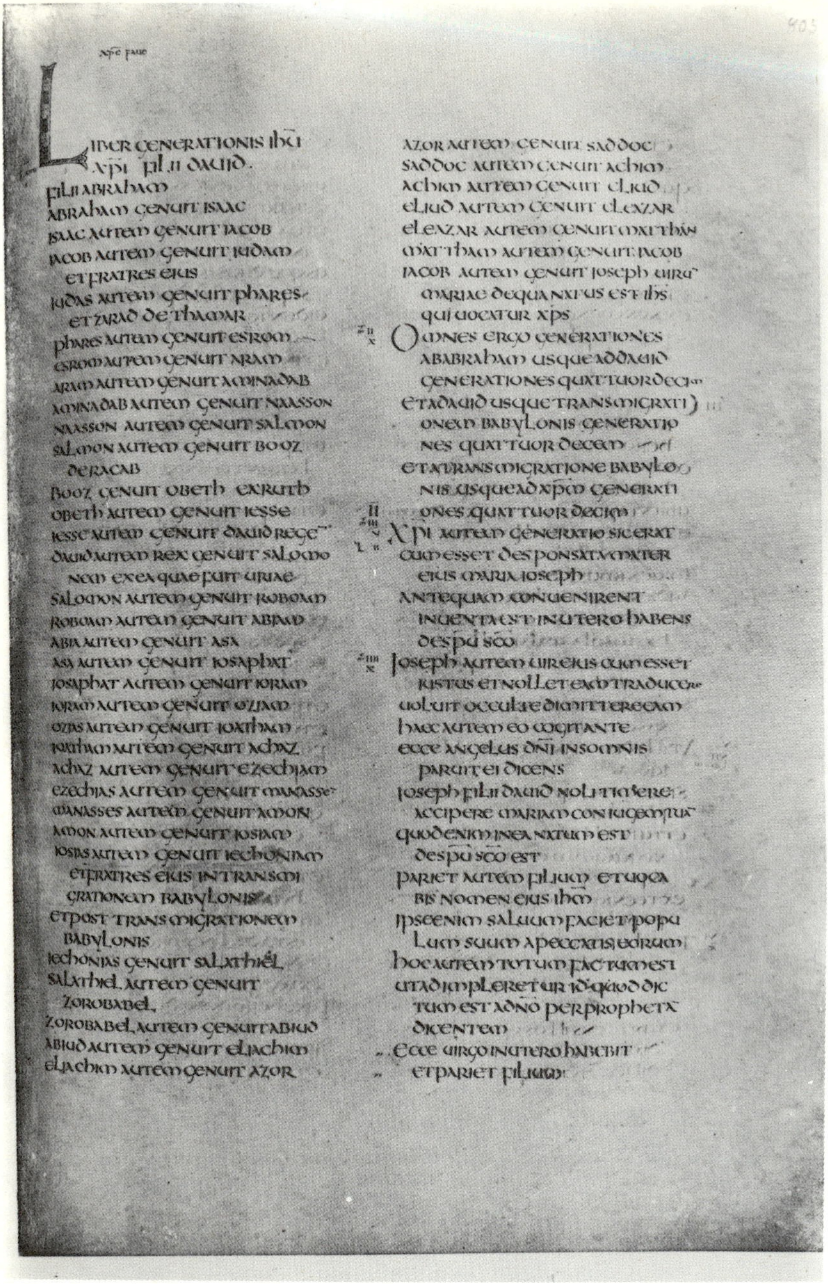
LIBER GENERATIONIS IHU XPI FILII DAUID.
FILII ABRAHAM
ABRAHAM GENUIT ISAAC
ISAAC AUTEM GENUIT IACOB
IACOB AUTEM GENUIT IUDAM
ET FRATRES EIUS
IUDAS AUTEM GENUIT PHARES
ET ZARAD DE THAMAR
PHARES AUTEM GENUIT ESROM
ESROM AUTEM GENUIT ARAM
ARAM AUTEM GENUIT AMINADAB
AMINADAB AUTEM GENUIT NAASSON
NAASSON AUTEM GENUIT SALMON
SALMON AUTEM GENUIT BOOZ
DE RACAB
BOOZ GENUIT OBETH EX RUTH
OBETH AUTEM GENUIT IESSE
IESSE AUTEM GENUIT DAUID REGE̅
DAUID AUTEM REX GENUIT SALOMO
NEM EX EA QUAE FUIT URIAE
SALOMON AUTEM GENUIT ROBOAM
ROBOAM AUTEM GENUIT ABIAM
ABIA AUTEM GENUIT ASA
ASA AUTEM GENUIT IOSAPHAT
IOSAPHAT AUTEM GENUIT IORAM
IORAM AUTEM GENUIT OZIAM
OZIAS AUTEM GENUIT IOATHAM
IOATHAM AUTEM GENUIT ACHAZ
ACHAZ AUTEM GENUIT EZECHIAM
EZECHIAS AUTEM GENUIT MANASSE̅
MANASSES AUTEM GENUIT AMON
AMON AUTEM GENUIT IOSIAM
IOSIAS AUTEM GENUIT IECHONIAM
ET FRATRES EIUS IN TRANSMI
GRATIONEM BABYLONIS
ET POST TRANSMIGRATIONEM
BABYLONIS
IECHONIAS GENUIT SALATHIEL
SALATHIEL AUTEM GENUIT
ZOROBABEL
ZOROBABEL AUTEM GENUIT ABIUD
ABIUD AUTEM GENUIT ELIACHIM
ELIACHIM AUTEM GENUIT AZOR
AZOR AUTEM GENUIT SADDOC
SADDOC AUTEM GENUIT ACHIM
ACHIM AUTEM GENUIT ELIUD
ELIUD AUTEM GENUIT ELEAZAR
ELEAZAR AUTEM GENUIT MATTHAN
MATTHAM AUTEM GENUIT IACOB
IACOB AUTEM GENUIT IOSEPH UIRU̅
MARIAE DE QUA NATUS EST IHS
QUI UOCATUR XPS
OMNES ERGO GENERATIONES
AB ABRAHAM USQUE AD DAUID
GENERATIONES QUATTUORDECIM
ET A DAUID USQUE TRANSMIGRATI
ONEM BABYLONIS GENERATIO
NES QUATTUOR DECEM
ET A TRANSMIGRATIONE BABYLO
NIS USQUE AD XPM GENERATI
ONES QUATTUOR DECIM
XPI AUTEM GENERATIO SIC ERAT
CUM ESSET DESPONSATA MATER
EIUS MARIA IOSEPH
ANTEQUAM CONUENIRENT
INUENTA EST IN UTERO HABENS
DE SPU SCO
IOSEPH AUTEM UIR EIUS CUM ESSET
IUSTUS ET NOLLET EAM TRADUCERE
UOLUIT OCCULTE DIMITTERE EAM
HAEC AUTEM EO COGITANTE
ECCE ANGELUS DNI IN SOMNIS
PARUIT EI DICENS
IOSEPH FILI DAUID NOLI TIMERE
ACCIPERE MARIAM CONIUGEM TUA̅
QUOD ENIM IN EA NATUM EST
DE SPU SCO EST
PARIET AUTEM FILIUM ET UOCA
BIS NOMEN EIUS IHM
IPSE ENIM SALUUM FACIET POPU
LUM SUUM A PECCATIS EORUM
HOC AUTEM TOTUM FACTUM EST
UT ADIMPLERETUR ID QUOD DIC
TUM EST A DNO PER PROPHETA̅
DICENTEM
ECCE UIRGO IN UTERO HABEBIT
ET PARIET FILIUM

Fig. 19. Oldest surviving MS of St Jerome's Vulgate

kings. Among the priesthood stood impregnable the primacy of the Roman Church. Thus the foundations of the medieval conception of the government of Christendom were laid in high-sounding phrases, that were to be developed and enlarged and diversely interpreted. Roman unity in the West was finding its refuge, as yet a matter of claim and influence, in the Papacy.

It was to a suggestion of Pope Damasus that the Latin Vulgate, the semi-official version of the Bible in the West, owed its inception. It was made by St Jerome (c. 347–420), a native of Istria, a rigid ascetic, a voluminous writer, an ardent controversialist, and the most learned Latin of his day. His own works, with their vivacity and honesty, place him high as an author, while he was one of the greatest of translators. Mainly at Rome he revised the old Latin translation of the New Testament; mainly at Bethlehem, whither he retired, he made a new translation of the Old Testament direct from the Hebrew instead of from the Greek Septuagint from which the old Latin version was taken. In spite of the resistance of conservatives the Vulgate, although never quite uncontaminated, gradually won its way to supremacy and has influenced the language and thought of Western Europe to this day.

To sum up the political effect of the ecclesiastical events of the fifth century. In the East they fostered provincial particularism, vastly enlarged the alienation of non-Hellenized lands from the Byzantines, and eventually contributed to their estrangement from Christianity altogether and their loss to the Empire. On the other hand they provided a national faith, identical with patriotism, for the Balkans and Asia Minor, which was not least among the forces which preserved the Eastern Empire. In the West they furnished the unifying culture and organization which gave its character to all subsequent history. Civilization, damaged and degraded as it might be, was preserved in the Dark Ages by the Latin Church, and the medieval civilization that was to arise was inspired and directed by that community and that inheritance.

CHAPTER 7

THE BARBARIAN KINGDOMS OF THE WEST

(1) COMMON CHARACTERISTICS

The new Germanic kingdoms founded on the ruins of the Western Empire varied according to the character of the invaders, the circumstances of their settlement, their relations with the conquered, the personality of their rulers, the religion they adopted, the institutions they evolved, their geographical situation, and their ultimate fate, but some characteristics they had in common which were fateful for their history. The ingrained strength of certain of these characteristics exercised a vigorous influence on the formation of medieval law and institutions. The lack or the modification of certain others goes far to account for the durability of the peoples of the Franks and Anglo-Saxons.

First among these common characteristics, and perhaps oldest, is the existence of the kindred, or group of kinsmen, called in the different tribal languages by such names as *maegth*, *aet*, *sippe*, *geschlecht*, or *fara*. It consisted both of the agnates by male descent, the 'spear' side, and of the cognates by female descent, the 'spindle' side. Their comparative importance is exemplified in the share they took of the *wergeld* or compensation for a slain kinsman; the agnates received two-thirds, the cognates one-third. This kinship-group was a natural and necessary institution, which gave the freeman some protection for life, limb, and property, and some status and weight in the community; even men of rank largely depended on their kindred for their power. Its solidarity and functions in a barbarous society are best shown by the primary duty, rooted in men's minds, of blood-revenge. If a member of a kindred was slain, wounded, or injured, it was the absolute duty and right of his kinsmen to inflict the same or greater injury on one of the kindred to which the inflicter of the wrong belonged. So close was the bond of kinship that it did not matter if vengeance was wreaked on the actual offender or on one of his kindred. Reciprocal revenge would be repeated in a *faida* or feud between the two kindreds, which produced a state of incessant private warfare in the community, and divided the kindreds themselves when the injury was committed by one member against another of the same group. Even among the barbarians, however, some mitigation of the custom, to which they were whole-heartedly bound, had crept in. Vengeance could, but need not, be remitted by the payment of *wergeld*, scaled according to the measure of the offence and the rank of the injured, by the kindred of the injurer. But even so the institution afforded a poor degree of protection in a society marked by

128

untamed passion and barbarous ideals. It is true that the settlement, as we shall see, broke up progressively the original kindreds, but new ones were formed by natural growth and by local or artificial associations. Almost throughout the Middle Ages the kinship-group and its feuds and the duty of revenge were to be main obstacles to the evolution of peace and order and the functioning of government.

As a second feature of these tribes may be reckoned the habit of assemblies of freemen to declare custom in disputes and to make decisions. They were called by some such name as *thing* (Scandinavian), *gemot* (moot, Anglo-Saxon), or *mall* (Frankish). As tribal assemblies these meetings hardly survived the settlement, but as local courts of justice they had a long and important life.

Thirdly, there was the vigorous insititution of lordship. King and great man still possessed some form of *comitatus*, the band of followers (*gasindi*) maintained by their lord, under his protection, and bound to his service in peace and war. This institution, blending with the late Roman custom in which a great man levied a bodyguard of so-called *bucellarii*, was to be fruitful not only of immediate uses but of the later development towards feudalism.

A fourth characteristic which conditioned the settlement of Goths, Burgundians and Vandals, and largely of the Franks was that the settlers became to a great extent landlords rather than peasants. This thin layer of barbarians, no longer a compact army but widely spread over a numerically superior 'Roman' population, of which an upper fraction at any rate still possessed a higher culture, was bound to be weakened thereby, to decay in solidarity and military power, to adopt the language of the majority around them, and to be absorbed by it as soon as the gulf of religion and race could be bridged, unless the destruction of the enfeebled kingdom first occurred.

The fifth and most debilitating characteristic which maintained the separation between the sparse, armed barbarians who ruled and the unarmed mass of their subjects was their Arian religion. The difference of faith accentuated the cleavage of race, language, and civilization. It affected the most ignorant 'Romans' as well as their natural leaders, the Catholic clergy, in the collapse of the Empire. Whatever other causes for mutual dislike and distrust existed—and they were obviously many—this exacerbated them. The barbarian might be inflamed to persecution, the 'Roman' to enmity, active or passive, towards his heretic rulers. Even after the conversion of the Arian Germans to Catholicism the memory of their misbelief might cling to them and hinder amalgamation. In fact in the early Germanic kingdoms two peoples, one privileged and armed, the other subject, dwelt side by side, kept hostile by religion, forbidden to intermarry, living under different laws, Germanic and Roman. The political edifice, if we may call

129

Fig. 20. San Apollinare Nuovo, Ravenna

it such, rested on a narrow and crumbling foundation. It was the good fortune of the Franks to be Catholics from their first conversion.

The conquest and settlement of vast provinces by the victorious tribesmen had naturally affected their own government and had increased the power of the kings who led them. From kinglets they had become autocratic rulers of powerful states, restricted only by custom, by the counsel of their landed nobles, and by the chances of murder and revolt. They soon appear as administrators, taxers, and legislators instead of as mere chiefs of a tribal army. In this development they stepped, however clumsily and ignorantly, into a Roman heritage.

The inheritance bequeathed to the now disrupted society by the civilization of the Empire, however depleted and maimed, was of the first importance. The methods and system of agriculture continued: the great and little estates; the *coloni*, whether free or servile, bound to their plots, dues, and services; the growing practice of a natural and almost closed economy, in which money and trade played but a minor part. The king succeeded to imperial prerogatives, as he did to imperial estates, even if his practical use of them was incoherent and tended to lapse. In various, ever more simplified degrees the Roman civil administration outlasted the conquest. So did the Roman Law for Romans: simplified, broken versions of it for

130

daily life were current and sanctioned by the kings. It influenced the evolution of barbaric codes and the far-away development of local custom in later centuries. Even a certain knowledge of Roman literature and the Christian Fathers and the Latin Bible lingered among the dwindling educated class, mainly Roman. While in Italy and Spain a proportion of these literates were laymen, elsewhere they belonged mainly to the clergy. The preservation of the elements of Roman and Christian civilization was preeminently the work of the clergy, the Benedictine monks, and the Catholic Church which enshrined in varying measure the spirit of both and, even if deformed by barbarism, supplied the life-giving germs of law and higher ideals in the reign of unabashed violence, passion, and anarchy.

(2) THE VANDALS IN AFRICA

Earliest to be fully formed and earliest to fall of the barbaric kingdoms was the Vandal state founded by the ruthless genius of Gaiseric. We have seen how he conquered the central African provinces, created a fleet and sea-power, and became the terror and plunderer of East and West. When he died in 477 he left the Vandal kingdom organized and seemingly strong, but resting on the narrowest basis. The separation between the Vandals and their conquered subjects was absolute. The Arian Vandals lived as proprietors on the confiscated estates of the 'Romans', principally in the fertile Africa proper, or Zeugitana, and degenerated rapidly in unaccustomed idleness and luxury. As an army they fought on horseback. They were tax-free, but the king was an autocrat. By the testament of Gaiseric the crown descended to the eldest male agnate among his descendants. Thus a minority was avoided at a cost of continuity. The king enjoyed the ex-imperial estates and revenues. He ruled with the aid of his *comitatus*, here named *domestici*. The Vandal districts were under the jurisdiction of the heads of thousands. The Arian clergy, to whom were given the church-lands, were directed by their Patriarch of Carthage, the capital. Like other officials their bishops were named by the king. A faint Latin culture began to show itself in court and nobility in the third generation after Gaiseric.

For the Romans the old civil administration in its provinces was maintained, manned by themselves. Indeed they filled many posts in the central royal bureaucracy. They were left to their own law and courts, save when a Vandal was a party to the suit. The *coloni*, whether within or without the Vandal allotments, continued in their former status. Probably their burdens were somewhat lightened by the Roman stewards (*conductores*) of their masters. On the frontiers, after Gaiseric's death, the vassal Moorish tribes renewed their raids and encroachments, steadily destroying the works and cities of ancient civilization.

131

4. The Kings of the Goths and Vandals

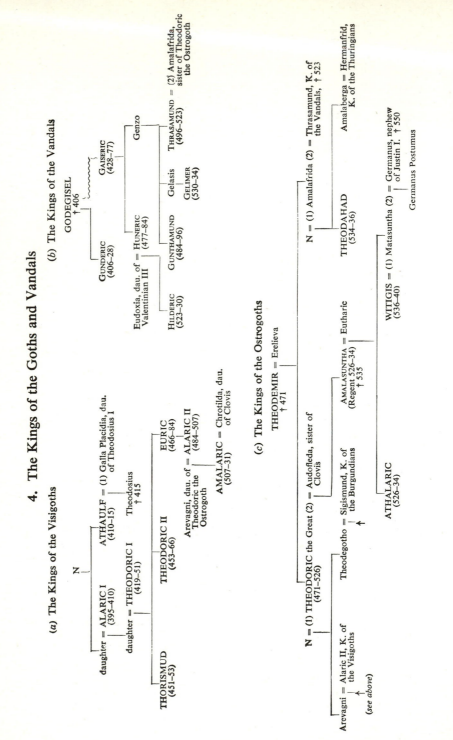

(a) The Kings of the Visigoths

(b) The Kings of the Vandals

(c) The Kings of the Ostrogoths

The worst grievance of the Romans was the intermittent religious persecution of the Catholics, which is closely interwoven with the political history of the kingdom. Outside the Vandal allotments Gaiseric practised a suspicious toleration. His eldest son, Huneric (477–84), who was a bloodthirsty tyrant, raging against rivals in his own family and their possible adherents, began a furious persecution in January 484. It lasted a year till his death. Catholicism was made a crime, like Arianism in the Empire. Churches and their property, outside the Vandal allotments, were confiscated. Deprivation, fines, and banishment were inflicted on those recalcitrant to conversion, and the Arian clergy outstripped the law in their cruel zeal. Huneric's nephew and successor, Gunthamund (484–96), relaxed the persecution (487)—the churches were reopened—but his brother Thrasamund (496–523), otherwise an amiable character, renewed from time to time, though in a less savage form, the persecution. His reign was marked by the shrinkage of the kingdom in unsuccessful Moorish warfare and his adhesion to the entente of Arian Germanic kings devised by Theodoric the Ostrogoth. With Hilderic (523–30), the elderly, utterly effeminate son of Huneric and Eudoxia, came toleration for the Catholics and the open decadence of the kingdom. He abandoned the Ostrogothic alliance, imprisoning Thrasamund's widow, Amalafrida, sister of the great Theodoric, and in some degree acknowledged Byzantine suzerainty. He was only saved from invasion by the death of Theodoric. Meantime the loss of inland Mauretania and Numidia to the Moors enraged his subjects, who deposed him and raised his cousin, Gelimer (530–34), against the order of succession devised by Gaiseric, to the throne. This revolution brought about the invasion of Justinian.

(3) THE OSTROGOTHS IN ITALY

A complete separation between the armed Germanic tribesmen and the Roman civilians was also the fundamental condition of the barbaric kingdoms in Italy, but there the barbarians were in theory in the old position of *foederati* employed under their chief, whether Odovacar or Theodoric, to garrison an imperial province. These kings were in theory Roman officials and generals, on the model of Ricimer, and in spite of its essential unreality this constitutional fiction did have practical results on their government and expressed genuine conditions in the world of fact. Italy had not altogether quitted the Roman Empire as Africa and Spain had done, and owned allegiance to the Emperor at Constantinople, from whom the kings received a revocable delegation.

Odovacar's reign in Italy was not unsuccessful, but he had become estranged from the East, and Zeno stirred up the Rugians on the upper Danube to attack him. Indeed they had long raided the derelict province

Map 2

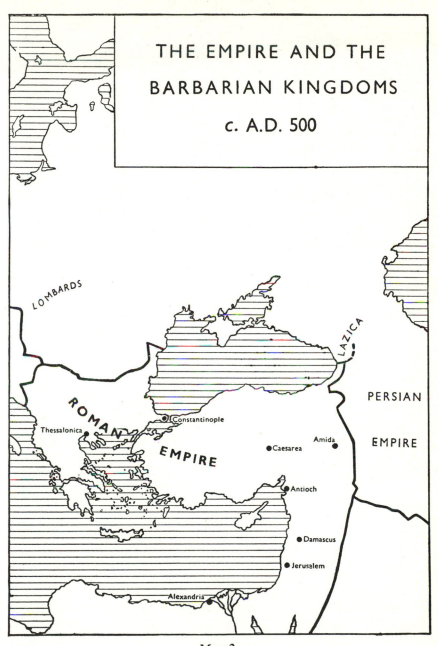

THE EMPIRE AND THE

BARBARIAN KINGDOMS

c. A.D. 500

LOMBARDS

LAZICA

ROMAN

PERSIAN

EMPIRE

EMPIRE

Thessalonica

Constantinople

Amida

Caesarea

Antioch

Damascus

Jerusalem

Alexandria

Map 2

Fig. 21. Ostrogothic nobles

of Noricum, where the saintly abbot Severinus had done his best to alleviate the misery of his rulerless co-provincials. Odovacar, however, crushed the Rugians so completely (487) that they soon after vanish from history. On the upper Danube they were succeeded by Germanic tribesmen from Bohemia, hence called Baiuvarii or Bavarians, who spread into Noricum and Rhaetia. But when Zeno authorized Theodoric the Ostrogoth to replace Odovacar it was a different matter. Odovacar and his veterans of fragmentary tribes fought hard; the three pitched battles of the Isonzo, Verona (489), and the Adda (490) were costly victories for Theodoric, who might have lost the third without Visigothic allies. Even then Odovacar held out two-and-a-half years in Ravenna. Theodoric only ended the siege by a treacherous treaty of alliance and co-regency (493). He then murdered his rival and guest at his own table. A carefully organized massacre of Odovacar's troops, many of whom were quartered in other towns, completed this atrocious proceeding, and Theodoric, satiated with revenge, could display himself as a wise and beneficent ruler.

The Ostrogothic king in his early years as a hostage at Constantinople had learnt to appreciate Roman civilization more thoroughly than most of his race, although his continued illiteracy and senseless ferocity when enraged showed his underlying barbaric mentality. We may believe that

136

the admirable professions of toleration, moderation, civilization and bene
volence put into his mouth by his Roman rescript writer, Cassiodorus,
and his panegyrists really express the considered purpose of their master.
His choice of ministers and actions speak for him. In the next generation
the Byzantine Procopius summarized his reign: 'His manner of ruling over
his subjects was worthy of a great Emperor; for he maintained justice,
made good laws, protected his country from invasion, and gave proof of
extraordinary prudence and valour.'

Theodoric owed a part of his victory to the fact that he came as an
imperial delegate, and thereby received the aid of the Italians and the
Catholic Church. Although he was an Arian, bishops opened the gates of
their cities to him, and one of them, Epiphanius of Pavia, induced him not
only to ransom 6000 Ligurians, whom Gundobad of Burgundy had
carried captive in a raid during the war, but also to remit two-thirds of the
year's taxes from the devastated districts. But full imperial confirmation
for his permanent position had yet to be got, and it was not till 497 that
the Emperor Anastasius made a definite treaty. Henceforward, Theodoric
named the western Consul in spite of friction amounting to hostilities on
occasion.

Theodoric was thus the ruler of two peoples. The Ostrogoths lived under
their own courts and their own customs. Where a Roman was the other
party to a lawsuit, the judge was a Goth with Roman assessors. Goths,
unlike Romans, were liable to military service. A third of the land formed
their allotments, but what with the vacant lands, e.g. in devastated Liguria,
the holdings taken over from Odovacar's dead soldiery, and, it has been
maintained, grants from imperial estates, the exaction was little felt by
the great Roman proprietors. In fact the Ostrogoths were not too numerous
and scarcely settled in Southern Italy. In land questions they were subject
to Roman law and taxation; in criminal matters the same subjection was
enforced. Tribal custom was evidently much restricted, and the king's
messengers (*saiones*) must have been busy in enforcing unwelcome
regulations.

The Roman civil administration was that of the late Empire. The pretorian prefecture and other high offices continued, and were held by
eminent Romans. From the official letters of his Quaestor, Cassiodorus,
the best picture of the time is to be obtained. The king-patrician himself
issued his *Edict*, derived entirely from Roman sources, as a Roman
magistrate; he did not infringe the Emperor's rights by calling it a law.
A friendly deference marked his intercourse with the Senate. He courted
leading senators with titles and flattery. So long as the estrangement between orthodox Italy and the Monophysite Anastasius existed, he acted,
although an Arian, as the tolerant protector of the Catholic Church. 'We
cannot impose a religion,' he said, 'since no one can be compelled to believe

Fig. 22. Theodoric's Mausoleum, Ravenna

against his will', and his control as ruler was accepted without question. The most difficult problem which arose was the schism in the Roman see provoked by the double election in 498 of Symmachus and Laurentius. It took years of synods and the stern commands of the king to secure the acknowledgement of Symmachus as rightful Pope. At this time, if Theodoric had distant hopes of an ultimate assimilation of Goths and Romans, it must have been on a basis of religious toleration, for his Arian convictions were strong and were shown by the churches he built for the Goths at his capital of Ravenna. Protection for the Jews was included in this programme, and a riot against them was severely punished.

Theodoric's good order and his care for the food-supply, both in the tradition of the Empire, gave Italy a last renewal of ancient prosperity and became almost a legend. His zeal for building, public works, and fortifications was on the same model. Late classic art and late classic literature testified in the mosaics of Ravenna, in the learned letters of Cassiodorus, in the works of Boethius, 'the last of the Romans', to the still living *civilitas*, the culture fostered if hardly shared by the king. Until near the close of his reign, Theodoric, Roman citizen, ex-consul, and patrician, endeavoured to act as the preserver and renovator of the past.

But he was also a Germanic and Arian king, and he based his foreign policy on the common interests of the new Germanic kingdoms. He aimed at an alliance of them all to preserve them both from imperial attempts of recovery and from the heedless ambitions of one another. To this end he formed a series of marriage alliances. His widowed sister, Amalafrida, was married (500) to Thrasamund the Vandal, to whom she brought a fraction of Sicily but not Odovacar's tribute, which Theodoric had thrown off. A niece was given to Hermanfrid the Thuringian of inner Germany. Of his daughters one was married to Alaric II the Visigoth, the second to Sigismund the Burgundian, and the third, Amalasuntha, to an Amal, Eutharic. Theodoric himself took for his second wife Audofleda, sister of Clovis the Frank. This elaborate scheme, however, too wide-minded for his world, broke down under the Catholic Clovis's separate ambitions. Such of the still heathen Alemanni who escaped from his overlordship were settled by Theodoric in his dominion. But of vital importance were the overthrow and death of Alaric II at the hands of Clovis (507), who possessed the sympathies of the Catholic Romans of Aquitaine. Theodoric's personal power was indeed increased, for his generals annexed Provence and defeated Clovis's expedition to conquer Septimania, the Gallic Mediterranean coastland, from the Visigoths. Since Theodoric now reigned over the Visigoths in Spain on behalf of his young grandson, it will be seen how large a portion of the Western Empire had fallen under his direct rule. But whereas Clovis the Catholic possessed the loyalty of the Gallo-Romans, Theodoric the Arian was only accepted by the Italians heartily while their rightful sovereign, the Emperor, was unorthodox and unpopular.

The breakdown of Theodoric's system began in 518 when the orthodox Justin ascended the throne of the East, although effusive amity was displayed between the two powers. While Hilderic the Vandal openly broke with the Ostrogothic alliance and courted the Emperor (523), Justin about the same time renewed the persecution of Arians in the Empire, and some senators of Old Rome were engaged in a correspondence with Byzantium which was open to suspicion. One, Albinus, was accused of high treason to Theodoric, and, when the imprudent Boethius, then Master of the Offices, but a novice in the court, declared that if the accused were guilty so were himself and all the Senate, he too was imprisoned and later cruelly put to death (524). So was his father-in-law Symmachus. Theodoric seems to have reverted to his earlier ferocity in his resolve to quell opposition. He compelled Pope John I (523–6), who was personally intolerant, to lead an embassy to Constantinople to demand the repeal of the persecution. The Pope was received with flattering honours and partially succeeded. But presumably the honours weighed more with Theodoric than the concessions: the ailing Pope on his return was arrested and died. The king is said to have ordered the closing of Catholic churches and was certainly preparing for war on Hilderic when he died of dysentery in August 526. These last years of his suggest that, soured and exasperated, he was adopting a new aggressive policy for which his own leadership would have been indispensable. His noble vision had shattered on the passions and prejudices of the time, and vanished from his subsequent legend. To the Germans he was the warrior hero, Dietrich of Bern (Verona), to the Italians the bloody tyrant, the Devil's prey.

From Theodoric's death the years of his system were numbered, but it outlived him owing to the influence of his widowed daughter, Amalasuntha, whom he had left regent for her young son, Athalaric (526–34). She was an able woman, bred in Roman culture and heir to her father's ideas, and she fought an unequal battle with persistence and little scruple. Although she retained the government, the leading Goths soon removed Athalaric from her tuition, and bred him a prematurely dissolute barbarian. She meanwhile sought the friendship of the Emperor Justinian, whose hopes for the reconquest of Italy began to grow.

(4) THE BURGUNDIANS

The Burgundian kingdom, although the weakest and shortest lived of these Germanic states, deserves a brief sketch, not only because of its earlier fame on the Rhine which inspired legend for centuries, but because it was the first to abandon Arianism for Catholicism and its Germanic dialect for the vulgar Latin of its Gallo-Roman subjects. The realm had increased from its settlement in Savoy until it extended from the Rhone and Saône to the Alps and the river Sarine, and from the northern shoulder of the Jura mountains to the river Durance: the tribesmen were most numerous round Lake Geneva. In the last decades of the fifth century three unfraternal brothers shared the land: Gundobad the ex-master of the soldiers in Italy, Godigisel and Chilperic. The last soon died, perhaps by fratricide. These Arian kings were tolerant and on friendly terms with the Catholic bishops and Gallo-Romans, but without acquiring their loyalty. The Catholic Clovis saw his advantage and defeated (500) Gundobad with the connivance of Godigisel. Then Gundobad murdered his brother in a church and became sole king. Although he eluded tribute, he found it best to be Clovis's ally against the Visigoths, to his own loss as it turned out, for he was forced to cede a district to the Ostrogoths. His son Sigismund (516–24) became a persecuting Catholic too late to weld his people into one. He was defeated and murdered by the sons of Clovis. He had already killed his own son. The tribal kingdom came to an end in 534 with the fall of his brother Godemar before the Franks.

In spite of their family history the Burgundian kings may count as enlightened. They had been far from revolutionary, if barbaric beside Theodoric. Some Latin culture persisted among Roman bishops and nobles. The allotment of lands to the tribesmen does not seem to have been oppressive. The kings allowed intermarriage between the two races and prided themselves on being vassals in name of the Empire. They were legislators. Gundobad issued (in Latin) the *Lex Gundobada* for both peoples, and a *Lex Romana Burgundionum*, which consisted of simplified, barbarized extracts of Roman Law, for Romans only. Traces of Burgundian descent are still obvious north of Lake Geneva, in Suisse Romande, where the use of a French dialect divides them from the Alemannian Swiss to the east.

(5) THE VISIGOTHS IN GAUL AND SPAIN

The history of the later Visigoths falls, in spite of overlapping, into two marked periods, the Gallic and the Spanish. In the first their destiny was decided by the cleavage between them and the Gallo-Romans, exacerbated by their fervent adherence to the Arian faith and the rawness of the wounds inflicted on their subjects by the extent of the confiscation of land. In the second the area confiscated was proportionately less, for there does not seem to have been so thick a settlement in so confined a territory, but the divergence of religion hindered not only the piecemeal conquest but subsequent amalgamation. The disjunctive geography of Spain, split up by mountain ranges, terrain, and climate, favoured provincial and sectional disunion even after the belated conversion of the Goths from Arianism. Rivalries and local independence prevented common action and common patriotism.

It was under King Euric (466–84) that the Visigothic dominion was consolidated in Gaul and established in Spain. He overcame the long and valiant resistance of Auvergne led by the Gallo-Roman noble, Ecdicius, the son of the Emperor Avitus. By a peace (475) with the Emperor Nepos,

141

the Loire, the Rhone, and the Mediterranean were acknowledged as his frontiers; by a treaty with Odovacar, Provence south of the river Durance was ceded to him. In 469 he began the conquest of Spain, and by the time of his death he ruled the best part of the east and centre from the Pyrenees to the straits of Gibraltar. The Basques, however, held out in the north, and the Suevi in the north-west, while some Hispano-Roman nobles seem each to have maintained a kind of autonomy in the centre.

Euric's great talents for peace and war are manifest, and his aim was the establishment of a Gothic empire in the West. He knew little Latin. He was a zealous Arian, hostile both to Catholicism and the Roman Empire, and this policy of his prepared the eventual failure of his isolated people. Like Gaiseric he refused even nominal subordination to the Empire; like Gaiseric he was on occasion a persecutor of the Catholic clergy, who from his point of view provoked him by open disloyalty. First of the Germanic kings, he issued a Code of Law additional to the Visigothic customs and adapted to their new relations among themselves and with the subject Romans. This appearance of written law, composed in Latin and tinged with Roman influences, was a sign of growing civilization among the Visigoths, while, in spite of some court favour to literature, that of the Gallo-Romans steadily decayed.

The separation of the two peoples was rigidly maintained; intermarriage was illegal, and each lived under their own law. The Gallo-Romans came off badly in the settlement of Aquitaine, for the numbers of the Goths required the surrender of two-thirds (not the traditional one-third) of their arable and one-half of their woodland as tax-free *sortes* for their Gothic *hospites*. Thus the Romans' burdens increased as their wealth diminished. Owing to their culture, they still manned the central administration organized on simplified Roman lines, and their *curiales* exercised their old functions in the towns under their chief, the *defensor*. Their bishops, unless in disgrace with the king, led their dioceses and public opinion as before. But supreme in each city was the Gothic count (*comes*), who was under the Gothic duke (*dux*) of larger areas. The Goths were grouped in thousands and hundreds, and under Euric were judged by Count and thousand-man (*millenarius*) jointly. Their Arian liturgy was in Gothic; their bishops were appointed by the king. Mutual propaganda, persecution and violence *versus* disaffection, embittered the minds of both peoples.

The king ruled his realm with little check, residing mostly in Toulouse, where his treasure was kept. He was installed by a kind of election or recognition of varying importance by his people from the line of Theodoric I, the son-in-law of the great Alaric. Under him the Goths lived as landlords, great and small, whose land was tilled by their *coloni*, while they hunted or went to war. Roman luxury made headway among these often idle barbarians, at least among their nobles who received the larger *sortes*.

Fig. 23. Lex Romana Wisigothorum

In spite of its imposing extent, the inner weakness of the kingdom became clear when Euric was succeeded by his feebler son, Alaric II (484–507). The new king dared not face an attack from Clovis the Frank, who was already on good terms with the Catholic bishops of north Gaul, although he was still a heathen. In 486 he surrendered to Clovis the fugitive Gallo-Roman 'king' Syagrius, whose state had just been conquered by the Frank. Evidently Alaric II knew he was no match for the conqueror. His efforts to obtain the loyalty of his Catholic subjects, if they were punctuated by disciplinary measures against disaffected bishops, were continuous and ineffectual, especially after Clovis was baptized in 496. He allowed their church councils to meet, and when the Frankish attack was imminent he issued the *Breviarium Alaricianum* (506) for their benefit. This was a compendium of Roman Law, carefully and intelligently simplified by experts and approved by a Gallo-Roman assembly for the use of Gallo-Romans. Roman Law was still a mystery to the unlearned, and the *Breviarium*, although merely practical in its aim, had merits of arrangement and clearness which kept it in general use west of the Alps for those who followed Roman Law.

Clovis was persistently aggressive, and in 507 he invaded Aquitaine, while Gundobad of Burgundy attacked from the east. At Vouglé in Poitou

Alaric was overthrown and himself slain by Clovis's own hand. It is noticeable that the Gallo-Romans of Auvergne fought hard at Vouglé for Alaric, but in general the Catholics welcomed their more barbaric Frankish deliverer. Theodoric the Ostrogoth, who had been held up from assisting Alaric in time by a hostile move of the Emperor Anastasius, did indeed preserve Provence and Septimania, the coastland from the Rhone to Spain, for the Goths, but otherwise the frontier now ran along the Pyrenees, and the second or Spanish period of Visigothic history began.

After overthrowing a bastard of Alaric II, Theodoric the Great took over the government on behalf of his grandson Amalaric (507–26), and ruled with his accustomed benevolent firmness. Under Amalaric (526–31) the perils of the Visigoths—Frankish aggression, their own insubordination, their persecuting Arianism, and their imperfect control of Spain—returned in full force. Amalaric, the last of his line, was murdered after receiving a defeat from the Franks, due to his ill treatment of his Catholic Frankish wife. The situation was saved by a new king, the Ostrogoth Theudis, an ex-viceroy of Theodoric (531–48), who victoriously repelled the invasions of the sons of Clovis. Other enemies now came to the fore. The great Spanish nobles, miniatures of Syagrius, who held most of Baetica (Andalusia), defeated King Agila (549–54). A rival Visigoth, Athanagild, called in Justinian, then in the full career of his recovery of the West. The East Roman troops easily conquered the pro-Roman south from Cartagena to the Atlantic, while Athanagild became king (554–67) with Toledo as his capital. Some revival took place: he repulsed the Franks from Septimania and married his two tragic daughters to Frankish kings, and he endeavoured to win over his Catholic subjects by his tolerance. His successor, Leovigild (568–86), was the greatest king of Visigothic Spain, pursuing by dint of wars on all sides the unification of the peninsula and the consolidation of the tottering royal authority. His adversaries were both within and without. There were the Suevi in the north-west, fortunately disunited, the Basques in the Cantabrian mountains, and the petty Hispano-Roman princes of the west-centre. There were the Byzantines in the south and the aggressive Franks to the north. Internally there were the discontented subject Catholics and, as hostile as any, the rival Visigothic nobles, all of them restive under royal control and each thinking that he had as good a right to seize the crown as the actual wearer.

Leovigild's earlier campaigns were directed towards enlarging or reasserting his dominion. The Suevi, now Catholic, had been encroaching under their king, Miron. Leovigild shore off land in the later province of León, and although he professed himself a Byzantine vassal, conquered Cordova from the Emperor and split the east Roman territory in two. On the death of his co-regent brother Liuva he showed too clearly his design of leaving the kingdom to his own two sons. This led to a widespread revolt from Cordova to Narbonne of Visigothic nobles and Roman subjects old and new, while Suevi, Basques, and Byzantines renewed the fray. Yet the king came out victorious from the contest, punishing the rebels with extreme severity. Executions and confiscations were his method of strengthening the monarchy: it seemed ferocious even to the Franks. By 578 he appeared to be supreme.

It was now that the religious question took the foremost place. Hitherto Leovigild had been a persecutor by the way, but in 579 his son Hermenegild married the Frankish princess Ingundis, a Catholic. The pair were sent to live at Seville, and there Hermenegild, instigated by his wife and the Archbishop Leander, abjured Arianism. Not only that, he rebelled with the support of the Andalusians. At first Leovigild tried to bridge the gulf by a joint synod of Arian and Catholic bishops at Toledo (580), in which easier terms of conversion were offered to the Catholics. When but few accepted them the king resorted to fierce persecution—banishment, death, and confiscation—without gaining many converts thereby. The war then blazed out with Suevi, Basques, Byzantines and Andalusians. Leovigild drove back the first two, building his new city of Vitoriá to hold down the Basques (581); he bribed the Byzantines to desist. Seville was captured after a two years' siege, when Hermenegild surrendered (585), and was killed in prison since he refused to revert to Arianism. Meanwhile, a new, usurping king of the Suevi, Andeca, was routed and the Suevic territory finally absorbed in Spain (585). The Franks, too, were being checked at sea and in Septimania by Recared, his second son, when Leovigild died in 586. It was the death-knell of the Arianism he had championed.

King Recared I (586–601) succeeded his father without difficulty, and at once set about a religious revolution. The personal inclination of the king and many other Visigoths after long-continued contact with their Roman neighbours probably had a share in his decision, but the political motive was overpowering: fusion into a united Spanish people was a necessity if the kingdom was to endure, and this was only possible if the Gothic minority, who were dropping their Germanic tongue, accepted the Catholicism of the Latin majority. After preparatory precautions against resistance, the king called a Council at Toledo (the third so-called), where after debates between the rival prelates Catholicism was formally adopted in May 589 in a declaration approved by Recared, five archbishops, sixty-two bishops, and many nobles. Henceforward the Catholic hierarchy was the mainstay of the royal power, and its authority in the divided state steadily grew. Not all the Visigoths were amenable to persuasion. A strong Arian faction remained to revolt and conspire, in spite of the burning of their doctrinal books, until the fall of the kingdom. Recared himself kept the upper hand over Arian rebels, the untamed Basques, and more Frankish incursions. His new faith procured him the mediation of Pope Gregory the Great in a peace with the Byzantine Emperor Maurice on the basis of the *status quo*. In short, his policy was directed to consolidation, not to expansion.

But Recared could not establish a lasting dynasty and with it a stable monarchy. It was in vain that to the regal pomp assumed by his father he added the unprecedented ceremony, borrowed from the Old Testament, of the sacring or anointing of the king at his installation by the bishops. It gave an ecclesiastical halo to the ruler which was to affect all medieval history, but it proved a poor defence against rival nobles who saw nothing sacrosanct in the upstart royal house. They clung to the right of free election, which was the safeguard of both their turbulence and ambitions. Recared's son fell before an Arian reaction under Witteric (603–10), which closed in the final victory of the Catholics. In 612 a man of mark ascended the throne in Sisebut, a warrior who was also a pious writer of Lives of the Saints, a sign of the Romanization of the Visigoths. Besides the usual Basque war, he forced the Emperor Heraclius to surrender eastern Andalusia. But his piety (or political and economic reasons now obscure), combined with the intolerance which had been nurtured in the Arian controversy, led him to initiate a persecution, fiercer than any heretofore, of the numerous and prosperous Jews of Spain. Up till then, by Roman Law and a canon of the Council of Chalcedon, the Jews had been treated as an inferior race, protected but excluded from Christian society. Sisebut ordered their immediate baptism on pain of banishment and confiscation. Some thousands migrated to Gaul; the majority submitted and originated the class of crypto-Jews which was long to endure in Spanish history. It is to the credit of Isidore of Seville that he with other prelates condemned these forcible conversions, but the sequel proved that Sisebut carried with him the general approval of his countrymen.

No more than his predecessors was Sisebut able to preserve his dynasty on the throne; the same unsuccess pursued later kings even when they avoided deposition or murder themselves. Of his successors, Swinthila conquered (629) the remaining Byzantine territory on the Atlantic coast, thus completing the occupation of Spain save for the indomitable Basques in their mountains. In the Fourth Council of Toledo, held in the reign of Sisenand (630–6), in which Isidore of Seville took the lead, the forcible conversion of Jews was temporarily condemned and the principle of free election to the crown by bishops and nobles unequivocally established. Under King Chintila (636–40) the Fifth Council of Toledo endeavoured to bolster up the royal authority, and the Sixth renewed the violent persecution of the Jews: the crypto-Jews were forced to sign a *placitum*, promising to act as zealous, persecuting Christians. With King Chindaswinth (642–53), a legislator, there was a vigorous reaction of the monarchy. He executed

700 nobles, while others fled the country to plot abroad. His son, Receswinth (649–72), whom he associated on the throne, allied himself firmly with the Church. From the outset the anti-Jewish canons were repeated in the Eighth Council of Toledo. They were evidently by no means effectual, and the king's personal animus was shown by his independent laws directed towards making the lot of the Jews intolerable. No doubt the unification of his people was a weighty motive in Receswinth's persecution. He endeavoured to appease the rebels, who were led by a great noble, Froja, by a general amnesty after their defeat. More important and more lasting was his legislation. Following up his father's law-making, and the continuous Romanization of Visigothic law, he abolished the *Breviarium Alaricianum* and issued a code for both Visigoths and Romans, the *Liber Iudiciorum* (654). Thus the disintegrative system by which personal or racial law depended on a man's descent, which became the rule in the West with the dissolution of the Empire and remained a fetter on the growth of jurisprudence for centuries, was replaced in Spain by the territorial law of the kingdom.

In spite of the imposing façade of king and law and the Councils of Toledo, that kingdom was more disunited and weaker than before. Regional antipathies took the place of racial, the nobles were no less unruly and ambitious, the peasantry were

Fig. 24. *Votive crown dedicated by King Receswinth*

oppressed serfs. Persecution had made the trading Jews with their widespread kin abroad deadly enemies of the state. And now a new and formidable foe was approaching as the armies of the Arabian Caliph were conquering and converting North Africa as far as the Atlantic Ocean. King Wamba (672–80) had to fight a Moslem fleet as well as to drive back the Basques. He subdued, too, a widespread rebellion under Duke Paulus north of the Ebro. How seriously degeneration was setting in is shown by his ineffectual laws to compel military service from nobles and the too numerous clergy. He was deposed by a trick of the malcontents, who dressed him as a monk during an illness, and the new king, Erwig, pardoned old rebels and submitted to restrictions on the royal power. A kind of reaction followed with the accession of Egica (687–701), who was busied as usual with rebellions, including a plot of the Archbishop of Toledo against his life. Far more ominous was the treason he laid to the charge of the Jews, intrigue with the Moslems, which was likely enough in view of the persecutions. The Seventeenth Council of Toledo replied by condemning all Jews to slavery and the education of their children as Christians. The law was not even nominally enforced in Septimania.

The routine of rebellion and decay was continued till Egica's grandson, Achila, was deposed immediately after his succession (710), when the chief rebel, Roderic, Duke of Andalusia, was elected to his ill-fated crown. Plentiful legend and scanty history remain of the last king of the Visigoths. The legend is of the traitor Julian (really Urban, the Berber ruler of Ceuta in Mauretania): what is certain is that Achila and his kinsmen took refuge with the Moslems. The result was the landing of the Moslem Tariq with a Berber army on the rock which still bears his name (Gibraltar, *Gebel Tariq*, 'Mount Tariq'). On 19 July 711, with some 12,000 men, he utterly defeated Roderic on the shore of Lake Janda nearby. The king disappeared, although it is claimed that he fought on a year or two. Tariq won a harder battle at Ecija, but as far as Toledo the towns easily surrendered: only Seville and Merida stood sieges. Jews and malcontents welcomed the invader. When Musa, the governor of North Africa, came to replace his victorious subordinate, a battle at Segoyuela (713) and some sieges of revolted towns completed the conquest of southern Spain for the Caliph. Basques and northerners held out in the Cantabrian mountains—the conquerors did not care to settle north of the olive-bearing lands—and it was not till 720 that they occupied Septimania, the limit of Moslem conquest.

There had been more room in Spain than in Gaul for the Visigothic invaders and their conquest had been slower. Hence there remained more great and small Roman landowners, although the principles of partition and settlement were the same as formerly. In general the Visigoths retained the late Roman social structure, although they were more rural, less civic, both in habitat and government. The inequality of classes was even enhanced. The country estates were tilled by oppressed *coloni*, free or servile, in the traditional fashion. The cities were still organized under their

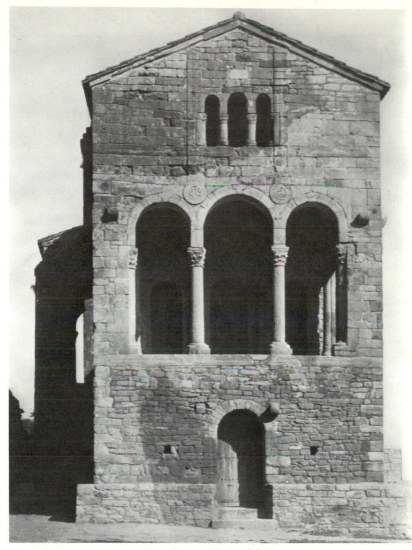

Fig. 25. Santa Maria del Naranco

curiae and compulsory gilds (*collegia*), but the burden on the *curiales* was lessened. The Visigoths themselves kept to their organization in the *Sippe*, the kindred-group, and their customs, which find parallels in far-off, primitive Scandinavia, proved in practical life long lived and infectious: they reappear remarkably in the early Fueros, or town charters, of medieval

Spain. But their formal law became more and more Romanized. Euric's Visigothic Code already shows Roman influences, and subsequent laws and changes were all in a Roman direction. The *Forum Iudiciorum* of Receswinth is overwhelmingly Roman in its sources, as are its revisions by Erwig and Egica and the unofficial revision, the *Forum Iudicum*, which was the law-book in the revival of Christian Spain.

While Gothic dukes and counts, etc. took the place of the Roman governors, the mainspring of government was the king, whose power in administration and law-making was autocratic so far as his unruly subjects allowed him to exercise it. Since Recared he was 'the Lord's anointed', and thereby the idea of the State and the lawful monarchy, sanctioned by God, which embodied it, was kept alive. But Church and nobles were also represented by the Councils of Toledo. Before them a new king took a detailed oath prescribing his conduct. They were composed of the bishops and of nobles, who owed their rank now to office or service under the king. The bishops filled the leading role. They alone passed ecclesiastical canons and could propose new legislation to the king. They had the chief share in codification; Braulio of Saragossa was a compiler of the *Forum Iudiciorum*. The laymen took part in lay affairs and the judicial business of the Councils, but the strict and often corrupt alliance of the bishops, royal nominees, and the crown gives the impression of a priest-ridden state. The clergy, indeed, possessed the decaying culture of the time, although there were literary laymen. It was Latin and preponderantly Christian and ecclesiastical. Its greatest figure was the Archbishop Isidore of Seville (*ob.* 636), whose encyclopedia, the *Etymologiae*, was copied and read throughout the West, and was a treasure-house of knowledge, infected indeed to puerility with decadence and barbarism. It was a potent formative influence during the Middle Ages.

It is obvious that Visigothic Spain presents the first, though unsuccessful blending of a battered classic and a nomad barbaric inheritance. This is exemplified, too, in its art, where we find degenerate Byzantine capitals as well as votive crowns and ornaments of fascinating skill and originality. Weland the Smith, the god of metal-workers, may have lost his worship but not his followers.

(6) THE FRANKS UNDER THE MEROVINGIANS

The invasion of Gaul by the Franks contrasts with those of the East Germanic tribes in that it was rather the overflow of long-settled neighbours of the province than the close of a series of migrations. Not only did this mean less displacement of the provincials, but it implied a far greater manpower undepleted by centuries of wandering and a solid block of territory both sides of the Rhine which even in the days of the Empire had been wholly Germanized, and which the Franks did not desert as they expanded. In 476 they were cantoned in two main groups. Round about Cologne on the middle Rhine was the kingdom of the Ripuarians; in modern Brabant and Flanders were the Salians, who had advanced as far as the river Somme. The latter were divided into fractions ruled by the descendants of Merovech, the Merovingians. The chief of them was Childeric, who had been the useful federate of the Gallo-Romans in northern Gaul. His son and successor (481) at Tournai was the famous Clovis (Chlodovech).

The talents and character of Clovis, become king as a boy of fifteen, can only be inferred from his achievements and his legend. To all appearance he was a treacherous barbarian, insatiable with dominion and conquest. Without attributing to him any uncanny foresight, we may perceive that he displayed a clear insight into the forces at work in his day, a shrewd calculation, a faithless diplomacy and a geographical instinct reminiscent of Constantine. At the outset he had the good fortune to be a heathen, untrammelled by the Arian convictions of the East Germanic tribes, and he early established friendly relations with the Catholic bishops of North Gaul, who were the natural leaders of the provincials. The death of the powerful Euric of the Visigoths gave him his opportunity. In 486 he attacked and overthrew near Soissons Syagrius, the Roman ruler of North Gaul. Within two or three years, all the cities north of the Loire had submitted to him as far as the frontiers of Brittany and Burgundy, and from a tribal kinglet he had become monarch of a wide state. It was now that his wisdom and his good luck were shown. The depopulated land gave ample room from which to endow numerous Frankish settlers as rewards of victory: no confiscation was needed at the expense of the remaining Gallo-Roman proprietors, and Clovis was able to employ the troops of Syagrius, themselves doubtless mainly Germanic mercenaries. Still more important, he courted and won the firm support of the Catholic bishops in his own territory and the good will of those elsewhere. That he transferred his residence to the Gallo-Roman land about Soissons was natural, yet symptomatic.

It was in 493 that Clovis made his next diplomatic success by his marriage with Clotilda, daughter of Chilperic the Burgundian, who happened to be a Catholic princess. This and the baptism of their children showed the trend of his policy. He then took up arms, as champion of all his neighbours, against the rival and powerful tribe of the Alemanni, who were pressing down the Rhine and west of the Vosges. Over them he won (496) a hard-fought victory near Strasbourg at the head of his composite army. By this time he was ripe for conversion. Clotilda's influence and his own interests coincided. At Christmas 496 he and 3000 Franks were baptized at Rheims by St Remi. 'Your faith is our victory', wrote Avitus, Bishop of Burgundian Vienne, and he voiced the thought of his contemporaries. It was only four years later that Clovis made his inconclusive attack on the Arian Burgundians. The Alemanni, however, remained formidable. From 505 Clovis waged furious war on them. By conquest and extermination he occupied Alsace and the valley of the Main, which was colonized by Franks. The Alemanni became his subjects, save a remnant who took refuge with Theodoric the Great. This conquest began an expansion of the Franks east of the Rhine, momentous for the future, but their centre of gravity was now in North Gaul.

Fig. 26. Gregory of Tours,
Historia Francorum, I, 1

The year 507 saw the rout of the Visigoths at Vouglé and the conquest of Aquitaine to the Pyrenees. How further advance was checked by Theodoric the Great has been told already. Beyond question Clovis was the aggressor. 'It grieves me that these Arians should hold a part of Gaul', he told his troops. The Gallo-Romans and their clergy rejoiced: there was no new confiscation, and the Frankish settlement was thin. Those Arians who did not emigrate Spainwards were soon obliged to conform to Catholicism. On his return north Clovis made a triumphal entry into Tours, wearing the purple, and flaunting the Roman title, seemingly of 'honorary consul', which he received from the Eastern Emperor Anastasius: evidently he was thought an excellent counterpoise to Theodoric. Then he proceeded to Paris (508) which he made his chief residence. It was an admirable choice, easily defensible on an island in the Seine, and on strategic and commercial cross-routes, the natural centre of a kingdom. From it the king of the Franks could reach out to all points of the compass. The Emperor Julian had once chosen it, as we have seen, but it was a stroke of genius in the barbaric Clovis, very little realized by his less gifted successors.

It seems strange that Clovis still ruled only a section of the Franks. Assassination rid him of the other Salian kinglets. As to the Ripuarians, he first incited the heir, Chloderic, an old ally, to kill the king, Sigebert the Lame, and then dispatched the parricide also as the avenger of his father. The Frankish tribes were thus united.

In 511, shortly before his death, Clovis set the seal on his new creation of Francia and on the principles (if they may be called so) of his rule by holding a Council at Orleans of his Gallic bishops: he was aware of the pillars which maintained his kingdom, built on the willing loyalty of Franks and Gallo-Romans, holding the same faith and steadily less separated by unequal civilization as the barbarization of the Romans progressed. It was a sign of episcopal influence and of some slight, but memorable, advance among the Franks that he issued in these years his written Latin codification of the customary law of his own division of the Franks, the Salian. It was primitive, of course, one of the 'personal' laws in vogue in his dominions, but the power which formulated could add to it. In this, as in his other achievements, Clovis was the ancestor rather than the founder of institutions and a realm.

The kingdom of Clovis had been created by his conquests and leadership. It was his property like the alod of the Frankish freeman, and as family property the sacrosanct and rapidly degenerating race of his descendants

Map 3

treated it. His four sons divided the 'regnum Francorum' into nearly equal shares, each taking a part of Gaul north of the Loire and a part south of it. All their capitals were in Gallo-Roman land: Theodoric (not a son of Clotilda) took Rheims, Chlodomir Orleans, Childebert Paris, and Chlotar I Soissons. Their greed made them bitter and faithless enemies. When Chlodomir died (524), Childebert and Chlotar murdered his sons and took his share. Yet Francia, though shared, was still one kingdom: Childebert's death in 558, and the extinction of Theodoric's line with his debauched grandson Theodebald in 555, left the remaining Merovingian, Chlotar I, sole king. Against external foes they had acted in concert. They conquered Burgundy and received Provence from the Ostrogothic Witigis

5. The Rulers of the Franks

(a) The Merovingian Dynasty

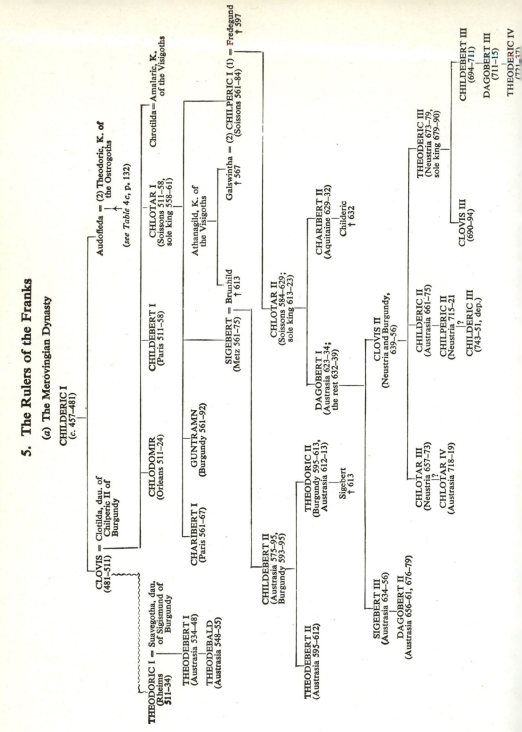

(b) The Arnulfing Mayors of the Palace

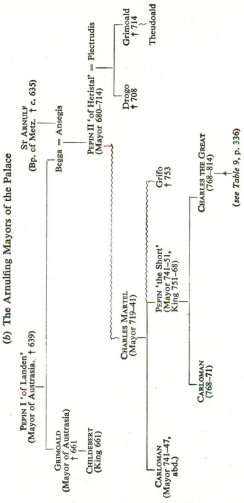

Pepin I 'of Landen,' (Mayor of Austrasia. † 639)

St Arnulf (Bp. of Metz. † c. 635)

Grimoald (Mayor of Austrasia) † 661

Childebert (King 661)

Begga = Ansegis

Pepin II 'of Heristal' = Plectrudis (Mayor 680–714)

Drogo † 708

Grimoald † 714

Theudoald

Charles Martel (Mayor 719–41)

Carloman (Mayor 741–47, abd.)

Pepin 'the Short' (Mayor 741–51, King 751–68)

Grifo † 753

Carloman (768–71)

Charles the Great (768–814)

(see Table 9, p. 336)

155

12-2

in 536. They vainly attacked the Visigoths. Theodoric, known in legend as Hugdietrich (*ob.* 534), and Chlotar I reduced the Thuringians of central Germany to subjection and attacked the Saxons. Theodebert (*ob.* 548), Theodoric's son, the ablest of the family, raided Italy, and even schemed for a coalition of barbarians against the Eastern Empire.

The death of Chlotar I in 561 brought about a new division of the kingdom among his sons. Charibert of Paris died early (567). Sigebert of Metz and Chilperic of Soissons were bitter rivals, with Guntramn of Burgundy as a faithless makeweight. The degeneracy and crimes of these grandsons of Clovis gives them the appearance of lustful ogres, sustained by the magic of their Merovingian blood. But the savage mutual hatred of their queens gives the interest of a drama of blood to events, and real political developments transpire in the close. Brunhild and Galswintha, richly dowried daughters of Athanagild of Spain, married respectively Sigebert of Metz and Chilperic of Soissons. Chilperic stands on an evil eminence even among the Merovingians. He was avaricious and debauched, gluttonous and cruel. He repudiated his first wife, whom he later murdered, to marry Galswintha. Before long he went back to a favourite concubine, the low-born Fredegund. Galswintha was strangled, and he married Fredegund. This crime produced an unassuageable blood-feud with Brunhild, who is almost attractive compared with her enemy. Vindictive, relentless, and domineering, she was highly educated, a patroness of the Italian Latin poet, Venantius Fortunatus, and a correspondent of Pope Gregory the Great. Her husband, Sigebert of Metz, had all but conquered his brother, whom he besieged in Tournai, when he too was assassinated by two slaves of Fredegund near Arras. Chilperic was restored, and Brunhild hardly escaped from prison to rule for her child son, Childebert II (575–95). This closed the first act of the tragedy.

Monster as he was, Chilperic possessed both brains and education, though they showed themselves in surprising ways. He desired that women should on occasion inherit land against the Salic Law. He declared against the dogma of the Trinity, and commanded the word God to be used instead of the orthodox formulas. This philosophic attitude did not prevent his embracing the most superstitious beliefs of the day, Christian and heathen. He set himself up as a Latin scholar, adding letters to the alphabet and composing hymns. He was, says Gregory of Tours, the Nero and Herod of his time. Blinding was the punishment for disobedience to his edicts. In 584 he too was murdered, and Fredegund ruled in the name of her child, Chlotar II.

Meanwhile Brunhild was maintaining herself by war and murder. She overcame at last the great nobles of her son's kingdom, who were now firmly rooted and grasping at power. She succeeded in gaining the succession to Burgundy for her son from the childless Guntramn (592). When

Childebert died young, she still reigned for her two grandsons, Theodebert of 'Austrasia' and Theodoric of Burgundy. Fredegund predeceased her (597), but the nobles of the Rhineland drove her out of Austrasia, while she mastered Burgundy. She then made Theodoric attack his brother, put him to death, and reign alone. Then Theodoric, like a true Merovingian, died young at Metz (613), and Brunhild endeavoured to reign in the name of her eldest son. This was too much. Arnulf, Bishop of Metz, and Pepin, the two founders of the later Carolingians, great men of Austrasia, called in Chlotar II. She was captured and dragged to death at the tail of a wild horse. Her great-grandsons disappeared.

Chlotar II (584–629) had now become the only King of the Franks, but this was due to the treason of the Austrasian and Burgundian nobles and not to his own capacity. He was obliged to accept the programme of the nobles and diminish his own authority. In the partitions and wars of the descendants of Clovis two general developments had taken place. First, the kingdom had fallen into three main territorial divisions, which were particularist although not national. The 'east land' of Austrasia stretched from Rheims to across the Rhine. It thus included nearly all the German-speaking part of Francia with a Gallo-Roman section where Franks were thickly settled. The 'newest land' of Neustria lay between the English Channel and the Loire. It was mainly inhabited by speakers of decadent Latin, which we might call the earliest 'Romance' dialects. To the south-east was the old Burgundian land from Langres to the Mediterranean. Brittany enjoyed practical independence under native counts. Aquitaine, where the Basques, reinforced from Spain, were turning the land south of the Gironde into Gascony (Basque-land), was loosely attached to Neustria. Secondly, in all three divisions there had grown up a powerful landed nobility, either by gifts of the Merovingians to their followers or by descent from the decreasing remnant of Roman senatorial families who played an important part in the State and still more in the Church and episcopate. These great nobles were greedy and tenacious of power, and particularist by reason of their local estates and the permanence of the three great divisions in which they lay. As a result of the bidding for support in the period of civil wars, boy-kings, and female rule, they had their opportunity. On 15 October 614 Chlotar II issued a constitution, supplemented later by an undated *praeceptio*, in which he proclaimed the freedom of episcopal elections, extended the competence of the ecclesiastical courts, and promised to respect wills made by his subjects in favour of the Church, already the greatest landowner. He agreed to suppress unjust taxes and to nominate as counts natives of the *pagus* or county, which meant handing over the office to the local nobles. Further, Neustria, Austrasia, and Burgundy were each to have their own mayor of the palace, who had become the chief administrative officer of the Crown and the leader of the nobles. In

623 he was obliged even to give the Austrasians his young heir Dagobert for their king, under whom Arnulf, Bishop of Metz, and Pepin, mayor of the palace, really ruled.

Some revival of the monarchy was effected by Dagobert (629–39), the last Merovingian who was more than a figure-head. He was sole king. He appointed one mayor of the palace, Aega. He perambulated and governed his realm. He recovered estates given to nobles and the Church, although he was a founder of new monasteries. Indeed he was a patron of the arts, and appointed his goldsmith-treasurer, Eligius (Eloi), to be Bishop of Noyon. Basques and Bretons were his vassals. He was the ally of the Eastern Emperor Heraclius against their common enemies the raiding Bulgars and Slavs. He left a great name behind him.

Even Dagobert, however, was obliged to yield to the great Austrasian nobles: in 634 he named his eldest son Sigebert their special king with a mayor of the palace in Ansegis, son of Arnulf of Metz and son-in-law of Pepin. On his death began the period of the *rois fainéants*. They were a dynasty of children, sometimes of apocryphal Merovingian blood, nominated by the mayors of the palace who ruled. They died young, worn out by precocious debauchery in their secluded *villae*. At long intervals they appeared before their people in the traditional chariot drawn by oxen. Otherwise they were shadows who provided dates for charters.

It was in Austrasia that the great nobles were most firmly in power and that two great allied houses furnished them with natural leaders. Ansegis, son of Bishop Arnulf of Metz, was succeeded as mayor of the palace by Grimoald, son of Pepin.[1] On King Sigebert's death, Grimoald thought the fruit was ripe for plucking. He had the king's young son, Dagobert, shorn of his long royal hair and sent to an Irish monastery. His own young son was proclaimed king. But the Franks could not yet endure a king who was not a Merovingian. They delivered the mayor to the King of Neustria to be put to death, and were content with a separate *roi fainéant* and an Austrasian mayor.

The field was thus left clear for the rivalry of Neustrian and Burgundian nobles. Ebroin, the Neustrian, who was ambitious of becoming sole mayor of the palace of the Franks, was resisted by the Burgundian Leodegar (Leger), Bishop of Autun. In 670 the bishop succeeded in shutting up his rival in the monastery of Luxeuil. He championed the principle that each division should have its native officials and that the two mayorships should go the round among the great men. But Ebroin escaped, captured Leodegar, whom he subsequently put to death, and was mayor for both Neustria and Burgundy till he himself was assassinated (681). It is no wonder that in these civil wars the Dukes of Aquitaine and Gascony made themselves independent.

---

[1] See Genealogical Table 5(*b*) above, p. 155.

Austrasia in this competition possessed the immense advantage of one noble house pre-eminent both by its possessions and the talents of its chiefs. Since Grimoald's fall, his nephew Pepin II of Heristal, son of Ansegis, took the lead and became mayor of the palace (680–714). He repelled Ebroin, whose ambitions he repeated. In 687 he won the decisive victory of Tertry near St Quentin over the Neustrian mayor Berthar, and became sole mayor of the palace for the *roi fainéant*. Only Aquitaine escaped him under its duke. The Franks were reunited under a new dynasty, soon to be named the Carolingians. Their supremacy across the Rhine over Alemanni and Bavarians was restored. It was significant for the future and for Pepin's policy that he was an encourager of missionaries among the heathen Frisians and Bavarians and the Austrasian Franks on the Main. In fact, although Pepin had gained much Neustrian support, the centre of gravity of the reunited realm shifted in an easterly direction, where the strength of the new dynasty lay. While parts of Austrasia, such as Metz, spoke Romance, the Rhineland as far as the coast spoke German. But this meant no division: the great men knew both tongues, and all were Franks.

Pepin II's work nearly fell to pieces at his death. His sons had predeceased him, and following the ineradicable Frankish custom he divided the kingdom among his boy grandsons as mayors, under the regency of his widow Plectrudis. This was to ask for civil war and anarchy, which duly came. Fortunately his illegitimate son Charles (Karl, 'the bold') seized on power as mayor of Austrasia. In three battles (716–19) he overcame the Neustrians. The Burgundians submitted and the realm was reconstituted. Even Eudo, the Duke of Aquitaine, acknowledged his subordination (719). For some years Charles even did without a Merovingian king. While his official style remained mayor of the palace, his contemporaries called him *princeps* or *subregulus*. He gave bishoprics and countships at his pleasure to his own sworn followers. He held the royal court of justice, issued decrees in his own name, summoned the assembly of great men, and commanded the army. From him his house was named the Carolingian.

His greatest victory was gained over the Moslems of Spain. Their northward progress was held for a few years by the able Eudo of Aquitaine, but in 732 a new governor, Abd-ar-Rahman, resumed the offensive. He defeated Eudo, burnt Bordeaux, and marched north past Poitiers to Tours. Here Charles came to Eudo's aid with the army of Francia. His victory was decisive: Abd-ar-Rahman was slain in the fighting, and Charles won, at least in later chronicles, the surname of *Martellus*, Martel, 'the Hammer', by which he is known. The invasion was not renewed; the Moslem onrush had spent itself and civil war occupied the energies of the Caliphs. Charles Martel could begin an ineffectual counter-offensive in alliance with Liutprand, King of the Lombards in Italy.

Charles Martel's record in Germany was that of the restorer of Frankish hegemony. He abolished the dukedom of Alemannia, intervened in Bavaria, and made punitive raids against his north-eastern neighbours, the Saxons. This collection of tribes had long been stirring as their numbers grew, and they retained the plundering habits of earlier times. The defence of the settled Franks on the east of the Rhine was a primary duty of Charles Martel. Like his father, he encouraged the Anglo-Saxon missionaries in their work among the heathen still predominant across the Rhine. But he was not to be led on new paths. When Pope Gregory III sent him the keys of the Confession (shrine) of St Peter and begged his aid against Liutprand (739–40), he turned a deaf, if friendly, ear. He had restored a transalpine realm. On his death (22 October 741) he divided it, in the usual unavoidable fashion, between his two sons, Carloman, who took Austrasia and the east, and Pepin ('the Short' of tradition), who took Neustria, Burgundy, and the west. The two mayors of the palace were to bring a new spirit, without discarding war and conquest, into Frankish government.

(7) FRANKISH INSTITUTIONS

The Merovingian Kings of the Franks, after the conquests of Clovis, were, as far as law went, almost absolute monarchs. The kingdom was their patrimony in which each king's son had an hereditary right to a share. On occasion, but not by necessity, they were raised on a shield on taking the kingship. They might wear a diadem. They declared, amended, and added to the laws, even the Salic Law, and made general decrees, their capitularies. They were supreme judges; they could put men to death without trial; crimes committed by their order were immune from punishment. They made war and peace, levied taxes, appointed all officials. Their orders or *banni* (bans) must be obeyed under sanction of a crushing fine. Their household followers (*antrustiones*) were protected by a triple *wergeld*. The only checks on them were revolt and assassination, to which indeed they were very liable.

The old tribal assemblies disappeared in the rapid expansion of the Franks, save when the host was mustered. Clovis himself, who had wished to preserve from the common loot a chalice of Soissons cathedral, was obliged to give way when a warrior refused: he could only cleave the objector's head at the next military review. The bishops, however, maintained their synods, and in the civil wars the great men of the three divisions of Francia held meetings, which under Pepin and Charles Martel coalesced into one, the annual Field of March; to it the magnates came with their followers-in-arms ready for a campaign. Under King Pepin in 755 the shortage of fodder in March turned the assembly into the Field of May. Those summoned brought the king gifts, soon compulsory and a principal source of revenue in cash; they tried cases of high treason; before them the capitularies were promulgated. They were thus an army, a council, and a tribunal. The Carolingians made the Field of May an institution of great importance.

Around the king were his household and officials, who carried on such central administration as still existed. The Merovingians aped the Empire with increasing inefficiency and inherited ancient Germanic habits. Out of the two elements a new amalgam ultimately arose. Their *Referendarii* drew up their diplomas; their *Cubicularii* had charge of their treasure, the royal hoard. The count of the palace regulated the royal tribunal. But the seneschal (a Germanic office) provided the royal table, and the marshals, with constables (*comites stabuli*) under them, administered the royal stud. Among these officials the foremost place was gradually taken by the mayor of the palace, an office peculiar to the Merovingians. It was a natural development, for the mayor of the palace was primarily the administrator of the royal estates, which in the breakdown of Roman bureaucracy and taxation became the chief source of revenue and power. He filled the king's purse and supported by the renders in kind the royal household. All depended on him; he had a share in the appointment of local dukes and counts and sent them orders to be obeyed. He was in charge of a boy-king's education. He presided for the king at the tribunal and often commanded the army. No wonder that the great men desired to elect the mayor of the palace, and to have one for each of the three divisions of the kingdom. He was the head of the government. When the Austrasian house of Arnulf and Pepin became hereditary mayors of the palace, they took the place of the shadowy Merovingians.

The court was frequented by large numbers. There were local officials come for business. Others were aspirants for office. There were bishops and clergy resident or visiting for like reasons. There were young nobles, 'commended to' and brought up by household officials as a preparation for employment. All these were the king's *optimates*, his *leudes* (his 'people', *Leute*), and by the time of Charles Martel they were the mayor's *leudes*, not the king's. Among them the *antrustiones*, the original Germanic *comitatus*, formed a trusty, if obsolescent, bodyguard.

The kingdom was divided into districts known as *pagi* (German, *Gaue*). These were the old Roman *civitates*, multiplied in northern Gaul and imitated beyond the Rhine. They were far more rural in character than their predecessors. Each was under a count (*comes*, German *Graf*). He was named by king or mayor from any class of society, even freedmen, and any race. He was a kind of viceroy. He kept such order as there was, arrested criminals, held the court of justice (the *mall*), levied the taxes, and executed the royal commands. He paid himself out of his receipts and from an allotted portion of the royal estates. The count's assistant was his 'vicar'; before long the county (*pagus*) was divided into several vicariates, where the 'vicar' took over the duties of the *centenarius* (hundred-man) or *thunginus* of the Salic Law. If occasion demanded it, several counties would be combined under a duke (*dux*) with mainly military functions, and in districts like Burgundy east of the Jura mountains this office was permanent. But dukes could be dangerously powerful.

We have already seen that 'personal' hereditary law prevailed. The Salic Law for Salian Franks and the *Breviarium Alaricianum* for Gallo-Romans were the most widespread. The laws of the Ripuarian Franks and the Alemanni were only partly written *c.* 700. All these customs, written or unwritten, were mainly concerned with scales of fines and procedure. Justice was administered by vicars for smaller cases, by counts for graver, in their courts (*placita* in Latin, *mall* or *mallberg* in German) at fixed dates. They were assisted by freemen (*rachimburgi* or *boni homines*), eventually seven in number, who declared the law and fixed the fines, but the counts could act alone in their perambulations. Above the count's *placitum* was the king's court, presided over by the king or mayor of the palace. It was composed of 'auditors', i.e. bishops, counts or the like. Appeals came to it—treason, questions of taxation, and cases of high officials or of those in the king's or mayor's special *mundium*, i.e. their protection, which included their *leudes*. But in this array of courts little success was attained against the disorder of blood-revenge and the oppression of the strong.

Justice was a source of royal profit owing to fines and confiscations. The army cost the king nothing, for the freeman armed himself. But the complicated Roman taxation, which demanded a civilized bureaucracy, went out of use in spite of the strenuous efforts of the early Merovingians. The remnants of the land-tax, the imperial *annona*, became limited to certain lands which had failed to escape it. Tolls, market dues, and other local exactions were multiplied, but they were depleted on their way to the royal hoard, or granted away to churches, monasteries, or great men. The minting of coin fell into complete disorder in the seventh century. More than 800 local names are found on Merovingian coins. The minters, provided with a licence, went from place to place with their trade, and put merely their own names with the place on their productions. The king's staple revenue, largely in kind, came from the large royal estates, on which he and his household subsisted in favourite *villae*. These scattered properties were administered by the mayor of the palace and his subordinates; some were allotted to the local counts. But at the close of the period, donations of land for good service or as bribes had seriously impoverished the monarchy. Germanic states, financed, so to say, by land, naturally tended to a land-bankruptcy in course of time. The king's gifts, *beneficia* as they were called, in spite of resumptions and confiscations, went to create and strengthen an aristocracy, which save for surviving senatorial Roman families was the product of royal favour and rewards.

The Frankish host underwent a curious development, in which the influence of precedent was marked. To his invading barbarians Clovis added the ci-devant soldiers of Syagrius, and these corps long retained their name and identity. Certain tribes, such as the Burgundians, were liable to special military obligations. Gallo-Romans volunteered and their descendants inherited military service. Others were summoned by the local count with the same hereditary effect. Thus military service of freemen became an hereditary duty, and there were also the followings of the great men. Naturally, when the king or mayor made gifts of land to his *leudes* he expected them to follow him well equipped in his wars with such force as their wealth in land allowed. Charles Martel was already short of land to give, and laid hands on the vast Church estates to endow his warriors. These new life tenancies carried the obligation of military service of a definite kind, that of the fully armed horseman, whose land was to enable him to bear the expense of equipment and campaign. It was part of the development towards the medieval feudal levy and the pre-eminence of mounted and mailed knight in medieval battles.

The Church was the most conservative and most powerful of Merovingian institutions. The king's permission was required for a man to enter the ranks of the clergy, and in theory the standard of selection was rigorous. Clerics were distinguished by their tonsure and a special garb; they adopted Roman Law on ordination, if not born to it. Each cleric was in theory attached to a special diocese (*parochia*). The dioceses corresponded as a rule to the old Roman *civitates*, although new were created and some old disappeared. The bishop was supposed to be elected by the clergy and people of his diocese. In practice the king's or mayor's consent was required, and in bad times the see was given or sold to the king's nominee in spite of the canons of synods. The bishop's power was great. He ordained his clergy, consecrated churches, confirmed the young, and was supposed to nominate incumbents. Under him the arch-priests alone baptized in their circumscriptions, which corresponded to modern English rural deaneries. Under them were the clerics who served the oratories of the *villae* (later parishes): they were presented by the proprietor to whom the estate belonged, and to whom (or to whose ancestors) the building of the oratory was probably due. The bishop's archdeacon superintended the clergy and adjudged disputes. It was the bishop who administered Church property, and that property grew enormously by gifts from wealthy bishops, from kings and from rich laymen, all of whom were anxious to compound for their flagrant sins. The Church always received and never gave back: its possessions were inalienable by canon law. There were other profitable privileges, granted by the kings, such as the right to levy dues at certain places or exemption from dues of toll or market. The Church claimed and largely got the Jewish tithe on the fruits of the earth and the increase of cattle. All this wealth the bishop managed. His secular functions as head of his flock were wide and often beneficent. As the town magistrates disappeared, he took their place. River-embankments, aqueducts might be renewed by him. He was the patron of his people, the protector of the poor, and the dispenser of charity. He could insist on the right of sanctuary for malefactors or victims. He himself could only be tried by a synod, his clergy (after 614) only by him on a criminal charge. In a grossly superstitious age, he was held in supernatural awe. Over the bishops were the metropolitans of provinces, and in distant Rome there was the Pope, but after the death of Gregory the Great (604) relations with the Papacy, never very effectual since Clovis, became very rare till the mid-eighth century.

Fig. 27. Gold coin of Justinian set in a Merovingian brooch

But with all this wealth, veneration, and power the Frankish Church, since Dagobert, was sunk into profound decadence. For eighty years no Council was called. Every vestige of education and civilization was being swamped. Morals and manners steadily degenerated from none too high a level. Charles Martel debased the Church further by giving bishoprics and abbeys to rude, unlettered laymen, who still preferred the sword to the chalice and dissipated church lands on their bastards. Other bishoprics were left vacant. Sees and abbeys were reduced to poverty by his seizure of their estates to supply benefices for his warriors. A complete reform was necessary.

The healthiest and most zealous life of the Frankish Church was to be found in the monasteries. The Merovingians had added to their number and their wealth, and so had wealthy laymen. But these foundations, even when well managed, enlightened only slightly the darkness outside them. Most austere were those founded from 585 onwards by the Irish monk, St Columbanus (*ob.* 615), and his disciples, such as Luxeuil and many others, which followed his sternly ascetic rule. These monks not only preserved learning and devotion, they were informed by a missionary spirit among Christians and heathen. It is true that their penitentials for the laity fostered by their scale of penances the compounding for errors and crimes by donations to the Church. None the less their zeal was an inspiring force for present and future.

Merovingian society was composed of definite gradations, marked by the *wergeld* at which each was assessed. The lowest was the slave. He might be born one, or have become one as a prisoner-of-war or a captive bought in the market. The word slave, which came eventually to replace the Latin *servus*, was due to the number of Slavs brought from the east as slaves. An insolvent debtor or a freeman who married a slave-girl fell into slavery. The slave was a mere chattel, often ill used. The fine paid to his owner for causing his death was that for the killing of a horse. But the Church declared his marriage before a priest a legitimate union. A slave could be enfranchised before the king or the Church, but usually his master merely gave him a written statement, which made him a *libertus* (freedman) or *lidus* (the half-freeman of ancient Germany). Above the *lidus* came the *colonus*, the peasant, theoretically free, but tied to his inalienable holding as in the Later Empire. In the gross these three classes were the inhabitants of the great estates.

Higher again came the freemen, each living under or 'professing' his hereditary law. A Salian Frank was rated at twice the *wergeld* of a Roman, but this did not prevent the intermingling of the two peoples, who were united in the same religion and equally eligible for office. If the Franks learned to speak 'Romance', the Romans adopted the customs and the Germanic names of the invaders. There had been no nobles among Clovis's Franks, but little by little there grew up an aristocracy of *potentes* or *priores*, who owed their status to the king's service and the ample lands he gave or allowed to them. The nucleus of this class, at least in Neustria and the West, was the remnant of the Gallo-Roman senatorial families, who still possessed vast estates. These families, though diminishing in number, filled bishoprics and offices, and were joined by well-endowed Franks, and others enriched and promoted by later kings. The amalgam formed the unruly aristocracy of the civil wars.

Their power had been much increased by the ever-rampant disorder. The poor and the weak sought security in their protection. They put themselves under the *mundeburdis* (Frankish) of, or in Latin 'commended' themselves to, a powerful neighbour: he promised to support and favour them; they promised to serve him in war and on all other occasions. To mark these new conditions a new sense was given to ancient terms. The protector was called the *senior* (*seigneur*, 'lord'), the client a *vassus* (vassal, originally 'servant'). The number of *vassi* which a king, great officer, or noble possessed became the true criterion of power, and the free population, as well as the servile, came to be composed of groups of men bound to each other by personal ties. This germ of the later feudalism was already present, although not omnipresent, in the seventh century.

The subordination of persons was supplemented by and often combined with a subordination of lands, which was pregnant of future history. The greater part of rural Gaul at the Frankish conquest was divided into great estates called *villáe* or *fundi*. So much was this the case that a preponderant number of inhabited centres were named from the original proprietor, and the names have descended to modern villages. Thus Victorius's *villa*, Victoriacus, has resulted in the modern Vitrac, Vitrec, Vitré, or Vitry according to the local dialect. The same thing happened with new Frankish proprietors: *Theodonis villa* has become Thionville, *Arnulfi curtis* Harcourt. The system may have been in vogue even before the Romans conquered Gaul. However, in the custom of the Later Empire, the proprietor would keep one part of his *villa* as the home-farm; the rest was divided into holdings, called *mansi*, cultivated by *coloni*, *lidi*, or slaves. Thus they were distinguished as *mansi ingenuiles*, *lidiles*, and *serviles*, according to the status of the cultivator. In return for his holding the peasant rendered dues and services on the home-farm, more or less according to his status. A *villa* was in the main self-sufficing with mill, wine-press, forge, and oratory or *capella*, the future parish church. Its woods and waste, generally extensive, belonged to the landowner, with a right of use left to the tenants. Over its inhabitants, free and unfree, the owner exercised a magisterial jurisdiction.

This economy was on the Late Roman pattern. Beside it there were the small estates of the plain freemen. But their number waned in the seventh century. The small landowners found safety in 'commending' themselves to a *senior*, and surrendered their land to him, receiving it back as a life-tenancy. From their *alod* (free inheritance) it became a *beneficium* (benefice) granted by the *senior*. The same thing happened with regard to the Church, which already let out part of its vast lands on a similar Roman tenure, the *precarium*, for cultivation and improvement. It is estimated that a third of the land of Gaul had become Church property by Charles Martel's time.

It is obvious how much a great man's power was increased by the number of *vassi* who held benefices of him. Hence kings, mayors of the palace, and nobles alike gave first alods and then benefices from their own lands in return for services rendered and in order to recruit and retain fighting *vassi*. Charles Martel, finding the stock of land he could give depleted by his predecessors, solved his problem by seizing on Church estates and granting them to his warriors not in full ownership but as life benefices. In this way a definite military service was attached to the benefice which supported its expense, and another characteristic of later feudalism took shape.

A third element in feudalism was growing at the same time—the exercise of State functions by the landowner. The royal estates had always been to some degree exempt from the ordinary public officials, such as the count, so far as their policing went. This privilege was retained by them when given away to Church or laity. It was a valuable right, for the count and his like could often be very oppressive. To churches certainly, to great landowners probably, the same rights could be given by charter for all their lands, the so-called *immunity*, which forbade public officials to enter them for taxation, policing or holding courts, or for levying for the host. Henceforward the 'immune' landowner did these things for the government, and though he was bound to produce accused tenants at the *placitum*, no one else could. For lesser matters his private court for his domain took the place of the public *placitum*. Immunity was not only given as a matter of privilege; it was also an easier means of keeping some sort of order by the interested activity of the local great man. Thus a set of new institutions was growing up beside those of the State: commendations, benefices, and immunities, ready to become feudalism when the State decayed. Tendencies similar to these were to be seen in other Germanic states, but nowhere else were they so clear and systematic as in Francia, which became by its extent and conquests the focus of a new order.

When it is compared with the Roman Empire it replaced, the Merovingian period appears as an eclipse of civilization. The old organized, centralized, bureaucratic government, with its hierarchy of officials, its penetrating control, its city-councils, gave way to turbulent counts and nobles and endemic disorder. Its civilized law, its security, its public works, and its intercommunication alike failed, while its heavy taxation dwindled to mere unrequited exactions. Public buildings fell into ruin; town population decreased still more, leaving vacant spaces within the walls, as trade withered away. Such commerce as remained was chiefly exercised by foreigners from the East—largely Syrians, who brought papyrus, ivories, and textiles, or Jews, whose connexions were to be found among Moslem countries as well as Christian, although there were Frankish merchants who dealt with inner Germany and the Slavs beyond it, such as the remarkable Samo who ruled a Slav kingdom on the upper Elbe in the early seventh century. Marseilles, Arles, Narbonne, Clermont-Ferrand, Bordeaux, Orleans and Verdun were still seats of trade. But most industry was practised in the *villae* for the local needs. As with the Visigoths, smith's work was the most living art, and showed a barbaric beauty of its own. Literacy almost vanished outside the Church. The only Merovingian poet in Latin was Fortunatus, an Italian immigrant under Queen Brunhild. Germanic lays have not been preserved. The native Bishop Gregory of Tours was a historian who could describe a character and tell a story with extraordinary vividness, but not in grammatical Latin. 'The world is growing old,' wrote some author of the time a little later, 'the keenness of intelligence is becoming blunted in us.' The best culture was not Frankish but that of the immigrant Irish monks. Under the surface, disguised by the various 'personal' laws, an amalgamated if barbarized people, thinned and toughened, was forming out of its diverse elements.

(8) THE ANGLO-SAXONS AND THEIR SETTLEMENT IN BRITAIN

The Germanic peoples who first raided and then settled in Roman Britain were divided into three main stocks of allied tribes speaking dialects closely akin. These stocks were the Angles from modern Slesvig, a part of which, Angeln, still preserves their name, the Saxons from Old Saxony by the rivers Elbe and Weser, and the more enigmatic Jutes, who may have originated in Jutland, but who in all probability had formed temporary settlements near the Franks and the Frisians. To judge from the scanty written and plentiful archaeological evidence there does not seem to have been a collective or homogeneous migration of any of these tribes. Save for the Angles in Slesvig, they had not had royal dynasties to hold each tribe together, and their invasions appear as the separate ventures of chiefs with their *comitatus* and other followers. In these ventures men of different tribes would take a share, and we find Saxons mingled with Jutes and with Angles, not to mention the closely allied Frisians and even Suevi. Their range was wider than Britain: Saxons had settled near Boulogne and Bayeux and on the Loire; an Angle chief, Wuffa, may, by a risky conjecture, have served Totila in Italy before settling on the Saxon Shore. The result was a piecemeal settlement in separated districts and tribelets which gradually coalesced into petty kingdoms.

Three main routes of penetration along estuaries and waterways stand out as early used, but they were supplemented by others on less inviting coastlines. They were along the Thames, the Wash and the Humber. The invasion by the Thames is linked with the name of the Jutish hero Hengest and with his dealings with the British ruler Vortigern in the mid-fifth century. A contemporary Gallic chronicle could even say that in 441–2 Britain was reduced to the dominion of the Saxons. This was doubtless the exaggerated report of refugees, but twenty years later the British Church appears to have been really cut off from those of the Continent. Bede, learned in Kentish tradition, placed the crucial invasion between 450 and 455. It was Hengest and his son or grandson Aesc who established the Jutish kingdom of Kent, the Cantwara, a name borrowed from the British tribe of the Cantii. Saxons, too, appear as working up the Thames in these years to Middlesex, Surrey and Berkshire, and on the coast of Essex. Another entry for the Saxons, early used, was the Wash and its river-systems. Hence they reached the Thames at Dorchester along the Icknield Way, while Angles from the same centre of dispersion formed settlements in the eastern Midlands. From the Humber Angles formed an expanding tribe, the Deirans, in the East Riding of Yorkshire, a less active kingship in Lindsey, and a far more aggressive people, the Mercians, up the Trent, whose name, 'the frontiermen', foretold their future, that of an expanding, aggressive border state.

The wars of Hengest and Aesc appear to have been chiefly concerned with the conquest and settlement of Kent, while independent bands took their way farther inland. But from the hortatory work on the calamities and sins of the Britons by a west British monk, Gildas, in the sixth century, we may dimly discern a great federated attack of the invaders in the later fifth century which ruined what remained of the Roman towns and spread devastation over vast stretches of the country. It has been plausibly suggested that this invasion should be associated with the Saxon Aelle, who over a century later was described by the English Bede as the first 'Bretwalda' (ruler of Britain)[1] and overlord of the lands south of Humber. Aelle's own settlement was in Sussex (the South Saxons), where he founded an isolated but comparatively populous kingdom between the uninhabited Forest of Anderida (the Weald) and the sea, probably between 477 and 491, when he sacked the fortified town of Anderida (Pevensey). In the long struggle with the invaders, the Britons had found a leader from the Roman-ized remnant, Aurelius Ambrosius, who made a successful resistance. This culminated in a signal victory at Mons Badonicus in the years round about 500, which was won over the Saxon host by the half-fabulous Arthur (Artorius), and some forty-four years of semi-peace for the western Britons ensued. They were divided into five or more tribal kingdoms, while the number and stability of the Anglo-Saxon kingships in the east was increasing. Jutes, who appear to have come from Kent, seized the Isle of Wight and the opposite coast. A Saxon chieftain, Cerdic, half-British in blood, penetrated farther into Hampshire at the head of his Gewissae. On the east coast a kingdom of East Anglia, with its centre near Ipswich, was founded. The Deirans spread to York. Little tribes, such as the Hiccas, round Hitchin, and the Wixna, perhaps near Uxbridge, were lodged in the eastern Midlands.

Among the five British kings denounced by Gildas, the most powerful was Maelgwn of Gwynedd (Venedotia), whose kingdom had been founded by his ancestor Cunedda, migrating from Gododin (north of the Wall, on the east coast) with his tribesmen towards 400. Maelgwn's death in the plague of 547 evidently gave the Anglo-Saxon kinglets their chance. In that year the Angle Ida is said to have landed at Bamborough and thence began to form the kingdom of Bernicia, which was extended by his sons against the fierce opposition of the British, or as the newcomers called them the Welsh (i.e. foreign), kings north of the Wall. Perhaps to this date belongs the Welsh defeat at Catterick at the hands of the Deirans, of whom a second Aelle appears as first king.

The Mercians, too, were clearly spreading around Repton to north and south, but the most victorious tribe was the West Saxons. Here the dispute

---

[1] The ancient word Bretwalda for these overlords does not, however, appear in Bede's Latin history.

is still unfinished as to whether this people arose round Dorchester-on-Thames coming from the Wash, as the archaeological evidence suggests, or whether we should follow the tradition of the *Anglo-Saxon Chronicle* which describes the advance of their dynasty from Hampshire. The best present solution of the difficulty is here adopted,[1] that the dynasty, though not the tribe as a whole, did really advance from Southampton Water in some alliance with the Hampshire Jutes. Cynric of the Gewissae defeated the Britons at Old Sarum in 552—the dates are not trustworthy—and again at Barbury Down (in 556?). The conquest of most of Wiltshire seems to be implied. His son Ceawlin was a warrior renowned enough to be considered the second Bretwalda, who dominated his neighbours south of the Humber. We are told of his victory over Kent (568?), and of his kinsman Cuthwulf's victory of Bedford (?) and his conquest of Aylesbury from the Welsh. If this version of events is admitted, by this time the Gewissae must have joined hands with the West Saxons on the Thames and added to their settlements. There followed a decisive victory as Ceawlin turned west. In 577 (?) he overthrew three British kings at Derham and brought his frontier to the Severn. It must have been about this date that the Hwicce, a West Saxon tribe, established themselves in Gloucestershire. Ceawlin's next aggression was northward. He fought the Britons (584?) at Fethanleag (Stoke Lyne in Oxfordshire) and looted the countryside. The battle may have been a defeat, and we hear of civil fighting at Wansborough in Wiltshire and Ceawlin's expulsion by his own people (592). His greatness was over, but his wide kingdom of Wessex, under princes of a prolific dynasty, remained. For a while his old enemy, Aethelberht of Kent, could figure as third Bretwalda of the south.

The expanding energy of the Anglo-Saxons next showed itself in the north, in the twin kingdoms of Deira and Bernicia, known jointly as Northumbria. Aethelfrith of Bernicia (593–617) became King of Deira also, driving the Deiran Edwin into exile. This conqueror extended his kingdom to the Irish Sea, exterminating or subduing the Britons. A victory at Dawston in Liddesdale (603) over the Scottish King Aidan from Argyll shows both his mastery of the north and the extent of the league against him. Some twelve years later he overthrew a league of more southerly British kings at Chester and finally split the Welsh of Wales from their kinsmen north of the Wall. This great and rapid extension of territory made Northumbria the most powerful Anglo-Saxon state, but at the expense of its solidarity.

The conquest of Britain by the Anglo-Saxons differs in some essential ways from those of the other Germanic tribes on the Continent. They re-

---

[1] Proposed by Mr J. N. L. Myres, *Roman Britain and the English Settlements*, and modified by Prof. Stenton in *Trans. Roy. Hist. Soc.* (1940) and in his *Anglo-Saxon England* (1943).

tained and imposed their own language; they kept their own barbaric institutions and customary laws with barely a vestige of the Roman fabric; Roman and Celtic systems of cultivation left few traces; like the Franks, they were heathens, but unlike them, Christianity was erased in the conquest; they were nearly untouched by Latin culture; their kingdoms were formed piecemeal, not as a unitary conquest.

The retention of their own language, the ancestor of modern English, with the smallest admixture of British or Latin words, runs parallel with the almost complete imposition of new place-names, not only in the earlier but in the later stages of the conquest. The few survivals of the older nomenclature consist mostly in river names and other natural geographical features, and are often generic, like 'Avon' ('river'), although it is possible that more lie concealed under an Anglo-Saxon name of similar sound, like Sorbiodunum under Searobyrg (Old Sarum). It is evident from these facts, coupled with the express literary evidence, that in the period just narrated wholesale massacre and flight of the Britons were frequent, and that the invasion was a real migration, however piecemeal, of the Anglo-Saxons. Yet there is other evidence in place-names and laws that Welsh communities and slaves survived among the conquerors: in some districts, such as the Fens and Chilterns, they were considerable, while the rapid extension of Aethelfrith's and later conquests resulted in subjugation more than in replacement of the conquered. Much of the land had always been uninhabited forest, much had been emptied by over a century of ravage since the raids of 365. Thus there was room for new settlement. In those ravages, too, the educated Romanized classes had been thinned out almost to extinction; their last efforts may be seen in the careers of Aurelius Ambrosius and Arthur. The new Welsh kings and tribes surviving in the west were Britons with but small tincture of Roman civilization or language. Those peasants and women who continued as subjects or slaves in the east were scarcely higher in civilization than their new masters and very likely still heathen, and contributed little or nothing to their cultural equipment.

Much the same breach with the Roman past was shown in economic life. The ruined villas and many towns were left deserted. The Anglo-Saxons were country-dwellers. They also preferred the lowlands beside rivers with their heavy but fertile soils for their cornfields, and they already used a heavy wheeled plough for their cultivation in long strip fields. The Celtic oblong fields have been revealed by air photographs on the light-soiled slopes of the downs and uplands. It is true that the southern Britons had known the heavy plough with its coulter, and their valley fields may have been effaced by the new Anglo-Saxon strips, but none the less the down fields were now deserted. In like manner the new colonists, earliest perhaps in Mercia, began the felling of the vast primeval forests for fresh settlements, where Roman clearances had but feebly preceded them. The process was to continue for centuries as the population grew, and to change the face of Britain.

Save in Kent, where conditions more like the past prevailed, the invaders in this early period settled mainly in little groups, 'nucleated' villages, and these villages were held largely by groups of kinsmen; indeed the solidarity of the *maegth*, the kinship, could hardly be maintained otherwise. But there were also the villages held by a lord or petty chief and his dependants, a method which did not exclude the kindred-group in the same place. In fact, the village names ending in *-ing*, which denote both relationships, are thickly clustered in the regions of the early, heathen, cemeteries. The villagers cultivated their arable largely on the two-field or even three-field system, which will be described later, with common pasture, waste, and woodland. Two ranks, above the slaves, were usual, the *eorl* or noble, and the *ceorl* (churl) or ordinary freeman. In Kent, which was first conquered by—the legend says ceded to—the more advanced Jutes, there was also an inferior class of half-free *laets*, presumably the British remnant. Indeed, Kent, with its Frankish affinities and neighbourhood to the Continent, preserved noticeably more of Romano-British ways than other kingdoms. Northumbria, especially Bernicia, kept up a village-system which showed markedly British rather than Roman affinities, and in later Wessex at any rate the Welsh freeman had a definite place in the social scale.

The villages were grouped in regions (*regiones*) which might be sub-tribes. In any case the Kentish *regio*, the later lathe, was an administrative division with a royal estate as its centre. The tribe, if it was to prosper, was ruled by its king, who claimed descent as a rule from Woden. These kingships were formed by the war-leaders of the conquest. They held the tribe together in peace and war, and were endowed with lands and the right to food renders from their subjects. Round the kings met the assembly of their folk, or at least its notables, for justice and the like. Presumably similar folk-moots existed for the 'regions'. Though far from democratic in the modern sense, there was a barbaric freedom in their tribal methods. The elaborate system of *wergeld* was in full vigour like the kinship feud it modified. It gave every advantage to the 'dear-born' man, but the penalty was declared by an assembly of neighbours.

The cultural equipment of the earlier immigrants outside Kent was poor enough, although metal-working, weaving, ploughing, and boat-building of considerable skill were parts of it. Vegetables and fruit trees came to them from the Roman world, perhaps in Britain. But, probably in Kent, their smith's work after the conquest acquired a remarkable excellence. In the decline of the Empire the Britons' native talent for artistic design of a curvilinear, symbolic type in pottery and the like had come again to the fore, and its tendencies and patterns seem now to have blended in some workshops with the smith's art born in the steppes and borrowed by the

Germanic tribes. Beautiful specimens of inlaid ornaments and bowls of the seventh century have been found in the graves of great men, e.g. the king's barrow at Sutton Hoo near Ipswich. Whether the workmen were Jutes or Britons, their art was both a mixed and a local one of unquestionable charm.

The influence of the British population and of continental neighbours is best seen in the burial customs of the invaders. The Angles and Saxons brought with them the custom of cremation, though the Jutes of Kent

Fig. 28. Purse with golden ornament

practised the inhumation of the Roman Empire. In the heathen cemeteries of the north, however, there was a steady growth of inhumation instead of cremation, which lingered longest in East Anglia and Northumbria, where on the whole a Romanized population had been small. All alike brought their gods from Germany. Woden, Thunor and Tiw are to be found in place-names south of the Humber as well as in our week days, Wednesday, Thursday and Tuesday. Their temples can sometimes be located by the meaning of a place-name, as at Harrow-on-the-Hill, and while we hear of special taboos for a priest, it is most likely that a chief was himself the priest of the temple he had built. There tribe or group met for sacrifice and feast in ancestral fashion.

(9) THE CONVERSION OF ENGLAND AND THE RISE OF MERCIA

To this people Christianity came not from their foes the Welsh but from overseas. The British Church, like its offspring the Irish Church, founded by St Patrick (*ob.* 461), had been cut off from close connexion with the continent after *c.* 460. The destruction of Roman organization and of town-life in Britain had had its repercussion on British Christianity. The Welsh were now under tribal kings, whose subjects were organized on a clan system of kindreds. In the south-west were the Dumnonii (Devon), divided from their kindred by Ceawlin; in South Wales the lead was taken by Demetia (Dyfed) and in the centre by Powis; the north was under the powerful kings of Gwynedd. North of the Wall the dominant British kingdom, sorely diminished by Aethelfrith, was Strathclyde with its capital at Dumbarton. In the north-west in Argyll and its islands was the kingdom of Dalriada, Gaelic speaking and founded by the immigrant Scots from Ireland in the sixth century, who brought eventually the name of Scotland to their new country. These were Christian, as were the men of Strathclyde after the missionary labours of St Ninian (*c.* 353– *c.* 413) and St Kentigern (527–612). Over the north-east spread the mainly heathen kingdom of the Picts. During the invasions the Britons from Dumnonia to Strathclyde, with their petty kingships, had constantly been forming confederations for resistance under various leaders. The most permanent headship was kept by the kings of Gwynedd. From their alliance came their later national name, the Cymry (*combrogii*, fellow-countrymen), but their actual organization was that of a crowd of princelings of greater or less power. To this situation the Celtic Church in Britain and Ireland accommodated itself. The bishop became a secondary personage. The real centres were the great monasteries ruled in tribal fashion by their abbots, and the strength of the Church lay in the fervour of ascetic monks. St Columba (*ob.* 597) founded his famous monastery in Iona, and soon (565) began the conversion of the northern Picts. It was from the Scottish Iona that zealous missionaries were to be drawn, not from the exasperated Welsh of the south.

It is significant that the conversion of the Anglo-Saxons to Christianity began in Kent, which was both most exposed to continental influences and the most apt to receive them from the former associations of the Jutes; and it was of the most far-reaching importance for the new Church that, like that of Ireland, it was founded and recruited for the most part by voluntary conversions and the free action of missionaries. There was a religious zeal and enthusiasm engendered which had a dynamic result. It so happened that after Ceawlin's fall Aethelberht of Kent (560–616) had acquired the sort of supremacy among the kingdoms south of the Humber which justified the ascription to him of the title of Bretwalda. His prestige is shown by his marriage to the Frankish princess Bertha, daughter of Charibert of Paris. She brought a bishop with her as her chaplain; we may notice that the family alliances between the various kings and the influence of their Christian queens evidently prepared the way for the spread of the new religion. The impulse, however, came from Rome. The great Pope Gregory, stirred years before, according to the story, by the sight of Deiran boys for sale in the slave-market, had burned with zeal for the conversion of these heathen. After becoming Pope, he seized the favourable opportunity and dispatched a monastic mission led by the second St Augustine which landed in Kent in 597. A friendly reception and a tolerant permission to preach were soon succeeded by the baptism of the king. His example was followed by his kinsmen Raedwald of East Anglia and Saeberht of Essex and by large numbers of his subjects, and St Augustine could become the first Archbishop of Canterbury, the Kentish royal town, while sees were set up in Rochester and London, which had by then become the East Saxon capital. But while Augustine, guided by Gregory's instructions, dealt wisely in his pastorship of lately heathen converts, he took an attitude of unbending superiority as the agent of the Pope towards the Welsh bishops, whom he was ordered to gain over for the enterprise. Each party, the Latin and the Celtic, attached immense importance to their particular usages. The Welsh computed the date of the Easter festival by a system which had been replaced in the West for over a hundred years by a cycle already adopted in the East, the Celtic clerical tonsure shaved the fore part of the head and the Roman a circle of the crown, and so forth. These differences and the call to join in the conversion, together with Augustine's haughty airs in conference, led to a complete breach, and the Roman mission was left unaided. Its success was less than appeared at Augustine's death (605), although it had struck lasting root. Its conscientious but rigid leader deserved the praise and the blame.

When Aethelberht died (616) his power had already waned in his old age, and his nephew Raedwald of East Anglia had gained the leadership south of the Humber. This eclectic, who worshipped Christ and the old gods together, was true to a manly code. The exiled Edwin of Deira had been harried from Wales to Mercia and last to East Anglia by the threats of his mighty supplanter, Aethelfrith. Raedwald refused to give him up, and took the offensive. Aethelfrith was slain in the battle of the river Idle close to his borders and Edwin was securely placed on the throne of all Northumbria (617). It seems probable that one of Raedwald's successors is the East Anglian king for whom the funeral barrow at Sutton Hoo near his hall at Rendlesham was constructed. It contained his state ship and arms, utensils, ornaments, and insignia fit for a Bretwalda.

Edwin's reign (617–33) in Northumbria was momentous. He annexed the little Welsh kingdom of Elmet in the West Riding to Deira, and since he subjected the Isle of Man and even Anglesey in Gwynedd to Northumbria he must have possessed a fleet. He was overlord, too, of his Anglo-Saxon neighbours, with the exception of Kent, becoming the fifth Bretwalda. The order he kept and his regal pomp were long remembered; the *tufa* borne before him may have been a ceremonial standard like that in the East Anglian barrow. But his most far-reaching act was his adoption of Christianity. There had been a serious set-back in the conversion. The new kings of Essex and East Anglia were heathen, and there was a strong party of their subjects firmly attached to the old gods. Even Eadbald of Kent, Aethelberht's son, apostatized for a time to marry his step-mother. The Bishop Mellitus was driven from London, a stronghold of paganism, and Archbishop Laurentius was only prevented from abandoning his see by a painful vision. In Kent, however, the mission regained the upper hand, and when Eadbald's sister Aethelburg became King Edwin's second wife, she brought her chaplain and bishop, Paulinus, with her. The king listened to persuasion, and a victory over the West Saxon Cwichelm clinched his convictions, like Clovis's. There was a debate among his Witan (wise men, the notables of the kingdom), which lives in Bede's history. The material argument of profit and loss was advanced by the chief priest Coifi—the gods he served had never rewarded him. Another chief spoke of the mystery of human life—it was like a bird flying from dark to dark through the fire-lit hall: the new faith might enlighten it. Both arguments, perhaps, bear witness to disbelief in the traditional gods in Northumbria. Then Edwin declared for the new faith, and the temple at Goodmanham was desecrated by Coifi himself (627).

Conversions came apace in the north. In East Anglia a Christian king, Sigeberht, erected a bishopric. But the foundations both of Edwin's power and of the Church were insecure. The rivalry of Deira and Bernicia, incarnate in the rival dynasties, was always a source of weakness; the large Welsh population there can hardly have been absorbed, and now there were Christian and heathen parties in both. Outside Northumbria there were heathen and Christian enemies. The central Anglian tribes were restive under any overlord, and they found a leader in the old warrior Penda, who became King of the Mercians. He was a fierce, fighting heathen of the ancient stock of Anglian kings, eager to build up a realm like Aethelfrith. Modern Shropshire and Herefordshire were added to Mercia, the Hwicce on the Severn were subdued (628), and the Middle Angles round Northampton were ready to join. Further, Cadwallon, King of Gwynedd and overlord of the Welsh, was eager for revenge. The heathen champion Penda and the Christian Cadwallon together routed and slew Edwin in the woodland Heathfield, near Doncaster (633). Cadwallon's aims were shown by his long ravage of Deira, whence Paulinus fled amid general apostasy. Penda had enlarged Mercia into a new central state, where he was overlord from the Humber and the Wash to Chester and Hereford. Its chief town was now Tamworth.

Mercia, if it could be consolidated, was in a far better position than Northumbria to dominate all England (Angle-land), under which common name Saxons and Jutes as well as Angles proper began to style their country. But its parts were yet discordant, while Penda had identified it with the losing cause of paganism and Northumbria was still powerful. Oswald, son of Aethelfrith, returned from exile in Iona to lead his countrymen. In 635 at Heavenfield on the Wall he overthrew Cadwallon, who perished in the battle, and then united Northumbria once more. At Iona he had become a fervent convert. He brought a Scottish monk, the gentle and devoted Aidan, to be first Bishop of Lindisfarne and to revive and extend the faith by his preaching journeys. The conversion now was permanent, and widespread. Not only did Anna of East Anglia, father of the famous abbess Aetheldreda (Audrey) of Ely, revive Christianity in his kingdom in spite of Penda's invasions, but the kings of Wessex established what, after some vacillations, proved a permanent bishopric at Dorchester-on-Thames for the independent Roman missionary Birinus. Backed by his coreligionists, who seem to have recognized him as Bretwalda, Oswald was able to press Penda hard, but he overreached himself by invading western Mercia. There Penda could join forces with Cadwalader of Gwynedd. Oswald was slain at Oswestry (Oswald's tree) in the rout of Maserfield (642), and Deira and Bernicia, ravaged by Penda, once more parted company.

Penda's second supremacy did little good for his creed. Wessex became finally Christian in 648; his own son Peada, King of the Middle Angles, was converted c. 653; Celtic missionaries entered the once obstinately heathen Essex. Native Englishmen were being elected to bishoprics and were leading missions, like the Northumbrian Cedd. At the back of all this progress stood Oswald's brother and successor in Bernicia, Oswy, who endeavoured to obtain Deira also by murdering its saintly king, Oswin (651). The threatened reunion of Northumbria sent Penda on the warpath again. In 654 he overthrew Anna of East Anglia, and gathering thirty vassal chiefs next year marched on Oswy's frontier. But his vassals were untrustworthy. At Winwaedsfield in Elmet he met defeat and death (655). Oswy became unquestioned Bretwalda, ruling even Mercia itself for a while.

The rout of Penda was the rout of paganism. Many heathen remained, but missionaries, like Cedd's brother Chad (ob. 672), could ply to and fro baptizing converts. Even isolated and heathen Sussex could at last (681) be attacked and won over by the exiled Northumbrian bishop, Wilfrid. The triumph of Christianity, however, brought to the front a long implicit dilemma. North and Central England had been converted by Irish-Scot monks and followed their usages and organization; Kent and Wessex by Roman missions in close connexion with the Continent. The two had worked side by side with considerable harmony, but with success it became imperative to decide which of the divergent teachings was the English Church to follow. Was it to remain in tribal isolation with the Celts or to fall into line with the common usages and methods of the West? The test question—the date of Easter—was pressed in Northumbria by the Deiran monk, Wilfrid, who had passed much of his youth in Rome and Gaul, and he had many supporters. On the other side Colman the Scot, Bishop of Lindisfarne, stood firmly for the traditions of his Church. King Oswy has the credit of deciding the dispute at the Synod of Whitby (663). He declared for the Roman Easter and thereby set the course of the English Church and secured its internal unity: it could become a unifying force. Further, the decision strengthened the links between primitive England and the civilization, such as it was, of the Continent, where the traditions of the Roman Empire were still alive, unlike the wild, almost prehistoric conditions of the Celtic lands. It also established in England the Roman conception of a bishop. The Celtic missionaries, homely and self-effacing, were succeeded by less attractive prince-prelates, who claimed and took a leading share in directing state-affairs. They brought practical benefits with them, although some of the unworldliness of the Church departed with Colman and his followers to Iona.

No less decisive an event than the Synod of Whitby was the appointment by Pope Vitalian of a new Archbishop of Canterbury, Theodore of Tarsus (669–90). A Greek, a scholar, and an organizer, an old man of inexhaustible energy, Theodore came with the fixed design of weaving the loose strands of the English Church into a united, orderly fabric, disciplined, endowed, and guiding kings and peoples. In 673 he held the Synod of Hertford, the first which took united action for all England. He subdivided the wide tribal, missionary bishoprics into manageable, administrative dioceses against the vain opposition of Wilfrid, whose see of York lost territory, and whose life was subsequently spent in alternate quarrels and reconciliations with kings, in exiles and restorations and intermediate missions which defy a brief history. The English Church was now really organized under Canterbury. Gifts were encouraged and sees and monasteries became large landowners. Theodore's friend, the African Abbot Hadrian, taught a numerous school in the learning of the age, while a Northumbrian, Benedict Biscop (*ob.* 690), set up a similar school at Wearmouth, to which and to his other monastic foundation at Jarrow he gave the books he collected in his journeys to Rome. One pupil of Biscop was the Venerable Bede (672–735), whose histories and theological writings became standard works for the Western Church. The English monks stepped into a leading place in Western culture when Francia was sinking deeper into barbarism.

Taken as a whole, the conversion worked a stimulating, progressive change in English society and government. The new clergy were literate and in close touch with Mediterranean civilization. Barbaric runes on beech wood were succeeded by the Latin alphabet on parchment, and documentary records and literature that was not merely oral began. The clergy formed a separate, superior class with more civilized ideas, which slowly penetrated the laity. They were shown at once in the promulgation in writing of amendments to the tribal customs. Aethelberht of Kent issued a code of amendments which has been preserved, and as Christianity spread he was imitated. It was a step of vital importance, for now there was a law-giving power, the king's, in the state. A small but growing stream of charters began to register gifts of lands and rights from the time of Theodore at least. They meant both record, definition, and slow innovation. The clergy, too, had a conception of an organized government with powers to tax its subjects like the Empire. By Bede's time the various kings had assessed their kingdoms in hides (*higid, hida*), each supposed to represent the normal holding of a family (*terra unius familiae*), reckoning each block of territory as so many hides on a duodecimal system, the 'long hundred' of 120, and then apportioning the total among its sub-districts for the incidence of dues. Thus Mercia proper was reckoned as 12,000 hides in two sections of 7000 and 5000 hides. King and clergy both benefited from their dues and the military levy.

A remarkable characteristic of the new literacy of the English was the use in it of the native dialects, whereas on the Continent Latin was the rule. Doubtless this was due to the absence in England of a Low Latin speaking majority around the invaders and to the speedy predominance of English over Old Welsh in the conquered districts. Save for ecclesiastical and learned needs, laws, documents, and the like were written in the native tongue until the Norman Conquest. Even English poems and lays, religious and secular, were written down. This meant a speedier permeation of the ruling classes by the new ideas, elsewhere secluded in Latin. It seconded the action of the clergy in the growth of English union. The clergy were almost always on the side of kingly authority and of extensive kingdoms. They supported the efforts after a Bretwalda-like dominion, for so the Church, whose structure was not local, would obtain better protection, wider lands, and a less obstructed range of influence in the propagation of Christian ideals. One result on customs of its teaching was the steady decline of the *maegth* of kinsmen as the primary factor in society. Christianity taught individual responsibility and the duty of forbearance. It set in train, bit by bit, if slowly, a movement which broke down the disastrous blood-feud of the group and reduced in the end the *maegth* to a useful instrument for police-purposes. Already under Aethelberht of Kent a crime was an offence against the king, who took his share of the *wergeld*. If not started by the Church, this was in line with its teaching.

To return from this future development to seventh-century politics, Oswy's supremacy was short lived. Mercia was too natural and too strong a combination not to last. On Peada's murder his brother Wulfhere (658–75), a zealous Christian, succeeded to his throne and at once expelled Oswy's officials from all Mercia. With Mercia's unity restored he aimed at a South English supremacy. In 661 the West Saxons were completely beaten, and the lands north of Thames became henceforward a Mercian province. The West Saxon advance just before to the river Parret at the expense of Welsh Dumnonia was for the moment a poor compensation. The submission of the East Saxon and South Saxon kings and the conquest of Surrey and the Hampshire Jutes further hemmed in Wessex. Wulf here was quite equal to a Bretwalda. The final clash with Northumbria came when his equally capable brother, Aethelred (675–704), succeeded to Mercia, and Ecgfrith (670–85) to his father Oswy. Aethelred first subjected Kent, when Theodore of Canterbury showed his foresight by allying himself to the king, who bid fair to be general overlord. Then the Mercian attacked Ecgfrith on the banks of the river Trent, winning so decisive a victory that for thirty-five years no Northumbrian king ventured to renew the war. The Humber was now the frontier. Northumbria was seeking compensation in northern conquests. Edwin had occupied Lothian, where Edinburgh bears his name; the land north of Solway round Whithorn became Bernician; Oswy was victorious over the Picts across the Forth; now Ecgfrith warred on Picts and Scots by land and sea. In 685, however, he met utter defeat and death at Nechtansmere near Forfar at the hands of Bruide, the Pictish king. English expansion northwards was finally checked. From that date Northumbria lost its vitality and gradually fell into chronic civil war. Only its pre-eminence in art and learning was left.

The unsubdued rival to Mercia was Wessex, which had hitherto been handicapped by the number of *aethelings* (i.e. princes of the house of Cerdic), who ruled shares and jostled for all the kingdom. One of these, the bloodthirsty heathen Ceadwalla, seized the throne (685–8). He re-invigorated Wessex, and his successor, Ine (688–726), was overlord of Sussex and a conqueror far into Devon. Like the Kentish kings of the time he issued a code of supplementary laws, which give glimpses of an advancing and partly Welsh society. His piety, like that of the new convert Ceadwalla, was shown by his pilgrimage to Rome to die. Piety and policy alike dictated his large gifts to the Church, and his erection of a bishopric at Sherborne, cut off from Winchester, for his western conquests, where his friend, the very learned and pedantic St Aldhelm, was first bishop.

Mercia, however, reached the height of its power under two great kings, Aethelbald (716–57) and Offa (757–96), the latter of whom took the style of King of all England. Kent, East Anglia, and Sussex were each rendered a submissive, Wessex a restive vassal. Essex and the Hwicce were fully absorbed in Mercia. Offa marked his Welsh conquests by the construction of the still existing Offa's Dyke from the Dee to the Wye, a safeguard against cattle-raids. But men do not fortify a boundary beyond which they hope to conquer. He improved the Mercian coinage, minting the

Map 4

Fig. 29: Offa's Dyke

silver penny imitated from Charlemagne's *denarius*, and even for show a gold *mancus* copied from the Arab dinar, a sign perhaps of the slave-trade. He, too, was a law-giver. Both kings evidently leaned on the clergy. Aethelbald freed the minsters' lands from all public burdens, so that the dues were paid to the churches, not to the king. Offa bought Pope Adrian's assent to the erection of Lichfield into an archbishopric for Mercia between Thames and Humber, as York already was farther north. The arrangement was dropped by his weaker successor, but it had been an unwise move, for it rendered the Archbishops of Canterbury lukewarm to Mercian supremacy.

At the close of the eighth century, as far as can be judged from the evidence, which is mainly southern, the general structure of English society was aristocratic and unequal. The marked distinction of classes and *wergelds* continued. At the top were the *aethelings* of the royal houses, below them the *eorls* in Kent, the *gesiths* in Wessex (a term which suggests that in Wessex service in the *comitatus* of the house of Cerdic, not original

182

nobility, made the 'dear-born' man), then the *ceorls*, then in Kent the half-free *laets*. In Wessex the ordinary *ceorls* were rated at similar values to the Kentish *laets*, which makes it likely that they too had once been half-freemen, whether invaders or Welsh, and there were numerous Welsh landholders, larger and smaller, in the later conquests. The possession of five hides gave *ceorl* and Welshman a higher *wergeld* in Wessex. It is clear that the mass of *ceorls* and Welshmen were rent-paying tenants, who rendered labour services to their lord (*hlaford*) as well as rents in kind for their free or servile holdings, although these were probably heritable, and for the free inalienable. The pressure of lay lord or church lord may have helped to produce or maintain a uniformity of size within the classes of peasant holdings, and so counteract the tendency to subdivision.

The king, like his compeers abroad, moved from estate to estate with his retinue, eating up the produce and the dues in kind which his subjects in the region owed him. In government and most certainly in law-making the king was counselled by his Witan (wise men) in their meeting (*gemot*), attended by bishops and the greatest laymen. They had a voice in and sometimes decided his election, or rather recognition, from the royal kindred. His real power depended on his warlike prestige and the landed wealth from which he could provide a numerous *comitatus*, a process which slowly drained the royal resources, and on the influence of the bishops. The kingdoms were divided into tribal or sub-tribal districts, in Wessex known as shires, whose rulers were commonly *aethelings*, with the West Saxon title of alderman or the Mercian of duke. These held the shire-moot twice a year, attended by *gesiths* and rich *ceorls*, for justice. In all probability the shires were composed of sub-districts, later at any rate called 'hundreds', meeting probably once a month, where lesser cases were dealt with. East and West Kent were composed of lathes, Sussex of rapes, the older *regiones*, and small shires of like character appear in Northumbria. Already in Offa's day some of the smaller districts were no longer supervised directly by alderman or duke, but their jurisdiction and its profits had been granted to a church. Here was a semi-feudalizing development, that was more efficient if disintegrating.

One common feature may be noted in the early Germanic kingdoms described in this chapter, the weakness which sooner or later overtook the efficient power of the kings. Diverse causes, such as the incapacity of barbaric administration, the dispersal of the conquering tribesmen in settling, or the extinction of an unquestioned royal house, may be ascribed for this decline, proportioned according to local circumstances, but one was always present: the impoverishment of the monarchy by its lavish gifts of land, the source of its wealth, to its warriors and to the Church which could ensure eternal salvation and temporal support. England was divided into petty states, and one by one the kingship was weakened in

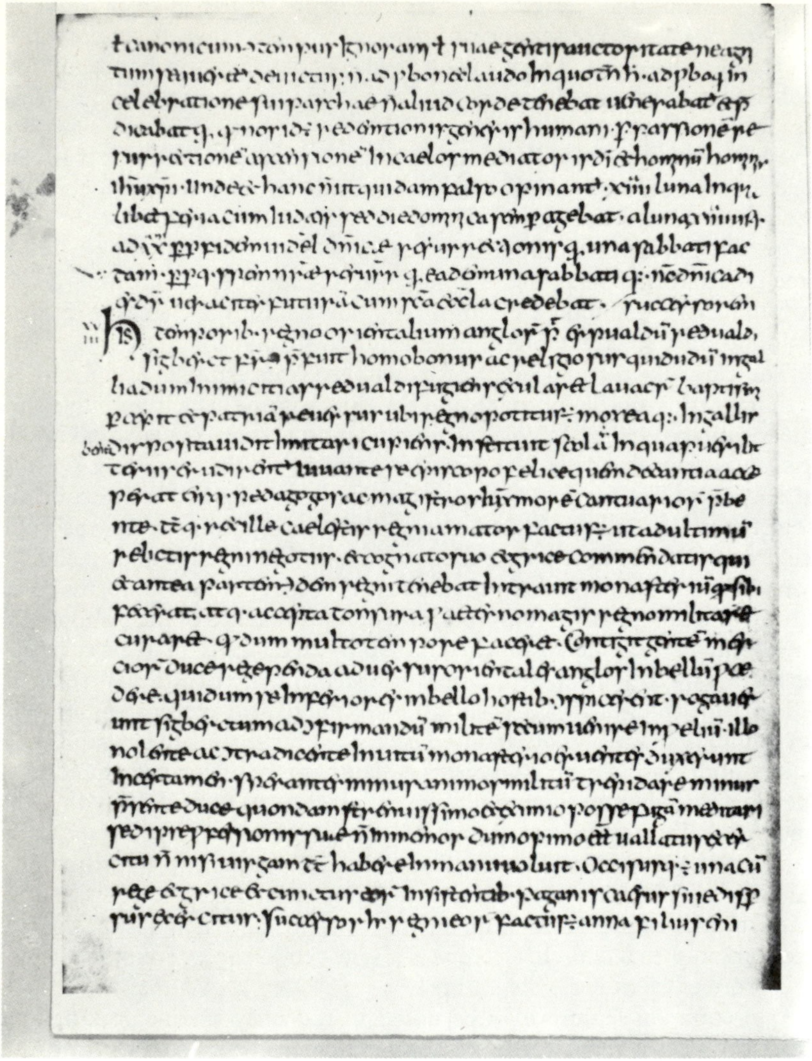

Fig. 30. Page of Bede, Historia Ecclesiastica

each, when no fresh conquests were available to replenish the royal stock
of land. Northumbria failed first, Mercia next (*c*. 800), and only Wessex,
with fresh Welsh annexations and with the extinction of rival lines of
aethelings, was still, so to say, a solvent monarchy.

184

BOOK III

BYZANTIUM AND ISLAM

CHAPTER 8

THE REIGN OF JUSTINIAN

(I) JUSTINIAN AND THEODORA

The death of Anastasius without an acknowledged heir left the succession open to a sordid competition, which ended in the acquisition of the throne by the aged Justin, the captain of a section of the guard, the Excubitors, the other section, the Scholarians, assenting. He was a Latin-speaking Illyrian, a peasant in origin with a creditable military record, but illiterate and incompetent as Emperor. He had two great assets, his orthodoxy and his nephew. Monophysitism had been the stumbling-block of Anastasius. Now the rebel Vitalian was reconciled, and duly murdered during his consulship (523); the disaffection of the Monophysite provinces was disregarded, and the policy of the Empire was now directed by Justin's nephew, Justinian.[1] Born near Scupi (Skoplie), he was a man of thirty-six, a Latin like his uncle, well educated in the capital and experienced in affairs. He was rapidly promoted and shortly before Justin's death was associated as Augustus (527).

Justinian was, in his lifetime, the subject of extravagant adulation and senseless invective, which make it difficult to give an estimate of a man who made history in his own age and who influences by his legislation the world to-day. Some features are clear. He was an emotional man, combining a passion for work—'The Emperor never sleeps', a courtier said—and an equal passion for autocratic rule in the minutest detail: everyone was to obey, everything to be done by, Church and State were to think by, his decisions. He had much of the needful ability; he was a shrewd politician, a tireless administrator, and a learned theologian. He was an instinctive judge of other men's capacities: even when we take account of the vast reservoir of talent in the Empire, it can be no accident that he commissioned the best generals, the best lawyers, the best architects, the best historian, and the deservedly most hated tax-gatherer of the day. He had, too, magnificent conceptions, an almost boundless ideal of the greatness and glory of the Roman Empire, of which he was God-given guide and

[1] See Genealogical Table 3 above, p. 78.

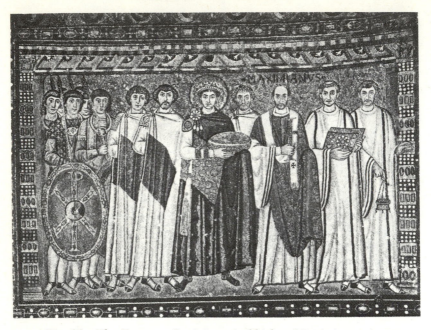

Fig. 31. The Emperor Justinian, Archbishop Maximian, priests and bodyguard

despot, the home of Christianity and civilization, of orthodoxy, of civilized order and government, of the arts, culture, and knowledge. To restore its ancient boundaries, to increase its splendour, to improve its law and administration, to unify its Christian faith, were the aims of his life, all pursued at once with a disastrous megalomania. The Empire paid in pernicious exhaustion for the glory and extravagance of its Emperor.

Yet he missed greatness himself. Vain, conceited, and devoid of genius, he did not measure his ambitions by his resources and overstrained the Empire. In spite of his despotic will, he was subject to moods and vacillation, and could be led by personal influences. Warlike but no warrior, he was jealous of the able men he used and could not outvie; indeed the Empire's history made suspicion of the most loyal generals almost inevitable. His fussy despotism combined with his turn for theology and his passion for uniformity to make him a bitter persecutor. Towards the close of his eighty-three years he neglected his secular duties for his studies in divinity. His defects were the more harmful because of the absolutism of his régime. 'He was the first of the Byzantine Emperors to show himself, by word and deed, the absolute master of the Romans', wrote the contemporary Agathias.

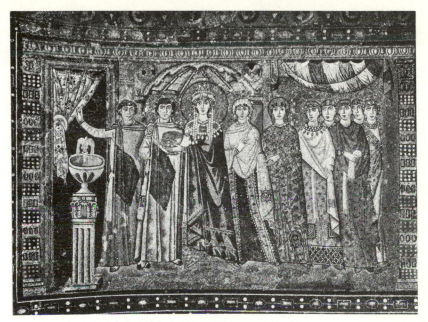

*Fig. 32. The Empress Theodora, priests, and
ladies-in-waiting*

Of all the personalities whose influence affected the unstable Emperor,
the most potent was his wife Theodora. Her career was almost unique, and
its strangeness and the furious animus of the historian Procopius in his
Secret History make it hard to distinguish between slander and fact. She
was the daughter of a bear-keeper of the Hippodrome, the great scene of
the shows of Constantinople, where she passed a scandalous youth as
actress, mime and courtesan. She was deserted by a lover at Alexandria.
There she came under the influence of leading Monophysites, who appear
to have led her to amend her life. Returning to Constantinople, by her
loveliness, charm and intellect she made a conquest of Justinian, who induced his uncle to change the law to enable him to marry one of her outcast class (523). She maintained her power over her husband till her death
in 548, bent his policy and gave a courage and resolution to his actions,
the loss of which was severely felt in his later years. But there was also
an evil report of her deceit, violence and cruelty, and of her implacable
enmities and her favouritism, which made the palace a hotbed of intrigues. Her influence was to be seen in appointments, dismissals and
diplomacy, as well as in the laws by which she improved the status of
women. Having lived in Egypt and Syria, she knew more of the Roman

world than her husband, who had not left the environs of the capital, and in religious questions she promoted a realistic pro-Monophysite policy which restrained and was wiser than the grandiose conformity and harmony with the West, dear to Justinian's theological ardour and bound up with his schemes of reconquest. Sometimes openly, sometimes covertly, she drove at home and abroad an independent policy, fundamentally the same as that of Zeno and Anastasius. Like them, she saw that Egypt, Syria and the easterners were mainstays of the Empire, and that their religious convictions, which gave an outlet for their separatist alienation from its Hellenized centre, must be appeased for its preservation.

For the satisfaction of Justinian's ambitions and of his theological convictions the healing of the schism between Rome and Constantinople was the first necessity. This was achieved under Justin, as we saw above. There was a Persian war, which was ended in 532 by Roman concessions. There was the unending defence of the Danube to be carried on. There was, above all, the treasury to be filled, and this Justinian's favourite, the cruel, vicious, and corrupt John of Cappadocia, who was made pretorian prefect (531), accomplished with the aid of his under-harpies. The result was that a stream of dispossessed peasants poured into the capital eager for revolution.

Riot was hatching there for another reason. For long the Hippodrome, where chariot races were run and shows given, had been the centre of the city's life, in which passions and opinions had their vent. It was dominated by two hostile factions, the Greens and the Blues, who inevitably took different sides on every contest and every public question, and whose disorders and outrages were most dangerous to public security. The Emperors themselves were unable to stand aloof, and Anastasius had been a Green. This made Justinian a Blue with the accompaniment of gross partiality in their mutual broils, while the Blues were enraged at any check. In January 532 the discontents merged in a formidable revolt of both factions and the immigrants together, with Nika (victory) for their slogan. Fires for three days burned famous buildings; the mob declared Hypatius, nephew of Anastasius, unwilling Emperor. Justinian had few troops to guard the palace, and prepared for flight. It was then that the indomitable Theodora nerved him. 'The purple', she said in council, 'is a good winding-sheet.' Bribes were hastily, secretly given; the generals Belisarius and Mundus made a surprise sally on the Hippodrome, and the slaughter of 30,000 of the packed crowd quelled the spirit of resistance for years. The home-front was secured.

(2) THE RECONQUEST OF THE WEST

Meanwhile, an opportunity for intervention, which became reconquest, occurred in the West. In 530 the pro-Roman Hilderic was deposed and succeeded by his cousin Gelimer as King of the Vandals. Justinian's remonstrances were rejected, and he prepared for invasion in spite of its risk and cost. The East Roman army was much below its nominal establishment. Most of it still consisted of the militia-like *limitanei* on the frontiers. The field-army included heavy infantry, recruited in the Empire, who played a subordinate part, and the all-important cataphracts, the mailed cavalry armed with lance and bow, mercenaries levied from every barbaric tribe, who decided battles. Some of these formed the private troops of the generals, their *bucellarii*. They were superb soldiers, but mutinous and pillagers, for which a corrupt commissariat and arrears of pay furnished constant excuse. But the Romans were scientists in warfare, and some of the generals were expert and brilliant. Such were Germanus, the Emperor's nephew, and Belisarius, the hero of the reign.

It was Belisarius who was sent to Africa. His army of 10,000 foot and 6000 cataphracts—a revealing figure—with a protecting war-fleet, was considered sufficient to attack the degenerate Vandals and their incompetent, sentimental king. Their Roman subjects were their enemies, the Ostrogoths stood neutral, and Gelimer dispersed his forces to deal with revolted Sardinia. A victory at Ad Decimum and the surrender of Carthage were gained by Belisarius in September 533; in December he finally routed the Vandals at Tricamarum. Next year the mournful Gelimer, chanting his misfortunes, surrendered on terms. But while the Vandals disappeared like a mist, their enemies, the Berber tribes, remained. Revolt within and raids from without the new-won provinces were complicated by mutiny of the troops (534–6). Belisarius, sent back to Africa, saved Carthage from the insurgents, and Germanus then crushed them (538). His successor, the patrician Solomon, restored peace and prosperity, but on his death revolts of Berbers and troops nearly lost the province. Two years of war under a new general, John Troglita, were needed to beat down resistance (546–8). Vandal Africa from Tripoli to Caesarea (Cherchell), with Sardinia, the Balearic Isles, and the distant outpost of Ceuta became a part of the Eastern Empire. It has been doubted whether the conquest was not a misfortune for the conquerors. It was a serious drain of treasure to make and to maintain. It was only a coastland exposed to the raids of the Moors, while even the inadequate garrison took up much-needed troops. It shared in the racking financial oppression of the Empire. Yet it increased the Byzantine command of the sea, and within a century provided the last stronghold against victorious invaders.

189

Fig. 33. Theodoric's daughter Amalasuntha and her son Athalaric

Long before the African wars were finished the Ostrogothic War had begun. The regent Amalasuntha, unpopular for her pro-Roman ways, was already thinking of refuge in the East when the young Athalaric died (October 534). To keep the throne she married and associated her cousin Theodahad, a miserable specimen of a Romanized Goth, an unreliable coward of literary pretensions. He speedily imprisoned and then murdered the queen in the teeth of her patron Justinian's remonstrances. The Emperor was still the legal sovereign, and the crime gave him a specious opportunity to change the delegated government of Italy. In 535 his troops under Mundus occupied Dalmatia, while those under Belisarius took Sicily. The craven Theodahad, at first ready to surrender, was encouraged by the revolt in Africa to resist, but Belisarius returned, welcomed by the Italians as a liberator, seized Naples, and entered Rome unopposed (December 536). The Goths, however, unlike the Vandals, had kept their fighting spirit. They dethroned Theodahad, and chose in his place the valiant Witigis. The new king bought off the hostile Franks with the cession of Provence, and then attacked Belisarius in Rome with his whole fighting force. The epic siege lasted a year (March 537–March 538). In it Belisarius, with 5000 men, defended the city victoriously against an overwhelming foe. But other imperial troops were landing. Some were sent towards the Adriatic, others to Milan which declared for the Empire. Witigis abandoned the vain siege of Rome, and turned on Rimini, now imperial. Justinian, however, had sent a fresh army, under the eunuch Narses, another genius of war, across the Adriatic. Unhappily he and Belisarius were soon at odds. They relieved Rimini, but their disputes allowed the Goths to recapture Milan, where they atrociously massacred the teeming inhabitants (539). To make matters worse, Theodebert of Austrasia led a Frankish army into the valley of the Po, playing a double game between the

190

combatants, and committing horrible ravage till disease in his barbaric army drove him back. Wherever the war was waged, Italy was depopulated by slaughter and famine. But Belisarius's hands were freed by the recall of the insubordinate Narses, and he could begin the siege of Witigis and the Goths in Ravenna. Their hopes of outside diversion from Persia were frustrated, and after six months the overcrowded city surrendered (540). Curiously enough, both Witigis and his Goths were eager to elect Belisarius their rebel Emperor. He deceived them, and the war seemed to Justinian at an end.

In this belief he recalled Belisarius, and installed a civil administration. It was a fatal mistake. The Goths recovered themselves north of the Po, choosing Hildibad for their king, while Justinian, at war on the Euphrates and the Danube, could do little beyond disillusioning the Italians by his taxation. At the end of 541 one of the few heroes of the time ascended the Gothic throne, the chivalrously brave and brilliant Totila. He marched victoriously to the unwasted south; the Byzantine generals attempted no common action; Naples fell in 543; he did not pillage, and his justice was proverbial. Belisarius, sent to Italy without an army, could only hold out in Ravenna and reprovision Otranto. Rome, which surrendered on 17 December 546, received strange treatment, for Totila ejected the inhabitants and left it a solitude. Spiritually, if not materially, this was the end of classic Rome. Inhabitants might filter back, ecclesiastics might flourish there, but the ancient cultured society with its secular traditions was gone. Yet the buildings were left standing—a military mistake—and Belisarius threw himself into the city and held it against vain attacks. Insubordinate lieutenants and sheer lack of means prevented an offensive till he begged for recall (548), when the triumphant Totila secured all Italy save four coast-towns and even subjected Sicily and Sardinia (551). Justinian was at last roused from his absorption in theology. By a supreme effort of his emptying treasury, he reconquered Sicily by sea, and dispatched the eunuch Narses with his largest army, perhaps 35,000 men, by land. In 552 Narses reached Ravenna, and then routed Totila at Busta Gallorum, not far from Taginae (Gualdo Tadino) in the Apennines. The Gothic king fell in his flight, but resistance was not over, for King Teias took up the struggle. The last battle was fought next year at Monte Lattere near Vesuvius, where he too was killed. There remained isolated garrisons such as Compsae (Consia) in the south to be reduced (555–63), and a devastating invasion of heathen Alemannic hordes to be repelled (554) at Capua, but Italy to the Alps was again Roman. We have seen above how Justinian recovered southern Spain.

Narses was really a viceroy at Ravenna. Under him a revised version of the former Roman administration was set up (554), as had been done in Africa. Dalmatia and Sicily were separated from the Italian diocese; Sardinia and Corsica belonged to Africa. Civil and military authority were kept distinct. On the frontiers of both Italy and Africa long strips of *limites* under military dukes were formed, as elsewhere, studded by a network of strong fortresses which were garrisoned by the *limitanei*, those peasant militiamen who held their allotted land on condition of defending their *limes*. In both Italy and Africa there was a *magister militum* in command. Most of the remnant of the Goths had emigrated across the Alps. They had shown themselves barbarians save for the exceptional policy of Theodoric and Totila. As for the Romans, they suffered even more in Italy than in Africa, where the effects of the wars, Berber raids, and Byzantine taxation were bad enough. Twenty years of war, pillage, and famine, followed by remorseless taxation, had reduced the country to a half desert. 'Nothing remained for the inhabitants but to die.' Naples, Milan, and Rome were nearly desolate. The rich were ruined or had fled to the East, the middle classes, crushed under their burdens, all starved. Justinian, if not his tax-gatherers, endeavoured to stimulate revival. He instituted public works. He built churches and fortresses. He encouraged trade. He favoured the aristocracy. He enriched the Church. In Africa his measures won some success, but Italy had been worse mangled, and, as it turned out, had less time in which to recuperate. The Gothic War makes a break in her history. Education, wealth, habits of life and thought sank to a lower level. At the close of Justinian's reign she was on the threshold of the Dark Ages.

(3) THE DEFENCE OF THE EAST

The cardinal error of Justinian was to attempt wide western reconquests and to reign and build with unexampled splendour, when the resources of the Eastern Empire required careful husbanding if they were to suffice for its mere defence. His defensive wars against Persia and the northern barbarians perpetually lamed and stinted his western enterprises as these did the more necessary maintenance of the oriental and northern frontiers. The Empire buckled under the strain. The danger from Persia was not of the Emperor's making, for the Sassanian kings, when their eastern frontier was quiet, never abandoned their dream of conquest to the Black Sea and the Mediterranean, and there was both religious and commercial friction. But Justinian's policy of peaceful penetration towards the Caucasus increased the unavoidable hostility. Byzantine diplomacy spread Christianity in Lazica and Iberia, which made them natural allies, and threatened Persarmenia. A first war, in which victory wavered, ended in the 'everlasting peace' of 532, when Justinian, intent on the West, made great concessions. He gave up his protectorate of inland Iberia, and paid a heavy tribute for the Persian guardianship of the Caucasian or Caspian Gates against the northern nomads. The new King of Persia, Kavad's son Chosroes I Anushirvan, was also anxious for peace until he was sure of his throne.

But he only awaited his opportunity. He was the ablest of his race, master of his kingdom, desirous of conquest and renown, and he employed the lull to centralize his government and reorganize his army. In 540, when Justinian's thoughts and forces were engaged in the Gothic war, he made a devastating raid to the Mediterranean, destroying the secondary capital of Antioch. Next year he captured the fortress of Petra on the coast of Lazica. Little was effected by the Roman generals, even Belisarius, to repair these losses and later ravages, and an invasion of Persarmenia ended in defeat (543). But the bubonic plague had appeared in Persia, so that a truce could be bought by Justinian, save with regard to Lazica. There the war continued for years with great intensity. At last a fifty years' peace was signed in 561. The Empire kept Christian Lazica; Chosroes was barred from the Black Sea; but Justinian paid an annual tribute of 30,000 gold pieces and discontinued his Christian propaganda; Nestorians in Persia were promised toleration. It seemed like a return to the *status quo ante*, but the suffering of the Roman provinces on the Euphrates had been immense and hard to repair.

Fig. 34. King Chosroes I of Persia

The Balkans, too, were given little respite from invasion. The Germanic tribes on the middle Danube, Lombards, Heruli and Gepids, did little harm: Justinian skilfully egged on their mutual wars. When the Ostrogothic kingdom broke down, the Lombards occupied derelict Pannonia, while the Marcomanni and others, who retained the name of their former home in Bohemia as the Baiuvarii (Bavarians), had taken over Rhaetia as far as the Brenner. Farther east, however, the nomads were a constant danger. Two Hunnish tribes, the Bulgars and the Kotrigurs, infested the Lower Danube and reached the Dnieper. Percolating among them and the Germans were Slav groups as plundering as they. Beyond the Dnieper were the Hunnish Utigurs and Sabirians, who threatened the Caucasus. Goths and the imperial city of Cherson occupied the Crimea. It was the Hunnish tribes and the Slavs who were now the curse of the Balkans. Their plundering raids, which pierced the defences of the Danube, lasted throughout the reign, becoming worse during the Gothic War. In 540 Huns reached the isthmus of Corinth, in 547 Slavs reached Dyrrachium. In 551 a force of 3000 Slavs advanced to the Aegean; in 558 a band of Kotrigurs looted outside Constantinople itself, to be turned back by Belisarius.

At the close of the reign a new horde of the same type, the Avars, migrated west of the Caspian and already threatened another avalanche of peoples. Yet under Justinian the invaders were each time obliged to recross the Danube, and his diplomacy was always busy, bribing their chiefs and embroiling each tribe with its neighbours.

All the same, the condition of the ravaged districts was terrible, their fields pillaged, their homes burnt, and the wretched provincials subjected to hideous atrocities and dragged off to slavery. Justinian's field-army was too small for its work and was employed elsewhere. The Emperor pinned his faith to fortifications. The system of *limites*, with their peasant militia, ruled by 'dukes', was extended to cover the whole frontier, as 'the wrapper of the Empire'. They were crowded with *castella* and fortified towns, big and little, old and new, as refuges and barriers, scientifically planned. They were raised in the inner provinces as well as in the *limites*: the Balkan peninsula resembled an entrenched camp. But the growing penury of the government led to neglect, undermanning, and disrepair, severely felt in his last days. The increase in the number of *magistri militum*, each with his section of the frontier, favoured readiness on the spot, but also disunion in the high command. Nor was the method of diplomatic bribery of barbarian neighbours without its perils. These heavily subsidized *foederati* were faithless vassals, who raided as the opportunity arose, and their knowledge of the Empire's wealth was an added temptation. The dissensions sown among them by the Byzantines as a further safeguard were, too, only a partial prophylactic. Altogether, these measures spread Justinian's influence from the Carpathians to Arabian Yemen and Abyssinia, but the depletion of the Empire's armies deprived them of solid backing.

(4) THE RELIGIOUS PROBLEM

The vital problem in internal government for the Emperor was his religious policy. Even more than his predecessors Justinian considered the control of the Church a part of his imperial office. He was the great representative of what has been called 'Caesaropapism'. He claimed to appoint and remove bishops, to convoke and direct councils, to sanction, amend, or annul their canons. He was a theologian, who set up as an autocratic doctor of the Church. He was an over-generous benefactor, a prolific founder of monasteries, churches, hospitals, and the like to an extent that impoverished the state, which lost in taxes as well as in property. Heresy was an odious crime, and persecution of heretics a public virtue. From the first he declared that for them 'to exist was sufficient'. Paganism was suppressed, its last temples in Egypt destroyed, and, above all, its last intellectual stronghold, the University of Athens, was abolished in 529. The surviving remnant of the Samaritans in Palestine was so illtreated that it revolted, only to be savagely crushed. The Jews fared badly enough, if better. Christian heretics were deprived of their civil rights, their worship forbidden, themselves hunted out. In Africa, Arianism was soon obliterated. But one form of Christian opinion in the East, Monophysitism, was too formidable for simple suppression.

Emperor and Empress represented different policies on this fundamental problem. By conviction and secular policy Justinian was a Chalcedonian, eager to secure the unity of the Empire and the support of the Westerners on that basis. Theodora, by sympathy and her knowledge of the Eastern provinces, was for reconciliation with the Monophysites and for a solidarity of the existing Empire on the lines of the Henoticon of Zeno and Anastasius. Between these views the government wavered; persecution, toleration, and attempts at compromise each had their turn, or sometimes contemporaneous application.

At first Justinian continued the fierce persecution of the Monophysites which he had begun under Justin. But they were masters of Egypt and powerful in Syria and Armenia. So he began his lifelong search for some common ground, which should yet be fundamentally Chalcedonian. On Theodora's advice he recalled the proscribed monks. Severus, ex-patriarch of Antioch, was invited to Constantinople as Theodora's guest. An amicable conference was vainly held in 533. Then Justinian went further. He issued what was called 'a new Henoticon', and the Monophysites were allowed to spread their doctrine. In 535 a Monophysite, Anthemius, was even made Patriarch of Constantinople. But a change came when the Pope Agapetus visited the capital. Anthemius was deposed (536), and Justinian fell under the influence of the papal legate, Pelagius. Fierce persecution began in 537, and even the Egyptian monks bent under a rod of iron.

Theodora, however, was far from beaten. In 537 she secured the deposition of Pope Silverius for alleged treason and the election of her protégé, the time-serving Vigilius. She procured court favour for the Monophysite leaders themselves, interned in the capital; they were useful missionaries abroad. Thanks to her, Jacob Baradaeus, Bishop of Edessa (543), in spite of the police who dogged his track, reorganized the Monophysite Church in Syria, which after him was called Jacobite. Once more Justinian changed his plans, and renewed the attempt at conciliation, this time on a side-issue which he hoped might beguile the Monophysites. Three theologians of Nestorian leanings, Theodore of Mopsuestia, Ibas of Edessa, and Theodoret of Cyrrhus, had been approved by the Council of Chalcedon. Their dubious pronouncements came to be known as the Three Chapters. If these could be condemned, the Monophysites might accept the phrasing of the Chalcedonian creed. Never was Justinian more arbitrary and despotic than in this new, almost trumped-up, controversy. In 543 he anathematized the Three Chapters by an edict of his own. To obtain the sanction of the Pope and the Western Church was the next aim. Vigilius was, perhaps by collusion, carried off under guard from Rome (545). When he at length arrived at Constantinople he soon yielded to pressure, and in 548 published his *Judicatum*, condemning the Three Chapters while maintaining Chalcedon. Theodora died soon after in triumph, but in the West there was a general protest. The effect on Justinian was to provoke him to force—he deposed recalcitrant bishops in Africa, and attempted to arrest Vigilius, who, in alarm at the ferment, was demanding a General Council. The arrest failed in a scandalous scene, when the altar to which the Pope was clinging for refuge in a church was overturned (551). He fled back to Chalcedon, but returned to Constantinople, where the Emperor held the Fifth Ecumenical Council in 553. The obedient bishops, almost all Easterners, condemned the Chapters, but the Pope, anxious for his lost prestige, now refused to attend and issued a hedging *Constitutum* of his own. Thereby he broke his word to the Emperor, and his entourage felt Justinian's wrath. In the end, in fear of deposition, the Pope solemnly confirmed the Conciliar decree. He died on his way home, and his successors were submissive. The Papacy had been deeply humiliated and shaken. Although persecution induced conformity, the metropolitans of Milan and Aquileia, with their suffragans, went into schism in support of the Three Chapters, which lasted 140 years. Nor was Justinian successful in his main object. In spite of conference after conference the Monophysites were never satisfied, not even by his adoption of a particular extremist heresy, that of the *Incorrupticolae*, in his last days. The cleft between the Monophysite and orthodox provinces, springing out of divergent racial temperaments, was only widened and deepened by the deplorable methods taken to close it. Loyalty to the Empire was sapped in Syria and Egypt.

(5) THE GOVERNMENT OF THE EMPIRE

Absorbing as theology became to Justinian's old age, and bent though he was on the reconquest and distracted by the defence of the East all his life, he showed the greatness of his conceptions and his zeal for good government in his internal administration. There was much to amend, much to reduce to order. By ancient custom, office was bought by the officials, who then recouped themselves with a profit out of its proceeds. This meant an all but universal corruption in administration, police, finance and taxation, and in the courts of justice. The chief sufferers were the peasants and townsmen, who were miserable under their burdens. The great proprietors could both evade oppression and inflict it; they bought and seized the land of the poorer; their private troops, *bucellarii*, pillaged their neighbours. Disorder and poverty grew. Only a third of the taxes reached the treasury.

One source of evils, which gave opening to unjust decisions, was the uncertainty of the Empire's best creation, the Law. Roman Law had grown slowly out of the decisions of the magistrates based on equity and on the amalgamation of the kindred customs of its chief peoples. The 'Praetor's Edict' which fixed the main lines of civil and private law was expanded, rationalized, and applied by the treatises of a marvellous succession of great juristic thinkers, such men as Papinian, Gaius, Paul, Ulpian and Modestinus, which came to an end in the middle of the third century. Further, there were the edicts, rescripts and constitutions of the Emperors which declared or amended the law, or made new law. The general fabric, mainly raised by the jurists, was magnificent and of wide-reaching influence. 'To Politics', wrote Sir Henry Maine, 'to Moral Philosophy, to Theology it contributed modes of thought, courses of reasoning, and a technical language.' In the West 'it supplied the only means of exactness of speech...and of exactness, subtlety and depth of thought'. In its own province it gave a reasoned, equitable framework and guide to the mutual relations of a highly civilized society.

But in detail the law was obscure. Its sources were multifarious, needing lifelong study and an ample library. The jurists often contradicted one another; so did the ever-growing enactments of successive Emperors. Even of the latter there was no complete collection, although the Theodosian Code did reproduce and classify the edicts of the Christian Emperors up to its date (438), and there were private compilations, the Gregorian and the Hermogenian, for those of heathen times. For the competing pronouncements of the all-important jurists Theodosius II had in 425 prescribed a rule of thumb: the judge was to follow the view of the majority of the great five named above and others of repute, or in case of equality to take the side on which stood Papinian, if he had expressed an opinion. This tangled excellence was a poor practical safeguard against the ignorant or corrupt judge and unscrupulous advocates.

The Theodosian Code itself, although covering the lesser part of the law, had great influence, and in the West simplified excerpts from it and the jurists formed the staple of the barbaric codes for Romans. But in full Roman territory the confusion and obscurity arising from the multifarious sources of valid law were only partially dispelled, and fresh imperial constitutions were constantly appearing to modify it. The knowledge of the law was being choked by its profusion. To reduce this accumulation of genius to order, harmony, fixity and accessibility was the task which at the beginning of his reign Justinian took in hand under the inspiration and chiefly by the efforts of his corrupt but most brilliant expert, the Quaestor Tribonian (*ob.* 546). In 529 the labours of a legal commission produced the first edition, now lost, of the *Codex Justinianus*, a classified, excerpted, and revised compilation of all still valid imperial Constitutions up to date.

This replaced the less perfect Theodosian Code, and was itself revised and perfected in its still extant second edition of 534. The next and most important task was to deal with the jurists, or as we may say from analogy the Common Law. For this purpose a new commission prepared in three years (530–3) the *Digest* or *Pandects*. It was a harmonized, excerpted, selected compilation from the jurists' works in their own words, mortised together and arranged in 432 titles according to subject. More than 3,000,000 lines from over 1600 rolls containing the treatises of 40 jurists were put under contribution in this single Codex of 150,000 lines. Neither the Digest nor the Code was a codification of the modern sort; they were the consolidation, combined with amendment, of the formless mass of the sources of law. They gave the Roman world a practical statement of the law in use, cleared of the obsolete, full in detail, yet terse and lucid, and of exclusive authority. It made manageable and thus secured the preservation of the wonderful legal achievement of generations of Roman jurists. The *Institutes*, published together with the Digest (533), was a manual for students founded largely on that of Gaius, and an authoritative course of study was ordained for the law schools of Constantinople, Rome, and Berytus in Syria, where only the law could be taught in future. Yet the changelessness implied was not in fact absolute. Justinian himself issued many new laws (*Novellae*), and provincial custom, Christian influence and the familiar Theodosian Code modified Justinian's Law in practice both in East and West. But in the long run Justinian's work was immortal, a fit reward for a great idea. His Law—and it was a Latin Law, although the Novellae were mainly in Greek—revived in Italy in the eleventh century, proved to be the tutor of the legal growth and much of the intellectual ripening of medieval Europe.

In his own law-making Justinian was largely concerned with administrative reform. In 535–6 he took this burning question in hand. General edicts abolished the sale of offices, and commanded mild and vigilant government with a rigid care of the revenue. The bishops were called upon to inspect the conduct of officials, probably a more effectual measure, and complaints were encouraged. In special edicts Justinian endeavoured to simplify provincial government, ceasing to adhere closely to the elaborate hierarchy of separate civil and military authorities devised by Diocletian. Near the frontiers and in troubled districts the military commander was made civil governor, an innovation with a future before it. The useless intermediate *vicarii* were suppressed in the East. Too small provinces were united in one, better organized; officials were reduced in number and better paid. Intermediate courts facilitated appeals. The police of the turbulent, dissolute capital was reformed. Under Theodora's influence prostitutes were reclaimed and protected as far as law went from the white-slave trade. Attempts were made to expel the undesirable immigrants who flocked to

Constantinople. With the riot-breeding games suspended, the capital was quiet for fifteen years after the Nika revolt.

There was the desire for public utility as well as for splendour and art in Justinian's passion for building. Roads, bridges, walls, theatres, aqueducts, reservoirs and public baths were constructed wholesale along with churches and monasteries. Even new cities were founded, like the Emperor's birthplace Justiniana Prima (Skoplie). When Antioch was ruined by the Persians, it was magnificently rebuilt. So were Syrian towns which suffered from earthquake. Above them all Constantinople was favoured after the destruction caused by the Nika riot. Churches, porticos, palaces, hospitals, vast reservoirs which exist to-day were constructed with lavish splendour; most beautiful among them was the peerless St Sophia, the masterpiece of Byzantine art. To the public usefulness of these works may be added the employment and education they gave to an industrious, art-loving population.

Trade, too, was favoured with paternal if not always helpful care. Justinian's diplomacy aimed at routes to the farther East in order to circumvent the Persian monopoly through which silk, spices, and Indian products came. The attempt to establish a southern sea-route through Abyssinian intermediaries failed owing to Persian opposition. More success, perhaps, was promised by the new route north of the Caspian to China, which was rendered possible by the emergence of a vast Turkish Empire over Central Asia: at any rate the Crimean ports flourished on their trade in northern raw products. The best help to industry was given by the introduction of silkworms, the eggs of which were smuggled in hollow wands from China by two patriotic missionaries. From 554 the Empire could produce its own raw silk as a government monopoly and check the exorbitance of Persian profits.

It would seem that the Empire was bound to prosper, but it did not as the reign closed. Great disasters befell it, such as earthquakes and the terrible outbreak of bubonic plague in 558, which thinned the population on its slow way through Europe. But the permanent canker was the incessant over-expenditure due to Justinian's simultaneous pursuit of his vast projects, and its consequence, the ruinous, racking taxation which exhausted his subjects and nullified the reforms. The disgrace of the hated John of Cappadocia in 541 by Theodora's means and the instrumentality of her favourite, Antonia, the wife who kept Belisarius in ignominious leading strings, gave no relief, for his successor, Peter Barsymes, was as bad. The sale of offices flourished; corruption grew; the Emperor repeated his edicts in vain, and he himself became neglectful in his old age. With increasing penury, the fortifications fell to ruin, the diminished army was starved, the frontier lay open to barbarian raids. The dispeopled Empire could not supply the empty treasury. Economies, sometimes wise in themselves, such as the discontinuance of the useless consulship after 541, were never sufficient to make up for imperial prodigality; and the neglect of the army was a fatal mistake. Justinian's death in 565 at the age of 83 was hailed with relief. He left the State bled white, the frontiers pillaged, the government weak before the great proprietors, the proletariat riotous and seditious, the Monophysites alienated. Yet he bequeathed great achievements to posterity, Byzantine art and the epoch-making Code which clarified and preserved Roman Law.

CHAPTER 9

BYZANTIUM AND THE AVARS, SLAVS AND LOMBARDS

(I) THE CRISIS OF THE EMPIRE

Justinian was succeeded without opposition by his favourite cousin, Justin II (565–78), who had the advantage of being the husband of Theodora's niece, the masterful Sophia. Unfortunately he was a rigid man, dazzled by his predecessor's glories, to whom fell the task of guiding an exhausted, ill-defended Empire through a crisis of the first magnitude and a new movement of peoples. In foreign affairs he took the attitude of the invincible, unbending Roman, and in the disasters which his lack of realism occasioned, his reason ultimately gave way. It was foreign powers which he underrated and hoped to bluff by a lofty inflexibility, for he was well aware of the desperate state of the finances and the army and of the need to reconcile the Monophysites. He, too, drew up an edict of compromise, but when Jacob Baradaeus and his followers refused to respond to his overtures, he fell back, like Justinian, on fierce persecution (571–2), which made matters worse.

External foes, however, were the occasions of his most fatal blunders. A new situation to both north and east had been created by the rise of a new, nomad Turkish empire in Central Asia in the middle of the sixth century. The destruction of the Ephthalites on the Oxus by the western khanate of the Turks in 553 relieved at least for a time the pressure on Persia's eastern frontier. More momentous was the migration of an Altaian tribe or conglomerate, known as Avars, which, defeated by the Turks, moved irresistibly westward from Central Asia to beyond the Caspian Sea. They subjected the Utigur and Sabirian Huns. Passing west, they subdued Kotrigurs, Bulgars, and various Slavonic tribes, whom they made their victims and tributaries. By 562 they had extended their range north of the Carpathians to the Elbe and Bohemia and were warring with the Merovingian, Sigebert of Austrasia, in Thuringia. Wherever they rode they spread devastation, like their forerunners the Huns. Justinian had subsidized these formidable newcomers, finding them useful allies against the nearer Hunnish tribes, and even offered Pannonia for their habitation. Now Justin II haughtily refused to give tribute to Baian, their Khagan. Baian, however, through the inter-Germanic tribal wars, obtained a new headquarters, a steppe land suitable for his mounted horde. Alboin, King of the Lombards, was at deadly grips with Kunimund, King of the

Gepids, long settled as quiet allies of Rome in modern Hungary and Transylvania. In 568 the Gepids were overthrown by the joint attack of Lombards and Avars. They disappear from history, and the Avars took possession of the Danube plain and of the serf inhabitants. They also occupied vacant Pannonia as the Lombards moved south to Italy. Here they remained in permanence. Justin II hurriedly threw a garrison into the key city of Sirmium on the Save, left derelict by the Gepids. Long negotiations, intermixed with defeat and pillage, ensued between Baian and the obstinate Justin, till at length he agreed to the blackmail demanded. It appears probable that Baian's patience was due to expansion northward, and that the area of his dominion and pillage over subject Slavs reached the Baltic during these years.

Meanwhile the Empire was preoccupied with a Persian war, almost insisted on by Justin II. There were two main inducements. First, the western Khan of the Turks was meditating war on Persia, and eager, like Justin, to establish a northern trade-route from the Empire to China. But the western section of this ran south of the Caucasus, exposed to Persian ambushes. Here there was a territorial dispute over the land east of Lazica. Further, Persarmenia, which was Christian, had risen in revolt against Zoroastrian persecution, and Justin assumed its patronage. In 572 he refused to continue Justinian's subsidy and struck the first blow. But Persian Nisibis held out, and Byzantine Dara was taken (573). The shock of the disaster upset the Emperor's reason. In December 574 the Empress induced him to create a trusted general, Tiberius, count of the Excubitors, Caesar or heir-presumptive; henceforth he reigned in fact until he was associated as Augustus in 578 just before the death of Justin II.

Tiberius II (578–82) was a Thracian, experienced in the Avar war. He was really the first of the Greek Emperors, and with him Byzantine becomes the fittest name for the Eastern Empire, which was still Roman in tradition. Thoroughly competent, he was free from the illusions of the past. He saw that the wasted Balkans must take the second place in imperial policy, and that the outlying and ruined conquest of Italy, then in the throes of the Lombard invasion, must be treated as relatively a subordinate interest. The strength and life of the Empire lay in the Greek-speaking Asiatic provinces, which were its core, and the Monophysites of Syria, Egypt, and the hardy Armenian borderland must be tolerated if they were to remain loyal. Till 598 persecution ceased.

In the Persian war Tiberius fought not for conquest but for an honourable peace. But this, in spite of continuous negotiations and a truce, was hard to get. In the fighting each side gained its victories; Chosroes was succeeded by his son Ormizd IV (579–90), and no treaty could be arranged. At this very time the peril in the Balkans was intense. Slav invaders were crossing the Danube and overrunning the country, and Baian chose the moment for a treacherous attack. There was no army with which to resist him, although Sirmium held out (580–82). Just before his death Tiberius agreed to cede the city and pay all the arrears of blackmail. During these years of war the Slavs poured over the Balkan provinces—a flood of murder and ravage, creating the vacancy they were soon to fill.

Tiberius II chose for his successor the Cappadocian Maurice (582–602), an experienced and sometimes victorious general who possessed insight, public spirit and courage. His fault was too much faith in his own excellent judgement without regard to the disagreement and unpopularity which he provoked by decisions in themselves right and wise. He was a better judge of policy than of men. Hence he could be fatally indulgent to time-servers who were incompetent, and overstrained the allegiance of his troops. He saw the dire need of economy—Tiberius had spent too freely—and forgot that the army did not. He was a strict disciplinarian and drew the reins too tightly without popular manners to ease the friction. He saw the most desirable strategic action without realizing the ferment among the overtried soldiery. So after resounding successes he came to his fall—one of the worst disasters of the Empire.

Successes in the long Persian war were nullified by the Emperor's ill-advised reduction of the soldiers' pay and the consequent friction, but here Maurice was helped by the equal unpopularity of his adversary, Ormizd IV, whose violence and insults provoked revolts. He was murdered in a palace plot, and his son Chosroes II was forced (590) to flee for his life before a usurping general, Bahram Chobin. He appealed to the Emperor, and against all advice Maurice became his champion. In 591 the Byzantine generals overthrew the usurper in two victories in Azarbaijan. Chosroes repaid his benefactor by large cessions: the Byzantine frontier was extended to Lake Van and the Araxes, and included vassal Iberia. It was a triumphant ending to the war, and gave the Empire an invaluable recruiting ground in the greater part of Christian Armenia.

Maurice could now (592) transfer his field-army to the Balkans, where was the greatest need. Italy and Africa he was still forced to leave to their garrisons and militia, but he reorganized the provinces of Africa and unified the defence and government of both countries by establishing in each a military viceroy, with the newly coined title of Exarch. In the Balkans he was determined to secure the frontier of the Danube against Baian with his Avars and Slavs. The war was by necessity long and chequered, but was rendered longer by the unaccountable favour shown by Maurice to incompetent or traitorous generals. Yet in the end victory was being won, when in 602 Maurice ordered the war-worn army, which was beyond the Danube, to remain in enemy country through the winter. It would save the treasury and drive home the success. It is perhaps some excuse for his unwisdom that Maurice, once a vigorous campaigner, who had restored the armies' morale, had since his accession obeyed the fatal, but almost canonized custom which since the days of Arcadius had forbidden the Emperor to quit the environs of Constantinople and the secluded pomp of the palace. He had ceased to know his army. The infuriated troops first mutinied against his order, and then marched on the capital in open revolt (October 602) with a brutal centurion, Phocas, at their head. On their approach Maurice sent the city militia, his only garrison, to man the walls, but he was unpopular, the Greens hated him, his own connexions had become restive, and the militia left their posts and joined in a riotous *émeute* against the Emperor, who taxed much and spent little. Maurice fled, while with the support of the Greens Phocas was crowned Emperor. Maurice and his sons were caught and massacred.

Then began a reign of tyranny, anarchy, and terror. The brute Phocas had neither capacity nor virtues; throughout the Balkans and Asia Minor civil war was raging, for men refused to recognize the usurper; the factions of Blues and Greens, which had spread to the provinces, fought out their hatred in Antioch, Alexandria, and Jerusalem; only the army as a whole remained faithful to their messmate, and the distant Pope Gregory, who had been at odds with Maurice, blotted his fame by approving the crowned assassin. Where he had the upper hand Phocas dealt out ferocious cruelty to his enemies, open and covert, without faith or mercy. Among the victims were the wife and daughter of Maurice. But a more formidable foe arose in the east. Chosroes II Parviz (the conqueror) declared himself the avenger of his benefactor Maurice and the patron of an impostor who pretended to be his murdered son Theodosius. Under this cloak he renewed the aspirations of Persia to the empire of Darius. He seized Roman Armenia, which was in the throes of civil war, captured the key-town of Dara, and, occupying Mesopotamia, overran Syria (607). Worse than all, his generals crossed the great barrier of the Taurus mountains and from Cappadocia raided northern Asia Minor to the Hellespont (608–9). The fissure in the Empire was not merely dynastic, for Phocas wooed orthodox support by attempting to suppress the openly resisting Monophysites. Defence was paralysed while the religious contest raged.

Fig. 35. Chosroes II, enthroned

Relief from this anarchic nightmare came from Africa. The Exarch

Heraclius, an old general of Maurice, planned rebellion. He had secret friends in the bureaucracy at Constantinople, including Priscus, another eminent general, who had become the tyrant's trustless son-in-law. The plan was that a subordinate friend, Nicetas, should invade Egypt from the west by land, while the aged Heraclius's like-named son sailed with an armament to Thessalonica and attacked the capital. In 608–9 Nicetas in vigorous fighting wrested Alexandria and Egypt from Phocas's adherents, and stopped the corn-supply which fed Constantinople. Probably the younger Heraclius established himself at Thessalonica. In any case in 610 his fleet appeared under the sea-walls of Constantinople. The Greens and the people rose in his favour, and on 5 October Phocas was dragged in chains on board the insurgent's ship. 'Is it thus, wretch, that you have governed the Empire?' said Heraclius. 'Will you govern it any better?' was the reply of the doomed Phocas. He was put to death, dismembered and burnt. His worst ministers shared his fate. The crown was offered to and accepted by the younger Heraclius, the founder of a new line.

(2) THE REIGN OF HERACLIUS, 610–641

The crisis did not end with the removal of Phocas, for the ills of the Empire admitted no sudden cure. The Slavs were still ravaging the Balkans; the treasury was empty; the army was demoralized, and the most influential general, Priscus, disappointed of the crown, was disaffected; the Persian foe was still bent on conquest. Years passed before the Emperor was sufficiently equipped to stem the invaders. It was not till December 612 that he treacherously made a monk of Priscus. His first attempt to repel the Persians was a failure (613). More disasters followed. In 614 Chosroes completed the conquest of Syria by the capture of Jerusalem and the Holy Cross, the most sacred relic of Christendom since its discovery by Helena, mother of Constantine the Great. It seemed that the Empire was falling, but with magnificent obstinacy it fought on. Although a Persian army under Shahin reached the Bosphorus and Chosroes refused to hear of peace, a desperate religious fervour, fostered by the stout-hearted Patriarch Sergius, animated the Byzantines and the government. Heraclius was in the utmost need for money for all his expedients. In 617 came an Avar invasion in full force. The Khagan hoped to take Constantinople by treachery. By his proposal Heraclius came to meet him at Heraclea (Eregli) on the Propontis to arrange a peace. At a signal given by the Khagan the Avars attacked. Heraclius saved himself at a gallop with his crown under his arm and closed the gates, but the suburbs were burnt and plundered, and many thousand captives led away. The Slavs were not only raiding but migrating into the depopulated Balkans. The Persian general, Shahrbaraz, invaded Egypt and added it to the dominions of his master. Constantinople lost the corn-supply once more. Heraclius in these straits planned to sail to Carthage as the best rallying point, but in a striking scene dominated by the Patriarch he was moved to swear not to abandon the capital.

From the emotion roused some gleams of hope began to appear. A peace was temporarily bought from the Khagan by tribute and hostages (619), and Byzantium still possessed an invaluable advantage, the command of the sea: when a new-collected Persian fleet appeared in the Propontis, it was decisively beaten. But money had to be raised for a fresh counter-offensive. At length, led by Sergius, the Church gave up its hoarded wealth, although only on loan at interest, for the crusade against the infidel. It was with a mystical conviction that he was under the protection of the Mother of God that Heraclius prepared to defy the tyrant custom and lead his armies against the Persians, who were overrunning Asia Minor. In April 622 he was ready, and solemnly commended the capital and his heir to the Patriarch and Bonus the *magister* during his absence. His strategy was always the same: to strike at the heart of Persia across their lines of communication, and thus force their invading armies to withdraw. In his first campaign, by skilful manœuvre, he marched into warlike Armenia and there defeated Shahrbaraz who had followed him. In 623 he occupied Dwin, the capital of Persian Armenia, and, crossing the Araxes, drove Chosroes himself from Ganzaca (Tabriz) in Azarbaijan, which was looted with other towns, while the fire-temples were destroyed. Under the threat of Persian armies gathering in Irāq, the Emperor returned to Armenia, where for two years the balance of the fighting was in his favour, but in 625 he returned along the Taurus mountains to Pontus, presumably because of the danger of exhausted Asia Minor from both Persians and raiding Slavs. It seems that Chosroes was imitating his enemy's strategy of attacking the heart, and he had a mighty ally. The Khagan of the Avars had gathered all his forces and on 29 July 626 began the siege of Constantinople. A Persian army under Shahrbaraz supported him from Chalcedon across the strait, and another collected pell-mell—a sign of exhaustion—under Shahin was in Asia Minor. Heraclius retained his central position himself, detaching reinforcements to the capital, and a force under his brother Theodore against Shahin. The defeat and death of Shahin was a valuable gain, but still more valuable was the Byzantine predominance at sea. The defeat of the swarm of the small boats of the Khagan's Slavs in the Golden Horn was almost a massacre, and Persian and Avar could not join hands. At the same time the great land assault of the Avars on the Theodosian Wall was hopelessly repulsed, and after eleven days' siege the Khagan, vowing vengeance, burnt his engines and retreated. He had not only failed; his marauding empire was shaken. Bonus and Sergius had served their country well. The veneration of the Mother of God became impassioned: she had saved her city and her shrine at Blachernae.

But the Balkans were becoming Slavonic and barbaric. On the coast-line of the Adriatic, Dalmatians might hold out in Spalato and Ragusa, and Illyrians in the Albanian mountains. There were Latin speakers, the later Kutzo-Vlachs, in the recesses of the Haemus, while Greeks maintained themselves in the cities of Thrace and along the coast of the Aegean Sea. But Croats and Serbs settled in solid blocks south of the Drave and the Danube to the outskirts of Thessalonica and Philippi. Other Slav tribes now populated Moesia and large parts of Thessaly and the Peloponnese. All that Heraclius could do later was to accept a nominal suzerainty. The Greek Empire only retained the fringes of the peninsula, and the ethnography of the Balkans took as new a shape as that of Western Europe.

But Constantinople had been saved, and Asia Minor could be. The Emperor prepared to strike again at Chosroes's own territory, exhausted and irritated by twenty years of incessant, profitless war. He gained a new ally in the Chazars, a Turkish tribe which had established itself on the Volga and between the Caspian and the Sea of Azov, and was now independent. The Khagan Dzebu Khan of the Khazars was the natural enemy of Persia and the ally of Byzantium. He joined in the war south of the Caucasus, although his aid was spasmodic. In 627 Heraclius again crossed the Araxes from Armenia. From Azarbaijan he turned west, marched through the Zagros mountains, then over the Greater Zab river to Nineveh. The Persian general, Rahzadh, had no choice but to follow from Azarbaijan

Fig. 36. Chosroes II, hunting

on a route whose supplies had been eaten already. On 9 December he lost a battle and his life at Nineveh. Heraclius now marched south and in January 628 seized the favourite palace of Chosroes at Dastagerd (near Shahraban) with his trophies, prisoners, and treasures. The Persian king fled to Ctesiphon, but he still refused overtures of peace and Heraclius did not attempt a doubtful battle. The winter had been mild, and he was able to recross the Zagros to Ganzaca before the snow made the passes impracticable. Soon came the news that Chosroes had been murdered by his exasperated subjects, and that his son Siroes (Kavad II) on a tottering throne was suing for peace. It was granted (April 628), and Heraclius could return to his Empire. It is probable that the frontier of Maurice (591) was accepted, and it is certain that the True Cross was restored to the devout Byzantines. Some fragments rewarded the Armenians and one was despatched to the exultant capital; the main relic was restored by the Emperor in person to Jerusalem. There was still Shahrbaraz and his army to deal with, but Heraclius gave him help to return from Asia Minor to Ctesiphon and usurp for a month the Persian throne. Thus the Persian danger came to an end. Amid anarchy and usurpations the Sassanian kingdom was dislocated ready for the Arab conquest.

The great Heraclius, with broken health, had still to face the reconstitution of an almost shattered Empire. The system of Diocletian, the sharp division of civil and military authority, was out of date; the great senatorial landowners, who had so long thwarted the monarchy, had been nearly broken by barbarian and Persian devastation, which made reconstruction easier; the veteran army, largely levied from Armenians and their neighbours, within and without the Empire, not to mention Slavs and others, required reward and could thereby be placed on a new basis. The orientalism of the Empire had increased, and, seconded by the hectic anxiety of the crisis, showed itself in an almost hysterical religious fervour, superstitious and enthralled to saints living and dead, which was at once the support and the disease of the later Empire.

Heraclius initiated, and his successors developed till its completion a century later, the military system of government of the themes. The themes (θέματα) were in origin divisions of the army, each under its general, the strategos, corresponding to the *magistri militum* increased in number by Justinian. They were cantoned in special provinces, the Armeniacs in Pontica, the Anatolics (Orientals) eventually in Cilicia and Cappadocia, the Thracesians (once levied in Thrace) farther west in Asia Minor, the Opsicians of the guard under their count in the north-west, the sailors (Carabisiani) along the south coast. Here, from imperial lands and ex-*latifundia*, the troops were endowed as military free tenants on condition that the holdings furnished recruits for their theme (θέμα) in perpetuity. Thus the free peasant-soldier farmer was re-established, and his offspring manned the reformed army. It was the system of the *limitanei* applied to the field-army and navy as well, and this landholding, warlike peasantry grew to form the basis, as long as it could be maintained, of the Byzantine Empire. Under the strategoi the civil governors withered away, until the theme became the name of the civil province as well as of its army division and the strategos became its governor. This military and social reform, when it was completed, was the salvation of the Empire. It gave a native army and an efficient administration. But its beginnings came too late to save the south-east provinces from the Arab invasion: the Anatolics clearly moved northwards after the loss of Syria.

A certain break with the Roman past, implying the predominance of the Eastern Greeks, was to be seen in the very imperial style, which was changed by Heraclius to celebrate his Persian victory. From being the colloquial Greek appellation, Basileus (properly 'king') became his official title, and it was qualified by 'the faithful in Christ our God', which we might almost paraphrase as Defender of the Faith. The official language was now Greek, not Latin even in the army, and Latin only appeared in conservative official titles, like that of Quaestor, most of them in Greek translation. Practical reform accompanied the change of style. If provincial administration tended to unification, the central was more departmentalized. The logothetes or like officials at the head of its divisions were becoming immediate ministers of the Emperor, not subordinated in the Constantinian fashion. It was still a time of transition, but the all-important bureaucracy was in course of being remodelled.

The chief internal danger to the Empire still lay in the religious conflict between orthodox and Monophysite and the provincial schism which it expressed and embittered. This Heraclius was bound to attempt to heal, and his failure in the task was complete and disastrous. Himself of Armenian extraction, commanding Armenian troops, and long resident in the East, he sought for concessions which might appease the Monophysites, who had in Syria and Egypt shown little resistance to Chosroes. The Patriarch Sergius, a Syrian by birth, thought (618) that he had discovered a suitable formula: there was but one Divine 'operation' ($\dot{\epsilon}\nu\acute{\epsilon}\rho\gamma\epsilon\iota\alpha$) in the Two Natures. His proposal was taken up by the Emperor. The Catholicus of the Armenian Church and many eminent Monophysites were induced to assent (631–3), but the opposition of the orthodox Sophronius, Patriarch of Jerusalem, caused Sergius to drop his formula and propose instead the doctrine of the Single Will in the Two Natures (Monotheletism). He secured the approval of Pope Honorius and defined his position in the document called the Ekthesis, which he induced Heraclius to promulgate (638). It declared the Single Will and forbade the dangerous discussion of the 'operations'. But it was no less dangerous. A new Pope, Severinus, denounced it, and the Monophysites were not satisfied; the whole Empire was embroiled. Already persecution had been renewed against the Monophysites in Syria and with especial harshness in Egypt. Along with it went heavier taxation to repay the loans from the remorseless Church. Syria had been lost to the Arabs, and Egypt was in process of conquest. In the midst of the controversy Heraclius, who had seen his army routed by the Moslems and the provinces he had wished to conciliate taken from him, disclaimed the Ekthesis and died (11 February 641).

Heraclius was one of the greatest and the most unfortunate of the East Roman Emperors. He had saved the Empire from ruin, he had begun a revivifying reorganization, only to be immediately attacked by the new migration of the Arabs and their religion, Islam, which revolutionized the Mediterranean lands. Italy was already half Lombard; the Balkans were more than half Slav; the remnant of Roman Spain was lost (629) in his days. He had really been compelled to oppress his subjects in order to refund its loans to the Church in accordance with the febrile, blind devotion of the time. Under the strain of his anxieties he himself had contracted a nervous disease which gave him a morbid fear of the sea. But his achievements had been immense, the work of rare talents for war and peace. He was the overtasked hero of a new and darker age.

(3) THE SUCCESSORS OF HERACLIUS

Pious though he was, Heraclius had incurred the disapproval of Church and people by marrying as a widower his own niece Martina, to whom he was devoted, and his plans for the succession were baulked by her unpopularity. His eldest son, by his first Empress, Constantine III, was consumptive, but had sons. He was left as co-Emperor with Heracleonas, one of the four sons of Martina. Constantine died almost at once, and people and army turned against Martina and her children in favour of his boy son Constans. They were degraded, and he was made Emperor. All this meant intrigue and disunion while the Arabs attacked and the frontiers receded. Asia Minor itself was raided across the Taurus. The worst danger was that the Syrian governor, the Arab Muawiya, had built a formidable fleet, which in 655 defeated the Emperor in person at sea. Fortunately for Byzantium, civil war among the Arabs produced a temporary treaty and breathing space (659).

Constans was a fighting, restless, unbalanced prince. He secured the throne for his sons by killing his brother. Received with hoots of 'Cain' in his capital, and realizing that Syria and Egypt were irrecoverable, he journeyed westward (661) to fortify the Empire there. He made no headway against the Lombards, but stripped the Roman Pantheon of its bronze tiles for supplies. None the less Sicily and Africa were preserved from the Arabs until his murder in 668 at Syracuse, but Asia Minor suffered again and again through the ever deeper raids of the Arabs. All the reign the useless religious dispute continued. Constans replaced the Ekthesis by the equally unacceptable Type (648), by which he endeavoured to impose silence on the parties. The West was up in arms against both; the contest was between Latin Rome and Greek Constantinople. Bishops and synods exchanged anathemas. At last Constans was strong enough in Italy to send a loyal Exarch of Ravenna to Rome with an army to arrest the recalcitrant Pope Martin (653) and hale him to Constantinople. Ill usage failed to bend the Pope, who was deposed and exiled to Cherson (654), where he died. Persecution was applied to the obstinate, but on Constans' death Pope Vitalian reverted to opposition. Nor were the Monophysites more pliable. After 662 no more was heard of the nominal reunion of the Armenian Church, although Armenia remained in the Empire.

Constantine IV (668–85), surnamed Pogonatus, inherited the stubborn ability of his house which could rise to heroism, its family discord, and an unusual degree of realism, fostered by the active life the Emperors now led and called out by the imminent danger of the Empire. He was only senior Emperor, but his two younger brothers were reduced to nonentity and finally deposed and their noses mutilated, which made them ineligible for sovereignty, in spite of the resistance of the Anatolics which was overcome by the accustomed treachery. Henceforth younger sons, though nominal Emperors, were powerless celibates. Constantine was faced by perils within and without, the religious schism and the renewed Arab advance under the Omayyad Caliph Muāwiya.

6. The House of Heraclius

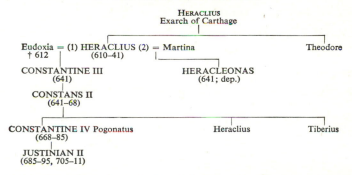

In Africa the failing but sturdy defence was left to the Exarchs of Carthage. In Asia Minor it was a matter of life and death. The Arab armies began to winter west of the Taurus; their raids reached the Aegean. Worst of all, the Moslem fleet was able from 670 to winter in the Aegean and Propontis. Through the summer of 674 it conducted the first siege of Constantinople. But now the Byzantines employed the terrible weapon of Greek fire, the secret invention of the Syrian Callinicus, that inflammable compound which could be projected on to the enemy's ships and consume them. Till 677 the Arabs renewed the assault every year. But in that year the Cibyrrhaeot theme of the Roman fleet annihilated their adversaries off Pamphylia, and the insurrection of the Mardaite Christians in Syria induced Muāwiya to buy a peace. When anarchy again broke out in the Caliphate (683), Constantine was even able to make an advance in the south-eastern Taurus.

But a fresh and dangerous foe had appeared in the Balkans. The Empire had made progress in taming the lesser Slav tribes in Thrace and Moesia. In 679 Constantine crossed the Danube to punish the raiding Bulgars of the Bessarabian steppes. During his absence owing to gout the Bulgar Khan Asparuch routed his army and crossed the Danube with his nomad people. The Emperor was obliged to pay blackmail to save Thrace. The result was that the Bulgars settled among the Slavs of Moesia between the Danube and Mount Haemus as deadly enemies of the Empire, for they formed a united state. They intermingled with the Slavs they ruled and before two centuries were over they were Slav-speaking as the Bulgarian nation, but their Hunnish blood differentiated them from the other southern Slavs and gave them a greater capacity for united action. The Empire's revival in the Balkans was more than checked.

To still the internal discord Constantine IV decided to abandon the hopeless compromise of Monotheletism and the Type. Most of the Monophysites were now irrecoverably outside the Empire; Monotheletism was a court creed without popular backing. The Patriarch of Constantinople was deposed, and thus encouraged, Pope Agatho, with the support of Western synods, including one at Hatfield in England held by Archbishop Theodore, issued a dogmatic letter on the Two Wills. In 680–1 the Emperor held at Constantinople the Sixth Ecumenical Council, which scarcely deserves its name. It declared Pope Vigilius's letters in his dealings on the Three Chapters to be forgeries and Honorius I to have been a favourer of heretics, and it condemned the Monotheletes; Pope Leo II rejoicingly confirmed its Acts (682). The danger of a lasting schism was thus averted, but the divergence between West and East, between Rome and Constantinople rested on other than purely doctrinal grounds. There were differences of discipline and usages, due to differing, isolated histories, differing temperaments, and differing levels of civilization: Italy was becoming barbarous to the Greeks. There was also the rivalry of the two great patriarchal sees. The Greeks willingly accepted their position as a State Church, and resisted the claims of the Pope to an authoritative headship of the Church. These differences were emphasized when in 691 the Emperor Justinian II held in the Trullan hall (*in Trullo*) an Eastern Council, the so-called Quinisext. Canons were needed after the convulsions of the Arab conquests, and the Quinisext passed many. They mainly confirmed old Eastern usages as against Western ways, e.g. they allowed priests to keep the wives they had married before ordination. More marked than all, a canon gave the Patriarch of Constantinople equal rights with the Pope. It was not likely that the canons would be accepted by the Papacy, nor were they, and Pope Sergius only escaped arrest through the support of the Italian army (695). So the breach between Eastern and Western Churches was rather covered over than healed, but the Eastern was united within.

The century-long tension of the Empire in its desperate defence had produced a lamentable decline in order and civilization. Manners had become brutal, discipline relaxed, superstition rampant, and literature dumb. Justinian II, the son of Constantine IV, shared this degeneration. He was active, able, reckless, and unbalanced to the verge of insanity. At first the disorders in the Caliphate favoured him. In 689 the Caliph Abd-al-Malik ceded more than the frontier of Maurice in the north, but Justinian unwisely removed his difficulties by agreeing to transport the insurgent Syrian Mardaites into the Empire. With the same unwisdom he utilized Macedonian Slavs he had just conquered as military colonists in north-west Asia Minor. His next mistake was to break the treaty with Abd-al-Malik, only to find his newly enlisted Slavs cause his defeat by defection in the crucial battle near Sebastea (Sivas) (693). He took his revenge by massacring their families, but Armenia was lost to the Empire and the raids recommenced.

These disasters added to the anger caused by the bitter oppression of Justinian's two ministers, a monk and a eunuch. The general Leontius, just released from a three years' imprisonment, led a sudden outbreak which placed him on the throne (695), and banished Justinian with the loss of his nose to Cherson. The revolution might be justifiable, but it opened the way to others as ill news discredited the government. When Lazica surrendered to the Arabs, and Carthage, just recaptured, was finally lost to the Caliphate, the Cibyrrhaeot fleet raised their *drungarius* (admiral) Apsimar to the throne under the name of Tiberius III (698), and Leontius in turn had his nose cut off to disqualify him for the future. Tiberius proved an able ruler. He repaired the sea-wall of the capital; his brother and generalissimo Heraclius fought hard on the receding eastern border. Meanwhile Justinian was brooding over revenge among the Chazars, where he married the Khan's sister. In 705 he suddenly gained over the Bulgarian Khan Tervel, and with him marched on Constantinople. He took the city by a bold surprise through an aqueduct, and reigned once more, satiating his revenge by the blood of his opponents. He did, how-ever, effect a reconciliation with the Pope, Constantine, on the last visit that a Western pontiff paid to his nominal sovereign at New Rome (710).

The restoration of Justinian was ruinous to the Empire. He was defeated by his quondam ally Tervel. The Arabs conquered Cilicia and crossed the Taurus once more, while the odious madman on the throne was perpetrating atrocities on the Chersonites, amongst whom he had once been exiled. Cherson itself was saved by the revolt of a general sent against it, Vardanes, who took the name of Philippicus. Justinian was beheaded and Philippicus reigned (711). He was quite incompetent: while the Empire was raided by Arabs and Bulgarians, he oddly declared for the effete Monotheletism, till a capable Emperor was found in the civilian Anastasius II in another revolution (713). Serious efforts were now made to strengthen defence against raids and against the great Moslem armament which was preparing to attack Constantinople by land and sea. But the soldiers were mutinous and divided. Anastasius was deposed and unwillingly succeeded by the tax-gatherer Theodosius III (716). This was the work of the Opsikian theme:

Fig. 37. Greek fire used by the imperial navy

the Anatolics and the Armeniacs under their generals, Leo and Artavasdus, refused to submit, while Maslama, the leader of the Moslem host, slowly forced his way across Asia Minor. Leo entered the capital and on 25 March 717 was crowned Emperor. He was a bold adventurer, a Syrian from Germanicea (Marash), whose resourceful courage and perfidious cunning made him fit to save the Empire in its utmost peril.

Maslama had held his hand in the hope that Leo might surrender. When this hope proved illusory he advanced (July 717) to Abydos, crossed with his army to Thrace, and began the siege of Constantinople from the land. It lasted over a year, and the decisive battles were fought at sea. Three Moslem fleets arrived one after another, but they suffered heavy losses by Greek fire, and their Egyptian Christian sailors deserted with valuable information to Leo. In the spring of 718 the sea-blockade was practically raised, and the besiegers in Thrace were starving. Meanwhile they had to fight Slavs and Bulgarians, incited by Leo, on the land. Their position became hopeless, and in September 718 the remnants of the Moslem host were recalled by Caliph Omar II. Even then its misfortunes were not over: most of the ships which conveyed it were lost in a storm. The disaster was complete, and due in the first instance to the Byzantine superiority at sea, which enabled Constantinople to be provisioned and starved the Arabs. The effects were epoch making, for it preserved the East Roman Empire and set a bound to the onrush of the Arab conquest and the spread of Islam. The flood of invasion was exhausted, and Christianity and classic civilization remained. Constantinople had taken up its task as the bulwark of Christendom. It was the most fateful event of the eighth century.

Maimed and degraded as it was, the Empire had won through. Its organization, its patriotism, and its fighting spirit had borne a most exacting test. The degeneracy of Justinian and his contemporaries had

214

indeed brought it near to extinction, but the healthier elements had at last prevailed, and within its natural fortifications of the Taurus, the Haemus, and the sea it could recuperate and be strengthened by a line of reforming Emperors.

(4) THE EXPANSION OF THE SLAVS

An ingenious philological argument has been employed to discover the original home where the Slavonic group of languages took shape and from which the Slavs spread. The Slavs had no native words for beech and yew, but they had for the hornbeam. The habitat of the hornbeam extended eastward in a wide curve over the Pripet marshes, the modern Polesie, beyond the range of the beech and yew. Therefore, it has been argued that in these marshes, which are still Slavonic, the earliest Slav communities grew up.[1] The marshland gave a peculiar isolation to the settlements within it, both from neighbouring tribes and from one another. It thus maintained a primitive way of life and imprinted a long-lasting incapacity for political organization beyond a patriarchal household in small villages and a somewhat formless tribal structure. The primitive Slavs were fish and millet eaters, swineherds, with an undeveloped method of agriculture. By all accounts they, in the marshlands, were unaggressive, ill armed and easy victims to their raiding neighbours, who found them most valuable slaves. In spite of all their disadvantages, however, the Slavs multiplied. In earlier prehistory their kinsmen, the Balts, had wandered north to the dense forests of Lithuania. The Slavs themselves later spread on all sides into the forests of central Russia, towards the Ukrainian steppe by modern Kiev, where a warlike tribe of them were known as the Antae, towards the Carpathian Mountains, and westward to the rivers Vistula and Oder. To the Germans they were known as Wends, a name derived perhaps from the earlier Celtic overlords; to themselves and the Byzantines they were Slavs, a native word of uncertain meaning. Part of this wide expansion was doubtless due to voluntary migrants filling the vacancies left by the Goths, Vandals and Suevi, and the forest depths of central Russia; but another part was caused by whole clans being carried captive as labouring serfs by the nomad Altaian tribes who came successively from Asia along the steppes, and of whom the Avars appear to have been the worst. It was round about 600 that Slavonic tribes reached to and beyond the Elbe in Old Germany, establishing a new frontier, and poured into Bohemia and Pannonia and along the northern bank of the lower Danube. All this movement seems to have been in the wake of the Avars under Baian, and, as we have seen, his Slavonic subjects first plundered and then settled in the Balkans.

---

[1] It has, however, been claimed, largely on archaeological grounds, that the early Slavs spread from central Poland and possessed a higher culture and organization than that of the marshland, here described.

No lot could have been worse than that of these western Slavs under their nomad masters. They were subject to every inhuman outrage and merciless exaction; they were forced to bear the brunt of battles in the van, while the Avars on their horses reserved themselves for the decisive blow at the close. But the Slavs under the yoke appear as doughty warriors, and they acquire a less rudimentary tribal organization either under a nomad aristocracy or in imitation of their masters. It can be no accident that their titles of government and honour were largely of Altaian origin, *zhupan, pan, ban* (this last from Baian), *gospodar* (sheep-owner, an Altaian quality, though a Persian word); when they were not, they were German (*knez*, king or prince, and later *kral*, king, from Charles the Great). As late as the ninth century we find certain northern Slav princes and nobles to be *kumiz*-drinkers, while their subjects drank mead. It may be due to the Avar deportations that Slav tribal names appear in widely separated areas in the west: Sorbs on the Elbe, Serbs in the Balkans, Croats on the Vistula and south of the middle Danube. Although in their extension the Slavonic languages remained closely allied, their tribes inevitably became variegated and mixed with other blood, Altaian, Germanic, Celtic, Alpine, in their new settlements: north of the Carpathians they were mainly blond, south of them black-haired brunettes. The Bulgarians are a recorded instance of intermixture, but obviously similar mingling took place elsewhere. Among the Romance-speaking Vlakhs (Rumanians) of the Balkans and Transylvania, as amongst the Greek speakers of Greece proper, there was clearly a large infusion of Slavonic blood, and many thousands of captives from the Balkans must have blent with the Slavs of Baian's realm north of the Danube.

The plundering empire of the Avars under their Khagan did not long maintain its extent. After the failure before Constantinople in 626 something like a break-up occurred. The Avars indeed retained their nomad kingdom, with its serf agriculturists, in the Hungarian steppe, raiding their neighbours, but the Bulgars under their Khans became independent in their tents by the rivers Pruth and Dniester, and so did Serbs and Croats and other Slavs in the Balkans. At about the same date the Slavs, who had spread into central Germany as far as the river Main, revolted under the Frankish merchant Samo, won victories over both Avars and Franks, and formed a transient kingdom of considerable size. North of the Carpathians there seems to have been a Slavonicized khanate.

Over the wide lands of east-central Europe the Slav settlements, whether little villages or hamlets or even fortified towns, according to the nature of the country, were increasing across mountain, plain, or forest. Where they were most oppressed on the steppes and their borderlands, the Slavs seem to have been almost vegetarian. Elsewhere they could add to their primitive agriculture of the hook-plough the possession of horses, sheep, and oxen as well as their swine. On the river-system of the eastern plains, they could even take to trade with foreign merchants like Samo; there were routes from Lake Ladoga to the Black Sea and the Volga. Their peasant communities, ruled by hereditary or elected zhupans and the like, might in Carinthia be almost equalitarian. More commonly under nobles and freemen there was an oppressed class, the Smerdy, i.e. the dirty. They were numerous, they extended from the Mediterranean to the Baltic and inner Russia, where they met the Finns, but their political instinct did not extend beyond the tribe, or rather the tribelet. Hence in most of their lands they played for centuries a passive, unrecorded role, and their heathen barbarism was profound. In their eastern territories their development was retarded by the vast forests in which they were sprinkled and by the rigours of the long winter, both of which secluded them. In the west they were long handicapped either by the aggression of more advanced neighbours or by the security of their mountains which favoured a conservative peasant life.

(5) LOMBARDS AND BYZANTINES IN ITALY

While the Empire was needing all its resources to defend its heart, it is little wonder that the exhausted province of Italy fell victim to a far from numerous tribe of barbarians. As we have seen, the Langobards or Lombards first appear as a small but fierce tribe on the west bank of the lower Elbe. Their nearest kin, as their law and location show, were the Anglo-Saxons, but in the course of their untracked wanderings to Pannonia their dialect had been transformed from the Low German of the north to the High German of their new neighbours. From some of these neighbours they had learned Arian Christianity, a change which had little effect on their savage manners, but a great influence on their subsequent history. They had also developed a kingship. By this time they already formed a fighting class with troops of unfree *aldiones*, like the *laten* of the Saxons, to till their lands. We have already seen how their king Alboin called in the Avars to crush the rival tribe of the Gepids. In so doing he could not hope to live on tolerable terms with the Avars in Pannonia, and on 1 April 568, reinforced by Saxon and other adventurers, the Lombards invaded Italy. It was a real migration. As if to ease their task, the aged Narses was recalled by Justin II at the same time with circumstances of opprobrium which created the legend that Narses invited their attack in revenge.

There was something irresistible but straggling in their piecemeal conquest. Cividale, Verona, Milan and Pavia fell in succession. The self-styled 'Patriarch' of Aquileia set up his see in the inaccessible island of Grado, the Archbishop of Milan fled to Genoa. Alboin conquered as far as the western Alps and may have raided beyond the Apennines, but the Romans held Padua and the line of the river Po, while refugees poured into the marshes and lagoons of Venetia, where they slowly grew into the future state of Venice. Alboin soon perished in a typically barbaric episode. He forced his wife, Rosamund, daughter of his slain foe, the Gepid Kunimund, to drink out of her father's skull, and the queen in revenge contrived his murder and fled to Ravenna (572). A new-elected king, Cleph, was soon murdered in his turn, and then for ten kingless years the thirty-five Lombard dukes, i.e. the commanders of clans (*fara*) and troops, ranged Italy, setting up little principalities in the Roman cities they conquered. Two of them, the Dukes of Benevento and Spoleto in the south, conquered more widely than their fellows, from whom they were separated by a band of unsubdued Roman territory which stretched from Ravenna to Rome. In this way the long-lasting political division between North and South Italy took its first beginnings.

Nothing could show more clearly the disorganization and weakness of the Roman defence than these wide, sporadic conquests of not many thousand invaders, who could not capture a garrisoned, well-fortified town. The Emperor Maurice did his best. He appointed a military viceroy with full powers for Italy, the Exarch of Ravenna, and he called in the Catholic Franks, always aggressive, against the Arian enemy (584). These steps brought reunion to the endangered Lombards. In 584 they elected a king, Authari, son of Cleph, and more, they endowed him. Each duke, save those of Benevento and Spoleto, gave up half of his share of land to provide the king with the necessary estates and income. The Franks were finally bought off with tribute and the cession of the entrance valleys of Aosta and Susa, after repeated invasions which nearly wrecked the new kingdom. Authari, too, secured himself by marrying the Catholic Theodelinda, daughter of the Duke of Bavaria, and descended from the Lethings, an older reigning house of the Lombards, a connexion which gave a certain hereditary sanction to his kingship. When he died (590), his elected successor, Agilulf, married his widow and took up the task of making a stable monarchy.

In this Agilulf (591–616) was successful. He warred down rebel dukes, he came to a friendly understanding with the dreaded Avars, and he resumed the conquest of Byzantine Italy. Duke Arichis of Benevento already ruled the south save Naples and the heel and toe of Italy; Duke Ariulf of Spoleto was attacking Rome, held back only by the personal influence of Pope Gregory the Great; the king himself forced the Pope to a private, invalid peace for the 'duchy' of Rome in 593. In the intervals of truces Agilulf took Padua, Parma, and Mantua from the Exarchate. At last in 605 a prolonged truce, on condition of tribute, was obtained by the Exarch Smaragdus. The Lombard kingdom was established.

The Lombards came into Italy, not as federates, but as enemies, and to them their Roman subjects were a conquered, rightless people. Authari and his successors displayed their sovereignty, and perhaps their Christianity, by assuming the imperial name of Flavius, but they were kings of the Lombard folk, and Lombard law was the law of their free subjects in their eyes, however much Roman, chiefly Theodosian, law might be practised among free or servile Romans within their territories. In fact, wholly free Romans were scarce in Lombard land. During the conquest, slaughter, enslavement or servitude, or exile had been the lot of the Roman land-owners. The mass of the conquered population remained or became *coloni* or the like, as the Lombard *aldiones*. It was a thin population in any case, although more numerous than the immigrant Lombards. Not to mention

Fig. 38. The Lombard King Agilulf

the dispeopled towns, great forests like that of Marengo had grown up or increased their extent on the countryside of North Italy, now called Lombardy. There was woodland and marsh for the Lombard herds of swine. Like other Germanic invaders, the Lombards became landowners, large and small, according to their rank and influence. The typical unit was the *curtis*, corresponding to the *villa*, and the *curtis*, though predominantly rural, might be the whole or part of a city. It was in large measure self-sufficing, itself cultivated and its simple domestic industries carried on by *aldiones* and slaves. The Lombards soon succumbed to Italian influences: their nobles and even their plain freemen would reside for at least part of the year in a town, which of course might be a convenient centre for much land within a certain radius. The free population formed the army, and were thus called *arimanni* (*exercitales*). The poorer freemen received their holdings more especially on the frontiers, whether in the ancient *limites* or in new formations on the edge of Byzantine territory. In these they inherited the obligations of the Roman *limitanei*, i.e. tenure on condition of special military service and dues to the crown on whose share of land they were settled. The frontiers shifted with fresh conquests in the north, but these specialized *arimanni* retained their somewhat tied freedom where they were placed at first, while fresh allotments on the same terms were made on the later *limites*. Town-life became naturally more agricultural and rudimentary in Lombard Italy, although here and there remnants of the Roman *collegia* of tradesmen might subsist, like the boatmen of Pavia or the soap-makers of Piacenza. The strongest survivals were probably ecclesiastical, after the first rush of Arian conquest was over: the Catholic or in Venetia the schismatic bishops seem to have been still elected in form by clergy and people. The Lombard settlement was naturally thick in the regions north of the river Po, which were soon divided into two main provinces, Austria to the east and Neustria to the west of the river Adda, but there was plentiful colonization in Tuscany also as well as in the two southern duchies of Spoleto and Benevento.

The rivalry of the provinces and the insubordination of the dukes, each in his city, made the elective Lombard kingship almost as unstable as that of the Visigoths. To this may be added differences in religious policy, for through intermixture and mere neighbourhood of Lombard and Latin a Catholicizing tendency began to show itself in the kingdom. Agilulf himself had tolerated the schismatics of Austria. The Arian party, however, was strong, and its leaders occupied the throne from 626. The second of them, Rothari, the Rother of legend, Duke of Brescia, reigned from 636 to 652, but he married Theodelinda's daughter Gundeberga, and allowed the Catholic hierarchy to be re-established in his kingdom. New lands, from which to reward his followers, were already necessary if the monarchy was not to be impoverished, and in renewed war with the Byzantines he conquered Genoa, where he placed no duke. He earned his chief fame as a legislator, through the *Edictus* which he published in 643. Its contents were essentially conservative and Germanic, although it stressed the royal power, but Roman influence was shown in the Latin in which it was written and in the fact that it was no mere string of amendments or restatements of custom, but a systematic codification of the law. The Lombards were already displaying their juristic aptitude.

Catholicism gained further ground in the reign of Aripert, the Catholic and Bavarian nephew of Theodelinda (653–61). Then came a revolution from the south. Grimoald, Duke of Benevento since 657, overthrew the quarrelling sons of Aripert and married their sister. The union of his duchy with the kingship made him more powerful than his predecessors (662–71). He repelled the Emperor Constans and the Franks and broke the power of the rebellious dukes. He failed, however, to found a royal dynasty. On his death Perctarit, the son of Aripert, ousted his young nephew, leaving Benevento to Romoald, elder son of Grimoald. Arianism was now dying a natural death. Both Perctarit (671–88) and Romoald were Catholics, and the opposition in Austria with which the king contended was no longer Arian but schismatic over the Three Chapters. When Perctarit died, Duke Alahis of Trent usurped the crown, but Perctarit's son Cunincpert (680–700), aided by the Catholic bishops and the Neustrians, won the battle of Coronate on the river Adda (689). This was a victory of the kingship over the dukedom and of Catholicism over the schismatics. Before Cunincpert died all Austria had renounced the schism, which left the two 'Patriarchates' of Grado and Aquileia (Cividale) as its only trace. About the same time a definite peace, not a truce, was concluded with the Empire on the basis of the *status quo*. The kingdom of the Lombards was now acknowledged even by the Byzantines as a legitimate foreign power.

The abandonment of Arianism and even of the Three Chapters schism gives a measure of the progressive italianization of the Lombards. Intermingling of races must have begun from the first, and as a Lombard could marry a freedwoman, intermarriage easily became frequent. Save in the highest classes mixed descent must have become the rule. The Lombards gradually adopted the romance speech of the majority, to which of course their own dying language contributed a number of legal and other words. A freed *aldio* or slave adopted the Lombard law of his master, but by 730 Roman law was not only practised but recognized by the kings for those who inherited it. The régime of personal law in short was admitted, although Lombard law had in the circumstances the greater vogue. In spite of this, Roman culture and art, however degenerate, gained, like Roman religion and town life, a firm hold on the conquering people. With his name of Flavius the king took over the rights and duties of head of the State. He legislated, dispensed justice and peace, controlled the bishops, took over the public lands, coined, levied state dues and tolls, appointed officials. Yet Germanic influence was strong. For all the kings' efforts the kinship's blood-feud and its solidarity in heirship and land were dominant social facts. Similarly, the regime of the dukes, parallel with the bishops, produced an extreme city particularism which gave medieval Italian history its peculiar character. It is true that the kings had estates in all the northern duchies and administered them by independent officials, called *gastalds*, who maintained the royal rights, but the centrifugal tendencies were always stronger than the centralizing, even when the dukes were nominees. Besides, the royal resources were always being sapped by grants of land. For the extension of cultivation, indeed, the ever-growing class of poorer freemen could be installed by landowners as lease-holders (*libellarii*) in Roman fashion to the profit of both parties, but, as well as large endowments of churches and monasteries—King Liutprand restored their vast patrimony in the Cottian Alps to the Popes—there were the kings' *gasindi*, who developed from the primeval *comitatus*, to be rewarded and provided for. These men and their descendants formed the new nobility, with the highest *wergeld*. From them were chosen the royal ministers and officials; their loyalty was secured by gifts of land. So times recurred when fresh conquests were needed to supply lands for their endowment and for the settlement of landless *arimanni*. The distribution of land was also necessary for the efficiency of the army. Although all *arimanni* were bound to serve, a law of 750 prescribed a scale of equipment based on property: the wealthier came as mailed, the next in means as light cavalry, while the poorer formed the ill-armed footmen, or even camp-followers, the last provision being a proof of a large free landless class. It is significant that there were landless traders in each of the three grades: Lombards, either by descent or enfranchisement, were already prosperous in commerce, whether landed or no. In this respect, too, coming events cast their shadows before.

Thus it was not only ambition and statesmanlike policy, but economic needs which prompted a belligerent period. When the Bavarian dynasty came to grief through its own dissension and civil war, King Liutprand (712–44), of a new house, though romanized and devoutly Catholic, aimed at conquering the Byzantine remnant as well as the semi-independent duchies of Spoleto and Benevento. He aspired to unite all Italy in the Lombard kingdom. The opportunity was given him by the Iconoclastic Schism, when Byzantine Italy, led by Pope Gregory II, rose in revolt against the Emperor Leo III in anger at his decree forbidding image-worship (727). Liutprand conquered Bologna from the Exarchate and Sutri from the Roman duchy. This last aggression, however, alienated the Pope, who entered into a separate league with the insubordinate Dukes of Spoleto and Benevento. The new Exarch, Eutychius, used the situation with Byzantine deftness. He allied with Liutprand, and the two together forced the dukes to submit to the king, and the Pope to the Emperor (729). But there was no stability in the three-cornered contest. In the strife Liutprand seized and lost Ravenna, made sure of Spoleto and Benevento, and took and restored four towns of the Roman duchy. He was about to reconquer Ravenna when perhaps in fear of the Franks he called a halt (743). He had been a legislator as well as a conqueror. The Lombard kingdom waned after his death (744), for divergent policies and disunion sapped it. Ratchis, Duke of Friuli, who led a peace party, relied on the Church, to which he was over-generous, and snatched the crown from Liutprand's nephew Hildeprand, only to be deposed by his own warlike brother Aistulf (749) and become a monk at Monte Cassino. War was already in progress against the Empire. Aistulf conquered Ravenna and the Romagna (751). This was the end of the Exarchate of Ravenna. Henceforward the only Byzantine possession in the north was the little semi-independent duchy of Venice in the lagoons. In the south the duchy of Benevento had absorbed all but Otranto, Calabria and the semi-independent coast-towns of Naples, Amalfi and Gaeta. In the centre, the Papacy, as we shall see, was the real ruler of the duchy of Rome under imperial suzerainty. It was Rome that Aistulf now attacked and thereby brought on the Frankish intervention and conquest.

In spite of the efforts of its kings the Lombard kingdom had remained radically weak. Its fighting powers had not been markedly increased by the growing amalgamation of Lombard and Roman. Its kings had never adequately replaced the landed wealth they lost by their grants to Church and laymen, in which public dues as well as land profits were sacrificed. Benevento and Spoleto were but mutinous vassals. In the north, besides the large-scale division into Austria, Neustria and Tuscany, the intense city particularism which the rule of the dukes had fostered was a fetter on common action. Most fatal of all, the effort at expansion brought on the enmity, irreconcilable, however propitiated, of the Papacy, which saw its temporal possessions attacked and its spiritual and temporal independence, so closely linked, threatened by a powerful Lombard neighbour, devout as he might be.

To the elaborate revival of Justinian there had succeeded by the middle of the seventh century a military administration in the fragments of Byzantine Italy. Under the Exarch there were *magistri militum* or dukes for the several military duchies (*ducatus*). These were like the themes which were emerging in the East. The troops to defend the duchies came to include a levy of the able-bodied male inhabitants; in fact they were a militia by 700. They were attached to definite towns and forts in corporations named *numerus* or *bandus* under the command of a tribune, who ruled his district in addition to his military authority. More and more commonly the tribune was the chief local landowner, and, though nominated by the Exarch, a quasi-hereditary lord. A rude, fighting aristocracy ruled Byzantine territory under the Exarch's supervision. Naturally more of the trading *collegia* of the towns survived as gilds than in Lombard land, but the ancient *curiales* faded, as at Naples, into a gild of notaries practising the law. For the law of Justinian was in force, although contaminated by older and newer custom.

Beside this military, aristocratic organization there was another, the wealthy Church, with estates and local troops independent of the tribunes under its own officials. Already favoured by the Emperors, ecclesiastics were liable to justice only in their own courts. The bishops were powerful public functionaries who took over municipal charges in their cities, once the burden of the *curiales*, and had rights of supervision over secular governors. Pre-eminent in power was the Papacy and the Roman Church. Endowed with vast estates round Rome, in Italy, in Sicily, and in Illyricum, the Papacy repaired the aqueducts and walls of Rome, supported the proletariat by its charities in succession to the vanished imperial dole, supervised the civil administration, fed and eventually paid the garrison and troops, and quite outweighed the dependent dukes appointed by the Exarch for the duchy of Rome. When after a long silence the prefect of the City reappears he is the Pope's subordinate. Gregory the Great (590–603) first acted as the real ruler of Rome and its duchy when warding off the Lombard invasions. He treated with Lombard chiefs effectually, even if his truce was disavowed by the Exarch, and his authority in his immediate ecclesiastical province south of the river Rubicon and in the papal estates was continuously exercised. With less prestige and effectiveness than he, his successors increased their legal functions, till in the iconoclastic schism Pope Gregory II refused to levy a new tax and headed the general revolt which turned out the imperial officials. Elected dukes replaced imperial nominees (727). The revolt, however, was subdued and the imperial officials returned (729). The Papacy suffered severely: its estates outside Italy were confiscated, and Illyricum, Sicily and the south were transferred to the Patriarch of Constantinople. But its local authority and its Italian prestige were undiminished. When the Exarchate fell (751), the Pope, like the dukes of Naples and Venice, assumed the so-called *dicio*, i.e. full powers of government, in the duchy of Rome, or as it now became, the Patrimony of St Peter, although he acknowledged the Emperor as his sovereign and dated documents by his regnal years. The long-developing States of the Church were nearly a legal fact, when Aistulf set out to conquer them. The imperial government of Italy was confined to its southern peninsulas, Calabria (a name now transferred to ancient Bruttium) and the Terra d'Otranto, both dependent on Sicily. But the Rome which the expanded papal bureaucracy ruled was barbaric to a degree. Fierce local nobles, uniting Lombard savagery with Byzantine riotousness, served the Papacy as clerks and laymen, strove in family feuds and political factions, and fought with violence and cruelty for the papal tiara itself. Yet ability, statesmanship, and even learning were still manifest at Rome in the midst of these repellent broils.

CHAPTER 10

ISLAM AND THE ARAB CONQUESTS

(I) ARABIA AND MAHOMET

While in the West the foes of the Roman Empire and the conquerors of its provinces had been migrating barbaric tribes, in the East, until the latter reign of Heraclius, its enemy, Persia, had been a long-established civilized realm. But in the seventh century Persia was replaced by a comparatively barbaric collection of Arabian tribes, who like the Germans burst their ancient bounds and flooded their civilized neighbours in an irresistible migration which changed the face of Nearer Asia and Africa, giving them a new religion, a new dominant language, and a new element in their population to rule them. This was the Arab conquest and the rise of Islam, which reinvigorated the Near East and forced back the European civilization which had spread by Greek and Roman conquest. Long brewing as were the revival and extension of oriental modes of life and thought, a new inspiration and impetus were given them by these fierce invaders and their creed. The break-up of the Mediterranean unity was completed, and with it the transition from ancient to medieval times.

Towards the close of the sixth century the condition of Arabia does not seem to have varied in most essentials from that of preceding millennia. There was the tropic desert of stone and sand sprinkled with oases and edged by coastal districts, which allowed rather than invited by a comparative fertility a settled population. This formidable land was the home of a tangled congeries of tribes and clans, mostly desert-wanderers or Bedouin, whose patriarchal society was bound together by the bond of kinship and the duty of the blood-feud. They were a mounted folk, restless and warlike; their wealth was in camels—the necessity of the desert—horses and date-plantations. Their speech was varieties of the typically Semitic Arabic. Their native religion, like their mode of life, had come down with little change save decadence from previous centuries: it was a primitive paganism of idols, sacred stones, shrines, and pilgrimages, held so loosely and so un-developed that in parts more accessible to the outer world there were to be found communities of immigrants and converts who professed Judaism or distorted Christianity. In some aspects their civilization, taken as a whole, appears to have declined from the past. The trading kingdom of the Himyarites in Yemen, successors of the Sabaeans of Sheba, had been broken by Abyssinian devastation and Persian rescue. The two northern border kingships, that of Lakhm, dependent on Persia, to the west of the Euphrates, and that of Ghassan, vassals of East Rome, in the Syrian desert, were

225

recently dissolved. But the Arabs themselves had lost none of the ancient qualities which many centuries earlier had sent out swarms of Semites to mingle with the races northward and imprint on them their characteristic energy and types of language. Fearless, fierce, and sensual, keen witted and materialistic, born traders and marauders, they only required a leader and union to make them conquerors of lands exhausted by long wars and divided by racial and religious antagonisms, as were both Persia and the Empire. Numbers for the migration were not lacking, for barren Arabia barely supported its inhabitants; the leader and the union were supplied by Mahomet and Islam.

The Arabians were almost wholly illiterate and our knowledge of the prophet's rise depends on his own allusive utterances in the Koran, which was compiled two years after his death without regard to chronology or subject-matter. It is supplemented by traditions recorded too late and too partisan to be trustworthy and by the meagre facts of the invasions to be gleaned from Byzantine chroniclers. The state of Arabia in his day is imperfectly known, and to separate history from legend is sometimes impossible. It appears that c. 570, the probable date of his birth, the town of Mecca in Hijaz, fifty miles from the Red Sea, was a prosperous community subsisting on the caravan trade north and south. It was also a sacred city, with a pagan sanctuary, the Ka'ba; a yearly festival, the Hajj or pilgrimage, was held annually in its neighbourhood. This place of old prestige was then occupied by the tribe of the Quraish, to a clan of which, the Banu Hashim, Mahomet (properly Muhammad) belonged. After a youth of poverty he entered the service of a wealthy trading widow, Khadija, successfully transacted a venture of hers in Syria c. 594, and then became her husband. He was now a prosperous trader, but his instincts turned to religious meditation. He practised fasts and solitary vigils. His nervous temperament showed itself in strange physical seizures, which he and others regarded as divine inspiration. From them and the revelations from God which he claimed to receive Islam was born.

There are traces of individual Arab monotheists before Mahomet, but the chief external influences which moulded his thoughts seem to have been Jewish and heretic Christian. It was not the reading of their sacred books which affected him—he probably only knew Arabic—but oral communications of dubious value. He clearly considered himself the last and greatest of a line of prophets commissioned by the One God to teach the true monotheistic faith. Jesus and the Hebrew prophets were his predecessors, but their teaching had been deformed by their followers. Now the definitive revelation had come: 'There is one God (Allah), and Mahomet is His prophet.' Three features mark the earliest passages of the Koran: (1) the One transcendent God, creator of all else, merciful and just, the divine despot; (2) the moral law laid down by Him for mankind; (3) the

*Fig. 39. The sacred enclosure at Mecca, with the
Ka'ba in the middle*

coming Judgement with Hell and Paradise, both conceived in the most materialistic form, the quintessence of the pains and delights of the senses in this life. Strictest of monotheists and foe to idolatry as Mahomet was, he yet retained a veneration for his native Mecca and the holy Ka'ba; God was 'Lord of this house', and perhaps in their polytheism an inchoate monarchic, monotheistic idea of Allah had floated in some Arabian minds. Mecca was to shape the career and religion of this Arabian prophet. At least as revolutionary was Mahomet's universalism, sprung from his monotheism, in his moral code. Hitherto the moral duties of the Arabs had been based on kinship and the tribe, with the corollary of blood-revenge. To some extent Mahomet recognized the older notions of honour, justice and propriety, but his moral duties regarded mankind, not limited by race or kin, and the duty of forgiveness, not of revenge, was laid down for his converts, a startling novelty for the Arab tribesmen. So, too, was his doctrine of a bodily future life with its accompaniments of Heaven and Hell, a Heaven which was the reward of martyrs who fell in battle for the faith. The new religion, which was to spread so widely, received the name of Islam ('surrender') and its adherents called themselves Moslems (Muslims), the 'self-surrenderers'.

For some years converts were few and secret; Mahomet's wife Khadija, his young cousin Ali, his friend Abu Bakr. When his preaching became public, it met with rigid opposition from the Quraish, who were attached to the profits at least of their ancient shrine. Persecution drove some of the Moslems to Abyssinia, but at last Mahomet won a sudden and notable convert, the future Caliph Omar. Yet the protection of his kindred became insufficient, and Mahomet cast about for a refuge. Eventually the town of Yathrib, later called Medina ('the city'), 200 miles north of Mecca, offered itself. There two rival pagan tribes held rule, but a large proportion of the inhabitants professed Judaism and evidently a number of converts had been gained on pilgrimages to Mecca. It was in 622 that the emigration of the Moslems to Yathrib was agreed under oath and effected. This was the Hegira (*hijra*, 'flight'), which has become the starting-point of the Moslem era. The Prophet was welcomed with enthusiasm in his new home. All the Medinese were not converts, but they were all his Helpers, in distinction from the Emigrants from Mecca. In no long time he became ruler of Medina, in spite of the opposition of its Jews, and was able to regulate the affairs of the town as well as to prescribe the religious and secular practices of Moslems. The institutions which he created were: (1) in ceremonial the five daily prayers, said towards Mecca, not Jerusalem as he had ordered before his breach with the Jews, the public service on Friday, the fast during daylight in the month of Ramadan, the annual pilgrimage, the prohibition of wine and certain foods; (2) each Moslem was bound to give 'alms', which became a tax to the State, and to fight for the Faith;

(3) for the betterment of society were commands in favour of women and slaves and to protect orphans and the weak against the strong and to limit the blood-feud as narrowly as possible, besides punishments for sexual offences. Altogether the Prophet was setting up a higher standard of life and enforcing it by religious law.

The progress of his dominion must be briefly told. His raids on caravans produced a war with Mecca. A victory, which seemed miraculous, at Badr, a defeat at Uhud, the successful resistance to the siege of Medina, ended (628) in the treaty of Hudaibiya by which Mahomet and his Moslems were allowed to perform the pilgrimage to Mecca. Mahomet had set his heart on return to his native town. He felt all the ancestral veneration for the sacred spot, and the pilgrimage allowed propaganda among the Quraish. When Mahomet himself made the pilgrimage (629), two of the future generals of Islam, Khālid and Amr, became converts. The final act came in 630. War seemed inevitable, for two Bedouin tribes, allies respectively of Mecca and of Medina, fell to blows; it was averted by the submission of the Quraish to Mahomet and Islam, and the Black Stone in the Ka'ba was the only remnant left of the old paganism of Mecca. Yet one more effort was made by neighbouring Bedouin tribes to safeguard their independence. Their coalition was overthrown in the hard-fought battle of Hunain, which was followed by their submission and conversion. From a fugitive teacher Mahomet had become monarch of a growing realm in west Arabia.

During these years of propaganda and conquest Mahomet had become aware of the irreconcilable opposition of the earlier monotheistic religions, Christianity and Judaism, which he hoped to supersede. The first to feel his hostility were the wealthy Jewish communities of Medina and its neighbourhood. They were ill hands at combining and fighting in the open, though they allied with his enemies. One by one (625–8) their clans were banished and their possessions seized. A massacre completed their expulsion, but when a remnant was conquered at Khaibar to the north they were allowed to remain there as tributaries; thus was formed the precedent of the treatment of the rival monotheistic religions, 'the peoples of the Book', by aggressive Islam. It was in 629 that Mahomet showed that he was not content to remain an Arabian prophet and ruler. He was aware, it seems, of the overflowing reservoir of strength that he was coming to possess in the Arab tribes he was uniting in Islam. His mission was world-wide and conquest was now his method of conversion. He began the Holy War by sending some 3000 men to attack the Byzantine frontier. They were defeated at Muta east of the Dead Sea, but the Prophet next year subjugated small settlements of Jews and Christians in north-west Arabia, and with superb self-confidence he was preparing another expedition against the Empire when he died at Medina on 7 June 632. He had created and launched in a few years a religious and national movement which was to have profound effects on history.

Doubtless the Arabs were ripe for a new faith and a national overflow, but this does not detract from the evident greatness of Mahomet himself. His character and work have been the subject of violently conflicting judgements, and there is no consensus of opinion. We hardly know how much of his doctrine and policy was due to his own personal qualities. It is clear that the change from the preacher to the conqueror and the spread of his religion were largely governed by factors over which he had no control. But the dominant nature of the man and his magnetic influence over voluntary and involuntary followers are likewise manifest. That influence was due in part to both moral and intellectual qualities, and it seems to have been overwhelming. It is only just to say that he used his immense power much more often to restrain than to stimulate the fanaticism of his converts.

(2) THE EXPANSION OF ISLAM

From the point of view of universal history the Arabian conquest is a fresh and decisive stage in the recovery of the autonomous civilization of the Near East. Alexander the Great had led a marvellous outburst eastward of the European civilization which the Greeks had created. It had overlaid its Near Eastern rival in the lands of the ancient Persian Empire and had been fortified and stabilized in the Mediterranean coastlands by Rome. There its impress was lasting, but beyond the Tigris and the Zagros mountains it steadily receded before the age-old native ethos. In the Mediterranean lands themselves the resurgence and counter-attack of orientalism had long been evident. Christianity itself was born in the East and retained and propagated, however Hellenized and cosmopolitan, an irreducible Eastern element, while the secular civilization of the East Roman Empire was deeply tinged even in the Balkan peninsula with an Eastern colouring. In Armenia, Syria and Egypt, as we have seen, the main body of the provincials had kept their ancient languages and literature and part of their customary pre-Roman law, and, what was still more important, had adhered to their congenial form of Christianity, Monophysitism, which estranged them from Western orthodoxy. Here was the rift which gave the Arabs their opportunity, though the military and financial exhaustion of the Empire played its part.

The Prophet's death, which to most was unexpected, bade fair to dissolve the new State of Islam, for the rivalries of Medinese Helpers and Meccan Emigrants, as well as the ambitions of Mahomet's cousin Ali, who was also husband of his daughter Fatima, were at once excited. It was only by the bold stand of leading Emigrants and almost a *coup de main* that a hasty election was made of the venerable and awe-inspiring Abu Bakr (632–4), eldest of the Prophet's companions, as his representative (Khalīfa, Caliph), which became the title of the chief of Islam. The new ruler was faced with a critical situation. Mahomet's actual realm consisted of Hijaz with a considerable fringe of vassal tribes only partially converted. These now refused to continue their tribute in the so-called Apostacy (Ar-Ridda), and they were joined by yet independent districts, such as Yemen, in war against the Islamic State. Abu Bakr had the advantages of the army assembled to attack the Roman Empire and of a born general, Khālid, the 'Sword of God'. In victory after victory, the most memorable of which was won at Aqraba over a rival prophet Musailima, Khālid subdued the Ridda, while other commanders conquered outlying Arabia to the sea. Both victors and vanquished were dangerous if unemployed, for the appetite of the Arabs for war, plunder, and conquest had been thoroughly aroused, and the expansion of the race under the banner of Islam, already preluded by Mahomet, was begun.

The penury of Heraclius, repaying its loans to the Church, had forced him to suspend the Byzantine subsidies to the Christian Arab tribes on the Syrian border. Some of them turned to the Moslems for help in the raids by which they hoped to recoup themselves. In 634 three small forces entered Palestine, one of which annihilated the local Byzantine army. Meanwhile Khālid, who had been raiding Babylonia (Irāq), made a rapid desert march across to Damascus, and thence effected a junction with the victors. There was now a dangerous foe to meet. Heraclius, then resident at Emesa, had concentrated a great army under his brother Theodore and sent it south. It was routed by the united Moslems at Ajnadain on 30 July, and Palestine was at the mercy of their plundering bands. They now had a new ruler, for Abu Bakr died, nominating the purposeful and stern states-man Omar to succeed him as Caliph (634-44). The southern Arabs were already astir migrating northward, and he was determined on conquest. Khālid took command, defeated the new Byzantine general Baanes at Marj-as-Suffar, and forced the surrender of Damascus and even Emesa in 635. The provincials, indeed, save the Greek towns, like Jerusalem and Caesarea, showed little will to resist. Heraclius, on his side, made a last effort in defence. Incapable himself of further campaigning, he placed a new army, largely composed of loyal border Arabs, under the leadership of another Theodore, surnamed Trithurios, who pressed Khālid southward. But 'the Sword of God' with much inferior numbers outmanœuvred his opponents, at odds among themselves; the border Arabs deserted; and on 20 August 636 the terrible defeat of the river Yarmuk decided the fate of Syria. The last troops of Heraclius had been destroyed; his frontier retreated to Mount Amanus. It was not merely that he lacked both men and money: the Aramaic and Arab Syrians were thoroughly alienated by taxation and religious persecution. The stubborn resistance of Jerusalem and Caesarea, which were Greek and orthodox, was isolated, and in 638 and 640 they surrendered in turn. The reduction of Roman Mesopotamia was a corollary effected without much opposition (639–46). The Caliph Omar himself joined his army to instal something of an administration and lay down rules for the government and taxation of conquered peoples and religions. On its surrender he entered Jerusalem, where the so-called mosque of Omar on the site of the Temple records his visit. Not the fierce soldier Khālid, but a shrewd chief of the Quraish, Muāwiya the Omayyad, was eventually (639) appointed governor of Syria.

During these campaigns a second momentous conquest by the Arabs was taking place in the East. With the fall of Chosroes II the exhausted Persian kingdom had fallen into anarchy. Fleeting, shadowy monarchs succeeded one another. This weakness and oppression provided fresh temptation to the predatory Arabs to the west of the Euphrates, especially to the Bakr and their sub-tribe, the Banu Shaiban, under their chief, Muthanna. They invited Khālid, the victor of the Ridda war, to join them in a raid on the fertile land of Babylonia which they called Irāq, perhaps because the new Moslem power seemed too formidable to be left a possible enemy in their rear. Together with Khālid's 500 volunteers they put the frontier town of Hira to ransom, but when their ally was called off to Syria they received a heavy defeat from the Persians at the battle of the Bridge (634). By this time Persia was reviving somewhat under Rustam,

Fig. 40. Yezdegerd III, defended by Ormuzd against a lion

the general of the last Sassanian Yezdegerd III (632–651/2), while the Caliph Omar was set at least on tentative aggression. A small victory won by Muthanna at Buwaib (635) kept the war alive, and in 636–7 Sa'd, the Caliph's representative, recruited with some difficulty a few thousand men. Rustam was by now seriously alarmed; he himself marched to the edge of the fertile land, and there at Qādisīya was routed and slain by Sa'd (May–June 637). The whole of Irāq now lay open to the Arabs, for Yezdegerd fled east across the Zagros: Ctesiphon (Madain) was captured with immense booty, and a victory at Jalula secured its possession. In fact the Aramaean peasants welcomed their Semitic conquerors, although the

Iranians of the eastern mountains held out. Basra and Kufa were founded as Arabian strongholds, the latter as a great armed camp and capital of Irāq.

After the victories of the Yarmuk and Qādisīya the great Arabian migrations assumed their full dimensions. Islam meant no longer a supremacy of Medina but a common empire of the Arabs. Expeditions became systematic conquests in which whole tribes shared. In 641 a fresh advance was made. Mosul on the Tigris was taken, Media was invaded, and the decisive victory of Nihavand was won over Yezdegerd III. That feeble monarch fled farther and farther east till his murder by a satrap took place at Marv in 651 or 652, but his people resisted stubbornly. The Median towns took some years to conquer; so did the province of Fars or Persia proper with its capital Istakhr, which fell in 649. Thence north-eastern Khurasan could be at last successfully invaded by Arab tribes and become part of the Caliphate. In spite of conquest, however, the national Iranian tradition lived on. Syria and Irāq easily adopted Arabic, a Semitic tongue like their own. Iran retained her native Indo-European language, interlarded indeed with borrowed Arabic words. When the majority of the Persians deserted their national Zoroastrianism for Islam, it was Islam with a difference, most unlike the orthodox form. Persia was the home of the Shi'a sect.

Meantime the Roman province of Egypt had attracted the ambitions of the Moslems. Its corn was already a necessity for Medina. Its great and wealthy port, Alexandria, with its dockyards and ships, offered both security and expansion by sea. Above all, it was bitterly disaffected to the Empire. The Monophysite Copts were undergoing severe persecution and ruthless taxation at the hands of Cyrus, who united the offices of Patriarch and governor. He is a dubious personage, who appears, blended with less known contemporaries, as the Muqauqis of Arabic tradition. The attack was led by Amr, now a veteran in the Syrian wars, at all times an unscrupulous politician with a gift for organization. In 640 he defeated the Byzantines at Heliopolis, and besieged Cyrus in the key town of Egyptian Babylon, close to the modern Cairo. Cyrus showed the cloven hoof, for he negotiated a treaty by which Egypt should be a province of the Caliphate. But when Cyrus went to obtain ratification from Heraclius, he was repudiated and banished by the enraged and dying Emperor. All chance of concerted resistance was lost by Heraclius's death (11 February 641), which left the government to faction and intrigue. Shortly afterwards the citadel of Babylon surrendered, and Amr could advance slowly on Alexandria, which, though the most Byzantine of Egyptian towns, was rent with the discord of orthodox and Monophysite, of Greek, Copt, and Jew. Too strongly fortified to be easily taken, its surrender on the usual terms of conversion or tribute after an interval for evacuation was privately arranged by the self-seeking and realistic Cyrus on his return, which was decreed by court defeatists. The Patriarch ran the risk of being lynched, but the treaty was accepted and the Byzantine troops sailed away on 17 September 642, when Cyrus was already dead. The rest of Egypt was by then subjected, and a new capital, an armed camp, Fustat ('the tent'), founded close to the Egyptian Babylon. The willing submission of the Copts allowed full scope for the Arab genius for assimilation. Roman administration and finance subsisted, little changed in native hands, under their Arab masters, isolated in Fustat by the provident Caliph.

Omar was not the man to allow his warrior captains to take root in conquered lands. Khālid was never governor of Syria; Amr was soon restricted to Lower Egypt only, and was recalled by the new Caliph Othman. When a Byzantine fleet suddenly came and raised Alexandria in revolt (645) Amr was needed to defeat the invaders and storm the city (646), but he declined the unprofitable reward of a mere command of the garrison: 'I might as well hold the cow by the horns while another milked her.' Egypt and Alexandria now became the chief Moslem naval base. With their aid Muāwiya of Syria fitted out a fleet and conquered Cyprus (649). From Egypt the further expeditions were dispatched.

The reign of the autocratic statesman Omar was brought to a sudden close by his murder at the hands of a Persian slave. His Caliphate with its beginnings of an organized state is well symbolized by his new and long-lasting title of Commander of the Faithful (Amir-al-Muminin). He left a board of electors to choose the new Caliph, and they promoted Othman (644–55), an Omayyad like Muāwiya, whose pliability promised a reaction from the stern rule of Omar. The choice proved a bad one, for Othman was a pronounced nepotist. Omayyads and their trusty adherents filled the offices of state to the general discontent. Further, there were financial, less justified grievances. Enormous booty as much as religious faith, which indeed grew with their marvellous victories, had lured the Arabs on to their migrations. Only a fifth of the spoil was reserved to the Caliph. But as the frontiers became permanent the booty diminished, and Omar decreed that confiscated lands and the regular taxes should be retained for his state treasury. From it he doled out impartially pay and pensions. Othman's nepotism made these rewards a preserve of the Omayyads. Revolts of the malcontents broke out, first among the men of Kufa. Then a number of the men of Fustat journeyed to Medina and murdered the defenceless old Caliph at his prayers in his own house. The crime was only made possible by the disloyal attitude of his quondam electors. One of them, the prophet's son-in-law Ali (655–61), took the Caliphate, but his reign was troubled and far from universal. Muāwiya, the Omayyad of Syria, led one opposition in revenge for Othman's death: another was headed by the Prophet's widow Aisha and two of the ex-electors. The unity of Islam and the Arabs broke up in this civil war. Ali was the choice of the men of

Kufa, and he overthrew Aisha and the men of Basra in the battle of the Camel (9 December 656). But Muāwiya held Syria and was backed by the wily veteran Amr. It was Amr who rendered the battle of Siffin in North Syria indecisive by playing on the pious scruples of the more rigid Moslems in Ali's army (657), and who obtained an agreement for arbitration. The rigid Moslems then revolted unreasonably enough from the Caliph and were routed by him in Irāq next year, but they survived under the name of Kharijites, or seceders, to give trouble to him and later rulers. In fact they represented the old disorderly, freebooting Arab instincts, fanatics though they might be. The arbitration meanwhile was abortive, but Amr conquered Egypt with its wealth for his own benefit (658), and in 660 Muāwiya could take the style of Caliph. The murder of Caliph Ali in January 661 and the submission of his son Hasan completed the victory of the Omayyads and the foundation of the Caliphate of Damascus, their capital.

This revolution ensured the ascendancy of the old Arab aristocracy and the Arab tribes settled in Syria. It was an Arabian empire, distinct in essence from the religious theocracy of Medina represented by the first four, or Orthodox, Caliphs. But the tribes of Irāq, more oriental than the Syrians, hated the usurping westerners, and the rule of the Omayyads was too political in its foundations to appeal to the growing cosmopolitanism of the Islamic religion, which was reinforced perpetually as converts streamed in from all the subject-races. Yet to strengthen the power of the political State, which was their own and their government's, the Omayyads were bound to foster the religious fervour of Islam, whose Caliphs they were. Muāwiya I (660–80) ruled like a patriarchal chief surrounded by other chiefs and nobles without the open absolutism and pomp of later Caliphs, but he knew well how to get his way. He avoided obvious nepotism and had a special talent for winning over able men. His aim was to found a dynasty and he nominated his son Yazīd I (680–3) to be his successor. This was against custom and tradition, and the new Caliph was at once met with revolts. The old-fashioned theocrats of Medina set up one of themselves, Abdallah (680–92), as Caliph; the men of Irāq rallied to Husain, the second son of Ali. They loathed the Syrian predominance, but as yet they were half-hearted, and the amiable Husain, who had sat on the Prophet's knees, was deserted by them and cut down by his enemies at Karbala (10 October 680). His martyrdom was more potent than his life: a theory of legitimacy—the divine right of the descendants of Ali and Fatima to the Caliphate—grew up in Irāq and became the leading dogma of the Shi'a sect, which spread to Persia, where it became national. The Fatimids were the heirs of the prophetic spirit, the only true Imāms or chiefs of the Faith and successors (Caliphs) of the Prophet.

This was for the future. The orthodox Caliph of Medina had to be subdued by a war against the Holy Cities, which brought odium on the

Omayyads, made worse by the extinction of Muāwiya's line. An elderly cousin, once Othman's confidant, Marwan I (683–5), succeeded at Damascus, but had to fight for his throne, for even the Syrians were divided; the Kalb tribes supported him, but the Qais tribes were for Abdallah, and their members were ramified throughout the empire. The rancorous and indelible feud became a contest between North and South Arabians, which disintegrated all Islam and its dominant race. Marwan I won the day at Marj-ar-Rabit (684) and conquered Egypt, but his son, Caliph Abd-al-Malik (685–705), hampered by the Christian Mardaites in Syria itself, had to wait before subduing the east. In Irāq the Medinese ruled, beset in their turn by a formidable Shi'ite rebellion under Mukhtar and by the ever-mutinous Kharijites. At last Abd-al-Malik overthrew the Medinese in Irāq on the Tigris (690), and his capable lieutenant Hajjaj captured Mecca and slew Abdallah (692). The Arab empire was reunited, while Hajjaj ruled Irāq and Persia for the Caliph.

The zenith of Omayyad power, although undermined by the tribal feud of Qais and Kalb, followed these successes. The constitutional principles of Islam were adumbrated by Omar, but Muāwiya and Abd-al-Malik had the chief share in their development. Omar made the Arabs supreme over their tax-paying subjects and founded the state treasury. Muāwiya made the Caliphate dynastic and introduced a political rather than religious government. Abd-al-Malik created an actual administration by the Arabs themselves. Hitherto they had only held the highest posts, while the native officials of subject Romans or Persians continued their ancient systems and routine. From Abd-al-Malik's reign Arabic becomes an administrative language in bilingual documents. He issued an Arabic coinage, gold and copper for ex-Roman, silver for ex-Persian provinces. Taxation was changed. Conversions to Islam had increased the tax-free Moslems and diminished the taxed infidels: emigration from the country to the new great camp-towns had made the burden on the stationary peasant heavier. Hajjaj made a beginning by retaining the tax on new converts. Under Caliph Hishām (724–43), it seems, a new system was brought into working order: all now paid the universal land-tax, but non-Moslems paid in addition the poll-tax of unbelievers. So, too, Arabs and Moslems generally became numerous in minor offices. Even in Egypt, where the Copts retained finance, conversions, immigration and inter-marriage were enlarging a mixed Arab population.

Under Abd-al-Malik and his son Walīd I (705–15) the Omayyads were at their greatest power. Buildings, like the Omayyad mosque at Damascus and the 'Dome of the Rock' at Jerusalem, showed their splendour and civilization, and expansion could begin again. The Moslems crossed the river Oxus and reached the river Indus on the east, and conquered Spain in the far west. The final conquest of Armenia, after half a century of wars,

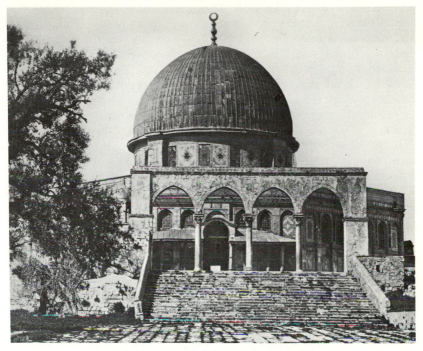

Fig. 41. Dome of the Rock, Jerusalem

brought the northern frontier to the Caucasus. The method of almost yearly attacks on Asia Minor found its culmination in the epoch-making failure to capture Constantinople in 716–17, but did not cease with that defeat. The subjection of Spain was the sequel to that of North Africa, which began in 642 by the occupation of Cyrenaica. Progress was made tempting by the discord between Romans and the wild Berber tribes—the exarch of Carthage, Gregory, was in revolt with Berber support—but one successful raid (647–8) was the only immediate result. A marked advance was achieved when Uqba, Amr's nephew, founded the armed camp of Qairawan, the later Moslem capital, south of Carthage in the heart of Roman Africa (670). But Uqba was of the old hectoring Arab type; he enraged the Berber chiefs whom he subdued or overawed, and undid the conciliatory work of Dinar, who replaced him for a time. Although he reached Tangier in a spectacular raid, he dispersed his forces and was cut down near Biskra on his return (683). The Berbers, led by their chief Kusaila, rose in a body and allied with their old enemies, the Byzantines. All Africa west of Cyrenaica was lost. The conquest was then renewed under Abd-al-Malik. First, Zuhair recovered Qairawan and over-

237

threw Kusaila at Mons Aurasius. Then came the real pacificator, Hassan ibn an-Nuʻman, who adopted Dinar's conciliatory policy. He combined severe discipline and astute diplomacy, and he saw that the Byzantines in the coast towns were the main enemy. With Syrian reinforcements he captured the Roman capital of Carthage in 697, only to lose it immediately. But the issue was decided by sea. In these evil days of the Eastern Empire the Arabs disposed of the more powerful fleet, and the defeat of the Patrician John at sea in 698 decided finally the fate of Carthage and Roman Africa.

There were still the Berbers, now led by a prophetess, the Kāhina, to deal with. At first defeated by her, Hassan gained over several tribes and won a decisive victory at Gafes. Henceforth the policy of fraternization was followed, in place of plundering. It was made easy by the resemblance in organization and mode of life, once the Berbers accepted congenial Islam. Under the next governor, Mūsā, Berbers as well as Arabs subdued their western kinsmen of Mauretania, now to be called Maghreb ('the West') or Morocco, and it was from Morocco that in 711 Arabs and Berbers proceeded to the conquest of Visigothic Spain.

It is remarkable how quickly and completely Latin and Christian civilization disappeared from North Africa and was replaced by oriental Islam. It seems that the Latin townsmen migrated to Sicily and Spain. The Berbers had always been barbaric and for over three centuries had been steadily ousting the Latins from the interior. With the Arab influx the process was completed, and the acceptance of Islam provided a religion and civilization more within the reach and to the taste of both settled and nomad tribesmen. The Moors, whether they adopted Arabic speech or retained their own tongue as Berbers, brought a fresh fanaticism and warlike fury to their new faith, which produced wars, sects, and revolutions inside and outside their own borders. The Mediterranean Sea had long ceased to be a peaceful Roman European highway; it now became a war-ridden frontier of opposed religions and civilizations.

(3) THE ABBASIDS AND MOSLEM CIVILIZATION

The Omayyad Caliphate was founded on a basis of Arab racial supremacy, and in particular on tribes settled in Syria, almost more than on the religious basis of Islam. The Caliphs and their court rarely showed any proselytizing ardour: they were tolerant, conservative, often pre-Islamic in their ways. In the end this attitude brought about their downfall. Conquests had resulted in mass conversions, and a new Moslem people had developed, Persian, Aramaic, Coptic, Berber, at first as clients of the dominant Arabs. These Mawāli ('clients') were more civilized and better educated than their masters. They brought a new, fanatic fervour into

238

Fig. 42. The Omayyad Mosque, Damascus

Islam, at least in the second generation. They knew nothing of a natural superiority of Arabs as such. To them the universal character of Islam was a reality: all Moslems were brothers and equals in the Faith. This political resurgence and religious transformation were made more potent by the divisions among the Arabs themselves, the rivalry of Syria and Irāq, the feud, which rent east and west, of Qais and Kalb, and the continuous fights of the tribes against the authority of the State. Finally, the Shi'a beliefs, becoming national and Persian, dealt the final blow to the tottering dynasty.

Most of the later Omayyads enjoyed but brief reigns. The eastern provinces were permanently mutinous, although Caliph Hishām, who dealt with the problem of the land-tax, restored some degree of order there with the help of an efficient viceroy. After him the Caliphs were victims of the feud of Qais and Kalb, and were mostly puppets. Four Omayyads succeeded one another in a year. The last, Marwan II (744–50), was a capable man, but the game was lost. All malcontent provinces and parties were against Syria and the Omayyads. Victorious insurrection began in the east-Persian land of Khurasan, the ancient Parthia, where Arab and Iranian had most intermingled and where the Shi'ite doctrines had taken the strongest hold. The true legitimist line, the descendants of Ali and Fatima, the real possessors of the Shi'ite divine right, were not of the stuff

239

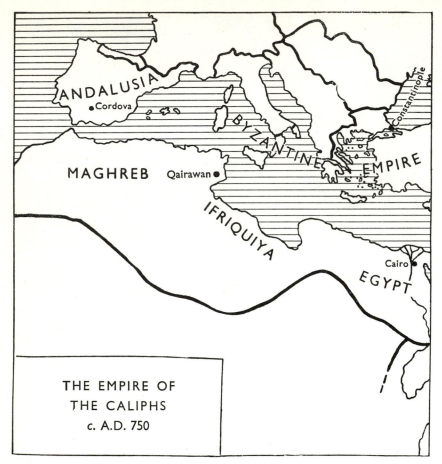

Map 5

of which successful pretenders are made, and their place as leaders was taken by their kinsmen, the Abbasids, descendants of the Prophet's uncle Abbās, by a sort of compromise which temporarily united the Shi'ites and the orthodox malcontents, the Sunni. Even so, it was their brilliant general, Abu Muslim, who won their battles and overthrew the Omayyads. Only Andalusia, the province of Spain, escaped the grasp of the new dynasty of Caliphs. There the survivor of the massacre of his kinsmen, Abd-ar-Rahman I, established an independent emirate.

The first Abbasid Caliph merely deserved his style of Saffah ('the bloody') (750–4); his brother Mansūr (754–75) reorganized the State. He built (762) the new capital of Baghdad on the Tigris, near the ancient Ctesiphon,

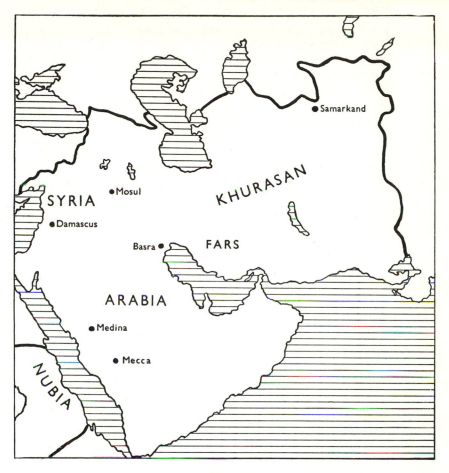

Map 5

in Irāq, and this typified the eastern, Persian trend of the new régime, which reached its apogee under his grandson, Hārūn-ar-Rashīd of legendary fame (786–809). Persian influence became predominant and the chief ministers were Persians. Such were the Barmecides for half a century till the jealous Hārūn destroyed them in 803. Now the Caliphs were autocrats surrounded by Persian pomp: as the central power grew weaker, the etiquette of the court grew more and more servile. On great occasions the Caliph wore the mantle of the Prophet. A new stress was laid on his religious authority, although he was not an Alid or a Shi'ite: he was the shadow of God on earth. His theoretic power was only limited by the prescriptions of the Koran, edited after Mahomet's death from his recorded oracles, with a supplement of accepted tradition of his utterances. The Caliph was supreme administrator, judge, and general. His duties were to defend the faith and Moslems, to war down unbelievers, to do justice, to levy and spend the taxes, and to appoint officials. He was the Imām, or leader in public worship, of all true believers, and as such could alone declare the Jihād or Holy War against the infidel. From him all legitimate authority was derived. Even when the Abbasid empire had broken up and the Caliph was a puppet, Moslem kings and emirs still sought a diploma of investiture from him to legalize their sway.

To head the administration the Abbasids created the office of the vizier (*wazīr*), who might under a weak or idle Caliph control the whole machinery of state, but it was a perilous eminence, as more than the Barmecides found, if an active master turned against his minister. One of the most important departments was the State Post, borrowed from Roman and Persian institutions. A network of highways, studded with posthouses, and thronged with couriers on swift mounts, kept the government daily informed of and in a position to control the provinces. It was supplemented by spies and a secret police. The prefect of police was a powerful and inquisitorial official, though the judges (*Kadi*), who tried cases, were independent of him. All this fabric of the Caliphate depended on finance by which its army and officials could be paid, and in the last resort its income depended on the virile industry of the dynasty, supported by a Moslem-united loyalty, which could keep the provincial governors as obedient instruments. After Hārūn-ar-Rashīd's death his sons fought for the throne, and the decay of the Abbasids began. Provincial particularism grew in the Islamic world-state, and the decline was both measured and partly caused by the decrease of the Caliph's revenue. Under Hārūn the revenue in cash amounted to some £21,000,000 of nineteenth-century value; it decreased under his sons, and after 900 was about £2,000,000. The sinews of war and government were withered.

Revenue was necessary for the upkeep of the army. There were the regular paid troops, and the volunteers with uncertain payments. With both of these the Caliphs kept up the almost annual warfare of raids with the East Roman Empire, and put down the frequent rebellions in their own lands. But the composition of the regulars changed. Persian troops from Khurasan formed an important division under the early Abbasids. Caliph Mutasim (833–42) levied a large, more trustworthy force of Turks from beyond the river Oxus, besides a corps of Berber slaves. The excesses of his Turkish troops led him to transfer his court to a new capital, Samarrā, higher up the Tigris (836). There the Turkish guards came to outnumber the rest of the army, the administration passed gradually into their hands, and the Caliphs were at their mercy. They broke into factions, while the provinces ceased to obey and send tribute. It was in vain that Caliph

Mutamid returned in 892 to Baghdad. In place of the standing army and a centralized government a system of military fiefs grew up, whose holders provided troops and tribute. The troops of both vassals and Caliphs largely consisted of white slaves (mamlūks), mainly Turkish, who thus became the arbiters of the free population. They did not give order to Irāq, to which the Caliph's dominion shrank. From 869 to 883 a slave revolt terrorized the delta of the Euphrates, sacking Basra and other wealthy towns. Far worse was the rebellion of the ultra-heretical Shi'ite sect of the Carmathians, which won over the Bedouins. For a century they spread terror not only over Irāq but Syria, Arabia and Egypt (890–990). In 930 Mecca itself fell a victim to their murderous campaigns of plunder.

Meantime the break-up of the empire proceeded apace. From 800 North Africa fell under the rule of its governors, the Aghlabids, who were practically independent. Morocco had already revolted under the Shi'ite Alid dynasty of the Idrisids. In the civil war which followed Hārun-ar-Rashīd's death between his sons Amin and Mamūn, the latter only won (813–33) by means of his Persian general, Tahir, who was rewarded with Khurasan. Egypt and Syria broke away under the Turkish Tulūnids and Ikhshīdids. The Arab Hamdanids ruled Mosul and Aleppo. Most of Persia fell under the native Shi'ite Buwaihids, who seized Baghdad and made the Caliph a cipher in 945. A new Shi'ite dynasty of Caliphs, the Fatimids, had already arisen in North Africa and in 969 conquered Egypt. It is no wonder that against divided Islam the Byzantine Emperors could pass from stubborn resistance to reconquest.

The transfer of the capital to Irāq had been followed by a period of commercial expansion. Wealth attracted silk from China and furs from North Europe. The width of the empire, the possession of an international tongue in Arabic, the honour given to the merchant in Moslem ethics, all contributed. Trade went by sea as well as land. Basra became the terminus for eastern voyages; the old ports of Egypt and Syria provided sailors and ships which were both merchantmen and men-of-war. If the Greek fire defended Constantinople, Arab fleets swept triumphant over the open Mediterranean.

In this abounding prosperity, centred round cultured Caliphs, learning, literature, art and civilization flourished in gorgeous profusion. Arabic gave them a splendid means of literary expression, but the authors and artists much more often than not belonged to the once subject-races, Persians, Aramaeans, Copts and Spaniards. Christians and Jews even wrote their works in Arabic. Much Roman Law found its way into Moslem legal treatises, and Greek science and philosophy were adopted as the basis of Moslem culture. The work of translation was organized under the half-Persian Caliph Mamūn. Greek works on philosophy, medicine, geometry, astronomy, engineering, music, and the like were turned into Arabic, often indirectly through Syriac. Algebra, the so-called Arabic numerals, and some astronomy and medicine came from India, and Moslem authors added to the store of knowledge. Arabic medicine culminated in the encyclopedic work of the famous Persian Avicenna (*ob.* 1037). Two other Persians were celebrated astronomers: Omar Khayyam, known in Europe for his quatrains, who reformed the Persian calendar in 1079, and Berūni (*ob.* 1048), one of the greatest intellects of his age. Moslem philosophy, founded on Aristotle, developed from Kindi in the ninth century and tended in an unorthodox direction. The thought, however, of Avicenna and of the twelfth-century Spanish philosophers who culminate in Averroes belongs almost as much as, if not more, to Western medieval development than to that of the Moslem East, and their influence was most profound in Christian Europe. The art of Persia lies outside our scope; that of the Near East has its place in the evolution of European art which will receive treatment later.

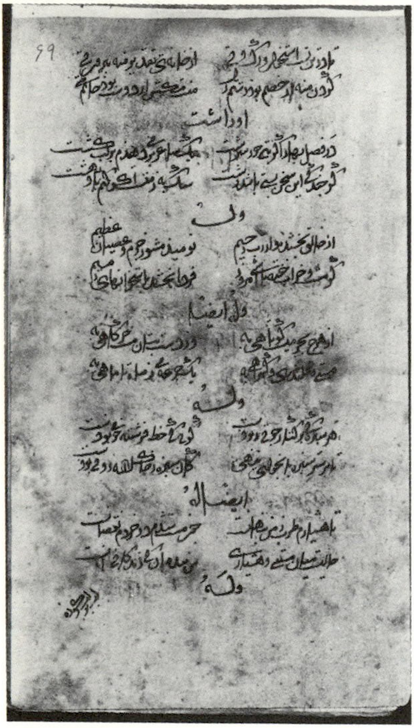

Fig. 43. Omar Khayyam's Rubā'iyyat

Although the dissolution of the Caliphate brought political weakness and turmoil to Moslem lands, it will be seen from the foregoing summary that it did not retard the growth and efflorescence of Moslem civilization. The Seljūk Turks and their like entered into the heritage of the past as patrons if not as full participants. It was the appalling devastation perpetrated by the Mongol conquerors in the thirteenth century that inflicted on the Moslem East a ruin from which it never recovered.

CHAPTER II

THE BYZANTINE REVIVAL

(I) THE ICONOCLASTS AND REFORM

The reign of Leo III 'the Isaurian' (717–40) marks the consummation of a rapid change in the Eastern Roman Empire which had been going on for a hundred years. It was then that the Empire fully entered on its Byzantine period, Greek in speech, deeply orientalized, with Christianity engrained in its thought and ethos. This Greek speech and mentality did not obliterate its inheritance from the older Roman phase of the Empire: its inhabitants thought of themselves as Romans ('Ρωμαῖοι)—to the Moslems their land was Rūm; their official language was tinged with borrowed Latin words; their institutions, bureaucracy, army and navy, law and finance were developments from the Roman State. The Basileus was the true successor of the Caesars; his titles of Autocrat and Sebastos were old translations of Imperator and Augustus, and though a despot, with power to associate his colleague and heir, he was on a vacancy still nominally elected by the Senate of New Rome (Constantinople) and acclaimed before or afterwards by his troops. If he had not been associated and crowned by his predecessor, and sometimes if he was, he was crowned by the Patriarch of Constantinople, a ceremony which well expresses the Christian imprint on the Empire and the religious character of his authority. There was an unbroken continuity, Christian, Greek and Roman from the ancient world. Life by law, bureaucratic organization, the very notion of the State apart from its rulers and races, were all hall-marks of this civilized island surrounded by oriental or barbaric monarchies and tribes. Unlike the barbarized Westerners, its upper class remained literate and educated. The masterpieces of the Hellenic past were preserved, copied and read. Literacy, theology and learning were not the monopoly of a small minority of clergy and monks as in the West. The advantages of science, training and system were understood by Byzantine society.

This civilized, European character was shown in the Byzantine appreciation of the art of war, which contrasts with the elementary, undisciplined, blundering valour of the West. The generals thought in terms of tactics and strategy; they varied their methods with the varying nature of their foes. The soldiers, a professional, scientifically equipped army, were efficiently drilled for their work, and formed the best fighting machine in Europe. No slander is more false than Gibbon's unhappy phrase that Byzantine victories were accidental. Till the irreparable disaster of Manzikert (1071) robbed the Empire of its best recruiting grounds, the Byzantine army, brave, well based, usually well led, was the bulwark of Europe against Asiatic aggression, and even later, when decayed, depopulated, and degenerating, the Empire held back the Turk for centuries, preserving the priceless inheritance of Greek and ancient civilization for the progressive West.

As will be seen in the ensuing narrative, the Byzantine Empire was by no means a changeless, fossilized State. Circumstances and problems kept changing, and had to be met by a series of usually able rulers as best they might. Its continuity and the helplessness of its final remnant after the mortal wound inflicted in 1204 by the Western brigands of the Fourth 'Crusade', have done much to create the false tradition of its immobility. Its changes indeed were always rather a reassortment of existing factors than fresh growth, but the forces of decay were curbed from time to time, and, thus reinvigorated, the Empire could revive morally and materially and thrust back its encroaching foes.

The rule of the Isaurian dynasty was the most decisive of these periods of revival. It is also the least known. Partly our lack of understanding is due to a real decay in the contemporary literature; there is a dark interval in historiography in the seventh and eighth centuries, which is one facet of the subsidence of secular, humane culture in those desperate times when existence was at stake. But a major reason is that the Emperors championed in Iconoclasm a religious and ecclesiastical reform which ran counter to the instincts and prepossessions of the majority of their subjects and which was ultimately defeated in its essentials, although it was not without enduring results and was accompanied by a secular reorganization which strengthened the Empire within and without. Iconoclastic writings were destroyed by their victorious adversaries, and we hardly know the Iconoclastic Emperors save by the impassioned reports of their opponents and victims, who vilified them with but rare recognition of the gratitude which the State and their subjects owed them.

Leo III succeeded to an Empire distracted by twenty years of revolution and invasion. It was his first task after the deliverance of Constantinople from the Arabs to suppress new revolts, and he was able in 720 to associate his infant son Constantine on the throne. Then there was military reorganization. He divided the overvast and dangerous Anatolic theme into two, as well as bisecting the maritime theme, which was the fleet. Later his son divided the theme of guards round the capital. The *Military Code*, which probably dates from Leo's reign, was designed to furnish a professional, specialized army. The careful appointment of able, loyal generals in the themes, each of which was at the same time a province and its territorial army corps, was the keystone in the reformation of these truly national troops. A full treasury was of course necessary for military and civil reform, and Leo did not fear to be oppressive to secure it. In 727–8 he made a double levy of the regular taxes, and in 739 raised an additional impost to rebuild the walls of Constantinople ruined by an earthquake. His social legislation, expressed in the *Ecloga* (740), was designed to simplify and Christianize the Civil Law. Certainly, in modern times its mutilations, which replaced in great measure the death penalty of Justinian, appear barbarously cruel, but they seemed more humane to the Byzantines of that day. Distinctions of rank before the law, once embedded in Roman institutions, were abolished, as was the legal condition of concubinage. The equal rights of both mother and father over their children were established as well as their mutual claims on each other's property. The strengthening of family life was one of the aims of the Isaurians.

His iconoclastic (image-breaking) policy, however, looms largest in the reign of Leo III. It had both its religious and social sides, and was destined to rend the internal harmony of the Empire and to lose it the remnants of Roman Italy. But it also arrested a dangerous disease. During the prolonged crisis of the seventh century, the all-powerful influence of religion had taken a dangerous direction in Byzantine society. Superstition and the belief in the marvellous had grown till men neglected their own exertions and left all to the interposition of the saints and the Virgin Mother of God. Above all, the cult offered to miracle-working images filled an enormous place in Byzantine minds. Everywhere the sacred icons (likenesses) were adored and besought for every desire. They were even made godparents at baptism. Theologians declared that it was the mystical presence of the saint in his icon which was invoked, but the populace drew no such distinction. It was the all-powerful image which worked continual miracles. Many devout minds had long denounced the worship of these Christian idols and urged their destruction. In Asia Minor, the armed core of the Empire, this antagonism was specially strong, and was shared by definite heretics, like the numerous Paulicians; the influence of the then proselytizing Jews and of the neighbouring Moslems with their horror of idolatry had also its effect. Leo III himself came from Asia Minor and was convinced of the iniquity of image-worship and the necessity of its abolition. Like all Byzantines he was a theologian at heart. With his iconoclasm was linked his alarm at the ill effects of the overgrowth of monasticism. The immunity from taxation enjoyed by the ever-increasing Church lands reduced the revenue; the swarming monks meant a loss of soldiers for the army and of husbandmen for the fields. The monasteries were dangerous foci of unrest, many depending on the miraculous icons they possessed; their control of education and their hold on popular opinion rendered them a formidable power in the State. Icons and monks were equally obstacles of the Isaurians' social reformation.

Leo III hesitated until the terrible volcanic eruption of Thera (Santorin) convinced him that the wrath of God was falling on the Empire. To propitiate it he issued in 726 the edict against images. The idols were to be destroyed. But he roused popular fury in the Balkans and the West. When the image of Christ above the palace gate was shattered, riot stormed in the capital. A short-lived revolt broke out in Greece proper, and, worse still, all Byzantine Italy drove out the imperial officers (727) with the sympathy of Pope Gregory II, who was already an opponent of Leo's new taxation. Leo's energetic counter-measures and the prudence of the Pope restored peace, but soon (731) Pope Gregory III in a Roman synod excommunicated the iconoclasts. Leo's punitive fleet was lost in an Adriatic tempest, and he had to be contented with confiscating the great papal estates in the Empire—a help to his finances—and with transferring Illyricum and the Byzantine fragments in Calabria and Sicily from the patriarchate of Rome to that of Constantinople. Save in the dating of documents by the Emperor's regnal years, the breach seemed complete: the Roman duchy was ruled by the Pope, Venice and Naples by native dukes.

Meanwhile the Eastern clergy were in opposition. Leo replied by deposing (730) the Patriarch of Constantinople in favour of an iconoclast, Anastasius, and closing the Church schools. An iconodule (image-serving) lead was taken by a monk outside the Empire, the Palestinian St John Damascene. He formulated not only the theological principles of image-worship but also that of the independence of the Church from the Caesaropapism of the Emperor. This became a cardinal doctrine in dispute. Yet in spite of some harsh acts Leo III enforced the edict and suppressed revolts with great moderation and laxity; it was his son Constantine V (740–75), slandered and abusively nicknamed Copronymus by the iconodules, who began late in his reign a real persecution. Constantine, if violent and autocratic, was great in administration and war, the idol of the army, 'the victorious and prophetic Emperor'. He took the offensive against the Arabs, then weakened by civil war; in ten victorious campaigns against the Bulgarians he restored the prestige of the Empire in Europe, and subjected the Slavs in Thrace and Macedonia. At home he carried on his father's work of reform and also his rigorous taxation, and he even began a revival of art, if only it was secular. His despotic bigotry was intensified by the revolt of his brother-in-law Artavasdus, who with the aid of the iconodules secured Constantinople.

Constantine, supported by the Asiatic themes, defeated his rival, and took Constantinople by storm (742), but rancour remained. He held the strongest iconoclastic views, condemning the cult of the Virgin and saints even without icons. He hated monks as shirkers and called their garb 'the raiment of darkness'. He was able to enlarge his party in Thrace by transporting Asiatics thither. When the outbreak of the plague in 746 dispeopled Constantinople, iconoclastic immigrants became the majority of its inhabitants. In 753 the Emperor could proceed to hold an icono-clastic Council. The bishops would not renounce the cult of the Saints, but they did condemn the worship of images as heretical and authorized an imperial persecution. Even so, Constantine waited until the worst of the Bulgarian war was over, and then for six years (765–71) an era of martyrs and furious repression set in. Images and mosaics were broken: 'all beauty disappeared from the churches'. Iconodules were hunted down. There was a real attempt, pursued with Byzantine cruelty, to destroy the monastic order. Monastic property was confiscated; monks were tortured, humiliated before the mob, or terrorized into marriage or flight or hiding.

7. The Isaurian and Amorian Dynasties

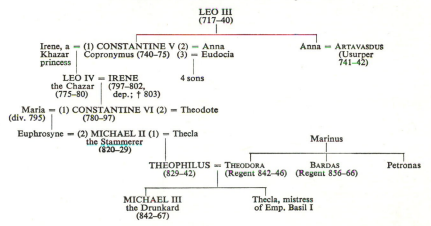

Courageous resistance merely exasperated the Emperor. His son Leo IV (775–80), surnamed 'the Chazar' from his barbarian mother, after an interval due to fears of his brothers' intrigues and to the influence of his Athenian wife Irene, who was a concealed iconodule, began in his last days to re-sharpen the persecution, but his untimely death left the throne to his ten-years-old son Constantine VI (780–97) with power in the hands of the Empress-mother.

The ruling passion of Irene was the lust for power. It was combined with a fervent devotion to images which made her think herself the chosen instrument of God and justified in all her actions. Her abilities for diplomacy and intrigue were great, although they were nearer to cunning than statesmanship, and her choice of ministers, especially from among her eunuchs, was directed to gaining and keeping power, not to the welfare of the State. The eunuch Stauracius, patrician and Logothete of the Dromos, was her faithful lieutenant. There were formidable obstacles in her path, which she skilfully overcame: the Caesars, her brothers-in-law, the iconoclastic officers of State and the army, the Patriarch and numerous bishops. The plotting Caesars were forced into the priesthood, the officials were changed, and the Patriarch was replaced by the iconodule Tarasius. Meantime toleration was the order of the day, while the Empress and Tarasius proposed to close the schism with Rome by a General Council of the Church. Its session was disturbed by the soldiers, but Irene gained over some provincial troops, and disbanded regiments of the guard. In September 787 the Seventh Œcumenical Council was finally opened at Nicaea in the presence of papal legates, amid a crowd of fervent monks. It promptly restored the cult of images, defining it as veneration not adoration. Ascetic discipline was re-enforced. The victorious monks could now aim at the complete freedom of the Church from the State, a striking departure from Byzantine traditions. They hailed Irene as the Christ-supporting (Christophoros) Empress.

But as Constantine VI grew up he wished to rule. A wife was forced on him, a first attempt (790) to oust Stauracius was ignominiously quelled—he himself was flogged—and Irene declared that she was the ruler. She was, however, unpopular with the army. Her regency had been marked by defeats at the hands of the Caliph Hārūn-ar-Rashīd, the Bulgars, and the Franks in Italy. The Pope had already renounced Byzantine suzerainty. At the end of 790 the troops rose and Irene abdicated. Constantine VI, now really Emperor, was martial and active, but he was credulous and devoid of constancy. He weakly replaced his mother and Stauracius, and then was the plaything of her diabolic cunning. She incited him to blind the general who had given him the throne and to estrange his angry troops by harsh repression. At her persuasion he cruelly mutilated his intriguing uncles. Finally, she encouraged him in his passion for her attendant Theodoté, and advised him to put away his wife and marry her (795). This was to outrage public opinion and the monks, whose consequent invectives were punished. Irene could safely plot against her isolated son. She had him seized, blinded and deposed, and proclaimed herself sole reigning Emperor (July 797).

The iconodules saw the hand of God in this unnatural crime of Irene, the rejoicing monks lauded their pious benefactress, who loaded them with endowments, and the populace were bribed by the lowering of the taxes. It was a hollow success amid public reverses. Humiliating treaties were accepted from the Caliph and the Franks. At Christmas 800 the Frank Charlemagne assumed the style of Emperor of the Romans, which to the Byzantines was an insulting usurpation and travesty of what was only theirs to bestow. In the palace Stauracius and his rival Aëtius were scheming to gain the throne for one of their relations. Stauracius died, and the many malcontents and the iconoclasts saw their chance. On 31 October 802 the Logothete-General Nicephorus seized the throne, while Irene, at a loss for intrigue, submitted to exile until her speedy death. Few so dis-creditable rulers have received such praise as she did from devout partisans. She had injured the Empire morally and materially by crime and unwisdom. Yet the Empire had been renovated by the Isaurians and their adversaries. The latter, too, had effected with all alloys a moral reformation in the Church. The monks had preached the Christian virtues as well as image-worship. Round about 800 in the famous Studion monastery, its Abbot Theodore had composed a practicable rule which combined manual work, prayer, and intellectual culture. The Emperors themselves had encouraged a picturesque art, which portrayed natural objects and secular events. The regrowth of civilization in its Byzantine phase had begun.

(2) THE END OF ICONOCLASM AND THE CAREER OF PHOTIUS

A heavy task lay on the financier Emperor, Nicephorus I (803–11). The State was in disturbance, the treasury impoverished by the popularity hunting Irene, and foreign foes were aggressive. Although abused by the iconodules, he was talented and moderate: he was resolved to be master and resigned to unpopularity. He triumphed over the short-lived insurrection of Bardanes Turcus (803). He reimposed the old taxes and in 810 reorganized the finances, making Church lands and Church tenants pay their share. This exasperated the monks no less than his resolute Caesaropapism. When he obtained from a synod the rehabilitation of the priest who had solemnized the second marriage of Constantine—still alive in obscurity—declaring an Emperor above Church law, Theodore of Studion refused communion with the compliant Patriarch and began the Moechian (adulterers') controversy. For two years the Studite monks were persecuted, while Theodore boldly appealed to the Pope, 'our apostolic head'. When Nicephorus fell against the Bulgarians, and his son Stauracius (811) soon died, his son-in-law Michael I Rangabé (811–13), an iconodule, reversed the rehabilitation, but thus offended army and iconoclasts. The defeat of Versinicia at the hands of the Bulgarian Khan Krum produced the revolt and enthronement of Leo V the Armenian (813–20), strategos of the Anatolics, and a supreme effort to impose iconoclasm. Not till after he had won a victory and Krum was dead, did the new Emperor show his hand. After some faltering he deposed the iconodule Patriarch and a synod at St Sophia reaffirmed the iconoclastic doctrine. The controversy was re-opened not only over icons, but still more over the Emperor's supremacy in the Byzantine Church. The Studites and their partisans aimed at freedom from the secular power, and to buy it were ready, against all Byzantine tradition, to acknowledge the effective primacy of Old Rome. Once again Theodore was exiled and the Studites persecuted, until a plot among the courtiers ended in the murder of Leo V in the Christmas service and the

*Fig. 44. The Emperor Leo V and Patriarch Nicephorus order
the destruction of an icon*

exaltation of Michael II the Stammerer, commander of the guards, to the throne (820–29).

Michael II, who came from Amorium in Phrygia, was inclined to toleration and abstained from violence, but the Studites would have none of his ecclesiastical supremacy. In 821 Thomas the Slavonian, who pretended to be Constantine VI, won over the iconodules and the aggrieved peasantry of Asia Minor to a formidable revolt. He had the support of Caliph Mamūn, and long besieged Constantinople by land and sea. Luckily the Bulgarian Khan Omurtag defeated him in Thrace (823), and thus enabled the Emperor, to whom the Armeniac and Opsikian themes were loyal, to overthrow him. Theodore of Studion retired to die in a Bithynian monastery (826). The iconoclasts were triumphant and misused their triumph. Michael's son, the pious Theophilus (829–42), was a relentless persecutor with the aid of the Patriarch John Hylilas. Convents were closed, the prisons were filled, and penalties of Byzantine cruelty were inflicted on the iconodules. But the results were ephemeral. Even the Empress Theodora and the court circle were of opposite sympathies: vainly the dying Emperor exacted an oath from her to maintain Hylilas and his work. Otherwise he had been a beneficent ruler. He had at least thwarted the Caliphs, he was economical in finance, he was eagerly just in judgement, his love of pomp encouraged the arts, and he renewed the wide web of Byzantine diplomacy. Not least important was his increase of the themes and provision for defence.

When Theophilus left the throne to a child, Michael III (842–67), later named the Drunkard, the Empress-mother Theodora took control. Her ministers and her brother Bardas were all anxious to restore orthodoxy, and only her loyalty to her dead husband made her hesitate for a while. Yet in 843 Hylilas was deposed and with a new Patriarch, Methodius, she called a new Council. The icons as pictures (not as statues) were for the last time solemnly reinstated, exiles were recalled or freed, the most famous iconoclasts anathematized. From 843 onwards the Festival of Orthodoxy and the Blessed Theodora has been celebrated on the First Sunday in Lent in the Eastern Church. The triumph of orthodoxy was in fact a compromise. Not to mention the pious fraud which invented a death-bed recantation of Theophilus, the imperial authority over the Church remained unimpaired in defiance of the 'free Church' demands of the Studites and the protests of the Roman Popes, who were unconsulted in the Council of 843. It was rooted in Byzantine habits as was image-worship in Byzantine beliefs. The two revolutionary counter-theses were both discarded. They were each alien to Byzantine mentality.

So, too, unhappily was toleration. The heretical Paulicians, whose doctrines were at least becoming Manichaean, although favoured by the earlier iconoclast Emperors, had already been persecuted by the rigid Theophilus: now Theodora gave them the choice of conversion or death. Blood was shed in torrents. The survivors, led by Carbeas, settled near Malatiya in Moslem territory as bitter foes, not defenders, of the Empire. It was one of the greatest political disasters of the century.

In other ways, the administration of Theodora and her confidant, the Logothete Theoctistus, was wiser. The finances were sound; the Slavs of the Peloponnesus were reduced to order, a preliminary to their Helleniza-tion; and missionary enterprise was revived. But her ill-conditioned son was growing restive, and her brother Bardas used him to grasp power by the murder of Theoctistus and her own supersession. Michael III was absorbed in pleasure, sport and the lowest society, but the Caesar Bardas, ambitious and unscrupulous as he was, had great qualities as a ruler (856–66) in his nephew's name. He was incorruptible and just and led an intellectual revival. He founded the school of Magnaura, where he gathered the best teachers of the day under the universally learned Leo of Thessalonica. Among them were Constantine (St Cyril), the apostle of the Slavs, and the brilliant Photius, whom Bardas made Patriarch (858), deposing for the purpose his enemy, the austere Ignatius. Byzantine culture under his auspices recovered, after the dark interval, never again to be obscured till the fall of Constantinople.

Ecclesiastical events of the greatest moment marked the rule of Bardas. The first was the Moravian mission, the invention of the Slavonic alphabet, and the translation of the liturgy into Slavonic through the agency of Constantine (St Cyril) and his brother St Methodius. The west Slav prince Rostislav, the centre of whose power lay in Moravia, and whose subjects had been partially converted by German missionaries, desired to stem the growing German influence in his country, and appealed to Constantinople for a Byzantine mission. By the advice of Photius his friend Constantine, already well known for his remarkable gifts and his knowledge of Slavonic, which as yet was not seriously differentiated into dialects, was selected for the task. He devised the new script and began the translation of liturgy and Scripture. It was all in the tradition of the Eastern Church and Eastern Christianity, which had never prescribed the use of one official language, as the Western Church among its barbarian converts did with Latin. In Moravia itself the work of St Cyril (as he was renamed shortly before his death at Rome in 869) and of Methodius was ephemeral—the German Western missionaries obtained the upper hand by 890—but their alphabet (the so-called Glagolitic), liturgy, and translations were carried by their disciples to the newly converted Bulgarians and other Slavs in succession, and became pan-Slavonic. The script in its revised form is the modern Cyrillic of Russia and Bulgaria. Meantime heathen Bulgaria had been gained for the orthodox Eastern Church. Christianity had already made some progress among its people when Bardas clinched the matter by an invasion. The Khan Boris submitted to be baptized in 864, and proceeded to force conversion on his subjects to the delight of Photius, who feared that Bulgaria might be acquired by the Latin Western Church. This nearly happened. Not getting a bishop, Boris made overtures to Rome, and Pope Nicholas I promptly sent two legates with much good advice (866). But the Popes, too, did not respond to Boris's wishes for autonomy, and in 870 the consecration by the Byzantines of an archbishop, next in precedence to the Patriarch, and ten bishops sealed his convictions. The Ecumenical Council of 869–70, in spite of the protests of the papal representatives, completed the adherence of Bulgaria to the Eastern Church.

The Bulgarian question was entangled with the so-called Photian Schism, which deepened the long-growing estrangement between the Greek and Latin Churches. This Schism was bound up with the personal fortunes of the ambitious Photius. His appointment had been irregular, and Nicholas I, insistent on papal primacy which the Studites supported, denounced it and championed the deposed Ignatius. In his defence Photius, with great diplomatic skill, raised all the Greek grievances against the Latins, both old and new. A Council, held by Michael III in 867, condemned Pope Nicholas. Photius made free use of the differences in customs between the Eastern and Western Churches, amongst which figured the recent Western addition of Filioque[1] to the 'Nicene' Creed. What was more fundamental in reality was the widespread feeling that Roman interference in the Byzantine patriarchate was unlawful. Here the dissidence was incurable.

The Council, however, did not save Photius. In spite of some success, Bardas had not been fortunate in war. Crete and Sicily were in Moslem

---

[1] Which expressed the Double Procession of the Holy Ghost from the Father and the Son (*ex Patre Filioque*).

hands, a danger to the Empire. The first Russian raid on the capital by sea had been baffled chiefly by the energy of Photius. Bardas, too, lost his hold on the drunken, capricious Emperor. Michael III had found a stalwart favourite in an adventurer, the peasant Basil, called the Macedonian from his birthplace, who consented to marry the Emperor's mistress, Eudocia Ingerina. In 866 the two atrociously murdered Bardas; next year Basil I was associated on the throne, and fearing a supplanter himself, hastened to assassinate his worthless benefactor (September 867). Thus did the Macedonian dynasty, which was to see the most glorious Byzantine period, begin its course. The immediate sequel in Church matters was the deposition of Photius by Basil, his enemy, and the restoration of Ignatius. Basil aimed at a superficial reconciliation with Rome without abandoning the independent position of the Eastern Church or Byzantine Caesaropapism. He and Pope Adrian II convoked the eighth Ecumenical Council at Constantinople (869–70) to settle the Photian question. He saluted Rome as 'the mother of all the Churches', and Bulgaria was formally abandoned by the Byzantines. It did not, however, pass under Rome, for its Khan Boris managed to maintain its ecclesiastical independence, and culturally it still looked to the East. Photius recovered court favour, was reinstated as Patriarch on Ignatius's death in 877, and was again deposed in 886. Out of these complex events was built up later the legend of a formal breach between the two Churches, which were drifting steadily apart in mentality, culture and organization.

(3) THE MACEDONIAN DYNASTY

Although he rose to power by base sycophancy and assassination, the Emperor Basil I (867–86) was a great ruler and benefactor of the State. He was both statesman and general. Apart from military and foreign affairs, he made his mark in administration and law. Here the indispensable preliminary was the appointment of incorrupt officials and just and learned judges. In finance the disorder and embezzlement since Bardas's murder were rectified, while endeavours were made to protect the peasant landowner from the encroachments of the wealthy proprietors. In law Basil's object was partly to return to Justinian's Code, partly to embody changes. The *Prochiron* (c. 878) and its second edition, the *Epanagoge* (c. 886), were intended as clear, simplified handbooks. A fuller codification was also initiated. Basil also figured as a patron of art. His New Church was celebrated for its mosaics, and illuminated manuscripts testify to an artistic revival, which was still more clearly shown in the continuous, yet varied tradition of Byzantine architecture.

Basil was unhappy in his family. His eldest and favourite son, Constantine, died before him. His second, Leo, whose mother was Eudocia, was really the offspring of Michael III, and was hated by his putative father.

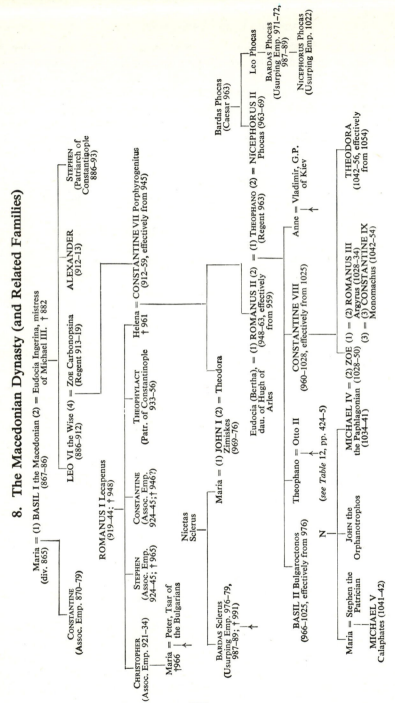

8. The Macedonian Dynasty (and Related Families)

The third, Alexander, was of no capacity. Yet when Constantine died in 879, Basil, who was beside himself with grief, was eager to make Alexander his successor. The courtiers took sides; Leo barely escaped blinding; and Basil may have met his end by murder. Leo VI the Wise (886–912), who reigned with Alexander as a powerless colleague, may have been Michael's son, but he carried out Basil's policies. Unlucky in war, he was distinguished in the arts of peace. He was a learned, legislating Emperor. To him belong the *Basilics* in its sixty books, a full codification of existing Byzantine law, written wholly in Greek, and supplementary Novels. They mark the completion of the development, influenced by Christian standards,

Fig. 45. The Emperor Leo VI

which had taken place since the days of Justinian. His hand was to be found in every branch of the administration in Church and State. Ceremonies, precedence, the policing and trade of Constantinople, and ecclesiastical organization were all dealt with. It was this stay-at-home Emperor who wrote a standard work on Byzantine military tactics, and he plumed himself on his sermons and hymns.

Marriage and the provision of a male heir were the stumbling-blocks in the path of the pious Leo. His first three marriages produced only daughters, and Byzantine law forbade a fourth marriage. None the less, when his mistress, Zoe Carbonopsina ('the black-eyed') bore him a son, Constantine Porphyrogenitus, in 905, Leo insisted on marrying her. The

257

Pope and the other Eastern Patriarchs condoned the breach of law, but Nicholas, the Patriarch of Constantinople, was obdurate and was deposed. The internal dispute was still active when Leo died, and Constantine VII (912–59) succeeded him. For a few months his uncle and co-regent Alexander held power (912–13), but fortunately died before he could oust him. Then a council of regency was the scene of rival ambitions until at last a soldier of the Armeniac theme, Romanus I Lecapenus (919–44), made himself master as Emperor-colleague. Constantine VII grew up as a political nonentity. He gave a halo of legitimacy to the government and retained popular sympathy, but he was a savant, an artist and a scholar, not a born ruler, in spite of his birth in the purple chamber which gave him his sobriquet.

Romanus I was an uneducated plebeian, ambitious to found a dynasty. One after another his three sons were made co-Emperors. In spite of his unpopularity he did service to the State. His foreign policy was successful both east and west; he continued in his Novels the endeavour to defend the peasant-proprietors, who formed the backbone of the Empire, from expropriation. But his sons were a liability. The youngest, Theophylact, whom he made Patriarch, was a disgrace to the Church. The two elder survivors suddenly deposed their father, and made him a monk. It was too much. In a month they shared his fate, and Constantine VII, ill fitted as he was, assumed the government. His personal influence is best seen in his encouragement of scholars and his encyclopedic learning. He was himself a voluminous author; his *Life of Basil I*, his works on the court ceremonies, the administration, and the themes of the Empire are even more valuable for history than they were as practical guides to the bureaucracy of his own times. But though he was not a cipher, the real strength and policy of the Empire lay in the hands of its firmly knit, well-trained and capable bureaucracy, and its efficient, organized army led by very able generals. Their merits are obscured by the treacherous, conscienceless intrigues of the court and leading officials, civil and military, for power, and the succession of conspiracies and rebellions for the next half-century veils, too, the danger to the State which the rise of a great landed nobility, bred to command in the army and mutinous to the central government, brought about.

Constantine Porphyrogenitus died in consequence of a poison given him by his son Romanus II (959–63) and the latter's wife, the low-born courtesan Theophano. Yet the ill-begun and brief reign of this worthless prince was marked by brilliant victories and the renewed expansion of the Empire. Partly this was due to the real ability of the criminal Theophano and her coadjutor, the eunuch Bringas, who directed the government, but the main reason was that the Byzantine army was now led by an eminent general, Nicephorus of the noble Cappadocian family of Phocas, who recovered

Crete and took the offensive beyond the Taurus range. When Romanus II died and Theophano and Bringas, ruling in the names of his infant sons Basil II and Constantine VIII, were rivals for power, his army declared Nicephorus II Phocas Emperor (963–9), and after street-fighting in the capital he was crowned in St Sophia. Being childless and a widower, the usurper could pose as colleague and guardian of the child Emperors, while he married their mother Theophano to the scandal of the monks, for he had vowed to join their order. A breach with the austere churchmen naturally followed, but the anti-ecclesiastical measures which Nicephorus took were probably more occasioned by the need of treasure for his triumphant wars than by mere rancour. He was of a harsh, ascetic temper, and could readily denounce the unevangelical greed and harmful wealth of his former friends. He confiscated old possessions and forbade new endowments of the monks, while his consent was made necessary for all episcopal appointments. But church treasures did not suffice for the Emperor's expenses; the taxes were made more rigorous, and, in spite of his victories, he met increasing disaffection. Revolt was simmering when it was anticipated by assassination. The Empress Theophano was passionately in love with the Armenian John Zimiskes, like Nicephorus a great noble of Asia Minor and a great general in the wars, but handsome and gracious, not rigid and austere, who had fallen into disfavour with the Emperor. In December 969 by his mistress's contrivance Zimiskes entered the guarded palace and brutally murdered Nicephorus. He was at once proclaimed Emperor and guardian of the two boys on the throne, for he too was a widower and childless. But the baseness of the plot gave the venerable Patriarch Polyeuctes the leverage to make terms. Before crowning the usurper he insisted on the banishment of the adulterous Theophano, penance from Zimiskes and punishment of his accomplices, and, not least, the abrogation of Nicephorus's ecclesiastical laws. His terms were accepted, and Zimiskes subsequently married an elderly daughter of Constantine VII to secure his throne.

The reign of John I Zimiskes (969–76) was as warlike and victorious as that of his victim, but less extortionate and more popular. He suppressed the revolts of the Phocas family, but the internal government was left to an old and experienced minister, the eunuch Basil, great chamberlain, an illegitimate son of Romanus I, who had been influential during four reigns. Although the Emperor could extend the frontiers, however, and buy off the enmity of the German Emperor Otto the Great by giving a Byzantine princess to be wife to Otto's son, the internal danger was constant. The great landed lords of Asia Minor, who were also generals of the armies, were rivals for the throne. The sudden death of Zimiskes let loose their ambitions, which it became the task of the chamberlain Basil, who now took charge of the State for the two young Emperors, to control. Bardas

Sclerus, brother-in-law of Zimiskes and his military coadjutor, struck for the crown almost at once. He gained Asia Minor at the head of its armies, but at sea his fleet was defeated by the loyalist navy, and the chamberlain boldly called in Sclerus's rival general, the ex-rebel Bardas Phocas. So two great Asiatic nobles were pitted against each other. After changes of fortune Bardas Phocas won in 979 the decisive victory of Pancalia near Amorium. Bardas Sclerus had no resource but to fly to the Moslems, among whom he was kept prisoner at Baghdad. The field seemed now open for rival generals and the chamberlain to keep the young Emperors in tutelage. Constantine VIII, a pleasure-loving trifler, was no obstacle, but the elder, Basil II, was of different stamp. Hitherto given to pleasure, he revealed suddenly a nature of granite. He had no taste for art or learning. He became a severe, ascetic, despotic soldier, 'haughty, reserved, suspicious, implacable', who raised the Byzantine Empire to its highest strength. He anticipated a general plot of officials and commanders in 985 by stripping with lightning speed the aged chamberlain Basil and Bardas Phocas of their powers. In the unrest and disloyalty that followed Bardas Sclerus escaped from Irāq in 987 and raised a revolt in the East. Bardas Phocas seized the opportunity to declare himself Emperor in Cappadocia and rallied the army round him. The two pretenders were to divide the Empire. But they were faithless to each other. Phocas made his fellow-rebel prisoner at an interview, and then proceeded to blockade Constantinople from the Asiatic shore. The resourcefulness of Basil II rose to the desperate occasion. He bought the aid of the Church by finally rescinding the edicts of Nicephorus Phocas, which the chamberlain had revived; he bought the aid of the Great Prince of Russia, Vladimir, by a promise of the hand of his sister. With 6000 Varangian (Russian) auxiliaries he won two bloody victories at Chrysopolis (Skutari) and Abydos. In the last Phocas himself fell. Sclerus, liberated by his captors, but old and nearly blind, quickly came to terms (989), and Basil II was master of his Empire. For the rest of his warlike reign the great Asiatic lords were kept in stern subordination. A brief revolt of the last Phocas was suppressed (1022). The peasant land-owner was, as we shall see, protected by Draconian laws, Basil's ministers and generals were only his instruments, and at his death in 1025 he left a superb army and a submissive State which stretched from the Danube to the Euphrates. He had earned the appellation of the Bulgar-slayer (Boulgaroctonos).

(4) THE MOSLEM WARS

The East Roman Emperors whose reigns have been epitomized above were almost incessantly at war with their neighbours, first defending and later extending their frontiers. Internal reform and conflict were carried on under the stress of this vital task of warfare. To segregate it in the

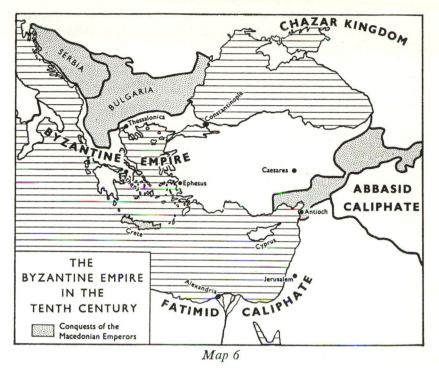

THE
BYZANTINE EMPIRE
IN THE
TENTH CENTURY

Conquests of the
Macedonian Emperors

Map 6

narrative makes for clearness, but diminishes the credit due to the rulers whose many-sided activity is blurred thereby, and their remarkable achievement in war alone is further decreased in appearance by the need to treat each neighbour and frontier separately, if some continuity in the history of events and policy is to be maintained. Due justice can only be done if we remember that the Empire was guarded on all its frontiers at the same time.

The salvation of Constantinople in 717 by no means ended the dangers and sufferings of the Moslem war. Cilicia had been recently lost. The Empire, indeed, could hold the natural barrier of the Taurus mountains by land, and its fleet could dominate the Aegean and sally from it by sea, but Moslem raids and sometimes real invading armies crossed the mountains almost yearly while the Caliphate maintained its power. For a century and more the Empire on its defence, besides forts and walled cities, kept up a chain of signal beacons from the frontier to the capital to give warning of invasions. The counter-raids which the Isaurian Emperors undertook were never so cruel as those of the Arabs, and did not reach so far into enemy territory. The transference of the Caliphate eastward to Irāq and Baghdad led to a decline in its navy, and the Byzantine naval themes did good service in the war. Yet by land, except during their frequent troubles with their own rebels, the Abbasids, especially Hārūn-ar-Rashīd and Mamūn, were as formidable and destructive as ever. It may seem strange that the Empire, attacked so long in its heart by so vast a monarchy, survived, but it was a centralized, homogeneous fabric with staying power and concentrated wealth, while the Caliphate was a collection of antagonistic provinces and peoples, loosely organized and ever harder to hold together. The disunion of Islam prevented even dangerous conquests from being fatal to Byzantium. In the ninth century the Empire lost its superiority at sea, for in 827 a fleet of Moslem adventurers from Spain seized the key-island of Crete, whence they ravaged the coasts and maintained a piratical dominion in spite of successive Byzantine attempts to repel them. Nor was this all, for in the same year the Aghlabid Emirs of Africa began the conquest of outlying Sicily. The attack was stubbornly resisted, and when there were forces to spare the Emperors sent help, but after Syracuse at last fell in 876, the island and its ports, with insignificant exceptions, was in Moslem hands. The mastery of the central Mediterranean and the Aegean belonged to the raiders and pirates of Africa and Crete. These Moors were practically independent of the Caliphate. None the less they made the severance between the Greek East and the Latin West of Christendom wider and deeper than it had ever been.

On land, however, the Empire was reviving, and the irremediable decadence of the Abbasid Caliphate and its dissolution into smaller, quarrelling emirates gave the opportunity to the Byzantines to pass to the offensive. It was the able Caesar Bardas who seized it. In 863 his brother Petronas won the decisive victory of Poson near the river Halys over the fighting Emir Omar of Malatiya. Henceforward Arab raids were on a pettier scale. Basil I, in spite of some reverses, drove the Paulicians from their strongholds and advanced the frontier to the upper Euphrates. He gained, too, a Christian semi-ally. In 885 the Bagratuni prince, Ashot I, refounded the kingdom of Armenia, and although he and his successors acknowledged the Caliph's suzerainty, their interests and their Christian, if Monophysite, faith drew them irresistibly towards Byzantium. These successes were clouded under Leo VI. The warfare with the frontier emirs produced as many checks as victories, while the Saracen piratical supremacy at sea produced disasters of great magnitude. In 904 the Greek renegade Leo of Tripoli, after capturing Abydos on the Hellespont, sacked Thessalonica itself, the second city of the Balkans. True, the Byzantine fleet was now improved, but victory alternated with defeat. Not till the rule of Romanus Lecapenus did the balance change. At sea in 924 his fleet destroyed the armament of Leo of Tripoli by Lemnos. On land, new generals, the Armenian noble John Curcuas and his lieutenants, won new victories over the divided Saracens. In 934 Malatiya was reunited to the

Empire, and, although among the petty Saracen princes Saif-ad-Daulah, the Hamdanid Emir of Aleppo (944–67), boldly resisted, he was hampered by his hostile neighbours who included the Caliph of Baghdad and the Ikhshidids of Egypt, and was only able to win intermittent victories. Expeditions on either side, however, had the character of triumphant raids rather than of conquests: a town captured while its citadel held out was not a permanent annexation. So, although the Byzantines reached Nisibis and the Tigris, their actual gains were far more restricted.

The effective Byzantine advance began in the reign of the worthless Romanus II and was due to the most brilliant of Byzantine soldiers, the future Emperor Nicephorus Phocas. Supremacy at sea was the preliminary. The indispensable recovery of Crete had long been the aim of the government, but great expeditions in 911 and 949 had proved ruinous failures, and the Moslem pirates remained the terror of sea and coast. Phocas in 961 redressed the balance by a complete naval victory and the reconquest of Crete. 'To me alone belongs the command of the sea', said Nicephorus when Emperor. A valuable corollary in 965 was the recovery of Cyprus, which, conquered by Muāwiya in 654, had later become a neutral island, paying tribute to both combatants since a treaty of 689. Meantime reconquest proceeded by land. Between 963 and 965 long-lost Cilicia with its plain and harbours was reduced. North Syria was attacked, the Emperor marched up the river Orontes to Hims, returning by the coast, and in 969 the great city of Antioch returned to Christian sway. At the time of Nicephorus's murder a humiliating treaty was imposed on the now tributary Emir of Aleppo. In the same year, however, a stronger power took control of Egypt and a little later of Moslem Syria. The Fatimite Caliph Muizz of Africa occupied Egypt, and transferred his capital from Qairawan to Cairo (972). Henceforward the petty emirs of Syria were Fatimite tributaries, for the much-vaunted invasion of the Emperor John Zimiskes in 975, which reached the Jordan without opposition, only added the coast as far as Jabala to Byzantine dominions. All the same the Empire was in the ascendant. In the border fighting Basil II himself twice intervened (995, 999) in much the same manner as Zimiskes. The truces he made with the Fatimites (988, 1000) were repeated in 1027 by Constantine VIII, when the Fatimite Caliphate was acknowledged and a Shi'ite mosque built in Constantinople.

Fortified by a friendly Armenia, whence many Byzantine soldiers came, the enlargement of the Empire had also been carried on eastwards. The frontier reached the Euphrates and the headwaters of the Tigris, while both Zimiskes and Basil II penetrated as far as Nisibis. The King of Iberia (Georgia) ceded a border district, Taikh, and Basil, who played on the quarrels of the Armenian dynasts, took over in 1022 the province of Vaspurakan beyond Lake Van, whose king abdicated rather than face a second invasion of the Seljūk Turks. The Emperor could not perhaps avoid taking up the championship of the Christian borderland, but the annexation brought the Empire into dangerous contact with a more formidable foe. Across the middle Euphrates even an advance was made by the capture of Edessa in 1031 by the general George Maniaces. Last of all, in 1046 came the treacherous seizure of the last king, Gagik II, of Armenia and his lands; fortresses were gained thereby and angry, ill-treated subjects in lieu of an ally.

(5) RUSSIANS AND BULGARIANS

During the greater part of the Saracenic wars the East Roman Empire was imperilled by foes and neighbours from the barbaric north. The Avars indeed, camped along the middle Danube, had ceased to be a menace in the east. At the close of the eighth century they were wiped out by the Frankish ruler Charlemagne and their lands left nearly vacant. The Turkish Chazars, who dominated the steppes north of the Black Sea, with their centre on the Volga, were nearly always friendly. They practised an unusual toleration in religion, and Jewish, Christian and Moslem converts were to be found among them. Their power, however, declined, subject tribes fell away, and newcoming tribes pressed on them. In 965 their town of Sarkel on the river Don was sacked by the Russian prince Svyatoslav: they were invaded by his son Vladimir: later they fade away. Of the tribes round them, the White Bulgars on the middle Volga remained a wealthy trading people, through whom the Baltic commerce ran eastward; the mixed Finno-Turkish tribe of Magyars migrated over the river Dnieper in the ninth century to the land round the river Dniester, and thence c. 895 to their final home in the Hungarian plain, vacated by the Avars. In both their new habitations they were fierce nomad marauders, the terror of settled peoples round. To each migration they had been forced by the onslaught of the Patzinak tribe, another Turkish neighbour of the Chazars, which in its turn had been driven westward by the Ghuzz Turks or Cumans. From 900 onwards the Patzinaks wandered between the Don and the Danube, raiding and plundering north and south for 200 years.

In strong contrast to the facile, if terrible, migrations of the Uralo-Altaic nomad tribes was the steady expansion of the East Slavs, or Russians as they came to be called. In the boundless forests and on the edge of the steppes the Slavs hunted and tilled. Homesteads became villages, and in favourable spots towns grew up along the Dnieper. Furs, honey and wax were their exports. A route existed from the Baltic to the Black Sea by way of Novgorod, Smolensk and Kiev, besides that to the Volga and the east. The Slav tribes to the south, like the Polyans of Kiev, found Chazar over-lordship a protection, but when Magyars and Patzinaks moved west across the route to the Black Sea, their towns needed fortification and defenders.

It was at this very time that Scandinavian adventurers and traders, principally Swedes, wandered in increasing numbers over the Baltic and along the trade-routes. They were known by the general name of Varangians, and one band of them assumed or were called by the name of Rus already in the early ninth century. Their leader was the legendary Rurik (Hraerekr) who became Prince (Sw. *konung*, Old Slav. *kunedsi*, whence Russian *knyaz'*) of Novgorod on Lake Ladoga. Other Scandinavians ruled at Kiev in the south as early as 839, when envoys of the 'khakan of the Rhos', coming *via* Constantinople, reached the Frankish court of Lewis the Pious. They appear to have had Slav imitators in other East Slav towns which were forming at the time. The organization of a town-state (*volost*) was simple enough. The prince was surrounded by his war-band or retinue (*druzhina*). They raised taxes in kind from their subject territory in the winter, and trafficked with the produce to Constantinople and elsewhere in the summer. But they were raiders and conquerors as well as merchants: in 860, as we have seen, they were already making a piratical attack on Constantinople, which failed. A generation later there was a consolidation of the power of these Swedish immigrants. Oleg (Helgi) of Novgorod, traditionally a son of Rurik, obtained possession of Kiev as well as other towns, and made it his capital: the state of Russia had been founded. In 907 he too attacked Constantinople in vain. This exploit was followed in 911 by a treaty regulating trade and subsidies. Oleg's son Igor (Ingvarr) made yet another assault in 941, but Greek fire destroyed his armament. His widow Olga (Helga), who succeeded him after a new treaty with the Byzantines, adopted another policy, for she came to Constantinople to be baptized in 954. Their son Svyatoslav bears witness by his Slavonic name to the change that was coming over the principality of Kiev. Hitherto the ruling class had been mainly Scandinavian: now they were becoming amalgamated with their Slav subjects, whose language they adopted and who took from them the name of Russians.

The Russian state was loosely compacted, for it was subdivided among the descendants of Rurik and the chiefs of the *druzhina*, but this did not hinder the Great Prince of Kiev from aggression on all sides. From 880, raids had been made as far as the Caspian Sea, and in 944 they once passed the Caucasus. Svyatoslav, a true viking, defeated the Chazars, as we have seen, and made Phanagoria a Russian town as Tmutorakan in the Taman peninsula on the Black Sea. But his ambitions aimed farther south. He attempted to transfer his throne to Bulgaria and even to Constantinople (967–71), and was beaten off with difficulty. The Patzinaks and Magyars of the steppes were redoubtable foes, while Russia tended to break up into petty chiefdoms. This danger was conjured by his son Vladimir (980–1015), a doughty heathen, who gained the throne of Kiev by fratricide and warred on all his neighbours, Russian, Polish, Bulgarian and Patzinak.

Fig. 46. Constantine IX receives the envoys of Vladimir of Kiev

But he felt the influence of Byzantine civilization. Christianity had made some way among the Russians even before Olga's baptism. Although a flagrant polygamist, Vladimir saw that Christianity and civilization were indissolubly united. Basil II bought his 6000 Varangian auxiliaries in 988 at the price of his sister Anne's marriage and the cession of Cherson. On his side Vladimir was baptized and enforced conversion on his boyars or nobles. His importance in Russian history is enormous. He reunited Russia; he made it part of the Byzantine Christian East, whence an imitative civilization, with missionaries, artists, architects, and culture flowed into his capital of Kiev; he held in check the Turkish nomads. As a statesman at any rate he earned his title of Saint.

To the Byzantine Empire, however, Bulgaria was the imminent and deadly foe. We have seen how the Black Bulgars settled south of the Danube in 679, and there slowly amalgamated with their Slav subjects, adopting their speech in course of time, and differentiating them in character from the other Slavs of the Balkans. Thenceforward they waged almost continuous war on the Empire under their Khans, Kovrat, Asparuch, Tervel, Bayan, and others, a war in which no battle was decisive. These Khans resided in their fortified camp at Pliska, near Shumla, and for long ruled both banks of the Danube. Underneath them were the two grades of nobles, *bolyarin* and *ugain*, chiefs of clans, whose turbulence they savagely repressed. The Isaurian Emperors from Leo III valiantly held the Khans at bay, but the great Krum captured Sofia (Sardica), and crossed the Haemus range. In 811 he annihilated the Emperor Nicephorus I and his army in the defiles and made his skull into a drinking goblet. In 813 he took Adrianople and laid siege to the capital itself, burning the suburbs. Then he received a crushing defeat from Leo the Armenian near Versinicia, and died (814) before he could renew his attack. His successor Omurtag concluded a thirty years' peace, and even helped Michael II in 823 against the rebel Thomas. The frontier, marked by a rampart, now ran between Adrianople and Philippopolis (Plovdiv). Omurtag had in fact turned westward, subduing the middle Danube Slavs. Those Slavs, however, the Serbs and Croats, offered a successful resistance under their native princes to the next two Khans, Malomir and Boris, and it was Boris (852–88) who began the civilization of his people, now Slav in speech, by adopting Orthodox Christianity, after hesitating between the Greek and Latin Churches. His conversion had been genuine, for he abdicated and lived as a monk in the odour of sanctity.

With Simeon (893–927), the cultured second son of Boris, who installed him after the ill-conditioned reign of his elder son Vladimir, the first Bulgarian state reached its zenith. Simeon made Great Preslav his capital, where he imitated Byzantine pomp, and imported a whole literature of translations from the Greek into his country. He took the quasi-imperial title of 'Tsar (Caesar) of the Bulgarians and Greeks', and raised the Bulgarian archbishop to the rank of Patriarch of Preslav. This was after a career of victory. Early in his reign he defeated the Byzantines and coped with a raid of the Magyars just before their last migration to Hungary. In a second war he won a crushing victory (917) over the Byzantines at Anchialus on the Black Sea, and in 923 vainly besieged Constantinople. Wider conquests were made to the west. He took most of Albania from the Empire; Belgrade and Nish were seized from the Serbians, though he was defeated by the Croats; at his death his kingdom stretched from the Black to the Ionian Sea.

Bulgaria's greatness was short lived. Simeon's younger son, the pacific Tsar Peter (927–69), made peace with the Emperor Romanus I, receiving the hand of a Byzantine princess in reward. But he had to fight first his warlike kinsmen and then a great noble, Shishman, who split the kingdom by establishing a western Bulgaria out of Simeon's conquests with its centre round Lake Ochrida (963). Serbs, Magyars and Patzinaks menaced the divided land, while the spread of the Bogomil heresy, with its Manichean doctrines, destroyed internal unity, both religious and political. When Tsar Peter unwisely demanded the tribute of Simeon's days from the soldier Nicephorus II a new disastrous war was unchained. Nicephorus called in the adventurous Svyatoslav of Russia, whose exploits in Bulgaria (967–9) reconciled the foes in a common alarm. At this juncture the death of Tsar Peter while his son Boris II was at Constantinople tempted the four sons of Shishman to seize on his kingdom. They were driven out, but the Russian enemy was not, for Svyatoslav returned, this time resolved to rule in the Balkans. He captured Great Preslav and the Tsar and threatened

Constantinople. The Emperor John Zimiskes was equal to the crisis in spite of the revolt of the Phocas. In 972 he recaptured Great Preslav and Boris II and expelled the Russians. But he was a faithless ally. He deposed Boris II and reannexed Eastern Bulgaria to the Empire.

Western Bulgaria, however, remained under Tsar Samuel, the surviving son of Shishman. He was an insatiable warrior, who reconstituted the dominion of Simeon and added the capture of Durazzo and the subjection of the Serbian prince (*zhupan*) of Dioclea, John-Vladimir. A first clash with the Empire in 986 ended in the rout of Basil II, whose noble generals were disaffected. Not till 996 were the Emperor's hands freed from the civil wars. Then he took up arms against Samuel. Year after year he attacked. First, Eastern Bulgaria was reconquered to the Danube, then Macedonia. Lastly, in July 1014 he won the decisive victory of Kleidíon in the Struma valley. He sent some 15,000 blinded prisoners, guided by 150 with one eye left, to Samuel, who fell dead at the sight. Four more years of this savage fighting, which gave Basil his surname of 'the Bulgar-slayer', completed the conquest of all Bulgaria. Basil II had extended the Empire once more to the Danube and the Adriatic. The petty Serbian princes, mainly in modern Bosnia, were his vassals. For 168 years Bulgaria was a Byzantine province.

Basil II turned most of his conquest into the theme of Bulgaria and the Danubian duchy of Paristrion. He followed the existing Bulgarian practice of levying the taxes in kind, which the conquered preferred, but greedy, annual officials and old memories kept the spirit of revolt alive and sometimes active for fifty years. The spread of the Bogomil heresy added to disaffection, although Basil kept hold of the Orthodox Church: it remained autonomous under the Archbishop, no longer Patriarch, of Ochrida, but its chiefs were Greeks. In sum, the recovered land was a dead limb of the Empire.

(6) GOVERNMENT OF THE EMPIRE: THE LAND QUESTION

The administration of the Empire underwent drastic change between the days of Justinian and Basil II, between the latest Roman and the fully Byzantine era. The Emperor, indeed, retained the same attributes: he was the omnicompetent master of the State and the Church. If his style was changed, it only expressed more clearly his sacred office, to which he was now anointed, like the Kings of Israel, by the Patriarch, as well as crowned. He was 'the Emperor ($\beta\alpha\sigma\iota\lambda\epsilon\acute{u}s$) faithful in Christ our God and autocrat of the Romans'. The daily, tedious ceremonial which surrounded him was designed to publish and exalt his unlimited power. Yet although a dynastic loyalty was always sprouting, there was no strict hereditary right to his office. He was at the mercy of plots and armed revolt. The bureaucracy, centred in the Senate, the army, and even the rabble of the capital could all be dangerous. The subservient Church could check him. His autocracy was tempered by revolution and assassination.

Although Greek in essence, the Eastern Empire retained the cosmopolitanism of the older Empire. It had a marvellous power of absorbing its alien subjects, immigrants, and mercenaries. Bound together by the orthodox faith and Byzantine culture, men felt an imperial, Christian patriotism which upheld and unified the State.

Under the Emperor were the bureaucracy and the army. It was the bureaucracy, ranging from senators to obscure secretaries, which administered the State and formulated its policy. To understand its mechanism, it must be borne in mind that every official had two titles, one denoting his rank, and the other his actual office. The rank indeed, was usually linked to the office, but it might be higher or lower than normal, or be given without the employment. Those near the throne took precedence as *Caesar*, *Nobilissimus*, or *Curopalates*. Below them came in order the titles of *Magister*, *Anthypatos* (*pro-consul*), *Patrician*, and so forth. The substantive offices of state had escaped from the hierarchic subordination of Diocletian's reforms. The heads of departments in the capital and the provincial governors were now directly responsible to the Emperor, by whom they and lesser officials were nominated. The government machine had been simplified. In the palace a high place was taken by the eunuch Great Chamberlain, whom we have seen ruling the Empire; there was a legion of court functionaries, high and low. Outside there were the four Logothetes. The Logothete of the Dromos (once the postal service) had become Chancellor, in charge of home and foreign affairs, and appropriately styled the Grand Logothete. A second Logothete was Treasurer, a third Paymaster of the Army. The Logothete of the Flocks managed the Crown lands and the important imperial studs. The Chartulary of the Sakellion managed the Emperor's private fortune, the Eidikos the arsenals and monopolies. The Sakellarios was Auditor-general. The Quaestor remained minister of justice, but the troops were now under the command of the Domestic of the Scholae, and the navy was the charge of the Grand Drungarius. The Prefect (Eparch) of Constantinople was loaded with the detailed administration of the capital in every aspect of its life. All these officers were assisted by bureaux of innumerable subordinates. The whole formed the solid framework of the State.

The Empire was now divided into some twenty-six to thirty themes, essentially military. Each theme was both a civil province and the army corps quartered and largely levied therein. Gone was the division between civil and military control. The *strategos* (general) of the theme was now its civil governor as well, although his civilian deputy, the protonotary, was in direct touch with the Emperor. The Empire in fact was reorganized for the pressing needs of defence. The whole armed force including the naval

269

Fig. 47. The Emperor Nicephorus III

themes may have numbered 120,000 men, small enough according to modern notions, but its separate foes were not overwhelmingly superior, and its quality was first rate. It was a standing, professional army, well paid, admirably organized, drilled and equipped, scientifically and skilfully led. Whether hereditary native soldiers or volunteers or foreign mercenaries, its men came of fighting stocks: Asia Minor, till the disaster of Manzikert, provided the best recruits from its highlands. The Asiatic nobles, often a danger to the government, gave them their best officers. The heavy

270

mailed cavalry, the cataphracts, were the backbone of the army, but light cavalry, heavy and light infantry, frontier guards, engineers and medical and transport services bore their due share. The navy was neglected for long intervals, but repaid its subsequent, if costly, renewals. Its Greek fire wrecked Russian as well as Arab fleets. The systematic study of war, unique then in Europe, saved the Empire in its continuous perils and showed its heritage of ancient civilization.

Such an army and administration could only be supported by a well-filled treasury. The world trade of Constantinople did much to replenish it. Situated at the point of contact between East and West, Constantinople, protected by nature and the fleet, was the central emporium of the known world whence commerce flowed out and in. It was, too, a great manu-facturing city of luxury wares in demand by the Empire and all its neigh-bours, and it was seconded by other towns like Thessalonica with their special products. From custom-dues, monopolies, and trading profits, the Treasury derived a large and stable revenue. The famous bezant or gold *nomisma* was wisely maintained at a constant purity for over 700 years, to the enormous benefit of trade, and with the Arabic dinar provided a standard of currency for Europe. Trade, indeed, in the strictly supervised gilds was only too much regulated; it was suited to a stationary market, not to mercantile initiative, and the State left the difficulties of transport and expansion to adventurous foreigners. The credit system was elementary, and the only outlet for accumulating capital lay in investment in land. Thus was exacerbated the chief internal peril of the Empire, the disap-pearance of the small landowner and the growth of a half-feudal nobility with vast estates.

In spite of trading wealth the main source of the imperial revenue continued to be the land-tax, and this was intimately bound up with the existence of free peasant proprietors who supplied recruits for the army. Bad seasons, the ravages of invaders, and oppressive taxation were always forcing the peasants to desert or sell their land, which was coveted by the great proprietors and the officials, classes which were allied in their wish to invest their wealth and often individually identical. Yet the Empire depended for its centralized, bureaucratic regime, for its State army, for its revenue, and for its very existence on the free peasant-proprietor, owing allegiance to the State alone. Two taxes formed the chief burden on the peasant population since Isaurian times. One was personal, the *kapnikon* or hearth-tax, the other was the *rhiza chorion* levied on the land. Both had come once more to be paid in money, except in reannexed Bulgaria. The commonest form of settlement was in a central village with its arable owned in severalty by the villagers and its unallotted pasture, wood, and waste used by them in common: the latter, too, could be turned into private arable by cultivation. There were obviously differences in wealth and some villagers might be leaseholders, not full owners, while detached farms might be outside the village complex. Outside it, too, were the independent properties of the great estates. The unity of the village community was mainly fiscal: it was the unit of assessment for the land-tax. If a member of the village could not pay his share or his land fell vacant, a neighbour was forced to take over land and tax. This was the system of *allelengyon*, most oppressive to the already overburdened peasant.

It was also the opportunity of the wealthy purchaser. In the ninth century the class of great landowner was rising again. Its members and the prosperous officials were called 'the powerful (οἱ δύνατοι)' in contrast to 'the poor (οἱ πένητες)', and the enlargement of their lands and the decrease of the free peasant-proprietor and of the soldier-peasant became a serious danger to the State. The peasant by sale or gift of his patrimony was turning into a less taxed tenant-serf of a lord or monastery. The 'powerful' could by exemption or influence be less oppressed than the 'poor' in his village community, and the revenue suffered. So did the army, for even if the great lord at the head of his valiant dependants fought well, he withdrew allegiance from the State to himself, as the civil wars of the tenth century, in which the rebel generals were great proprietors with local influence in their themes, bore witness. The foundations of the Empire established by Heraclius and the Isaurians were being undermined, and the tenth century was filled with a bitter struggle between the central government and the aristocracy. It was opened in 922 by a Novel of Romanus Lecapenus. He restored the right of pre-emption which peasant-owners had had in case their fellow-villager sold his land. He forbade purchase by a 'powerful' unless he already held land in the same village, and the reception by him of 'gifts' from the 'poor' in any case. The 'powerful' was not only to restore the land but to pay a fine, unless he was protected by prescription, in the case of a military holding of thirty years. A terrible famine produced so many infringements that a severer Novel was issued in 934. Further infringements were declared null, and land already purchased at a reasonable price was to be restored if the original owner repaid it within three years. The law, however, was clearly evaded, for Constantine VII extended the prescription period for military holdings to forty years and vainly strove to give the former owner of peasant land five years to repay the price he had sold it for. The officials in fact were commonly the 'powerful' themselves, and the peasant often found life easier under a lord. Nicephorus Phocas was himself a representative of the great lords, who were soldiers too. He abolished the villagers' rights of pre-emption, while he endeavoured to maintain more especially the military holdings. Henceforward, the noble was to acquire land only from a noble, the 'poor' only from the 'poor', the soldier only from the soldier, but the soldier's allotment was raised in minimum value; it made him no longer a peasant but a minor noble. It was only the wide monastic properties that Nicephorus was resolved to reduce, and that measure was repealed by Zimiskes, although his abolition of the hearth-tax may have helped the peasants to keep solvent. Basil II, on the other hand, when he had conquered the mutinous aristocrats, revived the defence of the peasant and the attack on the great landowners. In a Draconian Novel of 996 he decreed that prescription should protect no acquisition made by the 'powerful' from the 'poor' since 934. All such transactions were annulled, and the land restored to the peasant without compensation. The system of patronage, under cover of which the land really changed hands and its peasant owner became a serf, was forbidden. The burden of taxation was shifted by the provision that only the 'powerful' should pay the *allelengyon* for their insolvent peasant neighbours while they might not take over the debtor's land. The reform was completed by a cancellation of abusive titles to land under whatever sanction and by arbitrary confiscation of too formidable estates. While Basil II lived the situation was saved, but he alone could enforce his policy. The opposite tendency was too strong. Within a few years after his death the *allelengyon* was wholly abolished (1028). The land-laws were allowed to sleep. By farming out the taxes the government ceased to supervise their levy and the peasant-proprietor was squeezed out, while the privileged domains of nobles and Church, populated by serfs, increased. The 'powerful' had won, the strict centralization of government relaxed, and the economic and social foundations on which the Empire had rested collapsed before the advance of a quasi-feudal society.

(7) THE DECLINE OF THE EMPIRE, 1025–1068

The last, inglorious reigns of the Macedonian dynasty may be briefly told. Constantine VIII (1025–8), Basil's hitherto fainéant colleague, was active only for ill. He had two elderly daughters, Zoe and Theodora, heiresses to the prestige and genuine loyalty which surrounded their house. Neither, unhappily, possessed any capacity to rule, and on their passions and caprice hung the fate of the declining Empire. The voluptuous, extravagant Zoe was chosen to marry and thus provide an Emperor-colleague. This was Romanus III Argyrus (1028–34), a descendant of Romanus I, who was compelled to divorce his wife for the purpose and assume the purple. Worthy, vain and incompetent, he was also unlucky. Defeat in Syria, plague, locusts, famine, an earthquake at Constantinople, followed by palace plots, pursued him. Last of all, the Empress Zoe and her low-born paramour, Michael the Paphlagonian, had him murdered. Michael IV (1034–41) was at once made Emperor and husband of Zoe. He was an epileptic, tortured by remorse; perhaps the energy of his reign was mainly due to his greedy brother, the eunuch John the Orphanotrophos. Under his

Fig. 48. The Emperor Constantine IX and his Empress Zoe

able guidance victories were won in Italy and Bulgaria, but the sordid ambitions and mutual hatreds of the Paphlagonians ruined them. Zoe was induced to adopt the dying Emperor's nephew, Michael V (1041–2), nick-named Calaphates (the ship-calker). This capable ingrate turned on both the Orphanotrophos and the Empress, who were deported to monasteries. But the loyalist mob rose at the last outrage. After furious fighting the palace was stormed, the Emperor seized and blinded, and the two con-trasting sisters, Zoe and the pious, miserly Theodora, reigned together. A fresh Emperor-colleague and husband for Zoe was soon found in Constantine IX Monomachus (1042–54), a cultured, dissipated noble, whose reign possessed an importance in which he had little share. In 1050 Zoe closed her grotesque career. When Constantine died, the septuage-narian Theodora unexpectedly reigned alone for a year. With her death (1056) the Macedonian dynasty flickered out to its end.

From the court, where in reaction from Basil II's austere regime profligate, senseless extravagance reigned supreme, we turn to the momentous evolution of public affairs. Monomachus's chief personal merit was his interest in culture and law. It was a time of brilliant intellects, among whom Psellus, eloquent, learned Platonist, graphic historian, lawyer and wily courtier, stood foremost. There was a literary revival, and Monomachus was incited to renew the degenerating science of law in the reopened university of Constantinople. It was but a flash in the pan; co-operation was found impossible among these emulous, self-seeking scholars, who exhibited the decadence of the Empire's never high morale; and in five years the Schools were closed.

The event of European, if not world-wide, import which marked the reign of Constantine IX was the opening of the schism which divided and still divides the Eastern and Western Churches. Since the end of the Photian Schism in 898 a somewhat frigid amity had mainly existed between Rome and Constantinople. The Patriarch Sergius in 1009 had indeed formally revived the subjects in dispute raised by Photius, but his action seems to have had little result. But the practical rift between the two Churches had been steadily growing wider. The Papacy was only spasmodically and superficially recovering from the feebleness and corruption which beset it after Pope John VIII. The Patriarch on the contrary had become the spiritual head of a wider East: Russians, Bulgarians and Serbs acknowledged his authority. The East maintained its autonomy; the Papacy claimed effective dominion, no mere precedence. The Greeks, too, felt their superiority in civilization and inviolable orthodoxy: to them the Latins were ill-instructed, innovating barbarians. In 1024 Basil II and Patriarch Eustathius attempted a working compromise: the patriarchate was to be Ecumenic in its sphere as the Papacy was in the world. But the West, with its strong papalist views, rose in indignation against the proposal. So the matter rested until the advent of a new Patriarch and a new Pope precipitated the crisis. Michael Cerularius, promoted after a lay education from a monk to the patriarchal throne in 1043, was a man determined to domineer in Church and State. He shared to the full the dislike of his countrymen for the Latins and their ways. He aspired to direct the Emperor's policy and to be the Pope of the whole Eastern Church. On the other side Leo IX, become Pope in 1049, led the reforming party in the West with a firm conviction of the effective supremacy of the Roman See over all the Churches.

As it happened, political events led to a *rapprochement* of the Eastern Empire and the Papacy while alarming Cerularius and stimulating his ambitions. The conquests of the Normans in Southern Italy made both Pope and Emperor ready for an alliance to expel them, and the Emperor's deputy in the Byzantine province, Argyrus, 'duke of Italy', was a Lombard, who belonged like the majority in his province to the Latin rite. Cerularius saw the adherents of the Greek rite there dwindling. Possibly he feared the increase of papal influence in the East itself. He treated Argyrus as a heretic, and forcibly closed the churches and monasteries of the Latin rite at Constantinople. With his patronage Leo, Archbishop of Ochrida, addressed a polemic against the errors of the Latins to the Apulian Bishop of Trani, while a monk of Studion wrote a coarser attack. The Latin usages, such as unleavened bread at the Mass and the celibacy of the lower clergy, were denounced as heretical. But the Emperor's policy demanded conciliation, and a letter from the Patriarch to the Pope, while upholding the Greek position, was in a friendly tone. At this very time Leo IX was being defeated by the Normans and held captive (1053), but he was not the man

Fig. 49. Michael Cerularius's nomination as patriarch

to suffer his orthodoxy or his authority to be questioned. He replied by letters and by legates; he refused to treat with Cerularius as an equal, and the legates affronted the Greek's pride (1054). They, too, violently attacked the Greek usages. Constantine IX thought it best to side with them, when news of Pope Leo's death gave Cerularius his chance. He determined on a complete breach. He would not recognize the legates' powers and prepared a manifesto. The legates replied by excommunicating him in St Sophia itself. The Emperor still favoured them, but the Patriarch had the people behind him, and Constantine humbly surrendered. A representative synod denounced the Latin heresies in creed and usage. Thus in July 1054 the schism of East and West was consummated. It expressed a mutual aversion, which it exacerbated, and also different conceptions of the Church. The Latins espoused a single organization under papal dominion; the Greeks believed in a kind of federation of autonomous Churches, which coincided with political frontiers. Their own was the longest experiment of a State-Church that Christendom has ever seen. Politically, the dissidence, temperamental, cultural and religious, of the two halves of Europe was to be the fruitful parent of disasters.

Besides the wars in Italy and Sicily the Empire was embroiled on its other frontiers. The impolitic annexation of Armenia (1046) was due to

Byzantine aggression, elsewhere it was a case of defence. There were Patzinak raids across the Danube, worse still the last Russian invasion by sea sent by the Great Prince Yaroslav, which took years to repel (1043–6). Most serious of all were the military revolts led by discontented generals, Maniaces (1043) and Tornicius (1047), both of which were quelled with difficulty. These were evidence of growing disunion in the Empire.. Ever since the government allowed the extension of the great estates to take its

Fig. 50. A rebellious general attacks Constantinople

course, it had shown increasing distrust of the army and the nobles who commanded it. At the same time palace officials and eunuchs took control, and pursued an anti-militarist policy directed against the aristocrat generals. Matters came to crisis when on Theodora's death the civilian ministers carried through the elevation of an elderly puppet, Michael VI Stratioticus (1056–7), as Emperor. They soon provoked revolution. Eminent generals were disgraced and snubbed, and a dangerous enemy aroused by the exclusion from power of the Patriarch Cerularius, whose darling ambition, to rule Church and State, was whetted by the prestige acquired amid clergy and laity by the popular Schism. Hitherto the hold of the Macedonian dynasty on its subjects had placed the aristocrat generals at a disadvantage. Now under the leadership of Isaac Comnenus and secretly supported by the Patriarch they revolted in June 1057, defeated the imperialists, and at the end of August secured the capital by a popular outbreak. The feeble Stratioticus, at the command of the Patriarch, retired to a monastery to die. Isaac I Comnenus (1057–9) at once became Emperor.

This first of a new dynasty was the choice of the great nobles, to whom, by virtue of his estates in Paphlagonia, he belonged. But their triumph was fleeting. The civilian bureaucracy was strongly entrenched, and the times were critical. The treasury was emptied by past extravagance. Not only the Patzinaks but the Magyars from their final abode in Hungary were raiding the Balkans, while the danger from the new Asiatic power of the Seljūk Turks was threatening the east. Cerularius was not satisfied with the unfettered rule of the Church, which was his share of the spoils. The Emperor, who rested on the power of the sword but who had to govern through a disaffected bureaucracy, proved unequal, despite energy and insight, to his task. In his search for funds his taxes, economies, and confiscations of monastic lands raised a clamour against him. The leader of the malcontents was the egoistic Patriarch. He at least was defeated. Isaac suddenly arrested him with accusations of heresy (1058), and had the good fortune to be delivered from him by his natural death. Yet he was obliged to feign grief and repentance for his action against so popular an enemy, his own health gave way, and he found an escape in abdication and profession as a monk.

It was a surrender to the civilian bureaucracy, for Isaac chose for his successor Constantine X Ducas (1059–67), an aristocrat and soldier who adopted their policy. To save expense the army was now starved and reduced, and the generals kept out of the government. In its distrust the government had allowed the hereditary soldiers to buy themselves out of their obligation to serve, and hired barbarian mercenaries. The army was less Byzantine and was disorganized. Meantime the Patzinaks were raiding and the Balkan Serbs out of hand. A reaction came too late when Constantine X died, and his widow Eudocia Macrembolitissa married as Emperor-colleague for their son Michael the soldier Romanus IV Diogenes (1067–71). He was to meet the forces of eastern Islam now reunited and aggressive under the Seljūk Turks.

(8) THE SELJŪK TURKS

Turks as slaves, mercenaries, and officials had long played a leading part and founded dynasties in the lands of the Caliphate. Hordes of them, Chazars, Patzinaks, and Ghuzz or Cumans had successively crossed the Volga into the Black Sea steppes. Now a similar migration in force took place in Persia. A section of the Ghuzz, known as Seljūks from the ancestor of their chiefs, obtained a lodgement in Khurasan. Thence under the leadership of the brothers Tughril Beg and Chagri Beg they spread their conquests. They were continually reinforced by kindred clans. Tughril Beg (1038–63) united all Persia. He was an ardent and orthodox Moslem, and in 1055 rescued the Caliph Qaim of Baghdad from the Shi'ite governor who controlled him. In reward his rule was legitimized by the new titles of Sultan and 'Right Hand of the Commander of the Faithful'. Before his death he had pitiably ravaged Armenia. Ferocious as they were in war and rude tribesmen in peace, these immigrant Turks in Moslem Nearer Asia, or their leaders at any rate, were not impermeable barbarians like their nomad kinsmen of the northern steppes. Many of them had long been educated in the service of Moslem courts as slaves or mercenaries. Turks had already founded Moslem dynasties. Besides destruction the Seljūks brought revival, energy, and reunion to the Persian-Arab civilization of Islam and its fragmentary powers. The Seljūks, like their forerunner Mahmud of Ghazna, the conqueror of northern India, were patrons of art and literature. They used the acuter minds of their subjects. Tughril Beg's nephew and successor, Alp Arslan (the valiant lion) (1063–72), owed much of his triumphs to his famous Persian vizier, Nizam-al-Mulk, who founded the two Nizamiyah universities of Baghdad and Nishapur, and gathered round him eminent men, such as the astronomer Omar Khayyam, whose translated quatrains have become an English classic, the philosopher Ghazali, and the sinister founder of the Shi'ite sect of the Assassins, Hasan ibn Suffah. The Turkish rulers did anything but light the fire, but they fanned the flame.

What the Seljūks brought to their new empire was political capacity, fighting spirit and fanatical aggression. Their zeal to spread the faith and to conquer the infidel more than equalled that of the earlier converts. Their state was founded on a military basis. The Sultan was surrounded by his permanent bodyguard (*askaris*) of white slaves (*mamlūks*) and dependants, mostly Turks, who formed a heavy armed cavalry like the Byzantine cataphracts. These were rewarded by governorships and estates, great and small, for which they rendered military service. Each of these maintained a similar bodyguard of *askaris* of size varying with the extent of their 'fief', which they partitioned on like terms. Round the bodyguards were the swarms of light horsemen and expert bowmen of migrant Turkish clans, and the almost supernumerary levy of foot. Thus a semi-feudal system was set up; it was efficient, for the 'fiefs' were held at pleasure while gifted and strong Sultans sat on the throne, but decadence of the dynasty, civil wars, and rival ambitions gave endless opportunities for the loose structure of the empire and even of its provinces to crumble into fighting fragments.

Alp Arslan, however, was master of his dominions, which Nizam-al-Mulk administered in the best oriental tradition. He was almost a chivalrous conqueror, who kept a strict discipline over his troops. He turned on the Byzantine Empire. Armenia, Malatiya, Sivas (Sebastea) were subjugated. Romanus IV did his best. He drove back the Turkish bands in two campaigns; in the third he pushed forward to near Lake Van. There he was met by Alp Arslan, his army surrounded and destroyed through his own mistake, and himself captured in the fatal battle of Manzikert (19 August 1071). The Eastern Empire never recovered from this blow. The best of the troops were slain; the migrant Turkish bands

Fig. 51. The Emperor Romanus II and his Empress Eudocia

penetrated permanently through the Taurus frontier, conquering and looting; the uplands of Asia Minor, the Empire's constant source of recruits, changed masters. On all sides territory was being lost. Turkish chiefs were conquering in Syria Moslem and Christian alike; in 1084 Antioch itself fell by treason. In the strongholds of the Cicilian mountains an Armenian chief, Ruben, set up an emigrant principality of refugees,

Little Armenia, equally hostile to Greeks and Turks. Serbs and Bulgarians were in revolt. Magyars, Patzinaks and Cumans raided over the Danube. The Normans under their Duke, Robert Guiscard, completed their conquest of South Italy by taking Bari, the last Byzantine town (1071). When Romanus, freed by Alp Arslan, tried to recover his throne, he was so brutally blinded by his stepson Michael VII, nicknamed Parapinaces (1071–8), that he died. The Empire became the scene of military revolts of mercenaries, such as the Norman Roussel de Bailleul (1072), and of rival great nobles of Asia and Europe. Meanwhile Asia Minor was being subdued by Turkish chiefs, one of whom was a junior Seljūk, Sulaiman ibn Qutalmish, who fixed his residence at Nicaea and founded the line of the Sultans of Rūm, the name given by the Turks to the Empire and their conquests from it. Rival pretenders bought the aid of these enemies by the cession of towns. It was by dint of Turkish arms that an Asiatic rebel, Nicephorus III Botaniates, deposed the feeble Michael, married his wife Maria, and usurped the throne (1078–81). But Nicephorus made no better defence and was generally unpopular. In the midst of revolts the two houses of Comnenus and Ducas combined against him. He too became a monk, and Alexius I Comnenus, nephew of the Emperor Isaac, began his reign in February 1081. Alexius opened a new period of Byzantine history.

It was fortunate for the Eastern Empire that Malik Shah (1072–91), the son and successor of the murdered Alp Arslan, was content with the conquest of Syria and turned to that of Transoxiana and Samarqand, leaving to emirs the piecemeal occupation of Asia Minor. He was the last Great Seljūk who ruled a united empire. On his death civil war broke out among his sons, during which junior princes, like the Seljūks of Rūm, and provincial emirs attained practical independence of their nominal suzerain; after Sultan Sanjar of Khurasan died in 1156 they acknowledged no suzerain at all. The Seljūk realm was split into petty principalities, which warred with one another. The original dynasts of these, when represented by children or weaklings, were often supplanted by their tutors or ministers, Turkish slaves for the most part, who bore the title of Atabeg. It was the general scramble for possessions among these rival princes, paralysing further expansion and even defence, that allowed the survival of the Eastern Empire and the success of the First Crusade.

Amid the glories and disasters of the Byzantine Empire from Heraclius to the accession of Alexius one fact stands out pre-eminent: the shrinkage of ancient civilization both in area and content. Roman Asia passed step by step in spite of recoveries into the sphere of Islam. The Balkans became barbarized by the Slavs. Only the coastal fringe of the peninsula of Asia Minor, centred round impregnable Constantinople, retained its ancient heritage. Serbs, Bulgars and Russians were indeed won for the future by their acceptance of orthodox Christianity, but for centuries their civilization was to be an imperfect and mainly superficial copy. Cultural permeation, in any case tedious and slow, was disastrously retarded by the untoward course of their history. Nor did the Byzantine Empire itself, with all its splendid revivals and achievements, escape deterioration. Its methods were contaminated with barbarism, its thought, for all its subtlety, became hide-bound. No one would place its theologians and authors on a level with the past. Its distinctive inheritance of Roman Law decayed. The *Basilics* were but a reflexion of Justinian's *Corpus Iuris Civilis*, and after the *Basilics* legislators and jurists made successive endeavours to adapt the Code to the increasing feebleness of men's understanding. Yet in its decadence Byzantine society remained literate and cultured; the Empire was a bulwark of Christendom, a source of living, dexterous, magnificent art, and a storehouse of the traditional civilization of antiquity, the remnants of which it was to hand on to the slowly advancing West.

BOOK IV

THE DARK AGES IN THE WEST

~CPMCV~

CHAPTER 12

THE DEVELOPMENT OF THE WESTERN CHURCH UNTIL 741

(I) ST BENEDICT AND WESTERN MONASTICISM

Through the Dark Ages, which proceeded from the barbarization of Western Europe, it was the Church and the monks who preserved the remnants of ancient civilization and Christianity itself with its systematic thought and its ethic. They were the intellectual and spiritual leaven which at long last produced an upward movement once again. As we have seen, Christian asceticism in Western Europe had been an importation from the East, and it long retained the imprint of its Eastern origin. Hermit-life and extreme austerities were the ideal of its devotees. The Irish monasteries which had so dominant a share in the Irish-Scottish Church were almost hermit-villages. Such, too, was Marmoutiers, founded by St Martin of Tours, and many others in the West. Egyptian monasticism, however, had developed in a half-tropical climate, very different from northern conditions, and with difficulty compatible with them, although the Irish monks and hermits continued its traditions into the Middle Ages. From the too-hard endeavour more thoroughly cenobitic monasteries were liable to relax into an easy life, and the exemptions which the monastic profession secured led to unfit monks and monasteries, which were such only in name. Each monastery was autonomous under its abbot; it had its local rule and customs laid down by him. Reckless asceticism, reckless relaxation, and disorganized ideals tended to impair the institution as a whole.

The remedy was supplied by St Benedict, the father of later Western monasticism, in two ways, His Rule was an ordered and practical code of laws for the working of a monastery, and it adapted monasticism to Western ideas and Western needs. It was from its intrinsic excellence that it gradually spread from a single monastery to be the basic Rule of the West, which all subsequent reformers took as their common original for many centuries. This legislative genius was born *c.* 480 at Nursia in Umbria,

Fig. 52. Group of beehive cells of Skellig Michael monastery, Co. Kerry

appropriately in a noble, i.e. an official, family. He revolted in youth from the dissolute impotence of Roman society in those early days of barbarian rule, and fled *c.* 500 to lead a secret hermit's life in a cave near Subiaco, the famous Sacro Speco. His sanctity became known, and attracted followers. It was his own experience which convinced him that eremitism was not for them but for the perfect ascetic. He not only founded a ceno-bitic monastery ruled by himself but also directed twelve others round it. Somewhere about 520 he was obliged to migrate to Monte Cassino, which has become the mother house of the Black Monks, the Benedictine Order. There in 543 he died. He made no attempt from it to supervise other monasteries, although the Rule he composed could be adopted by any. The isolated, autonomous monastery of the past was still his ideal, and long continued to be the distinctive ideal of the Benedictines. He reinforced it by a provision which guaranteed the existence of each house as a con-tinuous, permanent society with its own traditions and quasi-personality. This was the vow of stability: no monk could leave the monastery where he had been professed. No other injunction contributed more to the solidarity and discipline of the monastery, or indeed to the difficulty of reforming it in decay.

Fig. 53. St Benedict handing his Rule to the monks of Monte Cassino

That discipline was austere, but not excessively or emulously ascetic. Chastity, poverty, and obedience were as usual the three vows. The black dress of tunic and cowl was simple, flesh food was forbidden, the life was busy, secluded, and hard, but its conditions and its clothing were not so unlike those of the Italian peasant as to be fiercely ascetic; it was 'a little Rule for beginners', not the mortification of the time-worn hermit. Roughly speaking, the monk's time was to be divided into three daily portions after allowing eight hours for sleep. First of all, and their essential duty, was the *Opus Dei*, the daily common services chanted in choir, taking some four and a half hours altogether. Second came manual work in field or cloister, an integral part of St Benedict's ideal, which occupied six or seven hours more. Last was reading of Scripture and the Fathers, to which were allotted three to five hours. It was a simple, busy life without ulterior ambitions. To make his monks good men practising the Christian virtues in obedience and humility was the aim of St Benedict.

The government of the abbey was to be the old Roman one, absolute authority exercised after counsel. The abbot was elected by the monks for life. He appointed all officials—later called obedientiaries—he took advice of all or of the seniors, all were to obey his commands. Under successive abbots, each monastery could develop its own customs on the basis of the Rule. This ordered life, elastic and practical, proved its worth by its long continuance. Its influence was immense. The monasteries were focuses of Christianity. It was not only their religious hold and the wealth that came to them which were influential. In a barbaric world of passion, impulse, violence, and disorder the monasteries at their best, and indeed when only perfunctory, were living examples of peaceful life by law and self-control. Their corruption, when it occurred, was an evil which spread far outside their walls.

As in the East, the Western monasteries rapidly accumulated endowments of land. To give by bequest or in their lifetime, to found fresh abbeys, were the favourite works of piety and penance of a devout or sinful laity. A new monk not infrequently gave his worldly possessions to his abbey. While the monk could own nothing personally, the corporate wealth of his abbey could become great. Changes in daily life were sure to follow. Manual labour would be abandoned to servants or to an inferior class of celibates. So, too, the practice of dedicating boys to the monastic life by their parents, while it produced shining examples of sanctity like Bede, also brought in monks little fitted for their profession, like the hare-hunting young monks whom Bede reproved in his old age. The tendency to a less austere practice was favoured by the half-secular motives of the donors. Monasteries were founded on the great roads to aid by their hospitality and civilizing influence traveller, trader, and pilgrim. Even when not founded in a town, an abbey might create one round it by its splendour, its needs, and its wise administration. Nor did the founder and his heirs lose all hold on it. The patron's kin provided the abbots; the abbey extended the family influence by an hereditary dependence. In Italy, however, the greatest danger to monastic discipline came from war and invasion. A monastery might be sacked and left desolate for years, and when its vagrant monks returned, it was unlikely that their pristine zeal and regular life returned with them.

These developments, with their beneficial and evil effects, were still mainly in the future when a fresh activity was added to Benedictine and Western monasticism, largely although not wholly by the efforts of a contemporary of St Benedict, Cassiodorus. That long-lived ex-Quaestor of Theodoric the Ostrogoth—he died in 583—if a supple and servile politician, was the greatest single contributor to the preservation of learning in the barbarized West. He was convinced that there ought to be an educated clergy, and failed c. 535 to found a Christian academy at Rome. About 540, amid the Gothic war, he became a monk in his own foundation of Vivarium, by Squillace in Calabria. There he created a library and wrote literary handbooks for his monks. But for him and the learned turn he gave to Benedictine labours it is possible that no Latin classic, save Virgil,

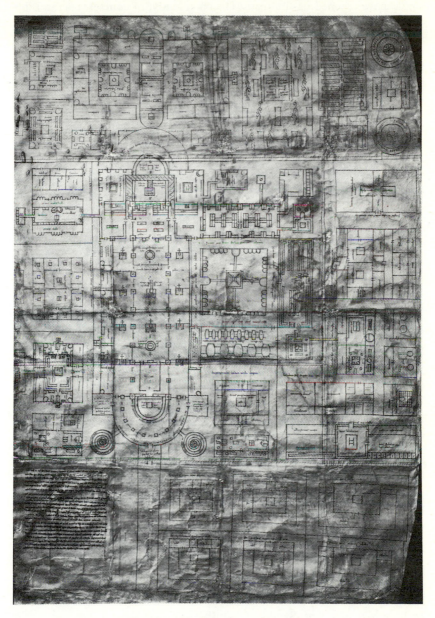

Fig. 54. Ideal lay-out of an abbey

would have reached us complete. The chief study, of course, was the Bible and the Fathers, the text of St Jerome's Vulgate being a subject of especial care. But ancillary to them were the study and preservation of ancient knowledge and culture. There was a recognition of the usefulness of secular learning, which clung thereafter to the Benedictine monks, and Cassiodorus's famous library and copies made from it or in emulation provided the tools, which thus outlasted the perilous eclipse of the Dark Ages. Vivarium and its disciples were, indeed, not alone. Influences and refugees from southern Gaul reached the new Irish monasteries of the sixth century, and there a tradition of learning continued until extinguished by the Northmen in the ninth century.

The Irish monks in fact, with their innate impulse to wander, exercised on the Continent a counter-influence to the spread of the Benedictine Rule.

Fig. 55. Legend of St Gall and the bear

The scholar-saint Columbanus (*ob.* 615), as we have seen, emigrated to Francia in 585. Three houses in the Vosges mountains, beginning with Luxeuil, were under the Rule he composed. Later he made his way to Alemannia, where his disciple St Gall was to start a great monastery, and last to Bobbio in the northern Apennines, where his famous abbey became a centre of learning. But the Rule of Columbanus was incredibly harsh, never sparing the rod; it stated principles and penances, but lacked the administrative framework, the ordered life, and practicable provisions of the law-maker, St Benedict. In the end, one by one, St Columbanus's monasteries accepted the rival Rule.

The decisive event for the dissemination of the Rule of St Benedict was the patronage accorded to it by St Gregory the Great. The settlement on the Lateran of the monks of Monte Cassino after the sack of their abbey by the Lombards (*c.* 577) is a legend, but many of the monks no doubt found their way to Rome, and when Gregory, then prefect of the city, became a monk and endowed his monastery on the Coelian, it was or soon became Benedictine. Thence the Rule was brought to England by the prior, St Augustine, the first missionary Archbishop of Canterbury, where the first non-Italian house was founded. The Rule took root in England largely by the work of Abbot Hadrian in Kent and of Benedict Biscop in Northumbria, and it ousted the Irish system after the Synod of Whitby. During the seventh century it spread over Francia, and in the eighth it was carried to Germany from England by the missionary saints, Boniface and his fellows. It was well adapted for its new environment, and, except in Ireland, quickly absorbed all Rules previously in vogue. It became an essential part of the fabric of Western Christendom.

(2) GREGORY THE GREAT AND THE PAPACY

From the monastic order it is a natural transition to the man who irrevocably allied the forces of monasticism to the Papacy, to one of the most celebrated of monks, Pope Gregory I, deservedly named the Great. He belonged to the Roman nobility, being the grandson of Pope Felix IV and the son of the wealthy *regionarius* Gordianus, and received the Latin education of his day, which clearly included law and music, but not Greek, a tongue he never learned. For literature and style he never showed any taste; indeed he prided himself on the rusticity of his own compositions. There is a gulf between him and the generation of Boethius and Cassiodorus before the outbreak of the Gothic war, the gulf which separates the Middle Ages from the ancient world. It was not due to lack of ability. As a young man he was appointed in 573 Prefect of Rome, the highest civilian official. But piety was in his blood. In 575 he became a monk at St Andrew's in Rome, once his palace, which he founded along with six other monasteries in Sicily out of his paternal lands. Fasts, vigils, and biblical and patristic studies now filled his time, but he was not to escape the life of affairs for which he was eminently endowed. He was made deacon of one of the seven urban regions, an administrative post, and in 579 was sent to Constantinople as the Pope's *apocrisiarius* or envoy. There he learnt imperial politics and diplomacy, and met in controversy or negotiation the rulers and ecclesiastics of the East. It is significant that he made no attempt to bridge the widening chasm between West and East; he remained ignorant of Greek during six years at Constantinople. Perhaps in his Roman pride, which despised the Greeklings, he was unaware of the decline of Western civilization. With nothing gained but experience he returned as abbot for his Roman monastery. It grew quickly as the home of devotion and theology, so that on the death of Pope Pelagius he was unanimously chosen by the Romans and accepted by the Emperor to be Pope, genuinely unwilling as he might be. Thus began an epoch-making pontificate of thirteen and a half years (590–604).

To Gregory his duties might all be aspects of his single office, the successor of St Peter, prince of the Apostles, in his primatial see of Rome. His favourite style 'bishop [without a qualification], servant of the servants of God (servus servorum Dei)', which has been kept by his successors, expresses his conception. But it is convenient to divide his activities into several inter-related spheres: (i) as bishop and metropolitan of the see of Rome; (ii) as a statesman perforce in the Lombard crisis and founder of the

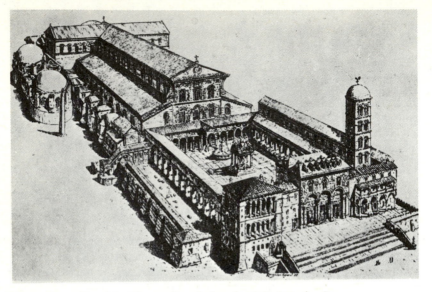

Fig. 56. The medieval church of St Peter's, Rome

Papal States; (iii) as Patriarch of the West, and claiming the special prerogative of Rome over all Churches; and (iv) as monk, theologian, and
author. In all these spheres he set a deep, enduring mark.

He began his career as Pope-elect during an onslaught of the plague,
and restored by his measures and his eloquence the morale of the city. He
was never at rest. The Register of his Letters, though incomplete, has been
preserved, and shows in numberless details his exceptional gifts as a ruler
and pastor. There were the vast papal estates in Italy, Sicily, and beyond
to be administered. No business was too small or too great for the Pope's
attention, in which practical good sense and a vigilant zeal for justice and
the repression of abuses were dominant. The revenue which flowed into
the papal treasury was used for the benefit of his flock and of the State. His
charity replaced the vanished imperial dole. His subventions helped the
local imperial administration. Over his metropolitan province of Italy
south of the Rubicon he exercised a strict ecclesiastical control, which had
its political side owing to the judicial and civil functions with which the
bishops were invested. He insisted on clerical privileges in the law-courts.
He supervised his suffragan bishops. He intervened in cases of oppression:
iniquity should not go unpunished. The evils of the times found a tireless
pastor to combat them.

The defence of Rome from the Lombard attacks, which Emperor and
Exarch failed to repel, made Gregory perforce a statesman and in effect

290

a secular ruler. He stimulated and directed the secular local officials and commanders both in Rome and Italy. To the Emperor Maurice's wrath he made, by his personal influence and negotiation, local truces with the Duke of Spoleto and the Lombard King Agilulf, until he rather than the imperial Duke of Rome was the real ruler of the City. The ancient Senate had expired in the Gothic war. The process by which in a century the 'Patrimony of St Peter' came to mean, not the wide-scattered papal estates, but the erstwhile Duchy of Rome, began with him, and in this sense he was the founder of the Papal States. He never pretended to be other than the holder of a sacred office, who as such was the greatest prelate and landowner of Italy. But that was enough. He remonstrated vigorously when Maurice forbade soldiers and officials to become monks, but he published the decree. He made an unanswerable reply to the Emperor's reproaches on his truce with the Lombards, but it was the reply of a loyal and injured subject, who 'amid the swords of the Lombards' and in defect of imperial aid stepped into the breach. His estrangement from Maurice led to his most questionable act. When the Emperor was murdered and succeeded by the ruffian Phocas, he addressed a paean of joy to the usurper at this dispensation of God, which was a disaster to the Empire.

Gregory's attitude to Maurice was partly connected with his views of the structure of the Church. He was in no way an innovator in ideas, but he had an unequalled gift for acting on them with a consistency, persistence, and tact which established them in the world of fact and precedent. He inherited the claims of Leo I and Gelasius I on the primacy of the Roman Church, that it was the guardian of the Faith, and that its consent was necessary for the universal validity of canons. He claimed, too, the right to supervise and correct all other bishops of whatever rank: 'I know of no bishop who is not subject to the Apostolic See, when a fault has been committed.' These were claims which placed the Papacy in quite a different rank from the other four Patriarchs, and they sharpened the latent discord between Rome and aspiring Constantinople. The Patriarchs of the imperial capital countered them by assuming the title of Ecumenic or Universal Patriarch, which carried with it an implicit claim to equality to Old Rome and a denial of subjection. The Popes were quick to take up the challenge. In 588 Pelagius II declared that the canons of an Eastern synod were null because they contained the offending title. When Patriarch John the Faster used it repeatedly in a letter to the Pope, Gregory in 595 denounced him 'sweetly and humbly' for his pride and presumption in taking a style so overweening, which Leo I had refused 'lest he should derogate from the honour of his brother bishops'. To the Emperor he wrote that St Peter had never called himself Universal Apostle. To claim to be Universal Bishop was to be a forerunner of Anti-Christ. The Patriarchs remained obstinate, and within a century the Popes also used the style with a more positive meaning. The Papal primacy won, as we have seen, few adherents in the East.

In the West, where there was no rival and primatial and patriarchal powers were united, the papal doctrine met with theoretical and some practical acceptance. Gregory forbade the bishops of Illyricum to attend a synod at Constantinople without his leave. In Italy north of the Rubicon, although he could not prevent the imperial candidate from becoming Archbishop of Ravenna, it was on condition of a penitential confession: 'I have sinned against God and the most blessed Pope Gregory.' In Lombard Italy he was checked not only by Arianism but by the schism of the Three Chapters which held the Catholics aloof from Rome. Theodelinda, the Catholic queen, was herself a schismatic. In Africa he appointed a local bishop his representative, and by persevering intervention established papal authority on a firm basis. He egged on the persecution of the surviving Donatist heretics in spite of tolerant officials. He continually corresponded with the African episcopate, defending 'the rights and privileges of St Peter'; no important decision was reached without his consent; the aggrieved applied to him; the officials were subdued by his strength of character and moral superiority; the people looked to Pope and bishops as their defenders. Thus by wise exercise and the habit of consent the right of supervision became a living doctrine.

In Francia influence and respect were more prominent than obedience. As a result of the Frankish conquest, ecclesiastical Gaul had become a collection of bishoprics, each a little monarchy, but all subject to the autocratic control of the Merovingian kings. Only the Bishop of Arles as papal vicar maintained close relations with Rome. Gregory took up his usual method of patient and discreet, but constant intervention. He directed and advised bishops and monks as opportunity offered. He corresponded with the Merovingians, and especially with the virago Brunhild, of whom he expressed, whether from diplomacy or wishful thinking, an unaccountably good opinion. The net result was the invigoration and amplification of the tradition of papal authority, if with little immediate effect on Francia.

In Spain Gregory contented himself with less. He saw with joy the conversion of the Arian Visigoths to Catholicism. He sent to his Catholic friend, Leander, Archbishop of Seville, the pallium, the woollen vestment given by the Popes to favoured prelates, especially metropolitans. But he made no attempt to intervene in the internal government of the Visigothic Church. In England the case was different. The Anglo-Saxon Church was a Roman mission, and Gregory took control from the first; indeed, as we have seen, he endeavoured through Augustine of Canterbury to absorb the existing British Church into his mission. It was in England that the tradition of papal authority took firmest root, that appeal was made to the Popes in disputes, and Gregory's conception of his prerogative had full sway.

But Gregory was not only a ruler and administrator of genius, he was also one of the four Doctors of the Latin Church. His *Moralia* on the Book of Job, written largely at Constantinople, remained a storehouse of theology for later thinkers, as did his homilies and other commentaries. Through him much of St Augustine filtered through in somewhat cruder form, for to him the visible Church was the *Civitas Dei*. His *Regula Pastoralis* on a bishop's duties became an indispensable work. His *Dialogues* gave a model for the hagiographers. They showed, indeed, in their wonders and credulity, as well as in their decadent Latin, the decline of rational thought which had come over Europe. Gregory was even hostile to ancient heathen culture as unworthy of Christians. Had he had his way, it would hardly have survived. Fortunate it was that secular learning had made a lodgement in monasticism.

Gregory's character is revealed in his letters. He was devoted to his task, filled with belief in the rights and duties of his office, stern to himself and others, dominating others, tireless in sickness and health, spurred by a passionate sense of justice and an active benevolence. He was eminently practical in all his works. He knew well the tragedy of his times when civilized government was crumbling and civilized behaviour was vanishing round him. Yet he never faltered in his desperate task. He ardently embraced the common notions of his age whether in his uncritical credulity or in his belief that asceticism was the truest Christian life. In his person and in his policy he closely linked the monastic institution and the monastic spirit in the West to the Papacy, with far-reaching consequences. To the Papacy he gave a practical programme in action which was to inspire and outlast the Middle Ages. In a barbarizing world he maintained higher standards and ideals, and preserved them by his deeds and writings for posterity.

His immediate successors were not men of like genius, but they continued his tradition. They saw the English mission triumphant at the Synod of Whitby (663); Archbishop Theodore was a papal nominee (669). By the close of the seventh century the Lombards had renounced Arianism, and the schism of the Three Chapters was ended. This was some compensation for the loss of Africa to Islam. The Popes' troubles mainly came from the East. We have seen how Honorius I hesitated at the beginning of the Monothelete controversy, and how Martin I was haled to Constantinople and banished. But the Papacy stood firm under Vitalian, and the Sixth General Council accepted Agatho's dogmatic letter, supported by the West, and condemned Monotheletism (681–2). It was at a cost, for the Council declared Honorius I, not a heretic, but a favourer of heretics; and dissidence was soon renewed when the Trullan Council (691) stood for Eastern usages and declared the Patriarch of Constantinople the Pope's equal. When Pope Sergius I refused to ratify the Council's acts, he escaped arrest by the intervention of the Roman troops (695). It was a sign how much weaker the Emperor's authority had become in Rome. Pope Constantine, who visited Constantinople to arrange a compromise, was received with veneration and returned in safety (710–11).

Renewed troubles divided East and West under the Iconoclastic Emperors. We have seen that Pope Gregory II (715–31) and Gregory III (731–41) successfully withstood the iconoclastic decrees, and that the Popes now appeared openly as the rulers of Rome. But they were escaping from Byzantine subjection only to run the risk of Lombard conquest. They were on the eve of momentous events, the conversion of inner Germany and the alliance with the Franks.

(3) ST BONIFACE AND THE CONVERSION OF GERMANY

The conversion of inner Germany was a backward wave from Rome's daughter-Church of England, not a direct missionary outburst from the Papacy itself. The conversion of the eastern Franks of Austrasia had in the nature of the case been skin deep over country areas. In their dependent tribes it was hardly nominal, when it occurred. Perhaps owing to the remnants of the Roman provincial population, the dukes of the Bavarians were Christians, but paganism still flourished among them. A change began with the emigrant Irish monks, like St Gall, who founded monasteries, supplemented by Franks like Emmeram of Ratisbon (Regensburg), but the effects were scanty and sporadic. Persevering, effective, organized work came from England, where the impulse to spread the Gospel and the practice of organizing a missionary Church were still in their first fervid strength.

A chief care of the English missionaries was that their work of conversion should be under the direct patronage of the Papacy, as their own Church was, with all the advantage of legal finality and sustained order which that patronage gave. Their first serious effort, among the heathen Frisians, was made with papal authorization by the monk Willibrord, who was later (695) consecrated at Rome Archbishop of Utrecht. It was under him that the real Apostle of Germany, Winfrid, the future St Boniface, began his missionary career.

Winfrid was born near Crediton c. 680, and bred in abbeys at Exeter and at Nursling in Hampshire. After a first essay in Frisia under Willibrord he refused an English abbacy, and journeyed to Rome to receive commission for his lifework from Pope Gregory II, who gave him the new name of Boniface (719). He spent some years in Thuringia and Frisia, but it was

Fig. 57. The martyrdom of St Boniface

when he removed to the heathen Frankish district of Hesse that he met with real success. Thousands were baptized. He was called again to Rome, and there consecrated bishop (722). He took, by a most significant innovation, an oath of obedience to the Pope modelled on that of the suburbicarian bishops round Rome, omitting the promise they made of fidelity to the Eastern Emperor. It was an oath with a long sequel. He came back to Hesse as a missionary statesman backed not only by Gregory II but by Charles Martel, the Carolingian Mayor of the Palace who ruled Francia. He could fell the sacred oak at Geismar. From Hesse he passed again to Thuringia. In 732 Pope Gregory III raised him to the rank of archbishop; and in 739 he was made papal legate, the first sent beyond the Alps, another step of vast significance in the growth of papal power. As such he divided Bavaria, where he had already journeyed, into dioceses, and did the same in Hesse, and Thuringia. He was the legislator and organizer of the wide province he had made Christian. His route was marked by the foundation of Benedictine monasteries, of which his favourite Fulda in Hesse became the most famous. The connexion of the mission with England and its monasteries was not broken: English monks and nuns came out to join him, and he may be said to have transplanted the special English reverence for the Papacy to the new Church in Germany. When Charles Martel died (741) and he was called to Francia itself by the new Mayors, Carloman and Pepin, for the reform of the disintegrated Church, he followed the same path under the aegis of the new Pope, Zacharias. He had already extended the boundaries of Latin Christendom, which had shrunk in Spain owing to the Moslem conquest. He had more than re-newed the effective authority of the Popes beyond the Alps. In 742 he began an epoch by undertaking the reform of the Frankish Church. The

single-minded Benedictine missionary, with his inborn gifts as a statesman and evangelist, was a maker of history, far greater than the able Popes
whose authority he used and extended. The unity of the Western Latin
Church began to be an effective reality through St Boniface. He ended his
career by martyrdom in half-heathen Frisia (754), but his work remained.
The Frankish Empire, papal supremacy, monastic foundations, and
ecclesiastical organization were the principal springs of medieval civilization. Each of these owed something of their strength to him.

CHAPTER 13

THE CAROLINGIAN EMPIRE

(i) PEPIN 'THE SHORT', 741–768[1]

By reuniting and reinvigorating the kingdom of the Franks and by checking permanently the onrush of Islam from Spain, Charles Martel had set the course of subsequent history. Not less profound, perhaps, was his influence on the future when he entrusted the education of his sons to the monks of St Denis close to Paris. The effects were epoch-making. The emotional Carloman was fervently religious; the cool-headed Pepin, while he was no less ruthless and dominating a warrior than his forerunners and successors —the Carolingians were a hard and grasping race—was chaste in private life and, as a statesman, was imbued with a conviction of a ruler's duties to his people which was new in Francia. Christianity, through the monks, was producing a new conception of kingship. 'To us', said Pepin, 'the Lord hath entrusted the care of government.' It was a trust which implied the defence and reform of the Church.

Charles Martel, in his career of victory, had been able to rule without a Merovingian figurehead, but his two sons, without his prestige, were taught by a year of turbulence that only the old aureole of kingship could give legitimacy to their power. They produced a Merovingian, Childeric III (743–51), the most shadowy of his line, to awake loyalty to their government as a submissive recluse, while they warred with the restive Swabians (Alemanni), with Odilo Duke of Bavaria from whom they took the Nordgau, with the Saxon raiders, and with the stubborn Dukes of Aquitaine, who were supported by an inveterate desire for provincial independence. The two Mayors acted in harmony, but when the passionate Carloman abdicated in 747 to become a monk in his new monastery of St Sylvester on Mount Soracte near Rome, Pepin took his dominions, to the exclusion of his nephew's claims. His half-brother Grifo, already a rebel, was freed from imprisonment only to be a refugee wherever rebellion simmered against the Frankish overlord. Yet from 749 to 751 there was peace, and Pepin could take the final step in the exaltation of his house and himself. Besides ambition and the love of power, always a ruling motive, to become king—not a hereditary official—was the only means to secure the Carolingians in the full possession of Frankish loyalty and to give permanence to them and more especially to Pepin and his sons over their competing kinsmen. Hitherto the long-haired Merovingians, the race of Clovis with their fabulous descent from heathen deities, had been the irreplaceable

---

[1] See Genealogical Table 5(b) above, p. 155.

bond of Frankish unity: their mere prestige had vanquished Grimoald's attempt to dethrone them. But since then it had waned. To live recluse and powerless on the single manor left them, to proceed once a year in an ox-drawn wagon to the assembly where they sat at gaze as puppets before their people, had at last dissolved the charm, and the time was ripe for revolution.

But a new sanction, a new supernatural halo was required if the new dynasty for all its long predominance was to gain the unquestioning allegiance of the old. That sanction was found in the Church and Christian belief. Pepin, like his brother Carloman, had been from his accession a devout reformer, fosterer, and chief of the Frankish Church. With reform and under the influence of St Boniface the traditional reverence for and links with the Papacy had grown stronger. The Church and the Papacy could give Pepin the consecration and authority he needed, the glamour he lacked. As it happened, the political as well as the ecclesiastical alliance of the Papacy was being prepared by events in Italy. In 751 the Exarchate of Ravenna finally fell to the Lombards, and King Aistulf was threatening to annex the Roman duchy ruled in fact, if not in legal theory, by the Pope. The Byzantine Emperor, expelled from North Italy, preoccupied in the East, was manifestly no protection. Already in 739 Pope Gregory III had appealed for aid to Charles Martel. Now his successor, the mild and diplomatic Greek Zacharias (741–52), whose ecclesiastical authority in Francia had been exalted by the reforms, would be all the more ready to forge fresh links with the pious Carolingian. To him in 751 Pepin's envoys, the English Bishop Burchard of Würzburg, and the arch-chaplain and Abbot of St Denis, Fulrad, journeyed with the momentous question: whether it were good or no that one man should bear the name of king while another really ruled. It was a question of morals addressed to the highest authority on Christian morals in the West. The Pope's reply was the desired one, that it was not, and Pepin could proceed. In November 751 the Frankish assembly was held at Soissons. There, on the Pope's pronouncement, Childeric III was deposed and interned as a monk, to die next year, and Pepin was elected king. He was not only elected: first of the Frankish kings, he was anointed in Biblical and Spanish fashion by St Boniface: he was king 'by the grace of God', like David 'the Lord's anointed', and a new mystical halo was given to the new dynasty and to the kingly office in Francia. As God's vicegerent he had public duties to God and the Church for the people committed to his care.

Following the lead of his brother Carloman, Pepin had already shown himself alive to his responsibilities. As we have seen, the Frankish Church under Charles Martel was corrupt and disorganized and its bishops and clergy very largely unfit for their office. Carloman in 742 invited St Boniface, who for three years had been papal legate beyond the Alps, to attend a synod in Austrasia for reform. This was followed by a synod for all

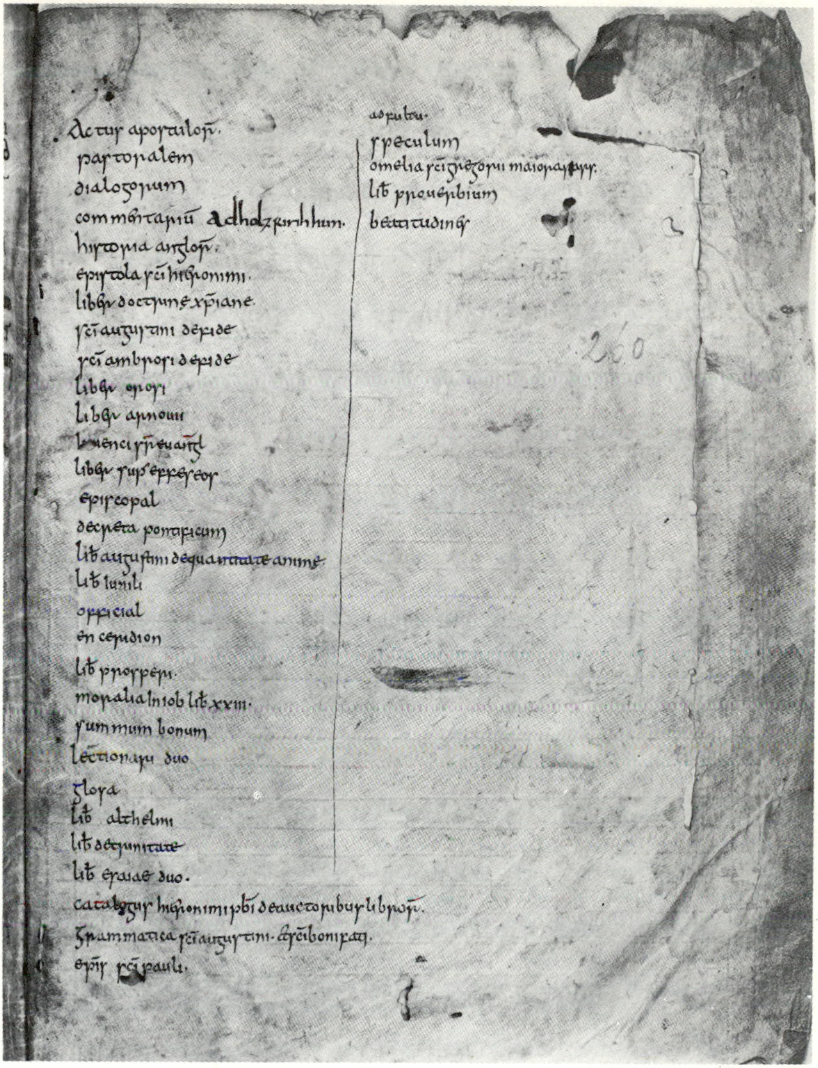

Fig. 58. Oldest library catalogue of Würzburg cathedral

Francia in 743 at Estinnes (*Liftinas*) in Hainault, and a synod for Neustria in 744. By their decrees, confirmed by the mayors, councils were to meet yearly, diocesan discipline was to be restored, unworthy bishops and priests were deposed, many new bishops were appointed, vacant sees were filled and new ones founded. The Church organization of bishoprics in provinces under archbishops was to be restored. In the end Boniface himself was appointed to the see of Mainz. The new archbishops were to receive the pallium from the Pope. In a final synod of 747 the bishops decreed their fidelity to Rome and regulated the rights of the new metropolitans. When St Boniface left Mainz in 752 for Frisia the reform was well under way. In all these proceedings, while the bonds with the Papacy were strengthened, the authority of the mayors was paramount: it was they who enforced the synodal decrees and appointed the bishops. They ruled the Frankish Church under the aegis of the Papacy. As king, Pepin convoked yearly synods to supervise the reform of discipline and the punishment of heathen practices among the laity. All Christians were to observe the Sunday rest and pay tithes to the Church, all marriages were to be public. 'Though at the moment', declared the king, 'our power does not suffice for everything... if later God shall grant us peace and leisure, we hope then to restore in all their scope the standards of the saints.'

It was necessary, however, if reform was to continue, to re-endow the Church, whose resources were depleted by the excessive expropriations of Charles Martel. The Church estates had been too vast, nor could the monarchy do without their seizure in order to provide lay 'benefices'. The two Mayors arrived at a kind of compromise, which Pepin systematized in 751. Some estates were given back to the Church; others and more were registered as leases (*precariae verbo regis*) at a rent of about one-fifth of their income and then conferred as royal 'benefices'. Thus the Church was sufficiently equipped for its work and authority. It was a skilful measure, but the evil of improvident gifts was bound to exist with its concomitants, overwealthy ecclesiastics and the land-grabbing of warrior laymen.

Soon after the assumption of the crown the Italian question demanded a momentous decision: was Pepin to intervene across the Alps or not? He was now the Pope's political debtor as well as his ecclesiastical ally. The Pope was in the utmost danger of subjection to the Lombard king. Stephen II (III), a Roman born, now sat in St Peter's chair (752–7). Aistulf (749–56), despite a forty years' peace just concluded with him, was demanding a poll-tax from the Romans as their suzerain. In vain the Pope sent first his own envoys and then a Byzantine official dispatched from Constantinople by his nominal sovereign, the Emperor, to protest. They were dismissed in turn with threats by the enraged Aistulf. Then the Pope turned to his last resource. Early in 753 he begged that Frankish envoys should be sent to invite himself to Francia to arrange for intervention. He appealed not only to Pepin but to the Frankish nobles to aid St Peter, who held the keys of Heaven. A not enthusiastic assembly agreed to King Pepin's consent. By a really remarkable timing, Pope Stephen was himself accredited, with a Byzantine official, in a new embassy of protest to Aistulf late in 754 at Pavia, just when the Frankish envoys, Duke Autchar (the legendary Ogier the Dane) and Bishop Chrodegang, were already there. Once more the request for peace and restitution was refused. Then the Franks demanded permission for the Pope to journey on to King Pepin. Aistulf might gnash his teeth, but he gave way. When in January 754 the Pope met his royal host, Pepin dismounted and led his horse like a groom, a fateful precedent for the future, but also a present magnification of the papal office. The Pope's authority was growing fast.

There were still negotiations and manœuvres to be gone through. A reluctant consent to a transalpine campaign was obtained at the Field of May. Vain embassies were sent to Aistulf. The mission of the monk Carloman from his last retirement at Monte Cassino to dissuade attack only produced his own detention by his brother and the relegation of his son to the cloister. A promise of territorial gains for the Pope was made by Pepin at his *villa* (manor) of Quierzy. Its contents are only known through an abstract, twenty years or more later, in the *Vita Hadriani*, but, however garbled they may be, they were evidently an ample promise of territory. Pepin showed no wish for transalpine annexations to Francia, and was possibly ill informed on Italian geography: it was dependants in Italy that he aimed at in his subsequent actions. He may, too, have been influenced by the most famous of forgeries, which was concocted at this time in the papal Curia. The *Donation of Constantine*, as the forged document is named, purported to be a grant made by Constantine the Great to Pope Sylvester. It embodied an older legendary tale of Constantine's disease of leprosy, his cure and baptism by St Sylvester, his gratitude and endowment of the Pope with the primacy, and his withdrawal to a new capital, Constantinople. The forgery made him give to the Pope the imperial insignia, lead his horse, and surrender to him the rule of Italy if not of all the western provinces. If this myth had become familiar to the Frankish king, his behaviour to the Pope has nothing puzzling in it, and the details of his promise given in the *Vita Hadriani* present nothing incredible.

Pepin did not go without a reward. In the abbey of St Denis, Pope Stephen anointed both him and his two sons, Charles and Carloman, confirming them as Kings of the Franks and creating them patricians of the Romans, and under penalty of excommunication and interdict forbidding the Franks ever to elect a king not descended from them. Thus a papal sanction consecrated the new dynasty, and gave a precedent to papal claims. It may be possible that the Pope had the Byzantine Emperor's authorization to invest Pepin with the rank of Patrician, but in any case the unction as such and the novel addition 'of the Romans' were his own device, and implied a hereditary protectorate of Rome, not at all compatible with the Emperor's sovereignty. It accords with Pepin's cautious temperament that he never took the compromising title in his diplomas.

Intervention beyond the Alps, in fact, was unpopular with the Frankish nobles, and Pepin endeavoured to do only what was absolutely necessary. One small victory at the *clusae*, the fortified outlet of the Mont Cenis Pass, sufficed to bring Aistulf to feigned submission. He accepted Pepin's overlordship, and promised to cede the Exarchate to the Pope. But he clearly thought that a second campaign would not be undertaken, for he kept Ravenna and late in 755 he was ravaging at the gates of Rome. So great was the emergency that Pope Stephen addressed a startling appeal to Frankish piety to overcome his allies' hesitation. It purported to be written—and many Franks may well have believed it—by St Peter himself to his 'adopted sons', offering Paradise for obedience and damnation for neglect. This was effectual. A second expedition besieged Aistulf in Pavia and enforced a real surrender. Even then the promise of Quierzy was not fully performed, but the Exarchate and the Pentapolis were given up to the Pope, while heavy payments were made to Pepin. The Donation of Pepin was made to St Peter and his successors, the Popes. On the march to Pavia a Byzantine envoy had asked that the Exarchate should be restored to the Emperor, and had received a peremptory refusal. No arguments from a lost dominion of an impotent third party would be likely to convince the Frank that he had not free disposal of his conquests from the Lombards. The Pope wisely continued to date by the Emperor's years, but he now ruled an enlarged Papal State under Frankish protection.

No reluctance for expansion was visible among the Franks when Pepin turned his arms to the West. In 752–9 Septimania was conquered from the Spanish Moslems. Thus Islam was expelled from Gaul, and the Franks held all its Mediterranean coast. More formidable was the resistance of Waifar, Duke of Aquitaine, who represented a long-lived provincial patriotism of a Gotho-Roman amalgam, unmixed with Frankish elements. Year after year Pepin attacked in force (760–8), and when Waifar's death ended the hopeless struggle, special privileges, which approached autonomy, were granted the conquered land. But Francia now effectually reached the Pyrenees.

Pepin himself died worn out in September 768. His epoch-making reign has been eclipsed unduly by the fame of his greater successor, but he was the initiator who gave a new direction to history. He was practical and persistent, relentless in his ambition but not needlessly cruel, never scheming more than he could safely carry out, and really resolved to do his duty to God and his people. A rise in Frankish culture began. Evidently at his request, Pope Paul I sent him books in Greek. Roman liturgic music spread. Bishop Chrodegang of Metz organized his cathedral clergy in a half-monastic fashion, which was the means and sign of zeal and efficiency. Pepin made the first steps in the Carolingian renaissance; he won for the Frankish kingdom the secular headship of the Christian West.

(2) THE CONQUESTS OF CHARLEMAGNE

Pepin divided his kingdom—he could hardly do otherwise in view of Frankish custom and the self-assertiveness of his house—between his sons, Charles and Carloman, but the division was new and significant. The north and the Atlantic coast and all true Francia, whether German or Romance in speech, were given to Charles the elder; the south, Burgundy, Swabia, Septimania, and east Aquitaine, fell to Carloman. It was a sign of renewed Frankish unity and perhaps hegemony, and it was not yet a disregard of natural forces at a time when speech counted for little and custom for much. Austrasia and Neustria together were pre-eminently Frankish land.

The division instituted by Pepin was evidently aimed at allotting the two brothers separate spheres of frontier policy, but personal rivalry prevented it working. Carloman would not aid his brother in subduing a brief revolt in Aquitaine. The efforts of their mother, Queen Bertrada, produced a reconciliation, and she endeavoured by measures of appeasement to prevent wars with the two remaining half-independent powers, the unruly vassals of the Lombards and Bavaria, which bordered Carloman's share. Her sons were both patricians of the Romans and unlikely to act in harmony. The chief danger-point lay in Italy and Rome.

Italian politics were more embroiled than ever. King Aistulf's death in 756 was followed by a disputed succession, which ended in the elevation of Desiderius, Duke of Tuscany, an adroit diplomatist, to the throne (756–74). The new king's policy was to avoid fresh Frankish intervention, and to raise up a pro-Lombard party in the Roman Curia by concessions and pressure, while he consolidated the Lombard kingdom and gained allies abroad. Perhaps he hoped to become the all-powerful protector of the Papacy, while he alienated it from King Pepin. The Pope, however, now Paul I (757–67), brother and successor of Stephen II, was a skilful opponent, who extorted the cession of Faenza and Ferrara, as well as the return of some papal estates elsewhere, in return for amity, with the support of Pepin always in the background. Desiderius, indeed, put loyal dukes into Spoleto and Benevento, and when Paul I died, nearly succeeded in carrying the election of his candidate in the unseemly, violent contest of Roman factions, which temporal dominion and barbarism had raised to a ferocious virulence. Then Bertrada's plans came to his help. Duke Tassilo of Bavaria was already the son-in-law of Desiderius. She arranged the marriage of the Lombard's other daughter to her son Charles. A family alliance should replace distrust. Even Pope Stephen III (768–71) tortuously submitted to see his chief supporter, the *primicerius* Christopher, who had perhaps composed the *Donation of Constantine*, overthrown and cruelly killed by the pro-Lombards amid civic fighting. Desiderius felt secure enough to refuse the price, his promised cession of estates to the Papacy. But now Stephen III died, and there was a sturdier Pope, the Roman Adrian I (771–95). More than all, changes took place in Francia. Charles broke with his Lombard queen, and married the Swabian Hildegarde. His discord with Carloman had nearly grown to war, and when his brother died in December 771 he seized the sole sovereignty of the Franks. Carloman's widow and her disinherited children fled to Lombardy. Bertrada's policy had come to grief, leaving the field clear to the dominating genius of her elder son.

Desiderius did not realize the strength of Charles, now his enemy. In 772 he conquered part of the Papal State, and endeavoured to force the Pope to anoint Carloman's sons. Although he retired from Viterbo on receiving Adrian's threats of excommunication, he was probably misled by the liberality of Charles's offer of money compensation, and he overrated his means of resistance to the Frankish invasion, which in answer to the Pope's entreaties was clearly coming. In spite of his gifts to supporters and the great monasteries, the Lombards were not united, and Francia was. The south held back, others deserted. The *clusae* at Susa were by-passed (773), Verona surrendered with Carloman's children, and Desiderius in Pavia was at last starved to surrender (774). Of Carloman's sons no more is heard; Desiderius was deported to Francia; his son and co-regent Adelgis fled into exile.

Meantime, Charles himself had journeyed to Rome. There in an interview on 6 April 774 he confirmed the Donation of Pepin at Quierzy, but either the account of it in the *Vita Hadriani* omits reservations and definitions or Charles subsequently modified its terms. The frontiers given in the *Vita* would surrender to the Papacy nearly all Italy south of the Apennines and the lower river Po; these were never later demanded by Adrian in his letters, but Charles did then make concessions of territory and income in Tuscany, Spoleto, and Benevento which suggest a compromise with papal claims.

With the capture of Pavia, the capital, Charles adopted a new solution of the Italian problem. He styled himself 'King of the Franks and Lombards and Patrician of the Romans'. This meant that Italy was to be a part of the Frankish realm, but an exceptional part. It was only gradually after a revolt that Lombard dukedoms were changed into Frankish counties, and Frank nobles settled in any number. Even then Italy was given (781) a provincial king in Charles's second son Pepin, still a child, with a regent, as a kind of viceroy for his father, who did not therefore cease to rule the land like his other territories. At the same time the title of Patrician, now used by the king himself, acquired in fact, if not by treaty, an enlarged meaning. Charles acted without contradiction as the suzerain of the Pope and his State. If he added southern Tuscany and Sabina to the papal lands, he issued orders to the Pope and supervised the administration of them all. The link with the Byzantine Empire was snapped. After 772 Adrian dated documents by the years of his own pontificate, not by those of the Eastern Emperor. This showed his wishes, but the enlarged Papal State was more subject to the king-patrician than it had been to the distant Caesar of Constantinople. The mutual understanding between the upright Adrian and his protector made the arrangement workable in spite of contradictions and recriminations, due to the fact that Charles was now the inheritor of the aim of his Lombard predecessors to rule all Italy.

This aim, however, was not achieved. On the fall of Pavia, Arichis of Benevento (758–87), the son-in-law of Desiderius, took the title of Prince as a sign of independence. The Byzantine Emperor, who still possessed Sicily, surrendered no claim. When the iconodule Empress Irene ruled as regent, an accord by which her son Constantine VI was betrothed to Charles's daughter Rotrudis was arranged (780), but she cancelled this treaty as her plans matured. Although Charles forced Arichis by a campaign (786) to submit to vassalage, the renewed hostility of the Byzantines led him to allow the prince's son Grimoald (787–806), who was in his hands, to succeed to Benevento, and to give him aid in repelling an invasion from Sicily, in which the exile Adelgis took part. But Grimoald reassumed independence, and later wars were ineffectual. The division of Italy into north and south grew steadily more marked.

The effects of Charles's conquest were none the less profound. He subjected and controlled the Pope he had saved from the Lombards. He had united North Italy to the Frankish realm, developing Francia as a Mediterranean power, with a long train of consequences, political, religious, and cultural, for all the West.

Yet the Italian conquest was only a part, and not the most cherished part, of the designs of Charles the Great, who passed into later memory as Charlemagne. The first place was held by the conquest of the Saxons, the last heathen and independent tribe of inner Germany, and their incorporation in Francia, which was the most hard fought of his wars and took up thirty-two years of his reign. Zeal to extend Christendom and its civilization was a powerful motive, but it was also due to the king's unflinching resolve to end an intolerable and dangerous situation, which imperilled the growth of the Frankish monarchy.

The Old Saxons had changed but little since their emigrants had joined in the Anglo-Saxon invasion of Britain. Although conscious of their tribal identity, even their three chief sub-tribes, the Westphalians, Engrians, and Eastphalians, were not political units. At most they acted together in time of war. Their country was a coagulation of smaller independent communities, composed in ancient fashion of nobles (*edelings*), full freemen (*frilings*), half-free (*laten*), and slaves. They had not developed even a local kingship, although they might elect a temporary leader for war. A marked characteristic was their firm attachment to their ancestral heathenism, so congenial to barbaric warriors, with its fanatical reverence for its ancient gods, its trust in their oracles, its sacrificial feasts, and its virile, fatalistic conception of human life. To raid peaceful or hostile neighbours was still the ideal exploit of these fierce tribesmen, made the more tempting by their own increase in number and the Franks' increase in wealth. Punitive reprisals had no effect; attempts at conversion were fruitless, and Charlemagne, like earlier Carolingians, found east Austrasia to be their favourite victim.

At first (772–5) he tried an intenser form of the usual reprisals, marching to the river Weser and destroying the column of Irminsul, adored as symbolizing the mythic tree which supported the world. But each time he was absent in Italy the Saxons renewed their incursions (774, 775), and by 776 Charlemagne was planning a gradual annexation. He was establishing strong fortresses as far as the river Lippe, forming a border province or march, where and whence Christianity could be extended by missionaries. In 777 he held the Frankish assembly at Paderborn in Engria. But a stubborn spirit of resistance was alive, and found a chief in the Westphalian chieftain Widukind. When Charlemagne was in Spain (778), fighting began again, which took three years to bring to a seeming end. The king reached the river Elbe in one campaign. He organized the Church in Saxony. In 782 he organized Saxony as a Frankish province. Conversion was enforced, the land was divided into counties, and submissive Saxon chiefs were made counts. The appearance, however, was delusive. Widukind could take refuge in Denmark, and the converts were heathen at heart. When in 782 the over-confident Charles sent a Frankish host with a Saxon contingent against the Slav Sorbs on the upper Elbe, there was a universal revolt with Widukind as its leader. The Franks were cut to pieces in the Süntel hills just beyond the Weser. The disaster moved Charles to the sternest and strongest measures. He marched himself to Saxony, rallying the submissive, and while Widukind fled to Denmark, he insisted on the surrender to him of 4500 rebels. He then massacred them at Verden on the Aller, a revenge which still blots his name. But it only enflamed resistance. Three furious campaigns were needed (783–5) before Saxony lay at the king's mercy. Then at last even Widukind submitted to be baptized and reconciled.

Severity was now the order of the day. Conversion was made compulsory on pain of death. The death penalty was imposed on heathen practices or attacks on the churches and clergy. Frankish political institutions were introduced along with Frankish counts and officials. Dioceses were established with bishops and clergy, and the hated payment of tithes was rigidly enforced. A rule of iron was set up, both political and ecclesiastical,

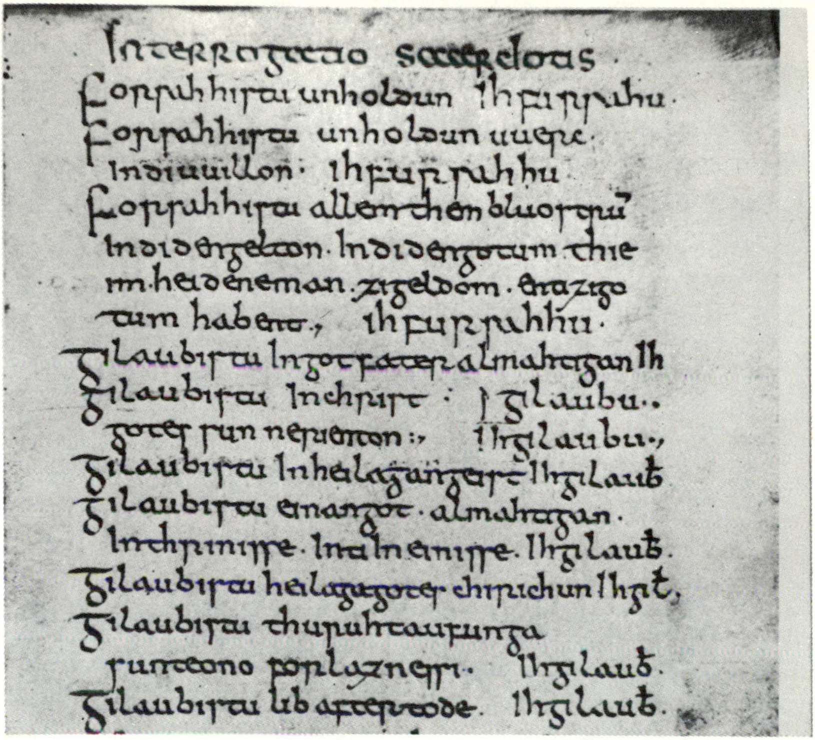
Interrogatio sacerdotis.
Forsachistu unholdun. ih forsachu.
Forsachistu unholdun uuerc.
Indi uuillon. ih forsachu
Forsachistu allem them bluostrum
indi den gelton. indi den gotum thie
im heideneman. zi geldom. enti zi go
tum habent. ih forsachu.
Gilaubistu in got fater almahtigan ih
Gilaubistu in christ. ih gilaubu..
gotes sun nerienton. ih gilaubu.
Gilaubistu in halagan geist. ih gilaub
Gilaubistu einan got. almahtigan.
in thrinisse. inti in einisse. ih gilaub.
Gilaubistu heliga gotes chirichun. ih gil.
Gilaubistu thuruh taufunga
sunteono forlaznessi. ih gilaub.
Gilaubistu lib after tode. ih gilaub.

Fig. 59. Baptismal vow imposed upon the Saxons

which was condemned in discreet phrase by Charlemagne's English mentor, Alcuin. It drove the Saxons to desperation. In 792 they rose again, and the yearly campaigns recommenced. Charles in 795 began a policy of deporting part of the population elsewhere, and replacing them with Franks. The final conquest of Nordalbingia (Holstein), which was Saxony beyond the Elbe, took place in 804, when its inhabitants were deported to make room for Charles's Slav allies, the heathen Obodrites. Already a milder law, like the Frankish, had been decreed for offences against Church and king. It had been a ruthless war, but its effects were permanent. The last independent German tribe had been forcibly made Christian and an integral part of the Frankish realm. Yet it retained its tribal identity and unity in the shape of an inextinguishable particularism.

Something of the same policy, in a less violent form, was pursued by Charlemagne towards the semi-independent duchy of Bavaria. He was determined to unite all Germany under the Franks, and his methods showed little respect for rights and scruples. But here the opposition was weak. Tassilo, Duke of Bavaria, construed his dependence on Francia as loosely as he dared, but he was no statesman—his interests lay in religion, in the furtherance of Bavarian monasteries. In 781 at the orders of king and Pope he was forced to renew to Charles the oaths he had sworn to

Pepin, but troubles soon arose on the disputed frontier on the river Adige, where Bavaria met Charles's Italian kingdom. In 787 he was overcome in a campaign without a battle, since the Bavarian bishops, at papal prompting, sided against him. He submitted to receive Bavaria as a Frankish vassal. It was now easy to trump up charges of treason against him, and this was done next year at the assembly at Ingelheim, which he unsuspectingly attended. He was condemned and compelled with his sons to become a monk, while Bavaria, like Saxony, was distributed among Frankish counts. Later the ex-duke was compelled to acknowledge his guilt to obtain a fresh pardon. But although annexed without difficulty, Bavaria retained, like Saxony and Swabia, its identity as a tribe. Submission to the king and particularism existed together.

Fig. 60. Golden chalice of Tassilo, Duke of Bavaria

The Bavarians in fact gained by the protection they received as well as by the good government of Charlemagne, for his annexations made him the defender of the eastern frontier against the barbaric Slavs and Avars. Both were heathens. The western Slavs had penetrated by this time deeply into central Germany. The river Elbe still marked the limits of the Obodrites (modern Mecklenburg) and the Lyutitzi or Wiltzes (modern Brandenburg), but the Sorbs further south reached the river Saale and even the river Main, and the Czechs and Moravians were a menace. In his later years Charles led or sent expeditions against all but the Obodrites, his allies; the frontier was defended if the submissions he received were vague. The war with the Avars, on the other hand, produced far-reaching results. Hitherto the duchy of Bavaria had reached the river Enns to the east, and had exercised a protectorate over the Slav peasant-principality of Carinthia, which had thrown off Avar rule. Both had been exposed to Avar raids, and Tassilo had possibly reckoned on an Avar alliance. In any case the Avars in 788 had advanced into Bavaria and Friuli (in north-east Venetia), and had been driven back. In 791 Charlemagne took the offensive in a campaign of reprisal as far as the river Raab, and in 795 proceeded with a war of conquest. The Avars were far decayed from the days of Baian. Most of the raided lands were closed to them. They kept to their primitive nomadic barbarism between the Danube and the Theiss, where their great fortified encampment or 'Ring' was situated, and they had lost their barbaric energy. To their weakness were added intestine quarrels. Thus Margrave Eric of Friuli, who had charge of the frontier, was able to cross the Danube, aided by the Slav prince Voinimir, and capture the Ring with its stored-up treasures. Next year King Pepin of Italy completed the work of conquest. The Avars were so wholly overthrown that they vanished as a people. The steppe-land they had wandered in was left nearly vacant. Their Slav subjects south of the Danube were included for the time at least in a great frontier-district or 'march'. South of the river Drave, Slovenes and Croats were made to submit to Frankish supremacy. The Danubian land was soon to become the East March (Austria proper) of Bavaria, the southern mountain region the duchy of Carinthia. Christian missions were busily at work, sent from Friuli and the Bavarian bishoprics. Meantime there began a German immigration, mainly from Bavaria, which was to continue for centuries until the south-eastern Alps were thoroughly Germanized. The colonists spread first in the fertile valleys, but it took long to absorb the Slavs among the mountains. Carinthia long after was still largely Slavonic, and Carniola to the south is still Slovene. Thus the south-eastern expansion of Germany began with the work of Charlemagne. There is no need to dilate on its historic importance.

Charlemagne was prompted both by political insight and by insatiable ambition, but his aggressions were redeemed by the sincere zeal to guard and extend Christendom and civilization. The indistinguishable interests of both were always in his thoughts and were no hypocritical pretext. All these motives led him to take advantage of the incessant civil wars of the Spanish Moslems to attempt the conquest of Spain. Thinking Saxony secure, he led an imposing army across the Pyrenees in 778 at the invitation of Ibn Ar-Arabi, who ruled Saragossa. But progress was small and he infuriated the Christian Basques of Navarre. When the Saxon revolt of Widukind and the power of the Omayyad Abd-ar-Rahman I compelled his retreat, his rear-guard was surrounded and destroyed by the Basques in the pass of Roncevalles in the Pyrenees. The disaster lived in popular imagination for centuries, and gave birth to famous epic poems, for the slain were eminent men among them Roland, warden of the Breton march, who is

Map 7

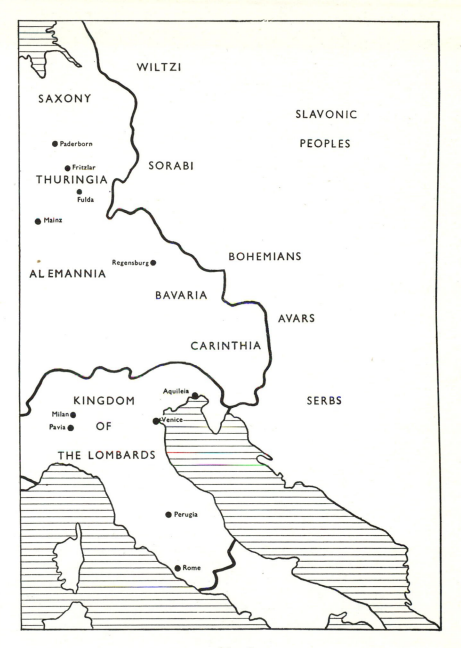

WILTZI

SAXONY

SLAVONIC

PEOPLES

● Paderborn

● Fritzlar

SORABI

THURINGIA

Fulda

● Mainz

BOHEMIANS

Regensburg ●

ALEMANNIA

BAVARIA

AVARS

CARINTHIA

Aquileia

KINGDOM

SERBS

Milan ●

OF

● Venice

Pavia ●

THE LOMBARDS

● Perugia

● Rome

Map 7

only really known to us by his death. Charles, however, by no means relinquished his designs. He conciliated Aquitanian particularism by placing his infant son Lewis (named after Clovis) as sub-King of Aquitaine (781), and local counts carried on the Spanish war. His cousin Duke William of Toulouse and Septimania (like Roland an epic hero as William of Orange), in spite of a Moslem counter-attack in 793, resumed the piece-meal invasion. In 801 the seaport of Barcelona was captured, and a Spanish March was formed beyond the Pyrenees. It was only a beginning and unwelcome to the Basques, but it led to a permanent immigration from Aquitaine into Catalonia, and divided it in language and institutions from central Spain. Catalan character and particularism owe their origin to Charlemagne's Spanish ambitions. For his own time, he had secured his frontier and recovered a province for Christendom.

With only one heathen neighbour did Charlemagne stand on the defensive, and this was ominous. Godefrid (Guthrödr) the Dane, who ruled a considerable Scandinavian kingdom where Widukind and Saxon exiles had often taken refuge, showed his suspicions of his new Frankish neighbour by building a fortification across the Slesvig isthmus, and his own aggressiveness by attacking the Obodrites. In 810 he anticipated a new era by sending a fleet of 200 ships to ravage the Frisian coast. Counter-measures produced less effect than the murder of Godefrid and the struggle of rivals for his kingdom, which somewhat relieved its foes. But Scandinavia was astir and the peril from the North Sea had begun.

(3) THE FOUNDATION OF THE WESTERN EMPIRE

Wars did not exhaust the immense activity and commanding genius of Charlemagne. He personally administered his vast realm which reached from the Elbe to beyond the Pyrenees and from the North Sea to the Beneventan frontier. The Christian provinces of the Western Roman Empire were united under him with the whole of inner Germany. He was suzerain of the Papal State. But his authority was not only secular, it was religious. It had taken on a theocratic and universal character. The Papacy had indeed rendered its primacy more effective in the West through its alliance with its Frankish protector. Its ecclesiastical headship was current doctrine throughout Francia. But Pope Adrian acted in submission to the King on whose political power he depended. His next successor placed a mosaic in the Lateran, depicting St Peter giving the pallium to the Pope and the banner to the king, with the prayer inscribed, 'Holy Peter, bestow life on Pope Leo and on King Charles victory!' This was the Gelasian doctrine of the two powers, priestly and royal, which were to govern the world. On their mutual relation Charles had no doubt: the priesthood were to pray, the kingship was to rule. The Church had been entrusted to his

*Fig. 61. Christ with the Emperor Constantine and Pope Silvester I;
St Peter with Charlemagne and Pope Leo III*

hand in the old Frankish fashion to govern and direct, not only to defend. His view resembled Byzantine Caesaropapism. He was to protect the Church from false doctrine, as Alcuin said, as well as from heathen on-slaught. 'With these two swords has God's power armed thy right hand and thy left.' His official scribe styles him in 796 'Lord and Father, King and Priest, the Leader and Guide of all Christians'. When the Adoptionist heresy spread from Spain, it was Charles who caused synods to be held in his presence (792, 794) and condemned it. This might please Pope Adrian, but when Charlemagne took umbrage at the decrees of the Council of Nicaea, convoked by the Empress-regent Irene in 787, which established image-worship, it was another matter. The king ordered the learned *Libri Carolini* to be compiled, denouncing the heresy of the Greeks, whose canons were for that matter mistranslated into less subtle Latin. He required the unwilling Pope to excommunicate the Emperor. Adrian compromised by defending the Nicaean canons and by excommunicating Constantine VI for occupying Papal estates. But Charles's Frankish Synod of Frankfurt roundly condemned the iconodule doctrine (794). To Charles it was a part of his constant supervision of and legislation for the Church of his realm.

This was a development of St Augustine's conception of the *Civitas Dei* as Christendom, the political state of the faithful on earth, and it combined with a similar identification of the unsanctified *Civitas Terrena*, exemplified in the four successive earthly empires of the *Book of Daniel*. The fourth was the Roman Empire. But had the Empire since the conversion of Constantine changed its character and become the secular embodiment of the City of God on earth? The controversial Frankish *Libri Carolini*

313

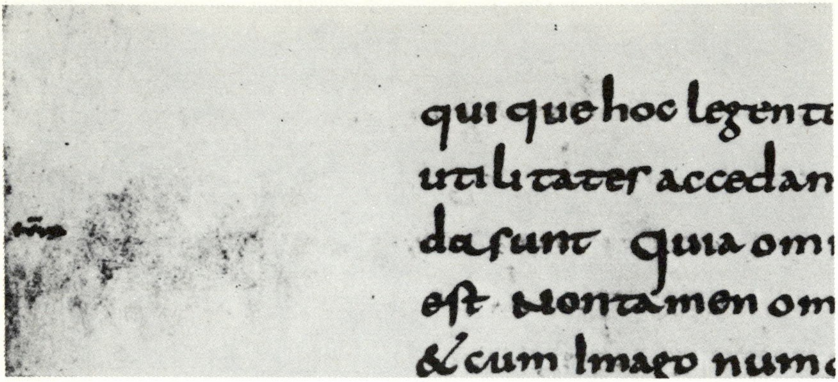

Fig. 62. Treatise on image worship showing marginal gloss representing Charlemagne's oral comment: it reads 'syllogistice'

stigmatized it still as heathen and idolatrous. In 800 Alcuin more moderately wrote of the three highest powers in the world, the Papacy at Rome, the Empire at New Rome, and the pre-eminent Kingship of Charles, appointed by Christ to be the Leader of the Christian people. But the tradition of the Roman Empire in popular memory and educated circles was still strong. Law and custom recalled it; its peace was glorified in retrospect amid the turbulent, hard-fisted life of the present; men read Virgil as well as St Augustine. It was hard for them to dissociate the idea of the unity and peace of Christendom from the world-wide Roman Empire, the home of law and civilization and legitimate rule. That Empire had its seat at Constantinople and its head in the successor of Augustus. The Franks were but strident claimants to a new hegemony, and for all its flatteries the Roman Curia was uneasy at the antithesis.

Thus the force of events and the force of convictions were alike urging a solution which might conciliate them and supply a consistent structure. The civilizing rule of Charles actually united the Christian West. That was the mission of the Roman Empire, which still survived in the East, and the divergence between the Greek East and the barbaric Latin West was profound. The time was growing ripe for Old Rome, the see of St Peter, to give traditional form to the revolutionary fact.

Fortuitous events paved the way. Pope Adrian I died on Christmas Day 795. The new Pope, the Roman Leo III (795–816), was disliked by his predecessor's kinsmen, who were powerful in the Curia, and was open at least to calumny. He showed his weakness at once by sending Charles the banner of Rome with a promise of fidelity and a request for Frankish envoys to receive the Romans' oath of allegiance. In as marked a way he dated his bulls by Charles's reign, an acknowledgement of sovereignty. The king-patrician warned him ominously to maintain the canons. But the enmity of the hostile faction increased till on 25 April 799 Leo was seized, maltreated to the danger of his sight and speech, and only saved by Frankish envoys. That he could see and speak seemed miraculous. He took refuge with Charles amid universal reverence, and was escorted back to Rome by Frankish envoys. There his opponents were brought to trial and exiled to Francia, while his own conduct was investigated. Charles himself followed (800) with a view to a permanent settlement. There was no judge, it was thought, who could try the Pope, but Leo agreed to take a public, 'voluntary' oath that he was guiltless of the charges brought against him (23 December). On the same day envoys from the Patriarch of Jerusalem brought Charles the keys of the Holy Sepulchre, a compliment suggestive of the headship of Christendom.

The restored Pope seized the opportunity to requite his benefactor and to magnify his own office. On Christmas Day 800, while Charles was kneeling in St Peter's during the mass, Leo suddenly placed a golden crown on his head, and the Roman notables chanted the acclamation from the ritual *Laudes*: 'To Charles, Augustus, crowned by God, the great and peace-bringing Emperor of the Romans, life and victory.' The Pope then performed the customary 'adoration' due to the Emperors, and later crowned Charles the Younger, the eldest of Charlemagne's sons, already a king. The patrician had become Emperor, and a new Roman Empire had been founded in the West.

Charlemagne did not scruple to declare publicly that he would not have entered St Peter's had he known the Pope's intentions, and doubtless the initiative had been wrested from his hands by that adroit diplomatist with far-reaching, unforeseen results in the future. But his policy could not have been wholly flouted by Leo, and it was surely the method and the illegality of the act which displeased him. It is clear from later proceedings that Byzantine ceremonial was anxiously observed and Byzantine recognition persistently sought by him. He wished to be Roman Emperor as far as legal form could make him, not a barbaric usurper of another's title. For that legal form, with the legal claims it might give—things of prime importance in a formalistic age—election by the Senate, acceptance by the people, and, if there was a reigning Emperor, recognition as co-regent were essential. For the first two conditions the acclamations in Old Rome were a substitute; the third, which might imply a claim to the true and Eastern Empire, was a harder problem. The semi-official Frankish *Annals* insisted on the previous deliberations of Pope, clergy, and Christian people, and on the facts that Charles possessed Old Rome and that the Empire was vacant through the usurpation of a woman, the Empress Irene. These preliminaries were natural, if they happened, but were only the beginning of a proceeding truncated by Leo's action. For the rest of his reign Charles was engaged in warlike and peaceful measures to obtain an arrangement with the Eastern Empire which would satisfy his territorial and constitutional ambitions. Co-existing Roman Emperors of East and West were quite in line of precedent. It was only when he had at last obtained recognition of his imperial title from the Emperor Michael that he associated his surviving son Lewis as Emperor co-regent, and it is worthy of note that he then commanded his son to take the imperial crown from the altar in his basilica at Aachen without the intervention of the Pope. The ceremony was a copy of Byzantine usage, and may have been partly designed to exclude over-great papal pretensions.

Yet at the time the Pope's act, as if by inspiration, well expressed the theocratic nature of Charlemagne's monarchy. He was the new David, the Lord's Anointed, chosen to guide the Christian people in the City of God on earth, and this imprint the new Empire of the West and its subsequent development, the Holy Roman Empire, never lost. It was the first political creation, the focus of political theory in the Middle Ages. It expressed in a secular institution the unity of Christendom as did the Papacy in the Christian Church. The Gelasian doctrine of the two powers, priestly and imperial, appointed by God to rule humanity, received a new embodiment, which long dominated men's conceptions of rightful rule. The mutual relations of the two powers were to be the subject of incessant controversy in fact and theory. Pope Leo had given the appearance that the imperial crown was awarded by the Papacy, and this suggestion was to acquire belief and to be enlarged, but Charlemagne himself, in fact and in theory, was master of Empire, Papacy, and Church. He was the God-given autocrat of Western Christendom.

Fact and theory, however, were still at discord although directed to one end. Charlemagne retained the titles which expressed the concrete foundations of his power. He was still King of the Franks and Lombards. Only in the Papal State was he solely Emperor of the Romans. In 802 he wove closer the strands of his authority by commanding all his subjects in all his lands to take a fresh oath of allegiance to him as Emperor; but when he executed a testament dividing his realm in 806, he merely followed Pepin's precedent and allotted true Francia and Saxony to his eldest son Charles (*ob*. 811), Italy and Swabia and Bavaria to Pepin (*ob*. 810), and Aquitaine with Burgundy and the Spanish March to Lewis, making no provision for any superiority or the imperial title. We do not know what scheme he had in view, for the situation was changed, when a decision came, by the deaths of his elder sons and by Byzantine recognition. When the Emperor Nicephorus refused his proposals (803), he proceeded to attack the only remaining Byzantine dependency in North Italy, Venice. The State of the lagoons had developed into a maritime and trading power under its elective native Doges or Dukes, but it was torn by internal feuds between the little towns of which it consisted, Heraclea, Jesolo, and Malamocco on the Lido. Charles had long desired the use of its fleet which might enable him to counter the Byzantine navy, and under his pressure there had grown up a Francophil party, which seized power and submitted to him in 805. At the same time he claimed Byzantine Dalmatia. A Greek fleet recovered both for the Eastern Empire. The retort of Charlemagne was to send King Pepin to conquer Venice. Its towns were sacked, the Doges were captured (809–10), but resistance was still kept up in the islets of Rialto, the core of the lagoons. Pepin withdrew to die, and Venice made a legend of his repulse. The Byzantines, whose fleet commanded the Adriatic, saw it was time to treat. Charlemagne offered to renounce Istria, Venice, and Dalmatia as the price for recognition. In 812 the Emperor Michael's ambassadors solemnly saluted him as Emperor. The sought-for legality had been won, and the aged Charlemagne in September 813 exalted his son King Lewis to be his co-regent Emperor.

Fig. 63. Memorial statue of Charlemagne

The war had completed the formation of the Venetian republic and given it a new centre. In 810 the Byzantine envoy on his way to Aachen appointed a new Doge, Agnello Particiaco, who resided in unconquered Rialto, the present Venice, where the inhabitants of the lagoons now concentrated. As an autonomous fragment of the Eastern Empire, yet Western in essentials and in faith and in constant treaty and trade relations with the rulers of Italy, Venice could slowly grow in practical independence. It was the one state in Italy which never received a Germanic imprint. Defended by the sea, Byzantine in its exterior, it remained a native development from the older Italy before the Lombards came.

Charlemagne died on 28 January 814 in his favourite palace at Aachen in the heart of Austrasia in the seventy-second year of his age, and was buried in the basilica hard by, for which he had despoiled Ravenna of its marbles. Well over six feet in height, his physical strength had been remarkable to the last. He was tireless in war, in the hunt, in the incessant task of ruling and in the intellectual activity which filled his waking hours. Like his father Pepin and with more creative genius, he felt his mission not only to give his Empire peace and good government but to revive the civilization, religion, and culture lost in the Dark Ages. In all parts, in law and judgement, in administration and war, his inspiring, irresistible personality kept control. He gathered round him a learned circle and a palace school; his cultured friends, immigrants like the Northumbrian Alcuin or the Lombard Paul, were the nucleus of the 'Carolingian Renaissance'. He himself spoke both his native German of Austrasia and a Latin which presumably was an early Neustrian Romance; we are told he could follow spoken Greek. In his old age he vainly tried to learn to write. He had read to him ancient chronicles and especially St Augustine's *De Civitate Dei*, which influenced his conception of his monarchy. Perhaps still more to his taste were the old Frankish lays of heroes and kings, of which he had a collection made. Its destruction by his monk-ruled son was an irreparable loss to literature. His exuberant vitality showed its darker side in his sexual licence, which set the tone of his corrupt court; it was perhaps the cause of his occasional cruelty as much as the influence of his third wife Fastrada, to whom it was ascribed. In the struggle for power and conquest he could be ruthless, as in his treatment of the Saxons; for to exile opponents or to thrust them into monasteries may be counted as his mercies. But these defects were blots on a character in the main kindly and genial; he had the will as he had the mental power to be beneficent. To him the Middle Ages owed not only the forms of their political development but also the resurgence, never cancelled, of civilization.

His conquests and their very limits moulded the future. In his Empire the effective unity of the Western Church was a fact. His theocracy was a model for the later Papacy. To their profit and loss Mediterranean Italy and the transalpine North were again linked in a common destiny not to be undone. By the union of all the German tribes in Francia the German-speaking Franks could be later drawn away from the Romance lands to form a new unity, Germany. His Avar war began German colonization eastward. His incomplete conquest of the Lombards was a stage in the division of Italy into North and South. His annexations in Spain gave Catalonia a separate language and being. His reign, with its deeds, its laws, and its civilization forms a climax to the slow changes of decay and renewal in the Dark Ages, and sets the stage of Europe for changes yet to come.

(4) FRANKISH INSTITUTIONS AND SOCIETY
UNDER CHARLEMAGNE

The powers and functions of the Carolingian monarchy were a development from those of the Merovingians, but transformed by the theocratic idea and enhanced by the personal genius of Charlemagne. The imperial title set a seal on his work, and, so to say, summarized the fusion of Germanic, Roman, and Christian elements in his authority. His Empire, like his kingship, seemed the visible embodiment of Christian society organized as State and Church under his sovereignty. The theocratic element raised the conception of the commonwealth, the *respublica Christiana*, above the sphere of private rule. God had bestowed authority on the anointed king in order that the people might be well ruled. The duties of the king were vastly extended. The Church was under his care and he was its head. Not only was he the defender of Christendom and maintainer of peace within it, but all questions of common life, everything that concerned his people's welfare, material and spiritual, came within his competence and were a state concern. It was an ideal that faded but never wholly died.

New ceremonies and insignia marked the exaltation of the monarch. The sacring or unction with holy oil by Pope or bishops expressed or gave the grace of God which hallowed him. The crown, now solemnly assumed, and sceptre were more secular, but Leo III's action in 800, which was the first Frankish coronation, formed a precedent of historic import, for the lay coronations of the Emperors Lewis and Lothar I by their respective fathers were each confirmed by a subsequent papal coronation. Thus the Church or rather the episcopate appeared as the source or sanction of the royal power, and was not slow to remember the superiority of the spiritual over the secular rulers of the earthly City of God.

Beneath the veneer of theocracy and Byzantine ceremonial, however, the powers of the Emperor-king were a development from the Frankish past, informed by a new and wider purpose. Charlemagne was an autocrat, to whom all subjects owed fidelity and obedience. The will and personality of its ruler gave to the Empire and Francia itself their coherence, their unity and directive force. The Carolingians had revivified the Fields of May, where they took counsel, obtained the consent, and prepared the campaigns of their subjects, whether they came in troops armed for immediate war or in smaller autumn assemblies of important personages. But these meetings of magnates only appear with independent initiative after Charles's death. The king was the guardian of justice and peace. The peace of the Empire was his peace, and the special protection that he granted to individuals increased the penalty for offences against them. The essence of the royal authority, however, lay in his power to issue coercive

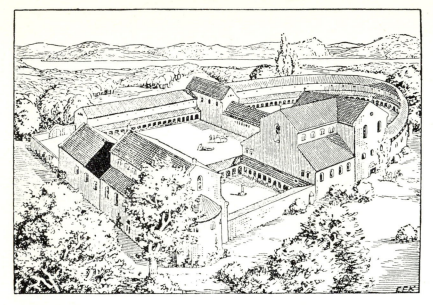

Fig. 64. Charlemagne's palace at Ingelheim

commands, the power of the 'ban', disobedience to which was disloyalty and incurred punishment of varying severity from fines to death or outlawry. Many transgressions against the law were defined as contempt of the king's command and liable to the old fine of 60 shillings, but this was a kind of minimum. The large legislation of the era, including the codifying and revision of the customary laws, as well as new enactments and administrative orders, was derived from this power of the ban even if alteration in tribal custom required a kind of assent.

Charlemagne did not inherit a court council or a departmental bureaucracy, nor did he create them. His 'palace' (*palatium*) was the royal residence where he happened to be in his continual peregrinations—Aachen with its new basilica, its medicinal springs, and its hunting-grounds was no capital even in his more stationary old age—and the *palatini* were his entourage. The old household officers, the seneschal, the butler, the marshal, and the chamberlain (who was in charge of the royal treasure), were great men in counsel and were employed in most various capacities in peace and war. The counts of the palace, of whom there were several, were in charge of the judicial business that came to the king and acted as his deputies, if need were, in cases that came before the royal court, but they were as little confined to that function as their fellows. The chancery was more specialized. It prepared and stored official documents. Its chief was always an ecclesiastic of the first importance, who had charge of the royal chapel—under Lewis the Pious he became known as arch-chaplain—and to the chapel his subordinate clerks and notaries, all ecclesiastics, were attached. But chancery and chapel were not identical, although manned by much the same personnel.

For counsel Charlemagne turned to his entourage, such as he chose or specially summoned, as well as to trusted friends at a distance. Nobles and ecclesiastics thronged the travelling 'palace' beside its more permanent members, even apart from the summoned assemblies. There were the household 'knights' at the king's disposition, teachers and scholars of the palace school, petitioners, merchants, and beggars. The court was the mainspring of political life and of the Church and intellectual culture of the Empire, deriving its own vitality from the inspiring, many-sided genius of its master. It was also a centre of very loose morals. Charlemagne himself was no model, and he allowed a similar licence to his friends and helpers. He could not bear to be separated from his daughters by their marriage, and was indulgent to their amours. Pious advisers, like Alcuin, shut their eyes to these defects, and it was not till the reign of his rigorist son that the open scandal of the court was done away. But, while Lewis might make a purge of vice, he could not supply his father's driving personality. Francia was still too barbaric and illiterate to provide an organized bureaucracy, even if Charlemagne himself had wished it. The Empire depended on the wisdom and energy of the monarch alone.

Wisdom and energy, however, were not sufficient without wealth. The monarchy had to pay its way, and here the Carolingian Empire, like other barbaric kingdoms, was radically defective in permanent resources. No revival of the ancient system of taxation was possible. The king still depended on revenue in kind, services, and money from his estates. Charlemagne and his son were the largest landowners in their Empire. Nevertheless, although vast increases in the royal domains were obtained by Charlemagne's conquests, there was the usual steady drain in gifts to the Church and in benefices to vassals, although it was mitigated by use of Church lands to reward the latter and by confiscations in conquered territory which could be dealt out to great Frankish nobles. Real danger of depletion, however, loomed as yet in the future. The king laid claim, too, to all land not in private possession or settled, to the rivers, forests and mountains and the minerals beneath the soil, and these were sources of profit to the Crown.

Towards the close of his reign Charlemagne compiled a register of the *fiscus*, an inventory of the crown-lands, and one ordinance, the *Capitulare de villis*, shows in detail the organization he prescribed for certain royal estates. In general only a small part of an estate was worked as a home-farm for the lord. The greater part was held by tenants under the ancient classification of *mansi serviles, lidiles,* or *ingenuiles,* according to the original occupiers, slaves, half-free, and free, who mainly continued. They worked their own portion (*mansus*) and performed services on the home-farm (*terra indominicata*) according to the status of their *mansus* and their personal condition. A *iudex* or *villicus* superintended the bigger estates; under him were the *maiores* (*meier*) of several home-farms. Those *fisci*, which were allotted for the support of the royal household, sold any surplus of their products to increase the revenue. Charlemagne in short was anxious to maintain the economic strength of the monarchy. There were of course great windfalls, like the treasure taken from the Avars, but a more constant income was derived from judicial fines, the various kinds of tolls, and the customary gifts brought to the Fields of May. The expenses of administration were lessened by the right to the services of all subjects. Hospitality to officials, work on forts and bridges and the like, were burdens which could be oppressive.

The heaviest burden was military service, to which the mass of the free-men were liable at their own cost in the continual wars, even if provinces which neighboured the seat of a particular war were most affected. The Emperor endeavoured to ease the burden for the small man by prescribing a minimum property, varying according to province and distance from the scene of action, for personal service. Freemen with less were clubbed together to provide equipment for one of them. Even so it was a hardship. The backbone of the army consisted in the mounted and mailed horsemen, who had to be sufficiently endowed to possess their costly armament. These were mainly the royal vassals, led either by the count of their district if they were lesser men or by the immunist lord who maintained them in his household or by benefices from his land on the royal model. Vassalage and benefices were definitely encouraged. Mobility and efficiency were thus procured, and the Frankish armies appeared more and more as collections of vassals and sub-vassals owing military service.

Charlemagne was the first king who attempted to lighten the burden of frequent attendance at the judicial assemblies of the counties, which weighed on the poorer freemen. He decreed that the 'unbidden' *placita* should only be held three times a year. Only those summoned need appear at special *placita* for business. This was made possible by the institution in his first year of a body of selected experts in law for each county, styled *scabini* (whence *échevins, Schöffen*) in the north and *iudices* in the south, who acted as the count's assessors, declared the law, and pronounced judgement. The office had a long life and survived the *placita* of freemen for which it had been created.

Local government continued on the old lines. Apart from the marches or frontier districts, where dukes or margraves ruled several counties, the normal unit was the *pagus* or *gau*, ruled by a nominated count, usually a local lord, who was remunerated by a portion of the royal *fiscus* and a third of judicial fines. He was judge, police-officer, and leader of the troops of his *pagus*. It was divided into several *centenae* (hundreds), which he perambulated to hold the *placita*. Under him were the officials normally called *centenarii* or vicars, and he could delegate his authority to a *missus* (envoy), or viscount. Beside him was the bishop of the diocese, whom he was to obey and assist in all things. And there were the immunist lords, largely ecclesiastics with their *advocati* or *Vögte* for their secular business, who were responsible for the policing and petty justice of their lands. Grants of immunity to Church lands were a part of Carolingian policy.

The problem of linking the administration of the local counts and immunist lords in his vast Empire to the central government, a problem which began with the dissolution of the Roman State and continued to the end of the Middle Ages, was met by a new device of Charlemagne, who even in peace-time could not personally inspect and control the provinces. The earlier Merovingians had employed envoys (*missi*) to carry out particular and limited duties. Charles Martel had revived that office in the shape of *missi discurrentes* (travelling envoys), who seem to have had more general functions. Charlemagne converted them into an institution of State. From 779 they appear charged to preserve the right in all ways. In 802 their duties were fully codified. The Empire was divided into *missatica*, to each of which two or three *missi dominici*, as they were styled, were sent every year with full powers to inspect, redress, and reform. They were now chosen from great prelates and lords. They were furnished with instructions, they communicated royal orders, and they made reports on their return. They held in May general meetings attended by all local magnates, ecclesiastical and lay, when they heard complaints, took evidence on oath (a royal prerogative), and punished the ill deeds of officials. Besides inspection they held *placita* to supplement those of the count during four months, and made a visitation of churches and abbeys in their *missaticum*. Their rank was supposed to make them immune to bribes. By their work the unity of the Empire was maintained and the direct power of the monarch made omnipresent. But their efficiency depended on the personal strength of the king. From the first the *missi* were frequently selected from bishops and counts of the *missaticum* they inspected, and under the weakened control of later rulers the value of the institution disappeared. Later, missatic power might be given to a bishop in his diocese as a mere increase of his jurisdiction.

In nothing are Charlemagne's resolve to civilize his government and people and also the limitations of a still half-barbarized age shown more clearly than in his perpetual legislative activity. The dissolution of the Roman State had left Western Europe under a regime of 'personal law', by which each man was subject to the customary law of the tribe or people to which he belonged. Salian Frank, Ripuarian Frank, Lombard,

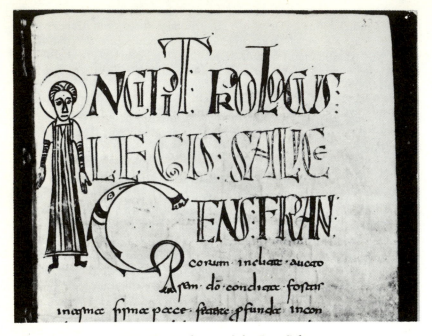

Fig. 65. Prologue of the Lex Salica

Bavarian, Roman, etc. all had their traditional codes, their 'Folkright', which were liable to development through the decisions of the courts, but no one questioned the right of the king to add and occasionally to alter legal ordinances, even if for alteration, at least among the Germanic tribesmen, some sort of consultation and consent was expected. Although in wide tracts, e.g. east of the Rhine, there were mainly homogeneous populations, yet elsewhere the sprinkling of Franks and others over all the Carolingian Empire during its formation resulted in a variety of laws held or 'professed' by the inhabitants of a particular district and produced a confused medley most alien to unity and good order. Charlemagne took the first steps towards reform—he seems to have aimed at more in fancy—in the great assembly of 802. By his command the unwritten customary law of certain tribes was reduced to writing, and that of others, like the Salic Law, was edited authoritatively. Amendment and extension, however, and the issue of laws cutting across the personal laws and binding on the whole Empire, were effected by the numerous capitularies (so-called from their internal division into *capitula*) issued by the king and his successors. These were in no way parts of a systematic code. Rather, the lack of a system was characteristic. They dealt with such questions of legal or administrative reform as came up year after year, and each contained a congeries of laws, regulations, and temporary or permanent commands according to need. The Frankish scribes themselves could only make a rough classification founded more on date and occasion than on watertight contents. The *Capitularia ecclesiastica* dealt only with Church matters; the *Capitula legibus addenda* added to the separate tribal codes; but the *Capitula per se scribenda* and the *Capitula missorum* (which were instructions to the *missi*) might also include matter belonging to the first two categories: they were all alike the king's commands. The most significant feature is that the State, embodied in the Emperor, was attempting to develop the law and provide a better life for its members.

It was in this spirit that Charlemagne paid special attention to economic conditions. Bridges and roads, tolls and customs, weights and measures, coinage and mints were regulated. For war and trade a grandiose project of a canal between the Rhine and Danube was attempted. Trade by night was forbidden, as well as the export of corn during dearth. Tariffs of prices were issued. To check speculation, corn and wine might not be sold before harvest and vintage. A kind of poor rate was instituted to which prelates, counts, and others were to contribute according to their degree. Saracenic piracy in the Mediterranean was assailed by sea, although not to that extent which would have led to the regular striking of the gold coins needed for a large foreign commerce. The Carolingians contented themselves with a reliable silver penny, the *denarius*. Francia, in short, was essentially a land power, based economically on agriculture.

(5) THE CAROLINGIAN RENAISSANCE

Not in its ephemeral political structure, but in the realm of thought did Charlemagne's Empire produce durable effects. Its unity was soon broken, its institutions were changed beyond recognition, its prosperity was ruined. Politically Western Europe had almost to start again. Only in the organization of the Church, which was renewed under its shadow, was there an abiding, if maimed, inheritance. But its conception of kingship remained to be an inspiration for the future, and its revival of learning and culture and its recovered touch with the remnants of ancient civilization, although much narrower than Charlemagne dreamed and intended, survived the dangers of the next two centuries and formed a foundation for the advance of the Middle Ages. It was the salvage of learning and ancient literature, sprinkled on the verges of the Empire, and now in the 'Carolingian Renaissance' spread over the monasteries and cathedral churches of Francia, that by its extension saved them for transmission to later times.

Between Boethius, 'the last of the Romans' according to a famous phrase, and the height of the Carolingian Renaissance three centuries had intervened. We have seen how Cassiodorus linked the study of Christian and also secular learning with monasticism, and how much of this was brought to English monasteries by Hadrian, Benedict Biscop, and their followers in the seventh century. The movement culminated in the persons of the Venerable Bede and St Aldhelm, perhaps the most learned men of their day in the West, but it continued with less creative vigour in the cathedral school of York, not to mention lesser centres, and its offshoots were already growing in eastern Francia in the monasteries of St Boniface and his fellows. England, however, was by no means the only refuge of literate culture. Manuscripts and some grammatical proficiency survived in Lombard Italy and the Papal Curia. In Visigothic Spain, reinforced by fugitives from Vandal Africa, there existed a living, if decadent, Christian learning and literature, of which St Isidore of Seville was the great exemplar. Further, there was a remarkable focus of ancient learning outside the Roman Empire in Celtic Ireland. There seems to have been an emigration thither of some scholars with books from Aquitaine even before St Patrick's mission. As Ireland became Christian, a knowledge of Latin and even a little Greek was acquired by Irish monks. St Columbanus was a real scholar. Indeed, there are Latin classics which have only survived through the medium at one time of Irish manuscripts. The emigration of Irish monks to the Continent brought Irish learning with it.

It was from these scattered centres of culture that Charlemagne began to develop a real system of education, an attempt to revive the past. His first desire was to obtain an educated clergy to maintain the Faith and the Church, but he himself possessed an eager thirst for knowledge, a vivid interest in literature and the things of the mind. The palace school, where his sons, young nobles, and others were brought up became a home of literary education for such as were apt. The educated layman, though a rarity, made his appearance. Cathedral and monastic schools arose; there was even an attempt to make parish priests undertake teaching. Books were multiplied and monastic libraries enlarged. From Corbie, St Martin of Tours and other abbeys, the clear and beautiful bookhand, the Caroline minuscule,[1] spread and replaced towards the close of the eighth century the decadent, ill-formed, divergent scripts which were current in the several lands of the West. Although some centuries later the Caroline minuscule gave way to pointed fashions of writing, it had imprinted a general unity on bookhands, which played its part in maintaining a unity of culture.

The best of Charlemagne's literary teachers, whom he made his friends, came from outside Francia. The central figure was the Northumbrian Alcuin (*ob.* 804), bred in the school of York, who came at Charlemagne's invitation, and was rewarded with the abbacy of St Martin of Tours. Although quite unoriginal, his wide reading and his accurate scholarship

[1] Of which our present roman type is an offshoot.

enabled him to be an excellent teacher with many disciples. His writings were voluminous, both verse, letters, school manuals, and theological treatises. In his last years he was busied in preparing a more correct text of the Vulgate Bible, which called a temporary halt to scribal corruption. In this revision he had a less effective rival in the Visigoth Theodulf, Bishop of Orleans (*ob.* 821), who was the best writer of Latin verse of the day. The best prose writer was the East Frank Einhard (*ob.* 840) from the Maingau: his *Vita Karoli*, succinct, clear, and picturesque, closely modelled in structure and wording on Suetonius, is a worthy monument of his master.

Fig. 66. Alcuin

Less classic and more spontaneous was the Lombard grammarian, Paul the Deacon (*ob.* 797?) from Friuli, who wrote a graphic history of his own people. The list of these men and their disciples might easily be extended, but in so short a summary it is enough to indicate their work. They restored grammatical Latin and established it in too many cathedral schools and abbeys for it to come to wreck completely again.

As might be expected of men with so much to learn and teach, the work of the Carolingians was rather in the acquisition and divulgation of ancient knowledge and literature than in any original contributions to thought. Only John Eriugena the Scot (*ob. c.* 877) was an original thinker. But they increased both the copies and the understanding of the Christian

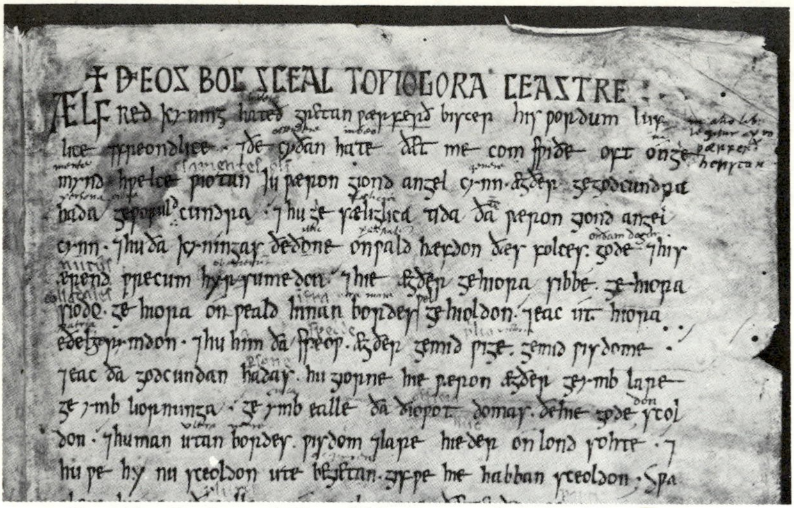

Fig. 67. Preface of King Alfred's translation of St Gregory's
Cura Pastoralis, *perhaps in the king's own hand*

Fathers and of the remnant of heathen classics: the oldest manuscripts
of most of these date from the Carolingian age. The spate of Carolingian
Latin verse was imitative to a degree. In thought, compendiums of excerpts from the Fathers, in which Bede had set an example, were their
forte. Hrabanus Maurus (*ob.* 856), Abbot of Fulda and later Archbishop
of Mainz, was the most assiduous and learned of this kind of commentator.
The Canon Law of the Church found its students, and, as will be seen,
its reforming forgers. Even doctrine had its controversialists. The Adop-
tionists of Spain, who held that Christ only became the Son of God at His
baptism, were countered by the orthodox Alcuin, and the *Libri Carolini*
dealt with the iconoclastic dispute. Paschasius Radbert (*ob. c.* 860) upheld
the doctrine of Transubstantiation in the Eucharist against Ratramn. The
unhappy Gottschalk (*ob.* 869), a compulsory monk and something of
a poet, suffered harsh persecution from the dominating Hincmar, Archbishop of Rheims, on account of his rigid view of predestination. This
unoriginal age could at least debate old problems.

Historical writing of a sort was practised in certain abbeys. Dry and
scrappy chronicles were jotted down—one by Charlemagne's grandson
Nithard soars a little higher. The official papal biographies in the *Liber
Pontificalis* give facts. But the vivacious *Gesta Karoli*, a repertoire of
legends, are more alive, if fabulous: the author was Notker the Stammerer (*ob.* 912) of St Gall, who by his sequences influenced the growth and
prosody of religious hymns, and through them of secular verse.

It is unfortunate that vernacular compositions of native subject-matter in the Frankish Empire before and during the Carolingian age are lacking. Charlemagne's collection of old Frankish lays was destroyed by his son. Only a fragment or so, like that of *Hildebrand*, remain of the old German poems, although Christian lays in native style, like the Saxon *Heliand* (*c.* 830), appeared, and the *Ludwigslied* celebrates a West Frankish victory of 881. The first specimen of Old French, consciously different from Latin, is the oath which Lewis the German took at Strasbourg to be understood of his brother Charles the Bald's West Frankish subjects. For the popular world of the age unhampered by a learned language and redolent of the new peoples, we must mainly go outside the Western Empire. England takes the most conspicuous place. The native codes and chronicles were there written in the native speech. The lay of *Beowulf* (*c.* 700?) preserves Teutonic traditions, only slightly Christianized. A small corpus of Christian poems keep the ancient outlook and technique. The translations made or inspired by King Alfred (*ob.* 899) from Gregory, Orosius, Bede, and Boethius are infused with something of his own great spirit. They were not intended to make his people erudite, but to equip them for a better practical life. The sermons of Aelfric (*ob. post* 1006) show the same purpose with an unaffected ease of style. A highly artificial technique and an unfettered imagination, on the contrary, mark the Irish poems and tales of this early period. The few early Welsh survivals have much the same quality. A more rugged artificiality appears to mark the earliest Scandinavian verse. A merit which they all have in common is to bring us vividly nearer to a barbaric but very human world than the laborious productions of learned, upward-striving cliques.

The history of the arts must be touched on, rather than traced, even more sketchily than that of literature. In Western Europe there were three main influences at work, the Romano-Christian tradition, the inborn native stock, and the steady pressure of Eastern ideas percolating westward by trade, travel, and territorial contact. To these we may add the needs to be satisfied in building, adornment, and instruction. First may be taken the influence of the East, in the main of the Byzantine Empire. It was not only an export from far away, but an existing model in the recently Byzantine lands in Italy.

Byzantine art was the creation of a long-descended and composite civilization still in full career. If it reached its apogee under Justinian, it continued to develop with fertile beauty and originality, while faithful to its dominant ideas. In the churches, the gathering-place of worship, the sacred drama, the gorgeous ritual procession, the chanting choirs, the atmosphere of supernatural awe were given their ideal setting, which demanded and enhanced them. Without pretence and without bungling the builders did what was required in a free and great way in noble materials and under the guidance of a fine tradition. Their principal means were the dome, many-

Fig. 68. Bishop celebrating Mass. Ivories, ninth century

coloured marbles, and mosaic decoration, whether the church were round, quadrangular, or cruciform in its main design. As in the masterpiece of St Sophia, designed by the architects Anthemius and Isidorus from Asia Minor, the outside was plain, if imposing. Within, St Sophia glistened with the many-coloured columns and their carved capitals and the walls and

330

dome encrusted with marble and mosaics, which set off one another with a harmony of contrast. All that could express the glory and the mystery of the cult was there on a magnificent scale. But lesser churches rivalled St Sophia in beauty of design and colour. The mosaics not only contained pictorial teaching with a solemn majesty but their golden backgrounds suffused the churches with a glowing atmosphere. This architecture could be seen in the West at Ravenna and Rome, to mention no other towns, while carved ivories and jewels journeyed westward along with illuminated manuscripts which furnished models for religious iconography.

The Roman-Christian tradition, however, was alive in the West apart from Byzantine novelties. Churches, monuments, and ruins of Roman provincial art (and the metropolitan art of Rome itself) were still extant in Gaul and Italy to give inspiration and guidance to the unpractised hands of barbarized generations. And those new peoples had something to give of their own. There was a barbaric element in their blood and traditions. The Anglo-Saxon school of art which arose in Christian Northumbria in the seventh century shows this blending to perfection. Arts and motives were brought from Italy by such men as Wilfrid and Benedict Biscop. Churches, if small, were built and decorated. Stone crosses were set up with sculptures, which were half-barbaric in their carving, yet so impressive in design that they have been claimed for a later century. The graceful illuminations and the calligraphy of the *Lindisfarne Gospels* (c. 700) testify to an exquisite feeling for colour and line. A similar artistic impulse is shown in Irish crosses and still more in the intricate decoration of the *Book of Kells* (c. 700) and the beautiful Irish script.

Much in the art of the Carolingian revival was directly derived from the Roman monuments, and men naturally made no distinction between provincial Roman of the West and Byzantine. The great fact was that barbarism took up the arts of civilization. Charlemagne and his court intended to renew ancient Rome. Romanesque art in his Empire is intentional in its use of Roman models. His round palace church at Aachen imitated churches like Justinian's San Vitale at Ravenna and was enriched with columns from Theodoric's palace. Its mosaics were of Italo-Byzantine inspiration. Decorative arts, like those of ivories and enamels, were developed by the impact of the East on the Teutonic craftsman. Superb illuminated gospels, like the *Golden Gospels* of Charlemagne, mingled influences from England and the south. The Frankish Rhineland became a focus of artistic influences. As in learning and literature, the Carolingian Renaissance was the parent of a growing art. Inexpertness and half-barbaric genius allowed the native impulses to break through the crust of borrowed models. Uncouth and stolid figures expressed a fierce and imaginative power. The artists betrayed themselves in attempting what they could not do, in grasping after conceptions which eluded their reach.

23-2

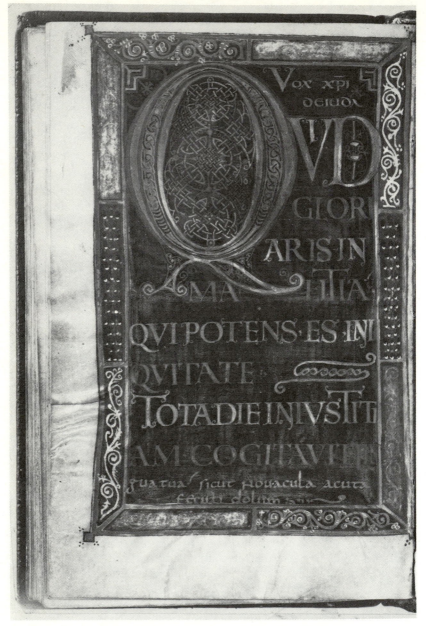

*Fig. 69 (and opposite). Pages from the Golden Psalter given to
Pope Adrian I by Charlemagne (Psalms 52 and 53)*

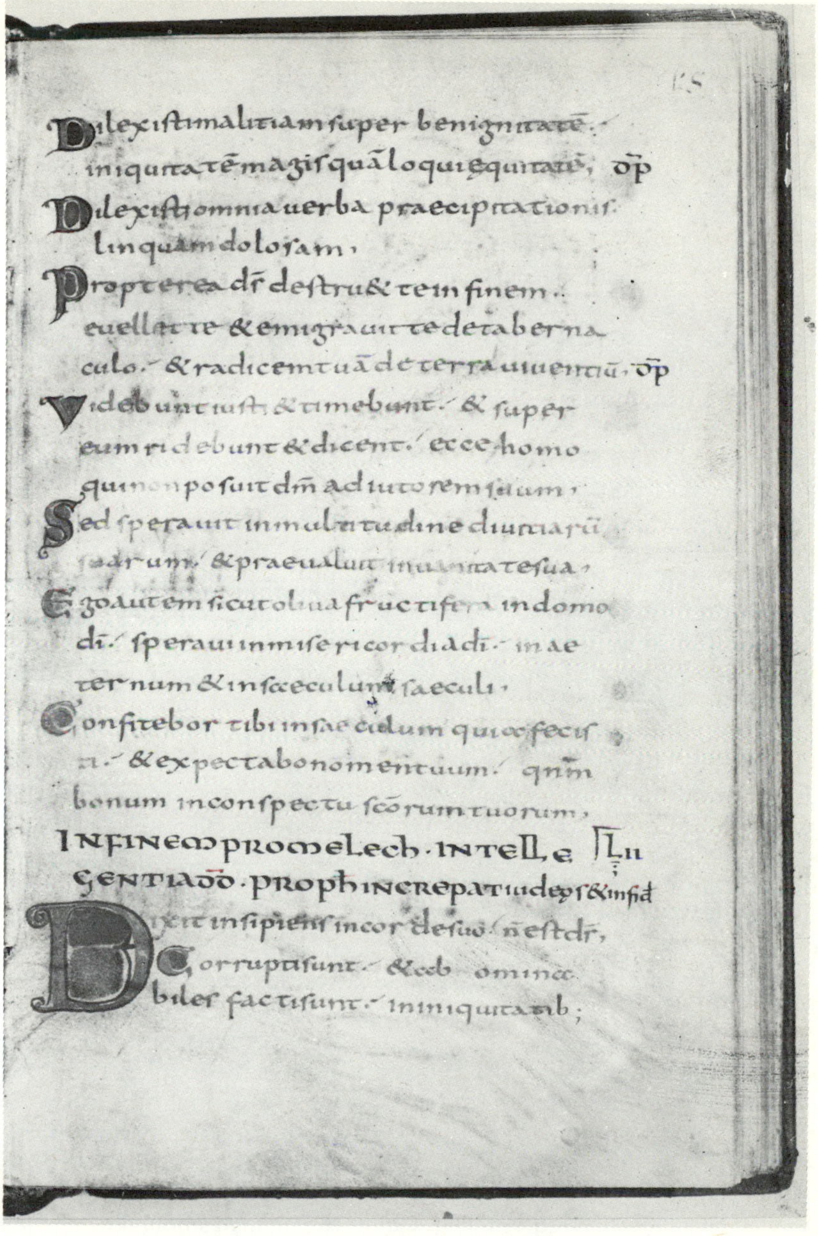

Fig. 69 (and opposite). Pages from the Golden Psalter given to Pope Adrian I by Charlemagne (Psalms 52 and 53)

CHAPTER 14

THE DISSOLUTION OF THE
CAROLINGIAN EMPIRE

Certain general causes may be assigned for the collapse of Charlemagne's precocious Empire. It was too vast. Only the tremendous, unique personality of Charlemagne could quell, defend, and administer territories so wide and separate and peoples so diverse and wild, linked so imperfectly by sparse Roman roads and untended rivers, and segregated by forest, marsh, moorland, and mountain. It was too barbarous. Not only its illiterate peasants, free and unfree, and its fighting lords and warriors, but its prelates and clergy and even its monasteries were incapable as a whole of rising above personal relations and justice, rough at best, to a conception of the State and its government and a reign of civilized law. Such a change in mentality could not be effected of a sudden by the compelling energy of one dominating genius, who himself imperfectly grasped the distant or legendary civilization he sought to recall. Its material basis consisted too exclusively of a fighting nobility and wealth in land. The king, the churchmen, the lay magnates and their armed followers all depended on the estates by which they maintained their households, provided their equipment, and rewarded services. Bishop, count, and the king as much as any needed lands if they were to be followed and obeyed. The whole machinery of public order and defence rested on this endowment. The Carolingian wars and administration fostered this ancient factor. Local lords added to their landed strength public functions, and in the long run it was impossible for the distant central kingship to supervise and control the near holders of immediate power. And they grew stronger while it grew weaker. Donations and benefices sapped the royal resources when once the era of conquests ended.

To these general causes, other particular causes have to be added: the Frankish custom of inheritance, the characteristics of the Carolingian house itself, and the barbarian invasions, the last of their kind in Western Europe, which overstrained the clumsy amalgam of the Empire. There was rooted in the Franks the custom that all sons had the right to a share of their father's inheritance, and this carried with it the division of the kingdom. The only modification introduced by King Pepin the Short had been the allotment of Francia proper to the eldest son. The division might help in the administration of the vast Empire, but it was bound to weaken it by the divergent interests and policies, to say nothing of the discontents and personal quarrels, of the co-heirs and the ambitions of excluded

334

bastards. Charlemagne's own eldest illegitimate son, Pepin the Hunchback, had conspired against his father; and it was not the happiest expedient for future peace when he allowed Bernard, the illegitimate son of Pepin of Italy, to succeed his father. The troubles which were almost inevitable under the custom of division were magnified to a pernicious degree by the characters of his descendants. Fraternal concord was rare in the barbaric kingdoms, but the Carolingians surpassed all but the Merovingians in their lack of natural affection and elementary good faith. It was seldom that they lacked either ability or energy, but their treacherous rivalry for land and power put them at the mercy of their vassals, who were no less selfish and more narrow-minded. The royal domains were squandered in lavish competitive bribes of offices and benefices, and lesser dynasties became rooted in the provinces where they were continuously endowed. In spite of its prestige the decay of the kingship was inevitable, and the pace was quickened by the new invaders by sea and land. The attacks of the Scandinavian pirates, the Northmen as they were called, unprepared for, expert, and quick-moving, baffled the kings of the unwieldy Empire and their slowly levied armies. It was the local lord, with his fortified castle or town and his mounted band of vassals and retainers, who finally was able to oppose a local, speedy resistance and appear as the champion of the population, to whom his present power was more formidable than the far-off, needy king. Much the same happened when Moslems from the south and Magyars from the east came later to the prey. The process was gradual, for the Carolingians were sturdy and persevering, but an anarchic century saw the central government decrepit almost to extinction, and Empire and kingdoms dissolved into petty feudal dominions, which themselves could hardly be held together in the general disintegration.

(i) THE REIGN OF LEWIS THE PIOUS, 813–840

The Emperor Lewis the Pious began the decay of the Empire both by his virtues and his faults. Probably no one but a second Charlemagne could have avoided doing so. Genuinely religious, virtuous, and merciful, he was subject to the influence of his clergy and his successive wives. He had neither the unbending resolution nor the shrewd sense to enable him to dominate his unruly sons and magnates. He could be too passionate and too conscience-stricken. Nevertheless at first the reign made a fair show: it had the inherited momentum behind it. Lewis 'cleansed' the court at Aachen of its disreputable elements, and, although the illegitimate descendants of Charles Martel, once favourites of Charlemagne, fell into disgrace, he retained or installed able ministers devoted to the imperial system. His first measures were directed to the reform of abuses and oppression in the provinces. His chief interest was to reform and protect

335

9. The Carolingian Dynasty (from Charlemagne)

For the ancestors of Charlemagne, see Table 5 *b*, p. 155.
The names of Emperors are printed in heavy type.

(*a*) Germany and Italy

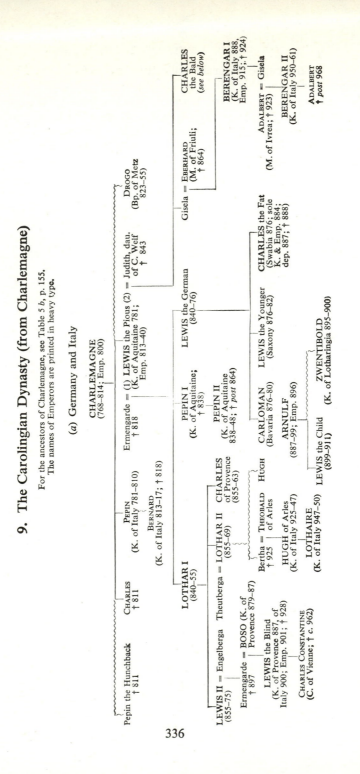

(b) France

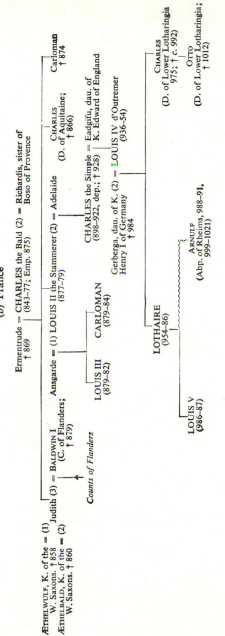

Fig. 70. Lewis the Pious

the Church, which was indeed essential for civilized government as well as for religion. There were two parallel institutions in the Church which concentrated its ideals and energies, the monasteries and the foundations of secular, i.e. non-monastic, clergy, or canons as they came to be called. The monasteries were composed of lay monks with a few clergy, who all

338

lived in common under a Rule ('Regula', hence they were called Regulars); the canons were all clergy attached to a cathedral or church, and by no means necessarily subjected to a life in common or even to celibacy. Both were more than liable to degeneration under the influence of wealth, external disorder, internal ill government, lay usurpation, and the mere relaxation of fervour as time went by. In both the evils were apparent and remedies devised in the eighth century. St Chrodegang, Bishop of Metz (*ob.* 766), imposed a quasi-monastic Rule on his canons, by which a common life and community of goods was enforced. He was widely imitated and his Rule became a type of reform. About 780 the Spanish noble Witiza, in religion St Benedict of Aniane (*ob.* 822), began the strict observance, with an increase of asceticism, of the Rule of the great St Benedict in his new foundation at Aniane. The movement spread. He became the mentor of Lewis the Pious in Aquitaine, and was called by him to be Abbot of Kornelimünster near Aachen to superintend the reform of Frankish monasteries in general. An endeavour was made to appoint only monks as abbots, thus avoiding the destructive gift of abbeys to great laymen. The crying evil to St Benedict of Aniane, however, was the diversity of monastic custom which allowed all kinds of relaxation of the Rules. He insisted on universal adherence to the strict Benedictine Rule. At last in 817, in an assembly at Aachen, Lewis decreed a more rigorous observance of the Rule to bring back the monks to the simple life. For all that, houses like St Denis near Paris refused to change from the separate life as canons which they had adopted. For canons too, however, the Rule of St Chrodegang was prescribed at Aachen. It was a programme hard to enforce.

In external relations the Empire for some years maintained its inherited prestige. Embassies came from the Byzantines and the tribes on the eastern frontier. A measure of success was attained in the alternating warfare with the border Slavs. Advantage was taken of the intestine quarrels of the Danes and efforts were made to gain them for Christianity. Their raids as yet were few. The Bretons were troublesome, but Lewis's agreement (826) with their chief, Nomenoë, if a dangerous substitute for conquest, at least secured a temporary peace. In Spain, in spite of reverses from Moslems and Basques, Barcelona was retained for the Empire. In short, the Empire was not threatened with disaster from without.

Eager as he was to promote ecclesiastical interests, Lewis was not minded to surrender his imperial rights over Rome. Successive Popes were loyal but restive in the pursuit of autonomy. They wished to deal with Romans as they pleased, while they bade them renew their oaths of allegiance to the Emperor. Leo III was forced to apologize for the unauthorized execution of conspirators (815), Paschal I to exculpate himself from the cruel deaths of two officials overloyal to the Frankish supremacy (823). On the election of Pope Eugenius II in 824, the young co-Emperor Lothar I was able to promulgate the *Constitutio Romana*. By this enactment permanent *missi* of Emperor and Pope superintended justice. The many Roman notables under imperial protection were not to suffer death without imperial leave. Romans like other subjects could 'profess' their hereditary law, a retrograde step, but the barbaric codes dealt less in the death-penalty than the Civil Law. The right of the laity in papal elections was strengthened. At the same time the right of the Emperor to confirm papal elections was established. Lothar, or rather his mentor, the monk Wala, grandson of Charles Martel, had won a diplomatic success for his father.

It was in diplomacy, in the creation of precedent and the opinion that followed it, that the Papacy and Curia excelled, not in the secular government of turbulent, barbarized Rome. Almost imperceptibly the Pope's claim to crown the Emperor was established. Pope Stephen IV took the occasion of his visit to Lewis at Rheims in 817 to crown and anoint him. Perhaps it was no accident that Lewis in the same year himself crowned his eldest son Lothar I co-regent Emperor, but Pope Paschal in 823 strengthened the papal tradition by recrowning and sacring him in Rome. In 817 he had already obtained from Lewis a comprehensive diploma confirming all the Carolingian grants of territory and autonomous jurisdiction. It is the earliest of these grants which has been preserved, and describes the geographical limits of the Papal States. The duchy of Rome on both sides of the Tiber (the 'Patrimony of St Peter'), Sabina, a slice of Lombard Tuscany, the Exarchate, the Pentapolis to Ancona, were acknowledged to be under the Pope's rule. Further, he was confirmed in the receipt of the royal revenue from the provinces of Tuscany and Spoleto, and his rights to the lost patrimonies in South Italy were admitted. Altogether, a wide avenue was opened to papal claims in the future which it would be hard to close to the undying, unforgetful Roman Curia.

The insoluble problem of combining the unity of the Empire with the Frankish custom of inheritance early revealed the defects of Lewis's character. At Aachen in 817 he attempted to arrange the succession on his father's principles. He associated his eldest son Lothar I in the Empire and in the government of Francia, with Saxony, Swabia, and Burgundy; on him was to devolve after his father's death a kind of mitigated suzerainty over his kinsmen. To the two younger sons, Pepin and Lewis (later called 'the German'), were allotted the frontier kingdoms of Aquitaine and Bavaria where border-warfare was continuous. Their cousin Bernard, son of Pepin, was to retain the more subject kingdom of Italy. Given the character of the princes, the settlement could only be durable while they were too young to rule. Bernard, who was eighteen, at once revolted, instigated by his entourage—he would not be subject to his cousin—and may have aimed for the Empire. He was easily quelled, and punished by his wrathful uncle with such a cruel blinding that he died (818). The deed, amid the general disapproval, left the kindly Lewis tormented by remorse. His grief was intensified by the death of his wife, his 'counsellor and helper', Ermengarde, soon after. To prevent his abdication, his advisers induced him to remarry; in 819 he chose Judith, the talented daughter of the Swabian Count Welf. Henceforth she governed him, and when she bore him in 823 a son Charles, later named 'the Bald', the history of his reign is dominated by his efforts to provide for his youngest born. He had earlier (822) severely damaged his personal authority by a public penance at Attigny for his treatment of Bernard and other kinsmen, which undermined the respect due to his office. There were signs, too, of the lack of control over the abuses due to an undisciplined aristocracy.

In 829 the storm began to break. The Emperor on his own initiative allotted a share, mainly Swabian, to the young Charles, and this was accompanied by a palace revolution. Count Bernard of Septimania and the Welfs took control, while Lothar, no longer co-regent, was sent to Italy nursing his grievances in the loss of territory and fearing worse. The dismissed counsellors looked on him as the hope of unity if only for his ambition. Pepin and Lewis the German were alike stirred by fear and greed to ally against their unstable father and his new advisers. He was deserted and a captive (830) when Lothar joined in the rebellion with intent to secure his abdication and his own succession. But Pepin and Lewis the German preferred their father as Emperor to their brother. A reaction quickly set in among the Frankish magnates. Lothar was forced to be content with the kingship of Italy only, while his three brothers were to share the rest of the Empire on their father's death. It was only a pause in turmoil. Pepin and Lewis revolted in turn with the same fears and hopes. In the civil wars the equally shifty Lothar, who came in on his father's side, made common cause with his brothers. He brought to them a new ally, the Pope Gregory IV (827–44), who was ready to further a stable peace and to magnify the Papacy. After long negotiations, Lewis the Pious with his supporters met his sons and the Pope in Alsace. The troublous years had done their work in the decay of loyalty and the tie of vassalage. In his encampment, thenceforward known as the Field of Lies, his army deserted him in a body and he became Lothar's prisoner (833) along with his wife and young Charles. Gregory IV took the opportunity to speak as a sovereign to the episcopate: 'Is not the authority over souls which belongs to the Pope above the imperial rule which is of this world?' The words marked the freeing of the Papacy from the trammels imposed by Charlemagne.

Lewis was deposed and forced by his hard-hearted son, aided by his satellite, the ungrateful Archbishop Ebbo of Rheims, to do humiliating penance at Compiègne for his sins of misgovernment. Mere faithlessness and greed were not alone the motives of Lothar's party. Old imperialists, like Wala, and bishops, like Agobard of Lyons, who exalted the power of the hierarchy, alike hoped for unity and the cure of anarchy and abuses from Lothar. But it was a delusion. Lands and bribes to the magnates, it was soon clear, were the prevailing factors. Meantime even the degenerating Franks became ashamed of their own treason. Sturdy loyalists, like Hrabanus Maurus of Fulda, defended Lewis, while Pepin and Lewis the German, whose only object was independent kingdoms, changed sides once more. On their march against him the overweening Lothar found himself betrayed as his father had been. Lewis the Pious was freed and restored (834), Lothar submitted to be merely King of Italy, and Ebbo, Agobard, and their like were deprived.

The harm done, however, was irreparable. Disorder had become endemic. The Northmen were yearly ravaging the coasts, while new plans of division were devised for the benefit of the favourite son, leading to fresh rebellions. On Pepin's death (838) his son Pepin II was disinherited. Lothar was reconciled and Lewis the German in revolt when the Emperor died near Ingelheim in 840. The death of Lewis the Pious, despite all his faults, snapped the link which held the Empire together.

(2) THE BREAK-UP OF THE EMPIRE

The Emperor Lothar I, with the support of the prelates, still hoped to maintain unity, but his character and record were against him. Besides, his brothers had each by now gained over the lay lords of East and West respectively by grants of honours and benefices; Lothar's party was in the old Carolingian land of central Austrasia. War was inevitable. Lewis and Charles the Bald effected a junction, and on 25 June 841 fought and won the desperate battle of Fontenoy against the Emperor. The slaughter of 'that accursed day' was immense, and the defeated side, the Carolingian homeland, lost for good and all the leadership in Western Europe which it had held since Charles Martel. As Lothar still showed fight, his brothers in 842 strengthened their alliance by the meeting and famous oaths of Strasbourg. The oaths, preserved by the chronicler Nithard, were taken in the two vernaculars of East and West, for they were addressed to and taken by the illiterate nobility. Lewis and his brother Charles's vassals swore to them in French, Charles and Lewis's vassals in German. It was a presage of the future. To make head against the coalition was beyond Lothar's power, nor could he be conquered, for there was a general weariness of the civil war. They came to terms and in August 843 concluded the definitive treaty of Verdun.

At Verdun the Empire of Charlemagne was broken up, for although Lothar retained the title of Emperor and the superiority over Rome, it implied no suzerainty over his brothers. They were all equally Kings of the

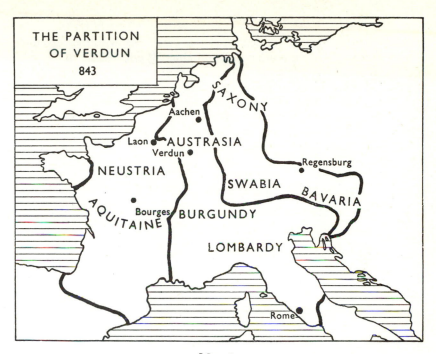

SAXONY

Aachen

Laon
Verdun
AUSTRASIA

NEUSTRIA

Regensburg

SWABIA
BAVARIA

Bourges
AQUITAINE
BURGUNDY

LOMBARDY

Rome

Map 8a

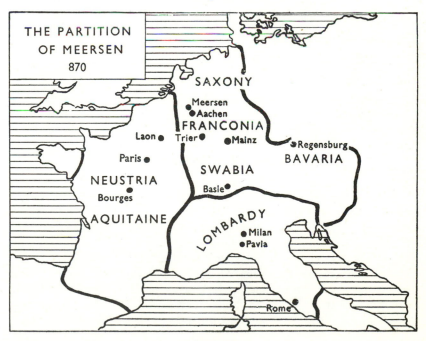

SAXONY

Meersen
Aachen
FRANCONIA

Laon
Trier
Mainz
Regensburg
BAVARIA

Paris

NEUSTRIA
SWABIA

Bourges
Basle

AQUITAINE
LOMBARDY

Milan
Pavia

Rome

Map 8b

Franks. The Empire was divided into three kingdoms, with their frontiers drawn so as to give each brother an approximately equal share of the royal estates, the material basis of rulership. Their actual possessions were likewise taken into account. Charles the Bald was allotted Neustria, Aquitaine, and the Spanish March, the kingdom of the West Franks as it

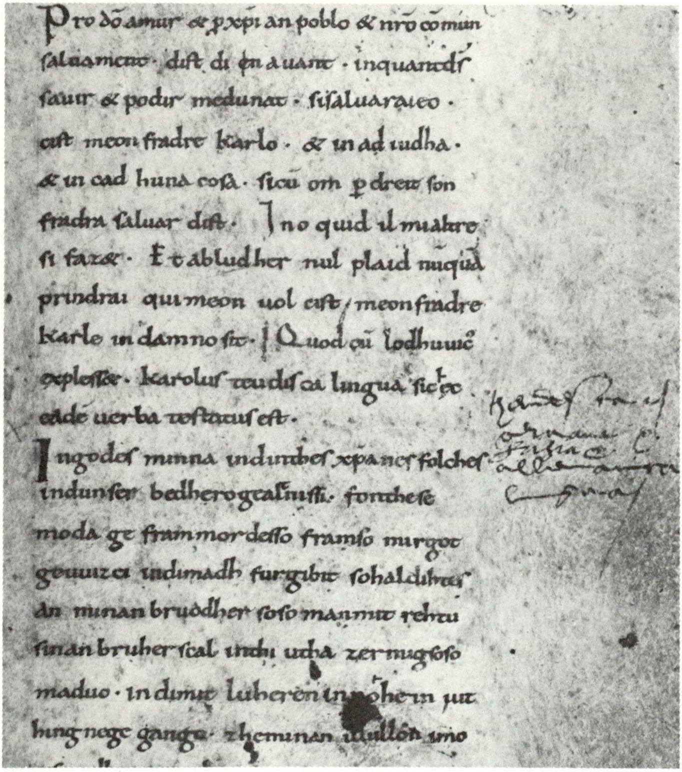
Pro do amur & xpi an poblo & nro comun
salųament. dist di en auant. in quant dr
sauir & podir me dunat. si saluarai eo.
cist meon fradre karlo. & in ad iudha.
& in cad huna cosa. sicu om p dreit son
fradra saluar dift. In o quid il mi altre
si fazet. Et ab ludher nul plaid nuqua
prindrai qui meon uol cist meon fradre
karle in damno sit. Quod cu lodhuuic
explesset. karolus teudisca lingua sic
ade uerba testatus est.
Ingodes minna indunthes xpanes folches
indunser bedhero gealtnissi. fonthese
moda ge frammordesso framso mir got
geuuizci indi mahd furgibit so hald ih tesan
an minan bruodher soso man mit rehtu
sinan bruher scal. in thiu thaz er mig soso
maduo. indi mit luheren in nohheiniu
thing ne gegango. the minan uuillon imo

Fig. 71. The Strasbourg Oaths

was called, which in time was to become the only France. His lands were almost all, save the extreme north-east, Romance-speaking. His eastern frontier roughly ran along the Scheldt, the Saône, and the Rhone. Lewis the German's lands were German-speaking: Bavaria, Swabia, Saxony, Thuringia, and easternmost Francia (Franconia), the kingdom of the East Franks that was to resume its ancient name of Germany. His southern and western frontiers lay along the Alps, the river Aar, the middle Rhine (overstepping it at Worms and Speyer), and then along the old border of Saxony. Lothar was left the lands between with Frisia, Mid-Francia (including Aachen), Burgundy and Provence, and his kingdom of Italy.

Although imposing, it was the worst share, for it was a long, heterogeneous strip, with no natural centre, no similarity of speech or climate, divided, not protected, by natural frontiers. All three realms were threatened by disintegration, but Lothar's was almost forced to dissolve. Its most solid portion, Mid-Francia (soon to be known as Lotharingia or Lorraine from the name of its second ruler), was exhausted, while Burgundy and Italy had nothing in common save Frankish counts. They were all to be the prey of stronger neighbours, and Lotharingia remained for centuries a debatable territory between France and Germany. Yet there was some suitability in its formation, as the emergence of the separate Netherlands was to show.

Modern France and Germany owe their beginning to the division of 843, but the division was then a matter of dynastic convenience, not of nationality. The Frankish nobility had no such consciousness. It was all but accident that the division, by assigning Romance lands to Charles and German lands to Lewis, provided a natural framework within which the French and German nations could acquire their identities and grow. But the dynastic separation followed obvious lines of least resistance, and thus could have the sequel which it encouraged. Not for nothing did contemporaries call Lewis 'the German'. What most and justly impressed them, however, was the disappearance of the Empire, the secular union of Western Christendom. That achievement of civilization was being replaced by dissolving, quarrelling, lacerated kingdoms. The ideal of unity in spite of all survived among thinking men, more powerful in the Church and for the Church, which possessed an admitted chief and centre in the Papacy. They still remembered with regret the vanished Empire.

The prelates were, both by interest and conviction, the champions of peace at any rate among the kings, the 'fraternal concord', and they helped to check quarrels until the death of Lothar I in 855. More effective perhaps were the troubles of the brothers. Besides the Northmen's attacks on all, Lewis the German was fighting the Slavs; Charles the Bald took years to eliminate his nephew Pepin II from Aquitaine and was obliged to admit the independence of the Breton kingdom, while unable to curb his own unruly magnates. The Emperor Lothar divided his dominions between his three sons: Lewis II, crowned Emperor at Rome in 850, kept Italy, Lothar II was given Lotharingia, which was now so called after its kings, with most of Burgundy, and the youngest, Charles, an epileptic cipher, was allotted Provence and Lyons. Of these only Lothar II had weight in northern politics. Lewis the German, whose hands were freest, was now the storm-centre; Charles the Bald, who had least control of his faithless vassals and was most harassed by the Northmen, was the victim. In 858 Lewis invaded West Francia. There was no question of fighting battles but merely of bribing the magnates. The bishops, led by Hincmar of Rheims, the one dominant statesman of the realm, stood firmly by Charles, but the lay lords deserted to Lewis, with one prelate, Ganelon (Wenilo) Archbishop of Sens, who, transmuted into a layman, became thereby the incarnation of treachery in the legends of after times. He crowned Lewis in vain, for the German lords were leaving for home, and the French were ready to be bribed to return to Charles. So the invasion ended in a resumption of 'concord', or rather a sordid rivalry for the succession to Lotharingia.

In these and subsequent broils, the surest support of each Carolingian king was to be found in his bishops, who almost alone retained an ideal of the Christian State as an institution for internal peace and good government amid the crude self-seeking and faithlessness of the time. Their spiritual prestige and their material power were great. But the bishops, filled with a sense of their responsibility and strength, claimed rather to be superiors than subjects. They summoned Charles the Bald to amend his government on Christian principles, and he declared himself ever ready to submit to their fatherly admonitions and sentences. To Lewis the German, Hincmar and his band of loyal bishops explained the text of the Psalm, 'Instead of thy fathers thou shalt have children', as meaning, 'Instead of the Apostles I have ordained Bishops that they may govern and instruct thee'. They produced an ecclesiastical theory of the State as the City of God on earth, which was expressed by Hincmar. Bishops make kings by the sacring: kings cannot consecrate bishops. The monarchy is an instrument in the hands of the Church, which directs it to its true end. And Archbishop Hincmar held the strongest views on his metropolitan authority: his suffragans, gathered round him, were to act obediently under his direction.

These were high claims, but archbishop and suffragans, although strong, were steadily confronted by the still greater strength and greed of the lay potentates, great and small, armed as the churchmen could hardly be. Nor were they united or disinterested among themselves: diocesan bishops were restive under a domineering archbishop, unable to control their own mutinous subordinates, and incapable of resisting unaided the attacks of the laity and the abuses in which they might be accomplices. Only a centralized Church, obeying a single head remote from local embarrassments, seemed to a section of the bishops a sufficient safeguard. They turned to the claims of Rome and the growing tradition of the papal Curia. It was under these influences that the famous collection of the *Forged Decretals* was concocted about 850 at some centre in West Francia. Some Frankish clerk, who assumed the name of Isidorus Mercator, using as his basis the ample so-called Isidorian collection of the Canon Law, which had originated in Spain, proceeded to forge, interpolate, misattribute, and rearrange a whole series of papal decretals, for papal decretals in the West were an essential part of Church Law along with the canons of councils. He composed 70 decretals for the venerated Popes before the Council of Nicaea (325), and inserted other spurious decretals among genuine material for later periods, whereas the earliest authentic decretal dates from Pope Siricius in 385. He made an ingenious and deceptive patchwork by misplacing genuine later quotations in a new and imposing context. His main object was to make the bishops legally impregnable against the archbishops, their own clergy, and the laity by means of the papal ecclesiastical monarchy. The pseudo-Isidore laid down the absolute and universal supremacy of the see of St Peter. The Pope is the sovereign lawgiver, without whose consent no council and no canon is valid. He is the supreme judge, without whose consent no bishop can be deposed, who finally decides 'major causes', which he can call to his tribunal in the first instance as well as on appeal. Thus the episcopate is freed from lay judgement and from their own metropolitans. The distant Pope appears as the supreme Head of Christendom.

Such a theory harmonized too well with the aspirations of the Popes not to find an echo in Rome. They had been working on parallel lines, and, too wise to rest on the *Forged Decretals*, could quote genuine later pronouncements. To the anxious inquiry of the learned canonist, Hincmar, on those newly circulated forgeries, Pope Nicholas truly replied that not every genuine papal document was preserved in the papal archives, and he forced even Hincmar to reinstate a mutinous suffragan, Rothad, for Hincmar did not deny the extra-legal, final power of the Pope. Hincmar, in fact, had already been using the supreme appellate authority of the Pope in a matter in which zeal for Christian morals was sharpened by political ambitions.

The dispute concerned the validity of the marriage between Lothar II of Lotharingia and Theutberga, sister of his vassal Hucbert, Duke of Jurane Burgundy, whom he had been compelled to marry by his father, the Emperor. Lothar II was devoted to his mistress, Waldrada, by whom he had a son, and as soon as he was his own master, repudiated and persecuted Theutberga, accusing her of incest. He, with the aid of his two archbishops, Günther of Cologne and Theutgaud of Mainz, induced a synod of his kingdom to condemn her, but not to divorce her (860). Now Hincmar stepped in as her champion in a treatise supported by his king, Charles the Bald. If Hincmar was honest, Charles the Bald at least hoped to annex Lotharingia if his nephew died without legitimate heirs, which was almost certain with regard to the barren Theutberga. Lothar extorted from a fresh synod of his bishops a decree of nullity, after which he married Waldrada, while Theutberga appealed to the Pope Nicholas I. It was an appeal to one of the ablest and most resolute of men.

Pope Nicholas I (858–67) was fortunately placed. The Italian Carolingian, the Emperor Lewis II, was the most amiable of the kings, and both he and the Pope derived strength from mutual support, while Nicholas overawed him by force of character. Nicholas could therefore act with the despotic freedom which he held to be the prerogative of the Apostolic See. He forbade aggression by the greedy uncles, while he sent legates to hold a Frankish Council in Lotharingia. The legates, however, were bribed, only Lothar's bishops appeared, and Lothar was falsely declared to have married Waldrada in his father's lifetime. But the cheat was revealed to Nicholas, who called an Italian synod to Rome, and there not only quashed the Lotharingian proceedings, but created precedent by summarily deposing Günther and Theutgaud and his own corrupt legates (863). Although Lewis II began hostilities, he was speedily brought to submission in a personal interview. A new legate reached Lotharingia, where Lothar II, isolated and threatened by his uncles, gave way (865). He took back Theutberga, and his uncles were curbed by the Pope's commands. By Nicholas's bold and skilful action, based on the weakness and feuds of the miserable kings, the Papacy had appeared as supreme arbiter of Christendom, and had advanced in practice the theory of its ecclesiastical sovereignty. The story had an end as sordid as its beginning. Lothar II was in hopes of obtaining from the next Pope, Adrian II (867–72), a reversal of the sentence when he died in 869 at Piacenza. The two uncles, disregarding the claims of his surviving brother, Lewis II, threw themselves on the prey in a bloodless war which ended in August 870 in the partition of Meersen, based on no other principle than an equal share of the royal estates. Provence had already been divided between Lewis II and Lothar II (863).

Both Charles the Bald and Lewis the German suffered deservedly from their sons, whom they were obliged to subdue, and their nobles whom they bought with counties, benefices, and lay abbacies, which disorganized the monasteries. Charles ended by blinding his brigand-like son, Carloman. Lewis in spite of revolts maintained his three sons as vassal kings of tribes. They both were now on the watch for the inheritance of their injured nephew, the sonless Lewis II.

Lewis II (855–75), whose imperial title was scoffed at by contemporaries, gallantly spent his life in the uphill task of defending his kingdom of Italy from the Saracens and of striving to rule it. He was nearly isolated from the north by the Alps, and was faced by great vassals hard to control. His most faithful allies were the successive Popes elected under the regime of 824, who looked to him for protection against their own subjects, while speaking as masters to the outside world. There were three specially formidable dynasts in Carolingian Italy, the Marquess of Friuli on the north-east, the Marquess of Tuscany, and the Duke of Spoleto. In the south were the practically independent Lombards of Benevento, and a little dynast owning allegiance to the Byzantines, the Duke of Naples, besides the seaport of Amalfi and the Byzantine duchy of Calabria. The Lombards in 840 disintegrated into the two principalities of Benevento and Salerno and the county of Capua, but were none the less persistent in resenting the claims of Lewis. All, however, were suffering from the terrible Moslem raiders, who since the conquest of Sicily (c. 831) and the capture of Bari (840) by them and their brief alliance with the Duke of Naples (837), had devastated all the south coastlands. In 846 they sacked the suburbs of Rome and the basilica of St Peter's. This was a shock to Christendom, and caused Pope Leo IV (847–8) to wall the suburb, the Vatican, round St Peter's, which took the name of the Leonine City. Lewis had been unable to prevent the sacrilege, but he continued to be the Pope's best friend: Nicholas I was his own choice.

We have seen Nicholas's achievements in the Frankish kingdoms and his unbending attitude, with its illusory successes, in the East. He demanded obedience from the Frankish kings with threats of his spiritual thunder and reminders of what they owed to his support. Basing himself on a growing tradition, he set a programme and theory for his successors which were never forgotten. Those successors, however, were weaker men, endangered by the growing turmoil of Italy and by the violent insubordination of the Roman nobles, who cared not for the Papacy or the bureaucratic Curia except as valuable prizes to seize. Their opportunity was coming. Lewis under all difficulties perseveringly fought the Moslems. In spite of being abandoned by the Byzantines, his momentary allies, he at last recaptured Bari (871). But he was then treacherously taken prisoner by the ungrateful Prince of Benevento, who feared he might become a vassal, and was only released on an oath not to return to South Italy. The Pope absolved him from his oath, but the subjection of Benevento could not be enforced. In 875 Lewis died, leaving only a daughter Ermengarde, and his kingdom vacant. Pope John VIII (872–82), with Italy and Rome imperilled, looked about for a Carolingian protector.

Charles the Bald and Lewis the German, who had since 871 been rivals for the new succession, entered the fratricidal lists once more. Charles, who was the Pope's candidate, set out at once. Lewis the German despatched two sons, Charles the Fat and Carloman, one after another, to Italy, and himself invaded West Francia. But Carloman was outmanoeuvred in the race of cunning, and his father won no ground. Charles the Bald received the imperial crown from the Pope, who now appeared as its donor, and returned home to negotiate. He was allured by the death of Lewis the German in August 876 to make an attempt on Lewis's Lotharingia. Lewis had left three sons, who already ruled their shares, Carloman in Bavaria, Lewis II the Younger in Saxony and Franconia, and Charles the Fat in Swabia. Of these, Lewis the Younger defeated at Andernach a meanly treacherous assault of his uncle and maintained the frontier of Meersen. Meantime Pope John VIII was loudly calling on the Emperor to come back to defend Italy. So Charles, bribing, not fighting, the raiding Northmen,

Fig. 72. Charles the Bald

set out. In 877, on leaving his eldest son, King Louis[1] II the Stammerer, as regent, he issued in a capitulary at Quierzy the celebrated decree that if a count should die on the expedition, Louis should continue his son in the honours which he held. This ordinance by no means established hereditary fiefs. Rather, it implied that honours (i.e. offices and benefices) were at the king's disposal when vacated by death, and its object was to prevent Louis from misuse of the royal rights for his impatient ambition in the usual Carolingian way. At the same time it displayed and recognized the prevalent custom that the son should succeed the father in his honours. It was a milestone in the progress of feudalism. The magnates of West France were steadily amassing counties, domains, lay abbacies, and the like as hereditary possessions to the enfeeblement of the impoverished crown.

As for Charles, he arrived in Lombardy with insufficient force, to find his

---

[1] Henceforward the French form Louis will be used for French kings, etc., Lewis for German and more eastern rulers. Both are variations from the original Chlodovech, Hludowic. The distinction is artificial but convenient, since it separates potentates of different lands and dynasties.

nephew Carloman of Bavaria already in the eastern march. The West Franks showed no zeal to succour their truant sovereign who neglected his own realm, and the shadow Emperor, retracing his steps, was overtaken by death in October 877 in Maurienne. Charles the Bald was a cultured patron of learning, who wanted neither ability nor courage, but he possessed even more than his share of his family's greed and lack of scruple. In a degenerate age, these last qualities, linked with a showy ambition, gave every encouragement to the anarchic, bargaining magnates, whose mounted vassals formed the Frankish armies. Adequate defence against the sudden, swiftly moving Northmen bands was in any event a Herculean task for the central monarchy: it was rendered impossible by the fratricidal strife of the Carolingians, who wasted their resources and mortgaged the future. In that Charles the Bald was one of the worst sinners.

The death of Charles deepened the embarrassments of Pope John VIII. Stouthearted as he was, he could not make head against the attacks of the Duke of Spoleto and Roman rebels and the predatory Moslems on all sides. Carloman of Bavaria, crowned King of Italy, withdrew smitten by a mortal disease. The Pope vainly journeyed to West Francia to induce Louis the Stammerer to take up his father's role. The king wisely refused, and so did Boso, the Duke of Lyons, Charles the Bald's brother-in-law, who had married Ermengarde, the only child of the Emperor Lewis II. Charles the Fat of Swabia was Pope John's next resource. He had taken over the claims of Carloman, and in 881 was crowned Emperor at Rome. But Charles, although a man of piety and learning, was devoid of energy: his various visits to Italy were totally ineffectual. At last in 884 John VIII was murdered in a Roman outbreak. His death marks an epoch. The bureaucracy of the Curia, which retained a tradition of civilized government, was broken. Rome became the prey of its barbaric nobles, who installed their discreditable candidates, creatures of faction, in the Lateran. What with scenes of savage revenge and dissoluteness in the next thirty years, which have won for the regime the name of the 'pornocracy', the prestige of the Papacy almost sank to zero, and it took another century before a revival was possible. Its horizon was restricted, if it kept its formal primacy. Only a thin, underground stream preserved the curial tradition.

The East Frankish, or German, kingship under Lewis the German was stronger than the West Frankish. Germany was less riddled with benefices and immunities than West Francia and Lotharingia; although the great families were firmly established, they had not laid such a hereditary grip on the countships. The danger lay in the strong cohesion of the ancient tribes, Bavarians, Saxons, Swabians, and to a less degree Franconians, but as yet the Carolingian prestige was fortified locally by each son taking a tribe to rule. The advantage was lost when Lewis II the Younger of Saxony took over the dead Carloman's Bavaria (880), giving the latter's illegitimate son

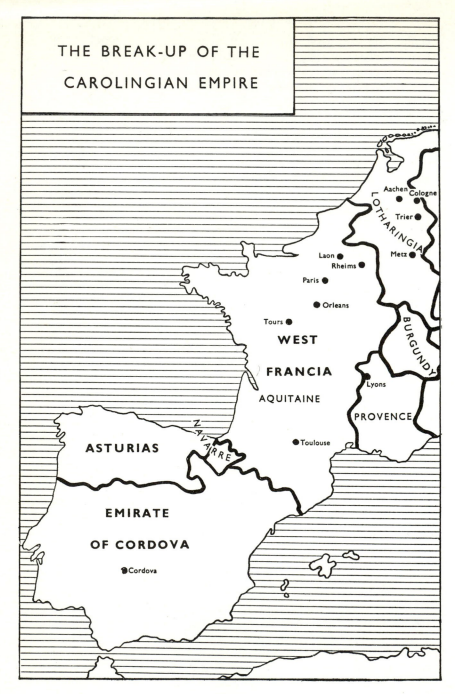

THE BREAK-UP OF THE CAROLINGIAN EMPIRE

Aachen Cologne

Trier

LOTHARINGIA

Metz

Laon
Rheims

Paris

Orleans

BURGUNDY

Tours

WEST

FRANCIA

Lyons

AQUITAINE

PROVENCE

NAVARRE

ASTURIAS

Toulouse

EMIRATE

OF CORDOVA

Cordova

Map 9

SLAVONIC

PEOPLES

Hamburg

Magdeburg

SAXONY   WENDS

EAST

FRANCONIA   BOHEMIA

Regensburg

MAGYARS

FRANCIA

SWABIA   BAVARIA

CARINTHIA

Milan

Pavia   Venice

KINGDOM   SERBS

BULGARIAN

KINGDOM

OF

ITALY

Rome

Benevento

Naples

BYZANTINE EMPIRE

Map 9

Arnulf the border duchy of Carinthia only, and then himself died (882) leaving the utterly incapable Charles the Fat to rule all Germany. It was a larger Germany, for in 880 the brothers, chiefly Lewis of Saxony, had wrested the West Frankish share of Lotharingia from the sons of Louis II the Stammerer by the treaty of Ribemont. King Louis had been only accepted by his magnates on promising to respect their possessions and rights after stern admonitions of Archbishop Hincmar (*ob.* 882), and even then the Marquess of Gothia (Septimania) was in revolt. On his death (879), his two elder sons, Louis III and Carloman, succeeded to West Francia. They were gallant youths, who fought well against the Northmen, if they had to buy off their cousin Lewis II of Saxony's attacks by yielding to him western Lotharingia. Another loss they tried in vain to prevent. On the Stammerer's death, Duke Boso of Lyons induced the counts and bishops under him to crown him King of Provence (879). In spite of a joint expedition of the Carolingian kings, united for once, he could not be wholly evicted. When he died (887), his young son Lewis was allowed to succeed him. It was a portent of the decay of loyalty to their house, although Boso was the husband of a Carolingian heiress. By an aggravation of misfortune both the young kings were carried off by accidents, Louis III in 882 and Carloman in 884, and their only heir was a child, their half-brother Charles, later named the Simple. The West Frankish magnates then elected the remaining German Carolingian, the Emperor Charles III the Fat, the very man to prove that a united Empire under one ruler was an impossibility.

Charles III was inefficient in all his realms. The defence against the Northmen was carried on by the great provincial nobles, among whom Eudes (Odo), Marquess of Neustria, had especially distinguished himself by the defence of the city of Paris. At last a general rising at the end of 887 deposed the Emperor, who died on 12 January 888. With him there vanished all but the semblance of united Christendom. Germany chose for king the only grown-up Carolingian, Arnulf of Carinthia (887–99), France the valiant Eudes (888–98); young Lewis continued in Provence, a Swabian Welf, named Rodolph, made himself king in Jurane Burgundy between the Alps and the Saône, Guido (Guy) of Spoleto, after an unsuccessful bid for France, went back to fight for the Italian crown against his rival Berengar of Friuli. They all of them acknowledged a kind of suzerainty in Arnulf, but in effect the kingdoms now chose kings, as the chronicler Regino said, from within themselves. Not that they felt themselves nations: the ruling class was mostly of Austrasian Frankish descent with widely scattered lands and without any provincial patriotism. But the rifts between the provinces were deep, their languages were separate, and they could only be ruled locally and apart. In the tumult of invasions, civil wars, feuds, and land grabbing, disruption and anarchy were the order of the day.

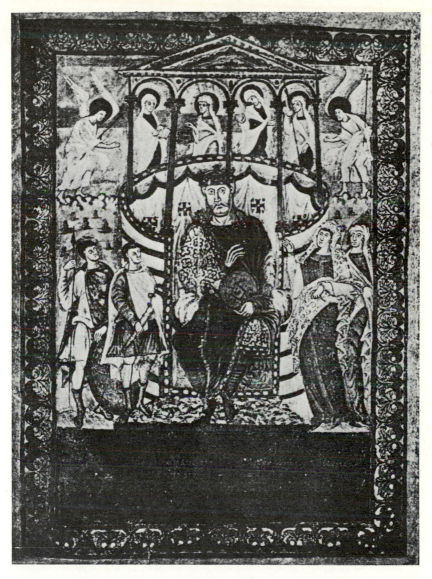

Fig. 73. Charles the Fat and his queen Richardis

King Arnulf proved his capacity and his desire to take up the task of defence. His decisive victory over the Northmen on the river Dyle on 1 November 891 ended their ravages in Lotharingia. The bloody defeat of the Saxons on the Lüneburg Heath in 880 had by its very slaughter deprived

355

the sea-rovers of any desire to win more battles there. Alternations of fortune attended the struggle with the south-eastern Slavs while Svatopluk I, who made Greater Moravia an extensive realm, the patron of St Cyril and St Methodius, was alive. When he died in 894, the quarrels of his sons and the other Slav princes gave up the discordant tribes to new enemies, the nomad Magyars, from the Ukraine, whom Arnulf in 892 had recklessly invited as allies. The Magyars destroyed Great Moravia, and became from their new abodes in the Danubian steppe a yearly scourge to Germany, Italy, and even France. Owing to the memories of the Huns they were given the name of Hungarians by their western neighbours, and the steppe became known as Hungary. Their settlement drove a cleft, not yet bridged, between the Balkan Slavs to the south and the Czechs of Bohemia and Moravia and the Slovenes of Carinthia, who belonged henceforth to Western Europe.

Meanwhile, civil war raged in North Italy between the rival kings, Berengar and Guido. The latter won a really hard-fought battle on the Trebbia (889)—a rare event in these intestine broils—and proceeded to force the unwilling Pope Stephen V to crown him Emperor in 891 and his son Lambert in the next year. The title was a mere travesty devoid of meaning: it did not even confer any control of Rome, and Berengar was unconquered in Friuli. But Guido's power led Formosus, the next Pope (891–6), a much-hated faction leader, to beg Arnulf to intervene. The German king led an army twice to Italy victoriously, but with little effect. In the first expedition against Guido he reached Piacenza; in the second, after Guido's death (894), he stormed Rome itself, which was hostile, in spite of Formosus, and in his turn received the imperial crown (896). He was then attacked by sickness, and withdrew to Germany, leaving the field clear for the Emperor Lambert, who came to an agreement with King Berengar. The river Adda was fixed upon as their common boundary.

There were troubles for Arnulf in his own kingdom, especially in Lotharingia, where the evolution towards feudalism was developing apace with its accompaniment of the private wars of powerful families. Franconia was little better. Arnulf hoped to restore order in Lotharingia and to rebut French claims by making his illegitimate son, Zwentibold, its king, but the experiment was not a success, and when Arnulf died in December 899 and his six-year-old son, Lewis III the Child, became King of Germany, disorder increased tenfold, while Magyar raids plundered the land. Zwentibold was killed in civil war and was followed by a duke of Lotharingia who could not restore obedience or peace. The lead in each tribe was now taken by great tribal magnates who assumed rather than were given the title of Duke; Liudolf of Saxony and Arnulf of Bavaria were overmighty subjects, if they defended their duchies and kept some sort of tribal peace. The advent of these tribal duchies marks a German epoch. They appealed to the strong particularism of past and present, and for nearly three centuries were a dominant factor in German history. In common they showed an aversion to the hegemony of the Franks of Franconia. Nevertheless in November 911, when Lewis the Child, the last German Carolingian, died, the Franconian, Saxon, Bavarian, and Swabian lords agreed at Forchheim to elect Conrad, Duke of Franconia, as their king.

King Conrad (911–18), a tireless warrior, strove in his troublous reign to maintain the Carolingian tradition of a central government. He at once lost Lotharingia, which, as the ancient Austrasia and home of the Carolingians, called in the Carolingian Charles the Simple of France, and repelled three attempts at reconquest. In Germany proper, besides the local feuds, one or other of the tribal dukes was always in insurrection, save when the Magyars produced some union. Basle was lost to Rodolph of Jurane Burgundy. Conrad in vain fulminated decrees against rebellion. To split up the realm into great principalities, tribal or merely feudal, owing little obedience to an elective king and keeping little peace among themselves, this became a constantly increasing tendency, fraught with ills, in medieval Germany. Conrad himself at least saw that the resources of his family and duchy were unequal to the task of kingship, and on his deathbed recommended the election of Henry, the powerful rebel Duke of Saxony, as his successor. A new era began with Henry's accession.

Among the West Franks, the French as we may begin to call them, there was no more concord than among the Germans. King Eudes's strength lay in his march of Neustria, i.e. between the Seine and the Loire, where he possessed counties and lay abbacies, but beyond the Seine, in the land which was at this time considered in the West Francia proper,[1] loyalty to the Carolingians was far from dead. The leader there was its greatest magnate, Fulk, Archbishop of Rheims, who had succeeded Hincmar in office and influence. Eudes, at first victorious against the Northmen, whom he had been compelled to bribe like any Carolingian, was routed by them at Wallers in Vermandois (891) and was losing ground among the magnates. Fulk thereupon crowned Charles III the Simple, then thirteen years of age, at Rheims (893). In the civil war that ensued King Eudes brought his rival to his knees, yet not so completely but that he allowed him some part of his inheritance and promised the succession. When Eudes died on 1 January 898, even his own heir and brother, Robert, Marquess of Neustria, along with all the magnates, recognized Charles III. The young king showed more energy than prudence to judge from his sobriquet. So long as he was guided and sustained by the loyal Fulk and his successor Hervé, he made more than a passable ruler. The great event of his reign was the treaty

[1] This special signification of *Francia* will be indicated by the use of italics, to distinguish it from the ancient Francia, the whole kingdom of West Francia or France, and Franconia.

357

of St-Clair-sur-Epte in 911 with the Northman Rollo by which coastal counties of Neustria along the Seine were ceded to Rollo as the vassal duchy of Normandy. This cession, if it did not satisfy the Northmen's desire for wider territory, made a virtual end of their deep incursions. It relieved France from the worst ravages and founded a feudal state of vast importance for the future. Soon after, the death of Lewis the Child (911) enabled Charles to obtain his hitherto vain ambition, the rule of Lotharingia. The land's loyalty to its native Carolingians made him its king and repelled Conrad of Germany. Charles preferred henceforward to live in Lotharingia. But the apparent prosperity was delusive. He angered the Neustrian lords

10. The House of Robert the Strong

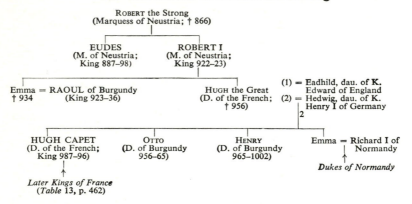

by his absence and his favour for a low-born Lotharingian, Hagano. The monarchy, too, was weak through the dissipation of nearly all its domains in France. The Marquess of Neustria with his wide lands was far more powerful. His father Marquess Robert the Strong, the champion of France against the Northmen, had laid the foundation of the power of his house. His brother Eudes began his career as Count of Paris and added the counties of Anjou, Blois, and Touraine before he became king. In 922 Robert roused his fellow-malcontents to revolt and crown him just as Hervé of Rheims lay dying, and then secured the archbishopric for a creature of his own. Charles, who put up a bold fight, was defeated near Soissons with his Lotharingians. Although the rebel king fell in the battle, he was at once replaced by his son-in-law Raoul (Radulf),[1] Duke of Burgundy, and the unfortunate Charles completed his own ruin by trusting the word of the faithless Herbert, Count of Vermandois, a Carolingian of

[1] As in the case of Lewis-Louis, an artificial distinction is made henceforward in the use of variants of the same name, Rudolf for Germans, Rodolph for Jurane Burgundians, and Raoul for Frenchmen. The Latin Rodulfus and Radulfus are used almost indifferently in the sources.

the line of Bernard of Italy. He was imprisoned, with a passing show of liberation, till his death at Péronne in 929. His wife and son escaped to his father-in-law, Edward of England. Raoul remained King of France, but after much fighting he was obliged (928) to consent to Lotharingia becoming a German duchy. Although there was a Carolingian restoration on his death (936), the recalled line never recovered any real hold on the great vassals.

The same sorry story of heathen ravage, faithless ambition and greed, and rampant disorder is exhibited in Italy and Provence. The death of Pope Formosus enabled his enemies to elect Stephen VI (896–7), who carried through a horrible travesty of law to debase his predecessor. The corpse of Formosus was exhumed, tried, and condemned as a perjured intruder: his acts and ordinations were annulled. In an anarchic reaction Stephen VI himself was strangled. After ephemeral Popes the Emperor Lambert was able to intervene and promote John IX (898–900) in spite of a violent opponent, Sergius. The new Pope and a Council reburied Formosus and revalidated his acts. Unhappily, Lambert, who gave promise of order, died heirless in a hunting accident (898), and Berengar took over his dominions. The weakness of his position tempted young Lewis of Provence to enter Italy (900), where the fickle magnates made him king, and he was even crowned at Rome (901), the most shadowy of all the Emperors. He was, however, quickly driven out again by Berengar, and on a second invasion, undertaken against his oath never to return, he was captured by his rival and blinded (905). Henceforward Lewis III the Blind reigned but did not govern in Provence. Real power was exercised, as far as the local counts could be governed, by Hugh of Arles, a descendant of Lothar II, the greatest of his nobles. As for Rome, the city fell under the domination of a truculent native chief, the Senator Theophylact, and his wife Theodora. So corrupt was the time that the sometime pretender, Sergius III (904–11), acquired the Papacy, a fierce tyrant to whom Marozia, a daughter of Theophylact, bore a son, later himself a Pope. Formosus and his acts were once again condemned. Great ladies, subjects of scandalous reports, were to play for many years important parts in the dynastic rivalries of Italy. It was Theodora who obtained the Papacy for a real statesman, John X (914–28), who took up the primary duty of war against the Moslem invaders.

In fact the condition of Italy, ravaged by the seafaring Moslems from the south and the Magyars from the north, and torn by civil strife of her princelings, was deplorable. In this renewed barbarism the land shared the lot of the other Carolingian kingdoms with even less sign of union. The *Regnum Italicum* of the north was invertebrate under the mild and cheatable Berengar I. The south was divided among warring competitors, the Lombard Princes of Capua-Benevento and of Salerno, the three coastal trading towns, Gaeta, Naples, and Amalfi, whose rulers were nominally Byzantine subjects, and lastly the Byzantines themselves. These at any rate were civilized, if oppressive, and they followed a consistent policy. The Emperor Basil I and his general Nicephorus Phocas had revived Byzantine power in Italy. By 901 there were themes, each under a *strategos*, Longobardia (around Bari) and half-Greek Calabria. The Lombard states seemed destined to fall, but men and money were always stinted in this fringe of the Eastern Empire. Even the Moslem danger, which extended to Provence, did not produce internal concord. One practical measure, however, was to be seen in Italy as in the northern lands. The cities were beginning to restore their ancient walls, mostly ruinous, under the direction of bishop, king, or magnate. Protection and co-operation could grow.

(3) THE NORTHMEN

In the decay of the Frankish Empire a chief factor was the invasions to which it was exposed on all sides by the latest of the barbaric peoples to expand or migrate westwards, the Northmen and Magyars, as well as from the seafaring western Moslems. Only incidental reference has hitherto been made to them. Now a brief account must be given of their attacks, both because of their immediate and destructive importance and because they added new elements, new states even, to Europe, which powerfully influenced its internal and external development. The effects of their conquests proved indelible. Among these newcomers the Northmen became an essential constituent of medieval peoples, a source of energy and of institutions as well.

The history of Scandinavia from *c.* 550 to *c.* 780 is almost a blank so far as definite events are concerned. About 520, a king of the Goths (Götar) in southern Sweden, named Chocilaicus (Hygelac in *Beowulf*), had been slain in a raid on Francia, but these attacks died away. The tribal settlements early fell into three or four main groups, the Norwegians on the western coast of the Scandinavian peninsula, the Danes in Jutland, the coastland of Scania across the Sound, and the islands between them, and the Swedes and Goths facing the Baltic only. The numbers of the three groups cannot be estimated from the mere areas of their seeming territories: Denmark, the smallest, was much the most populous because it provided a larger extent of cultivated plain; Sweden and Gothland, together the largest, were shrouded in untilled forests and only second in population; Norway was tree-clad, rugged, and mountainous to a degree, and the Norsemen were confined to settlements in innumerable bays on the sea-coast and in the narrow valleys. All these peoples were seafarers from of old, the boldest and most skilful in Europe. Fishing gave them a large part of their food-supply. The easiest communication between fiord and fiord, island and island, coast and coast, was by sea. Their trade with foreign lands lay across the sea, and by the end of the obscure period the Scandinavians were well known in the countries beyond the North Sea and the Baltic, and eagerly coveted the wealth they saw there. Their own civilization at this time showed a strange blend of primitive barbarism and culture. They had retained ancient Germanic institutions, ethos, and religion.

Their strongest organization was the kindred-group with its blood-feuds within the small folk, which held its *thing* of freemen for law and judgement; larger groups were very loosely held together if at all. Society was divided into nobles, plain freemen, and slaves (thralls). In the *thing* the hereditary *lawmen*, the repositories and expounders of custom, took the leading part, but the small folk would have its chief, with the title of king if his descent, like that of the Ynglings of Sweden, gave it to his family, or of earl (*jarl*) if less qualified. In Sweden, Gothland, and Denmark the kingly races were predominant. Farming their hereditary family freehold (*udal*) was the basic occupation, in severalty or in village communities according to the lie of the land and local custom. Seafaring and trade were common supplementary interludes. Free women, especially if heiresses, could hold a prominent position; there were queens on occasion. Along with a strong

Fig. 74. Vikings and a Viking ship. Stone of Stenkyrka

feeling of personal independence the aristocratic bias of the Scandinavian peoples was pronounced. The chief with his warband, the ancient *comitatus*, was the driving force. In contests for booty and territory and power Scandinavia was full of internecine wars before and during the period of the Viking raids. The term Viking given to men who sailed on raids at home or abroad means one who haunts a bay or creek (*vik*) as a base for this kind of warfare.

Their general philosophy of life was that every man must rely on himself and his own wisdom. The great aim was to attain fame and praise from men after death. A belief in Fate was overruling, a man must 'dree his weird'. Their wisdom was tarnished with cunning and deceit; it was unsafe to trust them. Their cruelty in warfare was ferocious—children might be tossed on their spears—and their courage was unsurpassed, on occasion rising to 'Berserk' fury of slaughter, when no wounds were felt. But the love of fighting was equalled by the love of gain, whether by trade or the more admired way of plunder or conquest. Profitless victories had little attraction for them. A Viking expedition was a search for land or treasure. Among the Scandinavians the ancient Germanic heathenism reached its latest development, and their gods reflected their character, Odin (Woden) the wily, warlike, and inspired chief of the warband, lover of battle, adventure, feasting, and minstrelsy, who called the slain heroes to his hall in Valhalla, and Thor, the rough, fighting farmer's god, with his invincible thunder-hammer, who protected boundaries and warred with the clumsy giants of frost and fell. They were appeased at times by human sacrifice. In accordance with Scandinavian fatalism the gods foreknew their own doom in the coming day of Ragnarök in their last fight with the anarchic powers, a belief perhaps tinged with the Christian Day of Judgement but quite native in conception. Much of their myths, however, pointed back to a more primitive savagery, and could be treated with a sense of rough comedy by their latest worshippers, from whom our knowledge is derived. Yet there is no trace of fading belief.

With all their barbarism the Scandinavians possessed an advancing civilization and culture. They had a strong and subtle grasp of law, and were skilful in its manipulation in disputes. The perpetration of crimes acknowledged as base branded the culprit as *nithing*, unworthy of comradeship. They were very ready to seize on new ideas and to learn and use the higher organization of societies they settled in; they were the most proficient of imitators. Born with an extraordinary capacity for bargaining and adaptation, they proved to be the most businesslike organizers of the states where they settled, if not of their native lands. In material things, their long, narrow ships, fitted with both oars and sail, were remarkably designed for speed and seaworthiness; in them they were capable of most adventurous voyages. Their weapons and shirts of mail were excellently wrought. They were fond of 'purple and fine raiment', and gaudy colours. Their carving and metalwork in silver and bronze displayed an inventive vigour and skill in ornament. To their native style of beasts' heads and interwoven limbs they added interlacing spirals derived from Ireland, and traces of English and Carolingian influence are to be found. The Oseberg ship and its furniture, buried with a dead Norse queen, shows what they could do in artistic luxury. In literature the poems of the *Elder Edda* on gods and heroes are inspired by a vivid, incisive, dramatic sense rare in the Middle Ages. If the court-poems in praise of chiefs are obscured by excessive conventions in construction and traditional, artificial metaphor, they at least testify to the quick apprehension of the audience, which could follow these masses of crossword clues.

The reasons for the sudden outburst of hostile activity abroad on the part of the Northmen are wrapped in much obscurity. Late Norman tradition ascribed it to overpopulation, and this is a very likely cause, for

Fig. 75. The Oseberg ship

it was not an inviting task to spread among the forests and mountains of Scandinavia. Polygamy, too, flourished among the chiefs and produced numerous younger sons ready to seek their fortunes. Further, the strife among the chiefs at home could produce malcontents and exiles, who took to the pirate's life in order to gain a following and re-establish themselves. Nothing, in fact, could be more natural in peoples, bred in the ethos of the warband, than raids and emigration when once they were straitened for room and independence. It is in harmony with this view that the earliest emigrants and Vikings came from the narrow settlements of Norway.

Norsemen appear early in the Shetlands, and are the first recorded to have raided Wessex in the eighth century; they were the ravagers of Ireland. Rival Danish princes troubled the Frankish coast. External events were also among the causes of the viking outburst. The Frisians had been the chief maritime folk of the North Sea: they had been crushed by the Carolingians and their ships were replaced by trading Northmen. The Saxons had held Danes and Franks apart: they had been subdued by Charlemagne. The Frankish Empire was a land power, and its coasts with their rich ports and undefended abbeys became familiar to the seamen of Scandinavia, rousing their appetite for plunder. A similar lack of sea-defence was to be found in the British Isles, absorbed in their domestic broils and studded with wealthy monasteries guarded only incompletely by their sanctity. At the same time adventurous Swedes, making journeys on the profitable trade-route between the Baltic and Constantinople, were founding colonies in the ill-organized towns and tribes of the eastern Slavs. All round them immense opportunities of wealth and land were opened to the overflowing Scandinavians.

The advance of the Swedes south-eastward which resulted in the formation of the Russian state and their absorption into their Slav subjects has been indicated in an earlier chapter. Their relations with the Frankish Empire were commercial, not usually by direct contact. Danes and Norsemen, however, although active in the trade and wars of the Baltic, made their main thrusts outward in the west. As we have seen, the Norsemen were the first to undertake formidable expeditions—in 793–4 they sacked the Northumbrian abbeys of Lindisfarne and Jarrow—but their chief route lay to the north. They colonized the Shetlands and Orkneys, and first ravaged and then settled in Sutherland and the Hebrides, which they called the Southern Islands (Sodor). In 802 the famous monastery of Iona fell a victim. But while Picts and Scots of North Britain suffered severely, Ireland, broken up in fact, if not in name, into quarrelling tribes, felt the full weight of their attacks. By 834 no place was safe from the incessant raids. They put an end to the 'Golden Age of art and learning'. It seems to have been largely Norsemen who by 821 wrecked the island abbeys of Noirmoutier and Rhé in the Bay of Biscay.

About 834 a wider scope and a greater intensity is apparent in the Viking raids. This was due in large part to the internal troubles of the Frankish Empire, which impaired the means of defence. Hitherto both Charlemagne and Lewis the Pious had mitigated the troublesome incursions by giving shelter to Danish princes in exile, while endeavouring to spread Christianity in Denmark in not unfriendly relations with the Danish king who was uppermost, and who feared the danger to himself of too successful pirate subjects. In 826 St Anskar was sent as a missionary, and if his efforts gained few permanent converts, he at least familiarized Danes and Swedes with the new religion. Now, however, Danes and Norwegians redoubled their raids in systematic fashion. In Ireland large Norse fleets began to anchor in the estuaries for the winter and build forts. The great Viking, Turgeis, conquered Ulster and plundered southwards until in 845 he was captured and drowned in Lough Owel. 'After this', say the chroniclers, 'there came great sea-cast floods of foreigners into Erin, so that there was not a point without a fleet.' Confusion became still more confused when in 849 a fleet of Danish Vikings arrived to dispute the prey with the Norsemen. Contests between these 'Black Foreigners' and the 'White Foreigners' (Norsemen) were complicated by the intermingling of native Irish feuds and the appearance of recreant Irish, called therefore the Gall-Gaedhil (the foreign Irish), with some intermixture of race. The result was the firm establishment of the Vikings in certain coast-towns, Dublin their chief stronghold, Waterford, and Limerick, all since 853 under the kingship of the Norse Yngling, Olaf the White, and his brother Ivar. They raided on all sides till 873, when Ivar died. There succeeded a newcomer from war in England, Halfdan, son of the legendary Ragnar Lothbrok, who sailed far and wide until he was luckily killed on Strangford Lough. After this there was comparative peace for forty years. Yet the mainly Norse colonies remained on the coast, active traders and pirates. They overflowed thence to western England.

Meantime the Danish Vikings in far greater numbers had been even more active in their favoured spheres of England and Francia. Their English conquests will be told in the next chapter, but here it should be noted that the fortification of a winter camp in Wessex began in 851, the first symptom of intended emigration, and that their attacks swung backward and forward across the Channel when they found resistance stiffen in either country and had exhausted it of portable booty in the shape of direct plunder or ransom on condition of departure. In Francia, Danish raids on the Frisian coast became incessant from 834. Some Danish exiles were employed to defend it by Lewis the Pious, but by his death (840) the rich inland port of Dorestad on the Rhine had been four times sacked, and Utrecht burnt. The Emperor Lothar even encouraged them to attack his brothers, granting the island of Walcheren to the Danish exile, Harald. By the time the ill-kept 'fraternal concord' was patched up, the invasions were extended far and wide. The Vikings reached Rouen, occupied Noirmoutier as a winter-camp, and ravaged Gascony. In 844 they circled Spain, and raided up the Guadalquivir from Cadiz to Cordova. Even Morocco was assaulted. Next year, probably under the famous Ragnar Lothbrok, a fleet sailed up the Seine and burnt Paris. The swarms of freebooters were, it seems, increased by the fact that the Danish chief kingship, which might have restrained them somewhat, was crippled by its dynastic dissensions. In 854 King Horic and most of his kinsmen fell in a disastrous battle. A boy son, Horic the Younger, was left, under whom the kingdom, such as it was, fell to pieces, and other lines ruled the fragments.

The years from 850 to 878 marked the widest extension of Viking ravage of Francia. Danish armies took almost permanent quarters on the Rhine, the Scheldt, the Somme, the Seine, the Loire, and the Garonne. Well armed, veteran, and adaptable, they had an enormous advantage over hasty local levies, even of mailed horsemen. They moved quickly, for besides penetrating on ship by rivers, they seized horses to traverse open country. In 859–62 a longer cruise was famous in tradition. Björn Ironside, a son of Ragnar, and Hasting sailed into the Mediterranean, ravaged Murcia, Septimania, and Provence, and sacked the ancient city of Luna in north Tuscany, which they thought to be Rome, and thence voyaged back to Brittany. Against the marauders Charles the Bald, when he was not at strife with his kindred and his vassals, displayed a laudable energy, but his designs were greater than his power. At best it took long to gather his unruly vassals, and then it was hard to keep them in array. Tours was sacked in 853. In 856 Björn and another chief built a fort on the island of Oscellum in the Seine near Mantes, whence they burnt Paris. Charles was besieging the island in 858, when Lewis the German attacked him. From 862 Charles employed a new device, that of building fortified bridges across the rivers to block the transit of the Viking fleets. He had some success; nevertheless in 866, after another sack of Paris, he only obtained their withdrawal by paying ransom, a remedy he repeated in 877. More effectual was the local warfare carried on against the Vikings of the Loire by Robert the Strong, Marquess of Neustria, ancestor of the later kings of France, until he died in battle with them in 866. Fighting with no booty and doubtful success had no allurement for the Northmen. They ceased after 865 to raid Aquitaine, and there was an alternative in England.

This did not mean that the Viking irruption had slackened in violence. By 879 the invaders had been checked in Wessex by King Alfred, but also whetted by their conquest and colonization of the English Danelaw. The yet unsatisfied turned once more to France and Germany. They fortified camps first on the Scheldt and then on the Meuse, whence they conducted great and small raids. In pitched battles their fortune was not great. In 881, at Saucourt on the Somme, young King Louis III won a famous victory over them which was celebrated in the contemporary *Ludwigslied*. In 880, on the Lüneburg Heath, they inflicted a memorable slaughter on the Saxons under Duke Bruno, but their own losses were so heavy that they soon left Saxony alone. But from their camp at Elsloo on the Meuse they burnt towns and abbeys to as far south as Trier (881–2), and reached Rheims and Amiens in France. King Carloman fought bravely, Charles the Fat negotiated. Both ended by paying enormous ransoms. Charles the Fat in addition gave Frisia as a fief to one chief, Godefrid, on condition of baptism, but he soon turned traitor and was murdered (885), when the chance of a Viking Frisia disappeared.

The peace did not survive the death of Carloman (884) and the succession of Charles the Fat to all Francia. The Northmen now held a strong camp at Louvain on the Meuse. They were resisted by the Lotharingian magnates, but not repelled. In 885 a great united Viking fleet, 300 ships strong, entered Rouen and sailed up the Seine under Sigefrid. Paris at this time had, like other Frankish cities, been rewalled by its count, Eudes, and its bishop, Joscelin. The city was on an island in the Seine, and two fortified bridges, connecting it with each bank, blocked the passage farther up the river. The Northmen besieged it for nearly a year, but they were baffled by a heroic defence led by Eudes. When Charles the Fat at length marched to the rescue, he dared not fight, and disgracefully not only paid a ransom, but gave the Vikings free passage to ravage Burgundy (886), a feebleness which ruined him and led to Eudes being elected King of the West Franks. The new king, however, had little luck in the war: he, too, was reduced to buying off the Northmen, and endured a defeat at Wallers (891). Some relief was obtained by the victory of King Arnulf of the East Franks. On 1 November 891 his troops stormed the Northmen's camp on the river Dyle by Louvain, and thereby freed Lotharingia at last from their incursions. Henceforward Germany was practically immune.

France secured a temporary respite by the renewal of the Danish attempt to conquer Wessex. This was defeated by 896, and the disappointed host turned to the Lower Seine with Rouen as their centre. By 910 their leader was a renowned Norse Viking, Rollo, but his men were predominantly Danes. King Charles the Simple put up a stout resistance, till at last an agreement was come to in 911 at St Clair-sur-Epte. By the treaty the basin of the lower Seine was ceded to Northmen settlement, like the Danelaw in England, as the duchy of Normandy. On his side Rollo received baptism, became Charles's vassal, and engaged to ward off other invaders. At first there was little change. The Northmen on the Loire ravaged and fought in Neustria for years in spite of the energetic defence of its marquesses, Robert and Hugh the Great. When Charles the Simple fell before his rebels, Duke Rollo extorted the cession of Bayeux (924), and his son Duke William Longsword (931–42) obtained the Cotentin and the land as far as Brittany from King Raoul (933). It was about the same time that the southern raids from the Loire finally ceased. In this lurid tract of history, with its pillage, massacre, and destruction, there were few alleviations for France, and those in a distant future. The thickly settled Normans in the new duchy introduced an extraordinarily capable, enterprising element into the population. With remarkable speed they adopted the language and institutions of their new country, and became a dynamic force in France and Europe.

If the later Normans owed much to their Northmen ancestors, however, they owed little less to the Franco-Gallic strain and its civilization. Their cousins in Scandinavia, unmixed and less under outside influence, showed small power of organizing or union. This was most obvious in the colony of Norwegians which settled in Iceland towards the close of the ninth century. 'We have no lord, we are all equal', said Rollo's Vikings. Their reckless individualism, left there to develop on its own lines, ended too often in social and political anarchy.

(4) THE MAGYARS

A much briefer account can be given of the Magyars, or Hungarians as they were named in the West, for their devastations and migration produced their most important effect in separating the south-western Slavs from their kinsmen in the Balkans and thus widening the cleft between West and East Europe. Their own development under Western influences added indeed a powerful nation to Europe, but they borrowed rather than gave. They were not a creative factor in the West.

As we have seen, this mixed Finno-Turkish collection of nomad clans moved over the Carpathians in 895-6 from the banks of the Dnieper into the half-vacant steppe of the middle Danube, at the instigation of the Emperor Arnulf. Great Moravia fell to ruin (906), and the Slavs and Vlakhs of 'Hungary' were reduced to servitude. The leader of the Magyars was the chief Arpád, who took the lion's share of the land and founded a long-lived dynasty of dukes and kings. But the Magyar horsemen by no means settled down or abandoned their marauding habits, and, although they were not too numerous, their speed, hardiness, and archery, characteristic of the nomad peoples, made them a scourge to the ill-prepared, discordant realms of the Frankish Empire. Only fortified towns and castles were an adequate defence.

The first country to suffer severely was Italy. In 899 a large Magyar horde devastated Lombardy. King Berengar summoned the whole force of the *Regnum Italicum*, some 15,000 troopers, and followed the retreating enemy to the river Brenta. There on 24 September they inflicted on him a disastrous overthrow. He was reduced to paying ransom after a year's plundering. They renewed their raids again and again, once (922) at Berengar's invitation against a rival. No more organized resistance was made to them by the competing kings and faithless, quarrelling marquesses of Italy. Their bands at times traversed the land as far as Apulia, which they plundered in 947. But, besides blackmail, another remedy began to reduce the harm. Citizens, led by their bishops, rebuilt their walls; nobles and peasants fortified country-towns as places of refuge (*castelli*), and these the raiders could not take. At last in 955 occurred the decisive victory of the German King Otto the Great over the whole Magyar host on the Lechfeld, and Italy participated in the general deliverance.

Germany had suffered even more during the half-century. From 900 their raids were annual affairs. All provinces were visited in turn, and victories over them were few. In 907 Margrave Liutpold of Bavaria was killed in a lost battle. In that year they crossed the Rhine to Alsace and France. Subsequently they made new raids through Germany on east and central France, burning the monasteries: in 937 a large band, after a wide pillage, devastated the kingdom of Burgundy and returned through north Italy. They reached Aquitaine in 951, and in 954 ravaged the north-east just before Otto's victory.

The beginnings of successful defence were to be seen in the tribal duchy of Saxony, whose duke, Henry, had been elected German King (919). In 924 a Magyar horde met no effectual defence, but by a stroke of luck a great Magyar chief was captured. He was freed by a treaty by which Saxony was to be immune for nine years in return for an annual tribute. The duchy was also subject to Slav raids, and Henry used the interval to build fortified towns and garrison them with serf troopers who were trained, unlike the old Saxon fashion, to fight on horseback. At the end of nine years, in 933, tribute was refused and a Magyar host appeared, to be routed by Henry on 15 March at Riade near Merseburg. The tide had turned, but civil strife in Germany allowed fresh incursions, although not so unresisted. The Magyars were beaten back from Saxony (937, 938) and defeated in Bavaria (948–9), although in 954 with the connivance of rebel dukes they ravaged the south and Lotharingia on their way to France. Next year they invaded Bavaria in full force. This time the German nobles of all the tribes united under King Otto the Great against the pest. In the battle of the Lechfeld (10 August 955) the Magyars suffered a ruinous defeat, one of the decisive events of medieval history. For three days they were pursued and slaughtered. The victory had far-reaching effects. The Magyars ventured no more on their invasions after their disaster, but took to a settled life in Hungary. Otto the Great appeared as the deliverer of Western Christendom, with Germany as its leading state.

(5) MOSLEM INVADERS OF THE EMPIRE

Unlike the Magyars, and like the Northmen, the Moslem invaders of Western Christendom were seamen who despoiled the coasts, making predatory incursions inland of terrible severity. Ever since 827, when exiled pirates from Moslem Spain had seized on Crete and the Aghlabid emirs of Africa had begun the conquest of Sicily, the Moslems of the west had dominated the greater part of the Mediterranean, and their piracy bade fair to abolish the already tenuous intercourse of Byzantium with Italy and

Francia. The suicidal folly of the South Italian dynasts attracted them from the sea to the shore. After Palermo fell into their hands (831) they possessed a magnificent harbour for aggression on the mainland, and henceforth Arab and Berber settlers in Sicily took a leading part in their depredations. Duke Andrew of Naples called them in as allies in a war with Benevento (837), and his example was followed by the other potentates. They occupied Taranto and Bari (840), where they formed a little Moslem state, and with this fresh base assaulted the Adriatic and Tyrrhenian coasts and scoured the land between. If they vainly besieged Naples and were beaten by a confederate fleet, they proceeded to burn the Roman suburbs and desecrate St Peter's, as we have seen already (846). The quarrelling Lombards and Campanians were incapable of preventing their ravages for years and indeed had recourse to them as allies. The Emperor Lewis II was appealed to more than once. In 852 he almost took Bari, but on his retreat the raids were as constant as before. The increasing plague led to an alliance between the Byzantine Emperor Basil and Lewis for a joint attack on Bari by sea and land. They could not agree, but Lewis persevered alone, and stormed the city at last from the land (871). The ungrateful Lombards then took him captive, destroying the prestige he had acquired, and his early death (875) left Pope and even princes looking for a new defender.

No help came from the shadow Emperors and rival kings in the north. Indeed, near this time Moslem pirates from Spain were raiding Provence and establishing a stronghold on its coast, Fraxinetum, whence they sallied inland to plunder, desolating the Alpine valleys far and near. In South Italy such relief as there was came from the vigorous policy of the Emperor Basil I. Yet it was not much, for if the Byzantines took over Bari and captured Taranto (880), they failed miserably to reconquer Sicily. Benevento and Naples allied with the marauders, who constantly raided the Roman Campagna and established an almost impregnable camp on the river Garigliano. In 881 they destroyed the famous abbeys of Monte Cassino and Volturno. The local dynasts, meanwhile, were engaged in wars and revolutions among themselves and against the advancing Byzantines. One competitor at least was eliminated in 899 by the conquest of Benevento by Atenolf I of Capua, who established a stable government. The danger from Sicily rose to its height when in 902 the half-mad Aghlabid, Ibrahim, who had wrested Taormina from the Byzantines, invaded Calabria in force, but his death before Cosenza ended his expedition and civil strife among the Sicilian Moslems gave a breathing space. Those of the Garigliano, however, ate like an ulcer into the land farther north. At last the warring Christians were so dismayed as to be reconciled and to accept Byzantine suzerainty. The warrior Pope, John X, took the lead. The strategos Picingli with all the princelings closed in from the south, the Pope and Marquess Alberic of Spoleto marched from the north and a Byzantine fleet guarded the river mouth. The Moslems were starved out and annihilated (915). With this victory of the Garigliano the very worst period of devastation was over, but piracy and coastal raids continued. In 909 the heretical Fatimite Caliphs secured the dominion of North Africa, in 917 the Caliph Mahdi conquered Sicily, and the Moslem depredations were renewed, only tempered by the payment of blackmail. Although the South Italian dynasts were now more stable, they did not cease from conflicts with one another which paralysed defence. In 935 an African fleet stormed Genoa in the north, and Byzantine lands suffered more. In 950–2 Fatimite troops overran Calabria and besieged Naples. Alternations of ravage and blackmail followed monotonously, for the reconquest of Crete in 961 by Nicephorus Phocas was counterbalanced by a disastrous invasion of Sicily to succour the last Byzantine hilltown (963) and an ignominious peace.

Meanwhile the Moslem pirates of Fraxinetum were no less a terror on each side of the Alps. Their brigandage extended even into Swabia; caravans were plundered in the Alpine passes, and some valleys were left uninhabited. A Byzantine reprisal by sea on Fraxinetum (931) produced no permanent effect. A joint attack on land by Hugh of Provence, King of Italy, and by sea by the Byzantine fleet failed likewise because Hugh found the Saracens useful allies (942). It was only when Otto the Great was Emperor that a crowning outrage produced deliverance. In 972 St Maiolus, the revered Abbot of Cluny, and a large caravan were captured in the Great St Bernard Pass. The Cluniac monks raised the ransom, but the local magnates were at length stirred to combined action. They extirpated the Moslem colony, freeing the passes for travellers, while the rescued districts could recover a meagre prosperity.

The conquest of Egypt by the Fatimite Caliphs (969) renewed their hostility to the Byzantine Empire, whose restive themes in Italy were ravaged and bought off their foes. Now a new competitor appeared, the German Emperor Otto II, who hoped to annex South Italy and defeat the infidel. Instead, he met with a crushing defeat near Stilo from the Sicilian emir, Abu'l-Qasim, which shook his own Empire (982), and the raids continued, while the Byzantine dominion was re-established. Rescue came at last from the growing sea-power of the trading Italian cities. In 1002 the Venetian fleet saved Bari from capture by a hard-fought victory; in 1005 the Pisans won a battle off Reggio in the Strait of Messina. When the Spanish Moslem, Mujahid, King of Denia, occupied the Sardinian coast in 1015, Genoa and Pisa allied under papal instigation to rout his fleet and drive him out (1016). It was the turn of the tide.

The effect of the Moslem raids had thus been finally to stimulate the growth of the local powers, while the Magyars had strengthened the new German kingship. In this the Saracens resembled the Northmen, but their invasions of this time added nothing to West European civilization except in Sicily. There, for all their ferocity, they transplanted the Arabic culture of Islam as it had formed in the courts of the Caliphs, and they left a deep imprint on the island and its people. The results were seen when the Normans reconquered Sicily for the West and Christendom passed to the offensive to dominate the Mediterranean.

(6) MOSLEM SPAIN

The Saracenic civilization of Sicily was much surpassed by that of Spain, a worthy rival to the Caliphate of Baghdad. But that culture was not accompanied by union or internal peace or even by the conquest of all Spain. The overthrow of the Visigoths had been achieved by discordant invaders. The Arabs, who took the best districts, and the Berbers (the true Moors) were always at enmity, and the Arabs were themselves divided by the bitter tribal feud of the Qais and the Kalb. Hence civil war was the order of the day. These divisions were accentuated by the geography of the peninsula, cut into provinces of diverse soil and climate by transverse mountain ranges and bordered by contrasted seas. Opportunity was thus given to the irreconcilable Christians in the Cantabrian and Pyrenean mountains of the north. In the Asturias, Pelayo was set up as king (718): other chieftains took the lead in Sobrarbe and Navarre on the spurs of the Pyrenees. They all maintained their autonomy the more easily because neither Arab nor Berber cared to settle beyond the northern limit of the olive, a climatic boundary. Accordingly by 756 we find them holding a line near latitude 41° in the west running from Coimbra and turning northwards from Guadalajara to Tudela and Pampeluna. The Christian Spaniards, headed by Alfonso I of the Asturias (739–57), maintained themselves in the northern mountains, and owing to the raids of both sides a wide uninhabited region surrounding the river Douro lay between them.

A change in the situation of faction-torn Andalusia (the name given by the Moors to their part of Spain) was made when Abd-ar-Rahman, the refugee Omayyad, landed in 755 on the south coast. With equal craft and courage he used and beat the factions and curbed the Christian princes. Charlemagne's invasions only nibbled, and that after the emir's death, at the extreme north-east, where Septimania had been lost for years. When he died in 788, Abd-ar-Rahman I left to his son, the pious Emir Hisham I (788–96), a military despotism, founded by his cruel and treacherous statesmanship, which made him admired and hated. The new emirate had, however, yet to be assured. Hisham gave excessive importance to the *faqihs* (professional theologians), who thronged the capital of Cordova and became as turbulent as their unlearned compatriots. A new faction, discontented like the others, had now appeared, the numerous renegades from Christianity or *Muladíes*, who were kept in powerless subjection. The

Fig. 76. Omayyad Mosque, Cordova

Emir Hakam I (796–822) dealt with the *faqihs* and other rebels in the spirit of his grandfather and with greater ferocity. Massacres at Cordova and Toledo tamed the two cities and many thousands were exiled. One body of 15,000 families emigrated to Alexandria, and, when expelled from Egypt, settled in Crete (827), to the long torment of the Byzantine Empire.

In spite of a great variety in events the reigns of Hakam I's successors, Abd-ar-Rahman II (822–52), Mahomet I (852–86), Mundhir (886–8), and Abdallah (888–912), were monotonous in their disorders, which assumed a provincial character. The Arabs in their two factions and the Berber tribes were settled in distinct districts; the *faqihs* were centered at Cordova; the renegades or Muladíes were strongest in certain cities, like Toledo and Seville, and in the mountains like the Sierra Nevada, while in city and countryside the staunch but subject Christians, the Mozarabs, who maintained their Church organization and special officials, were numerous and restive. They were apt to make common cause with the Muladíes in revolts. When submissive, they might be excited to provoke Moslem fanaticism to persecution, and might call for help on the Christians of the north. There was a period of martyrs (850–9), ended by the death of the zealous agitator, Eulogio, Archbishop of Toledo. Meantime provincial chiefs fought the emir and one another till the emirate seemed to be dissolving into petty dominions. The most formidable of the many foes of Abdallah was the ex-brigand, Omar ibn Hafsun, who led a revolt from the Sierra Nevada in

879, and became the leader of the Spaniards, Moslem and Christian. He dominated south Andalusia for years, whether at truce or war with the emir or with other dynasts, but he lost Moslem support eventually by turning Christian. Moslem Spain was rent by civil war when Abdallah died, and was endangered by external enemies. In the north the kingdom of León (as that of Asturias was now named), which claimed a kind of hegemony, had reached the Douro, the kingdom of Navarre was growing, and the Counts of Barcelona were consolidating the Spanish March into Catalonia. In the south there was an African danger. Although the Spanish Moslems did not recognize the Abbasid Caliphs of Baghdad, they were always orthodox. Now there was the heretic Fatimite Caliphate in Africa, and Shi'ite propaganda began. A local Mahdi for a time led the Berber tribes in the west.

From the long turmoil and disaster Andalusia was rescued by Abdallah's grandson, Abd-ar-Rahman III, the greatest of the Spanish Omayyads (912–61). In a few years everything had changed, for the emir was bold in war and equitable to the Mozarabs. The indomitable Omar ibn Hafsun was defeated, and after his death (917) his sons were gradually warred down till their last stronghold Bobastro was taken (928). It was not so difficult a task to put down the independent Arab and Berber princelings: in 930 the last was reduced. In 932 Toledo, which was a kind of republic protected by the Kings of León, surrendered to Abd-ar-Rahman, who thus achieved his aim of a united monarchy. In 929 he had assumed the titles of Caliph and Commander of the Faithful in rivalry with the Abbasids of Baghdad and the Fatimites of Africa. His success was partly due to his policy of promoting slaves to the highest offices instead of the great Moslem nobles. Hakam I had multiplied the foreign slaves in his bodyguard. They were called the 'mutes', for they knew no Arabic. Drawn from many countries by purchase or raiding, they included Galicians, Franks, Italians, and Slavs and others from the Black Sea, forming an important section of the troops and in the end a party in the State.

These successes were accompanied and followed by foreign wars to the north and south. That with the Christians to the north was chequered and stubborn. Ordoño II of León (914–24) and Sancho II (905–25) of Navarre were no contemptible foes, and they were aggressive. But they received a crushing defeat in 920, and on Ordoño II's death in 924 civil war in León lamed the Christians for some years. Then Ramiro II (931–50) vainly attempted to succour Toledo, and resumed the struggle in alliance with the rebel governor of Saragossa. In 937, however, the Caliph subdued Saragossa and forced Tota, Queen-regent of Navarre, to acknowledge his suzerainty. Yet two years later, owing to the resentments of the Arab nobles at their treatment by the Caliph, Ramiro gave him a terrible defeat. This reverse was without a sequel, since León was beset once more by internal discord. In the borderland round Burgos a great county, Castile, had been established under Fernán (Ferdinand) Gonzalez (923–70), who revolted against his overlord of León. He was subdued, but the enmity between León and Castile remained. Fernán, when Ramiro died, supported Sancho the Fat in rebellion. Although Ordoño III (950–7) won the contest with his half-brother, he sought peace with the Moslems. Sancho the Fat (957–66), become king, found Fernán at once his enemy. He was driven out and replaced by Ordoño IV the Bad. Abd-ar-Rahman intervened with success: his last achievement was to restore Sancho (960), and extort treaties from León, Navarre, and Castile.

The southern enemy was the Fatimite Caliph of Africa. Abd-ar-Rahman occupied Ceuta on the Moroccan coast, and set up a suzerainty on the littoral, but he made little headway, although he did forestall invasion, and it was the Fatimite's conquest of and removal to Egypt after his death which removed the danger. In all these years his fleet, not to mention Spanish pirates, controlled the western Mediterranean.

His internal government gave Andalusia a short-lived happiness. He established order and encouraged agriculture, industry, commerce, art, and science. He beautified Cordova until it rivalled Baghdad. 'Nothing', says Dozy, 'escaped that powerful, comprehensive intellect.' He grasped the smallest details and the loftiest conceptions. It was due to him that his son Caliph Hakam II (961–76), an ultra-learned bibliophile devoted to his library of 400,000 volumes, was nevertheless able to compel the faithless Sancho, Fernán Gonzalez, Navarre, and the Catalan counts to sue for peace. Civil war in León and the death of Fernán completed his security.

The most significant fact of Hakam's reign, however, was the rise to influence of a young Kalb noble, Mahomet ibn-Abi-Amir, a favourite of the Sultana Aurora. With her support, and after a campaign against the restless Christian states which revealed his signal military genius, he became within two years of Hakam's death *hajib*, or prime minister (978), of the child Caliph Hisham II (976–1009), who never issued from his tutelage as a spiritual figurehead. Aurora herself was excluded from power. The *hajib* proceeded to reform the army. He hired Berbers from Morocco and Spanish Christians from the north. More than all, to curb the power of the chiefs, the divisions of the army were no longer levied and commanded on the tribal system. He then took the offensive in the north in a victorious invasion (981), after which he assumed the title of Al-Mansur (the victorious) or Almanzor, by which he is known to history. The civil wars of León gave him every opportunity, while the Christians never ceased resistance. In his repeated campaigns he stormed Barcelona (985), León (987), and the holy shrine of Santiago de Compostela itself in Galicia (998), which he despoiled of its gates and the bells of its cathedral. In the year of his death (1002) he had marched into Castile.

375

Almanzor's tyranny and cruelty at home made him hated. The *faqihs* suspected his orthodoxy, but he outplayed them by burning the philosophical books in Hakam II's library. Loyalty to the Omayyads he tamed by dominating the all-but captive Caliph in spite of Aurora's efforts. He dazzled the people by his building—he himself worked as a labourer among a multitude of Christian captives to enlarge the great mosque of Cordova, now the cathedral. In it he placed the bells of Santiago as braziers. As king, for he took that title, he was strict in justice, a fosterer of prosperity, and a generous patron of letters. He was the idol of his soldiery. Of his greatness there can be no doubt.

Almanzor's son, Muzaffar, worthily continued his fighting tradition (1002–8), but was unable to turn the people from their loyalty to the Omayyads, their only bond of union, and when his brother, Abd-ar-Rahman, nicknamed Sanchuelo, a less able ruler, gained nomination as successor to the Caliphate from Hisham II, he fell in a revolution which promoted Mahomet II, an Omayyad, to the throne (1009). The new Caliph, however, emerging from nonentity, was incapable of uniting the factions, slaves, Berbers, and the rest. They fought for transitory candidates, while the reviving Christians of the north intervened in the internecine strife, in the course of which Cordova was pitilessly sacked by the Berbers. The welter became more confused until in December 1031 the last Omayyad, Hisham III, was deposed and the Caliphate was abolished. Moslem Spain split into warring provincial kingdoms (*reynos de Taifas*), which depended on mercenary soldiers.

The Christian states, in spite of their own dynastic rivalries, were progressive and rose to the occasion. They recovered and extended their territories. Alfonso V of León (999–1027) summoned a council and issued the *fuero* (code) of León with a view to reform. Sancho III the Great of Navarre (1000–35) conquered Castile and León proper, but divided his realm at his death among his sons. The eldest Garcia received Navarre, and thereby lost the opportunity of expansion, which a Moorish frontier gave. Ramiro I, who became first King of Aragon, although less well endowed, did possess such an outlet to the south of his narrow valley in the Pyrenees. Most fortunate and ablest was Ferdinand I (1035–65), whose share was the new and warlike kingdom of Castile. In 1037 he overthrew the rightful King of León, Bermudo III, and, lord of the two realms, could invade divided Andalusia. His contemporary, Raymond Berengar I of Barcelona (1035–76), was consolidating Catalonia. With them, not with the wealthy, wrangling Moors of the south, lay the future.

The brilliant Saracenic civilization of Moslem Spain rendered the Moors, even during their political decline under the *Reyes de Taifas*, the most cultured people of the West. They were a complex of varied races, tribes, and classes, which were usually at discord, but which each contributed something to the intellectual and material prosperity of Andalusia. The Arabs and Berbers preferred the country to the cities: hence Toledo, Seville, and the like were mainly inhabited by Muladíes and Mozarabs. There grew up a wealthy middle class from the profits of trade and industry, which held their workmen in subjection. Their manufactures, protected by the command of the sea, were exported over the Mediterranean, and enriched the Caliph's revenue by the duties paid. The Jews, relieved from Visigothic persecution, added greatly to the wealth of Cordova. The peasants, too, profited by the Moslem regime. Smallholders increased in number. Even the serfs, mostly Mozarabs, were better off. Their masters learnt the late Roman agricultural technique, which they improved by irrigation, and introduced plants as well as cattle-breeding. The Mozarabs, who, like Arabs and Berbers, dwelt in districts apart, were allowed their own local governor, the count, who administered the *Fuero Juzgo* of Visigothic times.

Fig. 77. Fuero Juzgo, *in Visio-gothic script (11th century)*

Literature and art were the glory of Moslem Spain, continuing after the fall of the Caliphate and finding their last refuge in the surviving kingdom of Granada, which was only conquered at the close of the Middle Ages. Literacy was far more widespread than in any other country of the West. Almost every branch of study was pursued, from poetry to medicine and philosophy. The literary tongue was Arabic, understood in all the Moslem world, although a vulgar Arabic and a vulgar Romance might be in common use, borrowing from one another. Arabic translations from the Greek and the philosophic and scientific works of eastern Moslems were imported, and Spain produced its own authors, of whom in the twelfth century the famous Averroes had the most enduring influence. The Jews shared in this enlightenment. When, from the tenth century onwards, Europeans from the north journeyed to Spain for access to oriental and ancient learning, it was to Jewish interpreters that they applied. For over two centuries Andalusia was a focus radiating intellectual progress.

The architecture of the Moors was an importation from the Moslem East, itself the offspring of early Byzantine and Persian building. The great mosque of Cordova, with its arches, columns, cupola, and decorated walls, is the most important survival from the Caliphate, but the style lived long and its devices, like the horse-shoe and cusped arch, spread northward to affect Languedoc. There spread, too, the Moslem arts and crafts. Carpets, curtains, cushions, silk embroidery, coloured glass and pottery, Cordovan leather-work (cordwain) and Toledo steel, found an avenue to the Christians from the Spanish Moors.

BOOK V

THE FOUNDATION OF WESTERN EUROPE

CHAPTER 15

THE FOUNDATION OF THE NORTHERN KINGDOMS

(I) ENGLAND IN THE NINTH CENTURY

King Offa of Mercia had united central and south-eastern England into a single state, for the subordinate rulers of Kent, etc., were kept in much subjection. There were, however, flaws in his edifice. Wessex and Northumbria were unlikely to admit Mercian supremacy longer than they could help, and in Kent, Sussex and Essex, as well as in East Anglia, there seems to have existed an aversion to the bloodily asserted Mercian dominion. Offa himself, to judge from the great work of Offa's Dyke, appears to have entertained little hope of expansion over Wales, and more conquests were needed for a stable kingdom. Further, it was unlucky that his son King Ecgfrith, for whom he had, in imitation of the Carolingians, introduced the ceremony of sacring, died within the year, and the approaching extinction of the royal house with its immemorial prestige was foreshadowed by the election of a distant kinsman, Coenwulf (796–821). Coenwulf did not lack energy, but there was a perceptible decline. He dropped the style of King of England. He at once fought the Welsh princes, a sign that they were no longer overawed. He overcame a revolt in Kent, and tried to conciliate the Archbishops of Canterbury by abolishing Offa's archbishopric of Lichfield, only to enter on a bitter quarrel with Archbishop Wulfred over some estates, a symptom perhaps of landed impoverishment. A war with Northumbria clearly brought no success. Later wars in Wales, which led to the passing conquest of Powys by his brother and successor, Ceolwulf I (821–3), evidently did not suffice to strengthen the kingship, for Ceolwulf was deposed and the new king, Beornwulf, was of a new stock. Every great noble might now think he could make a bid for the crown. The unity and solidity of Mercia disappeared with her age-old dynasty.

The opposite development was the destiny of Wessex. When Beorhtric, son-in-law and dependant of Offa, died in 802, his distant kinsman Egbert, who had been an exile at the court of Charlemagne, was elected king—we hear of no rival atheling—and revived his kingdom. He, too, attacked his Welsh neighbours of Cornwall, and, unlike the Mercians, found them conquerable (814). A revolt in 825 enabled him to deal with Cornwall as he pleased, to the increase of his own wealth and that of the West Saxon Church. There were but few immigrants, and the new shire remained a land of Cornish (i.e. West Welsh) speaking hamlets. Hardly was the conquest ended when Beornwulf of Mercia invaded Wiltshire and met with decisive overthrow at Ellendun (now Nether Wroughton). Events moved with dramatic speed. A West Saxon army was welcomed in Kent, Surrey, Sussex and Essex—probably Egbert's father Ealhmund had once been king in Kent—and Egbert's son Aethelwulf became sub-king of these districts, which felt more akin to Wessex than to Mercia. The change-over was complete, with Wessex now as the leading kingdom. The East Angles recovered their independence by slaying Beornwulf in battle. Egbert followed up the war, and in 829 drove Wiglaf, Beornwulf's second successor, from Mercia, while at Dore in the Peakland his supremacy was acknowledged by the Northumbrians. The West Saxon annalists vaunted him as the eighth Bretwalda. But it was a passing triumph. In two years Wiglaf was reigning again in Mercia and independent. Egbert's solid achievement was south of the Thames.

Aethelwulf (839–58) of Wessex bears a singular resemblance to Lewis the Pious; like him, he was fervently religious and devoid of the greed of conquest; but he was happier in his children, for his sons with one exception were dutiful and disposed to live in concord. Perhaps his conciliatory attitude towards Mercia, which he aided in a Welsh war (853), buried old rancours and eased a future union. Besides, the four remaining English kingdoms—Northumbria and East Anglia were the other two—had now to face a common and ever-growing danger. In 835 the Danish Vikings began their raids, their forces increasing almost yearly. In 838 a really large body landed in Cornwall and were joined by Cornish rebels. Over them Egbert won his last victory at Hingston Down by the river Tamar. In 841 a band ravaged Lindsey; in 844 another killed in a fray the King of Northumbria. These raids and their like, however destructive, were but a foretaste; they were hard to foresee and meet by local forces hastily gathered. It was in 851 that a fleet of 350 ships anchored in the Thames. The Danish army burnt Canterbury and London, and put Beorhtwulf of Mercia to flight. Then they recrossed the Thames, but they had given Aethelwulf time to muster the *fyrd* and lost heavily in their defeat at Aclea (unidentified). It was only a check, for they passed the winter in Thanet. The period of mere raids had closed.

Aethelwulf's devout disposition led him to quite exceptional acts in the comparative lull of Danish attacks on Wessex which ensued. In 855 he granted a tenth of his estates and the public dues and services from them to religious uses, a notable extension of Church wealth at the expense of the kingship. In the same year he departed on a long pilgrimage to Rome accompanied by his youngest son Alfred, who already as a child of four had made the journey and been decorated with consular insignia by the Pope. The journey was in the spirit of an elder time and may have knit Church and kingship more closely together, but Aethelwulf alienated men more alive to events by prolonging his absence and marrying a young wife in Judith, daughter of Charles the Bald. When he returned in 856, his warlike son Aethelbald took the crown, and civil war was only averted by a division, by which Aethelwulf was left with Kent and the east until his death (858). Aethelbald then created a scandal by marrying his stepmother —one may guess that her first marriage had never been consummated— while the next son, Aethelbert, took over their father's share. The division ended with Aethelbald's death (860), for happily the two next brothers, Aethelred and Alfred, put in no claim to sub-kingdoms. In 866 Aethelred I succeeded to the whole realm, when invasion and conquest loomed dark over England.

The Danes had already raided the coasts. Now in 865 a great Viking expedition for settlement as well as plunder was organized by the sons of Ragnar Lothbrok, Ivar the Boneless, Halfdan, and perhaps Ubbi, along with lesser kings and jarls. They disembarked in East Anglia, where they seized horses according to their wont, and proceeded northward to overthrow the rival kings of Northumbria and occupy the Vale of York (866). Anglian Northumbria never recovered its fighting strength or its civilization after this disaster, although native rulers held out in Bernicia, to which later the name of Northumberland was confined. The Viking host, however, was anything but satisfied. They forced Mercia into paying a ransom, Danegeld as it was called, one year, and in the next (869) made a long harrying march back to East Anglia. There is hardly a doubt that in it the famous abbeys of east Mercia went to ruin with their treasures and culture. The Anglo-Saxons had shown little mercy in their internal wars, but cathedral and monastery had been untouched sanctuaries. To the chronicler the Vikings were above all heathen foes. In November they crushed East Anglian resistance at Hoxne in Suffolk, when they martyred the valiant young King Edmund, steadfast to the Faith. He almost at once was venerated by his subjects, but they were helpless under heathen dominion. The leading Viking was now Halfdan, and yet unplundered England allured the host. Late in 870 they moved to Reading, which they turned into a fortified camp whence to harry the country. One victory was won by King Aethelred I and his brother Alfred (January 871), but other battles went against the West Saxons till Alfred, who had succeeded his brother, was forced to buy the departure of the still multiplying Vikings by a Danegeld. The hard fighting at any rate had saved Wessex from the fate of

11. England, 802–1066

(a) The House of Wessex, 802–1066

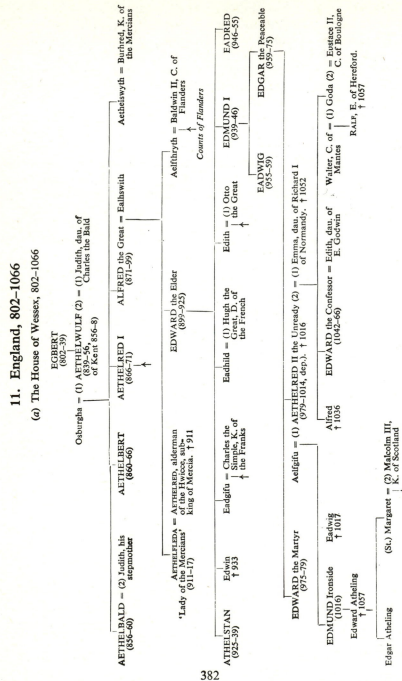

(b) The Danes in England, 1013–42

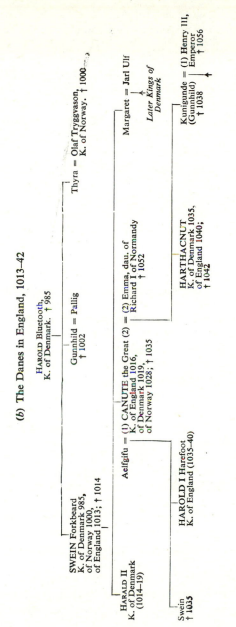

HAROLD Bluetooth,
K. of Denmark. † 985

SWEIN Forkbeard
K. of Denmark 985,
of Norway 1000,
of England 1013; † 1014

Gunnhild = Pallig
† 1002

Thyra = Olaf Tryggvason,
K. of Norway. † 1000

HARALD II
K. of Denmark
(1014–19)

Aelfgifu = (1) CANUTE the Great (2) = (2) Emma, dau. of
K. of England 1016,   Richard I of Normandy
of Denmark 1019,   † 1052
of Norway 1028; † 1035

Margaret = Jarl Ulf

Later Kings of
Denmark

Swein
† 1035

HAROLD I Harefoot
K. of England (1035–40)

HARTHACNUT
K. of Denmark 1035,
of England 1040;
† 1042

Kunigunde = (1) Henry III,
(Gunnhild)   Emperor
† 1038   † 1056

383

East Anglia, and the accession of Alfred the Great (871–99), one of the most remarkable men of all times, was a boon beyond price to his imperilled people.

Mercia became the principal victim of the army. A heavy Danegeld only bought a retreat from the south, first to York, where there was a revolt of the English vassal-king, and then to Lindsey, as headquarters for devastation. In 873 the Danes camped in the centre at Repton. Burhred of Mercia lost hope so completely that he abdicated and fled to Rome. In his stead the Danes set up a puppet-king, the 'unwise king's thane', Ceolwulf II, on the disgraceful terms that he should reign on their behalf and surrender Mercia when they demanded. Evidently fresh Vikings were expected, and evidently there was no united purpose in the army. Halfdan with part proceeded northward, where his wide and savage raids incidentally caused the Bishop of Lindisfarne to start on long wanderings with the relics of St Cuthbert. In 876 Halfdan 'dealt out' Deira, or rather the present Yorkshire, to his followers, 'who thenceforward continued ploughing and tilling it'. The settlement of Danes, 'holds', freemen, and freedmen, was a large and genuine migration, which made Yorkshire a half-Scandinavian kingdom. Halfdan the Viking did not remain as its king. Next year, to all seeming, he was slain by a Norse Viking in Ireland.

The other host of the Danes at Repton, led by three kings, of whom the chief was Guthrum, moved eastward to Cambridge. They were restless and less unanimous. In 877 they took from Ceolwulf the east of Mercia, and very large numbers thickly settled the land between the river Welland and the Humber in five disjointed divisions, each under a *jarl*, round Lincoln, Nottingham, Derby, Leicester, and Stamford, which became known as the Five Boroughs. But others under Guthrum hoped for more; they were in touch with kinsmen from Ireland. A first combined attempt by land and sea on Dorset came to grief, but Guthrum was able to retreat to Gloucester. A small force which had been harrying Dyved in South Wales under Ubbi now crossed to Devon, where it was destroyed by local levies. Even earlier in January 878 Guthrum made an unexpected onslaught on Alfred from Gloucester. The surprised king could just flee west of Selwood, while Guthrum ravaged the central shires of Wessex irresistibly. It seemed that the end had come. But Alfred held out among the herdsmen in the marsh-island of Athelney, where noble and churl gathered round him. In Selwoodshire lay much of the royal lands. In May he could make a sudden levy of the fyrd and fall on Guthrum at Edington in Wiltshire. So complete was the Danish defeat in this decisive battle that Guthrum made a peace at Chippenham (so-called of Wedmore). He was not only to evacuate Wessex but to become a Christian. Expulsion from England was obviously impossible, and conversion was the indispensable first step towards civilized intercourse.

384

Such a policy required time to bear its full fruit, but an immediate return was shown when Guthrum did not link up with a fresh Viking fleet in the Thames, and when in autumn 879 he left Gloucestershire for East Anglia. A change in western Mercia from the river Mersey to the Thames may have hastened him. The useless Ceolwulf II disappears, and his place was taken, not by a king but by an alderman, Aethelred of the Hwicce, who accepted King Alfred as his overlord and later married his daughter Aethelfleda. It was a substantial increase of Alfred's power and of English unity, voluntary, not enforced. The effect was seen when Alfred was impelled to take the offensive. For the time the Danish army was occupied with the allotment of lands, in which its lack of cohesion was manifest. King Guthrum and his men took East Anglia, Essex, and London at least; four *jarls* with theirs settled down round Northampton, Huntingdon, Cambridge, and Bedford. But Guthrum and his men could not keep the peace. When a Viking host, bought off from France, attacked the Thames estuary in 884, they joined in, and on its repulse received Alfred's counterblow. The result was 'Alfred and Guthrum's Peace' (*c*. 886), by which London and the districts west of the river Lea were ceded to Alfred, and the further frontier was drawn along Watling Street. Alfred re-fortified London, a gain of the utmost defensive value, and delivered these recovered Mercian districts to his son-in-law Aethelred, with a moderation as wise as it was honourable. 'All the English', we are told, 'submitted to him except those who were under the Danes.' The King of the West Saxons was becoming King of the English by common consent. The treaty gave, too, a boundary which was both racial and legal. East of it lay the Danelaw, densely settled by the Vikings, with its own Scandinavian institutions and law, and long influenced even in speech by the colonists.

There was yet one more Viking invasion to be repelled. Led by chiefs like Hasting, a restless host, which had endured hard measure on the Continent, made persistent raids from the Danelaw chiefly on western Mercia from 892 to 896. But the Danes reaped more blows than plunder, and at last sailed to more profitable warfare in France. On 26 October 899 King Alfred died in peace.

Alfred's victorious defence was due not only to his own heroic constancy and leadership and the loyalty of his people but also to his improvements in military organization in the intervals of peace. It was always difficult to hold the fyrds of the shires together for long; the needs of their farms drew the men away. Alfred divided the fyrd into two parts, which could relieve one another at convenient intervals and thus continue a campaign. More important still was the gradual erection of strongholds, some twenty-five, round Wessex, the only efficient means of protection against raids, just as on the Continent. In Mercia, too, the same policy began. These 'burhs' (boroughs) were mostly fortified by ditch, earthen rampart, and palisade.

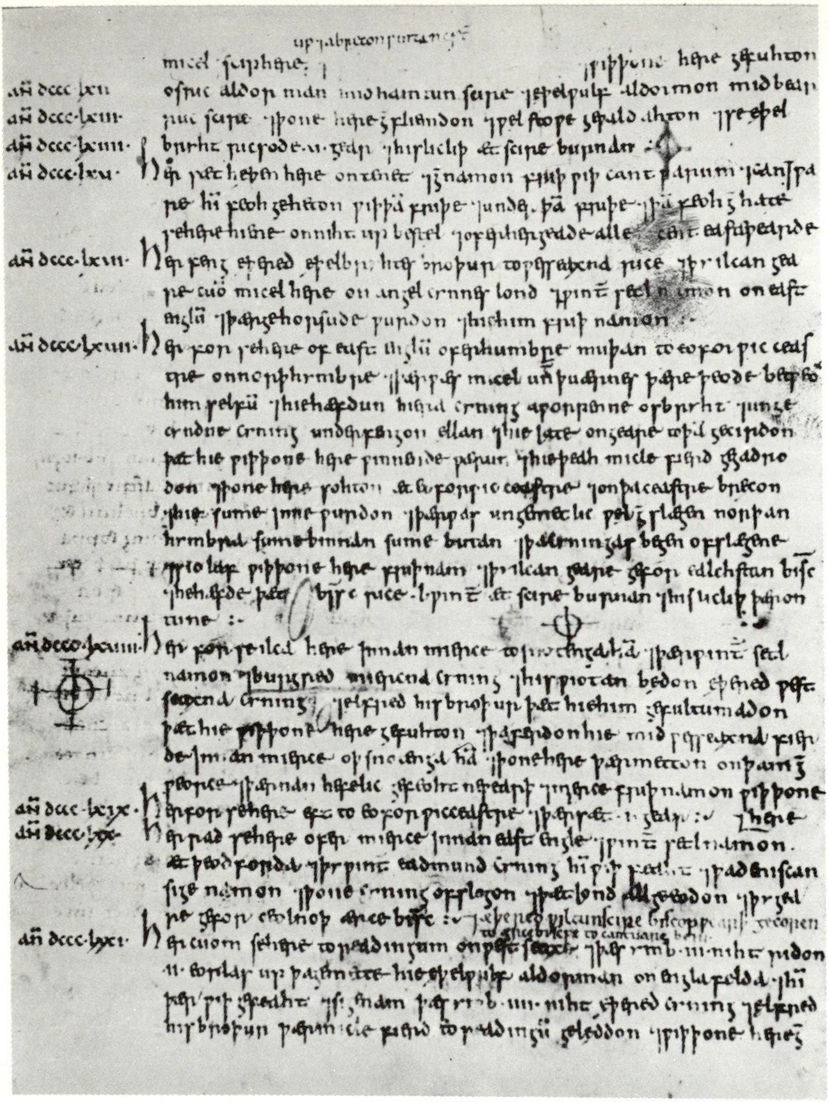

Fig. 78. *The* Anglo-Saxon Chronicle

Some were old towns. They were garrisoned by quotas levied from allotted districts round, which were also charged with their construction and repair. In spite of much harmful slackness, the measure slowly took effect and did much to encourage the growth of a true town-dwelling class. The best

386

defence of all, that by the long-neglected sea, was also undertaken by the king. He built improved warships and enlisted Frisian sailors, but a small royal navy, although it did good service, was not capable of warding-off the numberless, ubiquitous Viking ships which thronged the seas. None the less, Alfred's forces, the mounted thanes and their men, the more workable fyrd, the borough-men, and even the slender fleet were the indispensable basis of defence and future reconquest.

Most noteworthy, however, of all his reforms, the more marvellous because it was carried on amid his incessant activity in government and war, was his successful endeavour to revive religion and learning, which had been almost crushed out by the Viking inroads. He aimed not merely at revival, hard enough, but at a new and higher standard of secular culture. He was a man of thought and reflection as well as of action, and his early travels had perhaps shown him the way. He gathered round him from Mercia and elsewhere a group of scholars, one of whom, Bishop Asser the Welshman, wrote his *Life*, an intimate portrait. He himself learnt to read in youth, and late in life under torments of disease acquired Latin. With their help he issued English translations of Bede's *History*, Gregory's *Pastoral Care*, Orosius's *History of the World*, and Boethius's *Consolation of Philosophy*, and an adaptation from St Augustine's *Soliloquies*. They were intended to educate thane and priest. The scholarly were to proceed to Latin and wider learning. He did not hesitate to interpolate his authors —he inserted the geography of Scandinavia from merchants' reports in Orosius—and his personal views and character of rare nobility shine out in his writings. In them and the *Anglo-Saxon Chronicle*, which his influence inspired, we have the real starting-point of English prose. To these works Alfred added the arduous revision of the West Saxon, Kentish, and Mercian Laws. There are few lives in history which reach the level of this king of the Dark Ages.

(2) THE SUCCESSORS OF ALFRED, 899–975

The reign of Alfred's son Edward the Elder (899–925) proved the strength of the monarchy and the dynasty of Cerdic, the only survivor of the old Anglo-Saxon royal houses, and fortunate in producing a succession of able if short-lived rulers. The new king was soon involved in war with the Danelaw, to which his rebel cousin, Aethelwald, took to flight. When this was closed after the atheling's death in battle, hostilities broke out with the Danes of York, which resulted in a complete victory for Edward and Aethelred of Mercia at Tettenhall in Staffordshire (August 910), and marked the beginning of the reconquest of the Danelaw. This was furthered by the death of Aethelred, for he was succeeded anomalously by his wife, Edward's sister Aethelfleda, as 'Lady of the Mercians' (911–17), who rivalled her brother in war and organization. Edward, however, took over

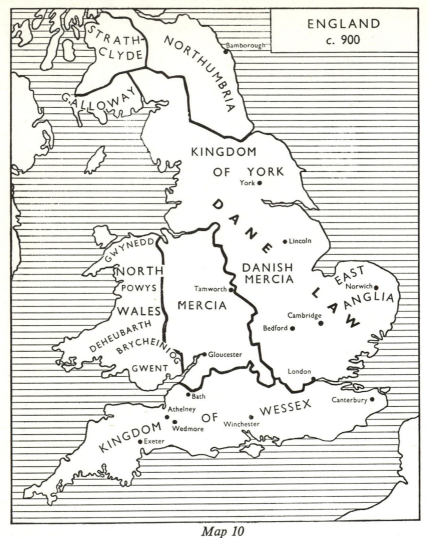

Map 10

London and Oxford. Their plan of reconquest was to move forward
gradually in the southern Danelaw, fortifying 'burhs', first within their own
frontier and then beyond it. Probably at this time, or soon after, English
Mercia was remapped in new shires, on the West Saxon model, each with
a 'burh' as its centre. The ancient tribal regions, small and great, vanished
in the process. In 917 the decisive campaign took place by which the
Danish *jarls* and their hosts were forced to submit to Edward and Aethelfleda. They retained their law and autonomy, but their territories could be

388

reckoned as shires. In fact, their resistance was crippled by their lack of cohesion; they kept the lands they had hungered for, Christianity was making peaceful headway, and the wilder spirits, who retained the Viking ethos, were finding a congenial outlet in the new duchy of Normandy, to which they drifted. Edward in 918 was able to exact allegiance as far as the Humber. Meantime, on his sister's death, he extended his direct rule over Mercia. He might well entitle himself King of the Anglo-Saxons.

Edward was now admitted by the Welsh kinglets to be their overlord; they had looked to his father for protection. But the Vikings of Northumbria were different neighbours to deal with. During his advance northward another contingent of invading settlers, this time from the mixed Norsemen of Ireland, had mingled in the broils. They occupied the coast of Lancashire and the Lake district, pushing inland over the Pennines into Yorkshire and south Bernicia, defeating both the English of Northumbria and the Scots and Britons of Strathclyde. In 919 their leader, Regnald of Waterford, made himself King of Danish York, while next year more Vikings from Dublin were active. Edward's bold advance in strength overawed all these mutual enemies, each eager for his support. At Bakewell he received envoys from all acknowledging his superiority. Such high feudal claims were based in a later age on these demonstrations of deferential friendship that the fact has been disputed. But probability is in favour of it as a natural move by competitors for Edward's valuable alliance.

When a real dominion beyond Humber was established by King Athelstan, Edward's equally gifted son (925–39), it was looked at askance by the northerners. In 927 he used civil war among the Northumbrian Danes and Norsemen to annex the kingdom of York. If for the moment Britons and Scots beyond it, as well as the Britons of Wales, were obsequious, Athelstan was soon (934) leading an expedition by land and sea beyond the Forth, and in 937 he had to meet a formidable coalition, in which Constantine of the Scots, the Britons of Strathclyde, and Olaf Guthfrithson of Dublin with his Viking fleet all took part. Athelstan overthrew the allies in his crowning victory of Brunanburh (still unidentified), and could use the vaunting title of King of All Britain till his death. He was renowned abroad, for his sisters were sought in marriage by the greatest potentates, the Carolingian Charles the Simple, Hugh the Great, Duke of the French, and Otto the Great, the future Emperor. Harald Fairhair of Norway wooed his friendship, and there are traces of English traders as far as Italy.

At home it is likely that he rearranged the local divisions and their assessment in the southern Danelaw, where the 'armies' were ruled by Danish 'earls' (the English form of *jarls*), while East Anglia proper was placed under an English noble, Athelstan the Half-king. North of the Welland the Danes were left to themselves. With all this, however, the

Fig. 79. King Athelstan presenting Bede's Life *to St Cuthbert*

lawlessness due to nearly a century of raiding warfare was obviously rampant. Athelstan's laws largely concern the peace and the repression of thieving. More bishoprics in Wessex, created by Edward and Athelstan, were another method of fostering civilization.

390

The testing-time of Athelstan's work was the reign of his young brother Edmund I (939–46). Could the union, even loose, of Anglo-Saxon England and the Danelaw be maintained? The most discordant and separatist element was provided by the Irish-Norse Vikings who were amalgamating with and dominating Danes and barbarized Angles north of the Humber: they were open to the Norsemen of Dublin and the Irish Sea. It was a question whether the Danes of the Five Boroughs between Humber and Welland, not to mention their kinsmen farther south, were sufficiently weaned by Christianity and settlement from the Viking instinct for raids and adventurous anarchy. Scarcely was Athelstan dead when Olaf Guth-frithson sailed from Dublin, seized the kingdom of York, significantly aided by its Anglian archbishop, Wulfstan, and marched southward. Edmund was obliged to consent to a peace which ceded to Olaf the Five Boroughs as far as Watling Street (940). The new-made union seemed to have foundered in disaster, but it was more seaworthy than appeared; perhaps there was even an English party in Yorkshire, and Danes of the Five Boroughs did not love their wild Norse conquerors. Luck helped, for Olaf died next year while raiding English Bernicia, and his successor was his cousin Olaf Cuaran Sihtricson, a feebler personage. Edmund fell on him, recovering the willing Five Boroughs, and soon after, while rival leaders paralysed the Vikings, annexed once more the kingdom of York (944). He abandoned his brother's more forward policy, and endeavoured to buy the alliance of the anti-Viking King of Scots, Malcolm, by ceding to him Strathclyde (Cumbria), which he had overrun (945). But it was not in fact his to give or Malcolm's to take.

Edmund was much influenced by churchmen, like Oda, the Dane whom he named Archbishop of Canterbury, a speaking fact for the conversion of the Danes, and St Dunstan, whom he made Abbot of Glastonbury. He even made an attempt to modify the pernicious blood-feud. In local government a dangerous change was becoming visible in his day. The English aldermen were ruling more than one shire—there were only three south of the Thames—and thus on the way to be overmighty subjects, while the king's predominance in landed wealth began to fail. Very probably the several shires were being also provided with king's reeves to look after royal interests, the later shire-reeves or sheriffs, but even when their office developed, they would hardly outweigh the aldermen without a strong local basis in land.

Edmund was murdered in a brawl, which pictures the times, in his own hall, and his brother Eadred (946–55) had to wrestle once more with the Viking anarchy of Northumbria. Turn and turn about he strove with the last great Viking of the ancient stamp, the exiled Eric Bloodaxe, son of Harald Fairhair, and Olaf Cuaran of Dublin, who alternated in seizing the kingdom of York. At last in 954 Eadred finally took possession, Eric being killed in the process, and granted all Northumbria as an earldom to the English Oswulf, who had ruled the remnant of Bernicia from Bamborough as 'high-reeve'. The welding, or rather the soldering, of England into a single kingdom had been achieved.

It seemed about to break in two when Eadred, a chronic invalid, died, leaving the kingdom to Edmund's elder son Eadwig, a boy of fifteen whose unlucky petulance alienated the northern nobles. He fell out with them at his coronation, and unwisely banished Abbot Dunstan, who intervened. In 957 Mercians and Northumbrians raised his younger brother Edgar to be their king, while Wessex, the stronghold of the house of Cerdic, remained faithful to Eadwig until his death (959), when Edgar 'the Peaceable' succeeded him. The two boys and their followers had never gone to war.

Edgar's reign (959–75) forms an epoch. The king had strength enough to control and the conciliatory wisdom to lead the powerful magnates. Besides, he and his sons were the only male heirs descended from Alfred, and both by real conviction and by policy he favoured the able churchmen on whose support he relied. The movement towards renewed religious zeal and Church reform, which had long been brewing, came to its own in his days. By his death the political power and the landed endowments of the Church, so impoverished by Danish conquest and wars, were not far from doubled. Oda of Canterbury (942–60) and Bishop Aelfheah of Winchester (934–51) headed the first stirrings for change, but St Dunstan proved the most influential, if not the most radical, leader of reform. From the time of his recall (958) to be first Bishop of Worcester, then of London, and finally Archbishop of Canterbury (960), he had the king's ear. A chief objective of the reformers was the restoration of monasticism, in which their endeavours ran parallel to the contemporary movement on the Continent and soon borrowed from it. From the time of Theodore the monasteries provided the homes of culture and devotion, whence religious education and zeal could spread to the secular clergy and even the laity. But since the coming of the Vikings, if not before, the monasteries had been ruined, and their lands, churches, and libraries lost within the Danelaw and beyond. Those that survived in Wessex and English Mercia as well as the colleges of clerks round cathedrals mostly no longer followed the Rule of St Benedict. The secular clerks who belonged to them were as often as not married men, living in their own houses a half-secular life and negligent of their duties. King Alfred, who draws a dismal picture of the destruction of learning and the disappearance of an educated clergy in his days, had made an essential beginning: it was now the time to develop what that benefactor of humanity had made possible.

Oda had attempted to enforce clerical celibacy. Aelfheah had persuaded St Dunstan to become a monk, and from Glastonbury the true monastic life spread. Two men were the most active reformers. The hard-handed

Aethelwold from Glastonbury, a harsh zealot, made the revived abbey of Abingdon a Benedictine model. As Bishop of Winchester (963–84) he violently ejected with Edgar's help the secular clerks from his cathedral, and others, too, in other churches he replaced by monks. But he did not stop with his diocese. With Edgar's benefactions and authority he refounded the fenland monasteries of Ely, Peterborough (Medeshamstede), and Thorney. It was both a testimony to the progress Christianity was making in the southern Danelaw and a potent means for overcoming Danish paganism. The English earls of East Anglia and Essex seconded the movement: Aethelwin, son of the 'Half-king', was joint founder of the new model abbey of Ramsey along with Oswald, Bishop of Worcester (961–92). The latter was a born administrator, possessed of a gentler temper than Aethelwold. His uncle Oda, when he decided on the monastic profession, had sent him to be trained at the abbey of Fleury on the Loire, then famous as an exemplar of Benedictine life, where he himself, although archbishop, took the vows. It was the usages of Fleury that Oswald introduced in his new foundation at Ramsey, but at Worcester he was content to bring in monks gradually as the secular clerks died off. The general result of Aethelwold's and Oswald's activities was a revival of strict Benedictine life in England. The seal was set on it at

Fig. 80. *King Edgar presenting the charter of New Minster, Winchester, to Christ*

Edgar's request by the promulgation at Winchester (*c.* 970) of the *Regularis Concordia Anglicae Nationis*, a composite Rule embodying customs promulgated by St Benedict of Aniane and in use at Fleury and at Ghent, where St Dunstan had spent his exile. Thus monasticism was revived and made uniform and its precepts made known in Alfred's fashion to those least equipped with Latinity.

The movement for reform was not confined to the advance of monasticism. St Dunstan in his diocese was concerned with the behaviour of parish priests and the laity as well. Nor did it cease with the death of its protagonists. Bishops, often drawn from the monks, continued busy. Aelfric, Abbot of Eynsham (*fl.* 1000), wrote sermons and lives of saints in skilful English for priest and layman, and he was not alone in his troublous times. One may guess that the presence among the later invaders of many Christians to a large extent protected monastery and cathedral from desecration and thus prevented the erasing of Christian culture in the lands they pillaged, as had happened when the Viking army could be best named 'the heathen host'.

Edgar's religious zeal did not divert him from his secular duties. To him is due the 'ordinance of the hundred', by which he prescribed the regular meeting and procedure of those local courts for the subdivisions of the shire which had come into being. For the Danelaw indeed he hardly dared to legislate, but privileges to the fenland abbeys had a secular as well as a religious purpose, which must have tended indirectly to the increase of royal control there and elsewhere. There are grounds for thinking that private jurisdiction in minor offences and the fines for them had earlier been granted to some lords of land, whether levied in the hundred-court or in a lord's court for the land involved, a jurisdiction denominated 'sake and soke'. In Edgar's day, besides the piecemeal kind of grant, we find blocks of hundreds, irrespective of ownership, given to Ely and Peterborough with all royal dues, services, and profits of jurisdiction. The monks would be more dutiful agents than Danish lords. Similar grants applying to his episcopal estates, thus turned into irregular hundreds, were made to Oswald of Worcester. In one way it was a dangerous retreat of the kingship from its direct rule, as well as a loss of income, and was parallel to the disintegration of government in favour of local lords in the Carolingian Empire, but it was also a check on the provincial magnates who had in reality dominated many hundred-courts or taken by grant the royal dues on their lands. After Edgar's death a violent reaction against the new monks was led by Aelfhere, alderman of Mercia, with some success in his shires but with failure in East Anglia.

While Edgar lived, the peace he maintained made a great impression. He strengthened the Church and his own power in the northern Danelaw by appointing Oswald to be Archbishop of York (971) while he kept his see of Worcester. It was an arrangement which rendered the rich, secure southern bishopric a prop to the weakened archdiocese, and was repeated later. Similarly, the diocese of Dorchester-on-Thames now extended to the Humber. Edgar himself exercised, it appears, some sort of superiority over the lesser kings of Britain, and it is probable that he secured its acceptance from Kenneth II, King of Scots, by ceding to him the ill-defended district of Lothian from the Forth to the river Tweed. It was a change big with future consequences. For Edgar it was no substantial loss: the only loser was the English earl of the Bernician remnant, an autonomous dynast, who won peace at any rate.

(3) ENGLISH AND DANISH KINGS

A latent danger to the English kingdom lay in the early deaths of the Alfredian house, hitherto concealed by hereditary ability. To it was now added the unfitness, complete and fatal, of its only heir. Edgar's elder son, Edward the Martyr, a mere boy (975–9), was treacherously murdered in cold blood in the interests of his stepbrother, a child of ten, Aethelred II, whom his subjects were to name with a bitter play on the meaning of his name ('noble counsel') 'the Unready' (*unred*) or 'Counsel-less'. When he grew up sluggish and weak with fits of stupid violence, yet secured by his birth from competition, he was incapable of giving a common purpose to the rival provincial nobles of southern England. North of the river Welland Edgar's personal ascendancy had veiled the weakness of the monarchy. There even he had little land or revenue; the Danish earls ruled as they pleased; the Church was poor and backward between Welland and Tees.

Meantime the danger from Scandinavia was recrudescent. Native dynasties were giving a new unity to Denmark and Norway, and while their first effect was to cause exiles and malcontents to seek fortune abroad as Vikings, their second was that the new kings turned to gratify their own ambitions and to reward their restless followers by organized invasions for conquest. England's weakness was soon realized. After sporadic descents the first serious raid was led in 991 by Olaf Tryggveson, an exile of the Norse royal house, who after defeating Brihtnoth, the earl of Essex, at Maldon, a combat described in a famous lay, ravaged Wessex till he was bought off by a Danegeld. The quality of Aethelred's government was now obvious. In 994 Olaf in league with Swein, the temporarily exiled King of Denmark, was repulsed from London by its sturdy citizens, but ravaged Wessex until he was bought off again. Happily, he was becoming a Christian, and this time he undertook to attack England no more, a promise he kept. He then sailed to make himself King of Norway, while the heathen Swein, his hereditary foe, likewise departed to recover Denmark. Their English spoils gave both the means they needed.

Severe, almost permanent, raiding by other Vikings continued. Such was English incompetence that Aethelred employed one, Pallig, Swein's brother-in-law, to repel them, but Pallig proved faithless, and another Danegeld bought off the host (1002). At the same time Aethelred made his second marriage with Emma, sister of the Duke of Normandy, possibly to gain a friend who was a power with the Vikings. The marriage was to give an unexpected turn to later history. Then Aethelred planned his crowning folly. On St Brice's Day (13 November) he ordered the massacre of the Danes in his service. Among them was Gunnhild, Pallig's wife and King Swein's sister, then held as a hostage. This atrocious, barbaric crime was the very thing to make Swein a mortal enemy and added to his ambition to conquer England.

He was ready for the war. He had regained Denmark and had conquered Norway from Olaf Tryggvason. The overflowing forces of both were at his call. He began an almost systematic campaign of remorseless harrying in 1003, which with small intermission lasted for ten years. The English rulers seemed dazed and were totally incapable of acting in concert. Heavy Danegelds were uselessly paid. Aethelred's contribution was to promote an intriguing turncoat, Eadric 'Streona' (probably 'the Grasper'), to be alderman of English Mercia, of which key-position he made unscrupulous use. Although Swein had reverted to Christianity, a large proportion of his Vikings were old-time heathens, and a body of them brutally murdered Alfheah (St Alphege), Archbishop of Canterbury, who refused to ransom himself. Their leader, Thorkell the Tall, thereupon took service with Aethelred. This brought Swein in person back (1013) to deal the finishing blows. He anchored in the Humber among friendly Danes, and marched south. Only London stoutly held out, and Aethelred fled to Normandy. Swein was really King of England when he suddenly died (1014). Norway was rising under Olaf II while his son Harald II succeeded in Denmark. Thither sailed his second son Canute (Knut) with the Danes to claim his share.

Aethelred was now recalled on promises of amendment, but he characteristically put his trust in the greedy Eadric, and rancorously attacked the Danes of the Five Boroughs, as if to widen the breaches in England. Here a new protagonist arose in his eldest son by his first marriage, Edmund Ironside, whose career showed at once that English and settled Danes only needed a sturdy leader instead of the 'redeless' king and the provincial potentates, engrossed in their lands and shires, to put up a gallant fight for their country. Edmund, however, had barely time to gain the support of the Five Boroughs by baffling Eadric's greedy schemes there when in 1015 Canute, now reconciled to his brother, returned with a formidable fleet to Wessex. Eadric's prompt treason enabled him to ravage unhindered as far as York, where he connived in the murder of the Yorkshire earl, Uhtred, and replaced him by the Norwegian Eric. He was now master of all England save London and the south-east, where at last Aethelred closed his baneful reign (1016). With this paralysing incubus removed, Edmund, chosen king by the Londoners, could rally the patriotic to the offensive. He roused the men of the old Alfredian land beyond Selwood once more, and drove Eadric and the Danes to retreat, relieved London which Canute was besieging, and received the perilous adhesion of the turncoat Eadric. This was his undoing, for Eadric deserted in the decisive battle of Ashingdon in Essex against Canute. Yet he was by no means overthrown, and Canute was content with Eadric's mediation to divide England with him by treaty. Edmund Ironside kept Wessex south of the Thames: the rest was Canute's. Future plans of either were cut short in a few weeks by Edmund's sudden death at Oxford, perhaps by foul play. The hopes of resistance vanished.

Canute was now King of England (1016–35). Viking as he was, and he late or never put off the barbaric ethos, he genuinely believed in the Christian faith and he was a statesman of great ability, who admired and aimed at the higher civilization he saw in the Christian West. He wooed the Church, and endeavoured to give his conquest the peace and justice it had lost in the degenerate days of Aethelred the Unready. First, however, he had rougher work to do, which it was not in his nature to shun. He hunted down Eadwig, Edmund's full brother, and Edmund's infant sons were only saved by exile and the mercy of their foreign hosts, who sent them out of reach to Hungary. Eadric Streona, always untrustworthy, was soon slain by his latest master, as well as others less unpopular. The two sons of Aethelred by his second marriage were safe in Normandy, being bred as Normans, but Canute made their kinsman, the duke, his ally by marrying their mother Emma, after repudiating his own half-wife, the English Aelfgifu. Viking earls held Northumbria, East Anglia, and key districts, while in less important parts pro-Danish English earls were promoted—earls, no longer aldermen. There was no systematic forfeiture, but an abundant sprinkling of Scandinavians and their followers were endowed over southern England. They were a garrison in effect, and the greater part of the remaining Vikings were paid off by an enormous Danegeld.

Fig. 81. King Canute and Queen Aelfgifu

The ravaged country must have been severely impoverished, for taxation continued to support forty ships and the permanent bodyguard of 'house-carls', not to mention further taxes for the wars. But Canute used his heavy hand to promote peace and justice in alliance with the Church. In 1019, before sailing to secure Denmark from competitors on his brother's death, he held a great moot at Oxford, where he declared he would govern by the law of Edgar. He was a master of the art of propaganda, all the more so because it was based on fact. When in 1020 he returned as King of

Denmark, killing the last Cerdicing in England and appointing the Sussex notable, Godwin, who had married his kinswoman, Gytha, to be earl of Wessex, he proclaimed his intention to rule England by the advice of the bishops, and this was really the keynote of his policy. He became a devout son of the Church; there were few minsters he did not enrich; he founded monasteries, turning the secular college of Bury St Edmunds into one of the wealthiest; and he richly atoned for St Alphege's murder by great gifts to Canterbury. England was his favourite residence. He renewed old legislation with additions in the footsteps of his predecessors. When he warred in Scandinavia with English aid, he claimed he was defending England, and after some vicissitudes he conquered Norway from the Christian Olaf II (1028), and maintained his grip on his native Denmark. In 1027 he went on pilgrimage to Rome, witnessing the imperial coronation of his mighty neighbour Conrad II. He characteristically took the occasion to publish in England the benefits he had secured for traders and pilgrims, and his own resolve to amend his sins and forbid oppression. Soon after he took up the defence of the north against the King of Scots, who had routed the Northumbrians at Carham some years earlier, and enforced some kind of submission, but the frontier remained at the Tweed. In short, he earned the title of 'the Great', which crowned his variegated career.

When Canute died in 1035, however, his composite dominion was already breaking up, for Norway had revolted under St Olaf's son, Magnus. His son and heir by Emma, Harthacnut, succeeded in Denmark with the Norwegian war on his hands, and this allowed an English faction, led by Leofric of Mercia, to set up Aelfgifu's son, Harold Harefoot, as king (1035–40). This worthless young man cruelly murdered Aethelred's eldest surviving son Alfred, who came to visit his mother Queen Emma and was captured and delivered to him by Earl Godwin, while Emma fled to Flanders. When Harthacnut at last appeared with a fleet Harold I opportunely died, and his brother's succession was not contested. He proved oppressive and disliked, but his early death in 1042 'as he stood at his drink' extinguished the line of Canute and the Danish rule.

While Denmark was in civil war, there was small choice before the English magnates. They elected the surviving son of Aethelred and Emma, Edward, later called 'the Confessor', who came over from his Norman exile. He was in a difficult position, bred abroad and heir of an uprooted, if still revered, dynasty, and faced by powerful nobles, who monopolized power in their earldoms and felt no hereditary loyalty. He was nearly forty years old and a confirmed bachelor, an unlucky trait for a depleted line. Nor had he the dominating character and youthful resilience which alone could have reversed the heavy odds against him. But he made a prolonged and sometimes skilful effort to overcome them. His bent towards religion and his attractive personality, combined with the evils which came after him, enshrined his memory as a saint to later generations. He naturally filled his court with Normans and Bretons whom he could trust, and this turned out to be a serious weakness, for they alienated native support. It ultimately led to the Norman Conquest, since Edward, stripped of English relatives by Canute, looked towards his French connexions and gave them a foothold for their ambitions. He did not, however, promote many to high positions—probably because the ruling cliques were not to be displaced from power. But he made his nephew, Ralf of the Vexin, an earl in the west, and a Breton Ralf his 'staller' with eastern estates, while his friend Robert, Abbot of Jumièges, became Bishop of London. At the same time the great magnates were stronger than ever. Leofric ruled northern Mercia, Siward all Northumbria. Most of all Godwin, in spite of the king's dislike, increased his territory. His eldest son Swein received a part of south-west Mercia, his second, Harold, East Anglia, his nephew Beorn from Denmark a south Midland earldom. Lands, including royal estates, were given them. Queen Emma was deprived of most of her dower. Edward himself was obliged to contract a nominal marriage with Godwin's daughter Edith (1045).

A chance of escape for the king was offered by the disgraceful conduct of Earl Swein, which culminated in the specially treacherous murder of his cousin, Earl Beorn. Godwin stupidly supported the culprit, and so lost influence that Edward could make his friend Robert Archbishop of Canterbury and another Norman, William, Bishop of London. Matters came to a head when Edward's brother-in-law, Count Eustace of Boulogne, Earl Ralf's step-father, paid a visit to England (1051). His men fell to fighting with the men of Dover, and Godwin disobeyed the king's command to punish the townsmen. Godwin prepared for civil war, but Leofric and Siward, far from wishing well to him, and perhaps aware of the danger of a fresh viking invasion from Norway, assembled greater forces for the king and his friends. Godwin and his sons gave way, lost their earldoms, and went into exile to plot revenge. It soon came. Edward took the occasion to bring in more unpopular French friends, and the question of the succession to the elderly, childless king, who dismissed his queen, was becoming more imminent. The rightful heir, Edward, son of Edmund Ironside, was far away in Hungary. Earl Ralf seems to have struck no roots in England. A new candidate now visited Edward. This was his maternal cousin, William, Duke of Normandy, who was determined to marry Matilda, daughter of the Count of Flanders, a descendant of King Alfred, and to him Edward made a promise of the crown. So unpopular a blunder turned the scales. In 1052 Godwin, no longer opposed by the northern earls, returned with a fleet and rallied his supporters. The king could make little resistance, and Godwin recovered most of his earldom of Wessex till his death in the next year. Robert of Canterbury and most of the French fled, while Edward, though never a puppet, was henceforth mainly occupied with the foundation of his abbey of Westminster, in harmony with his pious character.

The house of Godwin, however, had to buy its success at first. Harold, on succeeding to Wessex, agreed that Leofric's son Aelfgar should take over East Anglia while Ralf held Hereford. It is true that Stigand, Godwin's ally, was allowed to accumulate vast lands by adding Canterbury to his see of Winchester, but this uncanonical intrusion meant difficulties with the Papacy, which refused him the pallium, and displeased the English episcopate as well. More than his father Earl Harold stood for the greater consolidation of the kingdom under the supremacy of his family, but he had to reckon with the rivalry of the northern earls and the affectionate regard for the house of Alfred which lingered among lesser men in the south. A king whom all would acknowledge was only to be found there. Hence he took some trouble to bring back the Hungarian Edward Atheling to England as heir-presumptive. When the atheling died almost at once (1057), the infancy of his only son, Edgar Atheling, the last Cerdicing, opened up a possibility of his own eventual election. Meantime his plans with regard to his rivals underwent a change. The death of Earl Siward (1055) tempted both him and King Edward to link Northumbria more closely to the south by the appointment of his brother Tostig, a *persona grata* to the king, to the earldom. This alarming promotion led to wars and compromises with the Mercian earls, who were strong in their homeland and buttressed by the alliance of the great Welsh prince, Gruffydd. The deaths first of Earls Leofric and Ralf in 1057, and then of Earl Aelfgar (1062) and of Gruffydd, after a signal overthrow (1063), placed Harold at the height of his career and ambitions. The youthful Edwin, Aelfgar's son, could not be ousted from northern Mercia, but Harold ruled Wessex and south-west Mercia, while one brother, Gyrth, held East Anglia and another, Leofwine, the south-eastern counties round the Thames estuary. The crown was nearly in his grasp.

Then Harold's luck failed. In 1056, while crossing the Channel, he had been storm-driven to Ponthieu, whose count had delivered him as a prisoner to Duke William. He was only set free on condition of doing homage and swearing to assist the duke's pretensions when Edward the Confessor should die. It was on these terms, which, whether regarded or not, must lower his prestige and give more semblance of right to William, that he had returned to England. The Northumbrians resented the rule of the West Saxon Tostig, who had started a blood-feud with the Bamborough kindred. They elected as their earl Morcar, brother of Edwin of Mercia, and with Edwin's Mercian and Welsh forces marched as far as Oxford to enforce their demands. Edward and Harold gave way, even presenting Waltheof, Siward's young heir, with an earldom of Northampton. Tostig in high dudgeon left for Flanders, and shortly after, on 5 January 1066, King Edward died close to his abbey of Westminster.

There was now no chance for the youth, Edgar Atheling. Invasion threatened from three quarters, the angry Tostig who was the least formidable, the Viking King of Norway, Harald Hardrada, whose restless subjects had already made attacks, and ablest of all, Duke William of Normandy. Provincial disunion was dominant in England, but no province wished for a fresh conqueror. With the dying Edward's approval the Witan elected and crowned Harold II king. There was really no one else to turn to, and he fortified his position by marrying the widowed sister of Edwin and Morcar. He conciliated the bishops by being crowned by Ealdred, Archbishop of York, not by his dubious partisan, Archbishop Stigand. In this way the great house of Cerdic and Alfred, which had made the kingdom, ceased to rule in England.

(4) GOVERNMENT AND INSTITUTIONS ON THE EVE OF THE CONQUEST

The decline of the monarchy under the later Cerdicings was not only due to disastrous invasions and personal incapacity; it was due to the diminution of the royal estates and of consequent personal authority, coupled with the ever greater possessions of the higher local nobility. Harold's lands in 1066 nearly equalled those of King Edward. No doubt the growing ecclesiastical lands of bishops and abbots were a counterweight so long as the king really nominated or could rely upon them, but Stigand's appointments show that he could lose this resource. Bishops as well as earls and important thanes were called for the meetings of the Witan ('wise men'), without whose counsel the king could not properly perform a state-act. The *Witenagemot* (moot) was, indeed, a variable body, of an advisory kind save when a new king was to be recognized, but its real assent to laws, grants, and policy was essential if they were to be accepted in the provinces and carried out.

The chief authority in their groups of shires was exercised by the earls, but in the shire-courts the king, well before the Norman Conquest, had a personal representative in the sheriff (*scir-gerefa*), who was charged with his interests. The jurisdiction of both earl and sheriff was, however, broken into by the royal grants of 'sake and soke', whether these were for whole hundreds or for certain lands, and whether sake and soke included even the cases (the later pleas of the Crown) pertaining to royal justice, such as Canute granted to the Archbishop of Canterbury or to Queen Emma, or merely petty offences which belonged to the hundred-court. Such grants had become numerous by the time of the Confessor and were often held by landowners of no great note. Besides the 'private' hundreds, in fact, there were plentiful private judicial enclaves of the most varied kind, with a 'hall-moot' wholly or partly exempt from the hundred-court. It was a step towards feudalism, like immunity, but if the king lost profits, it was beneficial to order under a vigilant local proprietor.

Local order was the crying need, and here two parallel tendencies were visible. They both showed the short reach of the central government. One, appearing in Athelstan's reign, was the *frith-gild* (peace-gild), a local spontaneous league to prevent and punish wrongs. Its members were divided into tens and hundreds, each group (*frith-borh*) being responsible for one another's acts. These associations spread. The other was the growth of lordship, an origin of later feudalism. A lord was responsible for the good conduct of his men and their delivery, if accused, for trial. Athelstan ordered that lordless men should be placed under a lord by their kindred. At the close of the Confessor's reign most countrymen were under a lord of varying status from the king to a small thane. The tie might be voluntary and voidable or hereditary and lifelong. Its causes and effects were multiple. Very many English peasants had always been tenants of a lord. Crowds of others must have surrendered their freehold to a lord for protection in war and disaster and for means to pay the racking Danegelds, and have become his men and tenants. If the king's thanes were subject only to him, there were the numerous lesser thanes, who for land or necessity 'commended' themselves to magnates, lay and spiritual, on honourable terms. Bishop Oswald of Worcester (961–92), a systematic administrator, leased out his episcopal lands for three lives to small thanes, on condition of 'riding' service at his call in peace and war. It was a proto-feudal relation for these petty squires. The development did not mean that village and manor (to use the Norman term) had become conterminous and uniform when the Confessor died, although many had done so. The areas of sake and soke and the kinds of dependence on a lord were most varied, ranging from a merely personal 'commendation' apart from land-holding to a burdensome tenancy and subjection to the lord's private court, a long step towards a servile attachment to the soil.

The Danelaw presented a freer, more prosperous and populous society. Not that lordship and private sake and soke were unknown, for they were common and extensive, but the small freeholders called socmen, the descendants of the lesser Danish settlers, were still in 1066 very many in number. On their richer land they had filled the gaps left by harrying. They might have to attend a private hundred-court or a private hall-moot, and they probably had a personal lord irrespective of soke, but they chose their personal lord, and in law at least could change him. Even the lords' tenant-held lands would be sprinkled and intermingled in many different villages. The services owed from these scattered tenants and dependants were naturally lighter and less servile than west of Watling Street. How tenaciously the Danes kept to their own law (significantly enough the word 'law' is Scandinavian, not English) may be seen from the continuous existence in their shires of the twelve 'senior thanes' (the Scandinavian 'lawmen'), whose duty it was to accuse criminals to the courts, an institution which was a precedent for the later jury of indictment. It was the Danes, too, with their seafaring and trading instincts, who stimulated English trade overseas and the English traders themselves. Towns like London and York became flourishing ports. The fortified *burhs* and their burgesses develop a special status and customs and even a borough-court, of which London gives the eminent instance.

The mass of the countryside population west of Watling Street was, however, losing its freedom yearly. Not to mention the numerous class of actual slaves, employed in household and field work, the villager (the *villanus* of Norman times), although a freeman, fell into various degrees of economic and personal dependence. Even the lesser thane was commonly a lessee of his land on conditions of personal 'riding' service to his lord, king, bishop, or noble. Below him were roughly three grades of churls (*ceorlas*). The *geneats* performed only occasional services, harvesting, fencing, and all sorts of errands. The *geburs* ('boors', the typical *villani* of Domesday Book) held an average yardland of 30 acres, for which they did heavy week-work with their plough-oxen on the land their lord kept in hand, as well as rent and dues, and of course special harvest-work. At death, their heirs paid a death-tax, the *heriot*, to their lord, in recognition of the outfit originally given with the yardland. With the addition of dues to king and Church their lot was hard. Beneath them came the *cotsetlas* (cottars and bordars of Domesday), holding five acres more or less. Their services and dues were lighter because their plots were small and they did not possess plough-oxen, but were as servile in nature as the *geburs*', and their poverty was greater. All freemen were subject, at least indirectly, as far as law went, to the so-called *trimoda necessitas*, i.e. serving in the *fyrd* or host, repairing and garrisoning *burhs*. No doubt thanes and *geneats*, the men with the horses and weapons, bore the chief burden of this duty.

(5) THE CELTIC KINGDOMS

A common feature in the Celtic kingdoms of the British Isles was their long retention of a tribal organization, and with it the weakness of the impulse towards unity. They had mainly lain outside the direct rule of the Roman Empire and had missed its discipline in orderly government which was never forgotten in Western Europe. Even their Churches and monasteries were modelled on the clan-system, and when they conformed to the Roman reckoning for Easter, in Ireland 634–92, in Scotland 710–16, and in Wales 768, they did not change.

Fig. 82. Welsh homestead of the sixth century

Wales was broken up into tribal kingdoms, mutually hostile, which fell into the compartments of North and South. The North was divided between Gwynedd and Powys; the sections of the South tended to coagulate round the rulers of expanding Deheubarth. In the ninth century, however, in the face of constant Viking raids, a tendency to Welsh unity appeared. Rhodri Mawr ('the Great') of Gwynedd, belonging to a new dynasty, conquered Powys and much of Deheubarth (844–78). If his state broke up among his descendants, it was occasionally reunited, as by his grandson Howel the Good (Hywel Dda) (c. 904–50), to whom were attributed some of the Welsh laws. These tribal princes mostly owned the supremacy of the English kings with frequent intervals of harrying wars. Unification was once more achieved by the powerful Gruffydd ap Llywelyn (Griffith, son of Llywelyn) (1039–63) of Gwynedd. He was the formidable ally of Earl Aelfgar of Mercia and the foe of Earl Ralf and Earl Harold. At last Harold bestirred himself to a decisive campaign in Gwynedd, during which Griffith was deserted and murdered. Wales, although unconquered, split again into its old four principalities, Gwynedd, Powys, Deheubarth, and Morgannwg. A new situation was created by the coming of the Normans. Political divisions and mutual hostility were not favourable to resistance against the conquerors with their expert military system and their throttling ring of strategic castles, in spite of the strong geographical defences of Wales. It was not so much the Norman kings as their great border earls and adventurous barons who were dangerous. Although the Welsh princes

Fig. 83. The Chief Falconer and Iudex Curiae of Wales

fought fiercely and won occasional victories, like Mynydd Carn (1081), they went down piecemeal at long last. The death of Rhys ap Tewdwr of Deheubarth in 1093 opened the floodgates in South Wales, which as far as Pembroke was parcelled out among soldiers of fortune. The Earls of Chester and Shrewsbury seemed to be about to complete the conquest of

405

Gwynedd when a raiding Norwegian fleet under King Magnus Bareleg snapped their communications by sea, and since the coast defile then at Penmaen was impossible to secure, led to the Normans' retreat. Prince Griffith ap Cynan and the Prince of Powys recovered their lands.

King Henry I in person or by his vassals made himself master of all Wales but Gwynedd, which Griffith ap Cynan (*ob*. 1137) was actually enlarging round its core of Snowdonia and Anglesey. During the civil wars of Stephen, its princes Owain (*ob*. 1170) and Cadwaladr (*ob*. 1172) began a war of liberation. The Welsh had learned horsemanship and castle building and taking, and they regained much. They held out against Henry II. After 1172 the lead was taken by Lord Rhys ap Gruffydd (*ob*. 1197) in South Wales, but now Henry II, anxious at his Norman-Welsh vassals' invasion of Ireland, was bent on conciliation. At his death (1189) Wales was and long remained divided into two contrasted parts of shifting frontiers. In the north was Gwynedd, ruled by princes, who later took the title of Prince of Wales. Here was the last refuge of Welsh independence and of Welsh culture. In the south and east was Anglo-Norman Wales, the Welsh Marches, sometimes losing territory to Gwynedd, sometimes gaining it, roughly separated from England by Offa's Dyke. The fighting March, although Welsh enough in a way, was ruled by the lords marchers, with all but royal power. The forces of these great barons, Clares, Bohuns, Mortimers, and the like, were to be of vast importance in English civil wars.

To turn to North Britain. In the days of Egbert, there were three kingdoms, that of the Picts north of the Forth, that of the Scots or of Dalriada in Argyllshire, and that of Strathclyde or Cumbria (Cumberland, from Cymry) in the south-west. Perhaps one should add two more divisions: northern Bernicia or Lothian between the Forth and the Tweed, and the recent Norse settlements in the Orkney, Shetland, and Hebridean Islands. It was Viking ravages which produced a change. They so drained the Pictish kingdom of its strength that Kenneth I MacAlpin, King of the Scots, was able in 844 to make himself by conquest King of the Picts as well, a union which proved permanent. The Goidelic (Gaelic) tongue of the Scots, already widely spread, in course of time ousted any competing Pictish dialect north of the Forth, and the kingdom became Scotland to its neighbours, although for long the kings retained the ancient name of Alba (Albany) in their native style.

It became the object of the Scottish kings in the next century to extend their dominion from the barren Highlands to the richer soil southward, more accessible to the Christian world, as well as to defend themselves from Vikings. These two motives account for their alternate friendship and hostility to the new kingdom of England. They are obvious in 945 when Malcolm I of Scotland (943–54) accepted Welsh Strathclyde (Cumbria)

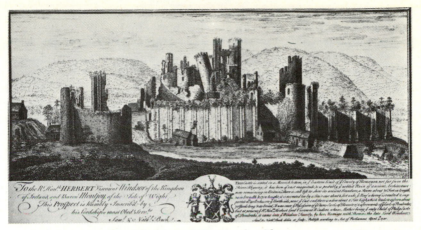

Fig. 84. Caerphilly Castle, Glamorgan

from King Edmund on condition of being his 'fellow-worker by land and sea'. The Welsh king Dunmail, however, soon recovered his land, and the first real Scottish advance was the annexation of Edinburgh by King Indulf (954–62). It was followed up by the cession of Lothian and the Tweed frontier by Edgar to King Kenneth II (971–95). The annexation, which was never reversed, was a turning-point in Scottish history. Lothian was the granary of the north. The Scottish kings resided there more and more. Its English tongue slowly prevailed over both Gaelic and Welsh, and its English polity was to transform the Lowlands and the kingship. Border wars continued furiously between the Northumbrians and Scots, and perhaps the victory at Carham (1018) of Malcolm II (1005–34) sealed the conquest. The next act of consolidation came by inheritance. In 1018 Owen the Bald, the last Welsh King of Strathclyde, was succeeded by Malcolm's grandson, Duncan, who inherited Scotland also in 1034. This time the union was lasting.

Although thus tacked together, Scotland was as yet anything but homogeneous. The most urgent need was to assimilate her populations and reconcile their cultural and political standards. It was not only the wide divergences between her component parts. The Gaelic tribes were loosely compacted together from patriarchal clans, which themselves were liable to fissure and always little concerned to obey the central kingship. There ensued 250 years of racial and civil turmoil. Duncan's accession (1034) provoked the first outburst, for it contravened the custom by which another branch of the MacAlpins alternately took the crown. Like Malcolm's, this branch was extinct in male heirs, but it possessed representatives in Gruoch and her husband Macbeth (the Thane and Lady

407

Macbeth of the play). Since Macbeth was 'Mormaer' of Moray in the north, he was the natural leader of the northern Picts. He overthrew Duncan and reigned (1040–57), till he was himself attacked by Duncan's son, Malcolm III Canmore, who defeated him with the aid of Earl Siward of Northumbria (1055), and finally slew both him and his stepson, Gruoch's heir, in Moray. Disaffection and a rival line of occasional pretenders continued among the northern tribes for two centuries.

Malcolm III (1057–93) had grown to manhood at Edward the Confessor's court in an English atmosphere, and his second wife (1070) was Margaret, sister and heiress of Edgar Atheling. Malcolm attempted several times to advance his southern frontier by fire and sword, but William the Conqueror and his son were too hard for him, and he was obliged to do them homage. Both exiles and captives produced an English infiltration meanwhile into southern Scotland, which was profound in its effects. The queen, St Margaret (*ob.* 1093), was its protagonist in culture and religion. This saintly, masterful woman dominated her husband, children, and court. She encouraged commerce and merchants. She brought the Church, in ritual and practices, into union with Roman Christendom. A rude society assumed the veneer of culture.

Although a Celtic reaction, under Malcolm III's brother Donald Bane (1093–7), gained a brief predominance, it was ended with the aid of an English force sent by William Rufus and led by Edgar Atheling. For nearly sixty years three of Margaret's sons, securely based on English-speaking Lothian, which saw in them heirs of Alfred as well as of Malcolm Canmore, continued the process of Anglicization, even if Celtic irreconcilables from Moray to Galloway were always ready to advance a pretender. Edgar (1097–1107) made Edinburgh the capital. Alexander I (1107–24) created or refashioned diocesan bishoprics, on the English model, at St Andrews, Glasgow, and elsewhere. The youngest brother, David I (1124–53), who had already ruled south of the Forth, conducted 'a bloodless Norman conquest' and transformed the Scottish monarchy. He introduced a new aristocracy of Anglo-Norman barons, Balliols, Bruces, FitzAlans (Stewarts), Lindsays and others. The Celtic population was not expelled; tenure by charter superseded the old lordship of chiefs of septs; the seven mormaers became earls. But ultimately the texture of Scottish society was changed. The cadets and servitors of the new barons received fiefs from them, and propagated the new culture and the English tongue. The greater part of the kingdom was held by feudal vassals, whether English or Celtic.

The Church bore its part, for David was 'a sair sanct for the Crown', as his descendant complained. Besides endowing bishoprics, he was a munificent founder of abbeys, peopled with Benedictines and the new Cistercians. Scotland fell into line with the West. A *curia regis* of the feudal type came into existence along with the great officers of state,

Fig. 85. David I and Malcolm IV, kings of Scots

constable, justiciar, and chancellor (these already under Alexander I), chamberlain, marshal, and steward (under David), of which the last was hereditary in the FitzAlans, who took therefrom the surname of Stewart. Royal sheriffs were appointed to administer military and fiscal affairs in districts based upon the king's castles, although the Celtic judges were left to function. But to all these changes there was a border-line. In the Highlands and in Galloway, the Celtic septs remained unchanged in their ancient, patriarchal, Gaelic tribalism.

David was ambitious to extend his kingdom, but here he failed. From the time of Earl Siward, probably, Cumberland, i.e. the strip of Strathclyde (Cumbria) south of the Solway Firth, had been ceded to Northumbria once more. In 1092 William Rufus re-fortified Carlisle, and this English boundary at the Solway lasted for good. David's schemes were wide-reaching, to annex the county of Northumberland and more. But savage raiding roused the population. He was routed at the Battle of the Standard near Northallerton in 1138, and although by adroit bargaining in the English civil war he obtained the earldoms of Northumberland and Cumberland for his heir Henry, as well as that of Huntingdon and Northampton, his grandson Malcolm IV was obliged to surrender the northern earldoms to Henry II (1157). A national frontier, in short, had emerged from these long hostilities before the Scots had fully become a nation.

Ireland, the centre of Gaeldom, had progressed far beyond Scotland in intellectual culture. The monasteries maintained a Latin learning fertilizing and fertilized by their connexions with their own emigrants on the Continent. Their illumination and script arrived at a wonderful excellence, combining motives derived from Italo-Byzantine art with prehistoric native traditions such as the interlacing spiral, and displaying the native artistry and genius of the craftsmen. The same gifts were to be seen in the metal-worker. The Gaels had long employed a native alphabet, the *ogham* script, for memorial sentences on tombstones. But there existed, too, a Gaelic literature of singular merit and charm among the hereditary bards and story-tellers. Like the Scandinavian, it was mainly barbaric in theme and in its elaborate, hampering conventions and exaggerations, but it was vivid, dramatic, and colourful with a delicate perception of nature and expression of emotion, hard to surpass.

A hierarchical pattern of tribal subordination had been evolved by the formulators of Irish customary law. The high-king (*ard-rí*) of Ireland was supreme over the five kings of the provinces, of whom he was one; these dominated their fellow-kings of tribal units, and these again the kings of small subject-clans. But this ideal system worked irregularly in practice. The high-king, almost always the head of one of the two chief branches of the descendants of Niall of the Nine Hostages, had much ado to enforce his authority, and the actual state of the island, amid wars, feuds, and general turbulence, provided a strong contrast to the legal theory. Kingdoms and septs fell into two traditional and deep-seated divisions of long-lasting significance, the northern Conn's Half (*Leth Cuinn*), roughly the provinces of Ulster, Meath, and Connaught, and Mogh's Half (*Leth Mogha*) in the south, roughly Munster and Leinster. Within them there were seven effective kingdoms: Cashel (Munster), Cruachan (Connaught), Ailech (central Ulster) under an O'Neill, Uriel (southern Ulster), Ulaidh (east Ulster), Tara (Meath) under an O'Neill, and Leinster. All males of a king's agnate kindred as far as second cousins were *rig-damna*, eligible to succeed him by election; in practice intrigues, violence, and bloodshed could decide the question. In spite of feuds and petty wars, however, a much chequered peace, unmolested by foreigners, allowed Ireland's 'Golden Age of Art and Learning' to flourish in monasteries and courts until the Norsemen came.

We have already seen how this prosperity foundered in the first period of Viking ravage. While groups of clans fought the invaders, no general resistance was organized, and indeed Felimy of Cashel endeavoured to seize the high-kingship from the O'Neills. The net result was that Viking

Fig. 86. The Rock of Cashel, Co. Tipperary

settlers under kings were securely seated in Dublin, Waterford, Limerick, etc. They intermarried much with the Irish as well as allying with and fighting them. From 914 a second period of invasion began. Fresh fleets sailed from Scandinavia and the Western Isles. Besides overflowing into Cumbria and Northumbria, as we have seen, they waged war with their Irish neighbours. In 919 King Sihtric slew the *ard-rí*, Niall Black-knee (Glundubh) in a battle on the river Liffey. In their English wars, however, they finally met with reverses. King Olaf Cuaran, son of Sihtric, after various vicissitudes was overthrown by Malachy II of Tara in 980, after which he became a monk at Iona.

A new champion of Ireland now appeared in the south. He was Brian Bórumha, leader of the Dál Cais of Thomond in Munster. In 967 his elder brother, Mahon, and he conquered the Vikings of Limerick. Mahon made himself King of Munster, ousting the Cashel dynasty of the Eoganacht, who in 976 succeeded in murdering him in alliance with the foreigners. They only cleared the way for Brian, who soon became King not only of Munster, but of all Mogh's Half. He now aimed, like some former Kings of Cashel, to be *ard-rí* by the usual method of compelling hostages to be given him by other kings. A purely Munster tradition claimed that the King of Cashel was ruler of all Mogh's Half and ought to be *ard-rí*. The existing *ard-rí*, Malachy II of Tara, naturally resisted, and vigorous warfare went on until 998, when it appears that the rivals agreed that Malachy should only be supreme in Conn's Half, and they then together defeated

28-2

Sihtric Olafson of Dublin and the King of Leinster. This was an interlude. In alliance with Sihtric (1000) Brian invaded Conn's Half. In 1005 he was recognized at Armagh as *imperator Scotorum* (the Gaels of Ireland), and at last in 1010 secured hostages from all the clans of Conn's Half.

Fig. 87. Cross of Monasterboice, Co. Louth

Brian Bórumha came nearer to uniting Ireland than any former *ard-rí*. Churches were built and restored, and there was some revival of art and learning. The *Book of Rights*, a code of law dating from about 900, was re-edited in his time. Henceforth the Scandinavian settlers were normally confined to their seaports and their environs. They had become Christians and were less prone to go on Viking raids. One last furious outburst occurred, a real attempt at conquest. Sihtric of Dublin allied with the Gael Maelmora of Leinster, with Sigurd Earl of Orkney and a Norse Viking Brodir. Supported by his Munstermen and his old foe, Malachy of Tara, Brian met them on Good Friday (23 April) 1014 in the epic battle of Clontarf. Most of the leaders, including Brian, were killed. Sihtric kept Dublin, but the few surviving Vikings fled to their ships.

Brian broke the monopoly of the high-kingship vested in the two branches of the O'Neills. The way to it was opened to other provincial kings, and for 150 years they strove to attain it, becoming at best *ard-rí* 'with opposition', i.e. with one province recalcitrant. Hence, besides the usual border-raids between clans, whole provinces were often engaged in mutual devastation. The aspirant usually would divide a conquered province between two kings. The uppermost hand was held till 1119 by the Dál Cais kings, of whom the last *ard-rí* was Murtough O'Brien. The struggle then intensified. From 1156 to 1166 Murtough O'Loughlin of the Ulster O'Neills was the most powerful king. Supported by Dermot MacMurrough of Leinster, he took hostages at last (1161) from his competitor, Rory

412

O'Conor of Connaught. But a gross breach of faith alienated his own people and the clergy, and he was slain in 1166 by the King of Uriel. Rory of Connaught then, by the customary campaign for hostages, secured the high-kingship.

Although there was little stability or union among the Irish kings and clans, there was in the Irish Church a vigorous effort towards both and towards pruning ancient barbarism. The Scandinavian settlers, exchanging piracy for trade and now zealous Christians, had revived communications with England and the south. Their bishops were suffragans of Canterbury. Church reformation entered Ireland through them. A Bishop of Limerick was papal legate; Bishop Malchus of Waterford presided over the famous school of Lismore, where one of his pupils was Maelmaedog, later known as St Malachy (*ob.* 1148). This lifelong friend of St Bernard went to Rome and was appointed papal legate (1139). He became the chief instrument of reform. A papal constitution (1152) after his death established the four metropolitan sees of Armagh, Dublin, Cashel, and Tuam, and he introduced Cistercian monks at Dublin and at Mellifont near Drogheda (1142). He was loud in his denunciations of barbarous practices and antiquated routine. His reforming movement had its share in the success of the Anglo-Norman invasion.

(6) THE SCANDINAVIAN KINGDOMS UNTIL *c.* 1130

The period of the Viking raids and emigrations was also the period when the Scandinavian peoples coalesced into three kingdoms and indeed nations, Denmark, Norway, and Sweden. We have seen that Denmark, the smallest but most populous and therefore the most powerful country of the three, had dissolved into warring fractions in the ninth century. It was finally united by the mighty warrior, Harald Bluetooth (*c.* 950–85). His son Swein Forkbeard (985–1014) and his grandson Canute the Great (1019–35), the conquerors of England, made it the paramount kingdom of the north for a time. Still earlier, Harald Fairhair, descended from the Ynglings of Sweden, but a petty king of Vestfold round Oslo, fought his way over the other kinglets and *jarls*, till he became first King of all Norway after his crowning victory of Hafrsfjord (*c.* 900). But his kingdom split among his numerous descendants and the powerful *jarls* of Trondheim in the north. Olaf Tryggveson (997–1000) made himself master for a while until overthrown by Swein Forkbeard, but it was the work of another heir of Harald, Olaf the Saint (1016–28), to unite Norway in resolute independence. Even he was ousted by the war and wily diplomacy of Canute the Great, and slain by Norwegian foes in his attempt to return. Canute's half-wife Aelfgifu and her son Swein, whom he sent to rule for him, soon roused such general resentment that St Olaf's son, Magnus the

Good (1035–47), was able to revolt successfully and even to conquer Denmark for a time, although Swein Estrithson, Canute's nephew, renewed the national Danish kingdom after his death. Meanwhile, *c.* 1000, Olaf the Tax-king had become by war or by inheritance from his father, Eric the Victorious, sole ruler of both Svealand and Gautland (Gothland) and thus King of Sweden. From about 1050 the three kingdoms, hitherto mutually hostile and aggressive turn and turn about, were fully formed and compelled to respect each other's independence.

Norway alone as yet had subjects of a foreign race, the Lapps, and oversea dependent colonies. The Faroe Islands, Orkneys, Shetlands, and Hebrides owned her dominion. The colony of Iceland, populated by exiles during Harald Fairhair's reign, was a free commonwealth, but purely Norwegian in tongue and customs. Norway, too, although politically behind Denmark, was, with Iceland, the most gifted in literature. Here were composed, for the most part in the tenth century, the heroic lays of the *Edda* and the best of the court-poems. In Iceland was to be developed the art of traditional story-telling, which produced prose history, biography, and romance.

In all Scandinavia the aristocracy was making a continuous advance. The free peasant-farmers were changing from landowners to lease-holders of the nobles. They still attended the *thing* or moot of their hundred (*herad*) and 'folk' or county for law and justice, but these were quite small districts, and even there their right to decide became insensibly a right to assent. The nobles themselves were for two centuries a rural aristocracy, local in interests and power. The law administered, though wider in area, was a local law. There were five law-districts in Norway, three in Denmark, and sixteen in Sweden. Only the king was a national institution. He had founded each kingdom by war, but he became an economic, military, administrative, and even spiritual force in the national life. His revenue, as elsewhere in the early Middle Ages, was derived in the first instance from his own wide estates, but this did not suffice to maintain his guard of companions and retainers. Accordingly, just as among the Anglo-Saxons, as he travelled from estate to estate consuming its produce, this had to be augmented by the food-dues of local landowners, in Norway the *veizla*, in Denmark the *stud*, in Sweden the *skot*. This was the basis of the earliest taxation. But he was also the guardian of justice. Hence to him was paid, as in England and Francia, a fixed share of judicial fines, and a special, heavy fine for disobedience to his commands. From his leadership in foreign war a new right sprang up, first of all in Denmark. This was the *leidang*. Almost all war was by sea, and the *leidang* was the conscription of a ship and men from each ship-district. In this way a national force was created under the king.

Beside and aiding the kingship there grew up another national institution and force, the Church, and this meant a foreign influence of the deepest import. The Viking emigrants in Christian Europe early accepted Christianity. In Scandinavia German and other missionaries made their way. The new national kings, desirous of admission into Western civilization, by which they were the more affected the more they knew of it, insisted on the conversion of their subjects, whether by persuasion or by brute force. Harald Bluetooth first made Denmark Christian, and his undutiful son Swein Forkbeard, after heading the heathen party, ended in tepid conversion. Canute the Great was devout. Olaf the Tax-king, who introduced *skot* in his Swedish realm, converted it also about 1000. In more insubordinate Norway the struggle in two acts was short and sharp. Olaf Tryggveson (997–1000) forced Christianity on his people at the sword's point. His cousin St Olaf (1016–28), who was also the national deliverer, repeated the process. He became the national saint. Meanwhile in kingless Iceland a Christian party formed and carried the day in the *Althing* while tolerating secret heathen sacrifices.

Superficial and political as was the conversion, it became real conviction in the next generation. True, the minor heathen practices and magic long continued, and the barbaric ethos was only slowly and partially tamed. But the Church became a power and its teaching gradually filtered into men's minds. While Christendom in the north as elsewhere was viewed as a world-Church, as a matter of fact the Church powerfully helped to organize the separate nations. The first truly nation-wide laws regulated men's duties to the Church and clergy; in each country the bishops were directly in the king's service. National devotion centred around saints who had been kings, St Olaf in Norway, St Canute in Denmark, and later still St Eric in Sweden. When in the eleventh century the Papacy constituted the German Archbishop of Hamburg-Bremen metropolitan of all Scandinavia, a move partly prompted by German ambitions, and when Archbishop Adalbert (1043–72) made great strides towards attaining an effective jurisdiction, he was roughly rebuffed by King Harald Hardrada (the 'Hard-ruler') of Norway. The authority of Bremen disappeared formally when in 1103 King Eric the Evergood of Denmark obtained the erection of the see of Lund in Scania as the Scandinavian metropolis. The Church was able to undertake tasks which the State could not, and its national organization and authority were favoured by the kings. Under Swein Estrithson (1047–74) eight dioceses appear in Denmark; in Norway Olaf the Peace-king (1067–93) organized four; before 1120 Sweden was divided into five.

Church power and State power at this time went hand in hand. King Canute of Denmark (1080–6), second son of Swein, besides exacting heavy services from the peasants, demanded a poll-tax for himself and tithes for the clergy. When he fell before the altar in a rebellion, and his brother

King Olaf Hunger's reign was afflicted by a famine, Canute's death was thought a martyrdom: he was sainted and his brother Eric the Evergood (1096–1103) could enforce the tithe. A little later the tithe was introduced into Norway and Sweden. St Canute, too, had recognized the independent ecclesiastical courts. In these ways the Church gained an economic and jurisdictional basis for its social activity. Its land and wealth grew. The religious movements of Western Europe entered Scandinavia. Pilgrims, crusaders (like King Sigurd of Norway, 1103–30), and missionaries issued from the country. Monasteries were founded. The links with the Papacy became more numerous and stronger, and favoured, if only for efficiency, the separatist spirit of the rival kingdoms. In 1152 the English papal legate, Nicholas Breakspear (later Pope Adrian IV), established the Norwegian archbishopric of Nidaros. A few years later in 1164 Sweden obtained her national archbishopric at Uppsala, Lund being left for Denmark. In each country the payment of Peter's Pence to Rome was ordained.

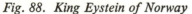

Fig. 88. King Eystein of Norway

The chief task of kings and clergy was to introduce peace and law, the clergy by penances, the kings by penal laws. The court-poets emphasized law, not war, and the era of law-books began. The laws show the changes in society. The kindred and its range of action have narrowed; landed property has become a family estate, not a possession of the kindred. Aristocracy and the individualistic nature of the Canon Law tended in the same direction. Social security began to depend on the State, not on the dissolving kindred. A new organization, the gilds, helped in the transition. It was borrowed perhaps, although modified, from England and the Netherlands. The gilds were plainly Christian; they bound neighbours together, often with the national king-saint as patron, for economic and legal protection, and they flourished for two centuries.

The attempts at greater internal peace did not mean the abandonment of foreign warfare under the leadership of the kings, but its objects grew more restricted after the conquests of Canute the Great. Magnus the Good of Norway (1035–47) had conquered Denmark and threatened England. His uncle Harald Hardrada, after an adventurous youth, in which he had reached Constantinople, met his death at Stamford Bridge whilst invading England (1066). Swein Estrithson and his sons were turned back from western conquests by the strength of the new Anglo-Norman monarchy. Germany to the south was an object of their dread. They looked for expansion to the Baltic, where Wendish pirates harassed them. King Magnus Bareleg of Norway (1093–1103), nicknamed from his kilt, enforced his sovereignty over the western islands, but met his death in Ireland. The Viking expansion was over. A premature movement towards the abandonment of aggression led to a meeting of the three Scandinavian kings in 1101, when they agreed on a perpetual, mutual peace, fortified by dynastic intermarriage, but *c.* 1130 the prospect was clouded over by the civil wars of pretenders, which involved all three countries. None the less they had formed national states, which now belonged to Christendom.

CHAPTER 16

THE HOLY ROMAN EMPIRE AND FRANCE

(I) THE FEUDALIZATION OF SOCIETY

We have seen how the evolution of internal government and social structure in the countries of Western Europe had been proceeding on parallel lines of development from its Roman and Germanic origins. In each a landed aristocracy, which included the church dignitaries, had taken local root, and besides furnishing the kings with their temporary officials, had acquired in different shapes a permanent devolution of public functions over their own and neighbouring lands: the 'immunities' of Francia, the 'private hundreds' and sake and soke among the Anglo-Saxons. It was indeed, as the kingdoms grew wider, the most efficient way of keeping local order in non-bureaucratic days and often of raising revenue as well as of rewarding service, while in any case the larger landowners would have the chief say in local assemblies and affairs. To this universal if variegated process the civil wars, invasions, and raids of the ninth century and the breakdown of central government gave an immense stimulus. But, although parallel, the developments in each country were diverse, and their outcome unlikely to be the same. It was in the Frankish Empire that the outcome was feudalism, which spread to its neighbours by conquest or imitation, and which even then was subject to innumerable variations from the general type.

Although full-grown feudalism was largely the result of the breakdown of older government and law, it both inherited law from the past and created it by a rapid growth of custom based on present fact. In one sense it may be defined as an arrangement of society based on contract, expressed or implied. The status of a person depended in every way on his position on the land, and on the other hand land-tenure determined political rights and duties. The acts constituting the feudal contract were called *homage* and *investiture*. The tenant or vassal knelt before the lord surrounded by his court (*curia*), placing his folded hands between those of the lord, and thus became his 'man' (*homme*, whence the word homage). He also took an oath of fealty (*fidelitas*) of special obligation. This of course was the ancient ceremony of commendation developed and specialized. The lord in his turn responded by 'investiture', handing to his vassal a banner, a staff, a clod of earth, a charter, or other symbol of the property or office conceded, the *fief* (*feodum* or *Lehn*) as it was termed, while the older word *benefice* went gradually out of use. This was the free and honourable tenure characterized by military service, but the peasant, whether free or serf, equally swore a form of fealty and was invested with the tenement he held of his lord.

The feudal nexus thus created essentially involved reciprocity. To the vassal were due from his lord gifts, if only of the land, and protection. If he thought he did not receive correct treatment, he could leave the estate (*déguerpissement*), and in France, the land of typical feudalism, he had the right to disavow his lord for breach of contract (*désaveu.*) The common result of this legal right was a trial of strength by private war between lord and man, but it was a genuine safeguard of the vassals' interests and the fruitful parent of constitutional progress in joint resistance to arbitrary kings in later days.

The vassal's duties to his lord, if they could be enforced, were many and onerous, and their neglect rendered his fief liable to forfeiture. The central and distinctive obligation was that of defined military service of one or more fully armed horsemen according to the terms of enfeoffment, which came to be limited to a certain number of days, generally forty, in the year. It shaded off into military serjeanties for castle-garrisons, archers, etc. Allied to it was the military service of the important class of serfs in Germany, the *ministeriales*, who rose to knighthood, although unfree in status, and held their small servile fiefs in return. To them corresponded the *servientes* (serjeants) of France, who were commonly free or were early freed.

A series of duties arose from the nature of the fief as a conditional grant of land. The conception of ownership (*dominium*), once unitary and exclusive in ancient Roman law, became bifurcated. There was the *dominium directum* (or *eminens*) of the superior from whom the land was held, and the *dominium utile* of the vassal who occupied and exploited it in return for feudal service. A vassal could freely parcel out his fief, or sub-enfeoff it to vassals of his own, provided that his due services were performed to the superior lord, thus becoming himself a mesne (*medius*, middle) lord. In this way a hierarchy of feudal tenants was evolved with its apex in the king. But the practice of sub-infeudation was harmful to the king and his tenants-in-chief, for the sub-vassals were bound to their own immediate mesne lord and not to his superior.

On the death of either contracting party, the feudal bond had to be renewed. If the lord died, his heir received the renewed homage and fealty of his vassals. Indeed, in the intensely concrete ideology of the time, when the physical, ceremonial act was necessary for a binding contract, they hardly felt bound to their new lord until they had performed them. If the vassal died, his heir, according to the growing custom of each country, had the right to succeed him in his fief, but the original nature of a grant for life or at pleasure left behind it the temporary resumption of the fief by the lord until he reinvested the heir after homage and fealty had been rendered and a *relief*, i.e. a more or less heavy payment, had been made to him. This payment was originally connected, too, with the *heriot*, the return of the military outfit given by the lord to his armed follower. In base tenure, the heriot (or *main-morte* in French) concerned the outfit of stock and the like for working the land, and was retained as a death-tax on the peasant.

Similar profitable rights accrued to the lord of a fief when the heir was a minor or an unmarried female. Neither could in person perform the services due, and the lord entered into possesion of the fief and its profits until the male heir came of age or the female was married. As their marriage might greatly affect the lord's interests, he had the choice of bride or bridegroom and made lucrative as well as political use of the opportunity. Demands for reasonable reliefs and for the mitigation of abuses arising from wardship and marriage recur in English medieval history.

None of these contingencies occurred for the fiefs held by the undying Church. The kings made up for the loss by entering on ecclesiastical fiefs during a vacancy, by taking the *spolia*, i.e. the personal property of deceased bishops, and in the earlier feudal age by sheer simony, the exaction of a money payment from a new bishop or abbot as the price of his appointment. When after bitter conflict all these abuses were either abolished or restricted, the danger of more land passing into the 'dead hand' (the English mortmain) of the Church roused powerful kings, like Edward I of England, to check or levy toll on the transfer.

Just as the lord owed support and protection to his vassal, the vassal was bound not to injure his lord in his person or rights or to impede his undertakings. But he owed also his counsel and aid (*consilium, auxilium*). The duty of counsel found its chief expression in attendance at his lord's court (*curia*), in which the lord's business of all kinds, administrative or judicial, was transacted. The duty was also a right: the lord was expected to act and decide after counsel with his vassals. The *curia* took cognizance of questions of land held of the lord and of other cases arising from the feudal tie, but by grant or usurpation much public justice, criminal or civil, relating to the lord's 'immunity', or 'franchise' as it came to be called, was dealt out in the *curia*, and a vassal had the right to be judged by his fellow-vassals, his peers or equals. There were gradations in the jurisdiction of such *curiae* according to the extent of the lord's powers, but all lords of fiefs with tenants under them had their court. The serfs within a single fief were suitors to and judged in their lord's court. They could only advise and had no redress. The free and noble suitor to the court of a franchise could insist on his privileges: the decision lay with his peers. In judicial cases in lay courts the right to appeal to a more authoritative tribunal in the modern way did not exist. But if the vassal could not get his case heard by his peers in the court of his immediate lord, he could ask the latter's suzerain to insist that it should be done. If he was dissatisfied, on the other hand, with the court's decision, he could appeal his peers for 'false judgement', a cumbrous and risky proceeding which involved perhaps a series of single combats with the members of the court, for ordeal by battle, an appeal to the judgement of God, was the typically feudal version of the half-barbaric notions of proof and evidence held by the times.

In other matters, too, the right to counsel became a right to consent. The king could not legislate or declare custom save with the consent of all his tenants-in-chief, and each subordinate lord stood in the same relation to his own vassals. Theoretically each vassal was only bound by his own consent. The majority principle took long to discover, and the absence of it had important practical effects in elections. But in practical legislation, the *stabilimenta* or *assizes*, unanimous consent could be taken as implied when the more powerful agreed: 'voices were rather weighed than counted'. In any case, the necessity of the participation of the *curia* was productive of much future development, and it went with the innate belief that custom, or rather law, was supreme and best known by the tradition of those who practised it.

The duty of aid (*auxilium*) produced a number of defined obligations besides that of military service. The castle held by the vassal was commonly liable to occupation by his lord on demand, and apart from that the lord had the right of *gîte* or *albergue*, i.e. of entertainment from the fief for himself and his household for some short period in his peregrinations through his territory. Aid in money was also due for the lord's exceptional needs: in the eleventh century such aid became limited by custom to payments for the lord's ransom if taken captive and on the occasions of the knighting of his eldest son and the marriage of his eldest daughter, to which in France was later added the aid if he joined in a crusade. This very definition of the obligatory money subsidies resulted in the payment of non-customary aids, which the kings later needed, becoming a case of a voluntary grant by the vassals, and thus leading to the formation of assemblies of estates and their constitutional rights.

In its heyday in France, feudalism, which made political subjection a matter of private contract, gave a legal form to the disruption of sovereignty. The greater part of the regalian rights and functions had been taken over for their territories by the tenants-in-chief of the Crown. But they themselves were unable to prevent those powers passing to their own vassals of importance, and so the process of devolution on the Continent ended in a host of *seigneurs* possessing most of the rights of jurisdiction and government in their estates. The higher rank of *seigneurs* judged the more serious crimes, involving the death-penalty (*haute justice*), but even the lesser lords held jurisdiction over lesser crimes (*basse justice*). All alike exercised the pernicious custom of private war with one another for offence or defence, revenge or gain. To limit or abolish it was to be one of the tasks of reviving monarchy.

The legal disintegration of the realm into fragmentary feudal dominions and the evolution of official counts and their subordinates into hereditary local dynasts was a gradual process, but the state of fact preceded its full formulation. The late Carolingian disasters and invasions produced an anarchy in which the local strong man, with the castles he fortified against the raiders, and with the complex round him of kinsmen, vassals, and retainers, took by grant or usurpation the full control of his district, large or small. It was in this fighting, anarchic society that the feudal contract and feudal jurisdiction were worked out. Count, viscount, and castellan became hereditary *seigneurs*. Not all the Carolingian *pagi* survived intact or even at all. Viscounts and castellans of fragments might in the end take the title of count of their fief. When bishop or abbey acquired criminal justice over Church lands, they not only needed vassals to defend them, but a lay advocate (*Vogt* in German) to exercise their functions over cases of blood, and these delegations produced fresh enfeoffments and loss of estates, and fresh lay dynasts or the increase of the power of those already established. Indeed, the wealthier monasteries were under the control of lay abbots. In West Francia, or France, the old popular *mallus* became by degrees the feudal *curia* of the count: the *scabini* were replaced by his vassals who gave him counsel. In Germany the two kinds of court continued separate. The inheritance of countships and the greater fiefs could hardly be denied in the tenth century. It took longer for lesser men and sub-vassals to establish absolutely the same right even with the payment of reliefs. In Germany and Italy it only became law in the eleventh century. Nor did every vassal-trooper obtain a fief. The household knight maintained by his lord in his castle lasted long.

The class of knights (*caballarii, milites, chevaliers, Ritter*) also took time to form. The original definition was that of the fully equipped horse-warrior. Among the well born at least, there existed a simple ceremony of admission to the degree, derived from the ancient custom of arming a young man when he came of full age. The ceremonial increased and in the twelfth century a religious element entered in, but the core in France remained the accolade, a blow with hand or sword from the grantor to the new knight. In the thirteenth century knighthood had become for the most part a privilege of rank, of men already considered noble.

Even after the cessation in the mid-tenth century of the foreign inroads, the instinct of the fighting—we may call it the feudal, knightly—class remained incurably anarchic. They had a ruling passion for conflict, echoed in the *Chansons de Geste* of the twelfth century, to gain, to retain, to avenge by war and pillage. In the incessant turmoil, as we have seen, the cohesion of lords and vassals in a feudal complex was a necessity of self-preservation and contributed to the formation of the reciprocal feudal contract. But the effective area of feudal control tended to be small and to decrease in size, for the vassal who felt himself strong enough would disregard the suzerain lord whom he did not urgently need. He could only be restrained by war, and the more circumscribed his territory the more prone he was to plunder the merchant, pilgrim, or traveller by unrightful exactions or plain brigandage. The usages of private war, too, were merciless to the unarmed peasant whose person, fields, and hovel were the prey of his lord's enemies and often of the greed of his lord. Yet even this turbulent early feudal society, or at any rate its chiefs, began to recognize its own disease. Churchmen, in spite of the decadence of the Church, took the lead. From 989 onwards, synods, beginning in Aquitaine and Burgundy, the most splintered provinces, anathematized ravagers of churches and despoilers of the poor. The movement spread, supported by the greater magnates; and sworn promises to abstain from violence to non-combatants and like misdeeds, and even from aggression in certain holy seasons, were made by the lords of a diocese or district for a term of years. The 'Peace of God', as it was called, needed renewal and was often broken, but it was a triumph of moral power over brute appetite. Amid outrage it was an effort of the better elements in society to recur to order and justice. About 1040 the 'Peace' was often supplemented by the more easily kept 'Truce of God' which forbade fighting from Thursday night to Monday morning all the year round. An analogous movement, the 'Indulgence' and the *Landfrieden*, which arose in Germany under Henry III, was designed to check the pernicious private feuds. If the practical success of the whole movement was small, it was a sign of a growing opinion which was to strengthen the hands of the greater potentates in controlling their tumultuous vassals and enforcing the quasi-orderly feudal obligations.

The dangers of keeping outside a feudal complex were self-evident. In the struggle for existence support had to be obtained by the individual. A real grant of land was far from being the only way of creating a fief. There was a constant spread of feudal tenure due to men's surrendering land they held in full ownership, their *alod* or *alleu*, to a powerful neighbour, lay or ecclesiastic, to be received back in fief. But the process of feudalization was never completed in all parts. If in England, after the Norman Conquest, all land was considered to be held, directly or indirectly, from the crown, and in northern France by 1200 it was the legal doctrine that all estates were held under feudal lords (*nulle terre sans seigneur*), in southern France allodial ownership remained common, and the rule was *nul seigneur sans titre*—no lordship was recognized without proof of title. Still more was allodial ownership of even wide lands long-lived in Germany beyond the Rhine and especially in the north-east. The great domains inherited by the Welfs in Saxony were only converted into a fief in the thirteenth century. But an allodial magnate could enfeoff parts of his land to others, although he owed no feudal service for it himself, and over it and more he might exercise the public powers and hold courts as an immunist lord, a Vogt (*advocatus*), or a count.

The small freeman, however, if he surrendered his allod to a powerful neighbour or bishopric or abbey, was unlikely to receive it back on terms of feudal service. He became a tenant on predial tenure and most probably, by degrees at least, sank into the ranks of the serfs tied to the land and personally unfree. By 1100 the mass of the peasantry were serfs, although freemen were to be found sprinkled everywhere and in some districts predominated. Bond or free, they held their land from the lord of their 'manor', in varying forms the typical rural organization. In spite of its manifold variations, the home of the 'typical' or 'textbook' manor was the corn-bearing plains of central and southern England, northern France, Germany, and Denmark. They lent themselves to the clustered village settlement with its open arable fields, its meadows, and its common 'waste' of woodland and pasture round it. Here labour-services, the two- or three-field system of agriculture, and serfdom itself had the most tenacious life. On the other hand, in hilly or pastoral country, the peasants lived in scattered hamlets, their dues to their lord were more in contributions of produce or money, and serfdom was rarely onerous and rapidly disappeared.

The most characteristic version of the manorial village, although narrowest in its distribution, was the English 'manor', which became the most closely organized and most durable of the type. It consisted of two once distinct elements, the economic and the administrative, and thus strove towards two intimately connected aims, the subsistence of the villagers, and the lord's profit and authority. The village community lay at the basis of the whole. In a brief description only an average account, subject to countless irregularities, can be given. The normal villager (*villanus, villein*) would hold a *yardland* or *virgate* of thirty acres (or its half, a *bovate*), distributed in scattered acre-strips in the three or two open fields of the manor, which might coincide with the village or be only a part of it. He followed the manor routine (its 'custom') in the cultivation, the ploughing, sowing, and reaping, of his strips; independent husbandry was barely possible in the open fields. In each year one field in rotation out of the two or three (as the case might be) was left fallow and unenclosed for beasts to graze in; the cultivated field or fields were fenced round. His own livestock up to a stated number were free to pasture in the 'waste'; he had his share of the hay-meadow. Intermingled with the tenants' strips in the open fields lay the strips kept by the lord of the manor in his own hands, his *demesne*. There was a strong tendency, however, to isolate the demesne in a home-farm. In this connexion arose the greater part of the labour services which the villager owed for his tenement. Each villein household owed *week-work* (one labourer) of usually three days a week on the demesne farm, which included its share of the ploughs, oxen, and implements for all kinds of work and cartage. The *cottars*, whose holdings were much smaller, owed of course less labour. At the peak periods of mowing and reaping, *boon-work* of all kinds was required in addition, and in this the freemen, socagers and others, who occupied their tenements for a rent or other terms implying free contract, took their part. A freeman, however, might hold land on villein tenure, and *vice versa*. The *assarts*, or reclamations from the waste, were commonly less burdened with the heavy dues of villeinage. Dues of all kinds, indeed, pressed on both villein and freeman of the manor, render of hens, eggs, special payments, etc. The villein, besides being tied to the soil, was subject to the servile fine of *merchet* (*formariage*) on his daughter's marriage and to the exaction of his best beast as heriot (*main-morte*) on his death; he paid the money levy of tallage at the lord's will; his corn was ground in the lord's mill; in France the lord's oven and his winepress were seigneurial monopolies. The villein might be selected as reeve or other petty official of rural manorial economy. His condition, however, was mitigated by the growth of the custom of the manor, which at any rate fixed the exactions he laboured under and secured him in his hereditary holding. Like the freeman he attended the manorial court, which declared the custom of the manor and its working. The lord of many manors would send round steward or bailiff to receive his profits and collect produce for his support in those in which he periodically resided. Besides the subsistence of the villagers, in short, their labour was to provide that of the warrior governing class and the allied ecclesiastical dignitaries, to both of whom they owed as a rule what little peace, justice, and enlightenment they had.

To oversee the performance of services, the render of dues, the inheritance of land, and the declaration of custom was a function of the lord's manor-court, but its judicial and policing powers were also far-reaching. In England, smaller misdemeanors were dealt with by it: cases of felony only if special franchises were obtained. There, too, its policing depended on the tithing system. In France, the area of non-seigneurial justice was much less, for there the disruption of the kingdom was more complete. The French baron ruled in arbitrary fashion over his serfs and was almost powerless with regard to his free *vassaux*.

The statement may be ventured in conclusion that the greatest feudal disintegration in western Francia was during the period when the typical feudal lay-out of society was in process of formation and feudal law still in crystallization. When in the twelfth century feudal custom, feudal rights and institutions as we generalize them were fully formulated, the anarchy in which they had received their impetus to grow was beginning to decline. The feudal reciprocity, the feudal bargain, which took shape from the mutual need of armed associates for self-preservation, had become a rigid bond enforceable on the faithless, and its very definition implied a renewed reign of order and legality, precise, limited, and artificial, for which it had once been the makeshift substitute.

(2) THE FOUNDING OF THE GERMAN MONARCHY

The kingdom of Germany was the first of the Frankish realms to recover from the anarchy of the late ninth century, and therefore to assume the lead in West European politics. This early recovery was largely due to the more conservative character of the German tribes east of the Rhine, compared with the territories to the west. Feudalism proper had made less progress. The public courts still subsisted in full working. The counts were doubtless vassals for their office and its endowment of land or as Vögte for ecclesiastics, but they were largely allodial proprietors of ancient stock. Their conservatism, however, implied and was partly due to the strong cohesion and tribal consciousness of the four German peoples, Saxons, Bavarians, Swabians, and East Franks or Franconians, which retained their tribal laws and divergent dialects, all the more easily because language, law, and tribe occupied relatively defined and solid areas. The rise of the tribal dukes, natives of their duchies, had given an increased strength to this particularism, while preserving in some degree the old official, not merely feudal, character of the administration. They had taken over the royal functions in their duchies, revolted from royal interference, and made the kingdom the most inharmonious of federations. Nor did their rule mean the end of private war within their duchies. Each was but one magnate among equals. The local dynasts waged their bitter feuds and grasped with the strong hand at the estates of their rivals and the Church. Franconia and Swabia were the scene of constant strife, and the Church in Bavaria was prostrate under the Duke, Arnulf 'the Bad'.

There were, however, two factors which made for union and the restoration of monarchical control. In spite of depletion, the royal estates, villages and forests, although inadequate, were still extensive in Franconia and Swabia, and while their scattered character prevented the formation of a solid royal domain (which happened in France), they gave the Crown (as in England) a wide possibility of local supervision and influence. Secondly, the churchmen, losing land yearly to their turbulent lay neighbours, either altogether or by advocateships and enfeoffment, were for the most part by tradition, education, and interest the powerful partisans of the monarchy, under which they had played the leading role in the unforgotten past. They still retained a conception of the orderly,

Fig. 89. Genealogical table of the Saxon, Salian and Hohenstaufen kings

civilized State, expressed in the kingship, and in spite of losses their spiritual prestige and their wealth and ability made them a power.

The election in 919 of Henry, Duke of Saxony, later nicknamed 'the Fowler,' as king of the Saxons and Franconians began the revival of the German monarchy. Materially, he brought to it his vast family estates in his duchy and the tribal loyalty of the warlike Saxons, who looked on him as their chief. Thus there was a solid foundation on which to build. Personally, he was a constructive statesman, strong and practical. Till his accession he had been a champion of ducal autonomy in his native Saxony and Thuringia, and he aimed at little more than being the effective head of a confederation. He showed for years no inclination to accept the centralizing ideas of the great ecclesiastics, whom he disliked, and he refused to be anointed and crowned by the Archbishop of Mainz. But he set himself to gain the recognition of his fellow dukes. Burchard of Swabia was easily reduced. He was confirmed in his duchy, but was forced to surrender the royal estates within it and to admit the royal nomination of its bishops. Arnulf 'the Bad' of Bavaria, popular with his nobles for his defence against the Magyars and whom the Bavarians had even proclaimed king in 919, made better terms. He was to appoint the Bavarian bishops, he struck coins, and he conducted his own foreign policy towards his Slav neighbours. Henry, however, was not satisfied with the four duchies: he was determined to recover Lotharingia for Germany. There was a strong current of loyalty to the Carolingians there, but also the faithless ambitions of its feudal lords. Gilbert, the duke, was an adept at changing sides. After long intermittent warfare the captivity (923) and then the death (929) of Charles the Simple of France decided the contest. It was easier for Henry to counter the non-Carolingian, King Raoul. In 925 Duke Gilbert was compelled to become his vassal and later married his daughter, Gerberga. Henceforward Lotharingia was an integral part of the German kingdom.

In six years Henry had established himself as unquestioned chief of the ducal confederation. It was his defence of his own duchy of Saxony and Thuringia and its repercussions on Germany as a whole which made him and his descendants something more. We have seen how he rescued Saxony from the Magyar raids, an object-lesson to the other tribes. His method of walling towns, like Goslar and Quedlinburg, was supplemented by his creation of a cavalry force, largely consisting of his own unfree *ministeriales*, which was imitated by other Saxon magnates. Both innovations were practised in the equally important warfare with the heathen Slav tribes, collectively called Wends, to the east. In the troublous times numbers of these had percolated west of the Elbe and Saale rivers, and fierce hostilities and mutual ravage were permanent between them and their German neighbours. Henry took up the merciless war in a spirit of conquest and expansion, thus beginning the *Drang nach Osten* (eastward thrust) at the expense of the Slavs which was to be a dominating force in German history. Of the enemy tribes those belonging to the Lyutitzi (Wiltzi) group were more resolute than the group of Sorb tribes to the south, but by the end of his reign Henry had obtained tribute and the nominal acceptance of Christianity from both. Merseburg on the frontier and Meissen amid the Sorbs were fortified. In conquered Wendish land he established military colonies of his *ministeriales*, the first steps in a vast colonizing movement. In addition he gained the overlordship of the Czech Dukes of Bohemia, now Christian, outplaying Arnulf of Bavaria. At the same time he recovered the Eider boundary against the heathen Gorm the Old of Denmark.

It was a sign of the development of Henry I's policy that he gave (928) the count's powers in his city to the Bishop of Toul in Lotharingia, imitating an expedient of the French Carolingians. It foreshadowed the alliance of the monarchy with the Church which was the key-note of the reign of his son Otto the Great. When Henry died in 936, the pre-eminence of Saxony was assured, and no one disputed the election of Otto I to succeed him. The new king at once signalized his conception of the kingship by his solemn sacring and coronation at Aachen, in Charlemagne's basilica, at the hands of the Archbishop of Mainz, when the four dukes of Lotharingia, Franconia, Swabia, and Bavaria acted as his chamberlain, steward, butler, and marshal at the State banquet. They were his vassals; he was the Lord's Anointed. He was renewing the unity of Germany and the Carolingian monarchy with the support of the episcopate. Ceremonial, seen and shared in by all, was then a most effective propaganda of ideas.

Nature had formed Otto the Great (936–73) equal to the task set by his ambitions. He had all his father's strength and practical wisdom with a persevering fortitude which carried him through the most dangerous crises. He was feared rather than loved, but could display a magnanimous tolerance and mercy on occasion. And he was a man of great conceptions. He was determined to be the real ruler of Germany, not the chief among her dukes. It meant an endeavour to bring internal peace and orderly justice. He not only used the Church as a loyal support; he furthered its ideals and culture and its civilizing mission in the turmoil of the time. He won his greatest triumph in rescuing Germany and all the West from the Magyars. But he was also intent on extending Germany and Christianity beyond the Elbe with fire and sword in the Wendish wars. His ambitions expanded with his fortunes. He early assumed the position of chief among the Western kings, and with the conquest of Italy and his new style of Emperor he aimed at the restoration of Charlemagne's Empire and the secular headship of Christendom.

To accomplish the union of Germany was a hard and lengthy task subject to many setbacks. The tribal dukes became disloyal at the symptoms of a new order. There were malcontents even in Saxony, of whom the most formidable were Otto's own brothers, the illegitimate and elder Thankmar, and the younger Henry, both aspirants for the crown. Lastly, the Carolingian Louis IV d'Outremer, overshadowed by his vassals in France, coveted Lotharingia, where some adherents still remained to him. The result was a widespread, if straggling and intermittent, rebellion in which the sons of the dead Arnulf of Bavaria (*ob.* 937), Eberhard of Franconia, Gilbert of Lotharingia, Thankmar and Henry, Louis d'Outremer, and even the slippery Frederick, Archbishop of Mainz, were protagonists (938–41). It was frustrated by the energy and diplomacy of Otto and by the fact that the rebels themselves were effectively lords only of their own lands, not masters in their duchies. Arnulf's brother, Berthold, was installed by Otto in Bavaria without the right to nominate the bishops, now resumed by the Crown. Thankmar was soon killed. Louis, who made spirited attacks, was at odds with his own chief vassals, Otto's allies. By a stroke of good fortune Gilbert and Eberhard both died in a fray with hostile Franconian counts (939). Henry submitted, to revolt and be pardoned again. This time he remained loyal, and was later rewarded (947) with the duchy of Bavaria. Louis desisted from his claim on Lotharingia, and became Otto's brother-in-law by marrying Gerberga, Gilbert's widow. It had been a war of raids and sieges. Otto now resorted to a system of family alliances for the control of the duchies. The dukes were his nominees; there was no question of hereditary right in the strict sense. Franconia he ruled directly: it was no longer the leading tribe, but an assemblage of counties. In his own Saxony he could safely entrust many of his ducal functions to his loyal kinsman, Herman Billung. In Swabia and Bavaria the new dukes were his eldest son by his English queen, Liudolf (949), and his brother Henry. Each was married to a daughter of a former duke of their tribe. Lotharingia was conferred (944) on a Franconian, Conrad the Red, who married Otto's daughter Liutgard. Thus the dukes were all strangers to their duchies and kinsmen of Otto. Time was to show that tribal particularism was unchanged: save Liudolf they were unpopular in their duchies; save Henry and the half-duke Herman they were disloyal to the king.

The result of this situation was a medley of cross-currents. The counts and nobles of the tribes chafed under the rule of their alien dukes, the dukes under the control of the Crown. The simmering discontent was brought to open conflict by the rivalries and ambitions of the dukes. As we shall see, Otto adopted in concert with his brother Henry the design of conquest in Italy. In the operations Duke Liudolf was unsuccessful, while Duke Henry and then Otto were victorious. In Pavia Otto took the Italian crown, and married his second wife, the widowed Italian queen, Adelaide, whose champion he had declared himself. Liudolf, fearing for his own

430

succession and at enmity with his uncle, withdrew to Germany to plot revolt. Otto also returned in haste (952) for counter-measures, while he charged Conrad of Lotharingia to complete the Italian campaign. But, when Conrad made an easy peace with the half-ousted King Berengar of Italy, he met with a stern reception from Otto and his treaty was drastically revised. Duke Henry, on the other hand, was rewarded by the rule of the March of Verona. Open revolt of the malcontents, Liudolf and Conrad,

soon followed (953). Otto, it seems, was taken by surprise: there were jealous malcontents in Saxony too. But the Lotharingians took arms against their duke, Conrad, whose real power was in Franconia, and Herman Billung broke the Saxon rebels. Still, the Swabians adhered to Liudolf, while the Bavarians turned against Henry, and the king failed to capture Mainz, where Archbishop Frederick was against him, as well as Regensburg. The cause of particularism, for the Lotharingians were more hostile to their duke than friendly to the king, was in the ascendant, when the folly of the dukes wrecked it. They had the unwisdom to aid, if not to invite, a fresh incursion of the Magyars, which roused their own supporters

Fig. 90. The Emperor Otto I dedicating Magdeburg cathedral to Christ

against them in the general suffering (954). Otto regained the upper hand even in Bavaria, and the rebels were lucky to obtain pardon at the cost of their dukedoms. Next year (955) the whole host of Magyars burst into Bavaria and besieged Augsburg. The danger rallied to Otto all five duchies, taught by bitter experience. Even Bohemia sent troops against the universal enemy. On 10 August 955 the Germans won the crushing, epoch-making victory of the Lechfeld, due largely to the ex-duke Conrad, now loyal, who fell in the battle.

After the revolt Otto tried fresh expedients with the dukedoms. Henry of course kept Bavaria, where he gradually took root. But Swabia was given to the native Burchard, and feud-ridden Lotharingia was conferred on the celibate youngest brother of the king, Bruno, since 953 Archbishop of Cologne. Bruno was a firm and prudent statesman, the very man to reduce the duchy to some sort of order, as well as an excellent bishop. His appointment, however, is merely an exceptional instance of Otto's Church policy, on which he relied to rule Germany. Large though his family

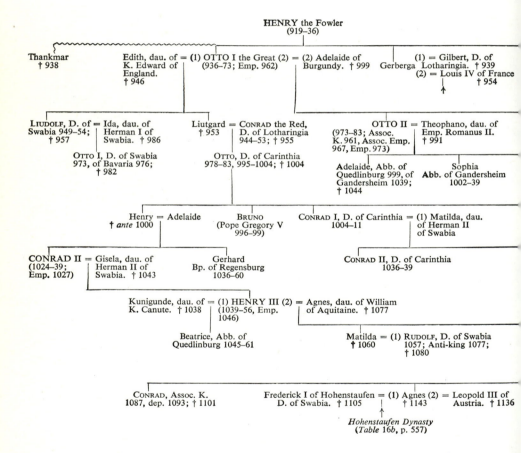

HENRY the Fowler
(919–36)

Thankmar
† 938

Edith, dau. of = (1) OTTO I the Great (2) = (2) Adelaide of
K. Edward of   (936–73; Emp. 962)   Burgundy. † 999
England.
† 946

Gerberga
(1) = Gilbert, D. of
Lotharingia. † 939
(2) = Louis IV of France
† 954

LIUDOLF, D. of = Ida, dau. of
Swabia 949–54;   Herman I of
† 957   Swabia. † 986

OTTO I, D. of Swabia
973, of Bavaria 976;
† 982

Liutgard = CONRAD the Red,
† 953   D. of Lotharingia
944–53; † 955

OTTO, D. of Carinthia
978–83, 995–1004; † 1004

OTTO II = Theophano, dau. of
(973–83; Assoc.   Emp. Romanus II.
K. 961, Assoc. Emp.   † 991
967, Emp. 973)

Adelaide, Abb. of
Quedlinburg 999, of
Gandersheim 1039;
† 1044

Sophia
Abb. of Gandersheim
1002–39

Henry = Adelaide
† ante 1000

BRUNO
(Pope Gregory V
996–99)

CONRAD I, D. of Carinthia = (1) Matilda, dau.
1004–11   of Herman II
                               of Swabia

CONRAD II = Gisela, dau. of
(1024–39;   Herman II of
Emp. 1027)   Swabia. † 1043

Gerhard
Bp. of Regensburg
1036–60

CONRAD II, D. of Carinthia
1036–39

Kunigunde, dau. of = (1) HENRY III (2) = Agnes, dau. of William
K. Canute. † 1038   (1039–56, Emp.   of Aquitaine. † 1077
                     1046)

Beatrice, Abb. of
Quedlinburg 1045–61

Matilda = (1) RUDOLF, D. of Swabia
† 1060   1057; Anti-king 1077;
             † 1080

CONRAD, Assoc. K.
1087, dep. 1093; † 1101

Frederick I of Hohenstaufen = (1) Agnes (2) = Leopold III of
D. of Swabia. † 1105   † 1143   Austria. † 1136

Hohenstaufen Dynasty
(*Table 16b*, p. 557)

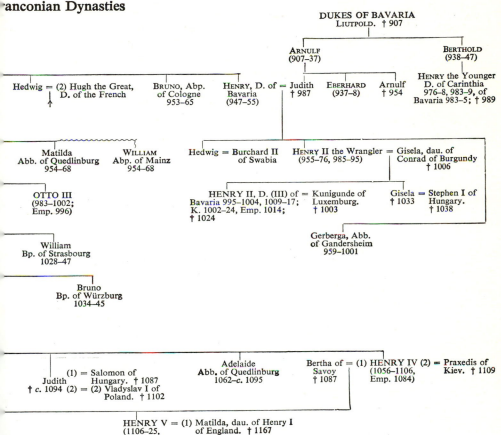

DUKES OF BAVARIA
LIUTPOLD. † 907

ARNULF
(907–37)

BERTHOLD
(938–47)

HENRY the Younger
D. of Carinthia
976–8, 983–9, of
Bavaria 983–5; † 989

Hedwig = (2) Hugh the Great,
D. of the French

BRUNO, Abp.
of Cologne
953–65

HENRY, D. of = Judith
Bavaria   † 987
(947–55)

EBERHARD
(937–8)

Arnulf
† 954

Matilda
Abb. of Quedlinburg
954–68

WILLIAM
Abp. of Mainz
954–68

Hedwig = Burchard II
of Swabia

HENRY II the Wrangler = Gisela, dau. of
(955–76, 985–95)   Conrad of Burgundy
                                    † 1006

OTTO III
(983–1002;
Emp. 996)

HENRY II, D. (III) of = Kunigunde of
Bavaria 995–1004, 1009–17;   Luxemburg.
K. 1002–24, Emp. 1014;   † 1003
† 1024

Gisela = Stephen I of
† 1033   Hungary.
            † 1038

Gerberga, Abb.
of Gandersheim
959–1001

William
Bp. of Strasbourg
1028–47

Bruno
Bp. of Würzburg
1034–45

Judith
† c. 1094

(1) = Salomon of
      Hungary. † 1087
(2) = (2) Vladyslav I of
      Poland. † 1102

Adelaide
Abb. of Quedlinburg
1062–c. 1095

Bertha of = (1) HENRY IV (2) = Praxedis of
Savoy   (1056–1106,   Kiev. † 1109
† 1087   Emp. 1084)

HENRY V = (1) Matilda, dau. of Henry I
(1106–25,   of England. † 1167
Emp. 1111)

433

estates and those still remaining to the Crown were, they were insufficient by themselves, even with the adjunct of the profits of fines, tolls, and other royal sources of income, to support his power, and the unfree *ministeriales* enfeoffed on them, although numerous, did not provide by themselves a sufficient armed force. The lay counts and magnates were practically hereditary local lords, intent on family aggrandisement, and the worst culprits in the reigning disorder; their loyalty could not be trusted, their contingents for the king's service were stinted, and their particularism was intense. In fact, hereditary feudalism was the chief danger of the monarchy. On the other hand, celibate bishops and abbots could not turn their ecclesiastical lands and the jurisdiction annexed to them into hereditary fiefs, the military service due from them to the Crown was heavier than that of the lay magnates,[1] they could be called on for the full performance of the duties of food-rents and *albergue* as the king passed to and fro in his ceaseless journeys from one domain to another through his kingdom. As a rule they were the firm allies of the protecting monarch against their encroaching lay neighbours and *Vögte*. Furthermore, in an illiterate society, the higher clergy formed the only educated class, and that an able one, which could keep the records and conduct the business of the king's household court. They manned his chapel and chancery. They were his counsellors, whom he could select for efficiency, his envoys abroad, his embryo bureaucracy at home. They could conceive a German kingdom and an orderly society. Hence Otto, in endowing bishoprics and abbeys with fresh lands, tolls, mints, and jurisdictions, which were, so to say, excised as enclaves from the counties, and made bishops and great abbots princes of the kingdom by the side of dukes and counts, was really increasing the resources and the power of the monarchy by what seemed reckless generosity. He was replacing untrustworthy lay officials by trusty ecclesiastics.

But the success of this policy depended on the royal control of the German Church. The king must nominate bishop and abbot and have the most binding claim known to the age on their constant loyalty. Otto revindicated for the Crown the right of appointment. The ancient form of election by 'clergy and people' might be maintained, though not always, but the real decision lay with him, and he appointed his trained chaplains and often kinsmen, like his bastard William to the see of Mainz (954). The bishopric or abbey was assimilated to the fief. The elect did homage and fealty to him and was invested with his office and lands by the king, who gave him his crozier with the words 'Accipe ecclesiam'—'Receive the Church' (of N.)—, a ceremony which appeared under Lewis the German. It offended ecclesiastical order, for the crozier symbolized the care of souls, which the

---

[1] In the Italian campaign of 981 the bishops and abbots sent 1504 knights, the lay vassals about 600.

metropolitan, not the king, should confer, but it was made easier by the sacredness of the royal office and the universal custom which made the founder of a church and his heirs its proprietors. Thus Otto, who did not otherwise intervene in the bishops' spiritual functions, was their master as State officials. The danger which was to emerge was the contradiction between the two sides of the bishops' duties, spiritual and secular. Did Church or king have the first claim on them? But the dislocation of the Western Church in the tenth century hid the flaw in Otto's system. Otherwise, his bishops were men of good repute, and in the time they could spare for their pastoral functions they performed them with pious zeal.

Throughout the period of internal broils there had been ceaseless warfare with the Wends. Otto chiefly worked through two able Saxon counts, Herman Billung and Gero. Time and time again there was furious war with the tribes between the Elbe and the Oder, a war which was accompanied by military colonization in half-conquered territory. Herman founded the Billung March among the Obodrite group round modern Mecklenburg; the March of Gero extended over the groups of the Lyutitzi up to the Oder and the Sorbs as far as the Lusatias. Otto himself in 950 enforced submission on the Christian Boleslav, Duke of Czech Bohemia. Here there was no attempt at direct German rule. On Gero's death (965) his sphere was divided into three Marches, but besides fortresses, garrisons, and colonists, Otto relied on the Church and the Christianization of the stubborn heathen Wends. Christianity and German dominion were twin aspects of the conquest. In 948 he erected missionary bishoprics at Brandenburg and Havelberg among the Lyutitzi. In 968, with papal approval, and after prolonged negotiations with the overgrown archbishopric of Mainz, he succeeded in founding an archbishopric at Magdeburg for his Slavonic conquest. Subject missionary sees were then set up in the lands of the Sorbs. It was a step never cancelled in the *Drang nach Osten*.

(3) OTTO I AND THE HOLY ROMAN EMPIRE

For all his activity in the east, Otto never lost sight of his ambition to reconstruct the Empire of Charlemagne. After their reconciliation in 940, King Louis d'Outremer was almost his client, though not his vassal. Otto supported him against his overmighty subjects both by expeditions which had no great success and by ecclesiastical pressure on his other brother-in-law, Hugh the Great, Duke of the French. At least Louis was able to recover his only town of Laon and to obtain the renewal of Hugh's homage (950). When he died his son Lothaire could succeed him as King of France without opposition (954). The unwieldy frontier duchy of Lotharingia was divided (959) for its better order by Archbishop Bruno between two powerful counts, Godfrey who oversaw the northern half, and Frederick, whose sphere was the southern half. On Bruno's death (965), they continued as dukes, Godfrey of Lower Lotharingia (Lothier) and Frederick of Upper Lotharingia (Lorraine), but they did not acquire the authority of the tribal dukes in their more feudalized territory. Meantime a diplomatic success of value was gained in the weak, anarchic realms of Burgundy and Provence. The history of the two kingdoms had been scanty and unhappy. Rodolph I (888–911) of Jurane Burgundy had maintained himself against the Emperor Arnulf. His son Rodolph II (911–37), besides annexing a small slice of Swabia, had been for a brief period King of Italy, where he was succeeded by Count Hugh of Arles, who ruled in Provence in Lewis the Blind's name and then in his own. When Rodolph II died, King Hugh married his widow Bertha himself and his daughter Adelaide to his own son Lothar. He no doubt hoped to rule Jurane Burgundy, but Otto contrived to kidnap Rodolph's son and heir Conrad (937–93), who remained at first his prisoner and afterwards his client. Conrad was gradually recognized in the southern kingdom, and c. 950 on King Hugh's death obtained the submission of the coastland, Provence proper south of the river Durance. In this way an enlarged kingdom of Burgundy was formed, but it was nearly a shadow. Conrad and his son Rodolph III were the most powerless kings in the West, and their nominal subjects were the victims of private war and the Saracen marauders.

Otto was wisely content to protect weak kings in a France and Burgundy disintegrated among the discordant magnates. The conquest of Italy seemed desirable and feasible. It was also alluring. The Dukes of Bavaria and Swabia could not be restrained from invasion. The land seemed richer than it was; its possession would extend Otto's dominions to the Mediterranean Sea and its civilized coasts, and restore contact with the fabulous wealth and splendour of the East, whereas the land route was severed by the Magyars. It would make closer relations possible with the Papacy and tighten the control Otto was exercising on the German Church. More than all perhaps, it was in the tradition of Charlemagne and Arnulf which Otto was reviving. It would crown his life's work.

From the date of the victory of the Garigliano (915) the state of Italy had been miserably embroiled. In the south, Lombard princes strove with the Byzantines; in the north, the *Regnum Italicum*, although King Berengar was crowned Emperor, it was a mere change of title—he was as weak as ever. Real power was in the hands of certain marquesses and counts, such as those of Tuscany and Ivrea, who preferred, it was said, two kings whom they could play off one against the other. In 922 they brought in Rodolph II of Jurane Burgundy, while Berengar was cooped up in his own march of Friuli till his murder in 924. But Rodolph, too, was ousted. In 926 the magnates raised Count Hugh of Arles, a descendant of the

Emperor Lothar, to the throne. Hugh was strong and wily. If he could not revive a central administration, he did by force and treachery endow his Provençal kinsmen with the great marches and bishoprics. He nearly achieved the rule of Rome and the imperial title. There the infamous Marozia, the daughter of Theophylact, overthrew in 928 Pope John X and in 931 raised her own illegitimate son, whose father was Pope Sergius III, to the Papacy. Her then husband was Marquess Guido of Tuscany, but he died and she found a successor in King Hugh, Guido's half-brother. The relationship was denied by the shameless king and the Tuscan house overthrown with brazen duplicity. Then there was a revolution. Her son Alberic, whom she bore to her first husband, Alberic of Spoleto, rose up against her and drove out King Hugh (932). For years Alberic governed despotically and well as Prince and Senator of the Romans. The Popes were his puppets, and King Hugh was unable to conquer him. Meantime Hugh with astute perfidy was making and unmaking the magnates; his most permanent promotion was that of his bastard Hubert to be Marquess of Tuscany. But he alarmed them all, and at last the most dangerous marquess left, Berengar of Ivrea, grandson of the Emperor Berengar, fled to Otto's court. In 945 he returned to meet with a general welcome from bishops and magnates, even those most recently favoured by Hugh. A singular compromise was effected, by which Hugh and his popular co-regent son, Lothar II, reigned in a kind of captivity and Berengar of Ivrea governed as 'chief-councillor'. Hugh was at last (947) allowed to retreat to Provence, where he died (948), and the way was cleared for Berengar by the sudden death (950) of Lothar II. Now Berengar II and his son Adalbert were elected joint kings, but their throne was most unstable. How little Berengar was ever master of the kingdom was shown by the civil war waged for five years by two rivals for the archbishopric of Milan. There was a large disaffected party among bishops and magnates, which collected round the wealthy widow of Lothar II, Adelaide of Jurane Burgundy. She was a beautiful woman of strong character, and Berengar, who was needy, seized on her dower-lands, while she fled to the impregnable castle of a friendly noble, Adalbert-Atto of Canossa. Her hand was the reward of rescue. Liudolf of Swabia and Henry of Bavaria both intervened, and in 951 Otto the Great himself undertook his first invasion of Italy in force. Bishops and nobles rallied to him; he declared himself King of Italy and married Adelaide. Then his difficulties began. Alberic and his Pope refused an imperial coronation at Rome, and the king was obliged to hasten back (952) to Germany to counter the plots of his jealous son Liudolf. His representative in Italy, Conrad the Red, came to terms with the unsubdued Berengar, which Otto, balked of his ambitions, made far more severe. Berengar was forced to cede Verona and Friuli to Duke Henry, and did homage to Otto for his mutilated kingdom.

Berengar's renewed reign was troublous throughout. He was at odds with the episcopate and suspicious of the lay magnates. In central Italy the death of Alberic in 954 deprived him of a possible ally. Alberic's son and successor, John-Octavian, who united princedom and Papacy by being chosen, following his dying father's command, to be Pope John XII in 955, was a dissolute and incompetent boy, whose pontificate was a glaring scandal and who manifested no friendship for the Italian king. The times were soon ripe for a fresh German invasion. It was victorious, but the death of its leader Liudolf (957) deprived it of effect. Exiles thronged to Otto's court, and war between John XII and Berengar precipitated Otto's return, for the imperial crown was offered him by the Pope. He easily occupied the *Regnum Italicum* (961), while Berengar held out in his strongest castle, S. Leo. On 2 February 962 he received the imperial crown and sacring in St Peter's.

There was still Berengar II to conquer in his fastness of S. Leo, and during the siege Emperor and Pope speedily fell out. Before his coronation Otto had sworn not to intervene in Rome without the Pope's assent; after it, in the diploma he granted John XII, while he surprisingly repeated the papal version of the pact of 774, he also renewed the *Constitutio Romana* laid down by the Emperor Lothar in 824 with its arrangements for imperial control. John XII had hoped for an ally, not an effective suzerain, although he had duly sworn fealty at the coronation; and he changed sides at once. Otto resolved to depose him. The scandal of his life weakened the Pope's position, in spite of the general belief that a Pope could be judged by no man. Otto drove him from Rome, from which he exacted a novel oath not to elect a Pope without his consent. Then from a synod of obedient bishops he obtained John's deposition and the election of a lay Roman, Leo VIII (December 963). Berengar's surrender and captivity followed immediately. But John scouted the synod and re-entered Rome. German rule was hated, and when John suddenly died, the Romans elected an irreproachable Pope, Benedict V (964). Otto promptly replied by starving the city to surrender, capturing Benedict, and reinstating Leo VIII, who was soon succeeded by John XIII. In spite of his charter the actual Papal State was reduced by Otto to the so-called Patrimony and the Sabina. The spirited young King Adalbert was expelled from Lombardy, as the land north of the Apennines was now called (965).

In this way Otto re-created the Empire of the West, or the Holy Roman Empire to give it its later style, which was to be the central fact of Europe for centuries. It was compounded of Germany and the *Regnum Italicum* and of the pre-eminent secular dignity of Roman Emperor. Resting on the tradition of Charlemagne, it was really new. Charlemagne had ruled the Church, Otto was only its protector. The Holy Roman Empire at its widest did not cover all Western Christendom. Within it, too, particularism was dominant, already stirred by instinctive national dislikes which were in the long run to give birth to nationality. Central government had become restricted: even in Germany officialism had given way to feudalism. Otto's aim, there and in Italy, was to be able to rely on and exploit the local potentates who possessed immediate power. In Italy he inaugurated a clever balancing of the lay and ecclesiastical magnates, who saw their best interest in obeying an often absentee Emperor. The bishops, often Germans, became his nominees. In an ancient land of cities they had in the days of anarchy headed their citizens. Like other magnates they had increased their 'immunity'; some already—and Otto increased their number —exercised the powers of a count within their cities and a radius round. Their importance for the monarchy rendered control of the Papacy the more essential. The leaders of the lay magnates were the marquesses. The Marquess of Tuscany and the Duke of Spoleto were almost viceroys over counts like the German dukes; the four northern marquesses were each counts of several counties, and their custom of division or compossession among male heirs soon began to weaken them, for they were prolific stocks.

Otto's embarrassments arose not in North Italy, which prospered under the comparative peace he gave, but in Rome which was restive under his Popes, and in the south which he desired to annex at the expense of the true Roman Empire of the East. At the same time he was eager for the recognition and friendship of the Byzantines, to whom his imperial title appeared a barbaric impertinence. He enforced on the Romans his choice of Pope John XIII (965–72), who seconded his policy by creating new Latin archbishoprics in the south. He secured the allegiance of Pandolf Ironhead, the Lombard Prince of Capua-Benevento, by granting him Spoleto, thus forming for a while a great southern dominion. With the Byzantine Emperor Nicephorus Phocas he tried a combination of war in Apulia and negotiation, the latter vividly described by his envoy, the scurrilous historian, Bishop Liudprand of Cremona. The final result was a treaty with the Emperor John Zimiskes, which gave a Byzantine princess, Theophano, daughter of Romanus II, to be the wife (972) of Otto II, the Western Emperor's surviving son by Adelaide, whom he had associated with himself (967) as co-regent Emperor, while Liudolf's son, also named Otto, was given Swabia by his uncle. The marriage was to have a share in producing singular innovations in imperial policy.

For six years Otto the Great himself was occupied in Italy. He only returned to Germany in 972, the year before his death. His epoch-making reign had closed the period of mere anarchy in central Europe and started the revival of Western civilization after its partial collapse. Even the Saracens of Fraxinetum were extirpated by a coalition of counts c. 972, and the west Alpine passes made reasonably safe for travellers and merchants. This had its influence on the new prosperity.

Óbodrites
(Billung Mark)

SAXONY

Liutitzi
(Nordmark)

THURINGIA

Brandenburg

FRISIA

LOTHARINGIA

●Cologne

Sorbs
(Ostmark)

(Lusatia)

Mainz●

FRANCONIA

NORD
GAU

(Zeitz)

(Meissen)

BOHEMIA

KINGDOM

OF

FRANCE

SWABIA

BAVARIA

OST-
MARK

CARINTHIA

KINGDOM

OF

BURGUNDY

KINGDOM

OF
ITALY

Pavia●

PATRIMONIUM PETRI

CROATIA

Ravenna

Ancona

Spoleto

Rome

(Byzantine)

Benevento

Naples

SICILY
(Fatimids)

THE WESTERN EMPIRE
IN THE TENTH CENTURY

Map 11

440

(4) OTTO II AND OTTO III

Otto II (973–83), ascending the throne at the unready age of eighteen, did not possess his father's genius, but he was not without vigour and resolution. His imagination, fostered by his brilliant wife Theophano, was captivated by the imperial idea of Otto the Great, which he pursued only too faithfully. But in fact there were many weaknesses in his father's edifice, within and without Germany, with which it was his lot to cope. Particularism was as strong as ever, especially in Bavaria, where his disloyal cousin Henry the Wrangler, who aimed at the crown, was duke. Lotharingia was honeycombed by the ambitions of its feudal lords as well as by a sneaking inclination towards the Carolingians of France. The newly annexed Wends were burning to revolt and return openly to their ancestral heathenism. The Czechs of Bohemia and the Poles on the rivers Oder and Vistula, recently united and Christianized, were alert to dissociate their Christianity from German domination. To the north the Viking spirit had risen to new heights and the Danes were yet uncertain whether Germany or England was the better prey. In Rome the instinct of disorderly independence was undiminished: its protagonists, the Crescentii, even thrust in an Anti-Pope, Boniface VII, for a few months, murdering the legitimate Benedict VI (974–5).

In repressing Henry the Wrangler Otto II relied on the support of his nephews, the two Ottos, sons of Liudolf and Conrad the Red, as well as on two Franconian brothers of Babenberg. In 976 the Wrangler was deposed and Liudolf's son, already Duke of Swabia, was given a reduced Bavaria; Berthold of Babenberg was made a margrave of the Nordgau, and his brother Liutpold margrave of the East Mark of Bavaria, the nucleus of the later Austria. As margraves (*markgrafen*) they were more independent of the duke than plain counts. Further, the duchy of Carinthia was severed from Bavaria and given to Henry the Younger, cousin of the Wrangler and belonging to the native Bavarian line. This was risky, and while Otto II was subduing Boleslav of Bohemia and cowing Mesco (Mieszko) of Poland, who had backed the Wrangler, the Carinthian Henry joined his cousin in a fresh revolt. Thereupon he was replaced (978) by Otto, son of Conrad the Red. Bavaria lost its exceptional independence in these events, but the two Henries retained their formidable possessions as magnates, while the revolts had estranged from the Emperor his mother, who hated her step-children.

Meantime the Danes were warded off in the north and Lothaire of France in the west. Otto II tried the device of appointing the Carolingian Charles, Lothaire's brother, Duke of Lower Lorraine, to pacify its troublesome counts (975), but this did not prevent a sudden raid of the French king, who captured Aachen and nearly took Otto himself (978). A counter-

Fig. 91. The Emperor Otto II and Empress Theophano

raid had little effect, and the two were nominally reconciled (980). The understanding, however, between the two dynasties had been terminated.

With some sort of order in Germany, Otto II now unhappily turned to Italian ambitions. The weakness of the Byzantines against the attacks of the Saracens of Sicily and the wars of the Lombard principalities after the death of Pandolf Ironhead furnished the opportunity. Otto made the

Fig. 92. Henry the Wrangler, Duke of Bavaria

Lombards his vassals, but failed to conquer Byzantine Apulia before a Saracen army landed in Calabria under the emir Abu'l-Qasim. In 982 the Emperor received a crushing defeat through sheer bad generalship near Stilo. He only escaped by swimming to a Byzantine ship and then leaping overboard to swim to his base at Rossano.

Not only the Italian scheme was frustrated; the Empire rocked to its foundations at this disaster, which had involved the loss of the flower of the German nobility. Swein Forkbeard of Denmark overran the border. Worst of all, the Slavs rose in a body. The Obodrites burnt Hamburg; the Lyutitzi destroyed Brandenburg, the Bohemians Zeitz in the Sorb territory. Although the Saxon margraves checked the Wends' advance west of the Elbe, all the northern part of Otto the Great's annexations was lost to Germany and Christendom for more than a century.

Otto II reacted with his usual energy, but Italy chained his personal interest. In an assembly or 'Diet' of princes at Verona (983), he gave way to his mother's influence. Otto of Swabia and Bavaria was just dead. Otto of Carinthia was deposed. Both Bavaria and Carinthia were now given to Henry the Younger. On the other hand, a Franconian Conrad received Swabia, and the Emperor's infant son Otto was elected German King. Otto II had just outraged Roman feeling by promoting his Lombard adviser, Bishop Peter of Pavia, to the Papacy as John XIV, and was waging war on the autonomous and wealthy Byzantine vassal, Venice, with a view to its subjugation, when he died on 7 December 983. In the *Regnum Italicum* his death produced no explosion. The magnates and bishops, led by Marquess Hugh of Tuscany, held by the Empresses Theophano and Adelaide to maintain the *status quo*. But in Rome Crescentius II seized power with the title of Patrician, sold the Papacy to the Anti-Pope Boniface VII, who murdered his Lombard predecessor (984), and on his death appointed the ill-reputed John XV. He did not, however, repudiate the Empire: Theophano could visit Rome as its sovereign (989).

In Germany there was an armed competition for the regency and indeed for the Crown. Henry the Wrangler, supported by some bishops and magnates, seized the child-king. Against him were ranged a group of Lotharingians, Conrad of Swabia, Archbishop Willigis of Mainz, and most Saxons, to whom Henry seemed a Bavarian alien. Lothaire of France, in hopes of Lotharingia, backed his own claim by invasion. But Lothaire was neutralized by his own great vassals; and the ablest ecclesiastic of the day, Gerbert of Aurillac, *scholasticus* of Rheims, a protégé of Otto and ex-Abbot of Bobbio, pulled every diplomatic wire. Even in Bavaria the Wrangler was opposed by his cousin of the native line, Duke Henry the Younger. He had been willing to win the crown by ceding Lotharingia to Lothaire. The end of the struggle was that the two Empresses were established as regents, while Henry the Wrangler was given back Bavaria without Carinthia, which was kept by the other Henry. Very soon Theophano ousted her mother-in-law and ruled with Willigis's help until her death in 991, when Adelaide took her place.

A minority was in any case an evil amid the self-willed, turbulent magnates; the dangers on the frontiers made matters worse. The Vikings renewed their raids on Saxony. The Wendish war raged on, with the general result that while the Lyutitzi and Obodrites were unsubdued, the Sorbs to the south were kept under, partly through Bohemian help. When Otto III at the age of fourteen took control in 994, the Wends formed a heathen block roughly between the Elbe and the Oder, fighting for their independence against the Germans on one side and the expanding Christian Slav state of Poland under Boleslav I the Great on the other, while Bohemia, likewise Slav and Christian, veered unwillingly between the two aggressive competitors.

Otto III, in spite of his youth, lacked neither strength nor ability, which was almost genius, nor a policy. He was half-Saxon, half-Byzantine. From Otto the Great he inherited the capacity to form wide political conceptions, from Theophano a Byzantine intellectualism and, so to say, a Byzantine nostalgia. He had been taught by a Calabrian Greek; he was profoundly influenced by that most learned scholar, the renowned Gerbert, now contesting the archbishopric of Rheims. He dreamed of a remodelled Roman Empire of the West, combining under his own headship, with the Papacy as his partner, a Christian federation of Germans, Italians, and Slavs. The scheme was grandiose, but in characteristic medieval fashion Gerbert and Otto took no account of distances and climates, rival, incompatible ambitions, peoples completely hostile or strangers to each other, ruling classes illiterate and undisciplined, and above all the narrow, weak basis of this ideal Empire in lands where central government and the mere beginnings of a bureaucracy were struggling to assert themselves with insufficient means over the strong provincial lords. By pompous assertion of his imperial claims and by a largely conceived policy of co-operation with neighbour rulers in the spread of Christianity, Otto hoped to transcend the limitations of his German kingship, the source of his real power, which indeed he scarcely realized. His sympathetic mentor, Gerbert, who knew Spain and Italy as well as France and Germany, was from his point of view more practical. The Western Church, much dislocated as it was, had remained a unity, an organization based on religious convictions, not on material power, and Otto's schemes, visionary in the secular realm, produced lasting, solid results in ecclesiastical politics.

In 996 Germany was quiet enough for Otto III to enter Italy and receive the imperial crown. Pope John XV died before he reached Rome, and the Romans submissively asked and obtained from him a new Pope. Otto made a bold choice. His father had nominated a Lombard; he selected the first German, his young cousin, Bruno, a son of Otto of Carinthia, to be Pope as Gregory V (996–9). Crescentius was deprived of his 'patriciate'. But when the confident Emperor left Italy, the Romans under Crescentius drove out the rash and hated young Pope, and set up in his stead John XVI Philagathus, the Calabrian, who had been Otto's tutor and was then

*Fig. 93 (and opposite). The Emperor Otto III, with representatives
of clergy and nobility, and the four nations*

returning from an embassy to gain his pupil a Byzantine bride. The election,
if cunning, did not placate Otto. In 998 he came back to Rome with
imposing forces. John XVI was degraded and mutilated; Crescentius II
was put to death: and Otto gave full play to his imperial ideas. His seal
bore the legend, 'Renovatio imperii Romanorum'. Hitherto the chanceries
of Germany and Italy had been distinct; now they were united under the
chancellor Heribert, who became Archbishop of Cologne in 999. The
Emperor's chosen counsellors were otherwise non-Germans; Gerbert,
since 998 Archbishop of Ravenna; Hugh, Marquess of Tuscany; Peter,
Bishop of Como, the titular arch-chancellor of Italy. In 999, Gerbert, the
Frenchman, was raised to the Papacy as Sylvester II, a significant name.

Otto's posturing as an idealized, theocratic Constantine and Charlemagne

446

*Fig. 93 (and opposite). The Emperor Otto III, with representatives
of clergy and nobility, and the four nations*

grew with the years. He entitled himself 'servant of Jesus Christ', 'servant
of the Apostles', in rivalry with the *servus servorum Dei* of the Popes. In
a scolding, argumentative diploma he denounced the Donation of Constantine as a forgery, that of Charles the Bald as invalid, and granted
Sylvester eight counties of the Pentapolis, hitherto under Hugh of Tuscany,
as a new gift. He numbered the Pope among his *optimates*, and treated
Rome itself as his own chief capital. Byzantine titles, sometimes written
in the Greek alphabet, were adopted by his courtiers. 'He would not see
delightful Germany, the land of his birth, so great a love possessed him of
dwelling in Italy.'

Imperial theocracy, however, was not Otto's only ideal. He had a genuine
religious enthusiasm and ascetic mentors, the Czech St Adalbert, the

Lombard St Romuald, and the Greek St Nilus of Calabria. By fits he went on pilgrimage or into monastic austerities. But there was a practical policy also involved. St Adalbert was slain in a mission to the heathen Prussians; St Romuald at Ravenna was the oracle of would-be missionaries. Otto divorced the aim of Christianization from that of Germanization. In his last journey north of the Alps (999–1000) he visited Duke Boleslav in Poland as an acknowledged suzerain, and there erected the Polish archbishopric of Gniezno (Gnesen). German Magdeburg found its missionary sphere of conquest restricted by a native Slav Church. In the same year the newly Christian 'Duke' of Hungary, Stephen I, obtained a royal crown and a native archbishopric for his country from Pope Sylvester. The ecclesiastical independence thus established for Poland and Hungary was never revoked, but the system of friendly co-operation with the Empire, wise as it might be, ran too counter to the instincts of all parties to last.

Meantime trouble was brewing in Lombardy. The Ottonian peace had brought prosperity, increase of population, assarts in the wide waste lands, trade in the cities. With prosperity came unrest among the country nobles and the citizens, two largely identical groups through the nobles being very commonly part-residents in the cities. Under the great magnates, bishops, abbots, marquesses, and counts, were ranged the *capitanei* or barons and the *secundi milites* or plain knights. Lower again were the traders of the cities or plebeians, the class distinction being due more to their not holding land on feudal tenure than to their origin. A resentment had arisen among all these discordant classes at the enlarging rule of the bishops, who were continuously favoured by the Ottos. The citizens of all ranks were restive, as when Milan, during the minority, warred with its archbishop. In spite of fresh imperial grants the prelates were losing ground, often owing to their family ties or to other difficulties. Nominal leases (*libellariae*) and over-enfeoffment were depleting the church estates. Ardoin, Marquess of Ivrea, was in sympathy with the lesser nobles and at odds with the Bishop of Vercelli, whom they killed. Otto III took the bishops' side. In 997 he enacted that no lease should outlast the grantor's life. In 999 he condemned Ardoin to confiscation and gave Leo, the new Bishop of Vercelli, the counties of Vercelli and Santhià, the first of such grants in Lombardy, although the whole province of Ravenna had been placed under its archbishop. It was an attempt to check the growth of hereditary feudalism, and Ardoin, although driven back, still resisted in his castles.

In the south nothing but formal submission could be gained from the Lombard princes, and in the centre the disaffection of the Romans was proof against the Emperor's courtship. In February 1001 they suddenly besieged him in his palace on the Aventine. Although his eloquence saved him, he left the city in revolt. Bad news reached him from the north. The neglected Germans were ready to rebel, only held back by his loyal cousin,

Henry of Bavaria, son of the Wrangler. On 23 January 1002 he died at Paterno near the Tiber, when preparing to besiege Rome with reinforcements. His Germans had to fight their way to Germany with the corpse. Ardoin seized the Italian crown; John Crescentius ruled Rome as patrician; but central Italy and part of Lombardy remained faithful to the Empire, while practically autonomous.

The confusion was really a sign of revival in the particularistic form which characterized medieval Italy. The lesser landholders were now more numerous; if enfeoffed or leaseholders they were striving for hereditary tenure, and for a share in the public authority. The seaport towns were making head against their Moslem foes: Venice in 1002 won a three days' sea-battle off Bari, which saved the town. In all this, as in similar internal changes in Germany, the megalomania of Otto III had no share.

(5) THE REVIVAL OF IMPERIAL POWER

The death of the childless Emperor left the throne vacant and extinguished the male line of Otto the Great. The principle of election to the crown naturally gathered strength. It was only after negotiations and a short civil war that Henry II, Duke of Bavaria and descendant of Henry I,[1] secured the prize. He was obliged to win recognition from Duke Bernard Billung and the Saxons by guaranteeing their tribal law, his Saxon rival, Eckhard, Margrave of Meissen, being disliked and soon murdered. A more widely supported competitor, the Franconian Herman II, Duke of Swabia, was isolated and subdued. In all these events the separate proceedings of the tribes and duchies were manifest, and throughout his reign Henry was busied with the uphill and endless task of holding the realm together and suppressing the feuds and rebellions (which were frequently the same thing) of the great nobles. The Luxemburgs, who were kinsmen of his wife, were specially rebellious; the Babenbergs were dangerous; the Franconian Conrad, heir in the female line of Otto the Great, took his turn at revolt late in the reign; and in Lower Lotharingia and Saxony disorder was endemic. Throughout, however, Henry II controlled the appointment of the dukes, who were his best lay lieutenants in the fight for order, although the tendency to heredity in the office could not be wholly disregarded. The loyal Billungs, hampered indeed by other turbulent magnates, were Dukes of Saxony. Bavaria, with intervals when the king ruled it directly like Franconia, was given to his discontented brother-in-law, Henry of Luxemburg. A Babenberg was installed in Swabia, and a local magnate Adalbero in Carinthia. The less important dukedom of Upper Lotharingia (Lorraine) was left in the hands of a native duke. Lower Lotharingia was placed successively under two brothers, Godfrey and Gozelo, counts in the Ardennes.

[1] See Genealogical Table 12 above, pp. 424–5.

Fig. 94. The Emperor Henry II

The character of the king himself was the decisive factor. Henry was active and persevering, pious and virtuous. His health was poor, he had been originally destined for the Church, and both from inclination and training Church affairs held a leading place in his mind, a fact which was later to earn him canonization (1146). But there was secular policy in him, too. He reverted to and exaggerated the system of Otto the Great before the Italian obsession of his cousins set in. In contrast to Otto III his seal bore the legend, 'Renovatio Regni Francorum'. Not that he abandoned the imperial idea, but with him Germany was his chief care. And his kingship was theocratic. He was ruler of the Church, inspirer of reforming synods, and to the Church he looked for unwavering support. He insisted on his right to nominate the bishops, and exacted the enfeoffment of his knights on Church lands and full service therefrom. But, relying on his complete control, he was lavish in his grants of land and jurisdiction: he gave whole countships to the bishops, who became more than ever indispensable servants of the Crown. They and the great abbots were formidable territorial powers, and Henry did not foresee the possibility that the Papacy might establish a first claim on their obedience. The new bishopric of Bamberg, which he endowed in East Franconia among a Wendish population, was exempted by his efforts from the metropolitan jurisdiction of Mainz.

At his accession Henry II was faced by war on every frontier. Most of Italy was lost to Ardoin. Boleslav the Great of Poland seized Lusatia and nearly conquered Meissen. In 1003 he added Bohemia to his dominions. The temporary disloyalty of the Babenbergs and some Saxons added to the danger, but in 1004 Henry reinstalled a loyal native Duke in Bohemia. Otherwise his campaigns brought little profit, and the peace of Bautzen (1018) ceded Lusatia to Boleslav on purely nominal terms of vassalage. The more northerly Wends enjoyed practical and heathen independence. Henry had not been minded to buy Polish friendship by accepting the Elbe as the German-Polish frontier.

In the west Henry was on good terms with the Capetian king of France, Robert, but recurrent war with the aggressive Count of Flanders only ended with the enfeoffment to him of the border scraps of Lotharingia he had occupied. With regard to the broken kingdom of Burgundy he did little better. He was nephew and natural heir of the childless and powerless king, Rodolph III, and in return for recognition of his claim to succeed and the cession of the frontier city of Basle attempted vainly to uphold him. His half-hearted efforts could not overthrow Otto-William, son of the exiled King Adalbert of Italy, who had built up round Besançon the 'County of Burgundy', the later Franche-Comté.

In the south, Italy and Ardoin presented a far more serious problem, which was bound up with the survival of the new Empire. As soon as possible in 1004 Henry staked out his claims by an expedition. In spite of fairly general submission and his coronation as King of Italy at Pavia, no real reconquest was effected. The mutual hostility of Germans and Italians caused a riot at and the burning of Pavia; Henry was called off to the Polish wars; and Ardoin resumed a much disputed sway. Not till 1013 did the German king find time and opportunity to invade Italy once more.

The immediate incentive was the situation of the Papacy. Since the death of Sylvester II (1003), the Crescentian faction had named the Popes, but in 1012 their candidate, Gregory, was defeated by the head of the rival house of the Counts of Tusculum (heirs of Prince Alberic), Pope Benedict VIII (1012–24). The Crescentian appealed to Henry, who was already the ally of Benedict, and grasped the moment for intervention and his imperial coronation. On his arrival in force in 1013 Ardoin withdrew to his castles, most bishops and the fervent monastic reformers were for him, and the lay magnates at least did not resist. On 14 February 1014 he was crowned Emperor by Pope Benedict in St Peter's. He had ensured the continuance of the Empire and the alliance with the Papacy, but his speedy exit to Germany left his work in Lombardy half done. His method had been to heap fresh grants and powers on loyal bishops and abbeys and to decree the return of alienated Church property. King Ardoin issued forth along with a motley throng of marquesses, counts, and vavassors, who were damaged thereby. But Bishop Leo of Vercelli, seconded by most bishops, gained the upper hand. Ardoin withdrew to a monastery, where he died (1015). The others asked for terms, which were allowed them, and Leo emerged enriched with forfeited lands (1018). When Henry paid his third visit to Italy (1021–2) he could exact the fealty of the Lombard princes in the south, and occupy himself with Church reforms. He failed to shake the Byzantine dominion in Apulia and Calabria. In June 1024 he lost his ally Benedict VIII, who was succeeded by his secular brother John XIX.

With Henry II's death in July 1024 the male line of the Saxon dynasty became extinct, but the hereditary principle was strong enough to limit the election of his successor to scions of the female line. There were two eligible candidates, both Franconians, both descendants of Otto the Great through his daughter Liutgard, and both named Conrad. The elder Conrad possessed a meagre inheritance, his cousin Conrad the Younger large estates. But popularity and force of character were on the elder Conrad's side, his cousin withdrew, and the three southern tribes elected him king. The Lotharingians, who had been for the younger Conrad, only submitted after the coronation, and the Saxons made terms before recognizing Conrad II (the Salic), just as they had done with Henry II. These delays were symptomatic of the fissures in Germany. Although the nobles of all the tribes were insubordinate, even to their dukes, the German king was able to exercise an amount of direct rule especially in the southern duchies which makes the contemporary kings of France seem impotent outside their narrow royal domain. But the turbulent Lotharingians were more feudalized and separatist, and the Saxons, who had been somewhat cool even to the Saxon Henry II because of his Bavarian surroundings, lost interest in the Empire when the crown passed to a Franconian. The provincial rights and the local defence of Saxony were their first consideration.

The king who thus succeeded to the Ottonian inheritance was endowed with a character strongly contrasting with his predecessor's. Unlike the devout, cautious, compromising Henry, he was harsh and domineering, inflexibly just, but grimly tenacious of his rights, grasping and passionate. The complex was well fitted to maintain the Empire, and it is noticeable that save in Church matters, in which he merely sought the profit of the Crown, he followed up in a workaday spirit the policies and schemes of Henry. It was perhaps chance which prompted him to give first public expression to the slow-forming and still infant conception of the permanent State apart from its ruler: 'if the steersman was dead, the ship remained'. He was eminently fitted to sail the ship.

Among the storms which beset him the self-seeking disaffection of the magnates was closely linked with the rivalries for the Burgundian succession. The childless Rodolph III was now ageing, and the death of the Emperor Henry II deprived him of an heir-designate. Conrad II, however, claimed that the designation included himself as Henry's successor in the Empire, and although he himself was not qualified by kinship, his queen Gisela of Swabia was Rodolph's niece. But other kinsmen advanced claims. There was Conrad's step-son, Duke Ernest II of Swabia, ambitious and insubordinate to the core, and there was the Frenchman Eudes II, Count of Champagne, half-brother of Robert II, King of France, and like him nephew of Rodolph III. Duke Ernest led two insurrections in Germany one after another, but Rodolph gave no help, and his own vassals in Swabia declared that their first allegiance was due to the German king. In 1027 Rodolph formally acknowledged Conrad's title to succeed, while a third revolt of Duke Ernest ended in his death in a fray (1030). His career had shown that, while certain great magnates like the two Dukes of Lotharingia and the Swabian Count Welf were ready for outbreaks, the lesser nobles and knights were loyal to the king; indeed Conrad won them by encouraging their hereditary succession in their fiefs, thereby developing the feudalization of south Germany and reinforcing the body of *ministeriales*, hitherto all unfree, who served the Crown.

The other aspirant to Burgundy, Count Eudes II of Champagne, was harder to quell. When Rodolph III at last died in 1032, he secured the northern part of his kingdom and raided Lotharingia. Conrad at first only obtained his own coronation as king. His second expedition was elaborately planned. He had gained over Count Humbert Whitehands of Savoy and Aosta, and this enabled him to send an Italian force over the Great St Bernard Pass, while he himself marched from the north. All resistance was crushed, and Burgundy became the third constituent kingdom of the Holy Roman Empire (1034). In 1038 his son Henry III was recognized as under-king. No domains and little authority were thus added to the imperial crown, but Burgundy was a barrier between France and Italy, and

Fig. 95. The Emperor Conrad II and Empress Gisela

the Alpine passes controlled by the Count of Savoy, who also now was Count of Maurienne leading to the Mont Cenis, provided a valuable alternative access to Italy. In government, Burgundy fell under its greater magnates and bishops; of the magnates the greatest were the 'Counts of Burgundy' in the north, the Counts of Savoy and the Counts of Albon (later the Dauphins) in the centre, and the powerful Counts of Provence in the south. These and less notable dynasts pursued their local wars and ambitions with small interference from their distant suzerain.

While the defeat and death of Eudes II at Bar (1037) put an end to his incursions into Lotharingia, and an amicable understanding with Canute the Great gave peace to the Danish frontier, the wars with Poland over the rival spheres of conquest and influence were waged with the customary ferocity. Mesco (Mieszko) II of Poland proved a redoubtable antagonist in spite of Conrad's alliance with the Russian Great Prince Yaroslav, and when Poland relapsed into civil war on Mesco's death (1034), Conrad found the Wendish Lyutitzi as hard to conquer however merciless his methods. Further south the Emperor owed much to the early capacity of his son Henry, already (1028) crowned, and appointed Duke of Bavaria. Internal dynastic disputes, dislike of German suzerainty, and enmity with Poland rendered Bohemia a thorny problem, only partly solved by the recognition of the gifted Bratislav as duke (1034). An unprosperous war with Hungary was concluded by a small cession (1031). Both confidence in his son and distrust of the German magnates dictated the appointment of young King Henry to be Duke of Swabia (1038). It marked an attempt to counter tribal particularism and the emulous local dynasts by uniting Crown and the dukedoms, but it implied a burden of incessant personal activity on the king.

Conrad's tendency to tread in his predecessor's footsteps without his religious zeal was clear in Italy also, but he was impelled to fresh expedients by the new conditions which had there come into being and which were not to be seen in Germany. The Empire was to endure, although a mutual hostility always broke out between Germans and Italians, of which evidence was at once given on Henry II's death, when the resentful Pavese openly revolted, and leading marquesses schemed vainly to introduce an anti-king in the person of Duke William of Aquitaine. But the episcopate, led by the masterful Aribert, Archbishop of Milan, stood firmly by the Empire. Conrad in 1026 entered Lombardy, punished Pavia, and was crowned at Milan and at Rome (1027). His prestige was heightened by the presence of Canute the Great and Rodolph III at the imperial coronation; the Lombard princes in the south did homage; it seemed a small, if ominous, drawback that fierce fighting occurred between his Germans and the citizens at Ravenna and Rome. So far, save in the neglect of religious interests, which made it easy for him to work with the Tusculan dynasty of Popes, the merely secular John XIX (1024–33) and his youthful and bad nephew

Fig. 96. Imperial crown of the Holy Roman Empire

Benedict (1033–46), Conrad was content to pursue the inherited policy, often appointing to vacant sees German bishops, who would maintain the union of Germany and the *Regnum Italicum*. But social changes in Italy were in rapid progress with the inevitable cross-currents. At the moment, the *secundi milites*, the plain knights, were the most dissatisfied class. Unlike their superiors, the magnates and *capitanei*, they had not attained heredity in their little fiefs, and this grievance was most alive in the episcopal estates, where the legislation of Otto III placed them at a disadvantage. In 1035, provoked by the confiscation of a fief by Archbishop Aribert of Milan, his petty vavassors took up arms. All joined the war, the vavassors of all Lombardy on one side, the magnates, spiritual and lay, and the plebeian citizens on the other. When a victory at Campo Malo was gained by a hair's breadth by the vavassors, both parties appealed to the Emperor for a legal decision. 'If Italy hungers for law, I will satiate her', he said, and crossed the Brenner in force. In a diet at Pavia (1037) he foreshadowed a constitution declaring and regulating the heredity of the petty fiefs. It was his German policy, and was not unwelcome to the lay magnates, jealous of the bishops,

455

but now Aribert could appeal to his suffragans and the town-plebeians, restive under the remnants of the feudal powers of the marquesses and hostile to the favoured vavassors. The arrest and escape of Aribert and the fruitless siege of Milan, which took his part, produced an impasse. If the young Pope was pliable to the Emperor, Conrad was already turning to the lay magnates and endeavouring to bind them to the German supremacy. The Marquesses Boniface of Tuscany and Albertazzo, leading member of the Obertine house, were given German wives, that of the latter being the eventual heiress of the famous Swabian race of Welf, while Adelaide, heiress of the power-ful Marquesses of Turin, was married to the Emperor's step-brother, Herman IV, Duke of Swabia. Disregarding the northern rebels, Conrad moved south in 1038 to intervene in the turmoil of the Lombard principalities. He enforced his suzerainty, and shared in the contemporary blindness to the import of the Norman emigrants then effecting a lodgement at Aversa. It was accidental, perhaps, that he recognized the trend of the times when as Emperor he decreed that in Rome and its territory Roman Law should decide all cases. As we have seen, personal inherited law had been a result of the barbarian invasions. Scattered settlement and migration had pro-duced an intolerable complexity of the varying law of litigants. It was slowly being replaced by the growth of a customary law of each district, but this decree was the first formal breach in the tradition of personal law as well as a sign of the study of Roman Law. In conservative Germany, where the tribes formed solid blocks, personal law by descent long survived.

Just as the riotous fighting in Italian cities as the army passed through witnessed to the unwelcome character of German rule in Italy, the pestilence which broke out in the army was an early instance of the invaders' lack of adaptation to the alien climate. Conrad II himself returned to Germany an invalid. He died in June 1039, leaving the Empire stronger indeed, for he had real capacity, but with none of its fundamental weaknesses on the way to being remedied.

(6) HENRY III AND HIS ACHIEVEMENTS

King Henry III inherited his father's energy and autocratic will along with a calmer temperament and a tenderer conscience. He had need of all his talents in the multiple task of keeping the vast, patchwork Empire together. There was the whole eastern frontier to defend, the centrifugal duchies to control, their ambitious, turbulent magnates to quell, Burgundy to retain at any rate in allegiance, the French king to neutralize, Italy to hold in obedience. He was devoid of genius; but he possessed plodding activity and austere good sense. His ruling passion was religion, and it led him, although he was no innovator, to precipitate a revolution in Church and Papacy which shaped the future and undermined the German monarchy.

No German king was more powerful than he, which makes his reign the apogee of the Empire, but the foundations were ineradicably weak. The attempt to shore them up by a reformed and friendly Papacy proved after his days to be an added danger, for it sapped the obedience of the bishops to their secular ruler, on which the Empire depended. Lay disloyalty and indiscipline, indeed, induced Henry to increase their already excessive endowments as princes of the Empire. The convictions of some, the selfish ambitions or the weakness of others, were to show the difficulty of finding fit pillars of the State in a time of ferment.

Henry shrewdly perceived the alienation of the Saxons, among whom great imperial domains were inherited from the Ottos, and he strove to remedy it by making his new town of Goslar a favourite residence. He made a gallant attempt to rule Swabia, Bavaria, and Carinthia in person, but events forced him to nominate fresh dukes, whom he chose, not too happily, from strangers to their duchies in the old tradition. It was probably due in part to this policy that private war was rampant. The devout Henry tried the heroic method of the 'Indulgence' of 1043, in which he and a long train of imitators solemnly forgave their enemies and renounced their feuds. Depending on inhuman perfectability, it had even less practical success than the Peace and Truce of God in France and Burgundy, with their more feasible alleviations of private warfare. Sheer mutiny among the magnates marred his later years. The Lotharingian Kuno, a bad choice, appointed Duke of Bavaria and then deposed (1049–53), was a pest to all neighbours till his death. Worse still was the situation in Lotharingia itself. Its two duchies had been reunited by Conrad II in 1033 under Duke Gozelo I. On his death Henry redivided them between his sons, giving to the nonentity Gozelo II (1044–6) Lower Lotharingia, and the Upper duchy only to the rancorous and grasping Godfrey II the Bearded. Thenceforward Godfrey was a recurrent rebel, raising up enemies in the duchies, France, and Burgundy. His power was great, his alliances and feuds widespread; he added to them by a stolen match (1054) with Beatrice, widow of the Marquess of Tuscany and regent for their daughter, the famous Matilda. Confiscation, imprisonment, and restoration were tried in turn by Henry with this redoubtable antagonist, but warfare was endemic among the Lotharingian dynasts whether rebels or loyalists at the moment. In spite of Henry's persistence in war and diplomacy he could only be sure of his nominee bishops in the disintegrating province, so laxly tied to the Empire. It was on the Archbishop of Hamburg-Bremen, too, his able, aspiring counsellor, Adalbert, that Henry relied to keep watch on alienated Saxony, its Billung dukes, and the northern frontier.

The eastern frontier was the king's personal charge and was the scene of his mediocre generalship and of his stubborn, if moderate, aims. He followed Conrad II's essentially defensive policy towards the Wends. If

Fig. 97. The Emperor Henry III and Empress Agnes

the Obodrites were partly converted, it was due to their native duke, Godescalc. The Lyutitzi were abandoned to their barbaric heathendom, with occasional hostilities. Casimir I of Poland, engaged in restoring order, was a nominal but amicable vassal, and only caused friction in the perennial frontier dispute with Bohemia. Bratislav of Bohemia was a real danger, partly because of his alliance with Hungary. However, he was brought under by a merciless invasion (1041), and kept the peace till his death (1055). The Czechs did not forgive their injuries; his son Spitignev II drove out all Germans from Bohemia. With Hungary there were the ancient causes of dispute, the raids and counter-raids of the fierce borderers, in which the Magyars, hereditary plunderers, did most harm, the fixing of a permanent frontier line, and the German wish to reduce Hungary to vassalage as a cure for the incessant friction. Henry's greatest efforts in the field obtained but poor results. He did advance (1043) the frontier of the Austrian march permanently to the river Leitha and the river March, up to which German colonization spread. But the vassal-kings he set up fell one after another, and Andrew I of Hungary was a vexatious enemy when he died. The past sixty years of peace and conflict, however, had linked Hungary to the West and the Western Church. The dividing line between the orthodox East and Western Europe was to run near Belgrade, not Vienna, just as Poland in the same period was secured for the Catholic, not the Orthodox, fold. Catholicism, in fact, had been something of a shield against the *Drang nach Osten*, whereas Orthodoxy warded off no foe, and could bring no pressure to bear.

In Italy and the Church, in contrast to his other dealings, Henry III's reign was epoch-making. Pacification appears to have been his earlier aim in Italy. He came to terms with Archbishop Aribert, a conservative force (1039). When a new fissure split the Milanese and the plebeians drove out (1042) *capitanei*, vavassors and the archbishop himself, who vainly besieged his city, Henry patronized a treaty which gave the plebeians some part in government (1044), and on the magnate Aribert's death made one of his frequent bad selections in the appointment of a vavassor, Guido, as archbishop (1045). The re-marriage of Adelaide of Turin to Oddo of Savoy was probably intended to secure the west Alpine passes under the single control of a loyal house. It was, however, events in Rome which, along with the pressing need of Church reform, finally drew King Henry to Italy to regulate the country and to celebrate his long-deferred imperial coronation. Benedict IX, the discreditable Tusculan, had for a while been expelled by an Anti-Pope, the Bishop of Sabina (Sylvester III), a Crescentian partisan, whom he was unable to subdue. He ended by ceding the Papacy to a virtuous reformer, the archpriest John Gratian, who became Gregory VI (1044). But Gregory's election was at least tainted with technical simony, and the confusion, with two men who had been Popes still living, was great.

Henry's desire for a reforming Pope, devoted to the Empire, and also willing to authorize *post factum* his own marriage, which was within the prohibited degrees, prompted him to copy the measures of Otto the Great. At the Synods of Sutri and Rome (1046) both Gregory VI, the Pope in possession, and the other two were declared deposed. An unexceptionable German was then elected Pope Clement II, and at once crowned Henry Emperor (Christmas 1046). As a further safeguard the Romans made the Emperor their 'Patrician', which gave him control of papal elections by the customs of the day. Clement and his successor fell speedy victims to the Roman climate, but in 1048 Henry found the Pope he desired in his cousin Leo IX. Meanwhile, after a none too prosperous intervention in South Italy, where he displayed his father's blindness to the growing Norman danger, the Emperor returned to Germany. Pope Leo's resurrection of Papal power belongs to the story of Church reform and his defeat at Civitate (1054) to that of the Normans in South Italy. When he died, Henry replaced him by his most loyal counsellor, Gebhard, Bishop of Eichstätt, as Pope Victor II (1055-7), whom he made Imperial Vicar for Italy. He was needed in both Italy and Germany, for the Emperor died in 1056, leaving his six-year-old son Henry IV under the regency of the Empress Agnes of Poitou, who was most unfit for her task and was surrounded by self-seeking prelates and nobles. A minority at that day was always detrimental. Henry III was evidently straitened to find men both able and loyal and of wide vision: some who united these qualities like his Popes, were not long lived. His judgement may have been at fault in others. But his strong hand and high ideals had maintained the imperial structure. 'With him died order and justice.' A dismal period for the secular empire began.

(7) FRANCE UNDER THE PROVINCIAL DYNASTIES

In no country was the development of feudalism so rapid, complete, and logical as in the kingdom of the West Franks or France, for there the decadence of the kingship gave it the greatest scope. After 888 the kings ceased to legislate. Foreign invasions, civil war, and the dissipation of the royal demesnes among the great vassals had disrupted the kingdom and destroyed the material foundations of the royal power. When King Raoul vacated the throne by death in 936, the most powerful magnate, Hugh the Great of Neustria (923-56), the son of King Robert I, prudently concurred in the recall from England and election of Charles the Simple's exiled son, Louis IV d'Outremer (936-54), to succeed him.[1] Louis' gallant and unconquerable spirit deserved a better fortune, but although he possessed the aureole of the crown and his Carolingian descent, he controlled only

[1] See Genealogical Table 9*b* above, p. 337.

one town, the hill-fortress of Laon, while his great vassals were masters of wide lands. South of the river Loire he was almost a foreigner: his title was sedulously acknowledged by laity and clergy, to whom his diplomas gave a legal cachet, but that was all. North of the Loire he was overshadowed by the mighty and able Duke of the French (*Dux Francorum*), Hugh the Great, and his treacherous rival, Herbert of Vermandois. His surest support lay in the Archbishop of Rheims, then Artaud. At first Louis was forced to subserve Hugh's ambitions. It is no wonder that he bid for the conquest (938) of Lotharingia and the leverage it might give him. His failure there was largely due to the open rebellion of Hugh and Herbert, who replaced Artaud by Herbert's young son Hugh, and he was only rescued by alliance (942) with his quondam foe, Otto the Great. The death of Herbert and the division of his lands, however, increased Duke Hugh's preponderance. In 945 he contrived to make the king his prisoner and extorted the cession of Laon as the price of his liberation. With King Otto's help and that of Pope and Church Louis was able to restore Artaud to Rheims, and even to recover Laon (949), but Hugh the Great, although he returned to his allegiance, remained not less formidable, if more cautious. When Louis d'Outremer died prematurely, he was foremost in electing his youthful son Lothaire (954–86) to the crown. The new king inherited capacity and perseverance, but did not learn from his father's experience. He had the unwisdom to strike another blow for Lotharingia (978) and thereby forfeited the alliance with the Emperor Otto II. It was the more unfortunate as the Archbishop of Rheims, Adalbero, a Lotharingian, was devoted to the Ottonian house, and the famous *scholasticus* of Rheims and future Pope, Gerbert, had long been its intimate. Lothaire's vain attempts to intervene in German politics brought about a crisis (985), when his endeavour to depose Adalbero was frustrated by the armed force of Hugh Capet, Duke of the French. Next year Lothaire died, leaving the hopeless struggle to his son Louis V, who in 979 had been already crowned and had failed to restore a royal authority in Aquitaine. A year after (987), Louis V, who was childless, died of a fall, the last Carolingian to reign.

Under these unlucky kings France had become a collection of provinces, wherein the great vassals strove for existence and territory. Of them the chief was the Duke of the French. Hugh the Great was direct lord or suzerain of Neustria from the Seine to Brittany as well as of numerous lands in *Francia*[1] east of the Seine. To his secular domain he added the 'lay abbacies' of St Martin of Tours, St Denis, and other wealthy monasteries. In Paris, of which he was count, he possessed a unique stronghold, the most secure and central of all the French cities. In 943 he obtained the suzerainty of the duchy of French Burgundy from Louis IV, and soon added that of the duchy of Normandy, henceforth a staunch ally. He obtained an

[1] See p. 357 n.

13. The Capetian Dynasty (to St Louis)

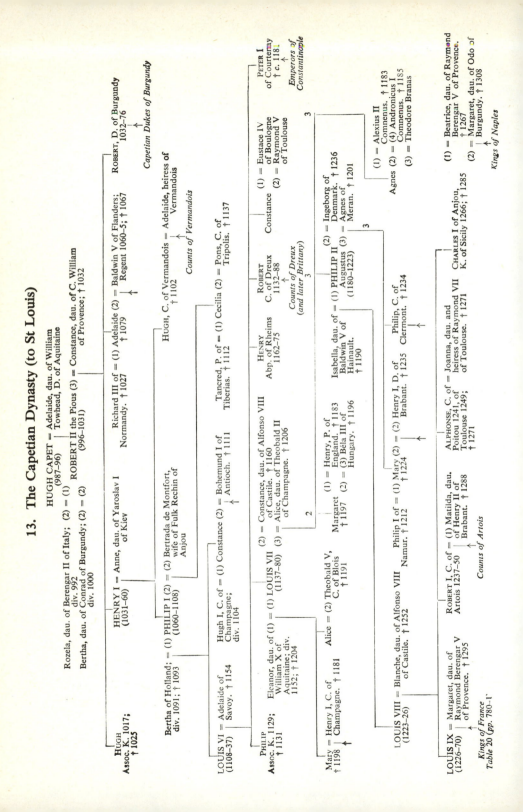

HUGH CAPET = Adelaide, dau. of William
(987–96) | Towhead, D. of Aquitaine
Rozela, dau. of Berengar II of Italy; (2) = (1) ROBERT II the Pious (3) = Constance, dau. of C. William
div. 992 (996–1031) of Provence; † 1032
Bertha, dau. of Conrad of Burgundy; (2) = (2)
div. 1000

HENRY I = Anne, dau. of Yaroslav I Richard III of = (1) Adelaide (2) = Baldwin V of Flanders; ROBERT, D. of Burgundy
(1031–60) of Kiev Normandy. † 1027 † 1079 Regent 1060–5; † 1067 1032–76

HUGH
Assoc. K. 1017;
† 1025

Capetian Dukes of Burgundy

HUGH, C. of Vermandois = Adelaide, heiress **of**
† 1102 Vermandois

Counts of Vermandois

Bertha of Holland; = (1) PHILIP I (2) = (2) Bertrada de Montfort,
div. 1091; † 1093 (1060–1108) wife of Fulk Rechin of
Anjou

Tancred, P. of = (1) Cecilia (2) = Pons, C. of
Tiberias. † 1112 Tripolis. † 1137

Hugh I, C. of = (1) Constance (2) = Bohemund I of
Champagne; Antioch. † 1111
div. 1104

LOUIS VI = Adelaide of
(1108–37) Savoy. † 1154

PETER I
of Courtenay
† c. 118[ ]
*Emperors of
Constantinople*

(1) = Eustace IV
of Boulogne
(2) = Raymond V
of Toulouse

HENRY ROBERT Constance
Abp. of Rheims C. of Dreux
1162–75 1132–88
*Counts of Dreux
(and later Brittany)*
3

(2) = Constance, dau. of Alfonso VIII
of Castile. † 1160
(3) = Alice, dau. of Theobald II
of Champagne. † 1206

PHILIP Eleanor, dau. of (1) = (1) LOUIS VII
Assoc. K. 1129; William X of (1137–80)
† 1131 Aquitaine; div.
1152; † 1204

Alexius II = (1)
Comnenus. † 1183
Andronicus I = (2) Agnes
Comnenus. † 1185
Theodore Branas = (3)

(1) = Henry, P. of
England. † 1183
(2) = Béla III of
Hungary. † 1196

(2) = Ingeborg of
Denmark. † 1236
(3) = Agnes of
Meran. † 1201

Isabella, dau. of = (1) PHILIP II
Baldwin V of Augustus
Hainault. (1180–1223)
† 1190

Philip, C. of
Clermont. † 1234
3

Alice = (2) Theobald V,
C. of Blois
† 1191

Margaret
† 1197

Philip I of = (1) Mary (2) = (2) Henry I, D. of
Namur. † 1212 † 1224 Brabant. † 1235

Mary = Henry I, C. of
† 1198 Champagne. † 1181

Theobald = (2) Matilda, dau. of Henry II of
† 1181 Brabant. † 1288

ALPHONSE, C. of = Joanna, dau. and
Poitou 1241, heiress of Raymond VII
† 1271 of Toulouse. † 1271

CHARLES I of Anjou,
K. of Sicily 1266; † 1285

(1) = Beatrice, dau. of Raymond
Berengar V of Provence.
† 1267
(2) = Margaret, dau. of Odo of
Burgundy. † 1308
Kings of Naples

LOUIS VIII = Blanche, dau. of Alfonso VIII
(1223–26) of Castile. † 1252

ROBERT I, C. of = (1) Matilda, dau.
Artois 1237–50 of Henry II of
Brabant. † 1288
Counts of Artois

LOUIS IX = Margaret, dau. of
(1226–70) Raymond Berengar V
of Provence. † 1295
*Kings of France
Table 20 (pp. 780–1)*

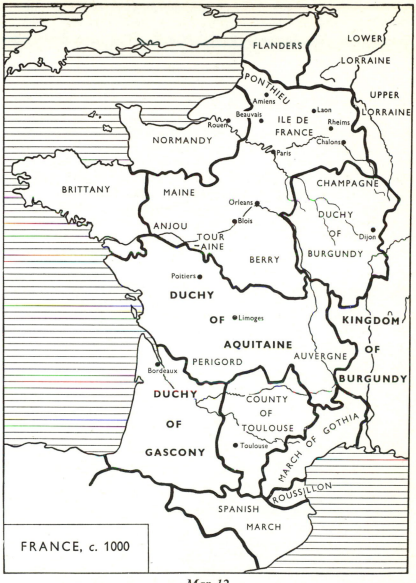

Map 12

ineffective grant of the suzerainty of Aquitaine. In this way he stood between the king and the greatest potentates of the realm. In the year of his death (956) he took actual possession of the vacant duchy of Burgundy. In short, far more than the king, he was the head of the kingdom. His son

463

Hugh Capet was no less able and aspiring. To some extent he suffered a diminution of material power. His younger brother Otto made good his claim to be Duke of Burgundy (960); the Count of Chartres and the Count of Anjou became very independent vassals, and the former gained (983) the nucleus of the later county of Champagne in Troyes, placing him astride of Hugh Capet's lands. The March of Neustria in fact was broken up among counts, as was *Francia* in the narrow sense. All the same, since the territories of the rival house of Vermandois were now subdivided, Hugh Capet remained the richest and most powerful great vassal.

One reason was that the other dynasts were in much the same case. Some were far removed from the centre of affairs. The Counts of Barcelona, who ruled Catalonia beyond the Pyrenees, were preoccupied with wars against the Moslems and almost dropped out of French history. The Counts of Toulouse were establishing their suzerainty over what had been once called Septimania and its northern neighbours. The duchy of Gascony, with its partly Basque population, was isolated. Between the Loire and the Atlantic the Counts of Poitou, in spite of rivals and the opposition of both the kings and the two Hughs, had won the dukedom of Aquitaine and a real superiority over its counts. In fact these southern districts, once Visigothic, formed as of old a distinct land, the later Langue d'oc, from the true France, the Langue d'oïl,[1] beyond the Loire: manners, customs, and dialects were akin to one another and strange to the north. For centuries the separation was to subsist.

North of the Loire, as we have seen, the country was split among its dukes and counts, whose ill-defined territories were being splintered among their turbulent vassals just as the kingdom was among themselves. Feudal custom and its reciprocal duties were still fluid and in growth, but the suzerains, who needed their vassals' aid, could not draw the reins too tightly. Their own authority was crumbling in their great fiefs like the king's. Most aloof from the rest was the half-Breton duchy of Brittany, never assimilated by the Carolingians. In the north-east lay the March or County of Flanders, where a dynasty, established by Charles the Bald, ruled in truculent independence as far south as Arras. The duchy of Normandy, founded by Rollo and now thoroughly French in tongue and institutions, while imbued to the full with the Viking spirit of war and adventure, was ruled, as far as rule was possible, in complete autonomy by the hard-bitten descendants of its founder. The fierce race of the Counts of Anjou were busy extending the limits of their little county towards Touraine. We have seen how the Counts of Chartres were forming a composite county of Champagne round Troyes. A number of other counties, Maine, Vermandois, and the like filled the gaps between the greater territories in

---

[1] Names derived from the characteristic words for 'yes': 'oc' in the south, and 'oïl' (the modern 'oui') in the north.

Neustria and *Francia*. The duchy of French Burgundy both had lost its northern borderlands to its neighbours and was slipping into anarchy within. Whatever their degree of power, all these great vassals, when they were not in rebellion, were unruly subjects of the king. Perhaps the most stable element, which kept alive the tradition of kingship, were the bishops of *Francia*. The Archbishop of Rheims, the Bishops of Châlons-sur-Marne, Langres, and Noyon, had become counts of their cathedral cities. They were great territorial lords, whose loyalty was increased by their losses to the lay magnates, disguised as enfeoffments. Their election required the king's consent, and to their support, moral and material, he owed what authority he could maintain in his incessant struggle with his overmighty vassals.

It was the defection of the bishops, not from the kingship but from the dynasty, which sealed the fate of the Carolingians. As it happened, the heir of Louis V was a weak candidate, his uncle Charles, Duke of Lower Lotharingia. At enmity with his brother Lothaire, he had lived as a German vassal, besides contracting a mésalliance which offended the haughty magnates. Only his descent pleaded for him. Hugh Capet could claim royal ancestors of fame; he was suzerain of the most powerful lords of France and of an array of bishops in his dukedom. He was a strong, long-proved personality. Now Adalbero of Rheims and the royal bishops were for him. He was elected at Senlis and crowned at Noyon (3 July 987), the third of his race to be King of France. He promptly crowned his eldest son Robert as his co-regent. But Duke Charles did not tamely allow his inheritance to go by default. He seized Laon and gained over the new Archbishop of Rheims, Arnulf, a bastard Carolingian. He might have held his own, had it not been for the infamous treachery of his host Asselin, Bishop of Laon, who took him and Arnulf prisoner and handed him over to King Hugh (991). Charles soon died in captivity, while Arnulf was deposed in favour of Gerbert to be restored as harmless years later. With the sons of Charles, Otto of Lower Lotharingia and his brothers, the house of Charlemagne vanished from history as the Merovingians had done before them.

The change of dynasty did not imply any change in men's conception of the kingship. Hugh inherited the theory and the aureole of the crown, and its lax control of the disintegrated realm. But he possessed at least a considerable, if much attenuated, royal domain, grouped round the important cities of Paris and Orleans in the very centre of France, fertile, on the main routes of intercourse, an admirable situation for politics, war, and trade. His was the alliance of the episcopate and Church in *Francia*, which he cherished. The permanence of his dynasty owed much to this, and much to the shrewd, practical character of successive kings, whose ambition did not o'erleap itself.

For all that, the Capetian monarchs were deplorably weak for many years. The expulsion of Arnulf from Rheims led to an embittered dispute with the Papacy, which even in its then discredited state could keep the Gallican Church in commotion over this grossly uncanonical affair. When Hugh Capet died in 996, King Robert II the Pious (987–1031), although he restored Arnulf, married a Burgundian princess well within the prohibited degrees, and only made his peace by deserting her for an allowed marriage years later. He was not able to exact ready obedience from the petty barons of his own domain. Yet he was energetic enough to recover a town or two and to occupy French Burgundy on an uncle's death. This cost ten years of war, and was a transitory gain, for on his death his crowned heir Henry I (1031–60) after a civil war bought out with the duchy the claims of his younger brother Robert, who founded a dynasty. The growth of Champagne could not be prevented, and on all sides the king lost ground, reduced to shifting alliances with his warring great vassals. He had inherited the friendship with the Duke of Normandy, but his very action in the fulfilment of it, although the most successful in his life, changed it into enduring enmity. In 1047 it was his aid which enabled the young Duke William the Bastard to win the decisive victory of Val-ès-dunes over his rebellious Norman vassals. For a while the two remained allies against the Count of Anjou, Geoffrey Martel, but the formidable and aggressive power of Duke William changed his overlord's interests and policy. He renewed his earlier league with Geoffrey, this time not against Champagne but against Normandy. Two campaigns involved two ugly defeats before Henry died. He had taken the precaution of crowning his son Philip I (1059), whom he left under the guardianship of his brother-in-law Baldwin V of Flanders.

The monarchy under the cynical Philip (1060–1108) appeared to be one, and not the most powerful, among the provincial dynasties. But the practical and inglorious king kept a shrewd look-out for the accretions to the royal domain which alone could render the kingship more than a title. He was never a nonentity, and used his suzerain rights with some skill. Henry I had absorbed the vacant county of Sens. Philip took advantage of a civil war in the house of Anjou to acquire the neighbouring Gâtinais. Among his acquisitions were the French Vexin on the Norman border, Corbie in Artois, and Bourges, all of value. His brother Hugh became Count of Vermandois by marriage. He exploited the discontent of Robert Curthose with his father William the Conqueror, now King of England, to fend off his too mighty *soi-disant* vassal, and played a similar part when Robert and his brother William Rufus were at odds. In all these broils he could generally count on the contingents, small enough, of the northern vassals who were not in active revolt. Of them the bishops were the most reliable contributors to the royal needs if they depended directly on the Crown. Philip received the revenues of vacant sees, and was the most unblushing simoniac in Europe in new appointments. When the enlarged movement for Church reform reached France he fiercely defended his rights of nomination, with which so much of his power and income was bound up. The question did not stand alone. The Capetian royal domain consisted of territories in which no count stood between the king and his subjects. His own demesne estates lay therein, but most was enfeoffed to petty barons, whose brigand-like disorders Philip made no effort to restrain, even when he was not an accomplice. He roused the enmity of Pope Gregory VII by this behaviour no less than by his simony. In 1092 he embittered the dispute with the Papacy by his abduction of and bigamous marriage with Bertrada, wife of Fulk Rechin, Count of Anjou. The consequent excommunications failed to move him or to affect the loyalty of bishops, who, even when reformers, were well aware of their common interest with the Crown against the anarchic nobility. At last in 1104 Philip was absolved on a pretence of separation. For some years he had, in failing health, left the government to his son Louis VI, who succeeded him, having escaped Bertrada's murderous plots, in 1108, and began a new era in the French monarchy.

The weakness of the preceding Kings of France is obvious. The estates they had retained in their hands provided a meagre subsistence even when supplemented by their rights of *gîte* in the royal abbeys. Their administration merely consisted of the officers, like the seneschal and chancellor, of their petty court, and the provosts and reeves of their manors. They could easily be defied by the barons of their royal domain. Yet they possessed a moral authority fostered by tradition and the Church and by the prevalent appeal of the feudal tie. They were anointed Kings of France, suzerains of all, vassals of none. Such as it was, they represented lawful government and the memory rather than the actuality of peace and justice. The great vassals were unwilling, even when rebellious, to flout the dignity on which their own legal title depended, or without excuse to disregard the fealty which bound their own vassals to them as well as themselves to the king. The age of lawlessness was being replaced by a growing feudal law which permeated men's ideas and bound their consciences. Thus these ill-provided kings among great vassals, who were running the same dangers of baronial turbulence in their fiefs, maintained an undisputed pre-eminence.

None the less, France was in fact divided into provincial dominions, whose lords, the direct vassals of the Crown, were hard put to it, like the kings, to assert their authority over the lower grades of the feudal hierarchy. The Counts of Anjou, Fulk Rechin (1067–1109) and his son Geoffrey II Martel (*ob*. 1106), were engaged in endless warfare with both their vassals and their neighbours. Yet they were successful, while the Dukes of Burgundy, impoverished and enfeebled, became as arrant bandits as their barons. The Dukes of Brittany were unable to tame rivals who were nominally their vassals. On the other hand the brilliant dynasty of the Williams of Poitou contrived with miraculous skill and activity to hold in leash the counts in their duchy of Aquitaine, to which they added Gascony (1039). William IX (1086–1126), a cultured, profligate knight and troubadour, was master of his scandalized bishops and an incessant danger to his neighbours. The Counts of Toulouse barely escaped ejection by him from their wealthy territories in years of war. They were, it is true, hampered by their crusading zeal and by their own restive and powerful vassals and the rival encroachments of the Counts of Barcelona. In the north the domination of the great vassals was less chequered. The Counts of Flanders, Baldwin V (1036–67) and Robert the Frisian (1071–93), were all-but independent potentates, who pursued the enlightened policy of extending cultivated land and fostering trade. Almost alone in France they quelled the anarchy of the petty barons and enforced their administration. The Flemish towns became thronged with weavers, the peasantry well-to-do in the peace given by the counts.

More homogeneous and nearly as straitly ruled was the duchy of Normandy. The dukes of the line of Rollo were men of mark. The legal, businesslike aptitudes of the Normans, in spite of their turbulence, favoured the logical development of a feudal organization, which did not omit the attributes of sovereignty vested in the duke by the possession of all the royal functions in his duchy. His estates were large, subordinate counts few and his near relatives and non-hereditary *vicomtes* (viscounts) watched over his local interests. Over his bishops, all suffragans of Rouen, he exercised unchallenged control. Duke Richard II the Good (996–1026) and his son Robert (1027–35) were both patrons of the revived monastic movement, and the abbeys they founded increased their predominance. Although the accession of Robert's bastard son, William (1035–87), at the age of eight inevitably meant a set-back, the future Conqueror, with the help of King Henry, overthrew the more undisciplined barons in 1047 at Val-ès-dunes. Henceforward he ruled his duchy with an iron hand, becoming an object of dread to his suzerain. By this time there appears in Normandy a regular organization of feudal service. Some 800 knights were due in the duke's wars from his tenants-in-chief; they themselves had enfeoffed about 1800. Below these were ranked the smaller freeholders or *vavassors*, who served on foot or horse with lighter equipment. The peasants were divided into serfs tied to the soil and *hospites* of freer tenure, a class due, it seems, to settlers invited to the manor and less burdened. The comparative peace of the duchy favoured the natural fecundity of the population, noble and peasant, and was shown in the plethora of younger sons who sought their fortunes in adventures abroad. From 1016 onwards there was a steady stream of emigrants to the wars of South Italy, which resulted in the foundation there of a Norman state; others went to fight the Moslems in Spain. Duke William looked for expansion elsewhere. His conquest of England in 1066, which entailed the greatest Norman emigration, belongs to another chapter, but he also contested the conquest of Maine to the south with the Count of Anjou. His marriage (1053) with his distant kinswoman, Matilda of Flanders, in defiance of the Church's ban, upset the balance of power in North France by allying Normandy and Flanders and turned King Henry into a foe. The two victories of Mortemer (1054) and Varaville (1058) checked the king, but Geoffrey I Martel of Anjou was hard to drive from Maine, whose rightful count fared ill between the two invaders. Geoffrey's death (1060) allowed William to master the county, and prepare for his invasion of England. Fulk Rechin, however, renewed the war, assisted by revolt in Maine, which left William at the close only part-possessor.

Thus by the end of the twelfth century the Capetian line had succeeded in maintaining itself in the kingship without a rival and even in enlarging its too scanty lands. It had been fortunate in an uninterrupted succession from father to son, in which each heir was cautiously crowned before the throne was vacant, and election with its perils went into oblivion. Hereditary prescriptive right sank into men's minds by force of custom. The monarchy, too, belonged to the new feudal order from which it had been born, and from which the Carolingians had been edged out, while at the same time it retained the prestige of the ancient kingship: the kings, who received the Church's sacring, were more than mere suzerains, for they represented and were the source of legal government. Even a rebel magnate, like Eudes II of Champagne, addressed his royal enemy with profound deference, for he held his fiefs and his rights from the king. Eminent bishops, like the saintly Fulbert of Chartres (*ob*. 1028) and his still more famous successor Ivo (*ob*. 1115), who guided what public opinion and enlightenment there was in their half-barbaric contemporaries, were royalists to the core. Nevertheless, the Capetians in power and resources had by 1100 been outdistanced by several of their vassals. The Duke of Normandy, become King of England, ruled far greater territories with a firmer hand; his administration was more advanced in its development. To a less degree and in a narrower sphere the same might be said of the wealthy Count of Flanders and the combative Count of Anjou. The Duke of Aquitaine and the Count of Toulouse, if quite uncontrolled and more civilized, were too remote to be dangerous as were their fellows in the north. But the upshot was that the Capetians were obliged to manœuvre among mightier combatants, who were growing in strength, while the kings seemed stationary.

All these potentates were striving with the forces of disorder incarnate in their lesser barons. It had been a century of castle-building in the incessant wars, and each castle was a focus of resistance and private war. Yet some progress was made by the rulers: the increase of population which manifests itself in the eleventh century, and the early growth here and there of trading towns, are witnesses to it. At the close of the century the crusading movement came to assist them. No doubt Gibbon was mis-stating the case when he spoke of the beneficial removal of 'the tall and barren trees of the forest'. Few of the greater nobles were so extinguished, and then with doubtful benefit. But the horde of lesser men was thinned of its most disorderly elements for a while: the bellicose spirit of the age was given an outlet. In their absence and its diversion, the princes had a freer opportunity to assert their authority, which the wiser of them well exploited.

CHAPTER 17

THE REFORM OF THE CHURCH

(I) THE FIRST PHASES OF CHURCH REFORM

During the anarchy and ravage which followed the reign of Charlemagne a lamentable degeneration overtook the Western Church in all its functions, pastoral and monastic. The bishops, with few exceptions, had grown to be as unscrupulous and violent and occasionally as hereditary as the lay magnates, from whose families they were largely recruited. As a class they possessed more education and a wider view, but their way of life showed little, if any, difference. As a class, too, although supported by their ecclesiastical office, and sometimes fighting men themselves, they were weaker than the warrior potentates, and by force or favour an immense alienation of the vast Church estates took place through the process of enfeoffment: a great part of the domains of the Archbishop of Rheims went thus towards making up the county of Champagne. The tithes on produce, which had been enforced as a Christian duty under the Carolingians, suffered the same fate. In most of France, as in Bavaria, the great vassals nominated their bishops at their pleasure. The primitive method by which bishops were elected by the clergy and 'people' of their diocese was almost everywhere out of use. At best it survived as a form, in which the cathedral clergy and leading laity were becoming the only participants. Those bishoprics which depended on the king were filled by his choice. By the tenth century, these facts were expressed and confirmed in a feudal ceremony, lay investiture. On a vacancy, the king or great vassal took possession of the lands of the see as a vacant fief, as well as of the personal property, the *spolia*, of the dead bishop. When he appointed or approved a successor, he received his homage and fealty, and invested him with his bishopric by handing him his episcopal staff and ring; to the metropolitan were left his consecration and profession of ecclesiastical obedience. The lands and attached jurisdiction were regarded as a fief held under feudal obligations, which took precedence of the strictly ecclesiastical. As a whole, royal appointments might be better than those by local magnates, but the general level was low, and almost all were tainted with simony, the payment of a sum down for promotion, which in feudal notions corresponded to the relief paid by an heir entering on his hereditary fief. The bishop recouped himself by fees, which were really sales, for conferring ordination and the like; the parish priests in the same way charged their flocks for the usual rites of religion. The whole Church was infected by simony, the open sale of its spiritual functions.

471

Fig. 98. Abbey Church of Cluny (reconstruction)

The position of the parish priests was more tied and subject still. By ancient custom, in great part of heathen German origin, the ownership of a church and its endowment belonged to their founder and donor, whether bishop, king, or more usually local landowner; the bishop of the diocese as such had merely the right of approval. The priest, commonly a married man in spite of the Canon Law, entered on his 'benefice' as his lord's vassal on such terms as he might impose. Much of the profits of the endowment and the fees (the *spiritualia*) were thus bargained away to the lord. In other cases, as often in Lombardy, well-endowed cures were almost a family inheritance. The married father was succeeded by his son. Like the bishop, too, he would fall to the temptation to enrich his family by enfeoffment or lease of lands with which his church was endowed. From one point of view the abuse might be regarded as a natural corrective of the over-endowment of the Church as a whole, but it was inevitably linked with the neglect or prostitution of the spiritual functions of the priestly office. The clergy had become a variety of the barbaric noble or henchman of a corrupt and brutal age, in whose vices they fully shared.

The state of the monasteries was the most deplorable of all. The spirit of the ascetic life seemed lost; the Rule of St Benedict was observed hardly anywhere; episcopal control, when attempted, was useless, especially as the bishops were so often themselves reprehensible. Invasion and rapine destroyed both zeal and discipline. Monks returning to their desolated abbeys were recruited more as ruffians than religious. The ghastly history of the wealthy and famous monastery of Farfa, with its poisoned abbots and dissolute monks, is a dramatic but not a lonely example in the tenth century. At Lobbes in Hainault a reforming abbot was blinded by the delinquents. Many monasteries had changed themselves into colleges of canons, and this generally implied the abandonment of a common life. The canons lived in their houses on their prebends, or share of the income, and were married as well. Their laxity compared favourably with the rank licence of disordered and corrupt monasteries. A potent cause of decline had been the appointment, which became often hereditary, of great nobles as lay abbots of the wealthiest monasteries. These abbots absorbed the greater part of the revenues, and the monks lingered on as a discredited and disillusioned remnant of relaxed discipline. The exceptional abbeys which retained some learning and order in the prevalent decay were not such examples of fervent zeal as to captivate the imagination of their contemporaries. The autonomy of each monastery, which was in one way a beneficent principle of the Benedictines, produced the local customs of each independent house, and these were usually relaxations of the strictness of the Rule. The regulations for abstinence from meat and for claustration within the abbey were softened to vanishing point. In short, the influence of these well-conducted men on the rugged world around them was likely to be small.

The age, however, barbarous, grossly superstitious, and semi-pagan in ethos as it was, was not dead to religion and piety if they came before it in a garb it could understand. Asceticism and devotion still commanded its reverence as the prime virtues, and inspired an infectious enthusiasm. The first glimmer of reform proceeded not from well-meaning members of the hierarchy from above but from the spontaneous fervour of a few devout souls seeking the way of salvation. In 910 Duke William I the Pious of Aquitaine founded a monastery at Cluny in French Burgundy to be a model of observance of the Rule. Its first abbot was a Burgundian noble, Berno (*ob.* 927), already known for his ability to rule an abbey, but the reform might have died away had not the second abbot, Odo (927–42), been the greatest religious force of his generation. He had a singular power of impressing the rough potentates of the day, who, whatever their own sins, desired perfect monks to pray for them. For fourteen years he was renowned as the reformer of Benedictine observance in France and Western Europe generally. In Italy Alberic entrusted to him the reform of the Roman monasteries. More durable was the reform of Fleury on the Loire, where he was called in by Hugh the Great (930), and which was thenceforth second only to Cluny as an influential pattern of monastic life. Abbot Maieul (Maiolus) (954–94), favoured by the Ottos, in his long life reformed

473

not only important Italian abbeys but celebrated French abbeys like Marmoûtier and St Bénigne of Dijon. So great was his prestige that, when his caravan was captured in the Alps by the Saracens of Fraxinetum, not only did his monks quickly raise a large ransom but the local nobles were roused to combine to exterminate the brigands. His equally long-lived successor, Odilo (994–1048), exalted Cluny to new heights of organization and influence. Duke William had surrendered his founder's rights. Odo had obtained from the Pope the then invaluable privilege of exemption from all episcopal authority. But Cluny, although so autonomous and wealthy, was as yet a monastery with only a few dependents. The abbeys, which accepted Odo and Maieul and their disciple William of Volpiano as autocratic reformers to remodel them, adopted the spirit and many customs of Cluny, but kept their Benedictine autonomy. Under Odilo Cluny expanded, and its 'Congregation' was all but a new monastic order. Old and new foundations over the West were affiliated to Cluny, and became as priories an integral part of its organization owing absolute obedience to the sovereign abbot. The priors met annually at Cluny in chapter, and their houses, which a little later numbered 200, were grouped in ten provinces for visitation. Cluny Abbey itself, the abode of over 300 monks, was splendidly rebuilt from the wealth which flowed in from the universal veneration—'from wood it became marble', said Odilo—while the daughter-monasteries, built or rebuilt, shared in the magnificence of the Congregation. The long rule of his successor, Hugh (1049–1109), was the high-water mark of the Cluniacs, who reached under him their greatest numbers. With piety and zeal unabated, they were becoming as an order the conservative wing of reform. Hugh, the godfather of Henry IV, preferred to influence rather than to browbeat the secular powers. Without abandonment of principle, he was a mediator rather than a combatant, and Gregory VII found him a lukewarm partisan when Papacy and Empire were at odds.

The Cluniac monks by Odilo's death had long been a power in Western Europe. Genuine monks, who lived up to the Rule, were what the religious instincts of the time desired. The spontaneity of the movement ensured its triumph: learning, ability, and devotion swelled the ranks of the Cluniacs. They were not the only reformers. Besides their imitators, as in England and Normandy, there came into being, from the same needs and impulses, quite independent groups of reformers. Good men in fact were revolting from the iniquity of the world still seething with anarchy. Gerard, lord of Brogne near Namur (*ob.* 959), turned as passionately to saintliness as he had to his former violent life. His abbey of Brogne became, like early Cluny, an inspiration to reform. His influence was in Lower Lotharingia and Flanders; in Upper Lotharingia the rôle of Brogne was taken by the abbey of Gorze. Unlike Cluny, these reformers were constant to the

Benedictine principle of autonomy, and they did not seek exemption from their diocesan bishop. They were in touch with the episcopate, which in the similar English movement took the lead. They were, however, more liable to ups and downs than the well-organized Cluniacs under their long-lived autocrats. A new outburst of reform was soon necessary. It was led by Richard of St Vannes (*ob.* 1046), through whose pupil, Abbot Poppo of Stavelot (1020–48), as well as from Cluny, the movement reached German monasteries beyond the Rhine.

About the same time champions of asceticism and renewed strictness arose in Italy. Nilus, the Calabrian Greek (*ob.* 1005), revived Basilian traditions in South Italy. The tendency in Italy, however, was towards a hermit life. Romuald of Ravenna (*ob.* 1027), the mentor of Otto III, was able to combine missionary fervour with the foundation of hermit-communities, like those of Egypt: the last was Camaldoli in the Apennines, which in 1072 was recognized as a distinct order. Not dissimilar was Vallombrosa, the foundation (*c.* 1038) of John Gualbert, a member of a noble family of Florence.

The instinct for Church reform in the desperately slow amelioration of society was in fact widely spread, and the advent of bishops who were conscientious and able furthered the cause among monks and even secular clergy. The appointments of the Ottonian dynasty showed a marked improvement, although efficiency as secular officials was still kept in the forefront. Archbishop Bruno of Cologne, the brother of Otto I, showed what a pious prelate could do, and there were many like him. The Lotharingian Ratherius (*ob.* 974), alternately Bishop of Verona and Liége, proved how ineffective against abuses a zealot could be, but his writings were influential. In France Bishop Fulbert of Chartres commanded everyone's respect. The promotion of the learned genius, Gerbert of Aurillac, even to the Papacy was a striking testimony to the force of ideas and to the desire for a better and civilized society.

The prevalent evil of contemporary Western Europe was seen by its leaders, and truly, as the reign of lawlessness, in which men followed the bent of their selfish passions as far as their power extended. To re-establish the rule of ancient law and order was the crying need and the ideal. To some extent a remedy was being supplied by the barely conscious growth of custom. Feudalism as a system of government and a social fabric was becoming formulated thereby, and Fulbert of Chartres could lay down the principles of a vassal's duty in his admired letter (*c.* 1020) to Duke William III of Aquitaine. The Peace and Truce of God were at any rate attempts to prescribe rules for more civilized warfare and baronial conduct. The study of the older laws was reviving in Italy at Pavia and elsewhere, as well as in Provence and the south of France, whose 'written law' already distinguished it from the lands of 'custom' in the north. The reform of monasticism itself was based on a return to the strict Rule of St Benedict and was built upon its implications. The new hermit-orders were modelled on the old. So with the struggle against the rampant corruption of the whole Church the renewed study of the Canon Law was the inevitable guide to current evils and its enforcement the proper means for their suppression. It established an orderly hierarchy of ecclesiastical government and the ancient legal methods of appointment; it forbade simony and clerical incontinence and marriage.

By this time the pseudo-Isidorian collection with its forgeries was generally received as authentic in the West. Like its predecessors it was not easy to consult for practical use, for synodal canons and decretals were arranged in chronological order, not in any way by subject-matter. A new kind of compilation came slowly into vogue with the publication (c. 1012) of the *Decretum* of Burchard, Bishop of Worms. It contained classified excerpts from the Canon Law, which a bishop should enforce. But while the law could thus be more easily known, its enforcement depended on the authorities and the public opinion of clergy and laity with which they had to deal: the reformers were a minority, even when personally revered.

The Emperor Henry II (1002–24) was the first secular ruler on the continent to take up seriously the question of the reform of the secular clergy. He was deeply imbued with the conviction of his powers over Church and State. More than Pope and archbishop he was the inspiring force in synods he held reviving Church discipline and forbidding under penalties simony and clerical marriage and concubinage. Conrad II (1024–39), however, was himself a simonist and indifferent to reform, which underwent a setback in the Empire during his reign. It was his religious son Henry III (1039–56) who worked a change. He was the friend of Hugh of Cluny. He held the same theocratic views of his office and its duties as Henry II, and to reform the Church was the highest aim of his life.

To abandon simony in the conferment of bishoprics and abbeys was his first step. More than that, his appointments were influenced by ecclesiastical fitness, a motive which also guided his contemporary, William of Normandy, in a narrower sphere. Since the death of Sylvester II in 1003 the Papal chair had been occupied by local potentates, chiefs first of the Crescentian and then of the Tusculan faction, whose interests at best were political. The partial improvement witnessed under the Ottos had given way to growing degradation, until in 1032 the young Tusculan, Benedict IX, completed it by his open profligacy. To the Emperors he was docile enough, but the Crescentian faction profited by his delinquency, and even in Rome there was a pious and reforming party, who held, as probably did the whole curia, the highest views of the papal authority as enunciated by Nicholas I and pseudo-Isidore. Benedict's riot, as we have seen, enabled his opponents among the nobility to replace him for a few months by the Anti-Pope Sylvester III. Then strangely Benedict, on recovering his see, sold the Papacy to his god-father, an honest reformer, John Gratian, the archpriest of the Lateran Basilica, who thereupon assumed the style of Gregory VI (1044). The price seems to have been the English Peter's Pence as an annuity. Gregory, a Jew perhaps by descent, was generally recognized, but the contract tinged his elevation with simony, although his virtues were acknowledged. It was in this distracted situation, with three Popes or ex-Popes co-existing, that Henry III descended into Italy to receive the imperial crown and cut the Gordian knot. It was clear that permanent and fundamental Church reform could not be achieved unless the Papacy and Curia were freed from their debasement and made partners in it. Henry's autocratic temper and his resolve to unify the Empire could not be satisfied without a trusted Papal partner and a German Pope. There were precedents for a non-Roman: Otto II had installed a Lombard, Otto III a German (Gregory V) and then a Frenchman (Sylvester II). We have seen how synods at Henry's command deposed the three Popes, and the German Clement II was elected to the Papacy, while Henry by obtaining the office of Roman Patrician secured the right to nominate future successors of St Peter.

Henry's action by no means obtained the approval of the stricter canonists. When Clement II died prematurely in October 1047, the loyal, reforming Bishop Wazo of Liége protested that no valid Pope could be elected in the lifetime of Gregory VI, then in exile at Hamburg, and Benedict IX was tempted to usurp his ancient dignity with the support of Boniface, Marquess of Tuscany. It required the threats of the Emperor to procure his expulsion and the enthronement of a new German nominee, Damasus II. This Pope (1048) fell a victim to the climate in a few weeks, but Gregory VI was by that time dead, and Benedict also disappeared, so that Henry's next choice, his cousin, Bruno, Bishop of Toul, was accepted without a murmur by both reformers and the Roman factions as Leo IX. A new era in papal history thus began.

(2) LEO IX AND PAPAL LEADERSHIP IN REFORM

The accomplished and distinguished Leo IX, who somehow narrowly missed being a great man, was peculiarly fitted both to carry out the reforms desired by the Emperor, to whom he was always a warm friend, and to start the Papacy on what was in practice a revolutionary career. Of high birth, handsome, commanding, an organizer, a tireless traveller, speaking several languages, fervently devout, he held fast to the now traditional views of his office in the Church and was resolved to turn the theory into an everyday reality. His very defects, his hot and combative temper, nerved him for his task, if they also precipitated disasters which a more patient statesman might have avoided. Fiery, uncompromising zeal was a common attribute of the reformers and the parent of strife. Bred in an atmosphere of reform, Leo had early become a royal chaplain, like many future bishops, and at the age of twenty-four had insisted on accepting the poor see of Toul, to which he had been canonically and freely elected. There he gained reputation in peace and war in the usual amphibious life of a bishop. Now he would not take up the Papacy until after an open election at Rome, to which he journeyed as a pilgrim (1049).

Leo saw his policy with perfect clearness. He would not be fixed at Rome as a distant, ultimate authority to ratify, when necessary, the decisions of the Emperor and independent synods. From this time Henry III gives place to him, even in Germany, as the presiding genius in ecclesiastical councils. Out of the years of his pontificate only six months altogether were spent at Rome. By continual travel and by the holding of numerous provincial Councils as he moved about, Leo brought papal prestige, steady papal intervention and control, home to the Western Church, with an active headship which it never lost. To his Councils he summoned abbots as well as bishops, thus securing in them a phalanx of monks ardent for reform and outweighing recalcitrant or lukewarm bishops. Popular veneration for the now visible Papacy and the ascetic champions added strength to his decrees. Two Councils especially in 1049 at Rheims and at Mainz marked out the main lines of the reform of the secular clergy. They were a programme and a first instalment. Simony and clerical marriage were to be rooted out. Bishops should be appointed only after election by clergy and people, an ominous beginning. At Rheims King Henry I of France vainly obstructed the assembly by calling on his bishops for their feudal service in a well-timed campaign, but those who obeyed him were excommunicated for non-attendance. The highest dignitaries were not spared. The Archbishop of Rheims and others were put on their defence for simony; one bishop was deposed; the Bishop of Langres took to flight. The effects of the Synod at Mainz were less striking, but in several Italian councils a start was made, which among much else included the exercise of papal authority in the all-but independent archbishopric and province of Milan. In disintegrated France the method was adopted of sending travelling papal legates to scour the country and enforce the synodal decrees. Summonses to Rome and attendance at the Easter Roman Synods, another innovation, worked in the same direction and towards the tightening of central papal control.

If the Papacy was to act continuously as the centre of Western Christendom, the Roman Curia could not remain a purely local body recruited from the Pope's immediate see and organized as such. Leo IX began the transformation of the papal Chancery on the model of that of the Empire, which was completed by his successors. The Cardinals could not continue to be merely the chiefs of the Roman clergy, the seven suburbicarian bishops, the priests and deacons of the Roman parishes. Leo recruited his cardinals, whom he treated as his Council, from ardent reformers, especially from north of the Alps and his native Lotharingia. They were men of a European outlook, well qualified to act as legates *a latere* with delegated power in distant missions and to keep the Papacy in touch with the provinces. Among them were Humbert, monk of Moyenmoûtier, created Bishop of Silva Candida, the protagonist of the movement to assert the independence of the Church from the laity; Frederick, brother of the disloyal Duke Godfrey of Lorraine, a theologian of the same party; and a young Tuscan relative of Gregory VI, Hildebrand, who had followed his kinsman into exile and there become a monk, and whose practical ability and force of character soon made their mark.

Leo IX was familiar with the conditions, ecclesiastical and secular, north of the Alps and in the *Regnum Italicum*, but he hardly grasped how different were those of the Eastern Roman Empire or realized the independence of its age-old civilization and traditions. He endeavoured to assert the papal theory in its full measure over the orthodox Eastern Church as a preliminary to a political alliance against the Norman invaders of South Italy. The rivalry of the two Churches in those territories and Leo's natural resolve to vindicate papal supremacy there sharpened the unavoidable dissidence, nor were his legates, two of whom were Cardinals Humbert and Frederick, fitted either by temperament or by convictions to temporize with the ambitious and adroit Greek Patriarch Michael Cerularius with his popular backing. The dispute ended in the lasting Schism of the Eastern and Western Churches (1054), a disaster for Europe as a whole. It has overshadowed the decisive success of Leo's ecclesiastical policy in the Latin West.

A temporal defeat in South Italy also darkened the Pope's closing years. Humane and upright, he was deeply stirred by the brigand-like atrocities of the Norman invaders of South Italy. He had the instincts, and in his earlier life some of the experience, of a warrior, and his remedy was to intervene in arms. When Henry III, with more essential tasks on his hands, declined to aid, and the project of a papal-Byzantine alliance was breaking down, Leo himself took the field. His motley army was routed and he was made prisoner by the Normans at Civitate (1053). His captors knelt before him, but did not set him free till he had agreed to their demands. Soon after his release he died at Rome (19 April 1054), closing in humiliation his memorable pontificate.

Henry III's next choice of a Pope, his most trusted minister, Gebhard, Bishop of Eichstätt, suggests some distaste for Leo's political independence. Victor II (1055–57), as he was renamed, was a peacemaker and in politics the Emperor's trusty lieutenant, ruling directly Spoleto and the later March of Ancona, and acting as imperial vicar in Italy. He was soon faced by the situation produced by the Emperor's death (1056) and the regency of the weak Empress Agnes of Poitou for her six-year-old son King Henry IV among the self-seeking nobles and bishops of Germany. Godfrey the Bearded, then in revolt, was pacified by being restored both to Lower Lorraine and to Tuscany, receiving the latter as husband of its dowager Beatrice, while his brother Cardinal Frederick was promoted to be abbot of the great and venerated frontier monastery of Monte Cassino. In this way peace might be maintained in Central Italy, but in Lombardy the first democratic storm of the Middle Ages was about to break.

The province of Milan under its archbishop, the successor of St Ambrose, had long maintained a proud independence of Rome. It was a stronghold of married and simoniacal clergy, who belonged to the feudal classes of *capitanei* and vavassors. But the traders and populace had already vindicated their claim to a share in government even against the mighty Aribert. About 1056 their democratic resentments and the new religious ferment coalesced. The agitation was started by a vavassor, the deacon Ariald, an idealist who zealously propagated the reformers' programme. He was seconded by two *capitanei*, the cleric Landulf and his layman brother Erlembald, both eloquent, ambitious demagogues. Class-warfare began under their influence in Lombardy. The old-fashioned clergy were denounced as simoniacs and Nicolaitans (i.e. married); the nobles nicknamed their opponents Patarines (i.e. ragpickers, the lowest class), which caused the whole reforming party to be called the Pataria. Guido, the archbishop, a weak man, and his fellow-bishops made no headway against the mob, nor was the promotion of a much-respected reformer, Anselm, to the Tuscan see of Lucca an adequate palliative.

Victor II's death in July 1057 dealt a fatal blow not only to local order in Lombardy but to the whole Empire and to the control, already relaxed, which Henry III had imposed on Papacy and Curia. Almost immediately, without any reference to Germany, a free election was made of Cardinal Frederick, who took the name of Stephen IX. He was an ardent reformer and his brother Duke Godfrey could be relied upon to support him. He did not address the German court till December, when Hildebrand undertook the mission. This, with the call to Peter Damiani, then the leader of Italian monasticism, to be a cardinal-bishop, and with the patronage of the Milanese reformers, was the chief event of his brief pontificate: the imperial leading-strings were snapped. But the severance and the Pope's early death in 1058 left the papal see at the mercy of its greatest danger, the turbulent Roman nobles, whose nominees, offsprings of faction, had so long discredited the Papacy. They seized the opportunity with one accord, and elected with much shrewdness a blameless cardinal-bishop, John of

Velletri, to be their Pope Benedict X. The reforming cardinals and curialists, however, were equal to the bold irregularities necessary for the occasion. They gathered in Florence, excommunicated Benedict as a usurper, and, protected by Duke Godfrey, elected a Burgundian, the guidable Gerard, Bishop of Florence, as Pope Nicholas II (December 1058). They then adroitly appealed to the Empress Agnes to authorize Godfrey to employ force. He entered Rome, drove out and captured Benedict X, and enthroned Nicholas II in January 1059.

It was the fate of Nicholas II, although verging on the status of a figure-head, to sanction radical developments in the freedom of the Papacy. He was guided by a group of reforming cardinals. Their leader at this time was Humbert of Silva Candida, who championed the complete severance of the official Church from secular domination, in which he saw the prime cause of corruption. In his book *Adversus Simoniacos* he argued that what was given to the Church was given to God and freed from earthly claims. The clergy were a holy class superior to the rest of humanity. Lay investiture, like simony and clerical marriage, was sinful; it was giving what no layman could give, the care of souls. Canonical election for bishops was essential. The duty of the laity was to carry out the instructions of the priesthood. Another of the group was Hildebrand. Less concerned than Humbert with these logical extremist theories, he had no doubt of the supreme dignity of the Papacy and the need for its complete independence, nor was he less ardent in the campaign for reform and for the consequent separation of the clergy from lay life. But his bent was practical and his expertness in affairs made him a frequent legate, an inspirer of political moves, and (1059) archdeacon of the Roman Church, an office which then included the charge of its estates and finance. The famous ascetic, St Peter Damiani, who was now by compulsion Cardinal-bishop of Ostia and most potent in the reformation of clerical and monastic manners, was quite outweighed by the extremists in the political sphere, in which he was a moderate.

These were determined to conjure the two political dangers which threatened the Papacy: imperial control and the elections by riotous Roman nobles. Hitherto elections to the Papacy had preserved the ancient canonical rule of choice by clergy and people. At the Lateran Council of April 1059 the revolutionary election decree of Nicholas II was issued. Elections to the Apostolic See were henceforth to be made, not necessarily at Rome, by the cardinals on the initiative of the cardinal-bishops, and from the act of election, not from consecration or enthronement, their choice was to possess full papal powers. The Roman 'people' was quite shut out. Only his 'due honour' was reserved for the boy King Henry IV, the future Emperor, a phrase which apparently meant a right or duty of formal confirmation. As the cardinals were appointed by the Popes, an oligarchy co-opted by its chief was set up. How unpalatable the decree was to the imperial court was soon to be seen in events and in a later garbled version of it which was produced.

But decrees without armed backing would be of little avail, and to provide it a startling reversal and expansion of papal policy was brought about. In August 1059 the Pope and his advisers held a council at Melfi. There the Norman leaders became vassals of the Papacy for their conquests on terms of tribute and military service. Presumably the forged Donation of Constantine furnished the grounds for this flat disregard of the rights and claims of Western and Eastern Empires alike. Thus the Papacy staked out claims and effected a reinsurance at the same time. The treaty was pregnant of a long future.

Meanwhile the tide of reform ran more strongly in conciliar decrees and in their enforcement. The clergy were removed from the judgement of laymen. The laity were forbidden to hear mass from an unchaste priest. The extreme and disputed opinion that simoniacal ordinations were void threatened a large part of the clergy with degradation: it was but a slight concession that unpurchased orders already received from a bishop guilty of simony should stand, although the like in future were to be null. Legates in France were busy repeating and enforcing the decrees against simony and clerical marriage. The most spectacular events occurred in Milan and Lombardy. In 1059 Peter Damiani and Anselm of Lucca came as legates to lead the reformers, who had gained over the plebeians. Guido and his clergy, although supported by the nobles, were powerless to resist. They confessed the universal simony, and vowed to avoid it and live celibate for the future. Guido sealed his submission by attending a Roman council. The cherished independence of the Ambrosian Church was gone.

The opposition, however, was overridden for the time only. The Lombard bishops, the Roman nobles, and the imperial court were all bitterly aggrieved. When Nicholas II died in July 1061, two months after Cardinal Humbert, a trial of strength began over the election decree. Roman nobles and Lombard bishops demanded from young King Henry, as patrician of Rome, the nomination of a Lombard bishop, Cadalus of Parma, to succeed him in the old fashion. Their wishes were granted in October, but the cardinals, led by Hildebrand, had already elected Anselm of Lucca to be Alexander II, and with Norman aid they forced him into Rome. The schism meant war. Cadalus, who took the name of Honorius II, fought his way, with his Lombards, into the city, where numbers were in his favour (March 1062). But Duke Godfrey intervened and induced both competitors to withdraw to their sees. A revolution in Germany turned the scales. In April 1062 Archbishop Anno of Cologne abducted the young king and overturned the feeble government of the Empress, who retired to the nunnery she had already entered. The German episcopate was divided save in disliking a Lombard, and Anno, selfish and vain, piqued himself on deciding who was Pope at the Synod of Augsburg (October 1062). Cadalus and his partisans fought on, even once re-entering Rome. A joint German and Italian synod at Mantua in 1064 was needed to re-acknowledge Alexander and to condemn his rival, who even then withdrew unquelled to his diocese of Parma until his death (1072). Anno had made a bad bargain for himself. His absence at Mantua enabled his rival, Archbishop Adalbert of Bremen, to gain control of the boy-king, and in his later years he was humiliated by the Pope he had helped to win.

Alexander II was no nonentity, like Nicholas II, but his minister, Archdeacon Hildebrand, was greater than he. Peter Damiani, the moderate, was allowed to retire. During the pontificate the increase of papal control and unsparing reform went hand in hand. Frequent local synods under zealous papal legates especially in France harassed the simoniac and married clergy. A vigorous attack was made on the customary rights of laymen to appoint parish priests instead of the bishop. Canonical election to sees was insisted upon. In Germany, while legates when sent were native reforming archbishops and much was left to the ordinary provincial synods, the conservative Anno and his colleague, Siegfried of Mainz, caught between papal urgency and the stubborn resistance of their clergy, became vainly eager for monastic retirement. In Lombardy the strife waxed furious. The leader at Milan was now the democratic *capitaneus* Erlembald, a tall, red-bearded, combative knight, pious and revengeful, a born revolutionary, the real founder of the commune of Milan. He obtained a banner with a red cross on a white ground from the Pope (1065). In these tumultuous proceedings Ariald aroused fresh enmity by using the Roman liturgy in place of the traditional Ambrosian. He was murdered by his enemies in June 1066, and his death, like his life, fanned the flame, which fresh papal legates could not quench. Guido was weary of the contest. Like most of his suffragans, he was a man of the old school, and his solution was to resign privately and ask the king to invest an eloquent young friend, Godfrey, with the archbishopric. Henry IV, now ruling himself, fell in with the plan, but Erlembald took up arms against the uncanonical intruder, while Alexander II, whose consent had not been asked, insisted that the wavering Guido should resume his see. The unhappy archbishop died during the civil war (1071), and a successor was found by Erlembald, with the Pope's approval, in a young noble, Atto (1072). The Patarines, or rather Erlembald, now ruled Milan itself in the spirit of faction, while the Pope urged Henry to accept his candidate. Henry's reply was to order Godfrey's consecration by his willing suffragans. So the war went on, and Alexander had only time to excommunicate the young king's counsellors before he died on 21 April 1073. He had outlived Godfrey the Bearded, Cadalus, and St Peter Damiani.

Although a thorough reformer, Alexander II had been a moderating influence in his party, adverse from the most extreme measures. He had not checked the tendency to political rather than purely ecclesiastical methods in the Curia, which had been growing since Leo IX, and became almost a necessity when dependence on the Empire was thrown off in Henry IV's minority if the Papacy was to maintain itself in the troubled waters of Italy. This tendency was seen when, at Hildebrand's instigation, a papal banner was given to William of Normandy on his invasion of England, a political enterprise to say the least, from which ecclesiastical profit might accrue to the reforming Papacy. It pairs off with the banner given to the democratic faction-leader Erlembald, whose victory would mean the subjugation of Milan to the reformers' programme and the reduction of imperial control over the Italian episcopate. Canonical election *versus* imperial appointment was an issue of fundamental importance. Was the bishops' first duty to the Church or to the State? It could lie dormant when the royal and priestly powers lived in rough harmony, not so in discord. And not only papal authority, but the whole movement the reformers urged so passionately required bishops devoted to reform and obedient to the Papacy.

(3) THE MINORITY AND EARLY YEARS OF ·HENRY IV

Part of the success of the Papacy in achieving both independence and ecclesiastical dominion was owing to the withering of the imperial control in the secular sphere. The king was a child, the regent a woman without capacity and beset by magnates who were blindly engrossed in personal or particularistic aims and insensible of the harm they were causing to the Empire as a whole. They could follow a leader, but one was lacking; by themselves they resented the discipline of a central government, the need of which they hardly conceived. Their turbulence and greed were not to be repressed. The dukes whom Agnes appointed, the Burgundian Rudolf of Rheinfelden to Swabia and the Saxon Otto of Nordheim to Bavaria, neither natives of their duchies and of poor service to the cause of order, pursued their own aggrandisement alone. Former Emperors had buttressed their authority by the bishops and abbots whom they had so prodigally endowed with lands and jurisdictions, and from whose *servitia*, more than from the scattered royal demesne, they derived the sinews of war and peace. Unhappily Henry III did not leave behind him unselfish statesmen in the episcopal office. He may, with his pious prepossessions, have misread their characters and their fitness as supports of the Crown. He had, too, used the best of the episcopate, naturally few, in appointing them to the Papacy, and in the uncongenial climate of Italy their lives were not long. At his death the leading archbishops were Anno of Cologne and Adalbert of Bremen. Both were earnest prelates in their way: Anno was a patron of monks, Adalbert, the primate of the north, of missionaries abroad; but to each the wealth and glory of their sees was a prime consideration. Archbishop Siegfried, whom Agnes appointed to Mainz in 1060, could not compete with them in personality.

After the death of Pope Victor II, affairs went from bad to worse. The independence of the Papacy was matched by that of Hungary and Poland. The inefficiency of the government perhaps justified Anno's *coup d'état* of April 1062, when he abducted young Henry at Kaiserswerth, and proceeded to rule in his name, admitting next year Archbishop Adalbert to a kind of

Fig. 99a. *Ring worn by the Emperor Henry IV*

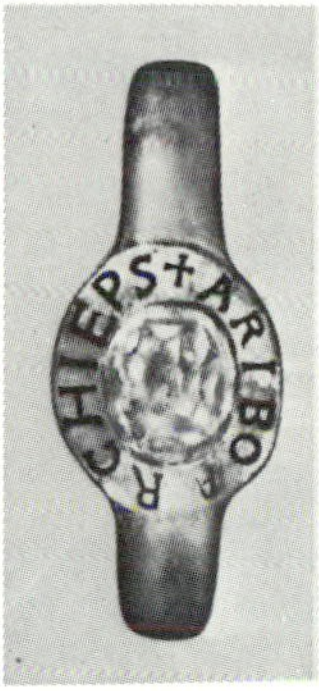

Fig. 99b. *Ring of Archbishop Aribo of Mainz*

partnership. But the two misused their trust. Henry was allowed to run wild, while Anno depleted the none too large royal revenues in order to enrich his monasteries. When Adalbert elbowed out Anno in 1064, his conduct was no better. He obtained lavish grants to his see from the royal demesne in Saxony, while it was further diminished by lax management and usurpations. His regency outlasted the king's majority (at the age of 15 by Frankish law) by a year, when early in 1066 the intrigues of Anno and other envious magnates secured his dismissal and spoliation. He died in 1072, Anno in 1075. Godfrey the Bearded, their lay counterpart, died in 1069, leaving Tuscany to the heiress, his step-daughter Countess Matilda, who by character and wealth was well fitted to dominate Central Italy.

Henry IV, 'King of the Romans' as he sometimes styled himself before his imperial coronation, was now his own master at sixteen. He made a bad start, incurring disrepute for his vicious life. He inherited the passionate, autocratic temper of Conrad II and not the religious self-control of Henry III. He had been married in boyhood to Bertha, daughter of Oddo of Savoy and Adelaide of Turin, an alliance of vital importance for the Empire in Italy and Burgundy. With headstrong folly he tried to repudiate her, quite in the manner of the lawless time. From this he was saved by Peter Damiani, sent as papal legate to enforce the new standards. The old saint insisted on the marriage being valid and becoming a reality. Queen Bertha quickly won over her tempestuous husband, and was his better angel in private life as long as she lived. But Henry was no mere pleasure-seeker. He was a statesman, clearly perceiving the ills of the Empire and resolved to restore the shattered royal power at all costs. He won enduring devotion, be it noted, from the rising class of townsmen along the Rhine, but he was only too much inclined to ride rough-shod over the Saxons in his demesne, where he and his South German *ministeriales* aroused a vivid hatred. Like many of his magnates he was untrustworthy; when in straits he would be humble and yielding, but when the danger passed, he would give way to arrogant overconfidence. He was more of an astute diplomatist than a prudent administrator.

Henry's first objective was to restore and secure the royal demesne in Saxony. The task was difficult and his harsh methods made it harder. He built castles and exacted all and more than his rights. But Saxony was particularist to the extent of isolation. Its lay magnates and its bishops were disaffected and alarmed at the looming prospect of South German control, and the large class of small freemen within it would follow them to maintain their tribal independence. The explosion came when Henry in 1070 not only removed the Saxon Otto of Nordheim from the dukedom of Bavaria (where he was replaced by the Swabian Welf IV, on his father's side a member of the Lombard house of Este) but also confiscated his Saxon lands. This turned the Billungs into rebels. A brief revolt was so easily suppressed that the king defied Pope Alexander over Milan and prepared to force Poland back into vassalage. But all Saxony suddenly gathered against Henry. He could hardly escape from his Saxon castle of Harzburg (1073). At a stroke he was powerless; the southern princes would mediate, not fight for him, for they feared his autocracy. Only the few Rhine towns desired a strong central government to keep the peace. Henry showed, now that he realized his position, his skill in political manoeuvre. He humbly propitiated the new Pope, Gregory VII, and backed by his own and episcopal forces came separately to terms with the Saxons (1074). The castles were to be destroyed; Saxon particularism was guaranteed. Then the Saxon peasants in their hatred played into his hands by wantonly wrecking his church at Harzburg. The treaty was broken, the Church offended; the south German magnates were already disappointed at Saxon indifference to their mediation and were estranged by a peasants' outrage which threatened their class. The result was that Henry could lead all the dukes against Saxony. On 9 June 1075 the charge of Duke Rudolf of Swabia's knights against the Saxon footmen won him the battle of the river Unstrut.

Henry reduced the rebels to ask for mercy, and that was small. In his elation his old faults took a free course. Imprisonment and confiscation were dealt out to the Saxon magnates and bishops; castles were rebuilt and the southern dukes alarmed. To crown all, Henry recklessly broke with the Pope.

(4) GREGORY VII AND THE FIRST STRUGGLE OF EMPIRE AND PAPACY

The death of Alexander II had been immediately followed (22 April 1073) by the election, at once tumultuary and regular, of Hildebrand as Pope Gregory VII. As archdeacon he had become popular in Rome and master of the Curia. His temperament was not that of the scholar or theologian, but that of a fiery champion of the Church endowed with an unbending will, great practical sagacity, and a zeal for righteousness (*iustitia*), as he saw it, in the Christian commonwealth, ecclesiastical and lay. He was bold and combative to the extreme in pursuit of an extreme ideal, but his practical sense made him moderate in his preliminary moves and unscrupulous when all was in jeopardy. His passionate belief in his cause strengthened him and also cloaked from him his own intense love of sway. He felt himself the representative of St Peter, and obedience to his just commands to be a part of Christian righteousness. He was carrying on a holy war against the rebellious forces of evil. He hardly understood the peace-loving attitude of Hugh of Cluny, whose sympathy he claimed; far more acceptable was the unswerving devotion to him of Countess Matilda, combined as it was with her virile ability to rule her great possessions, which comprised Tuscany and a block of counties across the Apennines along the lower Po.

He carried to new heights the doctrine, of which he was utterly convinced, of the Petrine supremacy over the Church and Christendom. He was in charge of all Christian souls with full power to correct the disobedient and unrighteous. The Pope was the judge of right and wrong in others, himself subject only to God. In the Church he was absolute master: all prelates must submit to his overriding authority; his powers of excommunication and absolution were unlimited; his legates' decrees were reversible only by him. In the true spirit of the age he appealed constantly to the existing Canon Law, but the Roman Church retained the inalienable power to add to it. As to the lay rulers he was at the outset a Gelasian. The *sacerdotium* and the *regnum* existed side by side by divine ordinance, like the sun and moon giving light to the physical world. But the sun of the *sacerdotium* far excelled the moon of the *regnum*; in fact, the supreme pastor, the successor of St Peter, was charged with the supervision of lay rulers, and with the duty

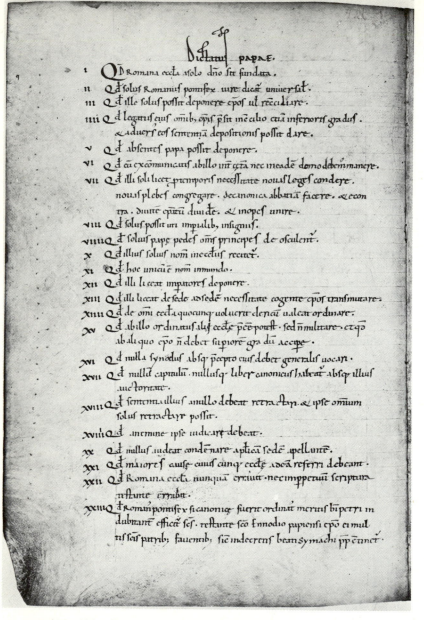

Fig. 100, 101. Dictatus Papae, principles of papal policy laid down by Gregory VII

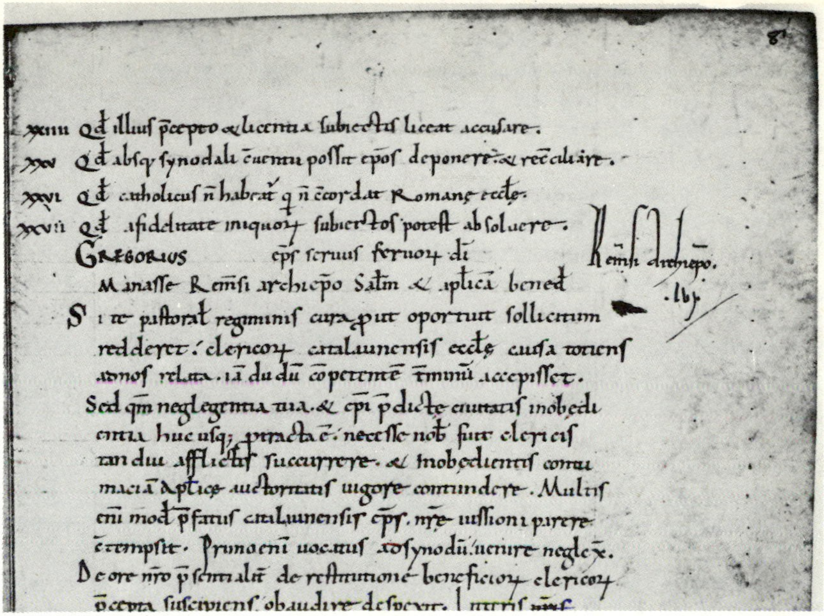

Fig. 101

of punishing, even of removing, them when disobedient or perverse. In his later days he thought of lay dominion in the sense of St Augustine as a human creation. The *Dictatus Papae* (1075), a list of useful canonical headings, sets forth in the most pointed terms the papal superiority and absolutism over what would now be called Church and State, or as they appeared in the Middle Ages the two sets of officials, spiritual and lay, who governed Christendom. No words could be more precise and emphatic.

Gregory began his pontificate with no desire for a breach with the King of the Romans but a firm, indeed impatient, resolve to spur on the lagging prelates of Germany to repress simony and clerical marriage and incontinence. Henry IV's humble apologies at the crisis of his first Saxon troubles lured him on to hope that the king would be another Henry III, a docile coadjutor in the reform campaign; he may have deferred his own consecration until assured of Henry's recognition; and he even indulged a dream of leading a crusade to the East, while Henry enforced reform at home. But save from the disloyal Saxon bishops, who were angling for papal favour, he met with obstruction from high and low in the enforcement of the reforming decrees. In Italy Henry took no steps to recognize Atto at Milan. To subdue the conservative German and Lombard episcopates and convert them from royal instruments into papal lieutenants was now a chief aim of the Pope. In the Lenten Synod of February 1075 he prepared for a crisis. Besides suspending recalcitrant German bishops, he commanded the laity to refuse to hear the mass of married priests, which was the surest way of coercing the lower clergy. Further, he drew up the *Dictatus Papae*, in itself a programme, and passed, with little publicity or record, the first Investiture Decree. It forbade, in general terms, the investiture of ecclesiastical office by laymen. That ceremony had become the means and safeguard of the royal prerogative of appointing to bishoprics and abbeys even without canonical election. It placed the king's choice in possession of the office and its rights and endowment: thus Henry IV had invested Godfrey with the staff and ring of Milan. Henry III and William of England might be careful in selecting their prelates, but Henry IV had thought only of his secular interests, and Philip I of France, like the majority of his great vassals, was an unabashed simoniac. Gregory VII was less moved by the theological arguments of Cardinal Humbert than by the desire to render impossible these arbitrary appointments by confining to ecclesiastical superiors the power to invest with ecclesiastical offices. He was willing to negotiate on the king's share in elections, but Henry here was adamant. The strength of his monarchy depended on his choice and control of his bishops with the wealth and jurisdictions attached to their sees; they counterbalanced the hereditary nobles. Overconfident after his Saxon victory, he proceeded to flout the Pope by discarding his former choice, Godfrey, disregarding the canonical Atto, and investing a fresh nominee, Tedald, with the see of Milan. The bishops in fact were the chief means left him of asserting his government in Lombardy. The murder of Erlembald and the loyalty of the bishops encouraged him to act.

Gregory answered the challenge with startling threats, verbally conveyed through Henry's envoys. In the spirit of the *Dictatus Papae* he would depose the proud, disobedient king. The effect on Henry was to excite him to a burst of fury. He assembled a hasty synod of his bishops at Worms on 24 January 1076, where they declared Gregory deposed in his turn as a criminal who exceeded his powers. The Lombard bishops followed suit, while the king in a violent letter recalled his own indelible sacring as the Lord's Anointed. It was a foolish stroke which missed its mark. Gregory was peculiarly strong in Rome, where an attempt on him by factious nobles had just been quelled by the Roman populace. At the Lenten Synod of February 1076 he fulfilled his threats. The rebellious bishops were deposed with a set time for repentance. In an address to St Peter he excommunicated Henry himself and forbade his exercise of kingship. No monarch had ever been excommunicated since Theodosius. In 1076 the sentence differed little, if obeyed, from removal from government, for excommunication was infectious; those who dealt with its victim incurred a similar boycott from Christian society. But both sentences were obeyed

490

in Germany; the Pope had proved the better calculator. In Lombardy the bishops were long hardened to papal excommunication; north of the Alps their knees knocked together and they vied in seeking forgiveness from the Pope they had defied. The Saxons of course rejoiced, but the lay nobles also, led by the southern dukes, partly from hostility to the revival of central government, partly from disbelief in Henry's violent assertion of ecclesiastical revolt, and partly from dread of spiritual reprɔbation, opposed or held aloof from the king. Henry found himself isolated. At a diet at Tribur in October 1076, attended by papal legates, the German princes (as the great vassals-in-chief were called) came to a decision, which Henry was compelled to accept. Unless he obtained absolution from Gregory within a year and a day from the papal sentence (i.e. by 22 February 1077), they would renounce their allegiance and elect another king. For this purpose a diet was to be called at Augsburg for 2 February, at which the Pope was invited to preside. To make assurance sure the rebel dukes, Rudolf, Welf, and the Swabian magnate, Berthold of Zähringen, titular Duke of Carinthia, blocked the Alpine passes into Italy, so that Henry should not reach Lombardy, and promised an escort to bring the Pope. Henry could hope for nothing from the assembly of his enemies at Augsburg. His one chance was to placate the Pope separately first at whatever cost in

Fig. 102. Emperor Henry IV in St Nicholas' chapel at Canossa

humiliation, and he took it. There was one pass left open and accessible, that of the Mont Cenis in the lands of Queen Bertha's kindred, the Counts of Savoy. Her mother Countess Adelaide, heiress of Turin, was herself a reformer and influential. In the depth of a severe winter Henry and his family crossed the mountains into Lombardy. The Pope had passed the Apennines and was awaiting the escort in Matilda's castle of Canossa, prevented from proceeding by his Lombard enemies. In front of its gate Henry stood as a barefooted penitent in the snow for three days until Gregory was moved by Hugh of Cluny, Adelaide, and Matilda herself and by his priestly duty to absolve him (January 1077). It was an immense surrender to the Pope's jurisdiction, a contrast to Henry III's lay supremacy; yet it was a diplomatic victory, for the Pope, still barred by the Lombards, could not reach Germany, while Henry, no longer an outcast, proceeded home through Carinthia to be welcomed by the loyal and the many enemies of the dukes.

The rebel dukes, however, persisted in their course. At Forchheim in Franconia they held their delayed diet in the presence of papal legates. There (March 1077) they declared Henry deposed—it was pretended later that he had broken the oath he had taken at Canossa—and elected Duke Rudolf king on condition that he renounced hereditary right and the control of episcopal elections. It was a precedent never forgotten. The Pope was placed somewhat in a quandary between the rivals, of which he endeavoured to make use by declaring that he would adjudge the crown to that claimant whose righteous conduct on trial deserved it. He lacked indeed the physical force to intervene. Meanwhile the civil war went on undecided and disastrous. Rudolf could rely on Saxony and his fellow rebels, but Henry had the majority behind him, including the growing Rhine towns. Although a papalist party made some gains in the south under ardent reforming clerics, Saxony became divided when the Billungs made terms with Henry, and his son-in-law Frederick of Staufen, whom he made Duke of Swabia (1079), helped to check Rudolf and the Welfs and Zähringens. He was still far from accepting the investiture decrees, which Gregory was making more precise, while he insisted that the Pope should recognize his indefeasible right to the oaths of fealty once taken to him. On the other side, Rudolf claimed that Henry had broken his obligations to his quondam vassals, and was resentful that the Pope did not accept the lawfulness of the election. By the assembly of the Lenten Roman Synod of 1080 Henry felt that the time was ripe and public opinion strong enough for an open breach with the Pope if Gregory could be made to seem the aggressor against ancient right. His envoys demanded with threats the excommunication of the rebels. The Pope was stirred to decisive action. In a solemn address to St Peter and St Paul he recounted his view of his dealings with Henry and the latter's conduct. He adjudged him excommunicated and expressly deposed for his sins. He entrusted the kingdom to Rudolf, the righteous elect of the German princes. He prayed the Apostles to vindicate his sentence. So complete was his confidence that he made a public prophecy on Easter Monday that Henry would be either dead or deposed by St Peter's Day (29 June).

This time it was Henry who knew his ground best. It was the Pope who had declared open war, and had plainly shown his doctrine that he was autocrat of Christendom, the lord and disposer of temporal monarchs and realms. All Germans, save the only too plentiful rancorous partisans and unruly particularist nobles whose public rebellion and ruthless private wars were making the land wretched, were rallying round the king. Henry stepped forth as the defender of law and order and peace, of government and ancient right. His plans now displayed forethought and preparation.

On 25 June he held a numerous council of German and Lombard bishops at Brixen, south of the Brenner Pass. Its business was to depose Gregory on counts old and new with small regard for fact, and to elect a fit successor, for it would not be wise to leave the new schism without an ecclesiastical head. Henry's choice was the Lombard Guibert, who assumed the style of Clement III. He was an irreproachable prelate, long influential as chancellor for Italy, and later Archbishop of Ravenna, where he had proved himself a steady opponent of Gregory VII. Neither he nor his king were now likely to be cowed. Pope Gregory on his side knew his danger and turned for fighting allies. The Normans in Italy, and more especially Robert Guiscard, had continued their conquests over south Lombard princes whom the Pope had recently acquired as vassals. They had turned deaf ears to his excommunications, but in June 1080 he met the culprits at Ceprano and bent his pride to enfeoff them with their usurpations in return for aid.

Meanwhile King Henry strove to overcome his German opponents. He was not fortunate in war, but his defeat on the river Grune near Pegau in Thuringia on 15 October 1080 turned out to be a political victory, since the mortal wound of the anti-king left his partisans without a chief, and their rivalries produced the election (1081) of a nonentity, the

Fig. 103. The anti-King Rudolf of Swabia

Lotharingian Count Herman of Salm. Outside Saxony the death of Rudolf appeared that judgement of God for which Gregory had prayed, and it was for Henry. It did not help matters when the Pope put forward a demand for an oath of fealty from the new anti-king.

*Fig. 104. Henry IV and Pope Clement III; Gregory VII's
expulsion from Rome and death at Salerno*

Henry could now prepare to attack the Pope at home. In 1081 he
appeared before Rome itself. Robert Guiscard was pursuing his own
schemes against the Eastern Empire, but the Romans held out for the
popular Pope both then and next year. However, Countess Matilda could
not resist in the open field, and the Eastern Emperor Alexius Comnenus
supplied his Western counterpart with funds. When Henry captured the
Leonine City with St Peter's in 1083, bribes were already having an effect
on Roman loyalty. Next year the Romans surrendered, while Gregory
stoutly held out in the castle of Sant' Angelo. Henry enthroned his Anti-
Pope, who duly crowned him Emperor (31 March 1084). But his triumph
was short-lived. Guiscard at last came to the rescue. The Emperor did not
venture a battle, and the Eternal City endured one of the worst of its many
storms. A large part, as far as the Capitol, was left in ruins in the brutal
sack. Rome was never again the marble city of antiquity which had
dazzled conqueror and pilgrim. Gregory himself lost once and for all the

affection of his people. He was taken in all-but captivity by his ally to Salerno, where on 25 May 1085 he died.

His last words, 'I have loved righteousness and hated iniquity; wherefore I die in exile', an ironic variant of a verse from the Psalms,[1] give the measure of his disappointment with events. Yet he had accomplished an immense work. The mastery of the Papacy over the Church was vindicated and gaining daily ground; so too was the extrusion of the lay powers from control, as far as laws could forbid it; even the particular abuse of lay investiture was to cease within a generation. The programme of the reformers, clerical celibacy and the prohibition of simony, was in a fair way to being accepted as law at any rate, and with it the sharp separation of the clergy from the laity, that cardinal point in his beliefs. And, what to him had become the great cause for which to battle, the supremacy of the Papacy over earthly potentates, of the *sacerdotium* over the *regnum*, was now a part of the papal tradition. It was to be reasserted in the future, and it had already shaken the Empire to its foundations.

(5) THE AFTERMATH OF THE STRUGGLE AND THE INVESTITURE CONTEST

The years after Gregory's death witnessed a slow advance of the Emperor's fortunes. His Anti-Pope Guibert held Rome. In Germany old foes died off or were reconciled. After 1088 Saxony submitted on terms of local autonomy. Except for the Welfs rebellion ceased. In 1087 he could crown his son Conrad as king. But the ambition of Henry to revive imperial power was not realized. It is noticeable that he had recourse to the Peace of God to mitigate private warfare. The death of the Empress Bertha (1087) was a serious loss in itself, and his second marriage to the Russian princess Praxedis (Adelaide) proved disastrous. Worst of all, the Gregorian reforming Curia and party triumphed over all its difficulties by its solid strength. Even in Germany there were bishops who would accept Henry but not his Anti-Pope. Countess Matilda remained unshaken. After the brief pontificate of the mild Victor III (1086–7), who as Desiderius had been for years Abbot of Monte Cassino, the Cardinals chose a statesman of the first rank in Otto, ex-prior of Cluny, to be Urban II (1088–99). A French noble by birth, he had long been a cardinal and legate, and he united his party and the Church under his vigorous leadership. He had all the adroitness which had been lacking in his great predecessor, a caution which did not mean any sacrifice of his principles, and a remarkable *flair* for opportunities as they presented themselves. To him the investiture question was weightier than it had appeared to Gregory. He was determined

---

[1] "Thou hast loved righteousness, and hated iniquity; wherefore God, even thy God, hath anointed thee with the oil of gladness above thy fellows" (Psalm xlv. 8).

to remove ecclesiastics from lay control to that of the Papacy, but except in dealings with Henry IV he went warily. In temporal affairs, without estranging lay opinion by demanding suzerainty as Gregory had done, he seized the secular leadership of Western Christendom by inaugurating the common enterprise of the First Crusade.

Urban passed his earlier years under the protection of the Normans of South Italy, while Guibert held Rome. But a new factor was coming into play. The Lombard cities were beginning to form communes or town-republics as a remedy for class and family warfare, and the power of the mainly imperialist bishops, like that of the marquesses, was on the wane. Autonomous cities were naturally against the Emperor. In 1088 the imperialist Archbishop of Milan was reconciled to the Pope. Next year the ageing Countess Matilda, long a widow of the loyal Duke of Lower Lotharingia, married the boy Welf V, who was heir to both Bavaria and Este. Henry IV then (1090) left Germany for Italy to combat the danger. He defeated Matilda's troops (1093), but the rebellion only grew. He lost the affection of his own family. King Conrad joined the papalists and was crowned at Pavia, only to remain a catspaw till his death (1101). Meanwhile the Pope was alternating at Rome with Guibert, who had become an uncancelled cipher. He could proceed northwards to Lombardy and France and take the initiative for the Crusade, while the Emperor, blocked on both sides of the Alps, was isolated at Verona, his character traduced more than ever by the accusations of his rebel son and the Empress, who fled from him to the Pope. The two Welfs, however, quarrelled with Matilda, and their reversion to his allegiance allowed his escape to Germany (1097), where he acknowledged their rights to Bavaria. Their kinsman Berthold (of Zähringen) became Duke in southern Swabia, while Frederick of Staufen kept the rest. All lay opposition ceased, but Henry was obliged to let his nobles go their own way, although they crowned his second son Henry king. He had failed to re-erect a centralizing monarchy.

The reforming party, in spite of all, continued to gain adherents in Germany. Politically their attitude may have been somewhat eased by the mitigation of the infectiousness of excommunication decreed in 1078 by Gregory VII. But Urban II sharpened the prohibition of lay investiture by forbidding even ecclesiastically invested bishops to do homage to laymen for their lands and jurisdictions. If he sought peace, he overstepped the mark. With Henry IV he was irreconcilable. The Emperor shrunk in power and prestige when the Pope, not he, stirred up the Crusade.

Urban's successor, the Tuscan monk, Paschal II (1099–1118), was unfortunate in lacking the shrewd, prompt insight and the courage needed for his tempestuous age, and he was handicapped by the rigid legislation of his predecessor, in which he devoutly believed. He was also politically weak. Although Guibert died in 1100, the turbulence of the Roman nobles made Rome insecure, haunted by Anti-Popes like fleeting spectres. Countess Matilda, although she had declared the Papacy heir to her alods, was no longer so fervid as she had once been. The Norman duchy of Apulia was relapsing into feudal anarchy. Paschal did not possess the personal influence of the French Cluniac Urban in France. None the less the momentum of the reform was sustained. In France, King Louis VI could afford to abandon the lay investiture and even the homage of his bishops for their temporalities, remaining content with the oath of fealty. Common interest and loyalty secured elections acceptable to the ruler and the performance of feudal duties by the prelates. Much the same happened to sees and abbeys dependent on the great vassals. In England and Normandy the kings had all along held firmly to their right of investiture and to the vassalage of ecclesiastical fiefs until the exile of Archbishop Anselm of Canterbury, the foremost of theologians, involved him in the synods which expressly forbade the practice. He entered on a stubborn contest with King Henry I, which was ended in 1107 by an ingenious Concordat. Due election under the king's influence was followed by the homage and fealty of the elect and his investiture by writ with his temporalities: then he was consecrated and given his ring and staff by the metropolitan. In England and France election was now made by the cathedral chapters, whether secular clergy or the monks of a cathedral abbey. Parish priests received episcopal institution. The actual influence of ruler or patron could not be banished by legal forms, but doctrinal theory was vindicated.

In Germany, however, the problem was different. Chapters and abbeys were filled with local nobles, peculiarly difficult for the Emperor to control; and the prelates were princes of the decentralized Empire, capable of holding their own without protection, yet essential for the effectiveness of the monarchy, which was poorly endowed for its too wide and uncemented realms. Further, the Papacy since Gregory VII was committed to a war to the death with the vainly deposed Henry IV. The curial tradition, as ever, could not admit defeat, and Paschal refused all reconciliation. The young King Henry had sworn not to act independently of his father, but his nature was hard and faithless, and he saw the kingship wither in the strife. The Emperor's proclamation of a 'land-peace' for four years (1103) angered the feud-loving nobles. Young Henry V took an early occasion to rebel at their head. In 1105 he gained easy absolution for himself, promised to act by the counsel of the princes, and with horrible treachery, perjury, and hypocrisy combined seized on his father's person. The Emperor promised to abdicate, but contrived to escape from prison, and with the aid of the townsmen of Lower Lotharingia won a victory over his unnatural son. Then he died, worn out, at Liége on 7 August 1106. The Pope refused him Christian burial. That Henry IV failed and died so miserably was due partly to his reigning during a long crisis of the monarchy which defied solution, partly to his own character which evoked hatred. Yet he was 'the father of the poor' and gained devotion from the townsmen oppressed by the anarchic nobility. He had fallen foul of the Papacy, the Saxons, and the magnates, and found them deadly foes.

Pope Paschal, however, was deceived, like other men, in the heartless, cunning Henry V, whose one merit was the desire to maintain the Empire. Negotiations went on, but the king resolutely invested bishops, elected under his influence, with the *regalia*, i.e. their fiefs and secular jurisdiction. The controversy came to a head when Henry V entered Italy with a formidable army (1110) to receive the imperial crown. Not even Matilda wished to oppose him. The Normans were disorganized, and the towns proffered formal submission. In face of him the Pope, with desperate idealism, proposed a radical solution: he would renounce the *regalia* possessed by the Empire's prelates, if the king would surrender lay investiture. Henry, who must have been alive to realities, agreed to the treaty. On 12 February 1111 he entered St Peter's and the terms were made public to the throng. Prelates who saw their wealth and power given away, nobles, their class-fellows, who saw their cherished rights as advocates and patrons vanishing, burst into uproar. In the tumult the king's following seized the Pope and cardinals and forced their way out of the city. Two months' imprisonment reduced Paschal to granting lay investiture and crowning the Emperor (13 April), who forthwith returned to Germany.

But he had overreached himself. The dynamic party in the Church outside Germany rose against the treaty and the unhappy Paschal, who was borne along by shifting currents of conscience and dread. Under dictation he retracted his concession which had been extorted by force. Meanwhile Henry V was deeply involved in civil war in Germany. Rigid or ambitious churchmen, particularist Saxons, and turbulent magnates joined hands against him, led by the egoist Adalbert, Archbishop of Mainz, and Lothar of Supplinburg, Duke of Saxony after the extinction of the Billungs. At best he avoided disaster. Like his predecessors, he was bent on increasing the royal demesne. For this purpose he left seething Germany for Italy in 1116 in order to acquire the vast fiefs and alods of Countess Matilda, who in 1115 died childless after making him her heir, a disposition hard to reconcile in fact, if feasible in feudal law, with her previous donation to the Papacy. The communal movement in her lands may have given her greater sympathy with the Emperor, against whom she felt no personal hatred. Henry, who now granted vague charters to some Lombard cities, took possession. By reason of his fleeting sojourns in Rome the Curia became migratory. When Paschal II died (January 1118), his successor, the South Italian Gelasius II, soon found refuge in France at Cluny, while the Emperor set up an Anti-Pope (Gregory VIII) in the person of the recreant Portuguese Archbishop of Braga. Thus the schism was renewed, and Henry returned to Germany for the unceasing civil war.

The death of Gelasius II brought to the papal throne a leader of the reforming party which had cowed Pope Paschal, for Guy, Archbishop of Vienne, became Calixtus II (February 1119). Not a curialist, but a provincial prelate of exceptionally high birth—he was cousin of most western potentates—he was fitted by strength of character and wide outlook to draw clergy and laity towards an accord. The negligible Anti-Pope was easily overthrown (1120), but negotiations with the Emperor had begun long before. The outrage to Pope Paschal had met with much disapproval in Germany, where the princes more and more held the upper hand and were happily themselves wearying of contention. In the natural distrust of Henry V the haggling over terms of settlement was a long and stubborn controversy, but at last under the guarantee and by the mediation of the German princes the famous Concordat of Worms was accepted by both sides on 23 September 1122. There was peace once more

Fig. 105. Wedding feast of King Henry V and Matilda at Mainz

between Empire and Papacy, and it was ratified next year at Rome by a Council which could be claimed as ecumenical in the West. The Diet at Bamberg had already made it imperial law. Calixtus II died in peace in December 1124. The Emperor's closing years were less happy. He was repulsed from Saxony by its autonomous duke, Lothar; an attack on France, in alliance with Henry I of England, whose daughter Matilda he had married, was an unmitigated failure. When in May 1125 he died childless, the starkly autocratic Salian line came to an end, defeated for all its struggles.

The Concordat of Worms consisted of an imperial diploma, granted to God and the Papacy, and a papal bull, addressed to the Emperor. Henry V guaranteed the canonical election of bishops and abbots, and renounced investiture of the elect with the spiritual symbols of ring and staff, which implied the cure of souls. Calixtus II conceded to the Emperor his right to be present at elections and to intervene when elections were disputed. Since there was no custom that a majority of votes carried an election, this faculty of supporting the sounder (*sanior*) party was of high value for the Emperor. Further, German prelates were not to be consecrated until the Emperor had invested them with the *regalia* by the lay sceptre, for which they should render their dues to him, i.e. homage, fealty, etc. Prelates of Italy and Burgundy, however, were to be invested by the sceptre and render their dues within six months after their consecration. In fact, their appointment and loyal service were of less importance to the Emperor owing to the communal movement in Italy and the laxity of his control of Burgundy. The diplomatic forms adopted allowed astute ecclesiastics to claim that the Pope's concessions were to Henry personally, but the imperial interpretation then and later insisted that they extended to his successors. The arrangement bore a marked resemblance to the accord between Henry I of England and Anselm.

Thus the strife between Empire and Papacy ended in a compromise. It had begun in the effort of the reformers to free prelates and Church from the control of the lay powers. It had been enlarged and brought to open war by Gregory VII's resolve to make the Papacy, holding the vicariate of God on earth, the supreme and autocratic ruler not only of the ecclesiastical hierarchy but of the secular potentates (the *regnum*), headed by the Emperor, as well. No compromise could be reached on that, and it was left to fester after Henry IV's death. The subsidiary abuse of lay investiture, which had once been the safeguard of royal predominance, was abolished, while recognition was made of royal rights over the secular functions and possessions of churchmen. In practice it was acknowledged that in such matters the control of kings and patrons over their ecclesiastical subjects could not be done away with. Nevertheless the Papacy had won a victory and had made a marked advance. The imperial theocracy was dead; no king retained a free hand over the Church. The papal theocracy in the Church was becoming a matter of daily fact; its leadership in Western Christendom had become more than an unaccepted claim.

The Concordat of Worms marks an epoch in the long movement to reform the secular clergy and the government of the Western Church. Its ideal was the separated, holy, ascetic class responsible only to its own officials, ruled by its own Canon Law, cut off from worldly domination, governed in hierarchical organization by the autocratic Papacy. The outward success of the movement was greater than the inward. There was developed a considerable, dynamic minority of devout and zealous clerics who enforced the acceptance of their ideals on society. Clerics were divided by law and privilege from the laity; they were brought under a different rule of life. The Western Church did act in large degree as a united body. Bishops were linked to and subordinated to the Papacy. It remained, as will be seen, to tighten the bonds between every diocese and province and the Papacy by the growth of appeals to Rome, through the series of revivified and graded Courts Christian of the Canon Law. The Roman Curia itself was developing to meet the situation. It was manned by ambitious, practical, legal-minded, businesslike administrators, who outnumbered the more enthusiastic elements. It was to show the West the example of a highly organized, able, and essentially worldly-minded bureaucracy. But in the Church as a whole human nature proved unconquerable. Simony in more covert forms flourished, nowhere more than in the Curia. Clerical incontinence was harder to subdue than clerical marriage, which itself did more than lurk among the recalcitrant clergy. The increase and the influence of those absorbed in their spiritual mission is manifest, but the concubinary or dissolute cleric was hardly an improvement on his predecessors, although less openly bound than they by the ties of this world and more brigaded in a vast and civilizing organization.

The 'righteousness' (*iustitia*), indeed, on which Gregory VII kept harping, included more than obedience to Church authority. It was a programme to combat the outrageous pagan lawlessness, ferocity, and oppression of the age. And the influence of the Church, however alloyed with fanaticism and ambition, was producing almost imperceptibly a less barbaric ethos. The knight was becoming chivalrous. To unflinching courage and fierce loyalty to kindred and lord he was adding a fierce

Fig. 106. Pope Calixtus II, treading underfoot the Anti-Pope Gregory VIII, standing with the Emperor Henry V, both holding the text of the Concordat of Worms

championship of the Cross and, slowly enough, courtesy and the protection of women, which the Church inculcated. Part of its moral appeal to its time lay in the fervent asceticism of its protagonists. Renunciation and austerity struck the imagination and called forth, willingly or unwillingly, the reverence of the rudest. On better moulded spirits they exercised an irresistible fascination. The growth of monasticism furnished the reforming Papacy with its most disciplined adherents and its most potent means of swaying opinion.

(6) THE NEW MONASTIC ORDERS

The impulse to asceticism, which so powerfully worked for the reform of the Church, found its most natural outlet in the monastic institution. Cluny and the old-fashioned Benedictines, with their conservatism, moderation, and splendour, no longer satisfied more zealous and aspiring minds. The hermit-orders of Italy and that of Grammont in France already showed this ascetic tendency. More successful in the same direction were the Carthusians, founded by Bruno from Cologne in 1084, when he obtained from the Bishop of Grenoble the desert mountain settlement of the Grande-Chartreuse. It had to be refounded in 1101, from which time the Order spread. Isolation and complete poverty were its principles; an ascetic life of solitary prayer, with the minimum of community, was long maintained. The rigorous selection of a limited number of inmates, the refusal of contact with the world and its wealth, preserved the Carthusians in their pristine zeal and reputation till the close of the Middle Ages.

It was not only the mounting tide of asceticism which led fervent men away from the older monasteries, it was the seemingly inevitable degeneration of a too wealthy and humanly attractive house. The lukewarm were sure to enter and the personality of a mediocre abbot, with his little-fettered power, could inflict lasting damage. This was exemplified on a large scale among the Cluniacs when the Abbot Pons (1109–22) succeeded to the great Hugh. His ambition and waywardness produced a violent domestic upheaval which was only partially remedied by the wisdom of Abbot Peter the Venerable (1122–56), whom everyone admired. Splendour and regularity and a high degree of comfort had come to replace the 'wrestling-school of the spirit'.

Against this magnificence and growing laxity the foundation of Cîteaux near Chalon was an ascetic reaction. In 1098 Robert, Abbot of Molesme, migrated there with six zealous monks to keep in austerity among the woods the literal rule of St Benedict. The legislator of the new abbey was his second successor, the Englishman Stephen Harding (1109–33), and its extraordinary growth began when in 1113 it was joined by a religious genius, St Bernard from French Burgundy. Rapidly increasing numbers led to colonization, the four daughter-abbeys of Cîteaux: La Ferté, Pontigny, Clairvaux, of which St Bernard was abbot, and Morimond. In 1119 the customs of what may be called a new monastic Order, the Charter of Charity (*Carta Caritatis*), were confirmed by Pope Calixtus II. The call to asceticism in the wilderness, combined with the apostolic career of St Bernard, who speedily became the true head of the Cistercians, exercised a marvellous fascination. Recruits poured in. Each of the four daughter-houses sent forth fresh colonies, and these and their offspring propagated the White Monks (as they were called from their habit contrasted with the Black Monks or older Benedictines and Cluniacs) over the waste lands of all Europe. In 1120 they entered Italy, in 1123 Germany, in 1128 England (at Waverley), in 1132 Spain, in 1142 Ireland, in 1143 Scandinavia, while in 1142–3 they reached the eastern lands of Poland and Hungary. By St Bernard's death, the Cistercian monasteries numbered 343, and, aided by accessions like that of Savigny, this figure was more than doubled by the end of the thirteenth century.

Fig. 107. Vézelay. Façade of the church before restoration

A new and happy constitutional system was devised for the Cistercians, avoiding the autocracy and over-centralization of the Cluniac congregation on the one hand and the independent isolation of the normal Benedictine house on the other. Cîteaux was the revered head of a family, arranged in a genealogical hierarchy. Every year a chapter-general of the abbots met at Cîteaux to regulate the Order. The important task of visitation to correct abuses was undertaken by the abbot of each house for its immediate

503

colonies, and so on down the line, so that each house was supervised by its immediate parent-house. Cîteaux itself was visited by the abbots of its four elder daughter-houses. Exemption from all but papal authority had impeded good relations between the Cluniacs and the episcopate, but although the Cistercians soon obtained a like exemption, their secluded sites and their refusal to accept endowments or functions of the secular Church enabled them to avoid conflict.

The search for solitude and austerity, which led the Cistercians to situations waste and wild, often therefore marked by singular natural beauty, and made them sedulously to avoid the magnificence and rich decoration and feudal endowments of the wealthy Benedictine houses, produced unforeseen effects. Their plain, severe buildings became models of sheer beauty of line and form. Their once barren lands, easily given as valueless, all within a prescribed distance from the monastery, became models of contemporary cultivation organized around 'granges' or farm-centres. By 1200 the English Cistercians were sheep-farmers deriving great wealth from their wool. The manual labour required was obtained by a systematic development of the class of *conversi* or lay brothers. These were under the monastic vows, but were forbidden to be literate; they lived in the monastery, and laboured there and in the granges, while the full monks' duties were in church, cell, or cloister. Thus, if the peasants could take their share in the Order, their separation from the educated or noble monk was manifest.

The attraction of the Cistercian Order to devout minds in that tumultuous age was immeasurably increased by the personal fascination of St Bernard (*ob.* 1153). A magnetic man, who dominated the fellow-men he loved, and whose extreme asceticism fulfilled their ideal of religion, he was indefatigable in travelling and preaching in the Church's cause. He was a thrilling orator and writer, who could sway an audience even if they were ignorant of his language. The most orthodox of men, he spoke plainly and with authority even to the Pope. For years he was the chief force in the Church. His mystical ardour and his intolerance of opposition led him into obscurantism and bitter unfairness; and his zeal for conversion crowded his Order with recruits, whose temporary fervour might fail when he was gone. But he upheld Christian civilization against barbaric violence and worldly legalism without fear of secular or ecclesiastical potentates. He was a beneficent influence in a world of passionate misdoing. He took the foremost share in its great events.

The Cistercian Order was not the only exemplar of cenobitic asceticism. The later eleventh century saw the evolution of the Augustinian Canons, collegiate priests who followed a Rule attributed to St Augustine of Hippo. Secular canons of cathedrals, who lived in their own houses on their prebends or share of the income, continued to exist, but numerous colleges of clerks adopted, or were founded for, the regular life in common. One reason for these communities had been the serving of a group of parish churches which were given to them, but the dispersion involved in this duty led to its being discountenanced until the Augustinians differed little from ordinary monks. This was not the case with a new Order of Canons, the Premonstratensian, founded in 1120 by Norbert of Xanten, a friend of St Bernard, who became (1126) Archbishop of Magdeburg (*ob.* 1144). It drew its name from its earliest abbey at Prémontré near Laon, and imitated both the austerity and the constitution of the Cistercians, while remaining a federated community of priests who were to serve parish churches. The Order spread over Europe in considerable numbers.

Naturally the progress of asceticism was shared by women, and the need for spiritual ministration and business-management led to special developments. The small Orders of Fontévrault in Anjou (1106) and Sempringham (1131) adopted the system of double monasteries of women and men, the populous abbeys of the former Order being ruled by the abbess, houses of the latter Order, which were all English, by the prior. There were also numerous nunneries which followed the Cistercian Rule. Many nunneries were but poorly endowed, but some of the older Benedictines, especially in Germany, were great landed foundations, tenanted by noble ladies and ruled by members of princely houses. There was a natural but not wholly beneficent tendency to devote superfluous daughters to the religious life.

Perhaps the most striking witness to the heyday of asceticism in the era of St Bernard was the adoption of monastic vows by the new military Orders which combated the infidel. The earliest of these were the Knights of the Hospital of St John of Jerusalem, reorganized or really founded early in the twelfth century to care for sick and poor pilgrims. In 1113 they made it their chief aim to fight in defence of the Holy Land, and thenceforward rapidly multiplied. In 1118 the Knights of the Temple (of Solomon) were instituted to protect the road to Jerusalem. Their aims and numbers expanded also, and their final Rule owed much to St Bernard. Hospitallers and Templars formed a permanent spearhead of celibate warriors to protect the Latin kingdom. They both acquired large lands scattered over the West as well as in Syria. After seventy years the Hospitallers could put 500 and the Templars 300 knights in the field. Besides the full knights, who were all of noble birth, they contained sergeants like the lay brothers of the Cistercians. Under the Pope each Order was governed by a grand-master and general chapter. Their valour was never questioned, but wealth and power brought corruption, greed, and suicidal rivalry with each other. The pride of the Templars in especial became proverbial and odious. Similar military Orders—Santiago, Calatrava, Alcántara—came into existence to fight the Moors in Spain; that of

505

Santiago, however, was not bound to celibacy. A still later imitation, the Teutonic Knights, made history in the Baltic lands.

The extraordinary growth of monasticism new and old in the century of Church reform undoubtedly brought too many into the cloister, whether as converts or as oblates, who had no true or lasting vocation for the ascetic life; and the enormous landed wealth lavished on them by the laity, either in devotion or in fear of Judgement Day, proved a dangerous ally of laxity and degeneration. Yet the multitude of abbeys provided a fit home for the pious and idealistic, and for some of the best and greatest. They were abodes of culture and of life by law in an orderly community, which impressed for the better their rough, not to say brutal, contemporaries. They were still homes of learning, in theology, history, and even the Latin classics. Even as lords and landowners the monks compared well with their lay neighbours. Their management might be selfish, but it was legal and often enlightened. Their splendour, even unconsciously, made them patrons of artistic advance. It was only too easy for them to be both grasping and unthrifty. A bad abbot and lax brethren easily fell into debt and disorder. Others might be more distinguished for business acumen than for ascetic fervour. The degeneration of monasticism, here less, there worse, was a recurrent theme of the later Middle Ages. But they had expressed the higher ideals of their times, which they overawed, and played no insignificant part in the painfully slow and chequered rise of civilization.

BOOK VI

THE TWELFTH CENTURY

❧❧❧

CHAPTER 18

THE MEDITERRANEAN POWERS AND THE EARLY CRUSADES

(1) THE NORMAN KINGDOM OF SICILY

The Moslem power in the western Mediterranean began to wane in the eleventh century by sea and land at a time when in the east the onrush of the Seljūk Turks was engulfing the Byzantine Empire. A large share in the shifting of the balance in the West was due to the formation of the singular Norman kingdom of Sicily.

Early in the eleventh century South Italy was in fractions. The Byzantine Empire ruled the 'heel and toe', Apulia and Calabria; there were three Lombard principalities, Salerno, Capua and Benevento, and three seaport republics, Naples, Gaeta and Amalfi. These petty states acknowledged Byzantine or the Western Empire's suzerainty according to the needs of the moment, and were nearly always at odds. Calabria had become mainly Greek, and the 'Lombard' Apulians hated Byzantine rule for its extortion and orthodoxy in spite of the quasi-autonomy of some towns. Insurrection and inter-state wars made the land a happy hunting ground for adventurous soldiers, and in 1016 a band of Norman pilgrims agreed to recruit mercenaries among their countrymen for the service of Melo, an Apulian rebel, and Guaimar IV, Prince of Salerno. Among the prolific and turbulent lesser nobles of Normandy they were easy to find; and an emigration began which soon became a steady stream. Melo indeed was overthrown at Cannae in 1017 by the Byzantine Catapan, Boioannes, but other employment was not lacking. About 1029 Duke Sergius of Naples, in fear of Prince Pandulf III of Capua, 'the wolf of the Abruzzi', granted to their ablest leader, Rainulf, the county of Aversa, and thus gave the Normans their first territorial foothold. Rainulf's personality, totally unscrupulous and self-seeking, did the rest, veering always with his peerless warriors to the stronger side. Among the swarming adventurers there arrived the numerous sons of a Norman vavassor of the Cotentin, Tancred de Hauteville, who came to the front in the incessant wars.

Fig. 108. Palermo. Cappella Palatina

In 1041 a new Apulian insurrection flared up, in which most of the Normans took part under successive leaders. Checked at first by a capable Catapan, Maniaces, they soon planned on his recall to divide Apulia among themselves. Their leaders were now the two eldest sons of Tancred, William and Drogo. The descent into Italy of the Western Emperor Henry III affected only the Lombard princes, not the Norman bands. It was about this time that another son of Tancred, Robert Guiscard ('the cunning'), took up his headquarters in Greek Calabria. This famous man, a fair blue-eyed giant, who was perhaps the most gifted soldier and states-man of his age, without faith or mercy, devoured by an insatiable ambition, led, like his fellows, the life of a robber-chief till he had carved himself a dominion by his invincible atrocities.

We have seen how Pope Leo IX, moved by the wretched lot of the natives, attempted to expel the invaders. He accepted the suzerainty of the city of Benevento and in concert with the ex-rebel Argyrus, son of Melo, endeavoured to arrange joint action with the Byzantine Emperor. That scheme broke down over the theological controversy which produced the Schism of the Eastern and Western Churches. His isolated attack ended in his defeat and capture at Civitate (1053).

The piecemeal conquests of the Normans now proceeded on all sides. Richard of Aversa extended his lands. Humphrey de Hauteville, third Count of Norman Apulia, did likewise. More than all, Guiscard was conquering in the south, aided from 1058 by his youngest brother Roger, only less able and ambitious than himself. In the year before he had seized on the 'County of Apulia' and begun his never-ending contest with his fellow adventurers, who resented his supremacy. To win his equally selfish brother Roger he went halves with him in Calabria; to gain a footing in Salerno he repudiated his Norman wife, by whom he had a son like himself, Bohemond, and married the sister, Sykelgaita, of the gallant and childless Gisulf, last Prince of Salerno. In the same year (1058) Richard of Aversa captured Capua.

In spite of their deserved ill-fame as godless, merciless brigands, the two Norman chiefs, Robert and Richard, were now firmly enough seated to be worth alliance to the Papacy in search of independence. By the Treaty of Melfi (1059), presumably on the strength of the forged Donation of Constantine, Pope Nicholas II enfeoffed Guiscard with the duchies of Apulia, Calabria, and Sicily (the last unwon) and Richard with the princi-pality of Capua. Homage, fealty, feudal aid and tribute were prescribed. In this way by a usurped authority the Norman states received a legal sanction, which was to be more a fetter than a protection.

The ensuing years were filled with wars. Robert fought the Greeks, landed with his brother Roger in Sicily (1060), and repressed the incessant rebellions of his Norman rivals and vassals. Neither the latter nor their descendants in fact ever looked on the upstart house of Hauteville as their natural lords, but only as grasping competitors in the scramble for land: the disloyalty of the Apulian baronage was their most permanent characteristic. None the less Guiscard always had the better. In 1071 he captured Bari, the last Byzantine city. Meanwhile with his brother Roger and a mixed company of mercenaries he proceeded to the slow conquest

14. The Normans and Hohenstaufen in South Italy and Sicily

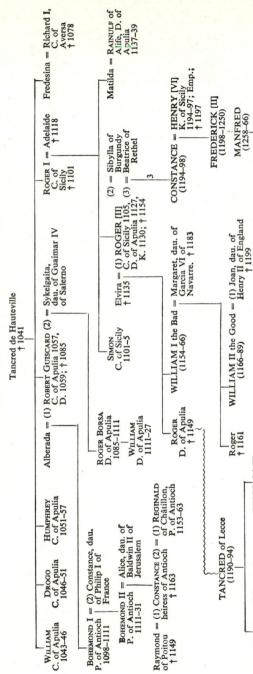

of Sicily. Fortunately the island was divided among three quarrelling Moslem emirs, and the Christians, who were still numerous enough to be a help, were naturally inclined to the new invaders. In 1061 Messina fell, in 1072 Palermo itself, each with a splendid harbour. Guiscard then enfeoffed his brother with the county of Sicily while retaining in demesne Palermo, half Messina, and the Val Demone or north-east province. Then Roger was left to prosecute the conquest. Both brothers now possessed a fleet levied from the seaports, but Roger's men-at-arms (i.e. his mailed cavalry) numbered only a few hundreds, and his progress against the Moslems of the south was slow, although the terms he granted were liberal. At last in 1091 the Saracens, even those of Malta, were all subdued. The new nobility, formed out of mercenaries and retainers and endowed with small fiefs, was of a very different temper from the resentful rivals on the mainland, and Roger's wise tolerance enabled him to levy trustworthy forces from his quondam foes.

Greater ambitions and greater dangers beset Duke Robert Guiscard. A fresh revolt of the Norman barons called him back from Sicily in 1072. Richard of Capua was his enemy, and the Papacy was hostile owing to the Norman conquest in the Abruzzi of lands both imperial and papal. He was excommunicated by Gregory VII in 1074, yet not only did he besiege and expropriate his brother-in-law Gisulf of Salerno but also Benevento, now a papal city (1077). Jordan of Capua, who reverted to the papal alliance recently quitted by his father Richard, rescued Benevento, and fostered a still greater rebellion in Apulia, which broke out (1079) when Guiscard had exacted an aid on his daughter's marriage. As usual Robert triumphed, while the Pope's need of a protector against Henry IV was urgent. In June 1080, by the treaty of Ceprano, Robert renewed his vassalage, this time under a hollow reserve, for his fresh conquests also. But he put his own schemes before his vassal's duties. He was aiming with Gregory's sanction at the conquest of the Eastern Empire in its time of trouble. The war begun in 1081 was hard fought, and he was hampered by the rebellion of his envious vassals and then by his tardy rescue of the Pope, when he perpetrated the terrible and characteristic devastation of Rome (1084). When he resumed the Byzantine war he died in July 1085, aged seventy. The death of the great brigand chief and born ruler closed the 'heroic' period of Norman adventure in Italy.

Guiscard's son by Sykelgaita, Duke Roger Borsa (1085–1111), witnessed the decay of the new-made duchy, only alleviated by the departure of his abler and elder half-brother Bohemond for the East, and by the homage extorted from Richard II of Capua, a useful precedent. Borsa's son, William (1111–27), retained little more than the title of Duke of Apulia. Count Roger I of Sicily, on the contrary, left at his death (1101) a well-organized state, with an administration in which Moslem and Byzantine

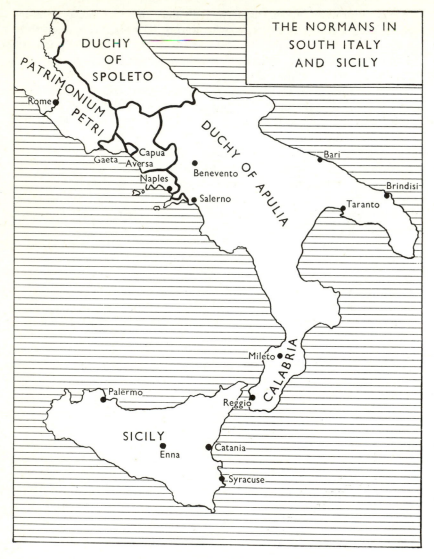

THE NORMANS IN
SOUTH ITALY
AND SICILY

DUCHY
OF
SPOLETO

PATRIMONIUM PETRI

Rome

Capua
Gaeta — Aversa
Naples
Salerno

Benevento

DUCHY OF APULIA

Bari

Brindisi

Taranto

Mileto

CALABRIA

Palermo

Reggio

SICILY

Enna

Catania

Syracuse

Map 13

elements were overlaid on feudalism, supported by troops largely Saracen.
In 1098 he obtained from Pope Urban II the hereditary legateship in his
dominions, a superior legate *a latere* being only admissible with the count's
consent. This made him master of the Latin Church, as he was of the
Greek Orthodox, to which as to the Saracens he displayed complete

512

toleration. By good fortune his Lombard widow Adelaide maintained the authority of their two young sons Simon and Roger II in succession until in 1112 Roger II (1105–54) took over control.

Roger II the Great inherited the ability and overweening ambition of his house. Less of a warrior, cruel and vindictive to his foes, he was a statesman and organizer of the first rank. A cultured autocrat and legislator on the Byzantine model, he made his court a centre of learning and magnificence. Although the harem he adopted from his Moslem predecessors inflicted irreparable harm on his dynasty, his own energy and invincible resolution never failed. His fleet and his half-Saracen army were always to be trusted among all the enemies his ambition raised against him. In a two years' campaign he conquered the inheritance left by his childless cousin at his death, and in the assembly of Melfi (1129) forbade private war and insisted on the rights of his courts in criminal jurisdiction. Next year the schism in the Papacy between Innocent II and Anacletus II gave him a rise in dignity. In return for recognition Anacletus granted him the title of king, and at Christmas 1130 he was crowned at Palermo.

The proclamation of the new Kingdom (*Regno*) of Sicily was an open defiance of the Eastern and Western Empires, in which both saw their territories reft from them and their sovereignty impeached. The strength of the new monarchy also raised up a more deadly foe. The Papacy was still bent on using the Normans as a protection against the power of the Western Empire, but was bitterly hostile to a unified power in the south, which might dominate Rome more stringently than the occasional intervention of the distant Germans. To use one against the other was the natural resource and the consistent motive in the inconsistent politics of the Curia as danger threatened from either side.

The strict control which Roger II established in Apulia produced a general revolt when Lothar III of Germany was approaching Rome with Pope Innocent to be crowned (1132). Fortunately for Roger the Emperor immediately withdrew, and the king could resume the up and down struggle with the rebels. But when Lothar returned in force, Roger could only cross to Sicily, while the chief rebel, Rainulf of Alife, was invested by Emperor and Pope with the duchy of Apulia (1137). Then the Emperor returned to Germany to die (1138), while Roger again began the reconquest of his lost territory. The schism was now moribund, for the Anti-Pope Anacletus died (1138) and his successor Victor IV was deserted. Innocent II was secure in Rome, and himself led an army to quell the Sicilian, the formidable Duke Rainulf, the soul of the Apulian rebels, being already dead (1139). But the Pope experienced the same disaster as Leo IX: he was defeated and captured on the river Garigliano by the king's son Roger (July 1139). He was forced to confirm the investiture of the kingdom of

Fig. 109. Christ crowning King Roger II of Sicily

Sicily by Anacletus to regain his liberty. Next year, however, the breach between Pope and king was renewed owing to fresh Norman aggressions in the Abruzzi. It was continued with long intervals of truce at need until 1151, when Roger II, who had all along kept a complete mastery of his Latin clergy, although successive Popes refused to sanction his appointments, directed the coronation of his surviving son William I at Palermo.

Pope Eugenius III then planned a German invasion by Lothar's successor, Conrad III, which the Emperor of the East, Manuel Comnenus, should favour. The Second Crusade had blocked the way only for a time. Roger's diplomacy, backed with bribes, secured a further respite. He gained over Louis VII of France and even St Bernard; he fostered civil war in Germany, and the death of Conrad III provided more delays.

One stimulus to the enmities which Roger encountered was his patent ambition from early in his reign to set up a kind of thalassocracy in the central Mediterranean. He possessed splendid ports in Sicily; his navy under his chief minister, the Grand Admiral (emir of emirs) George of Antioch, bade fair to command the sea. Hence the Italian sea-republics, Genoa and Pisa, were both his enemies and aided his rebels. Between 1134 and 1153 he succeeded in annexing the sea-coast of Africa from Tripoli to Bone, thus securing the trading outlets and dominating the Sicilian narrows. A wise tolerance in religion prevented revolt. But Roger was not content. During the Second Crusade, being already at odds with the Emperor Manuel, he had sent his fleet on a coastal raid which seized Corfù (soon lost) and plundered Thebes, the centre of the silk industry, whose captive workmen brought silk-weaving to Palermo. He was at the height of his power when in February 1154 he died. His unscrupulous political genius had organized the most advanced and orderly autocracy in the West, but left his kingdom surrounded by foes and honeycombed with disaffection. Exiles lay in wait, the subjected Norman vassals were furious at being ruled by low-born counsellors, the citizens hungered for their lost communal liberty, war was in progress with the Emperor Manuel, and a new King of the Romans, Frederick Barbarossa, was coming to Italy in alliance with a new and resolute Pope, Adrian IV.

William I, surnamed unfairly by his enemies 'the Bad' (1154–66), lacked his father's industry. Immersed in his harem, he left administration to his Grand Admiral, Maio of Bari, hated by the nobles. But at a crisis he displayed the warlike genius of the Hautevilles. Barbarossa proved less dangerous than was expected, for he retreated to Germany after his imperial coronation. Pope Adrian and Manuel, however, proceeded to joint action. A Byzantine army with many exiles occupied all the rebellious east coast of Apulia, while Adrian's troops in the west restored the exiled Prince of Capua. There was even a Norman revolt in Sicily. Then William, rising from his sick-bed, struck at his enemies in succession. Hardly was revolt in Sicily quelled when he routed the Byzantines at Brindisi (May 1156), wreaking terrible vengeance on rebels. The Prince of Capua fled and Adrian was besieged in Benevento. The Pope condescended to a *volte face* in policy (June 1156). The full investiture with the kingdom of Sicily and the royal legateship were renewed, more control of the Church being allowed in Sicily than on the mainland. The Pope, who had begun to look with dread on the revival of imperial power in North Italy, now placed his hopes on King William, whom he at last induced to a peace (1158) with the Eastern Empire. Yet the Sicilian king suffered a heavy loss in these years of conflict. The fanatical Moorish sect of the Almohades were setting up an empire in Barbary. The Moslems turned to them, and by January 1160 the Sicilian dominion in Africa was a thing of the past.

The king had to face one more conspiracy and revolt of the nobles (1160–1), in which he lost the Admiral Maio and his elder son, but his vigour and exemplary severity carried him through. He was a valuable ally to Pope Alexander III against Barbarossa, but only his strong hand kept the nobles in order. After he was dead they wrested for a time the government from his widow Margaret of Navarre, who ruled for her young son William II (1166–89). Luckily they were ousted in turn by the bureaucrats, led by the king's tutor, the Englishman Walter of the Mill, Archbishop of Palermo, who retained his pupil's confidence.

The reign of William 'the Good' was remembered as a golden age for its internal peace. The king lived in seclusion in his palace, but his ambitions were grandiose. As a papal ally he contributed to the Peace of Venice in 1177 between Barbarossa and Alexander III. He wished to be the leading power in the Mediterranean, and angered by the refusal of a promised Byzantine bride, undertook the conquest of the Eastern Empire. As a preliminary he bestowed (1184) the hand of his aunt and heiress-presumptive Constance on Barbarossa's son King Henry, a fatal marriage for his kingdom. But the Greek war ended in disaster at Mosinopolis on the Strymon (1185) and the enterprise was abandoned. Meanwhile William was aiding the Latins of Jerusalem against the Saracens of Egypt. He had become the son-in-law of Henry II of England, and was aspiring to lead the Third Crusade when he died childless.

Although they had sworn fealty to Constance, there was a strong patriotic party, which elected a bastard Hauteville, Tancred of Lecce, son of Duke Roger and grandson of Roger II, to the throne (January 1190). Short and ugly, the new king was a ruler worthy of the crown. He succeeded in buying a peace from his truculent creditor, Richard I of England, who had landed at Messina on his way to Palestine. He put down the usual rebels, held up the formidable German invasion at the siege of Naples (1191), and even made progress in recovering the mainland, taking prisoner the Empress Constance. He purchased papal recognition by surrendering the legateship and releasing Constance, but his death in February 1194, leaving only a child, William III, to succeed him, ruined all hope of resistance to the German conquest.

The organization of the unique Norman realm of Sicily was dominated by two factors: the conquerors were very few, especially in Sicily, and the conquered were sparse. Comrades and settlers were called in from all

Fig. 110. King William II of Sicily dedicating Monreale cathedral to the Virgin

parts, and the varied peoples of the land, Italians from north and south, the Greek element, and the Saracen had all to be conciliated. The autocracy of the monarch 'crowned by God' was like that of a Byzantine Emperor, but even the legislator Roger the Great in his Assize of Ariano (1140) confirmed the varying customs of his subjects if not in express conflict with

517

his decrees. In fact the public law was a mixture of the code of Justinian and Byzantine law with feudalism, which the Normans introduced into the conservative south. Toleration in religion was complete.

The feudal system of the Regno with its baronage holding fiefs of various rank by military service with certain jurisdiction was copied from Normandy. The knights, enfeoffed or not, formed a privileged caste. The mass of the peasantry were serfs, but freeholders, also, mainly townsmen, were common. The peasantry lived in little towns for security, as they do to-day. The *corvée*, resembling the English *trimoda necessitas*, weighed upon all the non-noble.

The central government wore a different complexion. The Lords of the Curia formed a privy council. The Grand Admiral till Maio's murder held the first place, but afterwards the Chancellor was chief minister. The wider *Curia Regis* was divided into departments for justice and finance, the latter under the Grand Chamberlain. In the provinces there were justiciars for royal and criminal pleas and chamberlains for finance. A count might be justiciar for his county, but it was a separate office from his feudal count-ship. Under-officials of ancient titles were numerous, including the governors of the towns. Through this non-feudal hierarchy the royal authority was kept in vigour everywhere. By aids (called *collectae*), by customs-duties in the great ports, by trade-profits in royal monopolies such as silk, the king's income was unusually large.

The civilization of this wealthy court and well-governed country was a mosaic of its variegated components. The king's diplomas were in Latin, Greek, or Arabic according to need; the court spoke northern French. There was no attempt at fusion save perhaps in art, but Arabic poets celebrated the kings, the geographer Idrīsī visited Roger II, and Sicilian bureaucrats made translations from the Greek into Latin, which were a stimulus in the twelfth-century Renaissance. The king, garbed like a Byzantine Basileus, was defended by one guard of Christian knights and another of Moslem negroes. The feudal levy was accompanied by Saracen archers. In art there was a more intimate combination of Norman, Byzantine, and Saracenic forms, which produced masterpieces of archi-tectural loveliness in marble and mosaics, like the Cappella Palatina of Palermo and the cathedrals of Cefalù and Monreale. Even ancient Greek art survived, if mangled, in the cathedral, once a temple, of Syracuse.

(2) THE FIRST CRUSADE

The Norman conquest of Sicily and the formation of a war-navy there were by no means the only way in which the Christians wrested the superiority in the western Mediterranean from the Moslems. In 1016 the Italian seaports, Genoa and Pisa, had rescued Sardinia from conquest by Spanish

Moors. Their fleets and trade grew together, as did those of Marseilles in Provence and of Barcelona in Catalonia. They co-operated in the conquest of Sicily. In 1087 Genoa and Pisa in alliance captured the chief Barbary port of Mahdiya and burnt its shipping. From this time the Italian fleets dominated the sea west of Sicily, while Venice, Amalfi, Genoa and Pisa traded actively to Constantinople and the East. In the same period the Spanish Christians were engaged in pressing south, with the aid of French and Norman adventurers: in 1085 Toledo was conquered. War with the infidel was in the air, and war was the occupation of the nobility. An inspiring religious cause, a battle-cry, and a vision of conquest would set in motion warriors from all the West.

It was the peril of the Byzantine Empire and the loss of Asia Minor, save for the little corner opposite Constantinople, which finally roused Western Europe. Pilgrimages to Jerusalem and the Holy Land had indeed long been a favourite exercise of devotion, and the reported destruction of the Holy Sepulchre by the abnormal Fatimite Caliph Hakim in 1009 occasioned the composition of the very dubious bull of Pope Sergius IV, the first intimation of a crusade. Pilgrimages *en masse* to Jerusalem in the eleventh century were not unknown, and the indignities which pilgrims suffered there became familiar. Meanwhile the Seljūk Turks were pushing south in Syria against local princes and Fatimites as well as west in Asia Minor. Their occupation of Jerusalem (1071) did not improve the conditions of pilgrimage, and their capture of Antioch (1085), the last Byzantine stronghold in Syria, was widely known from refugees. To aid the Eastern Christians and recover the Holy Places, so long in bondage to the Moslems, appealed to the religious conscience of Christendom.

It was Pope Gregory VII, stirred by the *débâcle* after the disastrous battle of Manzikert (1071), who first really planned a crusade to rescue both the Eastern Empire and the Holy Sepulchre (1074). But the scheme evaporated, and he even approved Robert Guiscard's attack on the Byzantines. The Emperor Alexius I Comnenus (1081–1118), however, survived his ordeals, and began to hope for the reconquest of Asia Minor now that the Seljūk Empire had broken up among quarrelling chieftains (1092). He knew from experience the fighting value of Western knights, and about 1089 had already asked for recruits from Count Robert of Flanders, whom he knew. His letter, made apocryphal by interpolations, was soon used as propaganda. In 1094 he sent envoys to Pope Urban II, the only authority who could appeal to the religious instincts of the Latin Church. No doubt he hoped for recruits on a larger scale than Count Robert could furnish. Nothing could have been more opportune for the statesman Pope. In the nature of things the Papacy was pledged to further the defence of Christendom and to aim at the recovery of the holiest shrines of the Faith from the infidel. And while the Empire, its theoretical coadjutor at least in things temporal, was paralysed under Henry IV, the Pope could and did stand forth as the head of the Christian Commonwealth. He alone was ruler of the Church, which extended over all the realms of the West, and possessed an organized hierarchy of officials and a militia of monks grouped round the Roman Curia, by means of which he could rouse religious zeal and direct its outlet. The star of the Anti-Pope Guibert was paling to vanishing point. Nor was Urban neglectful of the ills of his age: the swarm of warrior nobles, who tormented their own countries, might find a better use for their sheathless swords in the Holy War.

The decision to aid the Eastern Christians was first propounded in the synod of Piacenza in March 1095. By the time that Urban, journeying north, held the Council, crowded by laity as well as clergy, of Clermont in Auvergne in November 1095, the main features of the scheme must have been already blocked out. It was not only nor chiefly to aid the Byzantines but to deliver the Holy City, a Crusade to Palestine taking Asia Minor on the way—a very different object from that of Alexius. Peace at home was to be guaranteed by a three years' truce for crusaders' possessions; the cross on the clothing was to be the symbol of the crusader's vow. The Pope, an orator using his native tongue, harangued the assembly: they should remove the disgrace to Christendom, the Holy Land in Moslem hands. Instead of losing their souls in fratricidal wars, they should gain Paradise by fighting in God's cause. *Deus volt* (God wills it) should be their battle-cry. Death in the Crusade would be a sufficient penance, under the suitable qualifications, for their sins. The effect was electric: tumultuous shouts of *Deus volt* and a rush for crosses. In the next few months Urban traversed his native land of France, preaching and organizing the new movement which his political genius had created.

No monarch of the time was of the crusading temper. The leaders were great nobles, incited some by devotion, some by adventure, and more by hope of new princedoms. They had no chief—for the Pope's legate, Bishop Ademar of Puy, naturally held no military command—they were of diverse lands, and they were very soon jealous rivals for the spoils. Only his rank as the French king's brother gave Count Hugh of Vermandois any weight. Count Raymond of Toulouse possessed wealth, following, and experience, which procured him importance. The shiftless Duke Robert of Normandy, in spite of his warlike vassals, was a figure-head. Godfrey of Bouillon, Duke of Lower Lotharingia, and his talented brothers were influential but not too well provided. Robert II of Flanders played a secondary part, the vain Count Stephen of Blois not even that. Head and shoulders above the others in military and political ability stood Bohemond of Taranto, as ambitious and unprincipled as his father Guiscard. The rendezvous for all these was to be Constantinople in 1096, which was to be reached by three well-known routes, that by the Danube through Hungary and Serbia, that through North Italy and Dalmatia, and that across the Adriatic from Apulia to Durazzo.

There were many minor propagandists of the Crusade. One of the most successful was Peter the Hermit, who acquired a posthumous and fabulous fame. It was from him and his like that the sometimes discreditable, always ill-led, small independent bands of crusaders took their inspiration. Walter the Penniless, a Frenchman, and his men, Peter the Hermit himself with his French and Germans, both reached Constantinople after rough handling by the Bulgarians whom they had plundered. They were transported to Civitot, and, engaging the Turks against advice, were cut up in a defeat. Other bands from Germany behaved worse and came to grief in Hungary. The most evil record was that of Emico, Count of Leiningen, whose exploits were the massacre and plunder of the Jews in the Rhineland towns, the beginning of a terrible tradition of fanatical brutality in medieval history. Emico and his bands were refused the transit through Hungary, routed, and dispersed. In passing it should be observed that the numbers given by chroniclers to the crusaders are not even exaggerations: they are recklessly fanciful. A very few thousands would cover all these predatory bands taken together.

At the end of 1096 the chief crusaders were arriving one after another before Constantinople. The Emperor Alexius, confronted with this new barbarian invasion when he had wished for a mercenary levy, had supplied provisions and guarded the routes, but serious friction occurred and the main objects of the two parties were different. The crusading chiefs were bent on conquering Palestine and carving dominions for themselves: Alexius' aim was to recover his lost provinces. Both sides had something to contribute, Alexius the passage of the Straits, supplies, and guides, the crusaders their army. Hostilities and plunder were the accompaniment of the bargaining, and did much towards creating the rancorous enmity of Greeks and Latins. But agreements were come to. Almost all the crusading leaders swore fealty to the Emperor. His lands were to be restored to him. In return he was to lead an army to their assistance. In May 1097 they crossed the Bosphorus.

The first triumph was the capture of Nicaea, duly handed over to Alexius. Then followed the advance across Asia Minor. In the battle of Dorylaeum (1 July) took place the first trial of strength between the *askaris* and light horse-archers of the Turks, under the Seljūk Qilij Arslan of 'Rūm', and the mailed knights and sturdy infantry of the West. The crusading victory was decisive, and their further march to Iconium demanded more endurance of hunger, thirst and heat than of fighting. When they reached the Taurus range they found Christian allies in the newly settled Armenians. In fact, Baldwin, Godfrey's brother, was able with their assistance to set up the first crusading state, the County of Edessa beyond

521

the Euphrates. He had already come to blows with Tancred, Bohemond's nephew, over the possession of the Cilician plain, while the Armenian prince, Constantine (*ob.* 1100), held the mountains of the Taurus (Little Armenia).

Meanwhile the main crusading army began the difficult siege of Antioch (October 1097). Although the crusaders were helped by the native Christians nearby, they were not numerous enough to blockade and suffered the severest privations from lack of supplies until at last some reached them from Christian fleets *via* the port of St Simeon at the mouth of the Orontes. The Turkish princes, hitherto at odds, now assembled a joint army under Karbogha of Mosul just too late to prevent the capture of Antioch by Bohemond. In the battle outside which followed (28 June 1098), Bohemond's generalship won a complete victory, which decided the course of the war. To Bohemond, too, was mainly due a breach with Alexius. Stephen of Blois and other fugitives from the siege had found the Emperor on the march in Asia Minor, and their black report induced him to turn back to his own campaign. The treaty was broken, and in spite of the claims of Raymond of Toulouse Bohemond was acknowledged Prince of the ex-Byzantine Antioch.

What with their own quarrels and other hindrances it was only in 1099 that the other crusaders resumed their progress south and only in June that they reached Jerusalem. A year before the Holy City had been recovered from the Turks by the Fatimite Caliphate of Egypt, then really ruled by the Vizier Afdal (1094–1121). Although strongly fortified, it fell at the second general assault on 15 July, when the fervent joy of the victors in the Church of the Holy Sepulchre and the massacre of all and sundry expressed in combination the spirit of the Crusade. Raymond of Toulouse honourably preserved those who surrendered to him. A new government was at once necessary. Raymond refused election, believing a churchman to be the only fit head. The choice then fell on Godfrey of Bouillon (22 July), who styled himself 'Defender of the Holy Sepulchre'. It was no vain title, for Afdal was advancing from Egypt with 20,000 men. Godfrey led probably some 10,000, with whom he won the decisive victory at Ascalon (12 August). Perhaps some 25,000 to 30,000 is an approximate number for those who set out from Nicaea on the Crusade.

(3) THE KINGDOM OF JERUSALEM AND THE SECOND AND THIRD CRUSADES

Godfrey of Bouillon, whom romance numbered among the Nine Worthies of the world, reigned only long enough to begin the conquest of the new Latin kingdom of Jerusalem and its organization on the strictest model of French feudalism as a vassal state of the Church. His brother Baldwin I of Edessa (1100–18), a typical knight-errant, was elected to succeed him in spite of the new Latin Patriarch of Jerusalem, Daimbert, ex-Archbishop of Pisa, who none the less ended by crowning him king and receiving his homage. Baldwin lacked both money and men, although a steady stream of crusaders was now flowing, but he succeeded in taking the sea-ports, except Tyre, as far north as Beirut. These acquisitions were largely due to the fleets of the Italian trading cities, which were invaluable to the Latins from Antioch southwards. It was symptomatic that the Pisan Daimbert obtained the patriarchate, and Genoa, Venice and Pisa were all rewarded by exempt quarters and privileges, which placed them at the outlets of the caravan routes. Baldwin even built the castle of Montréal on the route to the Red Sea. He might have done more had all the fresh crusaders been well directed, or his fellows and vassals in Syria and the Byzantines been in full accord. But three crusading expeditions were successively shattered in Asia Minor in 1101. A fourth, of Scandinavians, attained Syria by sea in 1102. Bohemond of Antioch, the foe of Saracens and Byzantines, was a storm-centre. In 1100 he was made prisoner by the Turkish emir of Cappadocia. On his release he was defeated at Harran by the Turks (1104), while Alexius's fleet seized from him his towns in Cilicia. Next year he left his nephew Tancred in Antioch, and himself journeyed to the West to scatter charges against Alexius and collect an invading army against him. His failure and death must be told later. Meantime Tancred was creating and preserving his principality. Raymond of Toulouse on the other hand received Byzantine help in his campaign to form a county round Tripolis. After his death (1105) Tripolis fell (1109), and his son Bertrand ruled it. The county of Edessa was given to King Baldwin's kinsman, Baldwin du Bourg, who on ascending the throne gave it to Joscelin de Courtenay. The hold of the Franks (as they were called in the East) on this border-county across the Euphrates was always precarious, but it was a most valuable bastion.

The military position of the Latin states, thus formed, suffered from grave defects. True, they possessed all the Syrian coastline and, thanks to the Italian navies, the command of the sea. But inner Syria, the great towns of Damascus, Hamah, and Aleppo, they never gained. The core and best of the land remained Moslem. They endeavoured to secure their frontier strip by almost impregnable castles, adopting and improving the scientific fortification of the Eastern Empire. Their concentric walls and round towers were an immense advance on square, massive donjons, which were the best strongholds they had known in the West. But they were short of permanent man-power. Though the feudal levy was due for a year, the settled Latins were but a minority ruling over an alien race, and their fighting spirit deteriorated in an alien climate. The pilgrims and adventurers who reinforced them were more apt to cause untimely conflicts than to provide permanent accretions of strength. The best military force was

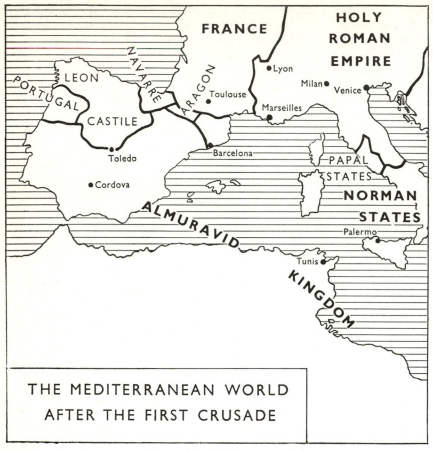

Map 14

formed by the Military Orders, the Templars and Hospitallers, whose castles were marvels of strength, but whose rivalry and fanatic ardour made them insubordinate and reckless allies. The conquest had been in greatest measure due to the division of the Turks into petty, mutually hostile principalities, each fighting for its own hand. Even temporary Moslem combinations had inflicted severe set-backs on the invaders. If they should unite once more under an able despot, their attack would be dangerous indeed.

The best energies of the veteran warrior, Baldwin II (1118–31), were spent in warfare to aid the three northern Latin states, Antioch, Edessa and Tripolis. They were bound to Jerusalem by the loosest tie of vassalage; indeed Bohemond I (*ob.* 1111) never admitted any but that to which he

524

HUNGARY

BYZANTINE EMPIRE

Bari

Constantinople

Nicaea

SELJŪKS

OF RŪM

Iconium

LITTLE ARMENIA

EDESSA

ANTIOCH

TRIPOLIS

Cyprus

Crete

JERUSALEM

Damietta

Ascalon

Alexandria

FATIMID KINGDOM

Cairo

Map 14

was forced in 1108 by Alexius. But their need for assistance led them to call in the King of Jerusalem. He acted as regent for Bohemond II from 1119 to 1126, and in 1123 suffered a year's captivity, warring for Edessa. In 1125 he secured the Edessan frontier by a victory over the Emir of Mosul. His greatest conquest, however, was won for him during his imprisonment in 1124 by the regent, Grenier, who captured Tyre with the help of a Venetian fleet. On his death the crusading Fulk, Count of Anjou, husband of his daughter Melissande, was elected king (1131–44), who by constant warfare with the Turks, complicated by the aggressive rivalry of the Emperor John Comnenus for the overlordship of Antioch and Edessa, maintained the Latin kingdom at its greatest extension.

Tradition declared that the earliest body of law and custom for the

525

kingdom of Jerusalem proper was drawn up at the order of Godfrey of Bouillon, but, if so, the collection has perished. Some assises (or decrees) of later kings, especially of Amaury, are preserved, and much of the older law must be contained, although altered, in the jurists' codes of Jean d'Ibelin and others in the thirteenth century. The oldest treatise, the *Livre du Roi*, dates from *c*. 1200, the Assise of the Burgesses between 1229 and 1244. In the *assises* as we have them, we have the picture of the ideal feudal state developed by Frenchmen when feudal theory was at its apex. The king, himself a vassal of the Church, was suzerain of his vassals with the customary rights and duties. Hereditary claims dominated the succession to the crown, yet the barons never entirely lost their share in the choice of a sovereign. To him they owed liege homage against all men, but by an assise of Amaury their sub-vassals did liege homage to the king also and only in the second place homage to their mesne lord. The power of the baronage lay in the Haute Cour, equivalent to the Curia Regis of the West. It dealt with justice and all political affairs. Without its consent neither assises nor treaties were valid; the king reigned as *primus inter pares*. There were the usual officers of state, the seneschal, marshal, chancellor and others. In their fiefs the barons held their seignorial courts. The trading burgesses of the towns possessed their own courts under viscounts; so did the native Syrians. Each of the Italian sea-cities enjoyed quarters in the chief ports, governed and judged by their own officials. The Latin hierarchy, led by the Patriarch, was richly endowed and was a power in the State. Daimbert had claimed to be lord of the kingdom, but his successors, save one, were content to co-operate with the kings. Their morale was open to criticism, as was that of the settled 'Franks', whether barons, Military Orders, or burgesses, the mongrel *Pullani*. The mass of the peasants were Moslems. The curse of the Latin states was their disunion. Clergy and laity, king and baron, knight and burgess, colonist and wandering newcomer pursued their separate interests. Templars and Hospitallers were bitter rivals. Venice, Pisa and Genoa, competitors for the Eastern trade, were consumed with mutual hatred, and carried their wars to the Levant. These evils lamed the Latins against the common Moslem foe in spite of the immense reserve of military power which they could summon from the enthusiasm of the West.

The reign of Baldwin III (1144–63), son of Fulk, and his mother Melissande (whom he deposed in 1152) began with disaster to the Latins. Since 1127 the most active Moslem ruler had been Zangi, Atabeg of Mosul. He was as fervid a champion of Islam as any crusader of Christianity, and his first object was to unite the Moslems under himself. He conquered Moslem North Syria, and in 1144 was at war with Damascus when another opening presented itself. Joscelin II of Edessa was indolent and negligent. On Christmas Day Zangi ended the brief siege of the ill-guarded town of

Edessa, thus beginning the Moslem conquest of the county, the bulwark of the Latin states, which was completed by his son the Sultan Nur-ad-Din (1146–73).

The news of the fall of Edessa created consternation in the West, where a new Crusade speedily took shape. King Louis VII of France assumed the Cross. Pope Eugenius III entrusted its propaganda to the great St Bernard, whose magnetic eloquence brought crowds of recruits, not only fighting men but women and non-combatants. The saint's visit to Germany roused an enthusiasm which carried away King Conrad III and great nobles alike. Unlike the First Crusade, the expedition was planned and led by monarchs and potentates, whose wisest counsellors thought that their first duty was at home. St Bernard saw in the rush to the Crusade a miracle. King Roger II of Sicily endeavoured to persuade Louis VII to cross the sea in alliance with himself—the wisest course, although his motive was the fear of a German, French and Byzantine coalition against him—but the old-fashioned route through the Balkans and Asia Minor was preferred at the instance of the Emperor Manuel Comnenus. The choice was unfortunate for the Second Crusade and for all concerned.

King Conrad started first (1147). Germans and Byzantines inevitably came to blows on his journey. He crossed into Asia Minor only to meet utter disaster from the Turks at Dorylaeum and on his retreat. Louis VII similarly fell out with the Byzantines. At Nicomedia he linked up with the wrecks of the Germans. Taking the coast road through Byzantine land, the mutual hatred of Latins and Greeks was redoubled in the quest for provisions. His misfortunes began when he left the secure route at Laodicea for the way over the mountains to the southern port of Attalia (Satalie). Terribly mauled by Turkish bands he reached the port and could only hire insufficient transport. The majority of the rank and file were left to Turkish captivity while he sailed to Antioch. Manuel's own fleet was resisting an attack by Roger II. Conrad had already proceeded by sea to Acre. The same ill judgement accompanied all the crusaders' decisions in Syria. Instead of aiding the Prince of Antioch, endangered by Sultan Nur-ad-Din, the formidable foe, the two kings resolved to besiege Damascus, which was ruled by the only Moslem emir who had escaped Nur-ad-Din's dominion. It would have been a valuable prize if conquered, but the Latins of Jerusalem were lukewarm—the emir was a useful buffer against Nur-ad-Din—and the usual disunion ended in total failure. The remnant of the crusaders drifted home with a crop of enmities: to St Bernard it was 'an abyss so deep that I must call him blessed who is not scandalized thereby'. In Syria it led to the acquisition of Damascus in 1154 by Nur-ad-Din, who led a confederacy of Turkish emirs on the quasi-feudal Seljūk model.

Baldwin III, a vigorous ruler, was able in 1153 to capture Ascalon, the last Egyptian possession in Palestine, from the decadent Fatimites, but

Fig. 111. The citadel of Aleppo

failed to gain Shaizar on the Orontes from Nur-ad-Din, largely owing to the dissensions which clung to the Latins. He was alive to the need for Byzantine co-operation, and formed an alliance with Manuel Comnenus, now suzerain of Antioch, which was continued by his able brother Amaury I (1163–74). Christian and Moslem, Amaury and Nur-ad-Din, stood face to face in Syria nearly at a stalemate; the conquest of Egypt with its wealth, its ports, and its defensible Delta would give a decisive advantage to either combatant. The Fatimite Caliphs of Cairo had long sunk to be puppets of their viziers. They paid a tribute to the Kings of Jerusalem. Two rivals, Shawar and Dirgham, strove for the vizierate, and alternately called in Nur-ad-Din and Amaury. Shawar, the latest victor with the help of Nur-ad-Din's general, Shirkuh, expelled him with the help of Amaury. Against his own better judgement Amaury was then (1167) persuaded by his counsellors to demand more extortionate terms, and by a fresh invasion to cause Shawar to invite Nur-ad-Din's alliance once more. This time Shirkuh had the better, forcing the Franks to retreat, and after Shawar's execution taking the vizierate himself. On his speedy death he was succeeded in his double function of Nur-ad-Din's deputy and the Caliph's vizier by his nephew, the famous Saladin (Salah-ad-Din). King Amaury did his utmost to retrieve the reverse, but his attempt in 1169 to capture the eastern port of the Delta, Damietta, with the assistance of a Byzantine fleet, ended in disaster. Egypt not only remained Moslem but became orthodox Sunnite, recognizing the Abbasid Caliph of Baghdad.

Worse for the Christians followed. In 1174 both Nur-ad-Din and Amaury died. Both were succeeded by boys, but while Baldwin IV (1174–85) was a leper and the Latins were inveterate in faction, the Moslems were united under an inspiring leader, Saladin, who in oriental fashion dispossessed his master's heir in Syria as well as Egypt, and renewed Nur-ad-Din's hegemony. He was a Kurd, not a Turk, by race, a mild governor, a good general who kept his vassal emirs in devotion and was intent on the holy war to drive the Christians into the sea. He could attack them on two sides. Meantime the Latin kingdom was distracted by personal feuds and opposed policies. Baldwin IV himself was at enmity with his cousin and ex-regent, Raymond III, Count of Tripolis (1152–87). In general, new immigrants backed by the Templars and Hospitallers, were for continual war, while the settled baronage, more orientalized and more aware of their weakness, were anxious for peace, if only by truces. One storm-centre was the robber-knight, come from the West, Reginald of Châtillon, who by his first marriage had been an always ill-advised Prince of Antioch (1153–63), and now by a second was lord of the impregnable castles of Krak and Montréal east of the Dead Sea, whence he raided the caravan-routes from Mecca and Egypt. Another storm-centre was the succession to the afflicted king. One of his sisters, Sibylla, was married to the Lombard Marquess William of Montferrat, who died leaving a child, Baldwin; the other, Isabella, to a local baron, Henfrid IV of Toron. Sibylla's second choice was another western adventurer, the unpopular and incompetent Guy de Lusignan from Poitou. Guy, being appointed *bailli* or vice-regent, aroused such enmity on all hands that his infant step-son Baldwin V (1183–6) was crowned prematurely with Raymond of Tripolis as bailli. During the preceding years no real advantage in the recurring hostilities had been gained, and Saladin's power had steadily grown over Moslem lands. He was now suzerain from the African Tripoli in the west and Arabian Yemen in the south to Mosul in the east and Mount Amanus in the north, while Egypt provided a fleet. When Baldwin IV died (1185), Raymond at once concluded a four years' truce with the redoubtable Sultan. But the child Baldwin V died next year, and the war-party forced the obvious election of Guy (1186–92) and Sibylla, to whom Count Raymond refused allegiance.

As if to play into Saladin's hands, Reginald followed his customary habit of flagrantly breaking the truce. On 1 May 1187 a Saracen force defeated the two Military Orders at Nazareth. The whole Latin army, their feuds suspended, was hastily assembled to resist Saladin in person. Against Count Raymond's advice, and pressed on by Gerard de Rideford, the Master of the Temple, Guy led his troops to give battle on the worst terms, and was overthrown in the disastrous defeat of Hittin on 4 July. Raymond was among the few who escaped, only to die of despair; Guy and his barons who survived were prisoners. The Latin kingdom was thus denuded of its defenders. Jerusalem surrendered on 2 October, and the only town left unconquered was Tyre. That was saved by the courage and skill of an unscrupulous adventurer, the Marquess Conrad of Montferrat, who arrived opportunely and took command. Saladin retired baffled from its siege.

In the West the news brought consternation coupled with a resolve to retrieve the disaster. Under the aegis of the Popes Gregory VIII and Clement III reconciliations, hollow enough, between hostile powers were the order of the day. The chief monarchs, led by the Emperor Frederick Barbarossa, took the Cross and made preparations, diplomatic and other,

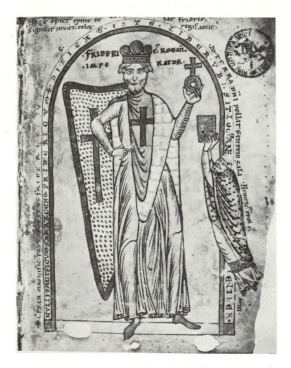

Fig. 112. The Emperor Frederick I as a crusader

for the Third Crusade. It almost seems infatuation that Barbarossa, who had accompanied Conrad III in 1147, chose the land route: his maritime subjects, who sailed with the Scandinavians round Portugal, where they fought the infidel, to Palestine, were almost flouted. The old Emperor's difficulties began when he entered the Byzantine Empire in 1189. The Emperor Isaac Angelus, enthroned by a revolution, had reason to dread the German invasion of his crumbling state, and, being of no capacity, first entered into negotiations with Saladin, and then obstructed the Germans in Thrace, which suffered from the crusaders. Frederick was already planning to conquer Constantinople, when Isaac at last gave way and transported his army to Asia Minor. The forward march after leaving Greek territory was a long fight with hunger and thirst as well as with the swarming Turkish light horse. Yet Frederick stormed Iconium, the capital of Rūm, and crossed the Taurus mountains under Armenian guidance. In Cilicia he was drowned (10 June 1190); his much-diminished force reached Antioch and eventually Acre.

King Guy had obtained his freedom on a promise, from which he was promptly absolved by the clergy, to fight no more against Saladin. At Tripolis, which with Antioch was still in Christian hands, he gathered an army of refugees and newcomers with which to renew the war. The first need was to regain the port of Acre, valuable in itself and the best base from which to regain Jerusalem. In August 1189 he began the siege and was soon besieged in his turn by Saladin, who was hampered by the periodic furlough of his emirs in winter, while fresh crusaders kept arriving from the West. For eighteen months of fierce fighting the obstinate double investment went on. The Turkish garrison began to starve, for the Italians held the sea; the crusaders were mown down by diseases, of which scurvy was one. At last the great armaments of Philip Augustus of France and Richard Cœur-de-lion of England appeared.

The two kings had sailed separately. Philip came first and fell ill. Richard compelled Tancred of Sicily to agree to his terms, and then tarried to conquer Cyprus from the rebel Comnenus who had provoked him. After his arrival the famished Turks surrendered (12 July 1191). Discord still rent the crusaders. Philip and Richard were enemies, and backed different candidates for the Latin throne, Guy, now a widower (1190), and Conrad of Montferrat. The former, gallant though he was, was unequal to the task; the latter, who possessed capacity, was distrusted and egoistic. Philip, shaken by sickness, soon returned to France, while Richard, whose heart was in the Crusade, marched south. His generalship won a victory over Saladin at Arsuf, captured Jaffa, refortified Ascalon, and vainly approached Jerusalem. The quarrels over the kingship had a curious ending. Guy was given Cyprus, renounced by the Templars; Conrad was married to Isabella, divorced from Henfrid of Toron, and made king, only to be murdered (1192) by the recent fanatical Moslem sect of the Assassins. Concord was re-established by the election of Henry of Champagne, who then married Isabella. Richard himself was needed at home, but his prowess rendered Saladin more yielding. By a three years' truce the Latins were left in possession of the coast from Ascalon to Acre with right of access to the Holy City. It was a miserable outcome of such an enormous effort, and a clear consequence of the feuds, rivalries and discord among the Christians. Richard at his best, however, and the real hero of the time, the merciful, chivalrous and upright zealot, Saladin, have cast a lustre on the Third Crusade.

Saladin's death (1193) produced civil war among his heirs, which was only closed when his brother Saphadin (Adil) restored his hegemony and reigned from Cairo (1199). The time was propitious for a new crusade. Guy was succeeded in Cyprus (1194) by his brother Amaury, who on Henry of Champagne's death (1197) married the widow Isabella and became King of Jerusalem. Cyprus was now an excellent base. Antioch, much diminished in extent, and Tripolis remained under their prince and count. The state of Little Armenia in the Taurus and Cilicia, attacked on all sides through the twelfth century by Greeks, Turks and Latins of Antioch, expelled the Byzantines for the last time in 1168 from Cilicia, and under Leo II (1185–1219) became a kingdom on the Latin model, although still Monophysite in religion. After the Third Crusade, the Latin kingdom itself was a remnant, whose few barons were eager for peace. All aggression came from the West, where a new imitative Military Order grew up, the Teutonic Knights of Germany. A new competitor appeared for the leadership, the Emperor Henry VI, who had just conquered Sicily (1194). He was full of vast schemes for world dominion, wherein the subjection of the Byzantine Empire and the recovery of Palestine were linked projects. Great preparations had been made and an army despatched to Acre, when the Emperor died on 28 September 1197. The imperial crusade collapsed; for a time the ardour of Western monarchs had burnt itself out and the lead returned to the Papacy.

(4) THE EASTERN EMPIRE UNDER THE COMNENI

The Emperor Alexius I Comnenus came to the throne in 1081 amid disasters and dangers of every kind within and without. He lacked a trustworthy army and an adequate revenue; he could not depend on the loyalty of his nobles or even of his kindred. The Empire was encircled by foes and was already shorn of its best provinces in Asia Minor. The Seljūk Turks were firmly established within the Taurus and ruled the Asiatic coastland. The Serbs on the middle Danube were hardly his subjects. The Patzinak nomads were likely to raid Bulgaria from across the lower Danube. Worst of all, Robert Guiscard, the Norman Duke of Apulia, setting up an impostor as the deposed Michael VII, was invading Epirus with the design of conquering the Empire. The fact that Alexius contrived to weather these and subsequent dangers, that he renewed the army and reorganized the administration, that he regained valuable territory in Asia and gave the Empire a new lease of life, is a title to fame which has been only grudgingly bestowed upon him.

This saviour of his country was a soldier and a diplomat of unusually varied talents. He excelled at setting one foe against another, at driving a good bargain by astute firmness. His generalship enabled him to survive defeats and, when his troops improved, to outmanœuvre his enemies and win victories. He vanquished his domestic foes with a cool adroitness and at need hypocrisy which confounded them and with a natural aversion to cruelty which was most unlike his age. Cultured and painstaking, he endeavoured to stop the dry-rot in Church and State. His tastes were for philosophy and theology, and he was perhaps the only ruler of his day who really strove to convert heretics, e.g. the dangerous Bogomils, by argument. The Empire suffered from the evils of his bankrupt finance and extortionate taxation, but the alternative was mere ruin.

Robert Guiscard was the first and most pressing danger. Alexius made peace with Sulaiman, the Seljūk of Rūm, and held off the Norman by allying with the naval power of Venice and subsidizing Henry IV and the rebellious barons of Apulia, confiscating Church treasure for the purpose. He fought Bohemond, Guiscard's son and lieutenant, unsuccessfully in Thessaly. When the Venetians were at last defeated (1084), the Empire was saved by the death of Guiscard himself and renewed rebellion in Apulia (1085).

The Patzinak invasions were next to be repelled. The fighting, which included a Bogomil revolt in Thrace, was indecisive, although the Patzinaks were attacked in their turn by the Cumans, their neighbours in the Ukraine. Not till 1091 did Alexius win the decisive victory of the river Leburnium. Even then he had to meet a serious raid of his late allies, the Cumans, who reached Adrianople (1095–6). The Patzinaks gave no more trouble in his day. The Cumans had to be repulsed again (1114).

The death of Sulaiman (1085), the mutual wars of the several Turkish emirs of Rūm (Asia Minor), and the general civil war among the Seljūks on the death of Malik Shah (1091), provided Alexius with an opening in Asia Minor. He recovered Nicomedia and endeavoured to levy soldiers in the West. We have seen how this contributed to the scheme of the First Crusade. By this time the Byzantine army was a singular mosaic. Alongside the native troops furnished by the military holdings and the great landlords it contained barbarian contingents, like the Bulgarians and Serbs, from within the Empire and a host of foreign mercenaries, Russians and English exiles (the Varangians), Turks, Alans, Germans and Normans from Italy. Although heterogeneous, it was once more formidable, and able to follow up the First Crusade. Joint operations with the Crusaders had given Nicaea back to the Empire. Alexius's own forces recovered the fertile coast districts as far as Attalia (Satalie) in Pamphylia, and the Byzantine fleet, which he had revived and which held Crete and Cyprus, obtained a footing on the Cilician coast. All these territories, however, were still exposed to severe Turkish invasions, and Alexius's quarrel with Bohemond over Antioch meant war with the Latins in North Syria and the Armenians of the Taurus and Cilicia. Not till 1115, after long defensive

Fig. 113 (a)

(*a*) *The Emperor John II Comnenus and his Empress Irene;*
(*b*) *opposite, their son, co-Emperor Alexius II*

warfare, was Alexius in a position to take the offensive against the Turks. His victory at Ampūn (1116) led to a peace with Sultan Malik Shah of Iconium (Rūm), which confirmed his possession of the coastline from Trebizond to Cilicia, and the interior west of Sinope, Ancyra, and Philomelium. A train of rescued captives returned to their homes. It was a great achievement.

In the interval the war with Bohemond had been a serious danger. The Prince of Antioch, hard pressed by the Turks and losing Cilician towns to the Byzantines, resolved in 1105 to rouse the West against Alexius, whose conduct throughout he painted, with much slander, in the darkest colours. In October 1107 his 'crusading' army disembarked at Valona in Epirus. But Alexius was ready. Without risking a battle he blocked Bohemond by land and sea, while he tampered with the Norman's commanders. Starved out, suspicious, and helpless, Bohemond came to terms (1108), by which he became the Emperor's vassal for Antioch and its once Byzantine territory: Cilicia he ceded to the Empire. Decorated and bribed, but broken in spirit, he returned to Taranto to die (1111). But he left a pernicious legacy of discord and distrust between Greeks and Latins.

These achievements were made at the cost of extreme financial oppression. The mainly mercenary army required large pay from the diminished and ravaged Empire. Alexius adopted, among other expedients, the harmful one of debasing the coinage. Before Manzikert the gold *nomisma* or bezant had been of a constant purity. Under the Comneni the ever-varying

534

Fig. 113 (b)

amounts of alloy rendered the bezant a mere name, confusing all business transactions, and an instrument of extortion when the government paid in bad money. Another means was the exploitation of the overgrown, inalienable property of the Church. At the crisis of the war with Guiscard, Alexius incurred universal odium by seizing on the Church treasures. For this patriotic confiscation he was obliged to atone by a permanent annual grant from the Treasury. By a more indirect and less profitable method, however, he contrived to make the enormous monastic estates contribute to his needs. Many monasteries were in decline or embarrassment. He would confide the administration of both decadent and prosperous to princes and nobles as *charistikarioi*, a method of rewarding service which did not burden his finances, while it agreed with his real desire to reform both monks and clergy. A more doubtful expedient was the recent device of the *pronoia*, which aimed at rewarding service and recruiting the army at the same time. A magnate would receive lands to administer, at first for life, on condition of providing a quota of soldiers. The *pronoetes* governed his district, like a Western fief, and took its profits, the resident peasants being his *paroikoi* on various terms. The bureaucratic Empire was thus largely feudalized, although Alexius tried to maintain control and avoid usurped exemptions by rigid surveys. Taxation fell all the more heavily on the non-exempt. It was poverty, too, which forced the Emperor to starve his fleet and introduce privileged, untaxed foreigners into the sea-going trade of Byzantium. In the Norman crisis he bought the invaluable aid of Venice by granting her merchants freedom from customs-duties and extraterritorial rights. He might lessen the uniqueness of these grants by favours to the Pisans, but his revenue was impaired and his subjects were placed at a disadvantage none the less. The decay of her navy was to make the Empire vulnerable.

Throughout his reign Alexius was threatened by the disaffection and plots of the ambitious magnates around him. He had not the legitimacy of the Macedonian dynasty. He deposed his nominal colleague, the young Constantine Ducas, to whose family he owed the throne, and elevated his own eldest son John to be joint-Emperor (1092). Conspiracies among the chief dignitaries to assassinate him were a natural Byzantine sequel, and were treated by Alexius with his accustomed clemency. Towards the close of his life a formidable intrigue in his own family was set afoot to change

15. The Houses of Ducas, Comnenus and Angelus

(a) The Houses of Ducas and Comnenus

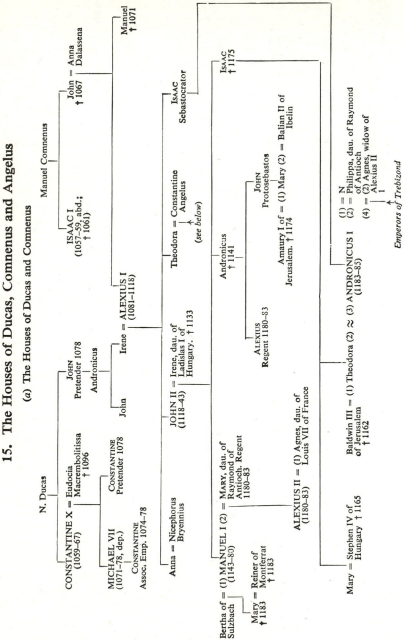

(b) The House of Angelus

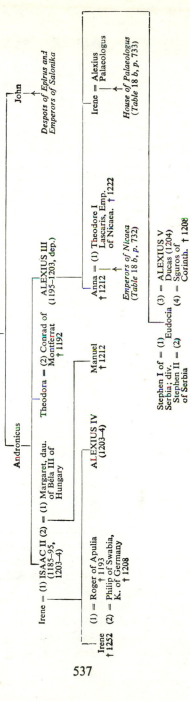

Constantine Angelus = Theodora Comnena,
dau. of Emp. Alexius I

Andronicus

John

ISAAC II (2) = (1) Margaret, dau. of Béla III of Hungary
(1185–95, 1203–4)

Theodora = (2) Conrad of Montferrat † 1192

ALEXIUS III (1195–1203, dep.)

Despots of Epirus and Emperors of Salonika

Irene = (1) Roger of Apulia † 1193
(2) = Philip of Swabia, K. of Germany † 1208

ALEXIUS IV (1203–4)

Irene † 1252

Manuel † 1212

Anna = (1) Theodore I Lascaris, Emp. of Nicaea. † 1222
† 1212

Emperors of Nicaea (Table 18 b, p. 732)

Stephen I of = (1) Serbia; div. Eudocia
Stephen II = (2) of Serbia

(3) = ALEXIUS V Ducas (1204)
(4) = Sguros of Corinth. † 1208

Irene = Alexius Palaeologus

House of Palaeologus (Table 18 b, p. 733)

the succession. The Empress Irene Ducas hated her son, the co-regent John; her daughter Anna Comnena longed to reign with her husband, the Caesar Nicephorus Bryennius; and the two used every effort to persuade the dying Emperor, while John wooed the Senate and people. The contest was decided by Alexius's connivance in a *coup d'état* by John, who took possession of the throne. The outwitted Empress could only upbraid her husband: 'All your life you have done nothing but deceive, and you are the same on your death-bed' (15 August 1118). A second conspiracy of Anna was easily dissipated and pardoned by her brother, and she retired to write her pedantic but valuable history, the *Alexiad*.

John II's reign was a continuation of his father's, modified by the austerely virtuous and upright character of the son. The Emperor, whose talent was in war, was served by a like-minded minister, a converted Turk, Azuch, who was his Grand Domestic, i.e. commander-in-chief. The civil wars of the Seljūks of Rūm and the rival Danishmandite Emirs of Sivas in eastern Cappadocia furnished the opportunities for Byzantine advance, which was indeed provoked by the constant incursions and infiltrations of the nomad Turks of the barren upland interior into the fertile valleys of the coast. John's campaigns in 1119, 1130–5, and 1139–40, although hampered by the disgraceful treasons of his brother, the Sebastocrator Isaac, were successful in maintaining the frontier and in annexing the region between Philomelium and Attalia, while curbing the powerful Danishmandites. But the Emperor made no real impression on the inland plateau, the stronghold of the Turkish tribes. He was besides more eager to take the Cilician plain from the Armenians, and to assert his suzerainty over the Latins of Antioch and Edessa. These were richer prizes, and threatened too by the Moslems from north and south. In 1137 John reconquered Cilicia from the Armenian Leo I, and, enforcing fealty from the Latins of North Syria, made a vain expedition up the river Orontes (1138). He came again in 1142, this time to demand the surrender of Antioch, but his death next year in Cilicia cut short his operations (April 1143).

John II's Asiatic ambitions had been long interrupted by the defence of his European territory. A Patzinak raid was ended by a victory at Beroea (Stara Zagora) in Thrace (1122), after which we hear no more of that tribe. The Magyar kingdom of Hungary, of which John's Empress Irene was a princess, also began a frontier war on the Danube, but had the worse (1128). The Empire's Serbian vassals were anything but docile, although their anarchic state kept them only troublesome. The serious foes were Venice and Sicily. John's attempt to revoke the harmful privileges of the Venetians led to a sea-war, from which he was glad to escape by restoring them (1126). To counter the ambitions of Roger II of Sicily, John sought the alliance of Conrad III of Germany and a German wife (Bertha of Sulzbach) for his son Manuel, a marriage which (1146) introduced a strong

Western influence in the Byzantine court. The Emperor himself, however, only toyed with western schemes. The East was essential and preoccupied his reign, which in spite of exhausting taxation was the happiest period of the Comnenian renaissance.

The full bloom of that period belonged to the time of Manuel I (1143–80) John II's youngest son, chosen by his father on his deathbed, and secured against his elder brother Isaac by the promptitude of the faithful Azuch. Born of a Hungarian mother, Manuel exhibited a singular mixture of Byzantine and Western characteristics. He was an adventurous and showy knight, delighting in single combat, rather than a general. He lacked fortitude in defeat. His two marriages, first to Bertha and then (1161) to Mary of Antioch, fostered his strong preference for the Latins, who filled his court to the wrath of the Greeks, and he wasted his resources in the vain pursuit of Western ambitions, conducted chiefly by an enormously expensive diplomacy, to the detriment of the all-important wars with the Turks. Yet he was a true Byzantine theologian, who considered himself the inspired arbiter of doctrine, which indeed he used to further his political projects, with regard to reunion both with the Western Church and with the Monophysite Armenians, in each case without success. His firm belief in astrology and magic had as much of the East as of the West in it; it was, after all, a groping after science. He and his whole court patronized the revival of literature; it was an age of historians, philosophic theologians, students, and literary men. In art the tradition of the Macedonian dynasty had been worthily followed by the Comneni, but Manuel was the most splendid patron. His building was secular in object. The palace of Blachernae, close to the junction of the Theodosian Wall with the Golden Horn, which Alexius I had made the imperial residence, was rebuilt and decorated by him, along with villas and works of public utility and defence. His splendour, like his diplomacy, cost the Empire dear. He forbade, indeed, further increase of the vast monastic lands, while confirming their existing extent. But the taxation of the non-exempt was severe, and the Empire was weakened by the substitution of a tax for the supply of ships and sailors by the maritime themes, and by the increase of the *pronoetai*.

His enmity with the Norman Kings of Sicily led Manuel astray in his foreign policy. Although the attack of Roger II on the Empire in 1147 was, after much damage, repelled with Venetian aid, Manuel allied with the German Conrad III for the conquest of Sicily. The Second Crusade, which exasperated Greeks and Latins against each other, delayed the scheme, while Roger raised up enemies against the allies. One consequence was Hungarian wars (1151–5, 1165–8) and Serbian revolts, which brought good results. Manuel acquired Dalmatia, and placed his own nominees Béla III (1173) in Hungary, and Stephen Nemanya in central Serbia. But the Norman war had fired the Emperor's ambition to reign in Italy, which

36-2

became his ruling motive. His attempt to conquer the Norman kingdom single-handed failed (1155–6), but only whetted his appetite. Alexius I and John II had already entertained schemes of reigning in Rome with the Pope's consent. Manuel incurred the hostility of Frederick Barbarossa in their pursuit. He became the ally of Pope Alexander III; he occupied Ancona (1166) and fell out with the Venetians, whose pride and privileges made them hated. In 1171 he arrested all Venetians in the Empire and seized their goods, inflicting enormous loss. Not until 1175, in fear of an attack from the republic and Sicily, did he make reparation and restore the Venetian privileges. But the injury rankled, and the gain had been nil. Alexander, too, made his peace with Barbarossa without Manuel's intervention.

The worst of these long, unprofitable diplomatic moves, backed more by money than arms, was that they diverted Manuel from his essential interests in the East, and lost him irretrievable opportunities. Like his father, he was most intent on the rich lands of Cilicia and North Syria and the subjection of Armenians and Latins. His first war reduced Raymond of Antioch to submission (1145). After the calamitous Second Crusade, he was faced by the Armenians' revolt under Thoros II which coincided with appeals of the Latins of Antioch for aid against Nur-ad-Din. On the defeat of his cousin Andronicus, he unwisely subsidized Ma'sūd of Iconium to attack Thoros, and then called in Reginald of Châtillon, at the time Prince of Antioch. But Reginald characteristically changed sides, and followed it up by a savage raid on Cyprus. Manuel was roused to a campaign in person (1158–9), which gained him the glory he wished. Thoros and Reginald were both subdued to vassalage—Baldwin III of Jerusalem was already his ally and husband of his niece—but his war with Nur-ad-Din was half-hearted. He neglected Cilicia, where Andronicus aroused hatred and revolt, which ended in the independence of Little Armenia under Thoros and Ruben III (1175–85). Manuel was more tempted by the hope of conquering Egypt in concert with King Amaury, as we have seen, but that project also came to grief. Showy successes and no permanent advantage were the results of the Emperor's dealings with the Latin States.

The war with the Turks of Asia Minor should by rights have absorbed the Emperor in the East, and it was in this he showed his lack of concentrated effort. His foes were grouped in two large states, the Seljūks of Rūm centred at Iconium and the Danishmandite emirs at Sivas, who formed a crescent round them stretching from the river Halys to the Euphrates at Malatiyah. At Manuel's accession, the bands of the Seljūk Mas'ud I were committing terrible ravages; Manuel fortified the frontier, subsidized the chief Danishmandite emir, and struck at but could not take Iconium itself (1146–7). On the eve of the Second Crusade he made a truce with Mas'ud.

Not until 1160 did he resume the war against Qilij Arslan, Mas'ud's son, in alliance with the Danishmandites, but again he was content with a peace (1162), missing the golden opportunity of Seljūk civil war. He even paid subsidies to Qilij Arslan, who made friends with Barbarossa, and did not curb the incursions of Turkish nomads. When Manuel at last took action, the Turks were united against his crusade. In 1176, of two Byzantine armies converging on Rūm, one was routed at Neo-Caesarea (Kayseri) south of Trebizond; the other, moving along the route of the First Crusade, led by Manuel himself, who like a Latin neglected all reconnaissance, was surrounded and met with utter disaster in the defiles of Myriocephalum. It was a second Manzikert. Manuel, who escaped, was allowed an easy peace by Qilij Arslan, which was soon broken. No hope of reconquest survived; Myriocephalum sealed the fate of the Comnenian revival.

Manuel died in September 1180. He had married his twelve-year-old son, Alexius II, to a French princess Agnes, daughter of Louis VII, and another Latin lady, the Empress Mary of Antioch, assumed the regency. This was a bad start, for the Latins were hated at Constantinople, where they filled all the chief posts, and Mary made the situation worse by choosing a foolish fop, her nephew-in-law, Alexius Comnenus, as her favourite, wholly incompetent to deal with the evils of the time, the legacy of Manuel's reign. The bureaucracy was corrupt, taxation and extortion were unbearable, and the great semi-feudal lords out of hand. The discontent in the capital crystallized in a plot contrived by the Empress's ambitious step-daughter Mary and her husband, the Caesar Renier of Montferrat, and the Empress only incurred odium by assaulting them vainly in St Sophia, where they had taken refuge (1182), and then by an equally vain attempt to depose the Patriarch Theodotus. A chance was thus given to the worst and ablest of the dynasty, Andronicus Comnenus, son of the sebastocrator Isaac, the same who had caused the loss of Cilicia, to set up as the saviour of the Empire. Treacherous, cruel, debauched, and fundamentally unstable, Andronicus possessed both talents and statesmanlike insight. His earlier life had been a mixture of treason, exile, and violent amours, which ended in retirement at Oenaeum on the Black Sea. Now he declared himself the protector of the Emperor. His march on Constantinople was the signal for defection of all save the Latins. Against them the populace of the capital broke out, massacring even the sick in hospital, although many were able to flee on shipboard. Andronicus, who embodied the vices of his house and people, used his victory with callous cruelty. He compelled the boy Alexius II to command his mother's execution. Mary and Renier died secretly. Andronicus became joint Emperor in September 1183, and murdered his ward in November. To crown all, he married his victim's widow Agnes.

An era of reform succeeded these atrocities. Corruption was violently halted. The great lords were harshly checked in their oppressions. So were the officials in their rapacity. 'You must choose between ceasing to cheat and ceasing to live', said the Emperor, who paid them well. Fugitives from extortion returned to populate the provinces, while Andronicus beautified the capital and patronized literature and law. But the aristocrats took up arms, and were repressed, even on suspicion, with horrible cruelty. An Isaac Comnenus remained unsubdued as Emperor in Cyprus, and the Empire was attacked on all sides. The Sultan of Rūm besieged Attalia, Béla III of Hungary recovered Dalmatia and crossed the Danube, Stephen Nemanya in Serbia and Kulin in Bosnia threw off their vassalage, and, worst of all, William II of Sicily sent an invading fleet and army which captured Thessalonica (1185). This danger raised hatred of the monster to its height, and Andronicus's universal suspicions led him to seize on a crowd of notables. Among them was a distant and insignificant cousin, Isaac Angelus. His flight to St Sophia was the signal for a tumultuous rebellion, which ended in his elevation to the throne, and in Andronicus suffering from the mob the death by torture he had so often inflicted (September 1185).

The reign of Isaac II (1185–95) was a succession of misfortunes, converted by incapacity into disasters. The inner decay of the Empire resumed an unimpeded course. One victory over the Norman-Sicilian army at Mosinopolis on the Strymon greeted his accession, and William II turned his thoughts elsewhere. But a new insurrection rent the Empire. The Slavonic-speaking Bulgarians and Latin (or Romance)-speaking Vlachs had seldom been more than sullenly submissive to their Greek conquerors. Now, spurred on by an extortionate tax in coin for the Emperor's pompous wedding, they rose (1186) under the two brothers, Tsars Peter and John Asen I. Isaac's folly, as we have seen, turned Barbarossa into an enemy and damaged his own resources in the Third Crusade. In 1190 he suffered a crushing defeat at the hands of Bulgarians and Cumans at Stara Zagora. When he was deposed and blinded by his brother Alexius III (1195–1203) in one of the familiar domestic Byzantine tragedies, anarchy and oppressive failure grew worse. The Bulgarian-Vlach Empire expanded under Tsar Johannitza (Kaloyan) (1197–1207), while the Greek contracted, losing all the inner Balkans. The Latin West was rancorously hostile. All was ready for the shattering disaster of the Fourth Crusade.

The degeneration of the Byzantine Empire, which is so marked at the close of the twelfth century and is mirrored in its Emperors, was partly due to the loss of virile populations in the heart of Asia Minor and the harried life of the peasantry in the coastlands that remained. Greater weight was given in its composition to the quick-witted, unstable, and febrile townsmen, whether luxurious nobles, rapacious bureaucrats, or tradesmen and artisans. The corrupt element, always prominent, made headway. This subtle, civilized people were the most oriental of Europeans. They loved magnificent spectacles, and above all those of the Church, whose festivals, icons, and holy men commanded their unquestioning devotion. They were a passionate people of a cruel mentality, subject to unbalanced alternations of favour and hatred, courage and servility. Cunning, adroit, hardhearted, and treacherous, yet always intellectual, they aroused the distrust and anger of the blunter, more barbaric Latins, who repaid them with a fixed hostility. The Latin element, too, which was added to the court and capital, was far from beneficial. The privileges which gave Venetians and others command of the sea-borne trade and diminished the revenue were a running sore. Western influences contributed to the megalomania, the lack of proportion, the dissipated energies, and the mis-directed policy of Manuel. The Empire suffered from the discord between East and West.

Yet, all deductions made, Constantinople was still the most wonderful city of Christendom, the most wealthy resort and mart, full of the treasures and products of all climes, the centre where all races met, a hive of industry, art, and learning; and the Empire was the most civilized of existing states. The exterior of the capital was yet unfaded. Its architecture, its mosaics, its marbles, the splendour of its churches and palaces were still in full bloom and were copied in Sicily and Venice by the envious West. The creative instinct was not lost, nor were patriotism and courage, although the political structure was crumbling. Byzantium, the bulwark of Christendom, was still qualified to teach the Slavonic East and to shed priceless influences on the self-taught Latins.

CHAPTER 19

THE HOLY ROMAN EMPIRE AND THE
WESTERN KINGDOMS

(I) THE GROWTH OF THE ITALIAN COMMUNES

The self-governing town was a characteristic phenomenon of the later Middle Ages, taking its rise in the eleventh century in the general revival after the miserable times of anarchy. It was the resurgence of trade, of manufacture for a wide or even a narrow market, which produced town and townsman, merchant and craft. They bore the character of their age. Safety and orderly life were only possible in association, in group-life, and the burghers replaced and competed with the feudal and kinship groups which preceded them. Local and personal law was the rule, and the laws of merchant and town took their place by the side of other local and class customs. Central authority was in greater or less degree in abeyance, and the town, like the baron, obtained its fraction of autonomy. Throughout the West, the towns bore a family resemblance, and created a new type of government, that of free co-operation, of elective magistrates, of popular assemblies, which could vote, discuss, and decree.

Akin as they all were in formation and institutions, the divergencies between the towns of different lands and districts were deep and wide. Within the same country, even, no town was the replica of another: each had its individual history: and the movement to self-government by association spread to places which were not towns at all. Most divergent, and presenting the most perfect type, were the Italian communes or city-states. In Italy, as elsewhere, geographical factors were the dominating causes of economic and social and thence political advance. Some, like Venice and Pisa, were ports, others were at fords or road-junctions or at the exit of mountain-passes, others were strongholds on the immemorial roads, the natural centres of a rich countryside. The whole land had the temporary advantage of being the half-way house, the key-point of the Mediterranean between the East with its civilization, its products, and its arts and the West, the eager purchaser and borrower. The struggle to command the sea to the west, the Ponent, and then to the east, the Levant, which was interlocked with the Crusades, has been already sketched. The effect was an immediate magnification of the citizens' wealth and activity. But the local advantages of site were permanent, and the Italian cities were old, remembering their ancient history and affected by it. Venice itself, almost the latest born, had belonged to the Eastern Empire, and never quite lost the traces of its direct descent from the ancient world, unblended with

544

Germanic invaders. Although traces of city institutions may be perceived earlier, it was only in the decades just before and after 1100 that the full-fledged commune appears in the *Regnum Italicum*. It was the breakdown of imperial and feudal government during the struggle of the Papacy and the Empire which gave the citizens the occasion to develop the sworn leagues of classes and whole towns, which had been growing for a century, into what was in practice a republic. At the base of the *commune*, as it was styled, was the *arengo* (*parlamento*), i.e. the general assembly of townsmen within the city wall. The *arengo* swore collectively to an agreement which included obedience to magistrates, the consuls (a title from Roman tradition), who in their turn took a reciprocal oath to observe the prescriptions laid down for them. Thus city legislation and government began. In the twelfth century a council of notables, whose most common name was the *Consiglio di Credenza* (council sworn to secrecy), with legislative and advisory functions, grew up round the consuls, and replaced for most purposes the formless *arengo*. In fact, although on a democratic foundation, the communes at this time were ruled by an oligarchy of consular families and notables. The counts, if they had not already lost their functions to the bishops, were ousted. The bishops lost control during the war between Empire and Papacy, and ceded their rights to or shared them with the upstart communes. The feudal viscounts did the same. By this means or by sheer usurpation the consuls took over the administrative and judicial functions of the ancient feudalized imperial officials, enlarging their original powers of arbitration into coercive jurisdiction of all kinds. In the growing complexity of organization these powers were soon delegated to special consuls of justice. By 1150 the public powers and revenues, the so-called *regalia*, had slipped into the cities' control.

Internecine warfare of classes or rival families had been a leading cause of the sworn leagues which developed into the commune, which was in its origin a private association, although it included, if necessary by compulsion, all citizens. The sectional beginning left the most obvious trace in the great commune of Milan, where *capitanei*, vavassors, and plebeians possessed their prescribed shares in the consulate and government, but variations of the same phenomenon were to be seen, less formulated perhaps, in multiform guise elsewhere.

External warfare was still more prevalent in the extension of a city's dominion. City nobles had always held lands in the countryside, its *contado*. But there were country nobles as well, who remained in their fortified castles or townlets, and their independence, exactions of tolls, often unwarranted, and predatory turbulence were a standing provocation to the aggrieved trading citizens. The early history of the Florentine commune is marked by petty wars to subdue these troublesome neighbours. The citizens needed, too, control of their food-supply. In result, though a

WESTERN EUROPE
IN THE
TWELFTH CENTURY

WALES

ENGLAND

Lincoln

London
Bristol
Canterbury

FLANDERS

NORMANDY

BRITTANY

KINGDOM

MAINE

OF

ANJOU

ANGEVIN

POITOU

FRANCE

CHAMPAGNE

EMPIRE

AUVERGNE

PERIGORD

KINGDOM OF NAVARRE

GASCONY

TOULOUSE

LANGUEDOC

KINGDOM
OF LEON

KINGDOM
OF
PORTUGAL

KINGDOM
OF
CASTILE

KINGDOM
OF
ARAGON

Saragossa

COUNTY
OF
BARCELONA

Barcelona

Lisbon

Toledo

ALMURAVID   KINGDOM

Cordova

Map 15

FRISIA

LOWER LOTHARINGIA

BRANDENBURG

SAXONY

LAUSITZ

THURINGIA

MEISSEN

FRANCONIA

HOLY

BOHEMIA

MORAVIA

UPPER LOTHAR-INGIA

BAVARIA

AUSTRIA

ROMAN

SWABIA

STYRIA

CARINTHIA

KINGDOM

OF

HUNGARY

KINGDOM OF BURGUNDY

EMPIRE

Milan ●

Verona ●

Venice

Pavia ●

LOMBARDY

Genoa ●

Florence ●

TUSCANY

Marseilles ●

Corsica

PAPAL

Rome ●

STATES

NORMAN

Brindisi ●

Sardinia

KINGDOM

OF

Palermo ●

SICILY

Messina ●

Map 15

547

number of feudal lords retained their independence in the Apennines and elsewhere, the cities conquered most, and forced them to become partly resident citizens. Thus a large increment was made to the fighting strength and also to the inner broils of the communes, for the habit of family feuds and vendetta received new stimulus from the incomers and became a characteristic of the whole population. Other nobles and little communes of rural townships became subjects of a city by entering into the vassalage of its bishop, whose own status was steadily being transmuted into privileged membership of his commune as the twelfth century wore on.

It was not only nobles who migrated into the cities. They were preceded and followed by a swarm of peasants, often of unfree status, who came to seek their fortune. In thirteenth-century Florence there were many who were still barely free in their native township while they were highly placed citizens in the city. The communes overflowed to suburbs, and in the twelfth century were building new circuits of walls to defend them and enlarge the citizen area.

With trade as the mainspring of the cities' advance and prosperity, the desire for secure outlets and commercial rivalry, combined with a local patriotism of amazing fervour, not to say virulence, rendered each city the enemy of those neighbours who blocked its routes with tolls and competed with it in outer markets and for stretches of the valuable countryside. Venice, Genoa, Pisa, and Amalfi fought incessantly for the sea-borne trade. The transit roads to Rome from the north and the exit to the sea at Pisa were an envenomed cause of the thirteenth-century enmity of land-locked, manufacturing Florence and her Tuscan neighbours. In Lombardy a kind of chequer-pattern of friends and foes was formed by the contest for the control of the river Po and its tributaries and of the great Emilian Way from Piacenza to Rimini and its southern offshoots, a pattern which was complicated by the ambitions of wealthy Milan with its three fertile counties. Thus each city possessed a foreign policy, alliances and enmities, which could only be modified, if at all, by the overwhelming pressure of a common danger to their autonomy. Inter-city war was almost endemic.

A large part of Italian trade consisted of the oriental traffic. The much desired spices and sugar which seasoned the coarse foods of the age, supplemented by silk, cotton, and textile fabrics, objects of art, dyewoods, and wine, and a little later by corn and fish from the Black Sea, were the Eastern exports, which were exchanged for Western iron, wood, hides, furs, linen, cloth, and slaves. Eastern products were handed on to the transalpines over the mountain-passes and along the rivers. This trade found its focus in the great fairs of Champagne, lasting most of the year, where merchants of all the North, including the separate trading system of the North Sea and the Baltic, met the southerners. Wool was the greatest product of the North, and the Italians either bought it to be woven at home or bought the rougher cloth of Flanders and North France to be dressed and made superfine by Italian workmen. In the later twelfth century the half-heretical, ascetic fraternity of the Umiliati in Lombardy improved the art of cloth-weaving, and the gild or 'Art' of Wool was one of the most important in each city. In Florence there flourished beside it the Art of Calimala, which specialized in the dressing of foreign cloth. .In the thirteenth century, such traders with businesses extending from London to the Levant were naturally specialists in money and credit. They then gained ill fame for their loans and usury forbidden to Christians by Canon Law, and by 1300 the Jews, whose scattered family connexions and faith had given them almost a monopoly in these transactions, were ousted by them from the field of high finance.

Externally, by sea the trade was well organized. Venice and her rivals possessed extraterritorial colonies in the Levant, where their officials (the forerunners of modern consuls) ruled and supplied ship repairs. Twice a year a fleet of each, escorted by war-galleys, voyaged to and fro, secure from sporadic pirates. By land the merchants travelled in companies and settled their disputes at the fairs by customary law-merchant. Internally, the increase of the trading classes in numbers and prosperity produced fresh organizations. The old division of the city into quarters and parishes and of its population into *milites* who served on horseback (the nobles) and *pedites* who served on foot (the plebeians or *popolani*) continued, but did not suffice. The merchants appear by the side of the *milites*, each with consuls of their organization. Jurists, money-changers, manufacturers, retail crafts formed gilds with consuls, whose functions were both trading and political. At the close of the twelfth century, the commune was an organism of many cells, represented, with the nobles in preponderance, in the Great Council. After the end of the contest with Barbarossa, disunion, partly due to class-conflicts, still more to the blood-feuds of the prolific noble houses in their *consorzerie* and societies, produced a constitutional change. The board of consuls was slowly superseded by a single executive, the *podestà*, usually an annual official elected from another city, while legislation, finance, and policy were retained by the Great Council. The change made for efficiency and expertness, for the *podestà* was almost professional. The citizen meantime played many parts. He might well be at the same time a noble of a *consorzeria*, a member of a trading gild, and an official of commune, quarter, and parish. He would serve in the army and travel on business. As time went on it was natural, not only from emulation and jealousy but from the drain on a man's time, that short terms of office in state and gild became the rule. City life, too, was not only busy, but turbulent. Real differences of policy, blended with family feuds and class rivalries and material interests, led to perpetual discord. Each city became a forest of towers, the strongholds of noble house and factions. But the average of ability and energy was high and produced a remarkable array of men eminent in jurisprudence, statesmanship, commerce, the Church, and eventually literature.

(2) TOWNS AND TRADE NORTH OF THE ALPS

Across the Alps four great territorial divisions are at once perceptible: the Midi of Langue d'oc speakers in France and the kingdom of Burgundy, the mass of Langue d'oïl in both kingdoms, the Netherlandish area in Flanders and Lower Lotharingia, and lastly the slow-developing towns of the Rhineland and inner Germany. Within all four, self-government grew in multitudinous variety, of which only the most general features can here be indicated. It need scarcely be mentioned that even the main divisions have shadowy boundaries, and hard and fast characteristics are few or none.

In the Midi, where on the whole the feudal yoke was light, Roman traditions better preserved, and prosperity more precocious, the leading type of town government which emerged was the *consulate*, so called from its officials. It commonly arose without a struggle. As in Italy, the local nobles, however given to private war among themselves, were influential members of the consulate, and the greater lords were glad to encourage these fortified and revenue-producing centres. To raise money for a crusade was a frequent inducement for the sale of charters of liberties. Sometimes, indeed, there were violent risings, as when Montpellier drove out its lord (1141) and replaced him by the King of Aragon. The greatest consulates were all-but free republics, like trading Marseilles which only owed military service to the Count of Provence, and was ruled by its *grand conseil* and its hundred heads of gilds, besides possessing a general assembly like the Italian *arengo*. Marseilles, too, was a seaport vying with Genoa, while Montpellier developed a university from its schools. Other towns, like Toulouse, submitted to some governmental rights of their feudal lord. Rural towns and sometimes small villages gained their communes with varying degrees of privilege. The beginnings of such often went back to ancient rights of managing common pastures and woods, but in the twelfth century monastic lords began to found privileged *sauvetés* to attract population to their land, and these were followed up, chiefly in the thirteenth century, by fortified *bastides*, of which the lay lords were the chief founders. Freedom from serfdom by custom, purchase, or free grant was naturally the basic privilege of all these communities. Fixed dues, their own officials, and the confirmation of their own customs came next. The real towns quickly developed merchant and craft gilds. All, however, admitted in greater or less degree the authority of their feudal suzerain.

In northern and central France, where feudalism was more short-sighted and oppressive, the picture is similar, but purely bourgeois and more chequered by violence, repression, and revolt. The true urban commune there was known as the *commune jurée*, owing to the mutual oath of association which was the essential feature in its foundation, as in Italy and the Midi, and made it a collective body. In its earlier history this was the league which often won or strove to win its liberties by the strong hand. Later in the twelfth century the privilege to form such a commune might be shrewdly granted among other rights by a complaisant and far-seeing lord, especially the king, for a consideration. The Counts of Champagne and the Dukes of French Burgundy were generous grantors. Insurrection and long conflict were most prevalent where towns were in the domain of the legal-minded Church, which regarded the cession of its powers and property as a sin. In 1077 the citizens of Cambrai set up a commune in defiance of their bishop-count. It was crushed in 1107, only to revive twenty years later. Laon revolted in like manner against the bishop-count, who was murdered in riotous strife. An accord, which left the townsmen still liable to servile dues, was but a truce, and after a stormy career of about a century the commune was annulled. Rheims, already a commune, in 1167 drove out its archbishop, who reclaimed his judicial powers. Twenty years later the city had its way. Full-grown communes, however, governed by their mayor and *jurats*, and electing their own *échevins* (derived from Carolingian *scabini*) for justice, were few and looked at askance even by potentates who favoured the townsmen. Most *communes jurées* were perforce content with less autonomy, and far more preferred by the rulers were the *villes de bourgeoisie*, which, however, are difficult to mark off from the less autonomous communes, for the commune of Rouen was not more exempt than the town of Senlis from its overlord's officials—perhaps the absence of the sworn league of townsmen furnished the criterion. King and great vassals were all the more willing to confer partial self-administration and personal liberty on bourgeois, when their own officials retained justice and surveillance. Paris itself was a *ville de bourgeoisie*, which was the common type of privilege in central France, and when *commune jurée* and consulate declined in the thirteenth century they sank into much the same position.

There also appeared in the twelfth century peasant communes of single villages or groups of villages. They were, however, less lasting than the *villes neuves* which, like the *bastides* of the Midi, were set up by king or lord to attract a rural population by granting personal freedom, elected officials, and easy dues. These were rural townlets, and their customs, which were non-political, imitated like the village communes those of older purely rural towns. Imitation was a marked characteristic in towns of the Langue d'oïl. The customs and privileges of certain model towns, such as Rouen in Normandy, Beauvais, and Soissons, were widely copied, as were those of Lorris and Beaumont in village charters. The common needs were the same.

In all these developments economic progress was the deciding factor. Increased, if far from perfect, security for the burgess at home or travelling with his goods allowed trade and manufacture to grow. Favourable geographic situation, as in Italy, caused old towns to revive and new ones to make their appearance. The burgesses were able to demand the liberties and customs they needed for their non-feudal, more advanced life, and they were capable of carrying on co-operative self-government and of devising a town and traders' law. The greater lords found their profit not only in the sale of charters but in their revenues from town and country. For rural prosperity and the increase of rural population flowed not only from greater security but also from the market for food-products in the growing towns. It was worth while to attract peasants to cultivate assarts and to populate the wastes and forests. No better expedient could be found than the grant of village-charters and the creation of *villes neuves*. The eleventh and twelfth centuries, as well as the thirteenth, were the age when the depleted population of the West multiplied. Peace and security revived, however slowly, and, freed from utter anarchy, natural fertility and natural energy were changing the face of western Europe.

The towns of the Midi and of most Langue d'oïl were largely stimulated by the trade which flowed up the Rhône and back between the Mediterranean and the fairs of Champagne. The Netherlandish area was itself the centre of another system of commerce, that of the North Sea. The Scandinavians, who had nearly destroyed Carolingian traffic, being themselves eager traders, ended in reviving it on a larger scale. They brought furs, etc., and oriental goods, which reached the Baltic Sea overland through Russia, to the Frankish coast and up the navigable rivers. The ancient weaving of Flanders and the metal work of the Meuse recovered, and were reinforced by supplies of English wool and German minerals. At the nodal points of rivers and roads and at natural ports, ancient cities, like Liége, revived, and new towns, like Bruges and Ghent, came into existence for trade and manufacture. Thence their merchants took their wares to Champagne or to England and Germany. By 1180 Bruges at the head of the then gulf of the Zwyn was the commercial pivot of the Netherlands, and the Flemish towns formed a joint Hansa or league in London.

These merchants inhabited the 'faubourgs' outside the old fortified cities and the new feudal castles for defence, and in the eleventh century were building walls for the defence of their settlements, the 'ports' (wharfs and warehouses), which were inland focuses of trade. Whether by strife as at Cambrai, or under the patronage of great lords like the strong Counts of Flanders, they were acquiring in the twelfth century communal governments of their own and were raising taxes for their fortifications and administering a new bourgeois law in place of the unsuitable or utterly inadequate feudal customs of the open country round them with their oppressive tolls and dues and half-barbaric judicial procedure. The Netherlandish towns were essentially oligarchic in government. The hereditary merchants (*poorters*) who imported the raw material, wool and metals, and exported the manufactured cloth and hardware, had the whip hand over the craftsmen. They have received the name of patricians from modern historians. Under them worked the subject craftsmen. The craft-gild (*métier*, *mistery*) of the twelfth century was an original creation of the bourgeois, although in Italy a few stray *scholae* or gilds may have survived from the ancient Empire. When applied to a local market—and in most towns and trades the market was mainly local—it safeguarded producer and consumer, for each closely organized gild of small masters supervised the purchase of its raw material and the sale of its products, and laid down the conditions of apprenticeship and membership. Abuses and evasions were doubtless continual, but by and large the system worked. Crafts which catered for a wide market, however, like the weavers and their allies, whose raw material was doled out by the importing merchant and whose productions were bought by him for distant export, were more in the position of employees. But these crafts were exceptional and in the twelfth and thirteenth centuries characterized only certain towns such as Bruges, Ghent, and Liége. The political dominance of the early oligarchies on the other hand was universal in the Netherlands. The patricians were energetic and public-spirited. They aimed at and largely succeeded in making their towns 'a world apart', with internal autonomy at least. The bourgeois there and elsewhere became a privileged class. Within limits, in spite of countless conflicts, they were valuable subjects to their suzerain; each commune was a 'collective seignory' with seal and governmental organs; in the Netherlands they developed local types of constitutions, such as the Flemish and the Liégeois. They took an essential part in the advance of medieval politics and civilization.

Meanwhile a similar development, due to the same causes, was to be seen in Germany. It was at first most active along the Rhine in episcopal cities, and the Jews with their wide connexions, in spite of envious persecution inflamed by fanaticism, took a leading share in their trade. Cologne, Worms, Speier, Mainz, Basle etc., obtained in the twelfth century chartered market-rights and freedom from toll and seignorial exactions. In the north, new-founded Lübeck, Hamburg, and Bremen gained equal privileges. The merchants of these Saxon ports went far to oust the Scandinavians from the fishing and carrying trade of the Baltic and North Sea. German constitutional progress, however, was slower than elsewhere. The town councils only appear at the close of the twelfth century. They and the government came into the hands of a merchant oligarchy, the patriciate of *Geschlechter*. The lesser gilds were subjects. In general they looked to the Emperor for favour; those on Church or seignorial land met with a sullen tolerance if not hostility from their overlords. The exception to these princes was Henry the Lion, who chartered Lübeck for the Baltic and his other foundation of Munich for the south-eastern trade.

Thus over Western Europe a new 'estate', that of the burgess and trader, had come into being alongside of the knight, ecclesiastic, and peasant. They ranked at first far below the feudal lord and prelate, but as much as any they linked Christendom together. Wealth and intercourse no longer depended only on arms, the land and the Church.

(3) GERMANY AND ITALY, 1125–1152

The death of Henry V without an agnate heir gave the German princes the opportunity to insist on their right of free election, which in 1077 they had stood for in the choice of the anti-king Rudolf. Owing partly to the wars and to the adoption of the celibate and profitable clerical career, the great houses tended to become extinct, and the princes now numbered among them new-risen dynasts. Such were the leading candidates for the crown: Frederick of Hohenstaufen, Duke of Swabia, son of Henry's sister and heir to the Salian lands, and Lothar of Supplinburg, Duke of Saxony since the extinction of the Billungs in 1106, whose wife Richenza was heiress of Nordheim and Brunswick. A century earlier, Frederick would have seemed the natural choice, but now the influence of the Church, led by Archbishop Adalbert of Mainz, and the dislike of hereditary right among the princes, combined with their particularism, led to the election of Lothar III[1] (1125–37), who was both elderly and sonless and a devout churchman. He showed energy and capacity both as rebel duke and king, and greatly

Fig. 114. The Emperor Lothar III presents the abbot of Vornbach with a privilege

strengthened his position by marrying his only daughter to Henry the Proud, Duke of Bavaria (1126–38), the head of the great Lombardo-Swabian house of the Welfs of Altdorf, and heir to the Billungs in Lüneburg.

---

[1] As Emperor he counted Lothar I and his son Lothar II as his predecessors.

554

The Church was satisfied by his relinquishing intervention in episcopal elections and receiving only the fealty, not the homage, of the elect.

None the less Lothar for most of his reign was hampered by the insubordination of the princes and by civil war caused by the revolt of the Hohenstaufen, whom he deprived of their new-won fiefs. Thereby he began the historic and pernicious feud of the Welfs and Hohenstaufen. Frederick the One-eyed of Swabia was a formidable antagonist. His younger brother Conrad was powerful in eastern Franconia and popular enough to be set up as anti-king (December 1127), and gained temporary if illusory support in Lombardy, where he was crowned King of Italy. In Germany the Hohenstaufen slowly had the worse, but both Lothar and Duke Henry contended with refractory magnates in their own duchies apart from the main civil war. Yet they came out the victors, though turbulence and private feuds were endemic. At last in 1135 the two Hohenstaufen submitted on easy terms, surprising after the ferocity displayed by their enemies on occasion.

Amid all the turmoil Lothar had found time and means to act outside Germany. His rival Conrad, in extending the battlefield to Italy, where Milan was in his favour, fell into conflict with Pope Honorius II (1124–30) over the inheritance of Countess Matilda. On her death in 1115 her counties and fiefs returned to the Emperor; her allodial lands she had converted in Gregory VII's time into fiefs of the Papacy and had confirmed the donation in 1102 by charter, while retaining full right of disposal. She had exercised the right in favour of Henry V, and Conrad now claimed possession. He failed and returned to the German civil war, but the Papacy meanwhile experienced an internal crisis of the first magnitude. There was a schism among the cardinals, which became a schism of the Western Church. One party elected Cardinal Peter Pierleoni as Anacletus II, the other Cardinal Gregory Papareschi as Innocent II (1130–43). The rivalries of the Roman noble houses, whose members were now leaders in the Curia, were responsible for the schism, for which the absence of a majority rule gave ample opportunity. Anacletus, whose following in Rome was greater, represented perhaps the ever-growing business element. Innocent, the weaker in the City, appealed to the ardent reformers in the Church. Fleeing to France, he gained over St Bernard, the greatest moral force in Christendom. From that moment the adhesion of the Transalpines was assured. The Kings of France and England accepted him as true Pope; Lothar met him and St Bernard at Liége (1131), led his horse (a compromising act in view of its public symbolism) like a later Carolingian, and entered into an alliance, although even he attempted to recover his right to intervene in elections. Baffled in this, he none the less undertook his first expedition to Italy (1132–3). His forces were too weak to overawe the Lombard communes—it was the magnetic St Bernard who reconciled

16. The Welfs and the Hohenstaufen

(a) The Welfs and their Kindred

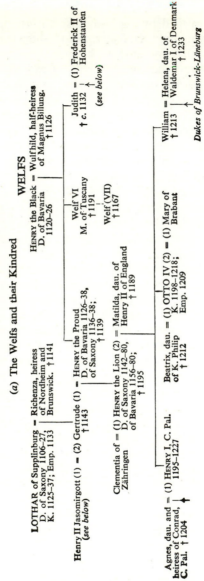

(b) The Hohenstaufen and their Kindred

HOHENSTAUFEN

BABENBERGS

FREDERICK I, = (1) Agnes, dau. of Henry IV (2) = LEOPOLD III,
D. of Swabia 1079–1105 · M. of Austria 1095–1136

Gertrude (2) = Henry II Jasomirgott (1) = Theodora,
of Supplinburg · D. of Bavaria 1142–56, · niece of
(see above) · M. of Austria 1141–77 · Emp. Manuel
(D. from 1156) · †1184
Dukes of Austria

Vladislav II (1) = Gertrude. †1151
of Bohemia. †1175

FREDERICK IV of Rothenburg
D. of Swabia. †1167

Agnes, †1157
= Wladislaw II of
Poland. †1159

CONRAD III
(K. 1138–52)

HENRY
(Assoc. K. 1147–50)

LEOPOLD IV,
M. of Austria 1136–41,
D. of Bavaria 1139–41

Judith = (1) FREDERICK II (2) = Agnes of Saarbrücken
(see above) · D. of Swabia · †1184
†c. 1132 · 1105–47

CONRAD
C. Pal. 1156–95

PHILIP of Swabia = (2) Irene, dau. of Emp.
(K. 1198–1208) · Isaac II. †1252

Elizabeth = Ferdinand III of
†1235 · Castile. †1252

ALFONSO X of Castile
Titular K. of Germany 1257; †1284

Beatrix = (1) Otto IV
†1212 · (see above)

Beatrix = (1) MANFRED (2) = Helena of
of Savoy · K. of Sicily · Epirus
1258–66

PETER III of = CONSTANCE
Aragon; K. of · Q. of Sicily
Sicily 1282–85 · 1282–1302
Aragonese kings of Sicily
(Table 19 b, p. 767)

Adelaide of = (1) FREDERICK I (2) = Beatrix, heiress of
Vohburg; · Barbarossa · Franche-Comté.
div. 1152 · (K. 1152–90; Emp. · †1184
1155)

HENRY VI = Constance, heiress of
(1190–97) · Sicily. †1198

Enzo
K. of Sardinia
1238; dep. 1249;
†1272

FREDERICK V
D. of Swabia
†1191

Constance, dau. of Alfonso II = (1) FREDERICK II (3) = Isabella, dau. of
of Aragon. †1222 · John of England
Yolande of Brienne, heiress = (2) K. of Sicily 1197, of · †1241
of Jerusalem. †1228 · Germany 1212;
Emp. 1220; †1250

CONRAD IV = (1) Elizabeth, dau.
K. 1250–54 · of Otto II of
(assoc. 1237) · Bavaria. †1273

HENRY [VII] = (1) Margaret, dau.
K. 1220; dep. · of Leopold VI of
1235; †1242 · Austria. †1267

CONRADIN
†1268

1

2

Genoa and Pisa and drew Milan from Anacletus—but strong enough to enter Rome and see him crowned Emperor. From Innocent he at last obtained a concession, for that matter of little effect, of Henry V's rights under the Concordat of Worms, as well as the enfeoffment of Matilda's lands to himself and Henry the Proud. That, too, was compromising, for Innocent in a tendentious wall-painting in the Lateran represented Lothar's homage as done for the imperial crown. The thesis of Gregory VII seemed triumphant. Innocent, however, was hardly the immediate gainer, for after the Emperor's departure he was once more driven from Rome by Anacletus and the Anti-Pope's partisan, King Roger II of Sicily. When in 1136 after the submission of the Hohenstaufen the Emperor could march into Italy with a large army, the case was altered. The Lombard communes dared not resist, and the objective was Roger II. Lothar proceeded along the Adriatic, Henry the Proud through Tuscany, accompanied by Pope Innocent, and they met at Bari (1137), while Roger retreated to Sicily. They set up the chief Apulian rebel, Rainulf, as Duke of Apulia. But the conflict of interests and claims was at once revealed. Both Emperor and Pope claimed to be Rainulf's suzerain, and the dispute was lamely adjusted by a joint investiture of the duke. The profound antagonism between the Empire which demanded all Italy, and the Papacy which feared to be encircled and desired a territorial balance, was not to be smothered. Lothar at any rate had increased his power when he returned to Germany to die in the Tyrol in December 1137.

In the north and east the Saxon Lothar, renewing the aggressive policy of the Ottos, revived the German *Drang nach Osten*. He tamed the Saxon magnates; in Bohemia, failing to install his own candidate, he made a loyal vassal of Duke Soběslav; but his main wish was to ensure the conversion and subjugation of the heathen Wends. The part-heir of the Billungs, Albert the Bear of Ballenstedt, received the Nordmark and Brandenburg. The Dane Canute of Slesvig was enfeoffed with the country of the Obodrites, and when he was murdered, two native princes submitted to vassalage. Even the Danes in their incessant civil wars thought it best to acknowledge the Emperor's superiority. The same course was taken by Duke Boleslav of Poland, who paid arrears of tribute and was enfeoffed with his acquisitions in Pomerania, while the Hungarian throne was filled by the Emperor's choice. The Empire's prestige was renewed.

Lothar III left his son-in-law Henry the Proud the most powerful man in Germany. He was Duke of Bavaria and Saxony, head of the house of Welf, with vast possessions in Germany and Italy. But the prelates, who had favoured Lothar, were against him, and the particularist lay princes had no mind to erect a new dynasty by electing him. The Saxon Albert the Bear of the Nordmark, the Babenberg Leopold IV, Margrave of Austria, Conrad, Duke of Zähringen, who was turning the rectorate of

Burgundy, conferred upon him by Lothar, into a reality east of the Jura, these and their like feared such an overwhelming suzerain. It was therefore easy for the leading prelate, Adalbero, Archbishop of Trier, to carry through the irregular election and coronation of the rival candidate, the well-liked Conrad III[1] of Hohenstaufen, in spite of the return to the older line which it implied. They knew they were choosing a weaker, poorer sovereign. Conrad began his reign (1138–52) with a great mistake, which revealed the lack of statesmanship that dogged his career. He reopened the feud of Welf and Hohenstaufen by depriving his overmighty subject of both his duchies, first of Saxony and then of Bavaria. Albert the Bear was promoted to the one, Leopold IV of Austria to the other. This was to begin a civil war. Henry drove his opponents out of Saxony, and was preparing to reconquer Bavaria when he suddenly died. His son and heir, Henry the Lion, was a boy of ten, in charge of his grandmother, the Empress Richenza, who also died (1141). His uncle Welf VI of Altdorf was defeated (1140) by King Conrad himself on the Neckar, where tradition said that the battlecries of 'Welf' and 'Waiblingen' (a Hohenstaufen castle) were first used by the contending factions. In 1142 a peace was patched up by which Henry the Lion kept Saxony, while Henry II Jasomirgott ('So help me God') brother of the dead Leopold, received Bavaria and married Henry the Proud's widow. The arrangement was 'a seed of discord', for only Jasomirgott was satisfied. Partisan warfare continued, and Duke Frederick of Swabia, Conrad's elder brother, who had married a Welf, was alienated. Lower Lotharingia, which had been disputed by two dukes since Lothar's time, continued in turmoil and really broke up into its component lordships. The king favoured especially his half-brothers and sisters, the Babenbergs, but although he succeeded in making the husband of one sister, Vladislav II, Duke of Bohemia, he failed to impose another brother-in-law on Poland, while Jasomirgott was routed by the Hungarians besides engaging in a feud with the Bavarian bishops. Germany was racked by war and famine when the Second Crusade and the influence of St Bernard put a brief stop to hostilities (1147).

Before starting on his disastrous expedition Conrad had taken the precaution of obtaining the election and coronation of his ten-year-old son Henry, but the centre of German events shifted to Saxony where Henry the Lion was showing his capacity to rule. The civil war had given the signal for a Wendish revolt which devastated the newly settled district of Wagria. The work of reconquest and resettlement was at once undertaken by Count Adolf of Holstein, who drew new colonists from Frisia and Westphalia. The town of Lübeck, with its natural harbour, was rebuilt. The colonization was seconded by a campaign to convert the heathen Wends, begun long before by the missionary Vicelin and now continued

---

[1] Conrad II as Emperor, since Conrad of Franconia had only been German King.

and made hateful by compulsion. When the Second Crusade was preached, the Saxon princes obtained the Pope's permission to turn their arms against the Wends with all the crusaders' privileges. The news roused those who had submitted to a fresh outbreak, and the Wendish Crusade of 1147, in which all the Welfic faction and the Danes participated, proved a failure. It was left to Henry the Lion in later years to resume the advance on his own account.

Conrad III came back to Germany in 1149 full of Italian schemes: the southern Hohenstaufen always looked southward, and he had not yet received the imperial crown. He had long been in treaty with the Emperor Manuel Comnenus for an alliance against their common enemy, Roger II of Sicily, and, as it happened, the plight of the Papacy in Italy rendered his expedition thither desirable to the Popes. After Lothar's withdrawal, as we have seen, Pope Innocent had fared ill in his contest with the Norman, although the schism hardly outlasted the death of Anacletus (1138). He had been defeated and captured, and was obliged to confirm Roger's royal title (1139). On his return to Rome new troubles awaited him. Rome, infested by malaria, without industries, and the prey of the fierce nobles and their fierce retainers from the Campagna, had once lagged behind the general progress. Now, as the seat of the Church's monarch and his bureaucracy, thronged with visiting prelates, clerics and pilgrims, she had developed a lesser nobility and a trading class. The communal movement entered the City with prosperity, and there assumed a particular form from her unique traditions. The Romans never forgot that their predecessors had been lords of the world and had made the Empire, whose continuance in German hands was an article of faith. Rome to them was still the capital of the Empire of the West and they themselves the rightful disposers of its crown. The legend distorted reality all the more easily because she was the Church's centre, but the Pope's temporal rule was a sore stumbling-block to a visionary sovereign people, and government through the ancient prefect of the City, the oldest official of the West, and the anarchic nobles was a superannuated abuse. The inter-city hatreds characteristic of Italy set light to this explosive situation. Rome's special enemy was her nearest neighbour in the Campagna, Tivoli. When in a bitter war Innocent accepted Tivoli's surrender and refused to destroy it, revolution broke out. The insurgent Romans 'renewed' the Senate, excluding the greater nobles, and proclaimed their independence of the Pope, who ought to be content with offerings and tithes (1143). After Innocent's death (1143), his second successor, Lucius II, attempted to subdue them by force, but he was wounded in assaulting the Capitol and died (1145), while Rome was governed by the 'patrician' Jordan Pierleoni, brother of Anacletus, a significant choice. Like the Senate without consuls, the patrician was a variation from communal practice.

With remarkable insight, and to everyone's surprise, the cardinals elected a Cistercian, of Pisan origin, who took the name of Eugenius III (1145–53) and proved capable of statesmanlike manœuvre in his stormy time. He was, however, twice forced to abandon Rome, where a new Church reformer was taking the lead. Arnold of Brescia, the staunch disciple of Abelard, who fulfilled all the contemporary ideals of ascetic holiness and was a born orator, had voiced for years the extreme wing of the Patarines, mainly consisting of the unprivileged poor. He demanded that the clergy should live in apostolic poverty without secular powers and lands, as Paschal II had once suggested. The wealthy, overbearing Church with its often hollow reforms was losing touch with the subject classes in Lombardy. His programme implied a social as well as an ecclesiastical revolution, but he was orthodox in doctrine, and although condemned to silence by Innocent II and denounced by St Bernard, was only sentenced by the milder Eugenius to a pilgrimage to Rome. This was to send fire to a volcano. Arnold included the Papacy in his propaganda of disendowment, as Paschal had not done, and became the oracle of the Romans, while the little cities of the Patrimony set up communes of their own. Eugenius turned to Conrad, and when, in spite of him, the King of the Romans went off on the Second Crusade, to Roger II, whose troops once more escorted him to the Lateran while the Senate remained in power at the Capitol. It was not long before he left Rome again and appealed to Conrad III.

Conrad, however, was impeded in his designs by his German opponents. Henry the Lion was claiming Bavaria in arms, and had gained allies. The Duke of Zähringen was for him. His uncle Welf VI was receiving a subsidy from the threatened King of Sicily, and although defeated by the young King Henry, the latter's death (1150) cancelled the reverse. Besides, negotiations with the Pope moved slowly, for if Eugenius wished for Conrad's help, he did not desire the intervention of his ally, the Emperor Manuel. When all was arranged, Conrad failed in a sudden stroke aimed to expel Henry the Lion from Saxony, and then himself died in February 1152. Although he was lavishly praised by his friends, failure was the keynote of his reign. He had exacerbated the feud of Welfs and Hohenstaufen, his greatest vassals were in revolt, and he died still King of the Romans, now the regular title used before coronation at Rome. He was in full concord with the Church, but he had taken even less part than Lothar in episcopal elections and suffered thereby. He left Germany so harassed by civil war that the princes themselves desired a stronger, shrewder king.

(4) FREDERICK BARBAROSSA AND ITALY

Fortunately for Germany the obvious candidate was the very man for the task. Conrad's surviving son was a child. Frederick, Duke of Swabia, the son of Conrad's elder brother, was half a Welf through his mother Judith, sister of Henry the Proud. He was therefore peculiarly fitted to compose the ruinous feud, and was elected King of the Romans at once with all-but unanimity. In the prime of life, tall, warlike and genial, he seemed the embodiment of knightly perfection to his day. For a layman he was well educated; he understood Latin and was interested in history and law. He was also a born ruler, sagacious, decided, tirelessly energetic and inexorably just, a compelling personality.

Frederick I, Barbarossa (Redbeard) as the Italians called him, was an experienced man of thirty at his accession, a survivor of the Second Crusade, and his aims, both general and particular, were defined from the start: he would restore royal authority and internal peace to Germany, and revive the Empire and with it peace in the nearly lost dependency of Italy. He was a backward-looking statesman determined to restore the past. He believed the legend of the Holy Roman Empire, and regarded himself as heir to the world-dominion of Augustus and Justinian. His politics were coloured by romance, perverted perhaps, for the Roman mirage tempted him away from humdrum progress in his native land. Yet the persuasion of Pope Eugenius was unable at once to divert him from the primary need of restoring the German monarchy. There three aims guided his policy: alliance with the Welfs in place of feud, the taming of the anarchy of private war, and the renewal of royal authority over the German Church and its resources. To these he bent his first efforts.

Henry the Lion was only to be won by the recovery of the Bavarian dukedom, but Henry Jasomirgott was not easily to be deprived. It was only in September 1156 that a final concord was achieved. Jasomirgott surrendered the duchy to his rival, and in return was created Duke, no longer Margrave, of Austria with unique privileges amounting to autonomy. It was the first step towards the fissure of the Danubian province from the rest of Germany. But Henry the Lion, too, now ruler of two duchies, became almost a viceroy in them. He could pursue his own policy within them and on the frontiers of the Elbe and the Eider. On his loyal friendship with his cousin the king the inner peace of Germany and the power of Frederick largely depended. Their uncle Welf VI was made Marquess of Tuscany, still a more than nominal dignity.

Backed by Henry and the greater princes and nerved by his own force of character, Frederick attacked the root of the prevalent anarchy. A general *Landfriede* for all Germany with penalties for breaches of the peace was promulgated. It was followed up by provincial *Landfrieden* of

Fig. 115. Duke Henry the Lion; his parents, Duke Henry the Proud and Gertrude; his maternal grand-parents Lothar III and Richenza; his wife, Matilda; her father, King Henry II of England; and her paternal grand-mother, the Empress Matilda

563

the old type, and at Roncaglia in 1158 a universal *Constitutio Pacis* pro-hibited private war altogether. But these decrees required Frederick's presence even for imperfect enforcement, and his absences in Italy always produced disorders. On his returns he quelled them with fire and slaughter, not unlike the disease, and it is significant that in the end, in 1186, he once more admitted the right of private war under conditions. Local government was too feudalized for the reform. Frederick did not attempt and probably had not the power or means to create bureaucratic officials to control counts, barons, and *Vögte*.

In the Church he achieved speedy and surprising success. St Bernard was dead and the Papacy in difficulties. Frederick was resolved from the outset to exercise his full rights over elections according to the imperial interpretation of the Concordat of Worms, and he found the German clergy, left to themselves, very willing to admit them. He quickly established the right to nominate a bishop in the frequent disputed elections. Thus in his accession year he appointed an Archbishop of Magdeburg in spite of the fact that his choice involved a translation from one see to another, which was canonically invalid without the Pope's consent. Eugenius's successor, Anastasius IV (1153–4), agreed not only to this but to the de-position on political grounds of the Archbishop of Mainz and other bishops. Without being usually present at elections, Frederick made his will prevail in their outcome, and the episcopate was manned by his confidants. Their secular duties, too, were strictly enforced. Failure to supply their feudal contingents entailed confiscation of the *regalia*, and on their deaths Frederick took over the *regalia* and *spolia* as aforetime for all the clergy's repining. In ability and usefulness to the Crown his bishops were well qualified—the more important, like Rainald of Dassel and Christian of Buch, had been his chancellors,—as prelates of the Church they were less satisfactory.

Two years had sufficed to establish Frederick's authority in Germany. In 1154 he could make the long-delayed expedition to Italy and Rome. While he was yet in Lombardy, on 5 December a new Pope, Adrian IV (1154–9), was elected to succeed Anastasius. Nicholas Breakspear was the only Englishman ever to sit in the papal chair. From an abbacy in Provence he had been promoted by Eugenius III to be a cardinal-bishop, and had displayed his capacity as legate in reorganizing the Church in Norway. Resolution and courage were his leading traits, and he was determined to regain the ground recently lost by the Papacy, for which he started a new period of expansion. He showed his quality almost at once. The Popes still held the Leonine City, while old Rome was held by the Senate. As a foreigner he was unpopular with the Romans fired by Arnold of Brescia's revolutionary teaching. The effect was that a violent mob seriously wounded an eminent cardinal and provoked Adrian to use an unexpected weapon.

In Holy Week he launched on the City for the first time in its history an interdict, which was to last until Arnold was expelled. The blow was deadly, not only because of men's religious horror, but because Rome depended in the last resort on the influx of pilgrims for the great festivals. Arnold was banished and took refuge with a baron of the Campàgna, while the Pope, triumphant and implacable, removed the interdict.

Adrian's tenacity was less rewarded in his dealings with William I of Sicily, whose royal title he did not recognize. Excommunication here proved a feeble retort to armed ravage. The aid of Frederick was therefore all the more necessary, and yet Empire and Papacy were based on rival political conceptions and were incompatible allies. No Pope could wish for a strong Empire to overawe him in Italy. Frederick on his entry into Italy had celebrated a diet on the plain of Roncaglia by the Po. The representatives of the cities offered their submission, and he began to act as sovereign by adjudicating on their disputes, but their submission was only in seeming save where the enemies of Milan sought to curb by his means her predominace. When Milan refused to obey, his force, inadequate for conquest, was expended in savagely sacking little towns, as in Germany, and in a long siege of her ally, Tortona, which was ruthlessly destroyed. All Lombardy rang with his vengeance as he hastened south. The Pope was already suspicious and held aloof until precise guarantees were given. First, and immediately granted, was the arrest of Arnold, who was thereupon condemned to the pyre. The heretic's courage never flinched, and the dispersal of his ashes in the Tiber did not quench his influence in North Italy; rather it let loose more revolutionary doctrines than his among the Patarines. When Pope and king met at Sutri a collision at once occurred between their opposed conceptions of their relationship. Frederick refused to lead the Pope's mule, until overborne by the force of precedent and Adrian's resolute persistence. It was an omen of future conflict. Yet each needed the other, and Frederick repulsed the vainglorious demands of the Romans. He entered the Leonine City by surprise and received the imperial crown the same day (18 June 1155). So enraged were the Romans that they attacked from across the Tiber and met with a bloody defeat. Frederick, however, withdrew from Rome. He was now Emperor, his army was suffering from malaria, and he retreated with speed to Germany. He had won much glory and much hatred. Milan resumed her prepotence, Tortona was rebuilt, and the Pope, left in the lurch, veered to other schemes.

A natural aim of Frederick Barbarossa was to build up the material resources of the Hohenstaufen in Germany. The imperial and Hohenstaufen domains did not sufficiently outvie the princes', and their extension was taken in hand. His cousin, Frederick of Rothenburg, was already Duke of Swabia; now he made his half-brother Conrad Count

Palatine of the Rhine, a great dignity and fief, opportunely vacant. He had divorced his first wife, and in 1156 was free to marry Beatrix, the heiress of the 'County' of Burgundy (Franche Comté). The acquisition gave him an authority in the dependent kingdom of Burgundy (or Arles) which had not been possessed since the time of Henry III. Prelates and magnates performed their long-neglected homage as far as Provence. The Duke of Zähringen, whose 'rectorship' had never been effective beyond the Jura, was compensated by the advocateship of the three bishoprics, Geneva, Lausanne, and Sion, round the Lake of Geneva, which fortified his ducal rule within the Jura, the first foreshadowing of modern Switzerland. Next year in October Frederick celebrated the eventful diet of Besançon in Franche Comté. It was attended by nobles of the whole Empire as well as by foreign envoys and legates from the Pope. Adrian IV took the occasion to complain of the unpunished ill usage of the Danish Archbishop of Lund by German brigands, but it was the singular language of his letter, or rather the way in which this was rendered into German, which roused a storm. The Pope wrote of '*conferring* the imperial crown' and of his willingness to confer even greater *beneficia*. In the Latin of feudal law, *conferre beneficium* meant to grant a benefice or fief, and Rainald of Dassel deliberately interpreted it as such when translating the letter for the benefit of the princes. The claim of Gregory VII to be suzerain of the Empire and the tendentious painting of Innocent II depicting Lothar as his vassal were well remembered, and when one of the legates, probably Cardinal Roland, asked, 'From whom does the Emperor hold the Empire if not from the Pope?' he barely escaped with his life. The whole theory of the Empire and its independence seemed at stake. The German episcopate repudiated the papal insinuation as they thought it, and Adrian, knowing that the Emperor was coming to Italy in great force to make his rule effective, was obliged to swallow the summary dismissal of his legates and to aver that his Latin was classical and meant that he had conferred a benefit, not a benefice.

The Pope's secular policy, however, had changed earlier than the diet of Besançon. Disappointed of the Emperor's help in 1155, he had yet made himself the pivot of the insurrection of the Apulian barons against William I, but, as we have seen, the Byzantine invasion of Apulia was defeated, and he himself was blockaded in Benevento and forced to agree to William's terms (June 1156). The treaty implied a change of alliances. The cardinals were divided into two parties, one desirous of co-operation with the Emperor, the other upholding the ideals of Gregory VII and inclined to bid for the support of the Sicilian king, Barbarossa's inevitable adversary. The latter party, headed by the eminent canon-lawyer, Roland, who was the chief legate at Besançon, was now the stronger.

Frederick prepared for the Italian expedition by a campaign to secure his eastern frontier. Duke Boleslav of Poland was compelled to do homage and to pay heavy fines for his recalcitrance. The submissive Vladislav of Bohemia was given the title of king in return for a large contingent for Italy. In July 1158 Barbarossa crossed the Alps by the Brenner in unprecedented strength. He found the Lombard cities, as ever, divided. Aggressive Milan had destroyed Lodi and Como. Her enemies Pavia and Cremona were for the Emperor. A brief siege induced the unprovisioned Milanese to yield, and Frederick proceeded to hold a memorable diet of the *Regnum Italicum* at Roncaglia. The study of Justinian's Code had flourished at Bologna for fifty years, and four celebrated doctors expounded the doctrine of the absolute rule of the Roman Emperor. Their pronouncement gave a theoretical support for his practical aims, which were to resume the direct rule of the cities and to obtain from their wealth the resources so much needed for the monarchy. The republican autonomy of the cities was the result of usurpation and prescription; it was rarely, and then vaguely, based on imperial charters. This unwarranted state was to be done away. Frederick reclaimed the *regalia*, the customs and tolls, mints, and jurisdiction, including the appointment of the consuls and above all of a single official, the *podestà*, to exercise the imperial rights of government in each. The clock was put back and more, for the podestàs were nominated officers, not like the bishops, counts, and viscounts of earlier, feudal administration. It was a death-blow to the hardly won and painfully developed autonomy of the cities.

Needless to say, the Emperor replaced the internecine civic wars by his decisions on their disputes. It was a benefit most unwelcome to their passions and ambitions, and was embittered to Milan and her allies by Barbarossa's hostile sentences. Milan was to lose half her territory, little Crema, the enemy of Cremona, her necessary walls. Resistance began immediately; Milan and Crema refused to obey and were put to the ban of the Empire. With reinforcements brought by Henry the Lion, Frederick ravaged the open country and in July 1159 besieged Crema. The little city held out with such heroism that he had recourse in vain to the cruel method of binding his captives to his siege-engines which were shot at, and only gained surrender through famine after six months. Meantime the breach with the Pope was widening. The *regalia* in the Papal State, the lands of Matilda (which Frederick had enfeoffed to Welf VI), the homage (as distinct from the fealty) of the Italian bishops, and even the nominal sovereignty of Sardinia and Corsica were in dispute. Adrian's terms would have erased all intervention of the Emperor in his nominal capital. In this discord Barbarossa attempted to link up with the Roman Senate with little success, while the Pope allied himself with the revolted Lombard cities. A direct conflict of Empire and Papacy was imminent when on 1 September 1159 Adrian IV died at Rome.

Feeling ran high in the College of Cardinals between the two parties and produced a stormy double election, which meant a fresh schism in the Western Church and a renewed war between the two heads of Christendom. In a tumultuous meeting on 7 September the imperialist minority chose Cardinal Octavian, an old friend of the Emperor, as Victor IV, while the majority proclaimed their ablest man, Cardinal Roland, who took the name of Alexander III (1159–81). Neither group was strong enough to remain in Rome, and it was their first task to win over the Western states, for each claimed to be the sounder, if not also the larger, party. Alexander and his following from the first showed an unbending confidence; Octavian knew himself a dependant and relied on his political value to the Emperor. On the news Frederick went warily. There was a schism, but he dared not openly dictate a solution. Rather he claimed that as Emperor it was his duty to summon a General Council which should decide between the rivals. But few prelates, save his vassals, attended his Council at Pavia in February 1160, and other monarchs did not commit themselves. Octavian of course appeared; Alexander in accordance with his principles firmly and wisely refused to submit his claims to its decision. The Council duly declared for Octavian, who was accepted by his patron Frederick, and the schism became an axiom of imperial policy inextricably involved with the revival of the Empire in Italy and the subjugation of the Lombard communes.

Undismayed, Alexander took up the challenge. He excommunicated Anti-Pope and Emperor and released Frederick's subjects from their allegiance. What was more effective, he assiduously won over the episcopate outside the Empire to his cause; even in Germany the Archbishop of Salzburg was an Alexandrine. All Barbarossa's energies were occupied by the Lombard war with the aid of Milan's rivals. In 1161, reinforcements from Germany enabled him to blockade the rebellious city, but it needed a year before she was starved into surrender. Rigour, excessive even to her enemies, was dealt out to her, for Frederick's aim was to quell his opponents by terror and to leave them helpless. Milan was razed to the ground and her citizens dispersed into four villages. Her allies, Brescia and Piacenza, lost their walls, and all Lombardy was placed under the yoke of imperial podestàs. Barbarossa seemed to have acquired the rich domain needed by the Emperors. An attack on Sicily, assisted by the fleets of his vassals, Pisa and Genoa, appeared feasible.

Alexander, however, knew where his strength lay. He left Campagna in a Sicilian galley for Genoa and France (1162). Through all the Midi he was received with devotion, and the kings of France and England were at least inclined to him. Frederick also turned northwards, in the hope of using the enmity between the French and English kings to persuade Louis VII to change sides at a personal meeting at St Jean-de-Losne on the frontier.

Louis very nearly committed himself, but at the last moment the influence and diplomacy of Alexander were victorious and the meeting fell through. He brought about an accord between Louis and Henry II, which resulted in the two solemnly recognizing him as true Pope at Coucy-sur-Loire. Frederick had been baffled. The cause of Octavian within the Empire itself was on the wane, and the essential struggle between Papacy and Empire was less and veiled by the papal schism.

In Italy the grievous yoke of Frederick's podestàs was rapidly ripening the germs of revolt, and dulling in the common suffering and indignation the inter-city hatreds which prevented union. A national patriotism was for the time overlaying and absorbing the intense city patriotism of the Lombards. Allies were ready-made in the threatened or ambitious powers outside, the Pope, the King of Sicily, the Byzantine Emperor and independent Venice. Barbarossa was in Italy in 1163 when Verona, Padua and Vicenza rose in joint rebellion, the nucleus of a league. He bribed Pavia and other cities with privileges without making headway against the rebels, when a further misfortune befell him in the death of his Anti-Pope (April 1164). Since 1156 Rainald of Dassel, first his chancellor and then (1159) Archbishop of Cologne, had been the congenial inspirer and ablest instrument of his policy. Now the headstrong minister egged him on to the hasty and outrageously uncanonical election of a new Anti-Pope Guido of Crema (Paschal III). The act was most unwelcome to the German episcopate, who had stood willingly by Victor IV, but now hoped for the closing of the schism and had no belief in the claims of Paschal. Only Rainald among the metropolitans was for him, and it required depositions and much compulsion to bring the German clergy to heel. By force of character and threats of severe punishment Frederick indeed extorted at Würzburg in 1165 an oath from the princes never to recognize Alexander, but even then the province of Salzburg was obstinate and punished by the confiscation of Church lands. The churchmen's support of the schism was henceforth reluctant. Alexander III felt strong enough to return to Rome, and the canonization of Charlemagne by the Anti-Pope was a feeble rejoinder.

Barbarossa, weakened in public opinion, and aware of Lombard exasperation, resolved to crush his adversaries by overwhelming force (November 1166). He was detained himself by the siege of Ancona, a necessary base, but two archbishops, Rainald and Christian of Mainz, routed the Romans, and Frederick was able in July 1167 to capture the Leonine City. Alexander was firm against compromise and fled from Rome, when the Romans wavered and submitted. With a fleet arriving from imperialist Pisa, it seemed as if the conquest of Sicily and the young King William II was certain. But Frederick had delayed too long. Caught in August heat of the malarious Campagna, the German army was

Fig. 116. Rainald of Dassel, Archbishop of Cologne, 1159–67

attacked by a deadly pestilence, which pursued it even when it made
a retreat in panic northwards. To the age it appeared a judgement of God.
The flower of Frederick's army and the best of his counsellors, including
Rainald, were dead before he reached the Apennines to cross a hostile
Lombardy. During his absence in the south, city after city had joined the
Lombard League of resistance. In April 1167, as a symbol of their union,
the Confederates began the swift rebuilding of Milan, which became as

570

great as ever. Hardly any cities, like Pavia, still held to the Emperor. When Frederick, as a hunted fugitive with a remnant of his soldiery, sought to escape to Germany, he could only do so over the Mont Cenis Pass by favour of the Count of Savoy.

The Lombards well knew Barbarossa would not abandon the struggle. Their League now embraced most of their cities, and in concert they founded a new town, Alessandria, named after their ally the Pope, at the junction of the rivers Bormida and Tanaro, where it commanded the routes of western Lombardy. Alexander deftly treated with the Mediterranean powers; he was as resolute against a compromise as ever, and a new Anti-Pope, John of Struma (Calixtus III), was feebler than the deceased (1168) Guido of Crema. Frederick meanwhile was pacifying the ever-recurrent feuds in Germany, especially those of Henry the Lion with Saxon magnates like Albert the Bear (*ob.* 1170), and in enlarging his own predominance. In 1169 he carried through the election of his second and ablest son Henry as King of the Romans. In central Italy the death of his cousin Welf VII left the elderly Welf VI childless, and he agreed to sell his fiefs, Tuscany, Spoleto and the Matildine lands, to the Emperor. Frederick was thus enabled to attempt a real imperial administration by the warrior archbishop Christian of Mainz, in a land where the communes had not been vexed by podestàs. But the acquisition had the unfortunate result of beginning a rift between him and Henry the Lion, which was exacerbated later when the impecunious Welf VI, having sold the succession of his family lands round Altdorf in Swabia to Henry and not obtained the price, resold it to his other nephew Frederick, who paid at once to clinch the bargain. Henry found himself ousted from half the family lands. His marriage to the daughter of Henry II of England and his pilgrimage to Jerusalem (1072) were also factors in a dislike of Frederick's Italian policy.

In 1174 Barbarossa crossed the western Alps to renew the conquest of Lombardy. Aversion to the campaign reduced his forces, from which Henry the Lion was conspicuously absent. The failure of the six months' siege of Alessandria induced him to enter into negotiations with the League and Alexander III. When these fell through, he again summoned troops from Germany, but the response was inadequate, for Henry stubbornly refused to come in spite of Frederick's humiliating prayers in a personal interview at Chiavenna. Nevertheless Frederick took the offensive, only to meet with a crushing defeat from the League on 29 May 1176 near Legnano. The Lombards, horse and foot, were at length victorious in a pitched battle against the furious charges of the German knights. Frederick lost his shield and banner, his treasure and the best part of his army, and fled to imperialist Pavia. The war of reconquest and the hope of the direct rule of the Lombard cities could not survive this decisive overthrow.

Frederick recognized at last that the policy of twenty years and the attempt to maintain a subservient Pope, which had spilt so much blood, had failed, but he meant to give up neither his authority over the German Church nor the project of controlling, if not exploiting, the Lombard republics. His talents as statesman and diplomatist, ripened with age, were never more displayed than when he changed his course and pursued his aims by conciliation and the skilful use of the formidable strength that was still his in law and arms. His first object was to effect reconciliation with the Pope. Alexander, too, was eager to end the disastrous conflict which divided the Western Church while events were in his favour, and less than three weeks were sufficient for the imperial envoys to come to an agreement with him in the preliminary Treaty of Anagni (November 1176). Barbarossa was to acknowledge Alexander as the true Pope and as possessor of the *regalia* in the Patrimony of St Peter, but Alexander conceded, what he had hitherto denied, that the schismatic German bishops should retain their sees. In secular matters there was to be a fifteen years' truce between the Emperor and Sicily, and one for six years between him and the Lombard League. Sicily might be satisfied, but the Lombards naturally felt that the Pope had left their autonomy unguaranteed in a separate peace. Thus, when Emperor and Pope and envoys gathered for a brilliant congress of all parties at Venice, it took some months of arduous and perilous negotiations before, by the efforts of Alexander and the Sicilians, a fresh breach was avoided. At last in July 1177 Frederick was absolved and came face to face in an emotional scene with the Pope, to whom he did customary reverence, and on 1 August the Treaty of Venice was solemnly ratified. The schism came to an end and the Pope could prepare for a General Council to repair the multiple disorders of the Church. One measure of the highest importance was the introduction of the majority rule in papal elections. Henceforward a two-thirds majority of the cardinals was prescribed, and their choice was thereby elevated to the Papacy. Although it was still possible that a vacancy, when two-thirds of the votes could not be mustered, might be prolonged, a double election should henceforward be out of the question. Alexander III's pontificate had manifested a political wisdom and capacity to rule more mature than Frederick's, just as his Church legislation was more civilized in mentality and method than the rude and clumsy secular laws of the time. Always a subtle lawyer, he had, without losing his native courage, exchanged the hot, overweening temper of his earlier days for a sober moderation in his victory over the schism. He closed his momentous pontificate on 30 August 1181.

(5) HENRY THE LION AND THE LAST YEARS OF BARBAROSSA'S REIGN

The last phase of the Lombard war had seen the breakdown of the accord between Welf and Hohenstaufen on which Frederick had based his power in Germany. The Emperor now did not need to bolster his authority by a kind of partnership, and was full of rancour at his cousin's desertion of his cause at Chiavenna. Henry the Lion's career had been that of a nearly independent ruler of his two duchies. Besides insisting on the obedience of their nobles, he threw himself into the work of German expansion, the *Drang nach Osten,* so recently revived, and into its concomitant, the promotion of commerce and of municipal life. It was he who intervened in the Danish civil wars, and became the protector of the victor, Waldemar I, whose disobedience he checked by a three years' war. The conquest of the Wends on the lower Elbe was systematically undertaken with the cooperation of the Danes, who were provoked by their piratic incursions. The old raids and massacres were superseded by the latest siege-warfare and organized campaigns. Submission was made inevitable. The years

Fig. 117. Lion monument erected by Henry the Lion in Brunswick in 1166

1160–2 saw the last serious revolt crushed after hard fighting by the allies. Compulsory Christianity made rapid progress after the conquest of the Obodrites, and Henry acquired the right to invest the three missionary bishops of Oldenburg (in Holstein), Mecklenburg, and Ratzeburg. The Wends worshipped as Henry, a hard taskmaster, directed. But Henry made the conquered region a Saxon and Netherlandish colony too. The Germans, with their fecundity and industry, were, like the Northmen earlier, the chief colonizing people of the later Middle Ages. Domestic oppression and feudal wars may have further incited them, but the practice of reclamation from marshy coasts and river estuaries and the density of their population sent forth a crowd of Frisian and Flemish emigrants to like waste and difficult lands eastwards on the favourable terms offered by the conquering and, later, the conquered lords. There was a system and organization in the adventure, which testifies to the singular advance in rationality and forethought in Western Europe which was, like the shadow of a dial, stealing 'from its figure and no pace perceived', and contrasted strangely with the elemental passions and cold-blooded ferocity glaringly obvious beside it. The most common method became the employment of a professional *locator*, usually a townsman, who gathered the colonists, allotted their shares on free, hereditary tenure, built the church, and took a privileged holding as *Bauermeister*. These rent-paying settlements without, and also within, old Saxony and Thuringia prospered and multiplied and were imitated by the Slavs themselves and even in Hungary. Henry's rival Albert the Bear was similarly busy in Germanizing his March of Brandenburg, and the Margraves of Meissen and Lusatia did the like, but treated the Wends better. Something like the same process was taking place in the Eastern Alps by Bavarians among the Slovenes and Ladins. They, too, assimilated their Slav neighbours, if with difficulty. The emigration and the fear of it benefited the peasants left behind. The lords were obliged to improve conditions lest they too should fly to the frontier, and the market for their produce grew with the growth of trading towns. Labour services began to be commuted, personal freedom granted. In northern Saxony the lord's bailiff (*Meier*) would prosper at both his expense and that of his fellow peasants. The process, not peculiar to Germany, was there set going by the movement of expansion. Other influences were more pacific and less arbitrary than magnates of Church and State. The Cistercians and the Premonstratensians sent colonies of monks and lay brothers to found abbeys among clearings in the vast forests beyond the Elbe. Like the laymen they brought a better agriculture and increased the cultivated land and its population, reaching the already Christian and expanding Poles. Nominal Christianity at least, as well as Germanic government and institutions, were overthrowing the paganism and tribalism of the Wends, and advancing the frontiers of Germany towards the east.

The patronage of trade and town life was no less an activity of Henry the Lion. He forced Count Adolf of Holstein to give up the port of Lübeck, which he had founded (1143), and transferred thither (1160) the see of Oldenburg. Lübeck soon became the chief centre of the rich Baltic trade and the immense fisheries of the Sound. In Bavaria he captured the profitable trade-route over the river Isar by building the bridge and founding the town of Munich, the duchy's future capital. But his predominance, in any case distasteful to the Saxon magnates, lay and ecclesiastical, was made hateful to them by his strictness and his unscrupulous greed of fresh possessions. In 1166 he had to fight a powerful combination of them. The death of Albert the Bear (1170) relieved the tension only for a time. In 1178 a feud broke out between him and the Bishop of Halberstadt, backed by Philip, Archbishop of Cologne. The Emperor, returned from Italy, was a vindictive arbiter.

The legal proceedings were long and complicated, for Henry was tried by two laws, tribal (the Swabian to which he was amenable by descent) and feudal, but they ended in 1180 in a complete deprivation of his duchies and fiefs of whomsoever held. The March of Styria was then shorn from Bavaria as a separate duchy like Austria, while the Bavarian dukedom was conferred on the Emperor's confidant, Count Otto of Wittelsbach, whose descendants held it until 1918. Saxony was even more drastically treated. It was divided into two, Westphalia being separated as a duchy for the Archbishops of Cologne, and the rest becoming a reduced duchy of Saxony for Bernard of Anhalt, a son of Albert the Bear. The Saxon and Bavarian bishoprics remained as before direct imperial fiefs. It was a revolutionary change in the map of Germany. Of the tribal duchies only Swabia (less the duchy of Zähringen) and reduced Bavaria retained some solidarity. Franconia and the two Lotharingias had already broken up. Now Saxony, the most important of all, was really dissolved. In place of the formidable tribes of the past, Germany was now parcelled among innumerable principalities, among which the few dukes were equalled in power by princes, ecclesiastical and lay, of lower rank. The Emperor was delivered from over-mighty vassals, but he was left with less means to control the numerous provincial magnates, who were as unruly as ever. Further, the German custom that fiefs which escheated to the Crown should again be granted out was confirmed. Frederick gained no increment to the royal demesne by the confiscations from Henry. Rather, it was less easy to strengthen the Crown by escheats than before; it would be against acknowledged law. Skilful in gaining his immediate ends, Frederick had blundered for the future.

During legal proceedings, in which Henry refused to appear and indeed was condemned for contumacy, he had been waging successful war against his Saxon foes, but when the Emperor took the field in 1180, his cause was lost. Foreign alliances were broken reeds, his own vassals deserted him, Lübeck surrendered, and he had no choice but to make humble submission. His reception was effusive, but the terms were hard: he might retain his wide allodial lands round Brunswick and Lüneburg in Saxony, but must go into banishment for three years (1182–5), which he spent with his father-in-law, Henry II of England. When he returned, Lower Germany was in something like anarchy. The Saxon magnates, at war among themselves, were united in rebellious particularism, in which the lead was taken by Philip, the Archbishop of Cologne, to whom ecclesiastical grievances, coming to a head in the disputed election to Trier, gave occasion for disloyalty. Frederick was able to dissolve the dangerous coalition, but Saxony was left to its own devices save that Henry the Lion, a potential rebel, was again (1189) sent into exile. Denmark renounced its nominal vassalage to the Empire, and encroached south of the river Eider. In the west, however, Frederick achieved one of his familiar diplomatic successes: he entered into a firm alliance with Philip Augustus of France, like him a steady enemy of the English king and therefore of the Welfs

(1187). In 1178, too, he had returned from Italy through Provence and had had himself crowned King of Burgundy at Arles, after a virtual inter-regnum since Henry IV.

Barbarossa's heart, however, was still set on Italy, where he still hoped to attain a control at least equal to what he possessed in Upper Germany. It was advantageous that Pope Lucius III (1181–5) felt unsafe even in the Campagna from the Roman commune and had not won back the trust of the Lombard cities forfeited by the Treaty of Anagni. Frederick now courted reconciliation with them. A final peace was negotiated at Piacenza and concluded at Constance in June 1183. The cities admitted his sove-reignty, and were invested by him or their bishops with the *regalia*. They were to elect their consuls, levy their taxes, make their laws, and administer justice. They could retain their league —even Alessandria, renamed for a few years Cesarea, was recognized— and were to occupy much the same position as the princes of the Empire. Frederick in his new course was seek-ing the alliance if not the succession of Sicily. In his role of a popular suzerain he met (1184) at Verona the Pope, who came for refuge as a friendly partner. He acquiesced in the Emperor's greatest diplomatic triumph, when the young Henry was betrothed to the elderly heiress-pre-

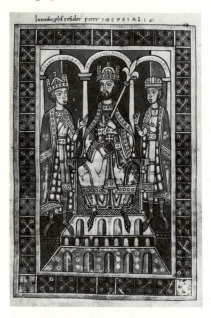

Fig. 118. The Emperor Frederick I with his sons, Duke Frederick of Swabia and King Henry VI

sumptive of Sicily, Constance, aunt of William II. There were, however, other crucial subjects of debate. The validity of the ordinations by Frederick's schismatic bishops and his right of nomination in the disputed election to Trier both involved his mastery of the German Church, and both were left unsolved. So was the question of Matilda's lands, of which the Emperor kept possession. The Pope, too, created a new precedent by re-fusing to crown King Henry Emperor in his father's lifetime—a coronation was a good asset in a bargain. This refusal was met by crowning Henry King of Italy and giving him the classic title of Caesar when he married Constance at Milan (27 January 1186). He was then left to act as his father's *alter ego* in Italy. Supported by the Milanese alliance, he was arbiter of Lombardy. An example was made of once imperialist

Cremona when she revolted; an imperial domain was built up in western Lombardy, and the Count of Savoy was driven back to the mountains. A more vigorous dominion was exercised in Tuscany, where communes like Florence were deprived of their *contadi* and the feudal lords encouraged. German garrisons and the Matildine lands backed up the revival of imperial government.

The chief obstacle in the way at first was the new Pope Urban III, a Milanese (1185–7), who attempted to resist on the inherited disputes but, unable to return to the Papal State, where Henry ravaged the Campagna, he was isolated from the Church by a kind of blockade at Verona and was forced to submit on all points. His successor Gregory VIII (1187) was an imperialist mainly concerned with the Third Crusade, and his policy was continued by the no less friendly Clement III (1187–91). The latter, however, succeeded in returning to Rome. The new imperial regime was in working order when Barbarossa left for the East in 1189. His reign closed in Cilicia (10 June 1190) in the height of his fame. The adroit diplomacy of his later years had secured more than frontal attack. Yet each of the small principalities and republics of the Empire was severally restive under imperial control. Their mutual enmities could be used to paralyse them, concessions could win momentary support, but fresh alliances incessantly sprang up, and it was hard to daunt so many potential adversaries with their obstinate particularism. The monolithic tribal structure of the past was ill replaced by a multitude of unmorticed bricks. Even the old large *Gaue* were divided by co-heirship and the feudal independence of great lords within them. There was no attempt outside Italy to construct a new central government by new royal officials to replace the now feudalized magnates. The German Church was still solid behind the Empire, but it too had its sectional grievances and its secular and particularist ambitions. Behind all was the Papacy, for the moment tethered, but unchanging in tradition and upheld by the convictions of Western Europe.

(6) THE FRENCH MONARCHY, 1108–1180[1]

In strong contrast to the dramatic events and European stage of Barbarossa's reign were the restricted activites of the kings of France. Yet their power steadily grew and provided a solid basis for future expansion more durable than the Empire's ill-knit edifice. Much was due to the hereditary nature of the kingship and the favourable location of the Capetian dynasty, much to the earlier advance of feudalism in France which had spent its most disruptive force there whereas in Germany it was still in its first vigour and reckless immaturity, much again to the fact that

---

[1] See Genealogical Table 13 above, p. 462.

the kings were too useful to the reforming Papacy to encounter its recurring enmity. But much, too, was due to the cautious, sober policy of the kings, who aimed at the immediately practicable, not the domination of Europe, and to their upright, loyal character, which gave them moral weight and inspired more trust in them than was the common lot of their contemporaries. They persistently, if with unequal talents, followed two main aims, the recovery of their authority first over the royal domain and then over the autonomous great fiefs; and opposition to the increase of the collection of territories amassed in France by the Norman-Angevin kings of England.

To reduce the royal domain, the Île de France, to order under their government was the essential preliminary, and this task was the life-work of the tireless warrior King Louis VI the Fat (1108–37). At his accession the condition of the domain was intolerably bad. Brigand barons oppressed their peasantry, plundered travellers and monasteries, and fought one another. The worst was Thomas of Marle, an ogre of insensate cruelty to all within his reach, but others vied with him in their careers of outrage. Year by year King Louis warred with these petty tyrants in battles and sieges of their castles. His perseverance and courage never flagged in enforcing at long last justice, security, and reparation. The anarchic lords were made to bow before the royal tribunal. He was the patron of trading townsman, peasant, and churchman, and a comparative order and prosperity reigned in the Île de France at his death. Its central government, the royal *Curia*, had been brought under the king's hand. At first the great household officers, the seneschal, chancellor, etc., had been members of baronial houses, greedy and unruly. The family of Garlande established almost a monopoly in curial dignities. It was only ousted in a three years' war (1128–30). Louis began the practice of either leaving these semi-feudal offices vacant or conferring them on distant great vassals, who could seldom exercise them. Actual administration was placed in the hands of lesser men dependent on the Crown, clerics for the most part or bourgeois. They were chosen for ability and fidelity. From 1130 onwards the famous monk Suger, Abbot of St Denis (*ob.* 1151), honest, orderly, and wise, was the chief adviser of the kings of France, helping by his capacity in business and government to bring about a better day.

If Louis VI devoted his main efforts to creating a solid monarchy in the Ile de France, which was the primary need, he did not neglect the prudent assertion of his rights and duties as suzerain of the great autonomous vassals of his kingdom. Their feudal service, if scanty, could still be relied on if their immediate, particularist instincts did not intervene, for the bond of feudal duty, on which they all depended, was growing stronger in spite of countless lapses. A kind of dynastic loyalty and pride in France was putting out its first shoots, and was shown on the memorable occasion in

August 1124, when the Emperor Henry V undertook an invasion in aid of his father-in-law Henry I of England and Normandy. The entire country rose eagerly and unanimously to repel the German invader, and the Emperor beat a hasty retreat. It was the first overt sign of a national feeling. Within the realm, Louis VI, when it was feasible, stood out as the champion of justice and protector of the oppressed. He restored the boy-lord of Bourbon, disinherited by his uncle. Twice over he vindicated the Bishop of Clermont against the attacks of the Count of Auvergne, the very thing

Fig. 119. Abbot Suger (d. 1151)

to rivet the loyalty of the episcopate. Less success attended him in the great and wealthy county of Flanders, which had developed a more than provincial self-consciousness. Its count, Charles the Good (1119–27), was sacrilegiously murdered at prayer in a church by a band of lawless nobles to the indignation of the townsmen. Louis hurried to the spot, punished the murderers, and insisted on his choice for an heir to the childless count among a crowd of claimants. He installed William Clito, nephew and enemy of his own foe Henry I of England, but the selection proved unwise. The blundering William ignored the townsmen, the strongest force, and relied on the retrograde country nobles in a feudal reaction. Louis' commands were flouted. The towns elected another claimant, Thierry

(Dietrich) of Alsace, William died in the civil war (1128), and Louis submitted to invest the victor.

This was evidence that the great vassals were not to be put in leading strings. Far more was provided by the recurrent war with Normandy. In 1106 Henry I of England had overthrown and captured its inept duke, his brother Robert Curthose (1087–1106), and began to tame the anarchic duchy. He soon fell out with his suzerain over the town of Gisors in the frontier district of the Vexin, which was divided between the two. Each allied with the other's enemies, Henry with the Count of Blois and Louis' pettier rebels, Louis with Fulk V of Anjou (1109–29) and Curthose's disinherited son, William Clito. In alternate raiding wars and treaties, Louis, although holding his own, had the worse. He was defeated at Brémule (1119) and acknowledged Henry's suzerainty of Brittany and Maine. The death of William Clito was another blow, and the marriage of Henry's heiress, the Empress Matilda, with Geoffrey the Fair, son and heir of Fulk, was a serious danger (1128), which was only partially allayed when (1135) Stephen of Boulogne, younger brother of Theobald of Blois, made good his claim to England and Normandy against Matilda on Henry I's death. War between Anjou and Normandy was an advantage to the French Crown, and Louis regained the loyalty of the Count of Blois and Champagne. At the same time an unexpected windfall appeared to place the French monarchy beyond the reach of competition. Duke William X of Aquitaine (1127–37) left his daughter and heiress Eleanor to his suzerain's care. Louis promptly married her to his son Louis VII, whom according to custom he had already crowned (1131), and who was taking up the inheritance of Aquitaine when his father died (1 August 1137). Louis VI had long suffered from such corpulence that he could not mount on horseback, but his energy had scarcely failed. His death was a loss to the monarchy, which he had so signally revived.

The young king inherited his father's probity and piety but not his political good sense. In his early years he was full of misdirected energy, in his later he displayed a pacific, yielding, gullible temper, which allowed him to be outmanœuvred by astute and powerful neighbours. Yet his virtues had their reward, and ended in preserving the traditional aureole of the kingship. 'He was a very Christian king, if somewhat simple-minded', was said of him. In the government of the royal domain at least he steadily followed his father's policy. He bestirred himself to punish oppression and defend the Church. He favoured peasant and bourgeois. He had no need of a guard among his direct subjects. As the reign went on the royal tribunal was able to take a more commanding tone towards the secondary rank of great vassals: they trusted in its decisions. He too gave his confidence to Abbot Suger and the able clerks and knights who staffed his Curia, and the administration such as it was grew in efficiency and strength.

In spite of his frequent mistakes in policy, the well-meaning monarch, backed by the growing force of feudal obligation, increased his prestige and called out a greater loyalty.

His mistakes, however, were many and a continual drag on the upward movement. In his early years, he neglected to oppose the conquest of Normandy (1136–44) from Stephen by the sturdy and shrewd Count of Anjou, Geoffrey the Fair (1129–51). Instead, he engaged in a twofold and sterile contest with the Papacy and with Theobald, Count of Champagne and Blois. Pope Innocent II insisted on an unwelcome Archbishop of Bourges. Count Theobald supported the Pope's legate in annulling the bigamous marriage of the Count of Vermandois with Queen Eleanor's sister to the detriment of his first wife, Theobald's niece. In the long war which followed, Louis perpetrated a massacre, typical of his time, at Vitry, but gained no decisive advantage and was moreover outwitted by St Bernard, who acted as a mediator for peace. At last he gave way on all points in dispute. His next aberration was to embark on the Second Crusade and to linger in the East after its collapse. Fortunately Abbot Suger, left as regent, ruled better than the absent king and preserved his throne.

A new political error of even greater danger succeeded the Crusade. Louis had been deeply in love with Queen Eleanor, but on the Crusade her conduct had been suspicious, and Louis obtained in 1152 the annulment of his marriage on grounds of consanguinity. He had not been able to control Aquitaine successfully, which diminished the immediate loss. Eleanor, however, who had only borne him daughters, promptly married the young Duke of Normandy, Henry II. Louis found himself suddenly confronted with a great vassal, whose collection of fiefs extended over Normandy, Maine, Anjou, and Aquitaine from the English Channel to the Pyrenees. Irresolution and inconsequence marred the whole of Louis' subsequent dealings with his rival. It is true that he was much inferior in resources of his own, and depended largely on unstable coalitions of the greater vassals, but his diplomacy also did not bear comparison with Henry's unscrupulous craft. His attempt (1152–3) to hinder Henry's campaign to win the English crown was a failure partly owing to the death of King Stephen's son and heir, Eustace of Boulogne, but mainly to his own ineptitude. Henry II, from 1154 King of England, was more formidable than ever.

Louis next endeavoured to live in peace and friendship with his too-powerful vassal. He reckoned without his host, who was then in his ambitious youth. The Norman Vexin had been the one compensation Louis had received from Count Geoffrey for the union of Normandy and Anjou. This was in 1158 made the dower of Louis's infant daughter on her betrothal to Henry's infant son, and given in trust to the Templars till their marriage, the future bride being handed over to Henry's care. The year before Louis had authorized the English king's annexation of part of and suzerainty of all Brittany. When Henry, however, besieged Toulouse in 1159 to enforce the suzerainty claimed by the dukes of Aquitaine over its count, Louis, his patience exhausted, made adroit use of his feudal rights in a feudally minded age. He entered the city in person. Henry flinched from besieging the suzerain to whom he had done homage, and retreated. He took his revenge in 1160 by suddenly marrying the two betrothed children and occupying the Norman Vexin. Once more the cheated Louis was forced in the end to acquiesce (September 1162).

This accord may have been partly due to the events of the papal schism. Louis, who had at first welcomed Alexander III, began to waver in his search for friends, and was nearly entrapped by Barbarossa into deserting him (August 1162). Henry II played a part in his escape from his entanglement, but Louis reaped most profit, for he henceforth acted as the host and ally of the Pope. With his pious instincts, moreover, it was natural for him to protect Archbishop Becket in his exile. The old grievances led to skirmishing wars until Henry II overreached himself. He was well aware that his motley fiefs could not long be held together and that his sons would demand shares. The younger, Richard, was to inherit Aquitaine, the elder, Henry, Louis's son-in-law, Normandy, Anjou and Maine with England. In 1169 Louis's sanction was given by his receiving the homage of the two young princes. This was to establish a direct feudal tie between him and them, which acquired a more than formal significance because Henry had lost or never gained the affection of his wife and sons, and their fierce and heedlessly grasping characters were a fatal flaw in the power of the Angevin dynasty, all the more dangerous as the fissures between its ill-assorted fiefs were deep and wide; only the iron hand and political genius of Henry II prevented disruption.

It was Henry's own diplomacy which first revealed the cracks in his ambitious edifice. In 1173, besides obtaining the homage of the Count of Toulouse, he secured for his youngest son John the betrothal of the child-heiress of Humbert III, Count of Savoy and Maurienne, thus extending his alliances beyond France into Burgundy and the Alps. Louis seemed hopelessly hemmed in, but Henry's three impatient, reckless sons, egged on by their mother, came to his rescue, while the Counts of Flanders and Champagne and others now looked askance at their formidable fellow-vassal. Young Henry, now nominally co-regent with his father, Richard, and Geoffrey, now Duke of Brittany, all fled to the French court to claim independence of Henry II in arms, and a widespread insurrection of malcontents broke out in England and Normandy. The peril to Henry II was great, for his neighbours attacked on all sides, but he and his able ministers and the bulk of his vassals stood firm and shattered the unwieldy, dislocated coalition led by the sluggish King of France. By September 1174 all Henry's rebels were imploring his pardon, the King of Scots was a captive, and Queen Eleanor was in prison. Beyond granting hospitality to his ever-undutiful son-in-law, the young King Henry, Louis henceforward lived in peace with the English king, even in amity. The death of the heiress of Savoy had removed one danger. Duke Richard ruled Aquitaine with small interference from his father since 1175, and the unstable, quarrelsome character of the young Angevins made their union in anything but rebellion remote. Louis's reign ended in a paralytic stroke on his return from a pilgrimage to Canterbury shortly before the coronation of his son Philip II (1 November 1179): his death occurred in September 1180. With all his errors he left the Crown stronger and more imposing, largely indeed owing to the general growth of feudal duty and orderly government, which was not his work, yet favoured by his own uprightness and benevolence.

(7) WILLIAM THE CONQUEROR AND THE SETTLEMENT OF ENGLAND

The two centuries following 1066 were a period of revolution and change which left a permanent mark on the English people.

The ease and speed of King Harold II's election on Edward the Confessor's death were a measure of the danger in which the English kingdom stood. William of Normandy was demanding the crown and reproaching Harold for his breach of fealty. With some difficulty he was rallying the Norman barons to the perilous adventure, he was sending to Rome to obtain Pope Alexander's blessing on it, and he was recruiting volunteers from Brittany, Flanders and even from central France by promises of a share in the spoil. Under Hildebrand's influence the Pope was induced to send a consecrated banner, which disguised the purely aggressive character of the enterprise. William had earned a good repute with the Church reformers, whose earlier programme he was carrying out in his duchy, making good appointments, enforcing discipline, and founding monasteries. Besides, his own private life was exemplary in strong contrast to his lawless contemporaries. Ships were built and provisions were collected for the Channel crossing after harvest. Altogether William gathered, it seems, something like 5000 men, of whom perhaps 2000 were knights and sergeants trained to fight either on horseback or on foot, while there was a large contingent of archers among the footmen, who themselves wore mail. The army was numerous for its day, and the more formidable through its expertness and the feudal discipline it possessed.

All through the summer Harold kept ships manned on the south coast to attack the Norman flotilla when it sailed, but with the harvest the crews disbanded to their fields. Contrary winds which prevented William sailing made Harold's wise sea defence premature, and fresh events dislocated his land defence. His brother Tostig joined forces with King Harald Hardrada and the two with a large Viking fleet entered the Humber. Harold was obliged to ride north with his housecarls in aid of Edwin and Morcar, who before he reached them had been defeated at Fulford. Over the invaders he won the splendid victory of Stamford Bridge (25 September 1066). Hardrada and Tostig both fell, and the remnant of the Vikings were glad to take ship homewards. But the English forces were depleted in the mutual slaughter, and the weather once more turned against Harold, for the wind veered and William's flotilla was able to cross the Channel unopposed. He disembarked at Pevensey (29 September). On the news Harold rode south, and unhappily, flushed with victory, hastened to give battle with only the south-eastern levies to reinforce the housecarls. When William attacked him (14 October) on the low ridge of the later Battle Abbey near Hastings, the repeated charges of the Normans won a hard-fought but complete victory over the English, whose greater number was offset by many of them being ill-armed peasants. The best of the vanquished fell on the field, but the fatal loss was the deaths of King Harold and his brothers Gyrth and Leofwine.

This decisive event determined the future course of English history. No national leader was left. The Witan in London, led by Stigand, declared for the boy Edgar Atheling, but they did not venture to crown him, and Edwin and Morcar, perhaps from weakness, made no effort to defend him. Duke William, with a generalship unusual in his age, reduced Kent, received the submission of Winchester, and then marched west to Wallingford, where he crossed the Thames, and cut off London from the north by advancing eastward. The party of surrender won the upper hand in London. They submitted, with Edgar Atheling, to the Conqueror, and on Christmas Day 1066 he was crowned at Westminster by Ealdred of York, for Stigand, although he made terms, was unrecognized by the Papacy.

William the Conqueror (1066–87) now looked on himself as the legitimate successor of King Edward. He rewarded his followers by distributing as fiefs the lands of those who fought against him at Hastings; he was busy building castles in the Norman fashion at key-points in the large stretch of the country which submitted. He assumed that all land, even Church estates, was held from him on feudal terms. Otherwise he claimed to maintain the laws and rights of the Confessor's day. He did not have long to wait for general recognition. The northern earls, Edwin, Morcar, and Waltheof, all made their submission, and in March 1067 he felt it safe to revisit Normandy, taking them and Edgar Atheling with him and leaving his half-brother Odo Bishop of Bayeux and his seneschal William Fitz Osbern to rule the conquered land.

Their government, however, and the bitterness of conquest fanned the embers of resistance into flame. In 1068 there were wide revolts in progress in the north and west, all but autonomous districts which had not yet felt the Conqueror's heavy hand. But the opposition was provincial, not national; there was no common cause to bind the English together; and men like Waltheof, Edwin, and Morcar, or the guerrilla chief Edric the Wild in Shropshire or the curiously colourless Edgar Atheling, who all took part, were not of a calibre to be leaders of a nation. The surrender of Devon and Cornwall was quickly effected by William; in Yorkshire and western Mercia the fighting, if desultory, was long and severe, and given fresh heart by a Danish fleet sent on his own account by Swein Estrithson, the heir of Canute. But William's generalship, based on a network of rapidly built, strategically placed castles, broke in detail the haphazard, ill-soldered coalition. In 1069–70 he took terrible revenge on his English foes, which rendered another uprising impossible. With a cold-blooded ferocity, surpassing Charlemagne's in Saxony, he systematically devastated the archdiocese of York from sea to sea, and with less completeness Cheshire, Shropshire, Staffordshire and Derbyshire. The aim—and it succeeded—was to exterminate the stubborn population. Twenty years later Domesday Book records that the greater part of the ravaged districts was uncultivated waste. The barbarous action has left an indelible and revealing stain on its perpetrator. One more forlorn hope was led by Hereward, a petty Lincolnshire thane, who held out heroically in the fens of the Isle of Ely for a year. It failed, and at the close of 1071 William was unquestioned master. Waltheof and Edric the Wild were submissive, Edwin was dead, Morcar a prisoner, and Edgar Atheling an exile in Scotland, to whose king, Malcolm III Canmore, he had married his saintly sister Margaret, the possessor of those ruler's gifts of which he himself, in spite of all his activity, seems to have been devoid. In 1072 Malcolm was forced to peace and some kind of homage by William in person, and the unlucky Atheling left for Flanders.

The prolonged resistance which William overcame produced changes of fundamental importance in the Norman Conquest of England. First, the ruling aristocracy, the baronage, became almost entirely Norman and French, and the theory, never so much as a half-truth, that the Conqueror had merely taken over the kingship of Edward the Confessor became more than half a fiction. In his early years William had been quite ready to retain the service of trusty English collaborators, whose knowledge of English laws and personal influence eased the transition and acted as a buffer between the natives and the newcomers. Such was Aethelwig, Abbot of Evesham (1058–77), who was entrusted with a general oversight over seven West Mercian shires, and who used his office to protect his unfortunate countrymen as well as the king's interests. But the vast confiscations after 1069 resulted in the transfer of land and power from English to Norman lords under the feudal system prevailing in Normandy. All English land was now held of the king, even the Church lands, on feudal terms with the usual feudal duties and rights, including for the most part defined knight-service in war, which provided an expert force of mailed cavalry, to act as a garrison of the conquered country and an army for offence and defence against neighbours and foes, for the knights were enfeoffed or retained in law for the king's service alone. Englishmen might find a place in the lower ranks of this feudal hierarchy, but they were swamped among the majority of invading settlers. Beneath the class which held by knight's service the condition of the conquered population altered for the worse even within the Danelaw south of Humber. The invaders were too few to cause much actual displacement of unimportant people. There were the free tenants, called *socmen*, who held of their lord by rents and light services, but the Normans were hostile to the system which allowed such to choose their lord—subjection became hereditary. The ordinary peasant was classed as a *villein* (*villanus*) if his holding were on the average a yard-land, as a *cottar* or *bordar* if it were but small. He was tied to the soil, and the free to a great extent were merged in the unfree. Serfdom in practice and in the next century in formal law became the dominant condition. The net outcome was increased exploitation of the peasantry in services and dues. At the same time, the new lords had a strong interest in the prosperity and larger population of their manors. They assarted woodlands, drained fens, built churches and mills. Revival went on apace. Black sheep, stupidly tyrannic and greedy, there were, but they were not typical nor encouraged by William. None the less the changes, carried out with such business-like, organized address amounted to a political, social, and economic revolution. England was changed into a fully feudal state. Courts of the 'honour', i.e. the assemblage of the baron's manors, determined the disputes of its knightly tenants and tried offences over which the baron had jurisdiction; the manor courts dealt with lesser men, the serfs, and their disputes and crimes. The manor indeed was still in 1086 in process of formation: it might be very large or very small: it was not yet rounded into self-contained, exclusive units, and its composition and organization at a much later date varied enormously between the Danelaw and Mercia or Wessex.

William, however, fully intended to preserve the prerogatives of his Anglo-Saxon predecessors, and their rights of legislation, jurisdiction and taxation, which were in such strong contrast to the powers of the Capetian kings of France, where the tenant-in-chief ruled unchallenged in his fief. William raised the Danegeld on landholders at his will. The sheriff represented him in the shires and held the county, or shire, court, in which the 'pleas of the Crown' and disputes between the tenants of different barons were dealt with, and the hundred courts for minor offences save when the hundred court had been granted to a baron or prelate. The Anglo-Saxon frith-gilds were developed into a system of frank-pledge, in which groups of ten, or *tithings*, were responsible for one another's behaviour. All freemen were liable to be called out in the fyrd as aforetime. The king, the warden of justice, never allowed himself to be excluded from any franchise or honour, however great, if he was implored to remedy wrong or his commands were disregarded. No barons were allowed the right of private war. His legislation, if scanty, was far reaching. Lord and hundred were fined if a Frenchman was found slain by an unknown hand, the crime of *murdrum*. The death-penalty of English laws was changed into mutilation. Ordeal by single combat came in with feudal law. Along with new regulations on Church matters, perhaps the most dynamic of William's innovations was the Carolingian prerogative, assumed by great vassals in France, of the right of inquest, i.e. that all men must answer the king's questions on their oath. It was on this principle that the famous Domesday Inquest was founded, and that unparalleled survey did in fact force every baron and subtenant to admit that they held their tenements by the king's grant and that his writ and seal were their only effective guarantee.

The central government of England, too, underwent a subtle and fruitful transformation. The Witan of former times became also a feudal court, which every tenant-in-chief of the Crown was bound on summons to attend, there to give his counsel and aid. But it retained its elastic character, and the usual meeting of household officers and two or three prelates and barons was as much the Curia Regis as was the large assembly for the most important business held on the three great festivals of the year when the king wore his crown. Thus the way was clear for future kings to utilize their feudal Curia as the chief organ of government, in which and from which departments of State for special functions were in due time developed.

Both by character and circumstances William the Conqueror was an absolute king, who established a new kind of feudal monarchy, whose nearest affinity was in his duchy of Normandy. His barons owed their own safety to him, and were chary of provoking their formidable overlord, whose interests were so largely theirs. The material backing for both was the judicious allotment of the land. It has been calculated from the returns in Domesday Book that in 1086 the total yearly revenue from the land, exclusive of the towns, may be reckoned in round numbers in the money of the period as £73,000. Of this £17,650 were reserved for the king and his kin, £1800 for personal servants, the royal sergeants, £19,200 for the Church, £4000 for the dwindling pre-Conquest landowners, and £30,350 for 170 incoming barons, great and small. The royal manors were more evenly distributed over the kingdom than the Confessor's had been, thus providing the king a foothold in most counties, and by hook or crook his

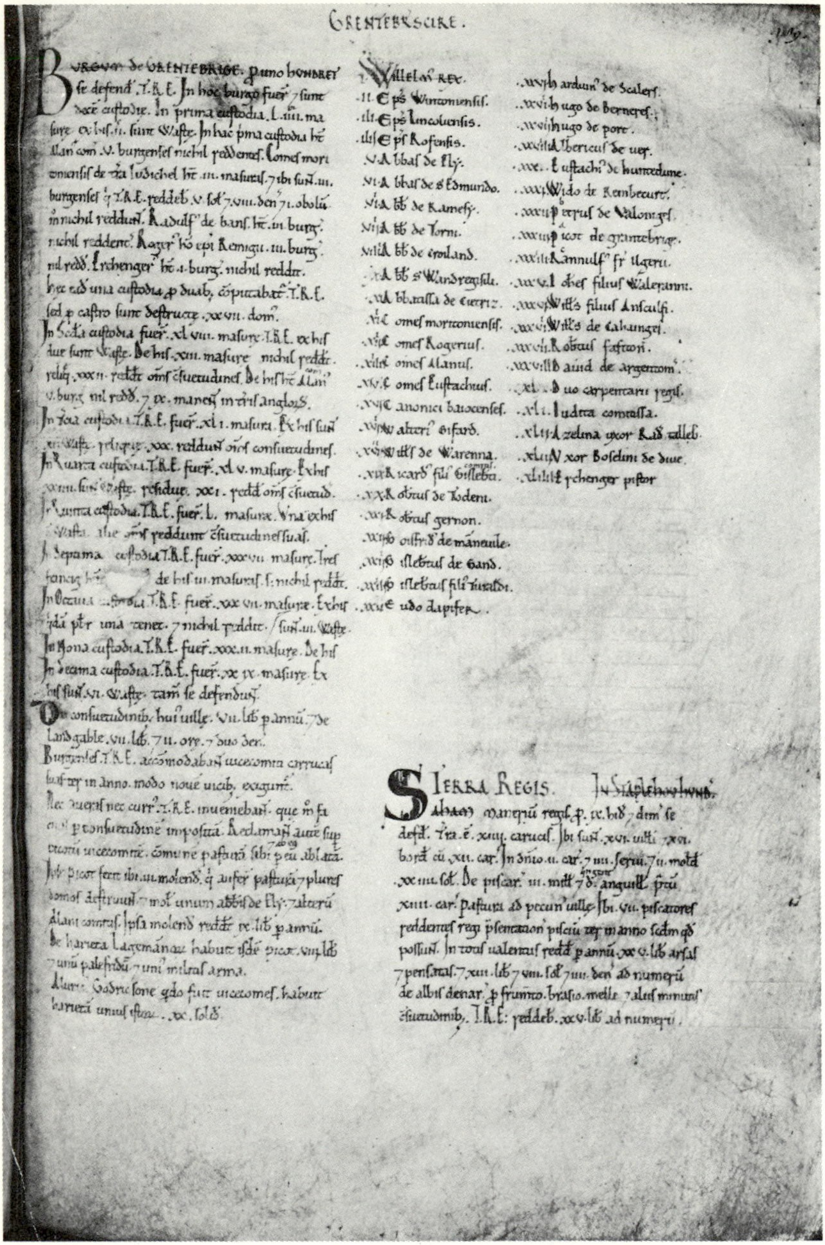
GRENTEBRSCIRE.

Fig. 120. Cambridgeshire in Domesday Book

sheriffs and reeves increased their returns. On the dangerous borders William granted compact fiefs with ample jurisdiction, against Wales for instance the three palatine earldoms of Chester, Shrewsbury and Hereford, and in Sussex some four great honours, but the marcher earls drew their best income from more profitable estates than their ravaged counties. The provincial earldoms of the past were abolished: William's few earls were of single counties and save on the frontier checked by the king's sheriffs. Their estates, too, like those of other barons were scattered far and wide. William, when he wished, concentrated land for a special purpose, but otherwise his distribution seems almost haphazard; perhaps he was merely reluctant to grant too many compact fiefs. The apportionment of knight-service also appears erratic: some barons were more heavily burdened than others of greater wealth: perhaps the value of the grants was only roughly estimated when they were made. The quotas of knights commonly ran from five upwards in round numbers to fit in with the organization of the feudal array of constabularies of ten men. There was no obligation on the baron to enfeoff the full number of his quota or to limit his enfeoffments to the knights he owed the king. On the contrary, in the eleventh century he would keep a number of his knights as unlanded retainers round him. 'Castle-guard', i.e. of the king's castles, was one of the knights' duties, for baronial castles (which needed a royal licence) were rare except in the marcher earldoms.

William dominated the English Church nearly as much as the baronage. This by no means corresponded with the ideals of the Church reformers, to which he zealously adhered. Synods had ceased to be held. Canons and clergy were married men. Bishops sat in the county courts to administer ecclesiastical law. Simony, plurality and worldliness abounded. Stigand, its head, was a greedy pluralist, uncanonically elected and unrecognized by the Papacy. If there were still learning in the great abbeys and certain worthy bishops, both organization and zeal had declined since the days of Edgar the Peaceable. In 1070, Ealdred of York being dead, the Conqueror undertook to bring the Church up to the Norman level, and incidentally to place its high offices, with their wealth and power, in trusty Norman hands. Three papal legates arrived, under whose auspices Stigand and three other bishops were deposed. Vacant sees were filled with eminent foreigners. Canterbury was given to the Lombard Lanfranc of Bec, Abbot of Caen, William's most intimate adviser, York to Thomas, a canon of Bayeux. As vacancies occurred, bishoprics and abbeys were one after another filled by carefully selected immigrants. Sees in villages, like Dorchester-on-Thames, were moved to towns, like Lincoln. Synods were revived. Monastic discipline was tightened up and learning, especially in Latin, encouraged. Canons were obliged to celibacy, and the same was, vainly enough, prescribed for parish priests in the future. Lanfranc started a movement for the building of more splendid churches. He secured for the time, backed by forged documents, the primacy of all England in spite of the reluctance of Thomas of York.

William himself aided the reform by a decree removing cases in Canon Law from the county courts to the Courts Christian of the bishops, now set up, which were free from lay interference. But he had no notion of abdicating his own royal control. Throughout he appointed and invested bishops and abbots. Like his friend Lanfranc, he belonged to the earlier type of reformers, not the Hildebrandine, and he insisted that no Pope should be recognized in England without his leave, that papal letters should have no force in England without his approval, and even that none of his barons or officers should be excommunicated without his consent. When in 1080 Gregory VII demanded the arrears of Peter's Pence and endeavoured to obtain his fealty, he paid the arrears but refused the innovation of the fealty, and the Pope avoided an open breach with a monarch and arch-bishop whose zeal for the Church was manifest.

William's later years were mainly occupied with an indecisive contest with the Counts of Anjou over Maine and the revolt of his eldest son Robert Curthose. Outstanding events in England were few but momentous. In 1075 three greater earls, Roger second Earl of Hereford, Ralf second Earl of East Anglia, and Waltheof, by William's favour husband of his niece and Earl of 'Northumberland' (the ancient Bernicia) as well as of his original east-Midland earldom of Northampton, rebelled for obscure reasons, perhaps connected with their diminished powers—the last two were pre-Conquest lords. They met with so little support from the barons that the king did not need to return from Normandy to suppress them. Their forfeiture completed the disappearance of the provincial earldoms; even that of Hereford was not renewed, and Waltheof, a popular figure, was executed, although he had never taken the field. Yet more unexplained is the sudden arrest and imprisonment in 1082 of the Conqueror's half-brother Odo, Bishop of Bayeux and Earl of Kent. It established a pre-cedent, for William, to avoid a breach of the Canon Law, insisted that he was proceeding against his English earl, not his Norman bishop. Whatever was the legal offence, it may be conjectured that Lanfranc's enmity (of old standing) and the king's increasing greed of money were motives for the confiscation of the bishop's vast estates; it was one over-endowed baron the less.

The last of William's great achievements—perhaps the greatest—was the compilation in 1086 of Domesday Book, which was designed to give the taxable capacity of the kingdom south of the Tees with a view to the Danegeld. Wealth was power, and the king's power depended on his ability to pay his way. This wonderful survey was made by bands of commissioners on circuit who convened the shire-moots and put a list of questions to juries of each hundred containing both Normans and Englishmen, questions eliciting the number of manors, their assessment in hides, their liability to Danegeld, their ownership and annual value in the Confessor's time and in 1086, their arable, meadow, pasture and woodland, their plough-oxen and ploughs, their livestock, and the number and grades of their peasant families. A sequel to this inventory of the king's vassals and their possessions was to enforce as strongly as possible their paramount obligations to him. All landowners 'that were worth aught' were summoned to Salisbury in August 1086 to swear fealty to him against all men, even their immediate lords. The oath set the seal on English feudal law, and was William's last public act in England. He died on 7 September 1087 of an injury received in warfare against his own overlord, King Philip of France.

The epoch-making character of William's career and his personal genius have cast a glamour over his posthumous fame. He is in the first rank of statesmen. He united England lastingly as never before and made the dissolving realm a powerful kingdom. He loved order. When master, he could be just. He was genuinely religious according to his lights. But he was ruthless in the pursuit of ambition and power and even of his pleasures. He introduced into England the cruel forest law of France to protect his hunting, which he enlarged without justice or compassion as in the New Forest. He was exceptionally merciless in his conquest. That his ferocity was not aimless may be set down to his intellect. The age, it is true, was hardhearted and fierce, but there were exceptions, not all ecclesiastics, which condemn him.

(8) THE SUCCESSORS OF WILLIAM THE CONQUEROR, 1087–1154

The Conqueror designated his second son William Rufus (the Red) to succeed him in England in preference to the valiant and feckless Robert Curthose, whom he could not prevent inheriting Normandy. Rufus (1087–1100) was crowned in haste by Lanfranc, but there was vivid discontent among a powerful party of the barons, landed in both countries, who detested the division. Their revolt, headed by Odo of Bayeux, in favour of Duke Robert was speedily overcome by the king, who was upheld by a majority of the magnates and notably by the native English, who preferred royal to baronial oppression. One of the rebels, the Bishop of Durham, again raised at his trial the issue of lay jurisdiction over ecclesiastics, but was answered by king and Lanfranc that he was tried as a baron. Only one more outbreak occurred (1095), which was easily put down.

William was as eager as the malcontents to rule on both sides of the Channel. He, too, had his partisans in Normandy, who had wide lands in

England. Eastern Normandy went over to him, and he then joined with Robert in evicting their youngest brother Henry from the Cotentin (1091). His war with Robert was soon resumed, but was ended when the duke, seeking money for the First Crusade, pledged his duchy to William (1096) for a loan. The change meant a stronger, better, more aggressive rule.

Rufus, too, has the credit of fixing his northern frontier at the Solway, in spite of the King of Scots, Malcolm Canmore, and it was his intervention (1096) which finally placed the half-English King Edgar on the throne of Scotland as his vassal. Meanwhile in Wales the work of Norman expansion went on. Here the marcher lords were protagonists. They were thrown back from Gwynedd, but became dominant in South Wales.

In his internal government the king earned an evil name. After Lanfranc's death in 1090, his favourite minister was one of his chaplains, Ranulf Flambard, whom he made Bishop of Durham. This man was an expert in ingenious and oppressive exactions, and won general hatred. He levied excessive and novel feudal dues, unjust fines and profits in the county courts, and increased the severity of the Forest Law, all to enhance the royal income. His congenial advice led to William's quarrel with the Church. First Canterbury and then other sees and dignities were left vacant, and their income was enjoyed by the Crown until they were filled by simony. In 1093 the fear of imminent death in an illness drove the venal king to invest the saintly Anselm of Aosta, Abbot of Bec, with the primacy, but on recovery he resumed his old ways and obstructed both synods and reform. In the conflict between the two, William was manœuvred (1095) into recognizing Urban II as rightful Pope, an admission that neither he nor his father had conceded. No reconciliation followed, and in 1097 Anselm departed into exile, universally regarded as a martyr, while the king again seized the lands of the archbishopric. By his firmness in resistance Anselm had set up a new standard for the English Church, which was to culminate in the first struggle of Church and State in England.

The reign came to a dramatic end when Rufus was killed by an arrow (2 August 1100) shot seemingly by a lesser baron, Walter Tirel, whether by accident or design; no enquiry was ever made. Men's aversion to the vicious, violent, extortionate king was manifest. But he had insisted that the king's peace should be kept and the king's will be supreme throughout the land: there was no break in the Conqueror's tradition.

Happily Duke Robert, preferred for his indolence and weakness by the anarchic members of the baronage, was far away in Sicily returning from the Crusade. Henry, the youngest brother, trained in adversity, cool headed, strong-willed and patient, was on the spot. He rode to Winchester, seized the royal treasure, won over such great and orderly barons as were there, and was crowned at Westminster two days later. Once king (1100–35) he rallied all the partisans of order and good government by an inno-

*Fig. 121. William the Conqueror, William Rufus, Henry I
and Stephen as benefactors of Westminster Abbey*

vation, the issue of a coronation charter for the redress of grievances, the
first step towards a limitation of the Crown. He promised to fill Church
benefices and refrain from simony, and to abolish the evil innovations in
extortionate feudal dues of his brother's time. In earnest of his pledges he
arrested the unpopular Flambard and requested Anselm to return from

exile. To please the native English he betrothed himself to Edgar Atheling's niece, Edith of Scotland, an act which united his own usurping dynasty with the ancient royal house. Anselm brushed aside the fable that she was a nun, and celebrated the marriage. The only concession made to Norman prejudice was the new name of Matilda given to the bride. It was a symptom of a rapprochement between conquerors and conquered, if Norman-French continued to be the aristocratic language and Latin the language of documents.

So strong was Henry in England that he easily baffled with false promises a belated attempt of his listless, impecunious brother to assert his claims (1101). He then turned on the most dangerous fomenters of disorder, the great house of Bellême. Its chief, the wicked Robert, third Earl of Shrewsbury, Count of Ponthieu, and richest of Norman barons, was egged into rebellion, overcome in a month, and banished along with his brothers, while vast fiefs were confiscated. Thus the most powerful and hated baronial house was eliminated from English politics (1102) with such effect that for thirty-three years no baron ventured on armed resistance to the king. In 1104 the Count of Mortain, lord of all Cornwall and much else, shared their fate without striking a blow. The time was now ripe for evicting Robert Curthose himself. Norman anarchy and the attacks of Bellême and Mortain on Henry's friends, who were barons both in England and the duchy, furnished the occasion. Invading Normandy, he closed the war by defeating and capturing Robert at Tinchebrai (28 September 1106). The ex-duke passed the rest of his long life as a prisoner: his infant son William Clito was left at liberty to become a thorn in the side of his uncle.

Meanwhile the contest between Church and king had been renewed, this time over the question of investitures. Anselm in his exile had become a convinced opponent of lay investiture, and had taken part in a Lateran Council which renewed the prohibition of it and forbade prelates to do homage to a layman. He refused to do homage himself and to consecrate new bishops and abbots whom the king had nominated without election and then invested with staff and ring. Henry on his side allowed the archbishop to hold a reforming Council, and was willing to negotiate with Pope Paschal II on the dispute. The Pope was obdurate, and when Anselm in person failed to obtain any concession at Rome (1103) and maintained his own refusal, Henry seized on the lands of his see. Fortunately king and archbishop felt no mutual enmity, and by 1105 Henry was aware that clerical opinion was against him. He met Anselm in his French exile, and they agreed to a compromise suggested by the canonist Bishop Ivo of Chartres. In 1106 Pope Paschal authorized the settlement, which was ratified by an assembly of magnates next year. Henry agreed to free elections, but in his presence. He was to receive the homage and fealty of the elect, but before consecration. He renounced investiture of their office

594

by ring and staff, but invested them with their lands by charter. In this way both sides upheld their main principles, but Henry in practice could impose his wishes on the electors and exact the performance of feudal duties from the prelates. None the less he had admitted the right of appeal to Rome and had given an opening for further papal intervention. The agreement had been extorted from him by Anselm's tenacity, and, most important of all, the newer generation of English ecclesiastics were becoming more and more imbued with Hildebrandine views on Church and Papacy.

The rest of the reign in England was notable for the erection of a system of government and a routine of law in place of the arbitrary despotism of Rufus. Henry was a hater of disorder and waste. As grasping as his brother, he preferred methodical pressure and definite rules in filling his coffers. He was better educated than most laymen, and desired a business-like administration of justice and finance by well-trained agents, whom he knew how to select for his officers and Curia. Seventeen of the years after 1106 he spent in Normandy, suppressing disorders, taming disloyalty, and baffling the attacks of King Louis VI and his nephew William Clito. He needed therefore a confidential deputy to act for him in the Curia Regis and the kingdom, and he found one in his treasurer, the Norman Roger, Bishop of Salisbury, a man of singular ability, who was styled justiciar of all England. So successful was the experiment that Bishop John of Lisieux occupied a like position in Normandy. To Bishop Roger may be credited the development within the Curia of a group of barons, charged with auditing the sheriffs' accounts and trying causes which concerned the revenue. It sat twice a year and was called the *Scaccarium* or Exchequer from the chequered tablecloth on which the counters, representing sums of money, were placed, an adaptation of the abacus for doing sums. The 'barons of the Exchequer' were Roger, the chancellor, marshal, and constable, and two chamberlains, assisted by sundry clerks, of whom one kept a written record of all the money accounted for, later known as the Pipe Roll. One roll of the reign (1130) survives to show the items of revenue due and their receipt with the deductions allowed. Thus the Exchequer acquired a grip on the local administration and the king's income.

Besides the institution of the Exchequer, Bishop Roger may have been responsible for the appearance in the Curia of a group of assistant justiciars, some of them quite new men, others sub-tenants or lesser barons. These dealt with purely royal concerns at first, but their skill and experience as judges led even great men to pay handsomely for the privilege of their complaints being heard before them. Further, the practice grew up of sending them on circuit to hear 'the Pleas of the Crown' in the county courts, and they maintained that all matters which endangered the King's Peace were subject to their jurisdiction. At the same time the rights of the sheriff and county and hundred-courts were preserved against the feudal courts, and tracts were written which attempted to describe the Anglo-Saxon laws and customs to the ruling Normans.

Henry himself was active in the government. He founded new dioceses at Ely and Carlisle. He accepted scutage, a money payment in lieu of the due knight-service, from Church fiefs. He restored capital punishment. But he had no intention of subverting baronial power and wealth once he had ejected the mutinous Robert of Bellême and his compeers. On the contrary he granted rich fiefs to old and new houses. Two barons were as well endowed as any of the Conqueror's. To his illegitimate son Robert the king gave (1122) the earldom of Gloucester with lands which fairly dominated the south-west, to his nephew Stephen of Blois, Count of Boulogne, three great honours in the north and east, as well as Mortain in Normandy. Evidently he looked on the baronage as a whole as normal and necessary coadjutors in the task of a feudal monarchy, which was able to insist on every tittle of its rights. Feudalism and the Church were the cement of the State.

A valuable source of profit to the king were the boroughs, some hundred in number, scattered over England, in some seventy of which he had the lion's share of house-rents and the control of their government, although in most there were areas belonging to other lords, making the so-called 'tenurial heterogeneity'. Altogether the Crown in 1086 received some £2400 from this source. But the average *burgus* was quite an insignificant community and often largely agricultural in character. As they prospered from peace and order, Henry increased his profits by abolishing their Danegeld and substituting much heavier 'aids'. In certain towns he allowed the burgesses to form merchant gilds, or voluntary societies for the regulation of trade: to the men of Lincoln he sold the 'farm' of his dues (i.e. the right of collecting and paying them to him) in their city without the rapacious intervention of the sheriff. But in his last years he made a singular innovation. London was the largest borough and in the smallest shire. Apart from London the sheriff had little to do; the king held no rural manors in Middlesex. Henry now allowed the Londoners to pay direct the farm of both London and Middlesex and to appoint the sheriffs of both. Their own justices were to try the pleas of the Crown, a privilege they were later to lose.

Henry planned to recover Maine by the marriage of his son William with the daughter of Fulk V of Anjou, but the arrangement was upset by William's death (1120) when the White Ship foundered in the Channel with him and other nobles. The king's second marriage was barren, and he set his heart on the succession of his widowed daughter, the Empress Matilda. He then made a match between her and the son and heir of Fulk, Geoffrey the Fair, sometimes called Plantagenet from the branch of broom he bore on his helmet. It was a brilliant stroke to unite the two dynasties, but was highly unpopular with the barons, who were compelled to swear fealty, all the more because of Matilda's haughty character and the novelty of a female reign. Henry, however, hoped that the birth of his grandson (1133), the future Henry II, would obviate the latter difficulty, when he died on 1 December 1135. Although his exactions and autocracy had rendered him unpopular, the systematic efficiency of his rule was soon regretted and left an ineffaceable tradition in the government of England and Normandy.

Scarcely was Henry I dead when an almost unanimous disregard of their forced oaths of fealty was shown among the Norman nobles on both sides of the Channel. The child Henry was out of the question: they would not accept an arrogant woman and her Angevin husband. The chance was seized by the late king's nephew Stephen, a great lord in France and England, and generally popular as brave, generous and religious; his wife, too, was a niece of Edgar Atheling, while his mother was daughter of William the Conqueror. London and Winchester declared for him. His brother, Bishop Henry of Winchester, won over the prelates, and he was crowned at Westminster (1135–54). He had, however, to buy the Churchmen's support by a charter (1136), which surrendered his financial rights in vacancies and promised free elections. The breach of his oath of fealty to Matilda was salved by his recognition as king by Pope Innocent II. His uncle's ministers, headed by Roger of Salisbury, had gone over to him. Even Earl Robert of Gloucester made his peace. He could cross to Normandy in 1137 and be invested with the duchy by King Louis VI. Yet in two years his star was on the wane. He became known as a mild and soft man, who could be defied with impunity, unable to enforce the king's peace or to maintain his own hasty resolves and actions with steady prudence. Against him were ranged the unyielding Empress and two sagacious captains, Geoffrey of Anjou and Robert of Gloucester.

The lasting effects of Stephen's reign and the civil war it engendered were the reaction which the average baron eventually felt towards the strong kingship of Henry I and the greater freedom from royal control of the English Church, which was coupled with a closer relation to the Hildebrandine Papacy. The events of the 'anarchy' can only be briefly summarized. Stephen gave a pretext for Robert of Gloucester to revolt in Normandy and England in 1138. He placated King David of Scotland in 1136 by enfeoffing the Scot's heir Henry with Huntingdon and Carlisle and in 1138 with Northumberland as well, and this after David's second invasion had been repelled by the rout inflicted on him in the Battle of the Standard near Northallerton by the northern barons. The Church, with Henry of Winchester as papal legate, was for Stephen, when in June 1139 he stupidly enraged it by arresting the overbearing Bishop Roger of

Salisbury and his nephew Bishop Alexander of Lincoln. The legate and the prelates were up in arms at this contempt for the ecclesiastical immunity they now claimed. The rebellion under the Empress and Gloucester gained ground from the south-west, and Stephen's attempt to stem it ended in his capture in the battle of Lincoln (1141): his new earls were playing for their own hand. But here the intolerable arrogance of the Empress came to his aid. After she had been joined by legate and Church, bought Geoffrey de Mandeville, Stephen's Earl of Essex, with extravagant grants, and entered London as 'Lady of England', she roused general disgust and was forced out by Stephen's queen. When the legate changed sides again, she besieged Winchester, only to be routed by a relieving army, which also captured the Earl of Gloucester. This spelt ruin to her hopes. The two prisoners, Stephen and Gloucester, were exchanged, and thenceforward the civil war went lingering on till Robert of Gloucester died (1147) and the Empress left for Normandy. There her husband Geoffrey had been conquering the duchy (1141–5). With singular wisdom he ruled as Norman duke through Normans, retaining the institutions and traditions of Henry I. In 1150 he even relinquished Normandy to its heir, his eldest son Henry II, now seventeen. Next year he died, leaving Anjou and Maine to the young duke, who, as we have seen, doubled his inheritance by marrying Eleanor, the heiress of Aquitaine (1152).

In 1143 King Stephen plucked up heart to deal with the strongest of the double-dealing barons, Earl Geoffrey of Essex. His power was exorbitant; besides his much-enlarged estates, he was hereditary sheriff and justiciar of Essex, Middlesex and Hertfordshire, and constable of the Tower of London. He was compelled to surrender his castles, and proceeded to rebel, making a stronghold in the Fenlands until his death next year. His career there was of the worst pattern of brigand barons of the anarchy; his terrible cruelties, extortions and use of torture inspired the picture of the reign in the Peterborough continuation of the Anglo-Saxon Chronicle. Even if his atrocities were exceptional, however, the slack rule of Stephen, although acknowledged in the bulk of England, meant a very low standard of order. Unlicensed (or 'adulterine') castles sprang up on all sides. Each petty baron could pursue his private feuds, and great lords of sounder instincts could provide for peace by private treaties. The king meanwhile was trying to recover some of Henry I's control of the Church in appointments and the like. Thereby he fell out with both Papacy and episcopate. Twice he was refused the coronation of his eldest son Eustace. Rather than obey, Archbishop Theobald of Canterbury fled overseas. At this point Duke Henry II arrived to rally his supporters in an unimpeded tour on truce (1153). When Eustace suddenly died, his father lost heart and made peace at Wallingford, by which Henry with his partisans did homage to Stephen at Winchester as heir to England and 'justiciar'; and Stephen's second son,

William of Boulogne, was guaranteed the earldom of Surrey and his father's fiefs. The barons thus secured their fiefs on both sides of the Channel, and were not ill pleased to see a strong monarchy restored. The Church had baffled Stephen, and like the mass of the people looked forward to the return of order and the destruction of the mushroom castles after fifteen years of licence. Stephen died next year, and Henry II was crowned without demur.

Although some districts suffered cruelly and some barons were turbulent ill-doers, the sombre character of Stephen's reign was due rather to a general lack of governance and justice than to oppression or extortion by the kindly king. Rather, he let the baronage assume too much power at their own will. They were not mere grasping tyrants. Out of their exactions they built monasteries as well as castles. There was a growth of the ideals, imperfect enough, of chivalry among them; tournaments became popular. There was an upward movement in architecture and the arts, even of learning under baronial and ecclesiastical patrons. Finally, French lords and English subjects began to blend into one nation.

(9) THE REIGN OF HENRY II

Thanks to his accumulation of territories, which was far from being an 'Angevin Empire', Henry II (1154–89) was the greatest and richest prince outside the Empire, but his European policy was concerned with France rather than with England, and his lack of any special aptitude for warfare restricted his desires for the expansion of his kingdom by feats of arms. But within England his dominating personality, his keen, legal intelligence, and his organizing powers made his reign an epoch, rivalling the Conqueror's. His creative genius shaped unconsciously the unknown future because it moulded the known present.

The reign started happily for a king determined to restore the strict control of Henry I. The two dangerous potentates, Ranulf Earl of Chester and David I, King of Scots, had both died in 1153, and their heirs were children. The way was open for Henry II to destroy the unlicensed castles or take them into his own hands with little resistance. David I's grandson, young Malcolm IV, surrendered Northumberland and Cumberland, and did homage for the earldom of Huntingdon (1157). Wales was a harder problem, for Owain of Gwynedd (1137–70) and Rhys ap Gruffydd of Deheubarth (1155–97) had checked the piecemeal conquest of the Norman marcher barons, and two expeditions of Henry himself (1157, 1165), the last of which was defeated, only produced the Welsh princes' homage and left them their autonomy in dominions they had enlarged.

With the driving force and restless energy of Henry II, behind them, and in spite of his absence on the Continent for over half his reign, the reorganization of the government and the tightening of the control over shires and sheriffs went on apace in the hands of capable men, inherited mostly from Stephen and now able to show their quality. Nigel, Bishop of Ely, a nephew of Roger of Salisbury, took charge of the Exchequer until he obtained the treasurership for his son Richard Fitz Nigel (or Fitz Neal), the author of the *Dialogus de Scaccario*. Two barons, Robert de Beaumont, second Earl of Leicester, and Richard de Luci, were joint justiciars, but more important was the king's intimate friend, Thomas Becket, appointed chancellor on the recommendation of Archbishop Theobald, in whose household he had begun his career. It was this very intimacy which led Henry in 1162 to choose Becket to succeed Theobald at Canterbury, the most flagrant mistake of his life.

Becket had an ardent, ambitious character, and saw himself whole-heartedly as primate and ruler of the English Church. Like Henry himself he was disposed to press every legal claim, however unsubstantial, a fact which partly explains their intimacy, but now they were his own, not Henry's claims. He looked back to Stephen's days when the Church had held the balance and overruled the king, and to Anselm, whose unyielding grasp of principle had won concessions from Henry I. He would be the perfect archbishop; from a splendid courtier he became a rigid ascetic. He showed no fear of the fits of furious rage which marred the dexterity of the king, but seemed to court them. After the first few irritating brushes between them, matters came to an open breach in 1163 over the question of criminous clerks, i.e. men in church orders who impeded the restoration of the king's peace. Were they only to be tried in a Court Christian and, if found guilty, only suffer the by no means inevitable ecclesiastical punishment of degradation? Henry proposed that on conviction and degradation they should be brought to his courts to be sentenced further to a secular penalty. To Becket this was a double judgement for the same offence. It was a nice problem for the canon lawyers. On Becket's opposition the king fell back on custom and demanded of the bishops their promise to observe the ancient customs of the kingdom, which in fact meant the regime in vogue under Henry I and Anselm. Although Pope Alexander III in his French exile temporized and the English bishops were not unfavourable, only a reluctant promise was obtained from Becket. The king, however, lawyer as he was, to clinch the matter, summoned a great council at Clarendon (January 1164), there to sanction the customs written down as Constitutions. All accepted them save the archbishop, who, assenting at first, resolved at last not to affix his seal.

The quarrel begun unnecessarily by Becket was pursued rancorously by the king. The archbishop, with his now extreme views of clerical immunity, incurred in a legal action the guilt of contempt of the king's court. He deepened his offence in a council at Northampton, where Henry, with the intention of forcing his hand, demanded security for the sums he had administered during his chancellorship. On his side Becket ordered his suffragans to refuse to join in judgement on him and to excommunicate those who obeyed the lay court's decisions on his case. He also appealed to the Pope, and fled across the Channel, while Henry spitefully exiled his numerous kinsfolk. Not till 1166 did Alexander feel safe enough to support the now fanatical champion of the freedom of the Church. He then made the

exile legate in England with authorization to excommunicate invaders of his lands. The Pope soon showed himself disposed for an accord, but Becket continued to scatter excommunications from France on his opponents, and demanded all arrears of his revenues. His bitterness was increased when Henry, providing for the succession, had his son Henry the Younger crowned king by the Archbishop of York, disregarding the rights of Canterbury (1170). Both antagonists were now beyond reason, and a reconciliation at Fréteval was a mere form, with every issue still unsettled, save that Becket was to return. The Pope, however, was arming the archbishop to fight them, suspending the prelates who had taken part in young Henry's coronation. Becket returned to Canterbury, publicly denouncing

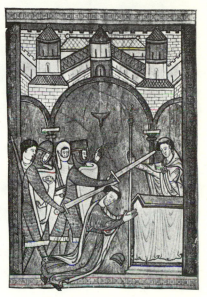

Fig. 122. *The murder of Thomas Becket*

the invaders of his see. The news drove Henry II into a transport of rage, which incited four household knights to murder the archbishop in his cathedral (29 December 1170). It is possible that Becket had aimed at a glorious martyrdom as an alternative to victory over the Constitutions. He became the most popular saint, and his shrine the most sought in England.

The murder placed both king and Pope in a quandary, for neither wished to break with the other. Henry sent envoys to clear himself, Alexander interdicted his continental lands, and after a time sent legates to arrange terms for reconciliation. Meanwhile the king made an expedition to Ireland, a long-cherished project of formidable consequences, to avoid both popular opinion and a too hasty settlement. At last he met the legates at Avranches (May 1172) and received absolution. The terms were really light. Henry did penance for his undesired responsibility for the

Fig. 123. Doorway of Clonfert Cathedral, Co. Galway, c. 1166

martyrdom, bound himself to hold fast to Alexander in the schism, vowed a crusade, surrendered the 'double punishment' of criminous clerks (a grievous gap in the repression of crime which lasted for centuries), and admitted the free course of appeals from the English Courts Christian to Rome. This last was a sign of the times. With the centralization and tighter linking of the Western Church under the Hildebrandine Papacy, the practice of appeals to the papal Curia had been logically growing. Checked in

England under Henry I by the need of royal permission, it had increased under the lax rule of Stephen and his resident legate, Henry of Winchester. Henry II had endeavoured to put the clock back, Becket to hasten it. Now papal intervention became a constant factor in Church affairs, and the papal decisions, which continually elaborated the Canon Law, operated as often and fast in England as in France. The validity of the remainder of the Constitutions of Clarendon was left to be worked out in a kind of anonymous friction between the royal and ecclesiastical courts.

The conflict over Becket, however, could not but damage Henry II's prestige and his hold over the malcontents irritated by the stern order he was introducing. As we have seen, his wife and ungrateful sons took the lead in widespread disaffection among barons and neighbours both French and insular. The powerful Earls of Chester, Derby, Leicester and Norfolk were leaders, allied with William the Lion, King of Scots. But Henry's luck and the stalwart, able loyalists triumphed over all. A straggling war, typical of the feudal age (1173–4), reduced the earls and forced the captured King of Scots to hold his kingdom as an English fief. There was no more trouble in England for the rest of the reign; restless spirits could seek adventure in the conquest of Ireland, and Henry at the head of his capable staff of bureaucrats could pursue his life-work in legislation and good government. The violent, hard-headed, lawyer king was to be justified by his deeds. The 'by the grace of God', which he added (1173) to his style (like an Emperor or King of France) emphasized the sanction and the duties of his kingship.

The reforms of Henry II may be grouped under the headings of administration, finance, and justice, although in their working they to a large extent overlap. The office of Justiciar developed during the reign until Richard de Luci (*ob.* 1179) and his successor Ranulf de Glanville, the probable author of the legal treatise *De Legibus Angliae*, became the king's deputies in all kinds of business, presiding in the Exchequer and in the king's court in justice, issuing writs in the king's absence, leading his troops according to need, as might be expected in the century. Like the king's their all-round ability had a legalistic bias. The *curiales* who worked under them were men of the same type, sometimes of baronial status, more often not. A feature of the reign was the gradual replacement of baronial sheriffs by such *curiales*. The office was being more strictly controlled by the Crown and a vast amount of fresh judicial and other business was being heaped upon it. A great local magnate was neither fit nor willing to endure the burden and constraint, while the *curialis* was trained at the centre and found his career in the king's service. Exploitation of the subject was the sheriff's vice. He collected the king's revenues in his shire, and what he could extort beyond the 'farm' he paid to the Exchequer was his profit. The amount he could make is suggested by the fact that the burgesses of Worcester paid up to £50 to the sheriff, and when, later, they paid their own 'farm' to the king, it was fixed at £24. In 1170 Henry sent commissioners to hold an Inquest of Sheriffs and officials who did his business in the shires, with the result that most sheriffdoms changed hands. Henry II inherited from the Norman kings the appointment of local justiciars for some royal judicial business, but this system he discontinued. The year 1166 is a turning-point. From that time he was experimenting in sending by very varied arrangements justices, chosen from household or Exchequer officials, to tour the shires, do justice, levy taxes, and inspect administration. From 1180 these justices itinerant (justices in eyre) visited the shires almost every year. They were intimately connected with the Exchequer at Westminister. There the Exchequer officials were the judges. Justice from the best experts was worth paying for. Whether justice was given by them in the county court, however, or in the Exchequer, or in the king's presence as he moved about, it was always in the king's court; he was the fountain of justice, and his court attracted more and more litigation on its merits, while the itinerant justices made it accessible in every shire. The result in the end was singular: the gradual supersession of the provincial and customary laws by the English Common Law, based on the successive decisions of the king's judges and developing by precedent from year to year into a national system. Ancient custom, Roman and Canon Law, might influence it, but growth was independent, a measure of advancing civilization and union.

With the advice of his barons the king could always make general statements of law and devise machinery to enforce it. He also possessed the prerogative to compel evidence on facts by oath in the shape of an 'inquest'. These powers lie at the root of his innovations designed to secure the king's peace, which were so fecund of social and institutional progress. His genius lay in subtly devising a single method capable of being applied to varying circumstances. In so doing he enlightened and trained the ruling class of landholders. In the Assize of Clarendon (1166) he opened a new period in criminal jurisdiction by instituting the accusing 'jury' drawn from hundred and village to name men suspected of murder and robbery, who were subsequently to be tried by the ordeal by water before the king's justices. If the ordeal acquitted men of bad repute, they were nevertheless to abjure the realm. It was a long stride towards centralization and uniformity. It also showed an infiltration of elementary proof by evidence of a sort into the primitive formalism of trials.

Among landholders the most frequent causes of disorder were disputes on the possession of land, leading easily to 'self help', a miniature form of private war. Henry now insisted that no man should be disseised of his free tenement unjustly and without judgement. Hence sprung the royal writs of Novel Disseisin and Mort d'Ancestor. The man put out of his tenement or prevented from succeeding to his inheritance could purchase these writs, which summoned a sworn jury of neighbours to state the facts; if their verdict went in his favour, he was reinstated. The procedure minimized the use of private force; it too involved evidence as proof, and it became most attractive. But it did not decide who owned the tenement by right. That was a question indubitably belonging to the feudal court of the lord. Yet feudal procedure admitted infinite delays in coming to trial and ended in the ordeal by the duel, generally by champions, which was primitive in its ideas of proof. About 1179, starting from the principle that no one need answer for his free tenement in his lord's court without the king's writ, which gave him a footing in all such cases, Henry devised the 'royal benefaction' of the Grand Assize to deliver his subjects from interminable delays and the haphazard of battle. When plaintiff brought his Writ of Right into the lord's court, the defendant could buy a writ placing himself on the Grand Assize, a specially elaborate and solemn form of a jury of inquest, whose verdict was final. Here again real evidence supplanted an ordeal, and the peace, even between two champions, was kept without formal prejudice to the baronial courts. Even so the process was long enough, and litigants might often prefer, in the course of proceedings in the king's court, to execute a compromise, the Final Concord, registered and guaranteed in the king's court.

One motive of these reforms was financial. The king's justice was the best and most resourceful to be had, and a rich revenue poured in from writs and amercements. Similarly, the strict control of the sheriff's administration enhanced the Exchequer's receipts. So did the census of enfeoffed sub-tenants in 1166, for those barons who enfeoffed more knights than they owed the king could be assessed for taxation on the actual number of knight's fees. But it also informed the king of the extent of these military forces. Wholly political was the Assize of Arms (1181), which prescribed the weapons a man must have according to his degree, and put into effective shape the ancient *fyrd*. On the other hand, it was for his personal pleasures that in 1184 Henry, a passionate hunter, re-enacted the cruel and oppressive Forest Assize. He extended the exorbitant area of the forests with their special courts to the detriment of his subjects of every degree in a majority of the counties. Yet if he was acquisitive, exacting, and tricky, they knew him to be a wise and beneficent master. The order, peace, and system of his creative rule bore fruit for centuries.

(10) GERMANY AND ITALY, 1189–1197 A.D.

The reign of Henry VI, the chosen heir of Barbarossa, was in a very real sense a continuation of his father's. The same methods and aims were pursued even to megalomania, for Henry dreamed of a universal Empire with the kings of Europe as his vassals and the Papacy as an overawed ally. Yet the men were singularly unlike. The genial, expansive Frederick, the model of German knighthood, was succeeded by the most unchivalrous of princes, a cold and calculating intellect, to whose honour no one could trust, capable of savage and revolting cruelty, without heart or scruple, yet an adroit diplomat and a masterful statesman who never faltered in his purpose, ready for all emergencies, whose learning, too, was vaunted by his courtiers. He was determined to follow up Barbarossa's achievement by dominating Italy and the Mediterranean as well as Germany, and he raised the Holy Roman Empire to the greatest height of at least its external power.

But Henry inherited the weak side of Frederick's policy as well as its strength. German rule only fostered the intense hatred of the Italians for their foreign, or indeed any master; only his sheer ability kept them obedient. The Papacy, seated firmly in men's belief, served by the best trained minds and disposing of the most advanced organization of the age, was merely waiting till the untoward current of events had spent its force. Worst of all, the foundation of the imperial structure in Germany was unsound. The feudal devolution of local government, slower and later in its growth in Germany than in France, was moving to its full efflorescence in the twelfth century. The magnates had established hereditary right to their countships and the like as vassals, while owing to the living tradition of their official character there were no royal nominees beside them, like the English sheriffs, nor justices itinerant to supervise them. It is true that the bishops could act as a check, but even if elected under the Emperor's influence they were great territorial princes in their own right and usually connected with neighbouring nobles. Only the Emperor's presence with armed force could enforce order, and more often than not he was absent. With the change-over from a mainly official to a strictly feudal conception of government, which had long taken place in France, a curious oligarchical narrowing appeared in the circle of 'princes of the realm'. After 1180 only those vassals who held at least one countship directly from the king and who did not hold any fief from another secular lord were reckoned as princes. This rule left only sixteen lay princes in Germany along with the bishops and abbots of royal abbeys, instead of the numerous princes of earlier times. The privilege of electing the king which belonged to the princes became all the more valuable, more an asset in bargaining, and less subject to popular feeling. The evils of the system were clearly seen by Barbarossa and Henry VI, but they were ruled by feudal ideas, and made no effort at centralization and bureaucracy. In fact the predominance of localized feudalism, absorbed in provincial broils, was the new expression of the particularism once expressed in the tribal duchies, and in especial of the mutual alienation of Low and High Germany, of the north and south, with their divergent aims and interests. The Emperors since Conrad III

Fig. 124. Illness and death of King William II of Sicily

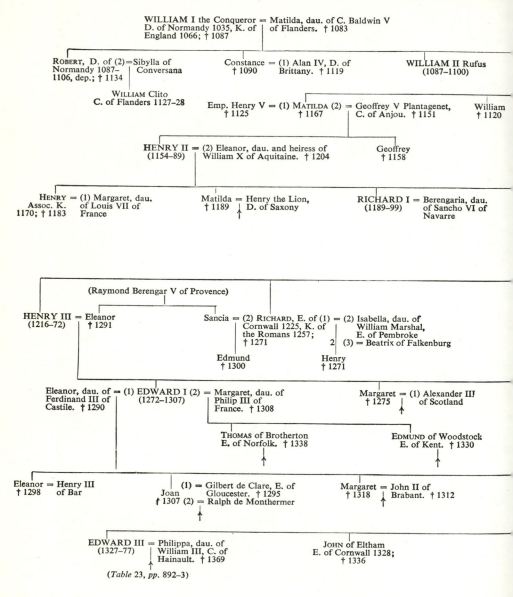

WILLIAM I the Conqueror = Matilda, dau. of C. Baldwin V
D. of Normandy 1035, K. of | of Flanders. † 1083
England 1066; † 1087

ROBERT, D. of (2)=Sibylla of   Constance = (1) Alan IV, D. of   WILLIAM II Rufus
Normandy 1087- | Conversana   † 1090   Brittany. † 1119   (1087–1100)
1106, dep.; † 1134

WILLIAM Clito
C. of Flanders 1127–28

Emp. Henry V = (1) MATILDA (2) = Geoffrey V Plantagenet,   William
† 1125   † 1167   C. of Anjou. † 1151   † 1120

HENRY II = (2) Eleanor, dau. and heiress of   Geoffrey
(1154–89) | William X of Aquitaine. † 1204   † 1158

HENRY = (1) Margaret, dau.   Matilda = Henry the Lion,   RICHARD I = Berengaria, dau.
Assoc. K. of Louis VII of   † 1189 | D. of Saxony   (1189–99) of Sancho VI of
1170; † 1183 France   Navarre

(Raymond Berengar V of Provence)

HENRY III = Eleanor   Sancia = (2) RICHARD, E. of (1) = (2) Isabella, dau. of
(1216–72) | † 1291   Cornwall 1225, K. of   William Marshal,
                            the Romans 1257;   E. of Pembroke
                             † 1271   2| (3) = Beatrix of Falkenburg

Edmund   Henry
† 1300   † 1271

Eleanor, dau. of = (1) EDWARD I (2) = Margaret, dau. of   Margaret = (1) Alexander III
Ferdinand III of (1272–1307) Philip III of   † 1275 | of Scotland
Castile. † 1290   France. † 1308

THOMAS of Brotherton   EDMUND of Woodstock
E. of Norfolk. † 1338   E. of Kent. † 1330

Eleanor = Henry III   (1) = Gilbert de Clare, E. of   Margaret = John II of
† 1298 of Bar   Gloucester. † 1295   † 1318 | Brabant. † 1312
                 Joan
             † 1307 (2) = Ralph de Monthermer

EDWARD III = Philippa, dau. of   JOHN of Eltham
(1327–77) | William III, C. of   E. of Cornwall 1328;
      Hainault. † 1369   † 1336

(*Table* 23, *pp.* 892–3)

Plantagenets (to Edward III)

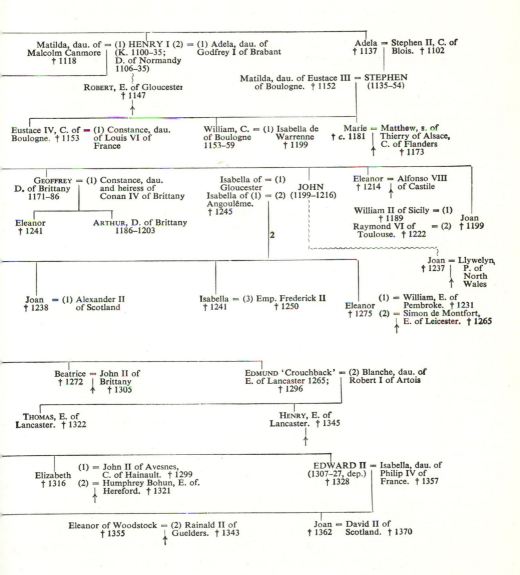

Matilda, dau. of = (1) HENRY I (2) = (1) Adela, dau. of   Adela = Stephen II, C. of
Malcolm Canmore   (K. 1100–35;   Godfrey I of Brabant   † 1137   Blois. † 1102
† 1118   D. of Normandy
          1106–35)

ROBERT, E. of Gloucester   Matilda, dau. of Eustace III = STEPHEN
† 1147   of Boulogne. † 1152   (1135–54)

Eustace IV, C. of = (1) Constance, dau.   William, C. = (1) Isabella de   Marie = Matthew, s. of
Boulogne. † 1153   of Louis VI of   of Boulogne   Warrenne   † c. 1181   Thierry of Alsace,
         France   1153–59   † 1199   C. of Flanders
                                            † 1173

GEOFFREY = (1) Constance, dau.   Isabella of = (1)   Eleanor = Alfonso VIII
D. of Brittany   and heiress of   Gloucester   JOHN   † 1214   of Castile
1171–86   Conan IV of Brittany   Isabella of (1) = (2) (1199–1216)
                        Angoulême.   William II of Sicily = (1)
                        † 1245   † 1189   Joan
Eleanor   ARTHUR, D. of Brittany   Raymond VI of   = (2) † 1199
† 1241   1186–1203   2   Toulouse. † 1222

                                                  Joan = Llywelyn,
                                             † 1237   P. of
                                                          North
                                                          Wales

Joan = (1) Alexander II   Isabella = (3) Emp. Frederick II   (1) = William, E. of
† 1238   of Scotland   † 1241   † 1250   Eleanor   Pembroke. † 1231
                                               † 1275   (2) = Simon de Montfort,
                                                       E. of Leicester. † 1265

Beatrice = John II of   EDMUND 'Crouchback' = (2) Blanche, dau. of
† 1272   Brittany   E. of Lancaster 1265;   Robert I of Artois
        † 1305   † 1296

THOMAS, E. of   HENRY, E. of
Lancaster. † 1322   Lancaster. † 1345

       (1) = John II of Avesnes,   EDWARD II = Isabella, dau. of
              C. of Hainault. † 1299   (1307–27, dep.)   Philip IV of
Elizabeth   (2) = Humphrey Bohun, E. of.   † 1328   France. † 1357
† 1316   Hereford. † 1321

Eleanor of Woodstock = (2) Rainald II of   Joan = David II of
† 1355   Guelders. † 1343   † 1362   Scotland. † 1370

609

were southern Germans with their eyes fixed on Italy; even in south Germany they were absentees for years, in the north they only were drawn in to repress rebellion.

From his father's departure (Easter 1189) Henry VI ruled the Empire. He was rapidly confronted with the old dilemma of action in the south and the north, the Sicilian inheritance and rebellion in Saxony. In October 1189 Henry the Lion returned from exile, made alarming progress against his foes, and was brought to an illusory halt by a treaty he did not keep, and which was followed by the wildest confusion of private, brigandlike wars amongst the Saxon magnates. Meantime Henry VI was engrossed with Italy. On 18 November 1189 William II of Sicily died childless, and Queen Constance was his legal heiress.[1] But neither the Sicilians nor the Papacy wished for a German master, although the nobles were divided between two claimants, Count Roger of Andria and Tancred, Count of Lecce, illegitimate son of Duke Roger, the eldest son of Roger II. Tancred secured the crown (January 1190). 'Behold an ape is crowned', said his enemies, but Tancred's brief reign justified his partisans. Henry VI himself was baffled in his first invasion (1191). On the way indeed he obtained his imperial coronation from Pope Celestine III, but at the price of delivering the town of Tusculum to the vindictive Romans, who destroyed their little neighbour with merciless cruelty. In so doing he reconciled the Romans to their octogenarian Pope. Thereby made secure at home, that experienced diplomatist was in a position to embarrass, if not check, the Emperor. With Tancred he made a bargain by which the Sicilian legation was abolished. But he made one mistake; he induced Tancred to set free his captive, the Empress Constance, and so give up the one effective fetter on Henry's actions.

No doubt the Pope trusted that Henry would be fully occupied in Germany, where disaffection was rife and compelled his return. The only compensation was the long-expected death (1191) of Duke Welf VI, which brought the great Swabian lands (Altdorf) of the Welfs to the Hohenstaufen as Barbarossa had planned. But although Count Adolf of Holstein and the sons of Albert the Bear were waging an equal war with Henry the Lion, a disputed election to the see of Liége was uniting the kindred discontents of Saxony and the erstwhile Lower Lotharingia or lower Rhineland. The anti-imperialist candidate, Albert of Brabant, whom the Pope shrewdly confirmed (a clear attack on the imperial claims), was murdered by German knights (1192). A definite breach with the Papacy was the consequence, and at the same time the Emperor was alienating several of the princes by his scandalous imprisonment of the crusading King Richard of England, the ally of the Welfs and of Tancred. Richard had been seized by his ignoble enemy, Duke Leopold V of Austria, as he journeyed home,

---

[1] See Genealogical Table 14 above, p. 510.

Fig. 125. Coronation of Henry VI by Pope Celestine III

611

and was by him handed over to Henry (February 1193). The disgraceful act, however, served to quench the rebellion it helped to inflame. Richard was an essential ally for the angry princes—money and trade bound north Germany to England—and Henry's move to sell his captive to his mortal enemies, his brother John and Philip Augustus of France, brought about an agreement in June 1193 at Worms, which resulted at last in Richard's release (February 1194). The terms were hard: an enormous ransom of 150,000 marks, the vassalage of England to the Empire (softened by a shadowy grant of the kingdom of Burgundy or Arles), the reconciliation of the Welfs, and the desertion of Richard's then ally, Tancred. After this Henry the Lion made his peace; he was near his end, which came in August 1195. The Emperor's hands were now free for Sicily. Yet there were prices to be paid. He had estranged his Capetian ally, and he was rather approving than choosing new bishops of the Netherlandish sees, where the Pope was freely using his appellate powers.

The task of the conquest of Sicily was now suddenly made easy by King Tancred's death (February 1194). His elder son Roger III was already dead, and his second William III was a mere boy. There was no one with authority or genius to unite the quarrelling nobles or direct defence. The Pope was unarmed; both Pisa and Genoa were lured to provide fleets. The furious battle between the two on the campaign provided the chief fighting in Henry's triumphal progress. Amid general surrender he was crowned on Christmas Day 1194 at Palermo. Shortly afterwards he sent the royal family and their chief adherents prisoners to Germany. The German dominion south of the Apennines was now made sure. The Empress was installed as governor of the Regno, Henry's brother Philip was created Duke of Tuscany, his ablest soldier, the freed *ministerialis* Markward of Anweiler, Duke of Ravenna with the Adriatic coastline, while other trusted Germans were placed in key posts in central Italy. As if to crown all, on 28 December the Empress bore her only child at Jesi on her way south, Frederick Roger, the heir of both Hautevilles and Hohenstaufen.

Master of the Regno and the immense treasure of its kings, Henry gave the loosest rein to his ambitions of world-dominion. In the background of his dream lay the vassalage of France and Aragon, in the foreground the old Norman scheme of hegemony in the Mediterranean, with the Barbary Moslems his tributaries, Little Armenia and Cyprus his vassals, and the Eastern Empire subservient at least. He married his captive, Isaac Angelus's daughter Irene, the widow of Roger III, to his brother Duke Philip, and arrogantly blackmailed the new Emperor Alexius III. There were, however, two preliminaries first to be achieved, the compulsory alliance of the hostile Pope and the conversion of the Empire itself into a hereditary monarchy; the latter scheme would unite Empire and Sicily

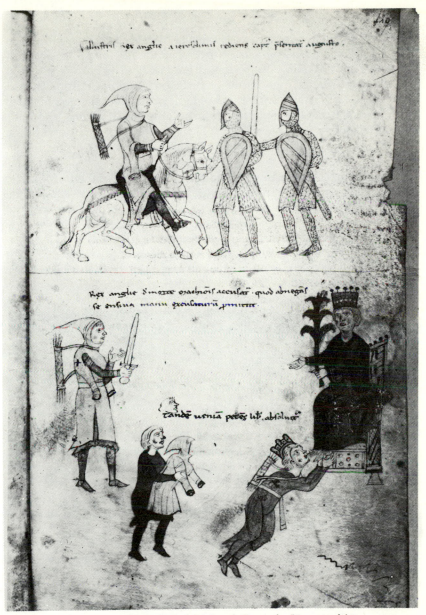

Fig. 126. *Capture of Richard Cœur-de-Lion, and his submission to Henry VI*

automatically in the same heir, besides eliminating the chances of election and bargaining which had so much impaired the German kingship. Henry displayed his highest political adroitness in his use of circumstances. The time was propitious and inviting for a new Crusade for the recovery of Jerusalem after Saladin's death, and at Easter 1195 Henry took the cross and actively prepared a great and German expedition. Celestine III had received no satisfaction for new and old grievances, the conquest of Sicily from his vassal and the continued occupation of the Matildine lands, nor any relief from the encirclement which Henry's rule over all Italy save Rome and the Patrimony involved, but he could hardly refuse to sanction so timely a Crusade.

Henry's moves to secure the second preliminary were less successful. The German princes at first refused to elect his two-year-old son King of the Romans. Then he unveiled his project of rendering the German, and therefore the imperial, crown hereditary. The events are imperfectly recorded, but under pressure a majority gave an approval of the scheme at a Diet of Würzburg (1196). In return for the loss of their cherished right of election, the lay princes were to receive unrestricted rights of inheritance in their fiefs, in male and female lines; hitherto the right of a brother to succeed to his childless brother was not absolutely inviolable, although consecrated by practice. The ecclesiastical princes were no longer to be subject to the *ius spolii* by which the Emperor took their personal property on their decease, and against which they had always protested. But the bribes were not sufficient, and opposition soon crystallized among the northern princes, led by the Archbishop of Cologne, whose right of crowning a new king, no mere formal privilege in an age when valid ceremonial carried legal weight, would lose its political importance. Henry therefore turned to the Pope to bargain for his assent. Threats would be out of place, so he journeyed to the neighbourhood of Rome with a small retinue. The establishment of a hereditary Empire could only be most unwelcome to the Papacy, and Henry made the widest proffers in return, though what they were is not really known. In any case, the wary Pope Celestine, who steadily maintained all the particular papal grievances, was too farsighted to agree to an arrangement for illusory gains which would rivet his encirclement and tie his successors' hands. On his definite refusal, Henry proceeded to Sicily in anger. In Germany he had met with a fresh defeat. The princes at Erfurt had finally declined his project. It may have been a sop to Henry that they in December 1196 elected the infant Frederick, which seemed to settle the succession, but the real limitations of Henry's control in Germany had been made clear as well as the unchanged, if cautious, enmity of the Pope.

It remained to press forward the Crusade with all its possibilities. But a widespread plot, the result of resentment at his harsh foreign rule, was weaving. The Empress herself, a Hauteville of Sicily, and even Pope Celestine may have had an inkling of it. The hated Emperor was to be murdered and a native king set up. The plot was betrayed, and Henry took ferocious vengeance, which shocked the West, on the rebels. Even his innocent prisoners in Germany were blinded. He evidently thought that terrorism made him secure, for he had despatched his crusaders to the East, when he suddenly died of fever in Sicily on 28 September 1197. The fragment of his hurried testament which has been preserved proves that he correctly rated the slenderness of the foundations on which his father and he had built, for it was an attempt by wide concessions to induce the Pope to continue the union of the Empire and Sicily under his infant son. The Regno should be held as a papal fief; the Matildine lands should be surrendered to the Papacy; and his most trusted general, Markward of Anweiler, should keep his Adriatic lands, the duchy of Ravenna and the March of Ancona, as a papal vassal. In short, Henry only hoped to maintain his structure by alliance with the strong-rooted Papacy. The masterly, if odious, statesmanship of his reign had roused too many hatreds for permanence. As it was, the acquisition of Sicily was a remediless obstacle to a sincere reconciliation with the Papacy, and a perpetual bar to the efficient government of feud-ridden Germany.

CHAPTER 20

THE TWELFTH-CENTURY RENAISSANCE AND ITS SEQUEL

(I) THE CHURCH AND PAPAL GOVERNMENT

Although the reform movement obtained only a partial and in secular matters an illusory success in its aim of freeing the Church and its hierarchy from secular control, and was rebuffed in its Hildebrandine endeavour to subject lay rulers to papal overlordship, its gains were both immediately great and capable of ready expansion in the ecclesiastical government of the Church itself and its unification under the Papacy. The Pope with his bureaucratic, legal Curia was now the administrative sovereign and the supreme court for ecclesiastics and 'spiritual' causes; he was also the living and universal source of the growing Canon Law. Whereas the canons of provincial synods, without him, had but a local validity, those in which he took part and his personal Decretals, which were mostly answers to episcopal enquiries, were in theory at any rate binding on the whole Church. Meantime for a century experts in Canon Law were following the example of Burchard of Worms in works which classified according to subject-matter the often contradictory prescriptions of synods and Popes. The three works of Bishop Ivo of Chartres (*ob.* 1115) were the most widely reputed of these, but they were all surpassed by the *Decretum*, originally named expressively the *Concordia Discordantium Canonum*, published *c.* 1141 by the Camaldulese monk Gratian, who taught Canon Law at Bologna. His arrangement and classification of excerpts produced a master-piece, a real code and treatise combined. To each excerpt that needed it he added a comment, the *Dicta Gratiani*. The whole work was rapidly treated as official, and was glossed by eminent jurists. It concluded the period of what came to be known as the *Ius Antiquum* of the Western Church, and, inaugurating the *Ius Novum*, exercised an immense influence on the future.

The Canon Law as declared by Gratian was not a finished, changeless product. Change, organization, and greater civilization demanded a perennial flow of new law to deal with problems as they arose, and this task was mainly performed by the Papacy, the fount of living law. Great lawyers filled the Curia, and in the persons of Alexander III and Innocent III sat on the papal throne. Their Decretals were almost all called for by specific cases, but they had general validity. This growth was due more especially to the increase of appeals to Rome from the lower Courts Christian or to enquiries from their doubting judges. Such appeals grew more frequent as the barriers imposed by royal resistance or episcopal independence melted away, until under Alexander III and Innocent III their free course was obtained. Thenceforward the *Ius Novum* of the Decretals became steadily more voluminous. Some five successive compilations of it came to be current, until in 1234 Pope Gregory IX published his *Decretals*, composed by the Catalan Raymond of Peñafort, which contained the papal legislation since Gratian, duly classified and dealing with most of the concrete problems of the day. Nor, as we shall see, did the growth of Church Law by fresh Decretals by any means then cease, while glosses and expositions (*Summae* as they were called) were written by celebrated jurists, among which the *Summa Aurea* of Henry of Susa, Cardinal of Ostia (*ob.* 1271), takes the highest place. The Canon Law, much influenced by the Civil Law of Justinian, which was thus evolved, was the most civilized of the age. It penetrated deeply into the daily life of the laity, for marriage, the performance of oaths, usury, legitimacy, tithes, all came within its province, and excommunication was a severe penalty. Its influence spread beyond its own limits, and it was a formative and vital element in medieval civilization.

As happened with the secular monarchs, judicial decisions and proceedings were one of the chief ways in which the government of the Church and its control by the Popes were carried on. Administrative control grew beside it. Dioceses were ruled by their bishops and, under them, by archdeacons and other officials, while they were grouped in provinces under the archbishops. The customary oaths of canonical obedience to immediate superiors bound the whole together. A whole network of ecclesiastical government covered the West. The aim of closely centralizing it at Rome was achieved by various means, possible for a literate bureaucracy, and at first against considerable resistance of kings and their prelates. One way was personal contact by the compulsory, periodic visits of the bishops to Rome *ad limina* or of metropolitans to receive the pallium. Another, most important method, was the despatch of legates for supervision, enforcement of decrees, and reform. They were given overriding authority, and so useful was this delegation that certain metropolitans, like Canterbury, were given permanent legatine routine powers, which also bound them more strictly to the Papacy. Still wider powers, however, were exercised by the frequent legates *a latere*, sent from Rome itself under special commissions. In fact, the practice of delegation proved to be a most efficient method of dealing with the mass of legal business on appeal to Rome. Local prelates were authorized, under directions, to hear and decide in the Pope's name cases of less and merely local import.

The holding of synods by bishops, archbishops, and legates was a further means of administration and solidarity. To mention nothing else, they secured the personal acceptance of new and old legislation by their participants—always a desirable aim in a time both crudely concrete and dislocated. Of pre-eminent importance were Councils held by the Pope at the Lateran, which summed up recent legislation and gave a direction for future policy. In his Ecumenical Council of 1179 Alexander introduced the novelty of a majority vote in papal elections, while leaving other elections, in case of dispute, to be settled by appeal; no better system could have beeen devised for the establishment of papal control. In his Fourth Lateran Council of 1215, Innocent III passed canons forbidding the priesthood to take part in the primitive practice of the ordeal—which killed it—making annual confession compulsory on every Christian, and restricting the bar of consanguinity in marriage from the seventh degree to the more practicable fourth. Such conciliar canons were specially suitable for a wide-reaching legislation.

The financial basis for the government of the Roman Curia was, however, as yet inadequate, although the Church as a whole was richly, if unevenly, endowed with lands and tithe, which by no means always or in greater part was paid for the benefit of the church or diocese where it was raised. The Pope's income from the Papal State was none too large, and the *census* (or tribute) from exempt or merely protected abbeys was but moderate when it was listed (1192) in the *Liber Censuum* of the papal Chamberlain Cencio, the future Honorius III. Offerings and above all fees on all the appeals, confirmations, privileges, translations of bishops (which were only valid with papal assent), etc., provided as yet the necessary funds for the papal court, and soon gave ground for the increasing complaints of its venality. In his contest with Barbarossa, Alexander III had recourse to borrowing, and thus sharpened the antithesis between the actual financial operations of the Papacy and the Church's prohibition of usury (i.e. the taking of interest on loans), which he repeated in his Council of 1179. The Crusades, on which depended so much of the moral leadership of the West assumed by the Papacy, were financed in two ways: by indulgences, which were commutations of the vow to go on a crusade in return for a money payment, a measure productive of perilous extension and abuse in all directions, and by the taxation of ecclesiastical income by kings with the consent of the Papacy, begun by Louis VI of France (1146) and repeated in England and France by the Saladin Tithe (1188), which under Innocent III developed into the claim to dispose of all Church property and to tax it at will, while excluding the lay powers from like behaviour. Further expedients by the Papacy to pay its way were to be devised in the next century. Thus with all their claims in theory and practice undiminished and championed by St Bernard in his tract to Pope Eugenius III, the *De Consideratione* (*c.* 1148), and summed up in the ample phrase 'plenitudo potestatis', the Popes of the thirteenth century were equipped for theocratic sway, while all the more immersed in that legal and political activity which St Bernard so bitterly condemned.

(2) THE REVIVAL OF ROMAN LAW AND ANCIENT LEARNING

Parallel to the growth of the Canon Law ran the revival of the study of ancient Roman Law, the *Codex Iuris Civilis*, i.e. the Code of Justinian. It was a strange phenomenon, for save in some fragments of Italy, and that imperfectly, the law of Justinian had barely penetrated the West, and it bears witness to the increase of civilization and the desire to reacquire the knowledge and culture of the still remembered, far distant past, which had made its first efforts under Charlemagne and reawoke in the era of Church Reform. Not all intellectual progress was confined to ecclesiastical matters or to men whose primary interests lay in the Church or religion.

It was in Italy that the intensive study of Justinian's Code began, and thence it spread across the Alps. There had always been more literate laymen in Italy than elsewhere, and in the eleventh century law was a favourite and lucrative study. There was a school at Pavia for Lombard and Roman Law, but the Code of Justinian was known at Rome and Ravenna. In the latter half of the century the centre of the study moved to Bologna, whose wealth and security and its central location on the crossing of trunk roads gave it the advantage. The story went that the manuscripts of the Code were transferred to Bologna from Ravenna. It was, however, a Tuscan, the illustrious Irnerius (*fl.* 1100), who gave renown to the school and began the succession of Glossators. The Gloss, or textual interpretation of the Law, became more and more elaborate. It settled the correct text, explained its meaning, resolved contradictions, deduced legal maxims, and discussed concrete cases, becoming in the end a real commentary. Its best service, perhaps, was its training in critical reasoning, however pedantic, which contributed to the mental advance of an immature age, but it also possessed an immediately practical utility. Although the *Corpus Iuris Civilis* was a dead law, the men who administered and improved the variegated local laws and customs in use were trained in it. Its more civilized prescriptions perpetually influenced the natural growth of the living laws as they were enlarged and amended to provide for the needs of societies progressing from semi-barbarism in the quest of civilization. Emperors like Barbarossa called in the doctors of Bologna to define their prerogative. The *Summa* of Azo (*fl.* 1190) was considered indispensable for a practising Italian lawyer. The Gloss of Accursius (*ob. c.* 1260) became the standard accompaniment of the text of Justinian. Nor was the study confined to Italy. In South France, the *pays du droit écrit*, the Code gradually superseded the older Roman law-books as the law of the land, modified only by local custom. In Northern France, the *pays de coûtumes*, it was in the thirteenth century mingled with the traditional usages. Even in Germany in the later Middle Ages the native tribal law began to be ousted by Roman Law, partly owing to the belief that Germany was the

Holy Roman Empire. In marked contrast England was producing, owing to the initiative of Henry II, a Common Law of its own manufacture.

The predominance of the Accursian Gloss was evidence that the Glossators' method of objective study of the text was in decay. Men wished more to apply the Civil Law to practice than to discover its plain meaning. Hence arose in Italy towards 1300 the school of the Commentators, whose brightest luminary was Bartolus of Sassoferrato (1314–57). It was the aim of the Commentators, by means of a fine-spun logic and dialectic modelled on the reasonings of the Schoolmen, to make the Civil Law applicable to court practice in their own day, to adapt it to living conditions, and to harmonize it with the very different feudal, municipal, Germanic, or Canon laws actually in vigour. By thus transforming it, they made it into a living code and deepened its practical influence, but at a cost. Casuistry, pedantry, and voluminous confusion followed, ending in the courts merely counting the number of Commentators for this or that opinion. In their endeavour to get back to the true features of Roman Law the Italian humanists in the fifteenth century attacked this degenerate science and even Justinian's Code itself, for was it not the mutilated fragments of the great original classic jurists of the golden, better age? None the less, the Commentators held their ground and indoctrinated France and Germany, until in modern times jurists with a historic sense on the one hand and with a philosophic view on the other slowly superseded them.

The twelfth-century quest for knowledge was not confined to the narrow field of law. Men sought to reacquire the remnants of ancient science. With regard to Latin, their studies resembled those of the Carolingians with a greater stress on information, such as Pliny's *Natural History*, and less on literature, although some elegant and much inelegant Latin verse was written beside splendid rhymed hymns and jaunty secular and satiric verse—the 'Goliardic' poems,—while a premature humanism appears in John of Salisbury (*ob.* 1180) and the school of Chartres only to wither again. But zealots for lost learning sought for it mainly in translations from the Arabic, often by the medium of the Jews, in Moslem Spain, as Gerbert of Aurillac (Pope Sylvester II), who introduced the abacus, had done long before. The twelfth and thirteenth centuries were a golden age of translators: Adelard of Bath (*fl.* 1140), Henry II's tutor, who translated Euclid and wrote on the astrolabe; James of Venice (*fl.* 1130), Burgundio the Pisan (*fl.* 1150), Henry Aristippus of Catania (*ob. c.* 1162), and Eugenius the Emir (*fl. c.* 1160), who all translated from the Greek; Gundisalvi (*fl.* 1140), Gerard of Cremona (*ob.* 1187), Herman the German (*fl.* 1240), Michael Scot (*ob. c.* 1234), and others, known and unknown, produced versions of Greek divinity, philosophy, medicine, astronomy, and mathematics (which brought in the Arabic numerals invented in India), mostly (save divinity) from Arabic translations along with Arabic commentaries and original works. The series closes with

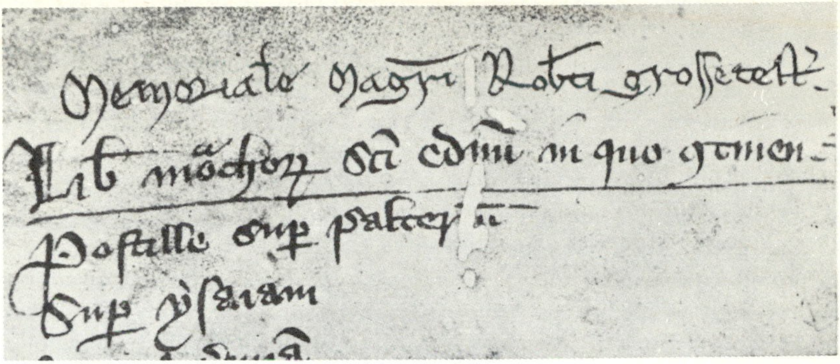

Fig. 127. Robert Grosseteste, holograph entry in Pembroke College Cambridge, MS. 7

the English Robert Grosseteste (*ob.* 1253), and the Flemish William of Moerbeke, Archbishop of Corinth (*ob.* 1286), both of whom translated direct from the Greek. On these translations a great part of the knowledge and indeed the thought of the time was based. It is true that the original Arabic versions were not faithful renderings of the Greek, and the direct Latin translations from the Greek were uncouth, crabbed, and difficult owing to their literal, word for word method in defiance of Latin grammar. But both were stimulating to thought, and the direct Latin translations were after all exact. Until the Fourth Crusade (1204) the chief centre of this transmission lay in Spain at Toledo, where Christian learners and Moslem and Jewish teachers met together. Much the same took place at the court of Palermo in Sicily, where first the Norman kings and then the Emperor Frederick II (*ob.* 1250) and his son Manfred promoted the advance. After the conquest of the Eastern Empire in 1204 by the Latins, direct contact with the Greeks facilitated direct translations of Aristotle and his compeers. To sum up, these medievals reacquired, not always intelligently, much of the information that Greek and Latin and Arab had to teach, including errors like astrology, alchemy, and magic. Very seldom did they, like Frederick II in falconry, add much from their own observation in these two centuries.

(3) THE UNIVERSITIES

From the time of Charlemagne higher and indeed lower literary education north of the Alps was sought in the monastic and cathedral schools, and during the eleventh century the cathedral schools began to outshine the monastic, the famous cathedral school of Chartres to surpass the famous monastic school of Bec. In the north it was from the cathedral schools that the universities, the most lasting of medieval creations, arose. They were assemblies of clerks with the privileges and restrictions of clergy. In Italy the universities, although containing clerks, were on the whole lay, arising from Schools of Law and Medicine. In both cases their appearance was the most organized embodiment of that reawakening of intellectual interests and change to a more civilized mentality which have not inaptly been named the Twelfth-Century Renaissance, an era of progress as momentous as the Italian Renaissance and the Reformation of a later age.

The origin of the name of Universities, which they acquired, may first be noted. *Universitas*, i.e. 'a whole', was the customary official address to any body of men—e.g. the Popes might address the body of believers as *universitas vestra* ('the whole of you')—but technically it was applied specially to particular associations of men, e.g. citizens of a town, a chapter of a cathedral, or members of a trade-gild. In the twelfth century the impulse of men below the ecclesiastical and feudal hierarchies was to seek security and strength by forming associations for mutual aid and to create in doing so modes and regulations of self-government. In essence the universities were like a craft-gild, an association for the protection and regulation of their craft of learning, and at long last they monopolized their name. At first, however, they were known by the more precise name of *Studia Generalia*, i.e. schools frequented from all parts, a term which came to have an official and limited meaning, recognized or conferred by Popes and Emperors, and which then implied the *ius ubique docendi*, the right of a graduate in a *Studium Generale* to teach in all universities.

The 'gild', which formed and ruled the earliest emerging universities, and was copied by their imitators, fell into two distinct types, the university of masters or teachers like that of Paris, or the university of scholars like that of Bologna. The first was the characteristic form north and the latter south of the Alps. Their difference in organization appears to have been due to the particular circumstances in the early history of the two models, Paris and Bologna.

The earliest school or *studium* which can be ranked as a university was, however, neither of these, but that of Salerno. As a meeting-place of Greek, Latin, Arabic, and Jewish culture, it was already famous in the tenth century for its physicians; the Hebrew element was probably strong. Its works on medicine, derived from ancient and Jewish authors, were the most reasonable of the Middle Ages. It was a College of Doctors of Medicine, and Frederick II made its examination a necessary preliminary for a licence to practise in the Regno (1231). With it may be grouped the old School of Medicine at Montpellier, which was a university by 1220, but of a more northern type.

The growth of a *studium* into a fully fledged university in the twelfth century is an obscure matter. It must have begun in the associated Doctors

622

or Masters—the titles were synonymous—of a great school who admitted
an aspirant as a fellow-teacher after some sort of probation and examination. When the Emperor Frederick I in 1158 issued his Authenticum *Habita*
to the Doctors of Bologna, it was a general privilege to the student-class of
the Empire, but he would hardly have given such the right of being tried
either by their bishop or by their Doctor if the Doctor were merely using
a self-assumed status. Yet only in the thirteenth century is it clear that the
two Colleges of Doctors of Civil and Canon Law, soon accompanied by
a College of Arts and Medicine, existed at Bologna. The Doctors taught,
examined, and granted degrees in their several Faculties. In 1219 Pope
Honorius III decreed that only the Archdeacon of Bologna was to confer
degrees, though his share in the graduations was never more than formal.
But these Colleges of Doctors, in which the actual right of teaching was
confined to Bolognese citizens, did not rule the University, which consisted
of students only. The students, who thronged in from all Europe to the
great Law School, found in both teachers and citizens their natural enemies
who preyed upon them. They formed already before 1200 their own
leagues or universities to protect themselves. There emerged eventually
the two Universities of (student) Jurists at Bologna, the Ultramontane
and the Cismontane, which acted together. Each was under an elected
Rector and Council, and further subdivided into 'Nations'. The student-
jurists, a large, cosmopolitan body, with influential connexions, and the
source of gain to teachers and city, succeeded in getting the whip-hand
over the Doctors, save in graduations to the doctorate. They made them
swear obedience to their Statutes, fined them for slackness or inefficiency
and restricted their movements. They were niggardly in paying fees, however, and when rival universities, like Padua (1222) or Naples (1224),
sprang up, the Bolognese came to the rescue with salaried chairs, which
established the class of Professors—a title in the north synonymous with
Doctor—and this reform, which was imitated by other Italian universities, but not beyond the Alps, killed the right of Doctors as such to
university teaching. In the same way non-Bolognese Doctors of Law were
excluded from the two Colleges. Meanwhile, the Bolognese University of
Medicine and Arts at last liberated itself from those of the Jurists (1306).
The combination therein and in other Italian universities of Aristotelian
science, grammar, and rhetoric had much to do with the appearance of
early Italian scientists and humanists. A strictly theological Faculty was
not installed until 1360 by the Pope, and was then a preserve of the
Friars. Secular culture was the contribution of Italy to the progress of
the human mind.

The progress of the northern universities was very different. They were
clerical and associations of teachers. In the cathedral schools, from which
they grew, the licence to teach was granted by a cathedral official, the

scholasticus or the Chancellor, but it was also necessary for the new Master (or Doctor) to 'incept', i.e. to be formally admitted (and soon tested) by the existing teachers in his Faculty. At first somewhat nebulous, these groups of Masters and their customs were definite bodies in the later twelfth century. They became the University and its rulers. A series of ranks was developed analogous to those of the craft-gilds; the scholar corresponded to the apprentice. After training and passing tests he was admitted to the degree of Bachelor (*Baccalaurius*, a term also applied to a knight who had no others serving under him), and then started as a subordinate teacher. Later again he became a Licentiate, and was finally admitted a full Master (or Doctor) of his Faculty. One characteristic of the 'inception' in early days had been the banquet given by the new Master to his colleagues; he 'paid his footing' after the degree had been solemnly conferred. It was soon imitated, with greater rudeness, by the undergraduates at the expense of new recruits, the *bejauni*.

The process of the formation of the University of Paris, the greatest of the medieval universities, was a slow one. William of Champeaux (*c.* 1070–1121) first gave the cathedral school some distinction, but it was in the time of his pupil, the famous Abelard (1079–1142), that Paris rose to the leading position. There was as yet no university. The masters who taught received their licences from the cathedral Chancellor; the custom of inception had, it seems, already begun. Thence grew a *de facto* university. But official recognition waited till 1200, when King Philip Augustus granted a charter of protection to masters and scholars. The earliest and simple statutes were passed by 1209, and a papal bull in favour of the university was obtained. It was already in conflict with its nominal head the Chancellor; in 1219 the Faculty of Arts seems to have appointed its four Proctors of the four 'Nations' into which the populous Faculty was divided. In 1245 a Rector of the whole Faculty was appointed, who acted as representative of all the University, for the other Faculties, Theology, Canon Law, and Medicine, each under a Dean, were small. The evolution of a settled and independent University was long and full of quarrels. In the final constitution, questions were decided by a majority of Faculties; the vote of the numerous Faculty of Arts was given by a majority of 'Nations'. The Nations were four, France (which included southern Europe), Normandy, Picardy, and England (which included Germany), an archaic classification, suggestive of the comparative numbers of masters who came from different lands. Independence of the Parisian Chancellor was furthered through many masters holding their classes within the jurisdiction of the abbey of St Geneviève, which also granted licences in Arts, but the method of 'dispersion' i.e. seceding from Paris, made easier by the fact that the University possessed no buildings of its own, was the most effectual. Thus the University gained its freedom from the Chancellor and won its bull of 1231; but against the Pope it failed (1251–7) to exclude intruding friars from teaching in Theology, although it kept them out of the Faculty of Arts. The University was by no means always in the right in its collisions with outside authorities. The undisciplined swarm of rowdy, irresponsible, and often dissolute boys and youths from fourteen upwards, who flocked to it for their education and chances in Church and State, were frequently a public nuisance through their riots and misdeeds. And the same defects accompanied other universities. Originally the students of Paris and other universities lived where they pleased, but the more usual fashion was for a party to take a common house, which one of them managed with his fellows' consent. Small endowments were given in aid of such. In 1258 Robert de Sorbon, St Louis's chaplain, made a new departure by founding an endowed college, the Sorbonne, for students in Theology. The example was rapidly imitated and at Paris some sixty Colleges existed by 1500 with officials, statutes, and some teaching and discipline. In 1457 the University forbade residence outside a college or approved boarding-house. Much turbulence was avoided thereby, and eventually college teaching superseded the unorganized, unendowed public lectures of individual masters, who had been a constantly changing body. The system which made the university a federation of colleges took root in other universities, like Oxford and Cambridge, where it has lasted to the present day.

The number of universities soon increased. Spontaneous development from pre-existing schools, secession of malcontents from older seats of teaching, and deliberate foundation were the chief means. Oxford was rising c. 1170, and Cambridge appears as a result of a migration from Oxford in 1209; both these came to be governed by an elected Chancellor, who was the Parisian Chancellor and Rector rolled into one, while their constitutions showed a general resemblance to that of Paris. Padua was a secession of students from Bologna. Orleans and Angers grew from cathedral schools. Foundation by authority became the most frequent origin. The Spanish universities are of this class. Naples was founded by Frederick II, Toulouse by Pope Gregory IX (1230), the Italian cities were prolific founders in the fourteenth century, and in France then and later fresh universities were created. The movement spread eastward when the Emperor Charles IV founded his German and Czech University of Prague (1348), which was followed by others like Heidelberg (1385), Erfurt, Vienna, and Louvain. Poland and Hungary created their universities in the fourteenth century. Others were founded in Germany, Scandinavia, and Scotland before 1495. In short, by the close of the Middle Ages there were universities throughout Western Christendom.

The course of studies at Paris furnishes a general type for those of the northern universities. In the twelfth century the study of Logic and Dialectic learnt from Aristotle ousted after a struggle the more humanistic interest in the Classics. Then round about 1200 the corpus of Aristotle's works was known by translations. It was in vain that in 1215 and later his physical and metaphysical writings were forbidden because of the heretical tendencies of them and their commentaries. It became the better way to weave their reasoning, whenever possible, into Christian theology and thought. From that time Aristotle became the staple of the Faculty of Arts. A knowledge of Latin was usually acquired first in grammar schools. The old division of subjects—the Trivium (grammar, rhetoric, dialectic or logic) and Quadrivium (arithmetic, geometry, music, and astronomy)—was perfunctorily adhered to, but for the B.A. degree the *Organon* of Aristotle and allied works of others were the real objects of study; for the Licence the *Physics* and *Metaphysics*, with lesser books, of Aristotle were the fundamental textbooks. The whole course in Arts took at least some five or six years, and no 'secular' cleric could enter the Faculties of Theology or Medicine without his M.A. degree. But the great majority never went further than the M.A., and perhaps two-thirds of the students never reached the B.A. The universities ensured some mental training, but did not produce a host of learned clergy. In the Theological Faculty the Bible and the *Sentences* of Peter the Lombard were the textbooks. Six years were consumed in attaining the B.D. and as much again in acquiring the Doctorate (D.D. or Sacrae Theologiae Professor). In all Faculties public disputations were as vital a part of the course as lectures or examinations. They gave ample opportunities for learning, ingenuity, and quick reasoning, before in the fifteenth century they were dwindling into mere routine. They have left an echo to-day in the title of Wranglers given to the first class of the Cambridge Mathematical Tripos, in which the word Tripos also recalls the three-legged stool on which the disputant sat.

It is hard to overrate the influence of the Universities on the life of the central Middle Ages, which gave rise to the dictum that there were three powers to guide the world, the Sacerdotium, the Regnum, and the Studium. As corporate bodies they were potent, the makers of public opinion. The theology of the Western Church was largely shaped at Paris, and the Canon Law, if not created at Bologna, was taught by its doctors and applied by their pupils, for both Roman and Canon Law wherever taught were the training-ground of lawyers in every country save England, where nevertheless the Canon Law was enforced in the Courts Christian. When the Great Schism disrupted Europe, it was the University of Paris which took the lead of the more than half-political Conciliar Movement in debate and in action. The universities were the homes of the advance in creative thought which was displayed in 'Scholasticism'. Finally, there is their educative influence on those who had undergone even a part of their training. They formed a large proportion of the men who directed affairs. It was chiefly through the universities that poor men, and even younger sons of nobles, rose to power and influence. They stocked the newly forming bureaucracies of Church and State. Although the numbers of students have been much exaggerated, they bear witness to the enormous intellectual enthusiasm of their time.

(4) THE SCHOOLMEN AND SCHOLASTICISM

Only a barren summary, more of great names than of thought, can here be attempted of that continuous effort to give rational form to their beliefs and to plan out by reason an intelligible framework of the world and man which has been called by the non-committal name of Scholasticism and might be described, haltingly enough, as the study of theological metaphysics and of metaphysical theology. The name is derived from its teachers, the Schoolmen (*Scholastici*), who taught in the cathedral schools and the later universities. It was natural that the explication of the Christian faith should produce a predominantly theological colour for their philosophy, and inevitable that the current of thought they developed should begin long before it could be described as Scholasticism.

The first great figure in medieval philosophy is the Irish genius, John the Scot (Eriugena), who left his native country for the court of Charles the Bald of France. He possessed the then exceedingly rare knowledge of Greek, and his thought was largely influenced by Neo-Platonic philosophy, which he derived especially from the Christian work of the Pseudo-Dionysius 'the Areopagite'. John himself was ardently Christian, but his views were not those of his own century. His first work, *De Praedestinatione*, was directed (851) against the fatalism of the unhappy monk, Gottschalk; his *De Divisione Naturae* is one of the most remarkable books of the world. It has been accused of pantheism: he conceived of the universe as one stupendous yet graded theophany, in which God appeared in, yet eternally transcended all his creatures. Mostly neglected, the book was always suspect, and in 1225 Pope Honorius III even condemned it, but in vain, to the flames. None the less it was a stimulus.

Dark centuries succeeded John the Scot, yet in them were preserved the ideas and the literary implements which accompanied the reawakening. With almost all their knowledge derived from past writings and from the texts of Scripture, combined with the treatises of the Christian Fathers and the accredited teachings of the Church, their most ambitious reasonings were essentially deductive. They worked from a mingled assemblage of articles of faith and *obiter dicta*, sacred and profane. Men accorded to the antique remnants they inherited an authority second only to Holy Writ and the Fathers of the Church. Aristotle they knew of as a logician, the master of dialectic. Their knowledge was limited to the translations by Boethius of two minor works (with the *Isagoge* of Porphyry), and to

Boethius's own commentaries. Plato was reverenced as a philosopher. If only a Latin version of part of one dialogue, the *Timaeus*, was read, his doctrines permeated medieval thought through the medium of Boethius, Porphyry, Macrobius, and St Augustine himself, to say nothing of others. Not till the thirteenth century did Aristotle become *the* Philosopher. Dialectic, however, was given a new importance by the controversy in terms of logic on the Real Presence in the Sacrament between the logician Berengar of Tours (*ob.* 1088) and Archbishop Lanfranc of Canterbury. The dispute was a landmark in the development of the doctrine of Transubstantiation.

The herald, if not the founder, of scholastic philosophy was the saintly Anselm (1033–1109), Abbot of Bec and Archbishop of Canterbury. He was an emigrant from the Alpine border-valley of Aosta, and could convert his patristic learning into original thought. His endeavour was to prove by reason the necessity of the existence and the perfection of the revealed Deity: faith seeking understanding (*Fides quaerens intellectum*) was his starting-point, his *sine qua non*. In the *Monologium*, the *Proslogion*, and the *De Fide Trinitatis* he sought to clothe the One with the attributes of an individual spirit, unbounded and perfect being. In *Cur Deus Homo* he attempted to rationalize, in terms almost legal, the mystery of the Incarnation. As a profound thinker he stands on a pinnacle rarely attained.

Curiously enough it was in controversy with Roscelin (*c.* 1050–*c.* 1120) that St Anselm had a share in the famous dispute between Nominalists and Realists, which was a favourite topic of the Schoolmen, although it by no means totally absorbed them. Were general notions or 'universals' true entities or were they merely words classifying individual things; was mankind a reality, or were only men realities? According to a nomenclature now confusing, the extreme Realists held a doctrine of 'universals' corresponding to the 'ideas' of Plato: 'universals' were real, and archetypes of their individual embodiments. The extreme Nominalists held that 'universals' were mere words (*nomina, flatus vocis*): individual things were the only real entities. But in between the extremists were many varieties. The prevailing tendency among them was to hold that 'universals' could not subsist except in association with individual things, but that they did express rationally that common element in allied things by which they are truly classified. The logical and metaphysical problems thus brought to light were perfectly genuine and could affect the doctrine of the Trinity and most philosophical questions.

In the early effort to apply free debate by the method of dialectic to these numberless problems, whether 'universals' were involved or not, the arresting and pathetic personality of Abelard (more correctly Abailard) is pre-eminent. He was born to fascinate or repel, and the tragedy of his romance with Héloïse makes him a living figure to-day. Pugnacity and his

628

bitter, irreverent attacks on his teachers and rivals were powerful reasons for the enmities he encountered in his philosophic career. He was a great teacher, whose thronging pupils gave renown to the incipient Paris University, a shrewd critic, a champion of dialectic, the mistress, as he declared, of all philosophical studies. As a constructive thinker he was less happy. His enemies could accuse him of heresy, and he had to contend with St Bernard, who had an autocratic detestation of the free use of argument in matters of doctrine. His condemnation was secured at Soissons (1121) and Sens (1140), and he ended his days as a devout monk in the friendly shelter of Cluny (1142). His famous book, the *Sic et Non* (Yes and No), proposed to solve by dialectic a long series of discrepancies in the authorities for the faith and is based on eminently sane principles of criticism. Some such authorities may be reconciled with one another, but no one outside Holy Writ is infallible. When dialectic fails to reconcile contradictions, the best alternative should be adhered to: they should not be swallowed or quoted indiscriminately. To many of the opposed statements that he listed Abelard did not offer a solution, but the method, which he had borrowed from the lawyers, won the day in spite of censure. He had set an example and inspired brilliant pupils. Uncritical dogmatism had seen its best days.

Abelard's contemporary, Hugh of St Victor (*ob.* 1141), was of another complexion. By temperament he was a genuine mystic: mystical insight surpassed the capacity of reason. Yet he was also a deeply learned scholar, for whom all knowledge was of value, loving to classify, arrange, and analyse. He, too, fostered the Church's inbred love of allegory in the interpretation of Scripture, its way of extracting the last grain of significance from the sacred text, which accorded with the medieval search for and submission to ancient, inspired, authoritative pronouncements, the citadel or the refuge of all partisans seeking to justify their cause in morals, politics, or creed.

More obviously influential was the transmitter of both Abelardian and Victorine methods, the great compiler, Peter the Lombard, Bishop of Paris (*ob. c.* 1160), the Master of the *Sentences* as he was named. His chief work, the *Libri Sententiarum IV*, was a systematic exposition of Christian doctrine discussed in the manner of *Sic et Non* by assembling the various authoritative statements (*sententiae*) of the Bible and the Fathers, and arriving at a conclusion on each subject by a dialectical process when they differed. Others were employing the same system, but Peter Lombard's book, orderly, subtle, and sober, surpassed them all, and became the textbook of theology on which innumerable schoolmen lectured and commented.

It took fifty years for the opponents of Peter Lombard to be silenced, but the defeat of the obscurantists had been sealed when St Bernard himself was unable to secure the condemnation of Gilbert de la Porrée, Bishop of Poitiers, in 1148. The philosophers, however, did not wholly justify their immunity. John of Salisbury could jibe at the endless, stale disputes on trifling logic and 'universals' at Paris. The revolution came when the gradual acquisition of a knowledge of Aristotle's works provided a new stimulus to thought, and ended in the Aristotelian invasion of Paris in the thirteenth century. Henceforward Aristotle was 'the Philosopher'. The change was due not only to the sage himself, but to the commentaries on him by the series of 'Arabic' thinkers (rarely Arabs in race), especially Avicenna (Ibn Sinā, *ob.* 1036), the Jews Avencebrol (Ibn Gabirol, *ob.* 1058) and Maimonides (*ob.* 1204), and the great Averroes (Ibn Rushd, *ob.* 1198), who wrote 'the great Comment'.

As we have seen, the Church was immediately alarmed at the intrusion of heathen, speculative philosophy into the Christian universities, where the growing Faculty of Arts was captivated by it. Prohibitions were vain, and the Dominican Friars, who at first shunned it, produced the greatest champions of a Christian Aristotelianism in Albert the Great of Cologne (*ob.* 1280) and his still more famous Neapolitan pupil, St Thomas Aquinas (*ob.* 1276). Both taught during certain periods at Paris. Albert, the pioneer, undertook the task of making the whole of Aristotle intelligible to the Latins in his encyclopedic works; St Thomas set out to show that philosophy as far as it went was consonant with the Faith, and that those who produced contradictory truths from Christian dogma and from philosophy were at fault in their reasoning.

A philosophic challenge was thus thrown down to the school of Averroists which became conspicuous in the thirteenth century. Theirs was the kind of rational scepticism which appealed to educated men. They exalted Aristotle to infallibility and followed the exposition of Averroes. In his train they accepted the eternity of the material world, the unity of the intellect in the world, and by consequence the mortality of the soul in individual men. Their protagonist Siger of Brabant (*ob. c.* 1283), Aquinas's contemporary, held these views to be proved philosophically though opposed to revelation. He claimed to submit to revelation, sincerely or not, and some Averroists declared for a 'double truth', that of philosophy and that of the Faith, a position that might seem designed to escape the charge and penalty of heresy. The sect survived the condemnation of Siger (1277) into the next century. Its existence excited a distrust of Aristotelianism which affected the reputation of Aquinas himself.

That remarkable genius of indefatigable industry constructed in his various works a whole system of rational theology and metaphysics. He commented on Aristotle with the aid of new, more accurate translations from the Greek; he wrote his two great *Summae*, and various minor works. He was the most constructive thinker of the widest view of the Middle

Ages. He was concerned to show that the 'Arabian' interpretations of Aristotle were wrong, and that the heathen Philosopher himself might err; that correct reasoning agreed with revealed truth, although revelation could surpass the reach of reason. In deductive fashion he strove to exhibit a four-square, complete, invulnerable edifice.

There was, however, an opposition to Aristotelianism and Aquinas. Besides the more old-fashioned Schoolmen and the more mystical philosophy of the Franciscans, Alexander of Hales (*ob.* 1245) and St Bonaventura (*ob.* 1274), there was a movement noticeable in England to follow a more progressive path. Its great figures were Robert Grosseteste, Bishop of Lincoln (*ob.* 1253), and his famous and unlucky pupil, Roger Bacon (*ob.* 1292). In Bacon, soon to become a legendary personage, there can be discerned beneath his critical onslaughts, complaints, and vaunts a profound discontent with the existing state of knowledge and with complacent deductive theorizing, and a conviction that no further advance was possible save by a kind of intellectual return to nature. Mathematics should be applied to physics, languages should be thoroughly learned,

Fig. 128. Franciscan friar teaching

translations be made by experts in the subject dealt with, knowledge of all sorts extended from the facts, and above all tested and increased by experiment. That this was the way of future science was clear, and Bacon's predictions of what could be done and found out by it were glamorous enough. But he himself, despite his efforts, had not the means required. He fell out with other teachers and his Franciscan Order. Although Pope Clement IV (*ob.* 1268) was his patron, he was condemned and imprisoned over his astrological views (1277). None the less his insight amounted to genius, and was almost prophetic. The school of thought of which he was the exponent survived, although in a confined circle in France, in the next century.

The general university public, however, developed on scholastic lines, and became divided into Thomists and Scotists. John Duns Scotus (*ob.* 1308)—he was a Lowland Scot—'the subtle Doctor', took up arms against the attempt of Aquinas to define a sphere for philosophy without detriment to the sovereign rights of theology. To Duns it was inexpedient to try to demonstrate the articles of faith, and improper to prove by reason that

God exists and is One, or that the soul is immortal. He differed, too, in his doctrine on matter and on the individuality of things, on what makes them what they are. Breaches thus appeared in Aquinas's edifice, and they were widened by William Ockham (*ob. c.* 1350) the Englishman. By 1400 the universites were divided among the *antiqui* or realists, who followed either Aquinas or Duns, and the *moderni* or nominalists, who derived from Ockham and his denial of the possibility of absolute proof in metaphysics and theology. The creative period of Scholasticism expired in their discord.

(5) THE VERNACULAR LITERATURES

The intellectual progress which marked the age was by no means confined to the dry studies of theology, law, the classics, and scholasticism. Its Latin hymns and 'Goliardic' verse have already been mentioned. To them should be added the Latin histories and chronicles, which flourished more especially in abbeys, telling of events in the past and present. Their authors grew more expert, full, and on the whole reliable as time went on. Too many achieved excellence even to be listed; few countries were without them; but some of the crusading histories perhaps hold the palm for wealth of accurate and vivid detail. A growing interest in documentary evidence is discernible, partly due to the political controversies and the accompanying wish to capture public opinion, but also owing to a sheer love of objective facts, which finds expression in the collection of records compiled by the English Matthew Paris.

More fundamental for men at large was the conscious emergence of literature in the vernaculars of Europe. The most striking and living was perhaps that of remote Iceland, where Latin learning had never taken root—the Old English prose and verse suffered a crushing blow at the Conquest; the Irish poets followed their secluded course away from the Continent. The Icelanders after the Viking age almost monopolized the literary tradition of Scandinavia. In their solitary homes the art of story-telling and hearing became almost a passion. Its material was ancient legend and their own historic past. The prose *saga*, preferably founded on fact, was born: pointed and picturesque, dramatic and realistic, with an unequalled gift for characterization; the personages speak and act themselves without the delays of probing and description. The most critical of the *sagamen* was the learned Snorri Sturluson (1179–1241), who told the history of the Norse dynasty of the Ynglings from mythical times downward, a masterpiece of vivid tradition in which kings and chiefs each live again. Throughout the thirteenth century family sagas were being written down, some at the highest level of story-telling, but legends borrowed from Germany were being told too, and imaginary heroes invented until the impulse evaporated.

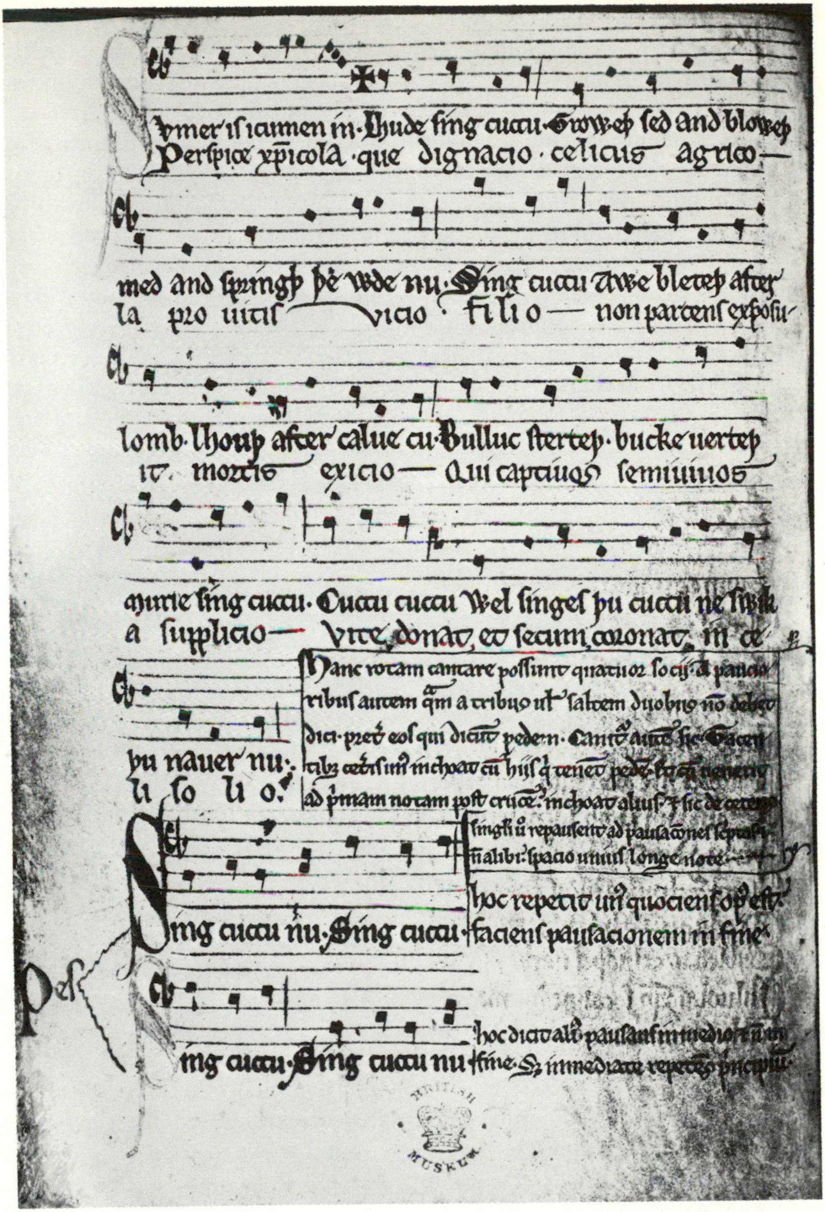

Fig. 129. Sumer is icumen in, c. *1240*

Of quite another ethos was the lyric poetry of the South of France which flourished in the twelfth and thirteenth centuries, the art of the troubadours, who composed their songs in the Langue d'oc (or Provençal) language, the chief dialect used being the Limousin. The first named troubadour was William IX, Duke of Aquitaine (1071–1127), but the art he practised was clearly past its infancy, although it did not reach its full growth until after his time. It was the offspring of the wealth and early civilization of the Midi, combined with the influence of feudal customs and of chivalrous notions fostered perhaps by the Crusades with which it synchronized. It was distinctively, whoever sang, an aristocratic art in a luxurious society in which the feudal lady, leisured and cultivated, played a leading part. Only in such a society could the intricate, elaborate, and varied versification of its lyrics and their subtlety of style, whether purposely obscure or plain, be evolved. Conscious style reappeared in Langue d'oc, and with it the extreme of artificiality in matter and manner. The predominant although not the only matter of the troubadours was the science of love, subject to as strait conventions as the verse. Here, too, the social environment was the prevailing factor. Unmarried girls were commonly kept in seclusion; it was the married dame who was the object of *amour courtois*, and the lover's suit was mainly pictured on Platonic lines. He wooed and served as a vassal of his chosen lady, whom he addressed almost as a patron-saint, under a pseudonym, for in this equivocal relation secrecy, real or feigned, was a fixed convention. A whole series of conventions, worship, desire, despair, delight, were the rule, so much so that monotony and frigidity in theme as well as in manner became the vice of the troubadours, in spite of all their ingenuity, and produced an early decline of their art irrespective of the horrors of the Albigensian Crusades which broke up their turbulent, prosperous society. None the less its Platonic tradition lived on and was transplanted to other lands to receive its death-blow in *Don Quixote*. It introduced in the West, whatever its theme, the æsthetic, artistic *motif* into poetry.

In Northern France (the Langue d'oïl), on the other hand, as well as in England and Germany, vernacular literature was dominated by the romantic story of adventure. Themes from age-old folk-lore, from early and recent tradition, even from all-but contemporary events were told and retold with plentiful variations, much mutual borrowing, and an amount of sheer invention. Incidents and situations were often at bottom of nearly primeval, sometimes mythological, antiquity, but they were developed, re-handled, re-clothed, shifted, and mingled until they seemed new, all the more easily because, in the absence of historical perspective, they were garbed in the ideas and likings of the audience and country in which they were retold.

Four great cycles of these legends in poetry and prose stand pre-eminent

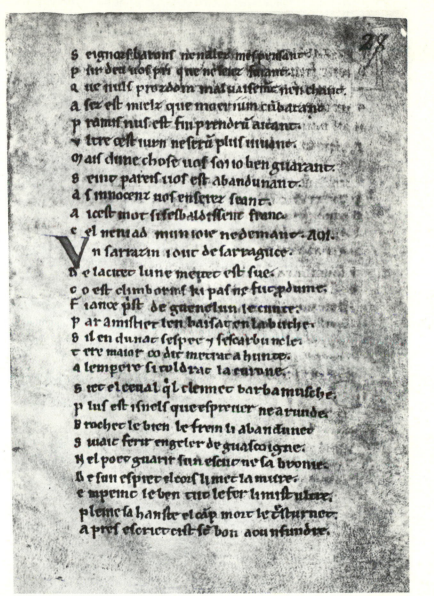

Fig. 130. Chanson de Roland

among them, the French tales of Charlemagne and his peers, the Arthurian tales, the classic romances of Alexander and of Troy, and the Germanic system of hero-tales. Each bears the impress of a glorified past and of an exaggerated, yet inevitably truthful present.

(i) *The Charlemagne Cycle.* Of this some seventy *Chansons de Geste*, as they are named, are preserved. Charlemagne, a composite figure of the Emperor himself and other Carolingians, as a rule is a minor figure in them. The real heroes are the paladins, typical figures of the warlike, in-dependent barons of the heyday of feudal disorder. Valour, loyalty to lord and kindred, zeal for the Faith against the infidel, an insatiable appetite for battle, and reckless pride mark their careers. They give the feudal ideal of the crusading years round 1100. Legendary or fictitious as their stories are, the personages were as often as not real nobles of the preceding cen-turies, bewilderingly transformed. Roland really fell at Roncesvalles in 778, the traitor Ganelon had once been Wenilo, the faithless Archbishop of Sens a century later, Guillaume d'Orange was a real fighting Count of Toulouse who ended as a holy hermit (*c.* 812). Whatever popular stories or songs may have existed, the vogue and rapid spread of the *Chansons de Geste* is indissolubly connected with the routes of pilgrimage and trade, with famous shrines and fairs. There the *trouvère* or *jongleur* chanted his lays to the throng. It was a mixed public of vassal, traveller, townsman, and peasant, which loved the violent, heady *geste* of fighting and adventure with its rough-hewn characters and sheer virility. In accordance with this simple mentality is the simple character of the verse, divided into *laisses*, i.e. groups of lines rhymed by a single assonance, where the identity of the final vowel was all that was needed. Yet high qualities of vigour and imagi-nation were to be found in the *Chansons* from the earliest known, the *Roland* and the *Willame*, till the exhaustion of the cycle.

(ii) *The Arthurian Cycle.* Only few years separate the appearance of the *Chansons de Geste* from that of its rival cycle, the Arthurian, but though contamination of the two occurred they remained remarkably distinct in matter, treatment, and largely in audience. In matter they derived largely from Celtic folk-lore, tales drifting in from Brittany and Wales and ex-panded by other similar material and by frank invention, all gradually associated with the legendary British King Arthur and his court. Some of these tales had already reached Italy by 1100, and the extraordinary pseudo-history of the British kings (*c.* 1135) of Geoffrey of Monmouth gave some kind of framework and won undeserved credulity. Arthur and his Knights of the Round Table became the theme of wonderful, adven-turous romance. Unlike the Charlemagne cycle it dealt with fairy-land, with lonely wanderings of errant knights amid magic and marvels. It was chivalric rather than feudal in ethos; the knights are famous jousters in combat and tournament. As the chivalric ideal grew higher, so did that of the Arthurian heroes. The order of knighthood became a noble fraternity. The treatment, too, was more artistic. The lays in French were composed in octosyllabic rhyming couplets. The first great artist of the cycle was Chrétien de Troyes (*fl.* 1170), who wrote his lengthy lays for the Countess of Champagne, the daughter of Queen Eleanor of Aquitaine, and who perhaps introduced the *motif* of the chivalric *amour courtois*, now quite deprived of its Platonic element, into the cycle. Others followed in his steps, ringing the changes and fishing up other fragments of folk-lore as well as extraneous legends. Their audience, like that of the troubadours, was a courtly circle in palace or castle, where the minstrel recited his repertoire. It was aristocratic, conventional, and in some degree educated, for round about 1200 the tales were written in prose, which could be read to and sometimes by the lady in her bower. The cycle soon made its way from France to Germany, to Spain and Italy, to Wales (where it met versions of some of the folk-tales from whence it arose), and of course to England, where its audience spoke Norman-French. In these lands (save Wales) the Arthurian tales were re-told still in verse—the fourteenth-century English *Sir Gawain and the Green Knight* is a fine example,—and Malory's famous prose compendium, the *Morte d'Arthur*, closes a poetic series.

With its diversified folk-lore ancestry and its close alliance with the growing cult of a fashionable chivalry, the Arthurian cycle underwent marked changes in its favourite characters and themes. Sir Gawain, perhaps the earliest leading knight, gives way to the French Sir Lancelot, the type of *amour courtois*, probably also an invention of Chrétien de Troyes; the Celtic love-tale of Tristan and Iseult, annexed to the cycle, was too much in harmony with the same prepossessions not to be a most popular member, and produced (*c.* 1210) the famous *Tristan* in German by Gottfried of Strasbourg; most transfigured and transfigurating was the series connected with the Holy Grail. In the last, Celtic magic objects and hero-stories took on a Christian colouring, largely due to the inventive genius of Robert de Borron in the late twelfth century; the Grail and its accompaniments became relics of the Passion in a long prose history of the conversion of Britain; the adventures of the heroes were Christianized. Another Christianized version appeared in the German poem, the *Parzival* of Wolfram of Eschenbach (*c.* 1210). In romances a little later all Arthur's knights were sent on the quest of the Grail, Lancelot among them and his son Galahad, the achiever with the traditional Percival of the quest. Although barely orthodox in their symbolism, the Grail stories were deeply transformed by the Christian element of chivalrous piety which they acquired. The ascetic ideal became predominant, and only the virgin Galahad and the chaste Percival were allowed full success.

(iii) *The Cycle of Rome and Alexander*. This is hardly so much a cycle as groups of poems and tales which drew their matter from late classic romance and pseudo-history and even more from the popular tales of the Near East, well stocked with marvels, enchantments, and boundless treasures. Apocryphal adventures of Alexander, long known, formed the staple of the *Roman d'Alexandre*, while tales of Troy, Aeneas, and Thebes also provided fables for the *trouvères*. The *Roman d'Alexandre* group kept to the metres of the *Chansons de Geste*, but the others used the octosyllabic couplets. The vogue of both was intimately connected with the Crusades and their revelation of the gorgeous and fanciful East, whether Byzantine or Moslem. The Greco-Trojan group turned its heroes into contemporary conventional knights, devoted to *amour courtois*, and much the same

happened to the adaptations from the popular Ovid, with results to be seen as late as Chaucer and Shakespeare. Translations and imitations appeared sooner or later in German and English. Their marvels caught the imagination, but ill replaced the home-grown Arthurian fairyland.

(iv) *The Germanic Cycle*. Thoroughly native and singularly primitive, on the other hand, were the poems of the Germanic Cycle. Lays had never ceased to be composed on its themes, some mythological in origin, others of heroes and events remembered in living folk-lore. Siegfried the Volsung, Gunther the Burgundian, Ermanric and Theodoric (Dietrich of Bern) the Goths, Attila the Hun, Lombard and Frankish kings, Woden and the old gods, not to mention some comparatively late potentates, were ready to

Fig. 131. Margrave Ekkehard and Marchioness Uta

hand, and their legends, intertwined or separate, were inexhaustible sources for the minstrel. By some the essentially heathen character of the folk-lore tradition was retained, by others the mythological incidents were curtailed and a superficial Christian and quasi-chivalrous varnish laid on. To the latter class the famous *Nibelungenlied* of the late twelfth century belongs. Composed in southern Germany, it may be ranked among the vernacular products of the contemporary renaissance, but its spirit belongs to the older time, the age of the migrations, of wandering tribes and kinglets, although decked with the trappings of twelfth-century knighthood. Fate is dominant. Unflinching courage, *Treue*, i.e. unalterable loyalty to lord and kin, and the grim duty of and joy in blood-revenge are the heroic virtues. There is no abstract code of right beyond these. Repulsive treachery and trickery against an enemy are compatible with them. The women are worthy of the men, passionate viragos, beautiful and fierce and unassuageable, at the opposite pole to the pious or wanton ladies and elusive fairies of the *amour courtois*. Superhuman strength and foreseen doom give a titanic grandeur to the tragedy. The appetite for marvels and prodigies, indeed, proved the bane of the cycle. Adventure heaped on adventure, feats grotesquely incredible were stuffed together in later compositions to the obliteration of the stark motives of the original legends and to the loss of their savage magnanimity.

One effect of this spontaneous outburst of vernacular poems was the emergence of a far more competent vernacular prose. Law-books in French and German, histories and biographies in French and Spanish appeared beside monkish and scholastic Latin in the thirteenth century. Poetry itself took a wider range; French verse, for instance, was applied to moral, allegoric, and satiric themes which appealed to a more sophisticated generation.

(6) ARCHITECTURE

In post-Carolingian times Romanesque architecture, diversified by local peculiarities, extended over Western Europe. Plain cylindrical vaults, massive walls and columns, round arches and small windows were the rule, practically enforced by the builders' inability to construct large edifices without the support of sheer weight and solidity. Even in the twelfth century this tradition remained unchanged in some parts, but in North Italy, North France, and by consequence in England a new inventive spirit was at work, which eventually transmuted Romanesque into the style which (due to a misplaced conviction of its barbarism) has received the name of Gothic. Architecture can do nothing if it does not obey the laws of engineering. It was the empirically increased knowledge of those laws which enabled forgotten men of genius to achieve stability in their experiments and to combine it with beauty and grace, fitted for the needs of the time and the purpose of the edifice, and expressing with a devout imagination their ideas and aspirations.

Three vital principles of structure made the Gothic style possible. First came the ribbed vault, a development of the plain groined vault (produced by two intersecting cylindrical vaults) which appeared in the mid-eleventh century in Lombardy and soon spread. The ribs were skeleton arches to be filled in afterwards. They saved the immense wooden frame required in building, and they concentrated the pressure of the finished vault. Concentration of the pressures of the superincumbent mass was to be the vital necessity of the Gothic style. Second was the use of the pointed arch, an ancient device. Whether in vaulting or elsewhere, it had less outward thrust than the round arch and was therefore easier to deal with. Third came the invention of the flying buttress to support a lofty, well-lit roof. A hall with side-aisles was the reigning plan of a church. The aisles would check the outward thrust of the main hall, but if it rose far above them lit with the windows of the clerestory, they could not do so, even when aided by their external buttresses, without being themselves blocked by the supporting arches built within them. After some experimentation the problem was solved by the external half-arch of the flying buttress, weighted by a heavy pinnacle, to make the thrust vertical.

By the end of the twelfth century these three factors had full sway in North France and England. The thrusts of roof and walls were concentrated by them, so that in the thirteenth century a great church appears to rest on pillars and buttresses only and its walls seem to be a mere screen, itself largely replaced by the huge windows.

The change from massiveness and gloom to delicacy and light went far beyond the fundamental structure of Gothic. Windows developed from pointed slits to long lancets and then to traceried spaces of endless variety filled with designs of coloured glass. The ornamental carving of doorway and capital could be light and undercut, while the sculptor's work grew, as his skill increased, into delicate imitations of foliage and of human figures full of life and grace. Variations of design were applied to general cruciform plan. The round apse became the polygonal chevet or the square end. Aisles, chapels, and towers were added. The style reached its height in the Île de France. No two of its great Gothic churches are alike, but they show the same science and the same intuition for form and beauty.

A divergence from the North French style may be seen in the countries to which Gothic architecture travelled. In thirteenth-century England this is shown in the 'Early English' style, as seen at Salisbury Cathedral and elsewhere, with its grouped and narrow lancet windows and prominent transepts, and this 'nationalism' continued in the next century, ending in the fan-vaulting and vast windows of the 'Perpendicular' period, of which King's College Chapel at Cambridge is a superb example. With that the creative impulse of Gothic appeared to exhaust itself. In contemporary France, on the other hand, the last effort of Gothic invention was the 'Flamboyant' style, in which ingenious devotion to detail ran riot to the detriment of the impressiveness of the whole.

In Italy, in spite of the Lombard ribbed vaulting, true Gothic was always something of an exotic. Romanesque was longlived, and it may almost be said that there only the fourteenth century was not dominated by it on the one side or the new Renaissance style on the other. The influence of Antiquity was too strong. The delicacy and charm of Italian Gothic are deservedly famous, but Gothic structural principles were never truly grasped. The flying buttress was almost unknown, and the outward thrust of the vaults was countered by iron rods to hold the buildings together. The essential beauty of these churches lies in their exquisite use of marbles, carving, and painting and only rarely in the logical plan of the building. The Byzantine style in Venice and Sicily and the Romanesque of the earlier time were after all more native to the soil, and could be masterly in design.

In Germany the Golden Age was the Romanesque, which lasted till the mid-thirteenth century. Gothic was a reluctant importation, often of great technical excellence but lacking in poetry and charm. In Bohemia Gothic was introduced by the Emperor Charles IV still later, with a French architect to build it. The Dukes of Burgundy were patrons of Flamboyant in the Netherlands, but on the whole the secular buildings in the Gothic manner there are more interesting than the churches.

In Spain, too, the native Romanesque took long to conquer. When in the thirteenth century Gothic won the day, the great cathedrals, such as Burgos, were closely copied from French models. But much-divided Spain was an aggregate of regions. A Spanish Gothic arose in Catalonia, of which one characteristic was that the buttresses were largely internal, separating a long row of side-chapels. As time went on, native tastes were shown in the extreme richness, in fact exuberance, of the decoration, which gave the churches a Spanish imprint, irrespective of their style.

It is evident that these varieties and growth of architecture responded to a universal feeling. They were shrines of the Faith, and shrines in which all in some degree could share. Rivalry and pride, penance and devotion all played their part, but there was a public which could appreciate the beauty and magnificence created for it.

In contrast it was direct utility which led to the development of military architecture. The barbaric ravages of the ninth and tenth centuries caused the restoration of ancient Roman town-walls, the erection of walls wholly new, and the construction of private castles. The last were the direct offspring of feudalism; they were the stronghold of the lord, and as feudal turbulence gained the upper hand, they increased in number and in strength. In the eleventh century the feudal castle was still in general a wooden *donjon* (or keep) on an artificial mound (*motte*), surrounded by the moat, the excavation of which supplied the earth of the mound. On one side of the mound a loop of the moat surrounded a court, the bailey. Both *motte* and bailey were fortified by an earthen rampart, topped by a stockade, within the ditch. Bridges crossed the moats from the bailey to the mound, and to the bailey from outside. Until the twelfth century stone castles were rare. In the main they imitated the motte-and-bailey type without the artificial mound and with ever-increasing elaboration. The keep would be massive and rectangular with jutting corner-towers; the gate-houses across the moats would be especially strong; drawbridges, battlements, a parapet-walk round the outer wall, and loopholes all facilitated defence. Knowledge of Byzantine fortification learned in the Crusades, as well as more formid-able weapons of attack, produced a change in design which manifested the intellectual progress of the age.

There were two main features in the thirteenth-century castle: first, the adoption of circular form for the donjon, when retained, and for the projecting towers in walls, which avoided dangerous angles and lessened the impact of the battering ram and the machine-hurled stones; second, the transfer of the main defence to the circumvallation of the bailey and whole castle. Among many striking examples, the crusading castles in Syria, such as the Hospitaller Krak des Chevaliers in the Lebanon, were eminent. The typical bailey of the year 1300 was divided into two or more wards, of which the outer might entirely surround the inner. The outer wall was built lower than the inner, so that from both missiles could be directed on the besiegers at the same time, and if the outer were taken, it was commanded by the loftier inner. Further, the main gateway was strongly defended by a fortified barbican, outside the moat, and furnished with a moat of its own; thus the entrance to the gates and portcullises was over two narrow and perilous passages even if the outer barbican were pierced. The walls were studded at intervals with semi-circular projecting towers, which provided a perfect cross-fire on the attackers of the 'curtain' between them. What with every device for missile-volleys and cover, such a castle within its water-filled moats could resist even the most powerful engine of the day, and would only yield to famine. The circumvallation of cities was improved on the same principles, and a successful storm of them became a great rarity.

It is probable that the invention of cannon in the fourteenth century worked no sudden change, but their improvement heralded the decline in medieval fortification. Perhaps the capture of Constantinople by breach and storm in 1453 is the outstanding event due to improved artillery in regard to walled towns. On the Anglo-Scottish border the castle reverted to the simple keep (or peel) and bailey, held against raids. In general the castle began to change into the country house with mimic fortifications. The true fortress developed later in the return to earthworks.

It has already been pointed out that a change in ideas, followed at a distance and most haltingly in conduct, took place among the feudal society of the twelfth and thirteenth centuries. The knight became chival-rous. Courtesy and fair play, protection of women and the weak were added to the ideal knightly virtues. The dubious *amour courtois* exercised a dominating influence. The knight was to be devoted to all ladies and to be a faithful, ecstatic lover. That there was a real effect in softening the fierce manners of the time is shown if we compare the first crusaders with

Louis VII, Earl William Marshall, and St Louis, but the common run were far below their level, just as the formal tournament was more knightly than the hurly-burly of war. Knighthood became the culmination of a training, the admission to the warrior, aristocratic class. The boy proceeded from page to squire, and the squire was knighted in peace-time by an elaborate ceremony, blessed by the Church, which seized the opportunity to inculcate a Christianized version of the warrior's ideal. With all deductions made—and they are formidable—chivalry took its share in the advance of civilization.

Fig. 132. The Bamberg Horseman